S0-DQZ-015

S T U D I E S   I N   S C R I P T U R E

Book of
Mormon

E D I T E D   B Y   K E N T   P .   J A C K S O N

Deseret Book Company, Salt Lake City, Utah

Book of Mormon

Part 1

1 Nephi to Alma 29

© 1987, 1988 Kent P. Jackson

All rights reserved.
No part of this book may be reproduced in any form or by any means without permission in writing from the publisher, Deseret Book Company, P. O. Box 30178, Salt Lake City, Utah 84130.

Deseret Book is a registered trademark of Deseret Book Company.

First printing *Studies in Scripture* volume seven, hardbound edition, November 1987

First printing *Studies in Scripture* volume eight, hardbound edition, August 1988

First printing combined paperbound edition, October 1999

Library of Congress Catalog Card Number 99-075003

ISBN 1-57345-602-0

Printed in the United States of America   72082-6599

10   9   8   7   6   5   4   3   2   1

CONTENTS

PREFACE

President Ezra Taft Benson, a modern prophet, has taught succinctly: "The Book of Mormon brings men to Christ."[1] As a testimony to the inspired mission of Joseph Smith and the divinity of The Church of Jesus Christ of Latter-day Saints, the Book of Mormon shows the world that God has opened the heavens in modern times and has restored truth and light to humanity. Most important, the Book of Mormon is a testimony of the work of the Savior; as its subtitle announces, it is "Another Testament of Jesus Christ." It brings people to Christ, not only by bearing testimony to his work, ancient and modern, but by teaching its readers how his works of creation and atonement touch their lives.

We Latter-day Saints gratefully acknowledge the Book of Mormon as the keystone of our religion, recognizing that the validity of our faith rests on the validity of the Book of Mormon. In the Church we accept not only the truthfulness of its doctrine, but also the historicity of the events it describes. We believe "that the Book of Mormon is just what it professes to be," as President J. Reuben Clark stated.[2] To teach less than this about it is to deny it.

Studies in Scripture, Vol. 7: 1 Nephi to Alma 29 is another book in a series intended to enhance and supplement the personal study of the truths found in the Standard Works of The Church of Jesus Christ of Latter-day Saints. Recognizing that there is no substitute for a careful study of the scriptures themselves, this series, *Studies in Scripture*, is presented as a resource, an aid in pointing members of the Church toward the profound realities to be discovered in sacred writings.

The reader will readily see that the emphasis in this volume is on the *teachings* of the Book of Mormon. The authors have stressed the messages contained in the sermons and writings of its prophets. At the same time, they have discussed Book of Mormon history to clarify the narrative and emphasize the lessons that are taught through the historical events it records. Since the primary purpose of the Book of Mormon itself is to teach and bear testimony of the gospel of Jesus Christ, our purpose in this volume has been to do likewise. Thus, we have considered external evidences of the Book of Mormon, as well as contextual and comparative studies, to be of lesser value for this work.

Each of the contributors is responsible for his or her own conclusions. This book is a private endeavor and not a production of either Brigham Young University or The Church of Jesus Christ of Latter-day Saints. Although the writers and the editor have sought to be in harmony with the teachings of the scriptures and the leaders of the Church, the reader should not regard this work as a primary source for gospel understanding but should turn instead to the scriptures and the words of modern prophets for authoritative doctrinal statements.

I express my appreciation to the management and staff of Deseret Book Company and to the contributors to this volume, whose spiritual sensitivities are apparent throughout its pages. I am also most thankful for the expert assistance of my colleagues Robert L. Millet, Monte S. Nyman, and Robert E. Parsons, whose wisdom and advice have added much to this book.

Kent P. Jackson

NOTES

1. *Ensign*, May 1987, p. 83.
2. Address of August 8, 1938, in David H. Yarn, Jr., ed., *J. Reuben Clark — Selected Papers* (Provo, Ut.: Brigham Young University Press, 1984), p. 256.

1

THE BOOK OF MORMON—
KEYSTONE OF OUR RELIGION

PRESIDENT EZRA TAFT BENSON

My beloved brethren and sisters, today I would like to speak about one of the most significant gifts given to the world in modern times. This gift I am thinking of is more important than any of the inventions that have come out of the industrial and technological revolutions. This is a gift of greater value to mankind than even the many wonderful advances we have seen in modern medicine. It is of greater worth to mankind than the development of flight or space travel. I speak of the gift of the Book of Mormon, given to mankind 156 years ago.

This gift was prepared by the hand of the Lord over a period of more than a thousand years, then hidden up by Him so that it would be preserved in its purity for our generation. Perhaps there is nothing that testifies more clearly of the importance of this modern book of scripture than what the Lord Himself has said about it.

The Lord's Witness of the Book of Mormon

By His own mouth He has borne witness (1) that it is true (D&C 17:6); (2) that it contains the truth and His words (D&C 19:26); (3) that it was translated by power from on high (D&C 20:8); (4) that

---

Ezra Taft Benson is president of The Church of Jesus Christ of Latter-day Saints.

it contains the fulness of the gospel of Jesus Christ (D&C 20:9; 42:12); (5) that it was given by inspiration and confirmed by the ministering of angels (D&C 20:10); (6) that it gives evidence that the holy scriptures are true (D&C 20:11); and (7) that those who receive it in faith shall receive eternal life (D&C 20:14).

A second powerful testimony to the importance of the Book of Mormon is to note where the Lord placed its coming forth in the timetable of the unfolding Restoration. The only thing that preceded it was the First Vision. In that marvelous manifestation, the Prophet Joseph Smith learned the true nature of God and that God had a work for him to do. The coming forth of the book of Mormon was the next thing to follow.

Think of that in terms of what it implies. The coming forth of the Book of Mormon preceded the restoration of the priesthood. It was published just a few days before the Church was organized. The Saints were given the Book of Mormon to read before they were given the revelations outlining such great doctrines as the three degrees of glory, celestial marriage, or work for the dead. It came before the priesthood quorums and Church organization. Doesn't this tell us something about how the Lord views this sacred work?

The Lord's Warnings

Once we realize how the Lord feels about this book, it should not surprise us that He also gives us solemn warnings about how we receive it. After indicating that those who receive the Book of Mormon with faith, working righteousness, will receive a crown of eternal glory (see D&C 20:14), the Lord follows with this warning: "But those who harden their hearts in unbelief, and reject it, it shall turn to their own condemnation" (D&C 20:15).

In 1829, the Lord warned the Saints that they are not to trifle with sacred things. (See D&C 6:12.) Surely the Book of Mormon is a sacred thing, and yet many trifle with it, or in other words, take it lightly, treat it as though it is of little importance.

In 1832, as some early missionaries returned from their fields of labor, the Lord reproved them for treating the Book of Mormon lightly. As a result of that attitude, he said, their minds had been darkened. Not only had treating this sacred book lightly brought a loss of light to themselves, it had also brought the whole Church under condemnation, even all the children of Zion. And then the Lord said, "And they shall remain under this condemnation until they repent and remember the new covenant, even the Book of Mormon." (D&C 84:54-57.)

Has the fact that we have had the Book of Mormon with us for over a century and a half made it seem less significant to us today? Do we remember the new covenant, even the Book of Mormon? In the Bible we have the Old Testament and the New Testament. The word *testament* is the English rendering of a Greek word that can also be translated as *covenant*. Is this what the Lord meant when He called the Book of Mormon the "new covenant"? It is indeed another testament or witness of Jesus. This is one of the reasons why we have recently added the words "Another Testament of Jesus Christ" to the title of the Book of Mormon.

If the early Saints were rebuked for treating the Book of Mormon lightly, are we under any less condemnation if we do the same? The Lord Himself bears testimony that it is of eternal significance. Can a small number of us bring the whole Church under condemnation because we trifle with sacred things? What will we say at the Judgment when we stand before Him and meet His probing gaze if we are among those described as forgetting the new covenant?

There are three great reasons why Latter-day Saints should make the study of the Book of Mormon a lifetime pursuit.

The Book of Mormon Is the Keystone

The *first* is that the Book of Mormon is the keystone of our religion. This was the Prophet Joseph Smith's statement. He testified that "the Book of Mormon was the most correct of any book on earth, and the keystone of our religion."[1] A keystone is the central stone in an arch. It holds all the other stones in place, and if removed, the arch crumbles.

There are three ways in which the Book of Mormon is the keystone of our religion. It is the keystone in our witness of Christ. It is the keystone of our doctrine. It is the keystone of testimony.

The Book of Mormon is the keystone in our witness of Jesus Christ, who is Himself the cornerstone of everything we do. It bears witness of His reality with power and clarity. Unlike the Bible, which passed through generations of copyists, translators, and corrupt religionists who tampered with the text, the Book of Mormon came from writer to reader in just one inspired step of translation. Therefore, its testimony of the Master is clear, undiluted, and full of power. But it does even more. Much of the Christian world today rejects the divinity of the Savior. They question His miraculous birth, His perfect life, and the reality of His glorious resurrection. The Book of Mormon teaches in plain and unmistakable terms about the truth of all of those. It also provides the most complete explanation of the doctrine of the Atonement. Truly, this divinely inspired book is a keystone in bearing witness to the world that Jesus is the Christ. (See the title page of the Book of Mormon.)

The Book of Mormon is also the keystone of the doctrine of the Resurrection. As mentioned before, the Lord Himself has stated that the Book of Mormon contains the "fulness of the gospel of Jesus Christ." (D&C 20:9.) That does not mean it contains every teaching, every doctrine ever revealed. Rather, it means that in the Book of Mormon we will find the fulness of those doctrines required for our salvation. And they are taught plainly and simply so that even children can learn the ways of salvation and exaltation. The Book of Mormon offers so much that broadens our understanding of the doctrines of salvation. Without it, much of what is taught in other scriptures would not be nearly so plain and precious.

Finally, the Book of Mormon is the keystone of testimony. Just as the arch crumbles if the keystone is removed, so does all the Church stand or fall with the truthfulness of the Book of Mormon. The enemies of the Church understand this clearly. This is why they go to such great lengths to try to disprove the Book of Mormon, for if it can be discredited, the Prophet Joseph Smith goes with it. So does our claim to priesthood keys, and revelation, and the restored Church. But in like manner, if the Book of Mormon be true—and millions have now testified that they have the witness of the Spirit that it is indeed true—then one must accept the claims of the Restoration and all that accompanies it.

Yes, my beloved brothers and sisters, the Book of Mormon is the keystone of our religion — the keystone of our testimony, the keystone of our doctrine, and the keystone in the witness of our Lord and Savior.

Written for Today

The *second* great reason why we must make the Book of Mormon a focus of study is that it was written for our day. The Nephites never had the book; neither did the Lamanites of ancient times. It was meant for us. Mormon wrote near the end of the Nephite civilization. Under the inspiration of God, who sees all things from the beginning, he abridged centuries of records, choosing the stories, speeches, and events that would be most helpful to us.

Each of the major writers of the Book of Mormon testified that he wrote for future generations. Nephi said: "The Lord God promised unto me that these things which I write shall be kept and preserved, and handed down unto my seed, from generation to generation." (2 Ne. 25:21.) His brother Jacob, who succeeded him, wrote similar words: "For [Nephi] said that the history of his people should be engraven upon his other plates, and that I should preserve these plates and hand them down unto my seed, from generation to generation." (Jacob 1:3.) Enos and Jarom both indicated that they too were writing not for their own peoples but for future generations. (See Enos 1:15-16; Jarom 1:2.)

Mormon himself said, "Yea, I speak unto you, ye remnant of the house of Israel." (Morm. 7:1.) And Moroni, the last of the inspired writers, actually saw our day and time. "Behold," he said, "the Lord hath shown unto me great and marvelous things concerning that which must shortly come, at that day when these things shall come forth among you.

"Behold, I speak unto you as if ye were present, and yet ye are not. But behold, Jesus Christ hath shown you unto me, and I know your doing." (Morm. 8:34-35.)

If they saw our day and chose those things that would be of greatest worth to us, is not that how we should study the Book of Mormon? We should constantly ask ourselves, "Why did the Lord inspire Mormon (or Moroni or Alma) to include that in his record?

What lesson can I learn from that to help me live in this day and age?"

And there is example after example of how that question will be answered. For example, in the Book of Mormon we find a pattern for preparing for the Second Coming. A major portion of the book centers on the few decades just prior to Christ's coming to America. By careful study of that time period, we can determine why some were destroyed in the terrible judgments that preceded His coming and what brought others to stand at the temple in the land of Bountiful and thrust their hands into the wounds of His hands and feet.

From the Book of Mormon we learn how disciples of Christ live in times of war. From the Book of Mormon we see the evils of secret combinations portrayed in graphic and chilling reality. In the Book of Mormon we find lessons for dealing with persecution and apostasy. We learn much about how to do missionary work. And more than anywhere else, we see in the Book of Mormon the dangers of materialism and setting our hearts on the things of the world. Can anyone doubt that this book was meant for us and that in it we find great power, great comfort, and great protection?

Drawing Nearer to God

The *third* reason why the Book of Mormon is of such value to Latter-day Saints is given in the same statement by the Prophet Joseph Smith cited previously. He said, "I told the brethren that the Book of Mormon was the most correct of any book on earth, and the keystone of our religion, and a man would get nearer to God by abiding by its precepts, than by any other book."[2] That is the third reason for studying the book. It helps us draw nearer to God. Is there not something deep in our hearts that longs to draw nearer to God, to be more like Him in our daily walk, to feel His presence with us constantly? If so, then the Book of Mormon will help us to do so more than any other book.

It is not just that the Book of Mormon teaches us truth, though it indeed does that. It is not just that the Book of Mormon bears testimony of Christ, though it indeed does that, too. But there is something more. There is a power in the book that will begin to flow into your life the moment you begin a serious study of the book. You will find greater power to resist temptation. You will find the power to avoid deception. You will find the power to stay on the strait and narrow path.

The scriptures are called "the words of life" (D&C 84:85), and nowhere is that more true than it is of the Book of Mormon. When you begin to hunger and thirst after those words, you will find life in greater and greater abundance.

Blessings of Reading the Book of Mormon

Our beloved brother President Marion G. Romney, who knows of himself of the power that resides in this book, testified of the blessings that can come into the lives of those who will read and study the Book of Mormon. He said: "I feel certain that if, in our homes, parents will read from the Book of Mormon prayerfully and regularly, both by themselves and with their children, the spirit of that great book will come to permeate our homes and all who dwell therein. The spirit of reverence will increase; mutual respect and consideration for each other will grow. The spirit of contention will depart. Parents will counsel their children in greater love and wisdom. Children will be more responsive and submissive to the counsel of their parents. Righteousness will increase. Faith, hope, and charity — the pure love of Christ — will abound in our homes and lives, bringing in their wake peace, joy, and happiness."[3]

These promises — increased love and harmony in the home, greater respect between parent and child, increased spirituality and righteousness — are not idle promises, but exactly what the Prophet Joseph Smith meant when he said the Book of Mormon will help us draw nearer to God.

Eternal Consequences

Brethren and sisters, I implore you with all my heart that you consider with great solemnity the importance of the Book of Mormon to you personally and to the Church collectively.

Over ten years ago I made the following statement regarding the

Book of Mormon: "Do eternal consequences rest upon our response to this book? Yes, either to our blessing or our condemnation.

"Every Latter-day Saint should make the study of this book a lifetime pursuit. Otherwise he is placing his soul in jeopardy and neglecting that which could give spiritual and intellectual unity to his whole life. There is a difference between a convert who is built on the rock of Christ through the Book of Mormon and stays hold of that iron rod, and one who is not."[4]

I reaffirm those words to you this day. Let us not remain under condemnation, with its scourge and judgment, by treating lightly this great and marvelous gift the Lord has given to us. Rather, let us win the promises associated with treasuring it up in our hearts.

In the Doctrine and Covenants, section 84, verses 54 and 58, we read: "Your minds in times past have been darkened because of unbelief, and because you have treated lightly the things you have received — which vanity and unbelief have brought the whole church under condemnation. And this condemnation resteth upon the children of Zion, even all. And they shall remain under this condemnation until they repent and remember the new covenant, even the Book of Mormon and the former commandments which I have given them, not only to say, but to do according to that which I have written — that they may bring forth fruit meet for their Father's kingdom; otherwise there remaineth a scourge and judgment to be poured out upon the children of Zion."

Since last general conference, I have received many letters from Saints, both young and old, from all over the world who accepted the challenge to read and study the Book of Mormon.

I have been thrilled by their accounts of how their lives have been changed and how they have drawn closer to the Lord as a result of their commitment. These glorious testimonies have reaffirmed to my soul the words of the Prophet Joseph Smith that the Book of Mormon is truly "the keystone of our religion" and that a man or a woman will "get nearer to God by abiding by its precepts, than by any other book."

This is my prayer, that the Book of Mormon may become the keystone of our lives.

NOTES

This chapter was originally an address in the October 1986 General Conference. Copyright © 1986 by Corporation of the President of The Church of Jesus Christ of Latter-day Saints. Used by permission.

1. Joseph Smith, *History of the Church of Jesus Christ of Latter-day Saints*, ed. B. H. Roberts, 7 vols. (Salt Lake City: The Church of Jesus Christ of Latter-day Saints, 1932–1951), 4:461.
   2. Ibid.
   3. *Conference Report*, April 1980, p. 90; *Ensign*, May 1980, p. 67.
   4. *Conference Report*, April 1975, p. 97; *Ensign*, May 1975, p. 65.

2

THE COMING FORTH OF THE BOOK OF MORMON

OLIVER COWDERY

In a series of articles published in the Church's Kirtland, Ohio, newspaper, The Messenger and Advocate, *Oliver Cowdery described in detail many aspects of the restoration of the gospel through the Prophet Joseph Smith. The following compilation, which draws from these articles, shows President Cowdery's testimony of these events. — Ed.*

On the evening of the 21st of September, 1823, previous to retiring to rest, Joseph Smith's mind[1] was unusually wrought up on the subject which had so long agitated his mind — his heart was drawn out in fervent prayer, and his whole soul was so lost to everything of a temporal nature, that earth, to him, had lost its claims, and all he desired was to be prepared in heart to commune with some kind messenger who could communicate to him the desired information of his acceptance with God.

At length the family retired, and he, as usual, bent his way, though in silence, where others might have rested their weary frames "locked fast in sleep's embrace;" but repose had fled, and accustomed slumber had spread her refreshing hand over others beside him — he continued still to pray — his heart, though once hard and obdurate, was softened, and that mind which had often flitted, like the "wild bird of passage,"

Oliver Cowdery was second elder of The Church of Jesus Christ of Latter-day Saints from 1830 to 1834, and assistant president of the Church from 1834 to 1837.

had settled upon a determined basis not be decoyed or driven from its purpose.

A Messenger from the Skies

In this situation hours passed unnumbered — how many or how few I know not, neither is he able to inform me; but supposes it must have been eleven or twelve, and perhaps later, as the noise and bustle of the family, in retiring, had long since ceased. — While continuing in prayer for a manifestation in some way that his sins were forgiven; endeavoring to exercise faith in the scriptures, on a sudden a light like that of day, only of a purer and far more glorious appearance and brightness, burst into the room. — Indeed, to use his own description, the first sight was as though the house was filled with consuming and unquenchable fire. This sudden appearance of a light so bright, as must naturally be expected, occasioned a shock or sensation, visible to the extremities of the body. It was, however, followed with a calmness and serenity of mind, and an overwhelming rapture of joy that surpassed understanding, and in a moment a personage stood before him.

Notwithstanding the room was previously filled with light above the brightness of the sun, as I have before described, yet there seemed to be an additional glory surrounding or accompanying this personage, which shone with an increased degree of brilliancy, of which he was in the midst; and though his countenance was as lightning, yet it was of a pleasing, innocent and glorious appearance, so much so, that every fear was banished from the heart, and nothing but calmness pervaded the soul.

It is no easy task to describe the appearance of a messenger from the skies — indeed, I doubt there being an individual clothed with perishable clay, who is capable to do this work. To be sure, the Lord appeared to his apostles after his resurrection, and we do not learn as they were in the least difficultied to look upon him; but from John's description upon Patmos, we learn that he is there represented as most glorious in appearance; and from other items in the sacred scriptures we have the fact recorded where *angels* appeared and conversed with men, and there was no difficulty on the part of the

11

individuals, to endure their presence; and others where their glory was so conspicuous that they could not endure. The last description or appearance is the one to which I refer, when I say that it is no easy task to describe their glory.

But it may be well to relate the particulars as far as given. — The stature of this personage was a little above the common size of men in this age; his garment was perfectly white, and had the appearance of being without seam.

Though fear was banished from his heart, yet his surprise was no less when he heard him declare himself to be a messenger sent by commandment of the Lord, to deliver a special message, and to witness to him that his sins were forgiven, and that his prayers were heard; and that the scriptures might be fulfilled, which say — "God has chosen the foolish things of the world to confound the things which are mighty; and base things of the world, and things which are despised, has God chosen; yea, and things which are not, to bring to nought things which are, that no flesh should glory in his presence. Therefore, says the Lord, I will proceed to do a marvelous work among this people, even a marvelous work and a wonder; the wisdom of their wise shall perish, and the understanding of their prudent shall be hid; for according to his covenant which he made with his ancient saints, his people, the house of Israel, must come to a knowledge of the gospel, and own that Messiah whom their fathers rejected, and with them the fulness of the Gentiles be gathered in, to rejoice in one fold under one Shepherd.

"This cannot be brought about until first certain preparatory things are accomplished, for so has the Lord purposed in his own mind. He has therefore chosen you as an instrument in his hand to bring to light that which shall perform his act, his strange act, and bring to pass a marvelous work and a wonder. Wherever the sound shall go it shall cause the ears of men to tingle, and wherever it shall be proclaimed, the pure in heart shall rejoice, while those who draw near to God with their mouths, and honor him with their lips, while their hearts are far from him, will seek its overthrow, and the destruction of those by whose hands it is carried. Therefore, marvel not if your name is made a derision, and had as a by-word among such, if you are the instrument in bringing it, by the gift of God, to the knowledge of the people."

He then proceeded and gave a general account of the promises made to the fathers, and also gave a history of the aborigines of this country, and said they were literal descendants of Abraham. He represented them as once being an enlightened and intelligent people, possessing a correct knowledge of the gospel, and the plan of restoration and redemption. He said this history was written and deposited not far from that place, and that it was our brother's privilege, if obedient to the commandments of the Lord, to obtain, and translate the same by the means of the Urim and Thummim, which were deposited for that purpose with the record.

"Yet," said he, "the scripture must be fulfilled before it is translated, which says that the words of a book, which were sealed, were presented to the learned; for thus has God determined to leave men without excuse, and show to the meek that his arm is not shortened that it cannot save."

A part of the book was sealed, and was not to be opened yet. The sealed part, said he, contains the same revelation which was given to John upon the isle of Patmos, and when the people of the Lord are prepared, and found worthy, then it will be unfolded unto them.

On the subject of bringing to light the unsealed part of this record, it may be proper to say, that our brother was expressly informed, that it must be done with an eye single to the glory of God; if this consideration did not wholly characterize all his proceedings in relation to it, the adversary of truth would overcome him, or at least prevent his making that proficiency in this glorious work which he otherwise would.[2]

For the Glory of the Lord

He was to remember that it was the work of the Lord, to fulfil certain promises previously made to a branch of the house of Israel, of the tribe of Joseph, and when it should be brought forth must be done expressly with an eye, as I said before, single to the glory of God, and the welfare and restoration of the house of Israel.

You will understand, then, that no motive of a pecuniary, or earthly nature, was to be suffered to take the lead of the heart of the man thus favored. The allurements of vice, the contaminating influence of wealth, without the direct guidance of the Holy Spirit, must have no place in the heart nor be suffered to take from it that warm desire for the glory and kingdom of the Lord, or, instead of obtaining, disappointment and reproof would most assuredly follow. Such was the instruction and this the caution.

Alternately, as we could naturally expect, the thought of the previous vision was ruminating in his mind, with a reflection of the brightness and glory of the heavenly messenger; but again a thought would start across the mind on the prospects of obtaining so desirable a treasure — one in all *human* probability sufficient to raise him above a level with the common earthly fortunes of his fellow men, and relieve his family from want, in which, by misfortune and sickness they were placed. . . .

Alternately did these, with a swift reflection of the words of the holy messenger, — "Remember, that he who does this work, who is thus favored of the Lord, must do it with his eye single to the glory of the same, and the welfare and restoration of the scattered remnants of the house of Israel" — rush upon his mind with the quickness of electricity. Here was a struggle indeed.[3]

An Open Vision

A remarkable fact is to be noticed with regard to this vision. In ancient time the Lord warned some of his servants in dreams. . . . But the one of which I have been speaking is what would have been called an open vision. And though it was in the night, yet it was not a dream. There is no room for conjecture in this matter, and to talk of deception would be to sport with the common sense of every man who knows when he is awake, when he sees and when he does not see.

He could not have been deceived in the fact that a being of some kind appeared to him; and that it was an heavenly one, the fulfillment of his words, so minutely, up to this time, in addition to the truth and word of salvation which has been developed to this generation, in the Book of Mormon, ought to be conclusive evidence to the mind of every man who is privileged to hear of the same. He was awake, and in solemn prayer, as you will bear in mind, when the angel made his appearance; from that glory which surrounded him the room was lit up to a perfect brilliancy, so that darkness wholly disappeared: he heard his words with his ears, and received a joy and happiness indescribable by hearing that his own sins were forgiven, and his former transgressions to be remembered against him no more, if he then continued to walk before the Lord according to his holy commandments. He also saw him depart, the light and glory withdraw, leaving a calmness and peace of soul past the language of man to paint—Was he deceived?

Far from this; for the vision was renewed twice before morning, unfolding farther and still farther the mysteries of godliness and those things to come. In the morning he went to his labor as usual, but soon the vision of the heavenly messenger was renewed, instructing him to go immediately and view those things of which he had been informed, with a promise that he should obtain them if he followed the directions and went with an eye single to the glory of God.[4]

Eternal Things

There is another item I wish to notice on the subject of visions. The Spirit you know, searches all things, even the deep things of God. When God manifests to his servants those things that are to come, or those which have been, he does it by unfolding them by the power of that Spirit which comprehends all things, always; and so much may be shown and made perfectly plain to the understanding in a short time, that to the world, who are occupied all their life to learn a little, look at the relation of it, and are disposed to call it false. You will understand then, by this, that while those glorious things were being rehearsed, the vision was also opened, so that our brother was permitted to see and understand much more full and perfect than I am able to communicate in writing. I know much may be conveyed to the understanding in writing, and many marvelous truths set forth with the pen, but after all it is but a shadow, compared to an open vision of seeing, hearing and realizing eternal things.[5]

By the Gift and Power of God

Near the time of the setting of the sun, Sabbath evening, April 5th, 1829, my natural eyes, for the first time beheld Joseph Smith.[6] He then resided in Harmony, Susquehanna county Pennsylvania. On Monday the 6th, I assisted him in arranging some business of a temporal nature, and on Tuesday the 7th, commenced to write the Book of Mormon.

These were days never to be forgotten—to sit under the sound of a voice dictated by the *inspiration* of heaven, awakened the utmost gratitude of this bosom! Day after day I continued, uninterrupted, to write from his mouth, as he translated, with the *Urim* and *Thummim*, or, as the Nephites would have said, "Interpreters," the history, or record, called "The Book of Mormon."[7]

I know that this Book of Mormon was translated by the gift and power of God. My eyes saw, my ears heard, and my understanding was touched, and I know that whereof I testify is true. It was no dream, no vain imagination of the mind—it was real.[8]

NOTES

1. "Our brother's mind" in the original.
2. *Messenger and Advocate*, February 1835, pp. 78-80.
3. Ibid., July 1835, p. 157.
4. Ibid., p. 156.
5. Ibid., April 1835, p. 112.
6. "This brother" in the original.
7. *Messenger and Advocate*, October 1834, p. 14.
8. Quoted by Jacob Gates, *Improvement Era* 15 (March 1912): 418-19.

3

ANSWERING THE LORD'S CALL
(1 Nephi 1-7)

D. KELLY OGDEN

First Nephi relates the ministry of Nephi—from his family's departure out of the land of Jerusalem to their arrival in the promised land. The first part of his "journal-history" is a synopsis of his father's record. "I make an abridgment of the record of my father, upon plates which I have made with mine own hands; wherefore, after I have abridged the record of my father then will I make an account of mine own life." (1 Ne. 1:17.)[1] His own account begins in chapter 10.

Nephi began with a note about his goodly parents, giving particular credit to his father, from whom he had learned of the goodness and mysteries of God. Generations of writers following Nephi bear similar testimony of the valuable instruction of their fathers. The first sentence cut into the plates by Enos was a eulogy of his father, Jacob, for having planted some seeds of eternal things deep in his heart: "I, Enos, knowing my father that he was a just man—for he taught me in his language, and also in the nurture and admonition of the Lord . . . " (Enos 1:1.) The revered King Benjamin caused his three sons to be "taught in all the language of his fathers, that thereby they might become men of understanding; and that they might know concerning the prophecies . . . " (Mosiah 1:2.) It appears to be a characteristic of goodly parents to spend an adequate portion of their

---

D. Kelly Ogden is assistant professor of ancient scripture (Jerusalem) at Brigham Young University.

time and energy teaching their children the things of God. In promising great blessings to Abraham, the father of hundreds of millions, the Lord said that "Abraham shall surely become a great and mighty nation. . . . For I know him, that he will command his children and his household after him, and they shall keep the way of the Lord, to do justice and judgment; that the Lord may bring upon Abraham that which he hath spoken of him." (Gen. 18:18-19.)

All of the above Book of Mormon passages refer to the *language* of the fathers. Language facility, the ability to communicate with others, is the breath of life to any civilization. We will see its importance again shortly when Lehi's sons were required to make a 500-mile trip to secure some metal plates, which would ensure their emigrant colony some cultural stability and continuity. For the moment we can say that Lehi's sons were taught in the learning of the Jews and the language of the Egyptians. The sons had likely been educated in Hebrew and Aramaic grammar and vocabulary (Aramaic being the *lingua franca* of diplomacy and commerce at the time), but it appears that they had learned to express their thoughts in written form in Egyptian characters. Lehi had been "taught in the language of the Egyptians therefore he could read [the brass plates'] engravings, and teach them to his children." (Mosiah 1:4.) Perhaps Lehi mastered the Egyptian language, as Joseph and Moses before him.

There appears to have been considerable commercial and cultural interchange between Judah and Egypt in the late 7th century B.C. Excavations show great Egyptian influence in this period, which influence rises out of that nation's rule over the land of Judah during some years prior to the opening of the Book of Mormon record. Egyptian soldiers, merchants, and travelers were present and active in those days.

Historical Background

Twenty years before the commencement of the Book of Mormon, the kingdom of Judah was experiencing its last period of greatness. The Assyrian Empire was rapidly disintegrating, and the righteous King Josiah expanded the political borders of the kingdom, instigated rigorous religious reforms, and established relative peace during his reign. Josiah's life ended tragically with his death at Megiddo. He had gone there at the head of his armies to stop the Egyptian advance under Pharaoh Nechoh toward the Euphrates, Nechoh wanting to support the last Assyrian king in a stand against the new Babylonian Empire. Josiah apparently intended to keep Egypt from acquiring total control over Judah, though upon Josiah's death, Pharaoh Nechoh proceeded to flex his military muscle and overran all phases of Judah's political life. That situation lasted for about four years, until the Babylonian invasions. Josiah's death marked the beginning of the end for the kingdom of Judah. (See 2 Kgs. 22-23.)

Josiah's son Jehoahaz was made king after his father's death in 609 B.C., but Pharaoh Nechoh took him away to Egypt and put his brother Eliakim on the throne. Eliakim's name was changed to Jehoiakim.

Jehoiakim reigned for eleven years, until 598 B.C., after which Nebuchadnezzar carried him away bound to Babylon, along with thousands of others, including Ezekiel. Jehoiakim's son was allowed to rule as a vassal or puppet king of the Babylonians. His name was Jehoiachin. He reigned only three months, and then Nebuchadnezzar summoned him to Babylon along with "ten thousand captives, and all the craftsmen and smiths" (2 Kgs. 24:14), and his uncle Mattaniah began to reign. His name was changed to Zedekiah. Book of Mormon history begins in the first year of Zedekiah's reign, which, according to Bible chronology, was 598 or 597 B.C. The Book of Mormon designates the year of its beginning, and the first year of Zedekiah's reign, as 600 years before the coming of Christ into the world.

Lehi and his family were living *at* Jerusalem. (See 1 Ne. 1:4,7 and 2 Ne. 25:6.) The preposition "at" in this case could mean on, in, within, close by, or near. Lehi could have lived several miles away and still lived at Jerusalem. It is recorded at least 33 times throughout the Book of Mormon that Lehi and Nephi went out from "the *land* of Jerusalem." Any satellite towns or villages that surrounded larger population or political centers were regarded in ancient times as belonging to those larger centers. That Lehi and his family lived outside of Jerusalem proper is also evidenced in the account of the

19

sons' attempt to obtain the plates with their abandoned wealth: "We went down to the land of our inheritance, and we did gather together our gold, and our silver, and our precious things. And after we gathered these things together, we went up again unto the house of Laban." (1 Ne. 3:22-23.)[2]

Nephi wrote that "there came many prophets, prophesying unto the people that they must repent, or the great city Jerusalem must be destroyed." (1 Ne. 1:4.) Amos taught that the Lord God would do nothing "but he revealeth his secret unto his servants the prophets." (Amos 3:7.) The Lord always gives sufficient warning; "never hath any of them been destroyed save it were foretold them by the prophets of the Lord." (2 Ne. 25:9.) For such a dramatic and devastating destruction that was coming, the cast of prophets was indeed, as the Book of Mormon says, "many." Lehi, Jeremiah, Huldah, Zephaniah, Habukkuk, Ezekiel, and one Urijah of Kirjath-jearim (Jer. 26:20) were all contemporaries.

"And the Lord God of their fathers sent to them by his messengers, rising up betimes, and sending; because he had compassion on his people, and on his dwelling place: but they mocked the messengers of God, and despised his words, and misused his prophets, until the wrath of the Lord arose against his people, till there was no remedy." (2 Chr. 36:15-16.)

While Lehi was out teaching in the city, he prayed earnestly in behalf of his people. As he prayed he saw and was taught many things through a spiritual manifestation that caused his whole body to tremble. Perhaps he was physically exhausted by the spiritual work;[3] he cast himself upon his bed and was overcome by the Spirit. He saw a heavenly court full of brilliant beings. One of them handed Lehi a book with the judgment to be passed upon Jerusalem: death, destruction, and deportation to Babylon. As with former prophets, Lehi then went forth to declare boldly what he had seen and heard. He detailed in the ears of Jerusalem's citizens a lengthy catalog of their sins; the result was mockery, anger, and violence. That the city of Jerusalem was doomed to destruction could not have been such shocking news to the Jews, as other prophets had been saying the same—Jeremiah had been sounding that warning for nearly three decades already.

What could be so difficult about believing that people would be taken captive to Babylon when thousands had already been taken? It would seem that someone would now be ready to listen! But people do not like to hear about their sins, especially when they are enjoying them and have no inclination to change. Lehi's hearers wanted to remove his antagonizing, grating voice.

Another significant witness Lehi bore to his Jerusalem audience was of the coming of a Messiah, for "none of the prophets have written, nor prophesied, save they have spoken concerning this Christ." (Jacob 7:11; see also 3 Ne. 20:24.) John later exclaimed that "the testimony of Jesus is the spirit of prophecy" (Rev. 19:10); that is, testifying of Jesus is the essence of prophecy. Even six hundred years before He would come in the flesh, the people needed to know to whom they should look for their redemption.

Into the Wilderness

The Lord warned Lehi in a dream to take his family and depart into the wilderness. Why Lehi? What qualified this Judahite[4] to lead a colony of Israelites through the wilderness to a new Promised Land? There are hints in the scriptural record that Lehi was wealthy. (1 Ne. 2:4; 3:16, 22.) The Mediterranean world was alive with mercantile activity in this period of time, Syria/Palestine being the hub of sea and commerce, the place where continents and cultures come together. Caravans traversed Judah from all directions: side roads off the Coastal Highway and the King's Highway, the distant Frankincense Trail, pilgrims' highways and trade routes connecting Moab, Edom, and Arabia with Gaza and Egypt. Lehi could have been a trained and experienced caravaneer and trader. He knew what provisions to prepare and what route to take. Knowing how God has worked in other periods of history, it is not unlikely that he selected a man who, in addition to his spiritual maturity and responsiveness, was already adapted to the particular task at hand, in this case one acquainted with the rigors of desert travel and survival. Here again was the right man for the right time.[5]

Lehi and his family abandoned all unnecessary possessions and gathered together appropriate provisions for an indefinite period of travel in the desert. Besides the tents especially mentioned, they would need food, emergency water, extra clothing, bedding, cooking equipment and eating utensils, weapons, and pack animals, probably camels.

The word *wilderness* occurs over 300 times in the Book of Mormon and may at some later time in the western hemisphere refer to the thick forests or jungle, but not while in Judah and its neighboring deserts. Two Hebrew terms for wilderness are *midbar* and *jeshimon.* *Midbar* is generally land to the east of the central hills, east of the agricultural fields, out into the rain shadow, with a feeble vegetation. These are tracts for pasturing flocks. *Jeshimon* is the desolate wasteland beyond, where little rain falls. The Judean Desert through which Lehi and his family probably journeyed is at first *midbar* and then *jeshimon.* It is known scripturally as a place of flight and refuge. It is a frightening, foreboding place for the uninitiated.

In recent years, researchers have ventured to describe the route Lehi and family took from Jerusalem to the Red Sea. Sidney B. Sperry wrote as follows: "As for a route to the Red Sea, they had two choices: they could go either directly south of Jerusalem by the road through Hebron and Beersheba and thence through the great wilderness to the northern tip of what is now the gulf of Aquaba, or they could go directly east across the Jordan until they struck the ancient 'King's Highway' and then proceed south, or nearly so, until the Gulf of Aquaba was reached. Lehi probably used the western route."[6] Lynn and Hope Hilton expanded the possibilities to three: (1) eastward from Jerusalem through the Judean Wilderness to the plateau on the eastern side of the Rift Valley to the King's Highway; (2) from Jerusalem southward past Hebron and Beersheba and then eastward to join the Rift Valley, called the Arabah; or (3) straight east to the northern end of the Dead Sea, past Qumran, En Gedi, Masada, and on south to the Red Sea.

The Hiltons objected to the first option, the King's Highway, because of passage through foreign lands with border complications, taxes, and so on. They also saw the second option as improbable since the route remains in the hill country, near population centers, instead of entering the wilderness as the account says. The Hiltons therefore concluded that the third option was the likely route.[7]

During 1986-1987, accompanied by students and faculty from

various Brigham Young University study groups, I walked the full distance from Jerusalem to the Red Sea and formulated certain opinions about the route from firsthand experience. It also seems to me unlikely that they would have used the King's Highway, or that they would have journeyed straight southward through populated centers like Hebron and Beersheba. The account specifically points to immediate entry into the wilderness. The Hiltons' preference, east to the area of Qumran, then south, however, is also most unlikely, as the fault escarpment of the Rift Valley drops down sharply and dramatically to the waters of the Dead Sea and allowed no passage to the south. There was no evidence of a road along the northwestern shore of the Dead Sea until the Israelis cut and paved one in 1967.

A viable course for Lehi's journey is southeast out of Jerusalem toward Tekoa and then along an ancient road to En Gedi (called the cliff or ascent of Ziz in 2 Chr. 20:16), and thence southward through the Rift Valley, and Arabah. An alternate route could have been from Tekoa southward, passing between Juttah and Carmel, down into and across the eastern Negev to Mampsis, then eastward to the Arabah.

Having arrived at the shores of the Red Sea, Lehi and his party decided to continue on for another three days, after which they established camp "in a valley by the side of a river of water." (1 Ne. 2:6.) The phrase "river of water" seems redundant to Western ears, since we are accustomed to thinking of rivers as logically consisting only of water. In the Middle East, however, most rivers are not perennial, but are *wadis*, an Arabic word meaning a valley or wash that contains water only in the rainy season, for relatively few days of the year; usually a wadi is dry and sandy and quite passable for travel. If they pitched their tents in a wadi near a flowing stream, it may tell us something about what time of year it was, perhaps spring, the time of winter runoff.

Lehi built an altar of stones to make an offering and give thanks. It was an altar of unhewn stones as stipulated in Exodus 20:25. The wording is intentional, again showing the Book of Mormon to be translated from an ancient Semitic record. It was not a stone altar (which might allow for cut, fitted stones), but an altar of stones.[8] Lehi then began naming various geographical features around the camp. All hills, rock outcroppings, wadis, and other topographical details were and are given names in the Near East. The ancient Hebrew people loved imagery and figures of speech. The most powerful way to illustrate a truth was to find something in human nature or conduct that corresponded to something in nature. If only Laman could be like this river, continuously flowing toward the source of righteousness! The prophet Amos pled with northern Israelites to "let judgment run down as waters, and righteousness as a mighty [or everflowing] stream." (Amos 5:24.) The two prophets wished that their people would be more constant and stable in their devotion and loyalty to God and his purposes.

Lehi's Sons

First Nephi 2:11-19 gives us insights into the character of Lehi's four sons. Laman and Lemuel are portrayed as stubborn, hard-hearted, lovers of money, faithless, and spiritually weak. Nephi and Sam, on the other hand, are humble seekers of knowledge and of God, faithful, and obedient to parents. The latter two are exemplary, deserving of being emulated, which, since we all need role-models, is one of the main purposes for the painstaking inscribing done on the metal plates — to preserve for us in modern times patterns for our lives. President Heber J. Grant wrote: "I read the Book of Mormon as a young man and fell in love with Nephi more than any other character in profane or sacred history that I ever read, except the Savior of the world. No other individual has made such a strong impression upon me as did Nephi. He has been one of the guiding stars in my life."[9]

By way of further tribute to Nephi in particular, we observe that the marvel is not that some complained about the hardships in leaving all and journeying into the wilderness, but that others did not! Conditions were such that *anyone* could have murmured. Murmuring we may define as half-suppressed or muttered complaint, or grumbling, maybe not even openly critical, but, behind the scenes, disloyal. What was the reason for Nephi's amazing ability to press forward positively and not join in the grumbling and rebellion? "I, Nephi, being exceedingly young, nevertheless being large in stature, and also having great desires to know of the mysteries of God, wherefore,

I did cry unto the Lord; and behold he did visit me, and did soften my heart that I did believe all the words which had been spoken by my father; wherefore, I did not rebel against him like unto my brothers." (1 Ne. 2:16.)

Faith and faithfulness are always rewarded. "The Lord spake unto me, saying: Blessed art thou, Nephi, because of thy faith, for thou hast sought me diligently, with lowliness of heart." (1 Ne. 2:19.) Nephi was promised a new land, and rulership of it, and prosperity in it. Nephi and all the others were called upon to make a great sacrifice, to leave behind practically all they had known; but the Lord promised, despite the sacrifice of the moment, that they would eventually possess more and greater blessings. We of modern times struggle with that principle also. One of the most dangerous problems we face is wanting immediate gratification. Few people, it seems, believe in postponement—if we want something, we want it now. Adam and Eve sacrificed a pleasant existence in the Garden for something ultimately and infinitely better, though immediately harder. Abraham was called on to sacrifice one of his most precious possessions, his beloved son. Moses sacrificed prestige in a kingly court for the noble task of suffering the sands and complaints of Sinai. Elijah, Amos, Isaiah, Jeremiah, and all the other prophets sacrificed comfort and security to fulfill a difficult duty with eternal rewards. There seems to be a follow-up principle to sacrificing: Whenever we give something up or go without, we find ourselves in eventual possession of *more* and *greater*. During the tests of his faithfulness, Job lost almost everything he had; his story concludes, however, with a simple note that he was blessed in the end with more than he had in the beginning. Lehi's family sacrificed their possessions, their riches, to follow the old patriarch into the great Arabian desert and over the sea; but after their journey, they possessed a land of amazingly abundant wealth. The promises of the Lord to Lehi and to Nephi (as with our own patriarchal blessings) must have encouraged and sustained them through the sometimes bitter trials they had to endure along the way.

As Lehi and his family traveled through the Arabah and near the Red Sea, they must have been inspired by the example of the prophet-hero Moses, who led their ancestors through some of the same terrain to their promised land. Lehi's wilderness journeys were shorter in time but greater in distance.

Obtaining the Plates of Brass

The Lord commanded Lehi in a dream to send his sons back to Jerusalem for the plates of brass, then in the possession of an elder of the Jews named Laban. (1 Ne. 3:1-4.) Lehi and his family did not have their own copy of the scriptures (roughly equivalent to our Old Testament), and Lehi did not want his children growing up without them, so the brothers had to go back. We might ask at this point, why did the Lord wait until they were more than two hundred miles away from home to command Lehi to get the plates? Could not arrangements have been made for them before they left Jerusalem? One more test! The older brothers immediately protested, saying it was a hard thing. We usually suppose that their foremost excuse for not wanting to go was their fear of Laban; but there is no doubt that the distance and topography also had some bearing on their resistance. The Book of Mormon itself and most Book of Mormon commentaries say little, if anything, about the distance and terrain involved. Professor Hugh Nibley refers to the two return trips as "quick visits" and "quick trips," noting that "Lehi's sons made a flying trip back to Jerusalem."[10] This writer and accompanying friends learned by walking it that the distance between Jerusalem and the Red Sea is 200 miles. (Some authors insert a figure of 150 miles or so, "as the crow flies," but ancient Judahites were not crows and they didn't fly, and it was 200 miles to the Red Sea!) An agreeable pace for a group of people on camels would be between twenty and thirty miles a day. So the journey was a minimum of seven or eight days. Add to that the three days they traveled after reaching the Red Sea, and the figures are up to 260-290 miles in ten or eleven days. That is one direction only. The round-trip that the Lord and Father Lehi were asking of the four sons was over 500 miles and at least three weeks through some of the most rugged terrain in the Near East! And they had no clue as to how they were going to obtain the plates. (And we, having the advantage of "knowing the end from the beginning," are amazed to think ahead and realize that Lehi, soon after his sons returned from their first assignment, would command them to go back again! That is over a thousand miles and many weeks on those desolate tracts of land — and we have often looked down on Laman and Lemuel for being chronic complainers.)

Having already worked things out with the Lord, Nephi responded positively to the Lord's command. In one of the most inspiring outpourings of faith in all of scripture, Nephi assured his father that he would go and do the things the Lord had commanded because he knew that the Lord never gives a command without providing some way to fulfill it. (1 Ne. 3:7.)

The brothers set out with their tents to go *up* to the land of Jerusalem. Approaching Jerusalem from any wilderness requires an ascent in elevation. All the locative adverbs in the next pages of scripture accurately depict the topography of Judah and the deserts to the south. After Laman's attempt to talk Laban out of the plates, the brothers agreed to go *down* to the land of their inheritance (which suggests that their homestead was outside of the city proper), gather the gold, silver, and other valuable objects they had left behind, and offer them to Laban in exchange for the plates. They went *up* again to Laban's house in Jerusalem, and upon their failure to secure the plates by that means, they fled for their lives and hid in a cave ("cavity of a rock" — caves are numerous in the Judean hills and desert). Having exhausted their resources and their patience, Laman and Lemuel had some hard words for their younger brothers; they even resorted to physical violence until stopped by an angel. The angel again commanded them to go up and get the plates, saying that the Lord would deliver Laban into their hands. After all human effort was expended, the Lord himself would help them to accomplish the task. One more time they went *up* to Jerusalem.

Nephi drew some parallels with Moses. The great deliverer from Egypt was backed up with his people against a wall of water. He had no further human recourse so the Lord took over. If the Lord could deliver all those Israelites from Pharaoh, he could also deliver these Israelites from Laban. The four approached the walls of Jerusalem at night; Nephi wrote that he "crept into the city and went forth towards the house of Laban." (1 Ne. 4:5.) He had no plan in mind but was led by the Spirit. He found Laban lying drunk in the road, and the Spirit told him to kill Laban. Nephi, never having shed human blood, was repulsed by the idea.

The Spirit's counsel came again: The Lord delivered Nephi; it was in answer to a prayer; Laban was a thief and a murderer anyway; and there was a precedent of the Lord's slaying wicked people to accomplish his righteous purposes (the Flood, the conquest of Canaan, etc.; 1 Ne. 4:11-13). As Joseph Smith taught, "Whatever God requires is right."[11] It would be better for this one man to die than for an entire (future) nation to dwindle and perish in unbelief (which would happen without those records).[12] Nephi continued to reason that future generations would need the commandments on the plates, and the Lord had devised this method for Nephi to obtain them. Having reasoned this out, Nephi obeyed the Spirit and carried out the unpleasant job of dispatching Laban into the next world by cutting off his head. He then disguised himself and imitated Laban well enough to convince Laban's servant to open the treasury, get the plates, and follow Nephi outside the walls of the city. Along the way there was talk about what the elders of the Jews had been discussing that night, possibly including the delicate political turmoil in which they were enveloped. Nephi reassured his frightened brothers that he was not Laban. He also convinced Zoram that he could stay with them and be a free man, and he bound him with an oath to do so. Then the five set out *down* through the wilderness on the long journey back to the main camp. (1 Ne. 4:18-33.)

During the long weeks of her sons' absence, Sariah had mourned for them, thinking that the worst had probably happened. She complained against her husband, telling him that he was a visionary man; they had lost their home, then lost their sons, and were now going to lose their own lives. The normal response to accusation is defense and counter-accusation. Lehi, however, responded to Sariah's complaint with comfort. When people complain, they often need comfort. Lehi's faith was Sariah's comfort. He had been promised that his sons would return, and he believed the promise. (1 Ne. 5:1-7.)

When the sons returned, the family rejoiced and gave thanks by offering up burnt offerings; then everyone's attention turned to examining their new treasure, the plates of brass.

Contents of the Plates of Brass

The plates that Lehi's sons had obtained at the peril of their lives would prove of inestimable value to prophets, historians, and numberless righteous people for a thousand years. Lehi and Nephi found them "of great worth . . . , insomuch that [they] could preserve the commandments of the Lord unto [their] children." (1 Ne. 5:21.) The brass plates were preserved for the Nephites just as the Book of Mormon was preserved for us. Not only that, but Lehi prophesied that "these plates of brass should go forth unto all nations, kindreds, tongues, and people" who were of his seed. He further prophesied "that these plates of brass should never perish." (1 Ne. 5:18-19.)

As Lehi's family and Zoram scrutinized the plates in their tent-camp on the shores of the Red Sea, they learned that they contained the five books of Moses (1 Ne. 5:11), including an account of the creation of the world, and of Adam and Eve. These five books presumably correspond to Genesis, Exodus, Leviticus, Numbers, and Deuteronomy in modern Bibles.

In addition to the five books of Moses, the brass plates also contained a record of the Jews and the prophecies of the holy prophets from the beginning down to the commencement of the reign of Zedekiah, even prophecies that had been spoken by Jeremiah. Laban was also a descendant of Joseph, as was Lehi. (1 Ne. 5:12-16.) Either he or some scribal assistants had been interested in recording two decades of Jeremiah's prophecies.

We know from later writings that it was not easy inscribing on metal plates. Nephi explained why he worked at it so earnestly: "The fulness of mine intent is that I may persuade men to come unto the God of Abraham, and the God of Isaac, and the God of Jacob, and be saved." (1 Ne. 6:4.) He later added: "We labor diligently to write, to persuade our children, and also our brethren, to believe in Christ. . . . We prophesy of Christ, and we write according to our prophecies, that our children may know to what source they may look for a remission of their sins." (2 Ne. 25:23, 26.) Nephi followed the example of the great patriarch Abraham, who noted in his own writings: "I shall endeavor to write some of these things upon this record, for the benefit of my posterity that shall come after me." (Abr. 1:31.)

The Family of Ishmael

Now Lehi had another revelation: the sons must go back to the land of Jerusalem once again! We repeat the query of the previous episode: Could not the Lord have arranged somehow for Ishmael's family to accompany the others into the wilderness on one of the two prior journeys? We have to repeat also the answer: Yet another test! But the record does not say that they murmured about having to return for their future brides; that was a fairer proposal—bringing marriageable women into the growing colony was apparently worth the aching bones and muscles of an additional long journey.

We might wonder how another family, without direct revelation from the Lord, would be so willing to abandon their home and all they had known to join these refugees in the wilderness. We can only surmise from the record of Nephi that Ishmael believed the words of the Lord that Jerusalem would soon be destroyed by the enemy armies who already occupied the city. Besides, Lehi's sons had quite a story to tell about how an angel had appeared and how the Lord had miraculously made it possible to secure their genealogical and scriptural records. The one reason given in Nephi's account for the family's willingness to go was that "the Lord did soften the heart of Ishmael, and also his household, insomuch that they took their journey with us down into the wilderness." (1 Ne. 7:5.)

Our tradition that Ishmael's ancestry went back to Ephraim, son of Joseph, is based on a discourse given by Elder Erastus Snow, in Logan, Utah, on May 6, 1882. He said, "The prophet Joseph informed us that the record of Lehi was contained on the 116 pages that were first translated and subsequently stolen, and of which an abridgment is given us in the First Book of Nephi, which is the record of Nephi individually, he himself being of the lineage of Manasseh; but that Ishmael was of the lineage of Ephraim, and that his sons married into Lehi's family, and Lehi's sons married Ishmael's daughters."[13]

From the above quotation and from 1 Nephi 7:6 we may propose that two of Ishmael's sons had married daughters of Lehi and Sariah. That would mean the two families were already related by marriage, which might explain Lehi's seeming nonchalance about instructing his sons to bring Ishmael's family down into the wilderness. There might already have been marriage plans between the two families — only the setting for the ceremonies would now have to change from the city to the desert. Another reason why Ishmael's family in particular was elected to join Lehi's was that Ishmael's had five unmarried daughters; the four sons of Lehi along with Zoram would in time marry Ishmael's daughters — a perfect five-way match set up in advance by the Lord.

The final journey from Jerusalem to the Red Sea was not without the usual friction, and even open conflict, between Nephi and his elder brothers. Laman and Lemuel again vented their anger on Nephi to the point of physical violence, and they were finally pacified only by the pleading of some of Ishmael's family. Their hearts were actually softened enough that they bowed down and asked Nephi's forgiveness. The greatness of Nephi's soul is again revealed in his terse summation of the episode: "I did frankly forgive them all that they had done." (1 Ne. 7:21.)

The Lord had now warned at least eighteen people to flee from the wrath to come over Jerusalem: Lehi, Sariah, Laman, Lemuel, Sam, Nephi, Zoram, Ishmael, his wife, five daughters, and two sons with their wives. (We do not know, but there may also have been children from the latter four.)

Two Reasons for Two Journeys

In some ways it must have been a sacrifice for Lehi and his family to leave Jerusalem, but their lives were spared by doing so. What about the other two trips? Besides the inevitable lesson that would come from submission and obedience to the will of God, to learn to respond no matter what the command and the conditions, what good reasons were there for commanding four men to trek a thousand miles through the inhospitable desert? The main reasons were two: records — of ancestry and prophecy — and marriages — posterity. What they were doing then was tied to the past as well as the future. They needed to preserve the knowledge and memory of one nation while producing with their wives another, that the covenants of the Lord would be fulfilled.

NOTES

1. See S. Kent Brown, "Lehi's Personal Record: Quest for a Missing Source," *BYU Studies* 24.1 (Winter 1984): 19-42.

2. For additional details see D. Kelly Ogden, "Why Does the Book of Mormon Say that Jesus Would Be Born in Jerusalem?" in *Ensign*, August 1984, pp. 51-52. See also Ian W.J. Hopkins, "The 'Daughters of Judah' Are Really Rural Satellites of an Urban Center," *Biblical Archeology Review*, September/October, 1980, pp. 44-45.

3. Spiritual work can be physically enervating: "I am full of the Spirit of God, insomuch that my frame has no strength." (1 Ne. 17:47.) "I have workings in the spirit, which doth weary me even that all my joints are weak." (1 Ne. 19:20.) "Ammon . . . was swallowed up in the joy of his God, even to the exhausting of his strength; and he fell again to the earth." (Alma 27:17.) "I was left alone, and saw this great vision, and there remained no strength in me." (Dan. 10:8.) "And the presence of God withdrew from Moses . . . and Moses was left unto himself. And as he was left unto himself, he fell unto the earth. And it came to pass that it was for the space of many hours before Moses did again receive his natural strength like unto man." (Moses 1:9-10.)

4. Lehi learned that he was a descendant of Joseph. But living in the kingdom of Judah, he was a Jew by nationality. We know that with Jeroboam's religious excesses in the North, righteous people from various tribes migrated to the southern kingdom. Especially with the fall of Israel in 721 B.C. did members of the other tribes take up residence in the land of Jerusalem. First Chronicles 9:3 adds: "In Jerusalem dwelt of the children of Judah, and of the children of Benjamin, and of the children of Ephraim, and Manasseh." Lehi, Laban, and Ishmael were all from the Joseph tribes.

5. For more insights into Lehi's qualifications and connections, see Hugh Nibley, *An Approach to the Book of Mormon*, 2nd ed. (Salt Lake City: Deseret Book Company, 1976), chapters 5 through 7, entitled "Lehi's Affairs." 1. "The Jews and the Caravan Trade." 2. "Lehi and the Arabs." and 3. "Dealings with Egypt."

6. Sidney B Sperry, *Book of Mormon Compendium* (Salt Lake City: Bookcraft, 1968), pp. 97-98.

7. Lynn and Hope Hilton, *In Search of Lehi's Trail* (Salt Lake City: Deseret Book Company, 1976), p. 38.

8. The form "altar of stones" instead of the customary English form "stone altar" conforms to standard Hebrew construction, called the "construct state." Examples from the Bible are "gods of gold" (Ex. 20:23), "altar

of stone" (Ex. 20:25), "bedstead of iron" (Deut. 3:11), "helmet of brass" (1 Sam. 17:5), "house of cedar" (2 Sam. 7:2), "throne of ivory" (1 Kgs. 10:18), "girdle of leather" (2 Kgs. 1:8), and "pulpit of wood" (Neh. 8:4). Other examples from the Book of Mormon include: "land of promise," "skin of blackness," "rod of iron," and "yoke of iron."

9. Heber J. Grant, *Improvement Era*, September 1941, p. 524.

10. *An Approach to the Book of Mormon*, pp. 87-88, and *Lehi in the Desert* (Salt Lake City: Bookcraft, 1952), p. 63.

11. *Teachings of the Prophet Joseph Smith*, selected by Joseph Fielding Smith (Salt Lake City: Deseret Book Company, 1938), pp. 255-56.

12. Compare the warning of Alma to Korihor: "Behold, it is better that thy soul should be lost than that thou shouldst be the means of bringing many souls down to destruction." (Alma 30:47.)

13. *Journal of Discourses* 23:184.

4

THE TREE OF LIFE AND THE MINISTRY OF CHRIST
(1 Nephi 8-11, 15)

Kent P. Jackson

When Martin Harris lost Joseph Smith's translation from the book of Lehi, contained on the first 116 pages of the Book of Mormon manuscript, the Prophet deeply regretted the loss. Not only was the divinely provided translation gone, but Joseph Smith felt the weight of an enormous burden of personal guilt as well.[1] While the loss and potential falsification of the manuscript was a serious situation (see D&C 3; 10:1-26), still the Lord had provided a solution for it.

The ninth chapter of 1 Nephi is an editorial note that Nephi inserted into his account of some significant doctrinal revelation. It explains the plates upon which the record was written. Nephi reported that on a smaller set of plates, which eventually would contain 1 Nephi to Omni, and possibly the Words of Mormon, he would record "the ministry of [his] people." (1 Ne. 9:3.) On larger plates he would record "the reign of the kings, and the wars and contentions of [his] people." (1 Ne. 9:4.)[2] The visions and revelations preserved in 1 Nephi were recorded on Nephi's small plates. These, including the great visionary material to be discussed in this chapter, are among the greatest contributions of the Book of Mormon.

Kent P. Jackson is associate professor of ancient scripture and Old Testament area coordinator at Brigham Young University.

The Visions of Lehi and Nephi

As Lehi and his family were preparing for their travels to the land that God had promised them, the Lord gave Lehi one of the most significant and well-known visions ever recorded. Chapter 8 of 1 Nephi contains Nephi's record of his father's vision of the dark and dreary waste, the tree of life and its precious fruit, the rod of iron and the path through the darkness, and the great and spacious building to which some apostatized.

Nephi, exercising faith in the Lord, desired to witness the things his father had seen. In response to his desire, he was "caught away" to "an exceedingly high mountain" (1 Ne. 11:1), where he was shown an impressive vision. Nephi saw what had been revealed to his father (1 Ne. 14:29), and he was also shown the interpretation of several of the major symbols of the vision, which he later recorded. Lehi's vision in 1 Nephi 8 is greatly clarified by the information gained from his son's experiences recorded in subsequent chapters. Nephi's vision provides the interpretation of the following:

1. The tree (1 Ne. 8:10-12): "the love of God, which sheddeth itself abroad in the hearts of the children of men." (1 Ne. 11:22; see also 15:22, 36.)

2. The fountain of living waters: "the love of God." (1 Ne. 11:25.)

3. The rod of iron (1 Ne. 8:19, 24, 30): "the word of God." (1 Ne. 11:25; see also 15:24.)

4. The mists of darkness (1 Ne. 8:23-24): "the temptations of the devil." (1 Ne. 12:17.)

5. The large and spacious building (1 Ne. 8:26-27, 31, 33): "the world and the wisdom thereof" (1 Ne. 11:35); "the pride of the world" (1 Ne. 11:36); "vain imaginations and the pride of the children of men" (1 Ne. 12:18).

6. The river of filthy water (1 Ne. 8:13-14, 32): "the depths of hell" (1 Ne. 12:16; see also 15:29); "filthiness" (1 Ne. 15:27); "an awful gulf, which separated the wicked from the tree of life, and also from the saints of God." (1 Ne. 15:28).

Nephi's vision consisted of much more than the scene of the tree of life and the efforts of some to obtain its fruits. That scene provided the setting and the backdrop for an even greater set of revelations —

an expanded prophecy of the future: the coming of Christ and his atoning mission, the future of Lehi's descendants, the restoration of the gospel in the last days, and the ongoing struggle between the forces of evil and righteousness. These revelations unfolded to Nephi great events of the future and used symbols from the vision of the tree of life to clarify events. They focus on Christ and his work and present the messages of the gospel that make the Book of Mormon indispensible as a witness for Jesus Christ. With the visions of the future interwoven into the tree of life scenes, Nephi's record in 1 Nephi 11-15 is one of the great revelatory and literary masterpieces of all time. This chapter will focus on a most important part of his vision: the vision of the mission of Christ. The following chapter will discuss Nephi's vision of Lehi's descendants and the Gentiles in later times, as revealed in 1 Nephi 12-13.[3]

The Coming Messiah

Through revelation, both Lehi and Nephi learned much about the mission of Christ. What was revealed to them was of great significance for their people in later generations. The information concerning the Savior that was revealed to Lehi, Nephi, and Jacob during the early years of their ministries, along with information concerning Christ found on the brass plates (see 1 Ne. 19), formed the foundation for later Nephite and Lamanite belief in Christ's mortal works. (See also 1 Ne. 10:4-5, 11; 19:8, 10; 2 Ne. 10:3; 25:19.)[4] Sadly, as the subsequent history in the book attests, not all Book of Mormon people believed their message, and a knowledge of the coming of Christ and a belief in him was not universally shared among them. (See, for example, Jacob 7:7, 9; Alma 30:6, 12-17, 22-27; 31:15-17.)

The visions of Lehi and Nephi included revelation concerning the Lord's mortal coming in Palestine as well as his glorified appearance in America. The information provided in chapters 10 and 11 gives a good overview of the Savior's ministry and provides confirming testimony to the accounts of Christ's life and message found in the Gospels. As such, the Book of Mormon fulfills one of its major roles as a witness to the Bible, "proving to the world that the holy scriptures are true." (D&C 20:11.) Among other things, Nephi's account of the visions tells us the following about Christ's mortal works:[5]

1. Jesus would be the Messiah, Savior of the world. (1 Ne. 10:4.)

2. All are lost, and none can be saved except through him. (1 Ne. 10:6.)

3. He would come six hundred years after Lehi's time. (1 Ne. 10:4.)

4. He would be the Son of God, born of Mary. (1 Ne. 11:13-21.)

5. John the Baptist would prepare the way for Christ's coming. (1 Ne. 10: 7-9.)

6. Jesus would be baptized by John. (1 Ne. 10:9; 11:27.)

7. Jesus would minister among men, performing great miracles. (1 Ne. 11:24, 28, 31.)

8. The twelve apostles would follow Christ. (1 Ne. 11:29.)

9. Jesus would be judged and slain by the Jews; he would rise from the dead. (1 Ne. 10:11; 11:32-33.)

Because of these and other things that were revealed concerning Jesus, the Book of Mormon people who looked forward in faith to his coming were Christians. Their record, therefore, is "Another Testament of Jesus Christ."

Nephi's revelation in 1 Nephi 11 contains not only a beautiful discussion of the mortal mission of Christ, the tree of life, the iron rod, and other things that his father had seen, but it also teaches significant gospel doctrine concerning both the Father and the Son. This vision, shown to Nephi by a heavenly messenger, uses striking symbols or images. Readers sometimes do not look beyond the surface of those images to learn what tremendous gospel truths this chapter contains. While the tree of life and the iron rod symbolize the love of God and his word that leads us to it, they also teach us of our ultimate goal of eternal life with the Father through the work and word of the Son. In this revelation, the messenger often gave Nephi a simple explanation of a symbol and then opened a vision that gave its fuller message. Through this means, the Lord tutored Nephi concerning the divine mission of the Savior. The following is a possible application of two of the major symbols:

Symbol	Message
Tree of Life = The Love of God	Eternal life in the presence of the Father
Rod of Iron = The Word of God	Christ and his gospel are the only means by which we can attain the presence of the Father

A focus of the vision is the sacred concept which the messenger called "the condescension of God." (1 Ne. 11:16.) "To condescend" means "to descend to the level of another"; "to descend from the privileges of superior rank or dignity, to do some act to an inferior, which strict justice or the ordinary rules of civility do not require. Hence, to submit or yield, as to an inferior, implying an occasional relinquishment of distinction."[6] As we shall see, the "condescension of God" has two profound implications—the condescension of the Father and the condescension of the Son.

The Condescension of the Father

Elder Bruce R. McConkie taught: "The condescension of God (meaning the Father) consists in the fact that though he is an exalted, perfected, glorified Personage, he became the personal and literal Father of a mortal Offspring born of mortal woman."[7] With this fact in mind, we can see why the messenger caused Nephi to see a vision of *Mary* to prepare him for the question, "Knowest thou the condescension of God?" (See 1 Ne. 11:13-17.) In the verses that follow, the messenger *showed* Nephi concerning the condescension of God, rather than simply telling him about it:

"He said unto me: Knowest thou the condescension of God? And I said unto him: I know that he loveth his children; nevertheless, I do not know the meaning of all things. And he said unto me: Behold, the virgin whom thou seest is the mother of the Son of God, after the manner of the flesh. And it came to pass that I beheld that she was carried away in the Spirit; and after she had been carried away in the Spirit for the space of a time the angel spake unto me, saying: Look! And I looked and beheld the virgin again, bearing a child in her arms. And the angel said unto me: Behold the Lamb of God, yea, even the son of the Eternal Father!" (1 Ne. 11:16-21.)

President Ezra Taft Benson has written concerning this aspect of the condescension of God the Father:

> The most fundamental doctrine of true Christianity is the divine birth of the child Jesus. This doctrine is not generally comprehended by the world. The paternity of Jesus Christ is one of the "mysteries of godliness" comprehended only by the spiritually-minded. . . .
>
> The testimonies of appointed witnesses leave no question as to the paternity of Jesus Christ. God was the Father of Jesus' mortal tabernacle, and Mary, a mortal woman, was His mother. He is therefore the only person born who rightfully deserves the title "the *Only* Begotten Son of God."[8]

After Nephi was shown "the Son of the Eternal Father," he was asked: "Knowest thou the meaning of the tree which thy father saw?" (1 Ne. 11:21.) Nephi answered: "Yea, it is the love of God, which sheddeth itself abroad in the hearts of the children of men; wherefore, it is the most desirable above all things." (1 Ne. 11:22; see also 11:25; 15:36; D&C 14:7.)

John taught: "For God so loved the world, that he gave his only begotten Son, that whosoever believeth in him should not perish, but have everlasting life." (John 3:16.) God's sending of his only begotten Son, so we can obtain eternal life, is the great expression of his love for us. Nephi was shown in vision the means by which we can obtain that goal: 1 Nephi 11:24: "I looked, and I beheld the son of God going forth among the children of men; and I saw many fall down at his feet and worship." Verse 25: "And it came to pass that I beheld that the rod of iron, which my father had seen, was the word of God, which led to the fountain of living waters, or to the tree of life." Verse 24, which describes Jesus' ministry among men, gives perspective and meaning to verse 25, which describes the iron rod leading to the source of eternal life: as the Father provided the iron rod to lead the people in the vision to the tree, he has provided for us a Savior, Jesus Christ, to lead us to life eternal.

The rod of iron is the word of God—the gospel plan, the scriptures, the words of living prophets. These are all called "the word of God" because they manifest the will of God. (See JST John 1:1.) In the scriptures Jesus Christ is also called the "Word of God" (Rev. 19:13; see also Moses 1:32; John 1:1-5, 10-14), because he is the living embodiment of the Father's will. The word that proceeds from him, in the scriptures and in the words of living prophets, is but an extension of his character and divine attributes.

In Lehi's dream, there was no way to get through the mists of darkness to obtain the goal of the tree without grasping and following the rod of iron. The scriptures clearly show that in our own pursuit of heavenly goals, we can overcome life's trials and temptations to obtain eternal life only through Christ. (See Acts 4:12; 1 Ne. 8:21-24; 10:6; John 14:6.) Jesus said, "I am the way, the truth, and the life: no man cometh unto the Father, but by me." (John 14:6.)

The Condescension of the Son

Nephi's guide next emphasized another aspect of the condescension of God by showing him rather than telling him what that condescension means:

> The angel said unto me . . . : Look and behold the condescension of God! And I looked and beheld the Redeemer of the world, of whom my father had spoken. . . . And I beheld that he went forth ministering unto the people, in power and great glory; and the multitudes were gathered together to hear him; and I beheld that they cast him out from among them. . . .
>
> And he spake unto me again, saying: Look! And I looked, and I beheld the Lamb of God going forth among the children of men. And I beheld multitudes of people who were sick, and who were afflicted with all manner of diseases, and with devils and unclean spirits; and the angel spake and showed all these things unto me. And they were healed by the power of the Lamb of God; and the devils and the unclean spirits were cast out.
>
> And it came to pass that the angel spake unto me again, saying: Look! And I looked and beheld the Lamb of God, that he was taken by the people; yea, the Son of the everlasting

God was judged of the world; and I saw and bear record. And I, Nephi, saw that he was lifted up upon the cross and slain for the sins of the world. (1 Ne. 11:26-28, 31-33.)

The condescension of God includes the condescension of Jehovah, Christ, the God of the world, who came down from his divine station to become flesh, to minister in mortality, and to suffer and die for the sins of the world. Concerning the Savior, King Benjamin taught:

> Behold, the time cometh, and is not far distant, that with power, *the Lord Omnipotent who reigneth, who was, and is from all eternity to all eternity, shall come down from heaven among the children of men, and shall dwell in a tabernacle of clay*, and shall go forth amongst men, working mighty miracles, such as healing the sick, raising the dead, causing the lame to walk, the blind to receive their sight, and the deaf to hear, and curing all manner of diseases. . . . And lo, he shall suffer temptations, and pain of body, hunger, thirst, and fatigue, even more than man can suffer, except it be unto death; for behold, blood cometh from every pore, so great shall be his anguish for the wickedness and the abominations of his people.
>
> And he shall be called Jesus Christ, *the Son of God, the Father of heaven and earth, the Creator of all things from the beginning;* and his mother shall be called Mary. . . . And even after all this they shall consider him a man, and say that he hath a devil, and shall scourge him, and shall crucify him. (Mosiah 3:5, 7-9, italics added; see also 1 Ne. 19:10; 2 Ne. 9:5; Alma 7:10-13.)

Elder Bruce R. McConkie wrote: "The condescension of God (meaning the Son) consists in the fact that though he himself is the Lord Omnipotent, the very Being who created the earth and all things in it, yet being born of mortal woman, he submitted to all the trials of mortality, suffering 'temptations, and pain of body, hunger, thirst, and fatigue, even more than man can suffer, except it be unto death' (Mosiah 3:5-8), finally being put to death in a most ignominious manner."[9]

The visions of Lehi and Nephi are a powerful testimony to the atoning mission of Jesus in mortality. But they testify of much more. The Book of Mormon, "Another Testament of Jesus Christ," bears solemn witness that he who was born of humble circumstances to Mary is in fact "the Lord Omnipotent who reigneth, who was, and is from all eternity to all eternity, ... the Father of heaven and earth, the Creator of all things from the beginning" (Mosiah 3:5, 8), "the God of our fathers, ... the God of Abraham, and of Isaac, and the God of Jacob" (1 Ne. 19:10), "the very Eternal Father of heaven and of earth, and all things which in them are; ... the beginning and the end, the first and the last" (Alma 11:39), "the ETERNAL GOD." (Title Page.) Being the Father's Agent in the governance of the universe, he into whose hands the Father has given all power, Christ and his atoning work also stand as the means by which we can obtain our goal of partaking of the tree of eternal life.

Latter-day Saints can see a profound application in the visions that were witnessed by Lehi and Nephi. The only way we can return to the Father is to grasp the iron rod—the word of God, the gospel of Jesus Christ. Only in living "by every word that proceedeth out of the mouth of God" (Matt. 4:4) can we obtain the glorious reward, "the love of God, which ... is the most desirable above all things." (1 Ne. 11:22.)

NOTES

1. Joseph Smith, *History of The Church of Jesus Christ of Latter-day Saints*, 7 vols., 2nd ed. rev., edited by B. H. Roberts (Salt Lake City: The Church of Jesus Christ of Latter-day Saints, 1932-51), 1:21-22; Lucy Mack Smith, *History of the Prophet Joseph Smith* (Salt Lake City: Bookcraft, 1979), pp. 128-29.

2. For a discussion of the nature and origin of the various plates used in the formation of the Book of Mormon, see Eldin Ricks, *Story of the Formation of the Book of Mormon Plates* (Salt Lake City: Olympus Publishing Co., 1966).

3. For information on Nephi's vision of the future, particularly concerning the Gentiles, see Robert E. Parsons, "The Great and Abominable Church," chapter 5 in this volume.

4. For a fuller discussion of the revelation of Christianity to Lehi and his sons, see Kent P. Jackson, "The Beginnings of Christianity in the Book of Mormon," in *First Annual Book of Mormon Symposium*, ed. Paul R. Cheesman (Provo, Utah: Brigham Young University Religious Studies Center). See also Robert E. Parsons, " The Prophecies of the Prophets," in *Second Annual Book of Mormon Symposium: First Nephi*, ed. Monte S. Nyman (Provo, Utah: Brigham Young University, Religious Studies Center).

5. In these accounts in 1 Nephi 10-11, the term *apostles* and the names *Jesus, Mary*, and *John* are not used. The identities are obvious to those familiar with the New Testament.

6. Noah Webster, *Dictionary of the American Language* (1828).

7. *Mormon Doctrine*, 2nd. ed. (Salt Lake City: Bookcraft, 1962), p. 155.

8. *Come unto Christ* (Salt Lake City, Deseret Book Company, 1983), pp. 2-3.

9. *Mormon Doctrine*, p. 155.

5

THE GREAT AND ABOMINABLE CHURCH
(1 Nephi 12-14)

ROBERT E. PARSONS

When Nephi was shown his father's vision of the tree of life, he was also shown future world events that Lehi's dream helped explain. For instance, as recorded in 1 Nephi 11, he saw the future New Testament scene and learned of the condescension of God. He saw the baptism, ministry, and crucifixion of the Lamb of God and the multitudes of the earth gathered against the twelve apostles. The angel taught Nephi that the tree of life was a representation of the love of God and tied the condescension of God and the life of the Savior to this symbol. The angel also taught Nephi that the multitudes who fought against the twelve apostles represented the wisdom of the world, represented by the great and spacious building. In 1 Nephi 12 Nephi saw the future Nephite and Lamanite scene in the land of promise. He beheld the righteousness, iniquity, and downfall of Lehi's descendants and the loathsome and filthy state of those who dwindled in unbelief. The symbols of the "mists of darkness" and the "great and spacious building" were used to show how the Nephites were overcome with pride and the temptation of the devil. With an understanding of the mission of Christ in the Holy Land, and with a seeric view of the future of his own people in the promised land to which they would be led, Nephi was prepared for the following

---

Robert E. Parsons is associate professor of ancient scripture at Brigham Young University.

scenes—the Dark Ages in Europe, the restoration of the gospel in America, and the end of the world. This chapter will concentrate on the concepts taught in chapters 13-14, particularly as they relate to the Great and Abominable Church.

When Adam was placed on the earth, the kingdom or church of God was also established. "In relation to the kingdom of God," Joseph Smith said, "the devil always sets up his kingdom at the very same time in opposition to God."[1] "And since the kingdom of God or true church has been on earth from age to age, so also has the kingdom of the devil or the church of the devil."[2] The kingdom of God consists of priesthood, organization, and teachings. It becomes immediately apparent if one examines the church or kingdom of God at specific periods in world history, that at each point the church or kingdom contained priesthood, organization, and teachings. However, it is also apparent that these kingdoms differed from time to time in the specifics of these three things. Adam's priesthood organization was patriarchal. As far as we know, he did not have a First Presidency, Quorum of the Twelve, Relief Society, or Primary, but he had the Kingdom. Similarly the kingdom of God organized in the days of Enoch, Abraham, and the Nephites had its unique features with each group of people. When God established his kingdom, the devil established his. The Book of Moses speaks of secret combinations and Master Mahan as part of the devil's kingdom in the days of Adam. (Moses 5:29-31.) No doubt his kingdom or church was organized with priestcraft instead of priesthood, an organization to suit the times, and teachings consisting of untruths mingled with scripture to deceive the people. If one were to look at the kingdom of the devil in other ages (those of Noah, Abraham, Nephi, and so on) one would find the kingdom organized similarly but not exactly the same in each period of time. This is important to understand, since 1 Nephi 13 is concerned with the church or kingdom of the devil as it was organized in a certain geographical area of the world during a certain time.

The Great and Abominable Church of 1 Nephi 13

The geographical area that Nephi beheld in 1 Nephi 13 is described as "many nations and kingdoms" (v. 2) and "the nations and

45

kingdoms of the Gentiles" (v. 3). He was shown that the great and abominable church was formed among these nations of the Gentiles (v. 4). In verse 10 Nephi learned that the many waters divided the Gentiles that he beheld from the descendents of his brethren (the Lamanites). In verse 12 he specified that the seed of his brethren were in the promised land, which is identified over and over in the Book of Mormon as the Americas. Since the Gentiles were across the waters from the promised land, this just leaves the problem of identifying whether they were West or East. This is taken care of in verse 12, where we learn that a man, Columbus, who was among the Gentiles, had the Spirit of God come down upon him and went forth upon the waters to the promised land.

It was Christopher Columbus whom he saw, and he observed further that the discoverer was guided by divine power on his journey.

Go to any public library, read almost any detailed biography of the discoverer, and it becomes immediately clear that he felt himself an inspired man, sent of heaven to make the voyage. For example, *Christopher, Don Quixote of the Seas*, written in German by Jacob Wassermann and translated into English by Eric Sutton, tells the story very well:

"From my first youth onward, I was a seaman and have so continued until this day. . . . Wherever on the earth a ship has been, I have been. I have spoken and treated with learned men, priests, and laymen, Latins and Greeks, Jews and Moors, and with many men of other faiths. The Lord was well disposed to my desire, and He bestowed upon me courage and understanding; knowledge of seafaring He gave me in abundance, of astrology as much as was needed, and of geometry and astronomy likewise. Further, He gave me joy and cunning in drawing maps and thereon cities, mountains, rivers, islands, and harbors, each one in its place. I have seen and truly I have studied all books — cosmographies, which our Lord unlocked my mind, sent me upon the sea, and gave me fire for the deed. Those who heard of my enterprise called it foolish, mocked me, and laughed. But who can doubt that the Holy Ghost inspired me?"[3]

We know that Columbus made his journey from Europe to America by sailing west. Since Columbus was "among the Gentiles," it is obvious that Europe was part of the "nations of the Gentiles" that Nephi saw, but since he saw "many nations and kingdoms," his view could well have included Asia Minor, the Middle East, and all of the Mediterranean area. We are concerned with this point since we learned earlier that the church of the devil was organized among the nations of the Gentiles, or, as now shown, in lands across the waters and east of the promised land.

Following this line of reasoning, many members of the Church have identified to themselves what this great and abominable church was. We should emphasize at this point that The Church of Jesus Christ of Latter-day Saints has not officially identified the great and abominable church. We are left to our own supposition and conclusion. If a person identifies it as one church in Europe, that is his personal opinion. If another person identifies it as all churches in Europe and Asia Minor except the true, restored church, that is his opinion. And if another wishes to define it as all organizations in Europe, Asia Minor, and the Middle East through which the devil operated, that is his opinion. The scriptures are before us to study, but in the absence of an official declaration from the Church, our conclusions remain our private views and should not be taught as Church doctrine.

As one studies chapter 13, one should be more concerned with what the great and abominable church did than with who or what the great and abominable church was. Beginning in verse 20, the angel showed Nephi a book (the Bible) being carried forth among the Gentiles of the promised land. Since the Bible had not been written in 600 B.C., it is not surprising that when the angel asked Nephi if he knew the meaning of the book, he responded with a no. The angel then told him, "[It] is a record of the Jews, which contains the covenants of the Lord . . . and it also containeth many of the prophecies of the holy prophets; and it is a record like unto . . . the plates of brass, save there are not so many." (1 Ne. 13:23.) This would be understandable to Nephi, for he had a good knowledge of what was on the brass plates. For us it is important to understand that the brass plates are a more complete record of the history and prophecies of the Jews than what has been retained in our current Old Testament. We can look forward with eagerness and anticipation to receiving this ancient record, for Lehi prophesied that "these plates of brass should go forth unto all nations, kindreds, tongues, and people who were of his seed. Wherefore, he said that these plates of brass should never perish; neither should they be dimmed any more by time. And he prophesied many things concerning his seed." (1 Ne. 5:18-19.)

The angel continued to give Nephi valuable information about the Bible, which culminated in Nephi's assignment to begin the record we call the Book of Mormon. In 1 Nephi 13:24 the angel told Nephi that when the "book [the Bible] proceeded from the mouth of a Jew it contained the fulness of the gospel of the Lord." We are left to our own interpretation as to what is meant by "the mouth of a Jew." Some early church writers felt that this had to do with Ezra's collection of scripture and his reading it to the Jews (hence it proceeded forth from his mouth).

For example, in their *Commentary on the Book of Mormon,* George Reynolds and Janne Sjodahl wrote:

> The prophet is here [1 Nephi 13:32] speaking on the Old Testament, as it was to appear through the labors of Ezra and his associates and successors. Ezra undertook the work of collecting all the sacred writings that existed at his time. This work included not only the discovery of copies in various places, the rejection of those that were not authentic and the copying of manuscripts the contents of which could not otherwise be secured, but also the correction of the text, after careful examination of the variations that must have been found. It was this work that was shown to Nephi in his vision of the Old Testament, and therefore, he, very properly, says he beheld it coming "out of the mouth of a Jew."[4]

If we accept this meaning of "proceeded forth from the mouth of a Jew," we would have to accept the idea that Ezra's collection of writings more nearly approached what was in the brass plates than the writings now contained in our Old Testament, since the angel also told Nephi that the book contained the fulness of the gospel.

The fulness of the gospel of necessity would include a correct understanding of the creation, the fall, the atonement, and the principles of faith, repentance, baptism, and the Holy Ghost. All of these are essential for one to enter the celestial kingdom, and the fulness of the gospel prepares and qualifies one to enter that kingdom. Since the Pearl of Great Price and the Joseph Smith Translation of the Bible make it abundantly clear that much has been lost from the Old Testament, and since our King James Version of the Bible agrees to a great extent with the Dead Sea Scrolls, it seems apparent that many Old Testament losses occurred before the time of Christ. However, since Paul seems familiar with the Tame and Wild Olive Tree allegory (Rom.11:17), and since Jude refers to writings in the book of Enoch (Jude 1:14), perhaps losses after the time of Christ also occurred. Elder Mark E. Petersen wrote: "When Nephi spoke of the 'plain and precious' parts of the scripture which were eliminated he spoke of the witness of Christ which is no longer in the Old Testament."[5]

In light of all we know today, perhaps a better interpretation of "the book that proceeded forth from the mouth of a Jew" would be to identify it as the Bible, which came from the mouth of Jesus and also the mouths of many Jews. This would be consistent with 1 Nephi 13:24, which states that the book contained the fulness of the gospel of the Lord, of whom the twelve apostles bore record, and verse 25, which states that "these things [the book] go forth from the Jews in purity unto the Gentiles." However, a distinction should probably be made between the Old Testament and the New Testament. The Greek Septuagint translation (around 250 B.C.) and the Dead Sea Scroll Old Testament manuscripts (around 200 B.C. to A.D. 70) were already corrupted before the New Testament was written. The New Testament was pure at first but was later corrupted. Thus, there never was a time in which both the Old Testament and the New Testament were uncorrupted at the same time, though the component parts of each of the testaments were pure when they "came from the pen of the original writers." First Nephi 13:26 makes it quite clear that it was after the Bible went forth by the hand of the twelve apostles, in other words, after or during the latter part of the first century, that several important things would happen. The great and abominable church was formed, which took away from the gospel "many parts which are plain and most precious; and also many covenants of the Lord have they taken away." Verse 27 informs us that this was not done accidentally or ignorantly, but that "all this have they done that they might pervert the right ways of the Lord, that they might blind the eyes and harden the hearts of the children of men."

What, then, was the great and abominable church that began and finished this work as described in 1 Nephi 13? Was it the apostate Christian churches of the first three centuries? Was it the church that grew out of the apostate Christian church of the first three centuries? Or is it every organization, political, ecclesiastical, and fraternal, that had a hand in corrupting the writings of the apostles and the scriptures they used? Again, it seems that the identity of that great and abominable church is not as important as an understanding of what happened to the scriptures that fell into the hands of that church.

It seems clear that the changes made in the Bible by this great and abominable church were made between the time of the apostles (1st century), and the invention of the printing press (15th century), for it was the invention of the printing press that enabled the Bible to go forth to all the nations of the Gentiles. Prior to that invention, the Bible was in the custody of the early Christian church of the apostles, the apostate Christian church, and the later Roman Catholic Church. Somewhere and sometime during that period, the Bible passed through the hands of the great and abominable church, and many plain and precious things were taken away. As we shall see later, the evidence seems to indicate that the changes took place in the earlier part of this time period — probably within the first two centuries after Christ. Nephi wrote:

> Thou seest that after the book hath gone forth through the hands of the great and abominable church, that there are many plain and precious things taken away from the book, which is the book of the Lamb of God. And after these plain and precious things were taken away it goeth forth unto all the nations of the Gentiles; and after it goeth forth unto all the nations of the Gentiles, yea, even across the many waters which thou hast seen with the Gentiles which have gone forth

out of captivity, thou seest—because of the many plain and precious things which have been taken out of the book, which were plain unto the understanding of the children of men, according to the plainness which is in the Lamb of God—because of these things which are taken away out of the gospel of the Lamb, an exceedingly great many do stumble, yea, insomuch that Satan hath great power over them. (1 Ne. 13:28-29.)

This now brings us to the reason why Nephi was shown all of this: so that he would understand the importance and necessity of the angel's charge to him that he and his descendants were to write a book (the Book of Mormon) that would contain the plainness of the gospel and that would be brought forth in the last days to restore the gospel to the earth. He wrote:

It came to pass that the angel of the Lord spake unto me, saying: Behold, saith the Lamb of God, after I have visited the remnant of the house of Israel—and this remnant of whom I speak is the seed of thy father—wherefore, after I have visited them in judgment, and smitten them by the hand of the Gentiles, and after the Gentiles do stumble exceedingly, because of the most plain and precious parts of the gospel of the Lamb which have been kept back by that abominable church, which is the mother of harlots, saith the Lamb—I will be merciful unto the Gentiles in that day, insomuch that I will bring forth unto them, in mine own power, much of my gospel, which shall be plain and precious, saith the Lamb.

For, behold, saith the Lamb: I will manifest myself unto thy seed, that they shall write many things which I shall minister unto them, which shall be plain and precious; and after thy seed shall be destroyed, and dwindle in unbelief, and also the seed of thy brethren, behold, these things shall be hid up, to come forth unto the Gentiles, by the gift and power of the Lamb. And in them shall be written my gospel, saith the Lamb, and my rock and my salvation. (1 Ne. 13:34-36.)

The Loss of Plain and Precious Parts

Let us now consider what happened to the "plain and precious" teachings and to the "covenants" of the Lord. If scholarship has made a correct assessment of what happened, we can conclude that the changes in the scripture began at a very early period — the first century after Christ. The fourth-century historian Eusebius recorded the words of an even earlier writer:

> For this purpose they fearlessly lay their hands upon the holy Scriptures saying that they have corrected them. And that I do not say this against them without foundation, whoever wishes may learn; for should any one collect and compare their copies one with another, he would find them greatly at variance among themselves. For the copies of Asclepiodotus will be found to differ from those of Theodotus. Copies of many you may find in abundance, altered, by the eagerness of their disciples to insert each one his own corrections, as they call them, i.e. their corruptions. Again, the copies of Hermophilus do not agree with these, for those of Appollonius are not consistent with themselves. For one may compare those which were prepared before by them, with those which they afterwards perverted for their own objects, and you will find them widely differing. But what a stretch of audacity this aberration indicates, it is hardly probable themselves can be ignorant. For either they do not believe that the holy Scriptures were uttered by the holy Spirit, and they are thus infidels, or they deem themselves wiser than the holy Spirit, and what alternative is there but to pronounce them demoniacs?[5]

Hugh Nibley wrote: "In our day the experts have reached the reluctant consensus that the Christian message has not come down to us in its original form. 'The present generation,' writes a leading authority on New Testament documents, 'stands at the beginning of a new cycle, in the search for the original Greek New Testament.' And it stands perplexed, not knowing which way to turn: 'Any substantial effort to improve the basic critical text must "mark time" until the whole complex of textual studies reveals a new integrating pattern . . . we know only that the traditional theory of the New Testament text is faulty but cannot yet see clearly to correct the fault.' "[7]

In regards to those who manipulated the early Bible text, Dr. Nibley has written: "Today the experts think they have a pretty good idea of the sort of people responsible. They were people who had received the gospel from the apostles, but immediately after the passing of the apostles proceeded to make basic alterations, deliberately disregarding some of the most important teachings. They were not the old Jewish-Christian communities, but various local churches of gentile composition, into whose hands the record came at an early time (in the 70's and 80's A.D.), and by whom the alterations — especially deletions — were made."[8]

This seems consistent with what we know about the Bible, for if we compare our modern Bible with the earliest manuscripts (the Vatican, Sinaitic, and Alexandrian) and the earliest version (the Latin Vulgate being the most important), we find that they are quite similar. From this we must conclude that the covenants that were lost and the plain and precious truths that were removed were lost and removed before the writing of our oldest manuscripts and versions. The manuscripts are dated from A.D. 300 to 450, and St. Jerome's Latin Vulgate was finished by A.D. 382. We believe that Jerome would have used the earliest manuscripts he could find for his work. What this leads us to is that if Jerome's Latin Vulgate and the Vatican, Sinaitic, and Alexandrian manuscripts basically agree with our King James Authorized Version, then what Nephi saw the great and abominable church do to the Bible began very early — prior to the 4th century. Joseph Smith stated: "I believe the Bible as it read when it came from the pen of the original writers. Ignorant translators, careless transcribers, or designing and corrupt priests have committed many errors."[9]

Kent P. Jackson has stated: "Scholars who have examined the biblical texts found among the Dead Sea Scrolls have noted with considerable interest the fact that Old Testament texts have changed very little since 100 B.C. This means that the removal of plain and precious truths from the Old Testament took place *before* that time. Since whole books like those of Zenos and Zenock were lost from the Bible entirely, while Isaiah on the Brass Plates shows only minimal difference from Isaiah in current texts, it seems likely that the loss of precious things from the Old Testament perhaps involved more deletion of text, including entire books or sections of books, than corruption of the existing text."[10]

What does the Book of Mormon say about the Bible? Most people generally familiar with Nephi's prophecy understand that the Bible, which "proceeded forth from the mouth of a Jew," originally came forth in purity (1 Ne. 13:24-25); but as it was handed down, important parts were lost, removed, or obscured. A more detailed picture than this alone, however, can be gleaned from the words of 1 Nephi 13:24-25.

These words of the angel seem to identify *three* stages in this process — not just one. First, it is said that the Gentiles would take "away *from the gospel* of the Lamb many parts which are plain and most precious" (13:26). It is possible that this stage could have occurred by altering the meaning of the things taught by the Lord, without necessarily changing the words themselves.

Second, the Gentiles would take away "many *covenants* of the Lord" (13:26). This step, too, could be taken without deleting any words from the Bible as such. The knowledge and benefit of the covenants of God could become lost simply by neglecting the performance of ordinances, or priesthood functions, or individual covenants as the Lord had taught.

Third, Nephi beheld that there were "many plain and precious things taken away *from the book*" (13:28). It appears that this step was a consequence of the first two, since 13:28 begins with the word "wherefore." Thus, the eventual physical loss of things from the Bible was perhaps less a cause than a result of the fact that, first, the gospel, and second, the covenants had been lost or taken away.[11]

The Great and Abominable Church of 1 Nephi 14

Having seen the work of the great and abominable church among the nations and kingdoms of the Gentiles between the time of the apostles and the time the Bible went forth "unto all the nations of the Gentiles" (1 Ne. 13:29), and having received his heavenly charge to write a record that would contain the plain and precious parts of the gospel, Nephi was shown in chapter 14 the work of the great and abominable church in the last days. Unlike in chapter 13, where Nephi was shown that the great and abominable church is "most abominable above all other churches" (v. 26), Nephi now learned that in the latter days, when the gospel is restored, "there are save two churches only; the one is the church of the Lamb of God, and the other is the church of the devil" (v. 10). In verses 11-21, the angel told Nephi that in the last days the church of the devil would have dominion over all the earth, among all nations; that the church of the Lamb of God would number few but would also be found upon all the face of earth; that the church of the devil would gather together multitudes among all nations to fight against the Lamb of God; that the power of the Lamb of God would descend upon the members of the Church, who would be scattered upon all the face of the earth; and that there would be wars and rumors of wars among all nations that belong to the church of the devil. At this point Nephi was shown John the Revelator and was told that John would see and write the remainder of these things.

Elder Bruce R. McConkie wrote: "The church of the devil is the world; it is all the carnality and evil to which fallen man is heir, it is every unholy and wicked practice; it is every false religion, every supposed system of salvation which does not actually save and exalt man in the highest heaven of the celestial world. It is every church except the true church, whether parading under a Christian or a pagan banner."[12]

Shortly after the death of the Prophet Joseph Smith, Elder John Taylor wrote of the great organization John had described in Revelation 13, 17, and 18.

> It will readily be perceived in the foregoing extract that John had no more reference to the Roman Catholic, and Protestant churches, who had a form of godliness, denying the power, than he had to all Babylon from Nimrod down. The old woman, Satan's wife, was "drunken with the blood of the Saints, and with the blood of the martyrs of Jesus," and the account actually includes all, whose "names were not written in the book of life, from the foundation of the world." Babylon, literally understood, is the gay world; spiritual wickedness, the golden city, and the glory of the world. The priests of Egypt, who received a portion gratis from Pharaoh, the priests of Baal, and the Pharisees, and Sadducees, with their "long

robes," among the Jews are equally included in their mother's family, with the Roman Catholics, Protestants, and all that have not had the keys of the kingdom and power thereof, according to the ordinances of God.[13]

Elder James E. Talmage developed this idea:

> I do not understand that when the Lord states that those churches shall be overthrown — I mean the church of the devil, using his expression as he says — I do not understand that all members of those churches are to meet destruction, physically or otherwise. He is speaking there of the church collectively, and he is not pleased with it; but individually he may be well pleased with many of his sons and the daughters who have been born under an environment that has led them into those churches which are not of God . . . . But the Lord is not pleased with those churches that have been constructed by men and then labeled with his name. He is not pleased with those doctrines that are being taught as being his doctrines when they are only the effusion of men's brains, undirected by inspiration and utterly lacking in revelation.[14]

President Ezra Taft Benson said:

> In 1845, the Quorum of the Twelve issued an epistle to the heads of state in the world. I quote from one paragraph:
>
> "As this work progresses in its onward course, and becomes more and more an object of political and religious interest and excitement, no kin, ruler, or subject, no community or individual, will stand neutral. All will at length be influenced by one spirit or the other; and will take sides either for or against the kingdom of God." (James R. Clark, comp. *Messages of the First Presidency of The Church of Jesus Christ of Latter-day Saints*, 6 vols. [Salt Lake City: Bookcraft, 1965-75], 1:257.)
>
> That day is now here. Opposition has been and will be the lot of the Saints of the kingdom in any age. The finger of scorn has been pointed at us in the past, and we may expect it in the future. We also expect to see men in high places defend the Church; there will also be "pharaohs" who know neither Joseph nor his brethren. The seed planted and watered

in 1830 has now matured to a fully grown tree for all to see. Some will seek the refuge of its shade in the heat of the day, but none will be neutral in their appraisal of its fruit.

The Church will continue its opposition to error, falsehood, and immorality. The mission of the Church is to herald the message of salvation and make unmistakably clear the pathway to exaltation. Our mission is to prepare a people for the coming of the Lord. As the world drifts further away from God and standards of virtue and honor, we may expect opposition to the work of the Church. We may expect to see the time, as the Book of Mormon forecasts, when "multitudes . . . among all the nations of the Gentiles [will gather] to fight against the Lamb of God." (1 Ne. 14:13.) The power of God and the righteousness of the Saints will be the means by which the Church will be spared. (See 1 Ne. 14:14-15.)[15]

The Fall of the Great and Abominable Church

In chapter 14 Nephi was shown that when God's wrath would be poured out upon the great and abominable church in the latter days, war would cover the earth. "I beheld that the wrath of God was poured out upon that great and abominable church, insomuch that there were wars and rumors of wars among all the nations and kindreds of the earth." (1 Ne. 14:15.)

Although Nephi was shown further events of the last days (v. 26), he was forbidden to write what he had seen, for that mission had been reserved for John (vv. 19-22, 27). In his later writings, Nephi did allude to what he had seen concerning the final destruction of the great and abominable church, that it would be destroyed by internal war:

> The blood of that great and abominable church, which is the whore of all the earth, shall turn upon their own heads; for they shall war among themselves, and the sword of their own hands shall fall upon their own heads, and they shall be drunken with their own blood. And every nation which shall war against thee, O house of Israel, shall be turned one against another, and they shall fall into the pit which they digged to ensnare the people of the Lord. And all that fight against Zion

shall be destroyed, and that great whore, who hath perverted the right ways of the Lord, yea, that great and abominable church, shall tumble to the dust and great shall be the fall of it. (1 Ne. 22:13-14.)

Nephi vividly described this great and abominable church as follows:

> The righteous need not fear, for they are those who shall not be confounded. But it is the kingdom of the devil, which shall be built up among the children of men, which kingdom is established among them which are in the flesh — for the time speedily shall come that all churches which are built up to get gain, and all those who are built up to get power over the flesh, and those who are built up to become popular in the eyes of the world, and those who seek the lusts of the flesh and the things of the world, and to do all manner of iniquity; yea, in fine, all those who belong to the kingdom of the devil are they who need fear, and tremble, and quake; they are those who must be brought low in the dust; they are those who must be consumed as stubble; and this is according to the words of the prophet. (1 Ne. 22:22-23.)

Whenever the kingdom or church of God has been on the earth, the kingdom or church of the devil has also been established. Nephi saw the work of the church of the devil among the nations of the Gentiles during the time that plain and precious teachings of the Bible were lost and at the time when one church was most abominable above all others. (1 Ne. 13.) He also saw the latter days when there would be "save two churches only; the one is the church of the Lamb of God, and the other is the church of the devil." (1 Ne. 14:10.)

Although Nephi did not write in detail about the end of the world, he did inform us that the great and abominable church would be destroyed when the wrath of God was poured out upon it, and that those who belonged to this church would war among themselves. Following this, God's people will have rest, and the millennium will be established:

> The time cometh speedily that the righteous must be led up as calves to the stall, and the Holy One of Israel must reign

in dominion and might, and power, and great glory. And he gathereth his children from the four quarters of the earth; and he numbereth his sheep, and they know him, and there shall be one fold and one shepherd; and he shall feed his sheep, and in him they shall find pasture. And because of the righteousness of his people, Satan has no power; wherefore, he cannot be loosed for the space of many years; for he hath no power over the hearts of the people, for they dwell in righteousness, and the Holy One of Israel reigneth." (1 Ne. 22:24-26.)

NOTES

1. Joseph Smith, *Teachings of the Prophet Joseph Smith*, selected by Joseph Fielding Smith (Salt Lake City: Deseret Book Company, 1938), p. 365.

2. Bruce R. McConkie, *A New Witness for the Articles of Faith* (Salt Lake City: Deseret Book Company, 1985), p. 340.

3. Mark E. Petersen, *The Great Prologue* (Salt Lake City: Deseret Book Company, 1975), pp. 3, 26.

4. George Reynolds and Janne Sjodahl, *Commentary on the Book of Mormon*, 7 vols. (Salt Lake City: Deseret Book Company, 1961), 4:262.

5. *Church News*, January 22, 1966, p. 16.

6. Eusebius, *Ecclesiastical History*, trans. C.F. Cruse, V. 28.16-18 (Grand Rapids: Baker, 1955), pp. 215-16.

7. K.W. Clark, cited in Hugh W. Nibley, *Since Cumorah*, (Salt Lake City: Deseret Book Company, 1967), pp. 27-28.

8. *Since Cumorah*, pp. 29-30.

9. *Teachings of the Prophet Joseph Smith*, p. 327, Oct. 13, 1843.

10. Kent P. Jackson, personal communication.

11. *F.A.R.M.S. Update*, January 1987 (Provo, Utah).

12. Bruce R. McConkie, *Doctrinal New Testament Commentary*, 3 vols. (Salt Lake City: Bookcraft, 1965), 3:551.

13. *Times and Seasons* 6:939 (June 15, 1845).

14. Conference Report, October 1928, pp. 120-21.

15. Conference Report, April 1980, pp. 46-47.

6

TO A LAND OF PROMISE
(1 Nephi 16-18)

TERRENCE L. SZINK

Chapters 16 through 18 of 1 Nephi contain some of the best-known stories in the Book of Mormon. This section has received a fair amount of attention from Latter-day Saint writers.[1] It is for the most part historical narrative recounting the arduous journey of Lehi and his family from the valley of Lemuel to the New World. This journey compares with the Exodus of the Israelites from Egypt and the Saints' trek to the intermountain region in difficulty, importance, and miraculous nature.

To better understand any writing, we need to consider several issues: when it was written, who wrote it, what the author's purpose was, and what ideas or attitudes may have influenced the author. First, it is important to understand that our record of Lehi's wilderness experience was taken from the small plates of Nephi and was written some thirty years after the fact. (2 Ne. 5:28-31.) Thus Nephi was free to pick and choose his material, putting it together in any way he saw fit. The result does not represent a day-to-day or even a year-to-year account, but rather a highlighting of main events with special emphasis on "the things of God" and a desire to "persuade men to come unto the God of Abraham, and the God of Isaac, and the God of Jacob, and be saved." (1 Ne. 6:3-4.)

Terrence L. Szink is a doctoral student in ancient Near Eastern studies at the University of California at Los Angeles.

The first six verses of chapter 16 can best be understood when seen as the conclusion of the previous section, 1 Nephi 8 through 15. These chapters contain visions, prophecies, and finally an explanation by Nephi to his hardhearted brothers. Laman and Lemuel complained that Nephi had spoken "hard things" to them. He responded by reasoning that the teachings were hard only to those who were condemned by them. Verse 6 seems to conclude this section.

When the narrative from chapter 7 picks up again, Lehi and his family are camped in the valley of Lemuel. The valley of Lemuel was "in the wilderness in the borders which are nearer the Red Sea." (1 Ne. 2:5-6.)[2] Although it did not offer the family the comforts of Jerusalem, it at least provided them a sure source of water (1 Ne. 2:6) and possibly some amount of security.[3]

The valley of Lemuel probably held some good memories for several members of the group: Sariah had "rejoiced exceedingly" at the return of her sons from Jerusalem; further, her testimony of her husband's calling had been strengthened there. (1 Ne. 5:8-9.) Nephi and Lehi had received several important visions there. Finally, Lehi's sons had taken Ishmael's daughters to wife there. (1 Ne. 16:7.) While the group had no doubt also suffered some hardship in that valley, more severe challenges awaited them in the wilderness of the Arabian peninsula. In 1 Nephi 16:9 are recorded Lehi's "marching orders" from the Lord — he and his family were to leave the valley of Lemuel and take up their journey into the wilderness.

The Liahona

Perhaps the object that comes to mind most readily in any discussion of Lehi's wilderness journey is the Liahona. Lehi found this "round ball of curious workmanship" at the door of his tent on the morning the group broke camp and resumed their journey. (1 Ne. 16:9-10.) Alma, noting that the Liahona was prepared by God, said: "Behold, there cannot any man work after the manner of so curious a workmanship." (Alma 37:39.) The Liahona served as a kind of compass and is even called such. (1 Ne. 18:21.) It was, however, different from a modern compass in at least one important way. As the family would soon learn, it operated according to their righteousness and faith. When they exercised their faith, the Liahona showed them which way to go in the wilderness, led Nephi to food, and apparently gave the group special instructions when they were needed. "And thus we see," Nephi observed, "that by small means the Lord can bring about great things." (1 Ne. 16:29.)

Apparently the family did not always use this spiritual compass to its full potential; some five hundred years later, while delivering the Liahona to his son, Alma said: "Because those miracles were worked by small means it did show unto them marvelous works. They were slothful, and forgot to exercise their faith and diligence and then those marvelous works ceased, and they did not progress in their journey; therefore, they tarried in the wilderness, or did not travel a direct course, and were afflicted with hunger and thirst, because of their transgressions." (Alma 37:41-42.) This disobedience contributed to the group's eight years of wandering in the wilderness. (1 Ne. 17:4.)

Finally, since the relationship between Lehi's party, the Liahona, and the Lord was one of faith and trust, the Liahona served well as a Christological symbol. Alma compared it to the words of Christ: "Behold, it is as easy to give heed to the word of Christ, which will point to you a straight course to eternal bliss, as it was for our fathers to give heed to this compass, which would point unto them a straight course to the promised land. And now I say, is there not a type in this thing? For just as surely as this director did bring our fathers, by following its course, to the promised land, shall the words of Christ, if we follow their course, carry us beyond this vale of sorrow into a far better land of promise." (Alma 37:44-45.)

Two Wilderness Incidents

As mentioned above, the family was in the wilderness for eight years, during which time they had a variety of experiences. Nephi wrote: "We had suffered many afflictions and much difficulty, yea, even so much that we cannot write them all." (1 Ne. 17:6.) Since he could not write about everything that happened to the group, he may have chosen for inclusion those experiences he felt represented the trip as a whole. He began his account with a general description of their route and an explanation about how they obtained food. Occasionally they would pitch a base camp and launch hunting expeditions from it. At other times they would hunt food "along the way," always trying to stay in the "more fertile parts" of the wilderness where game was more plentiful. This description of their life as nomadic hunters serves as a prelude to the first of two stories. These stories not only demonstrate the type of problems the family had to overcome and the manner in which the Lord helped them, but they also give important clues about the character of the individual family members.

Verse 17 of chapter 16 separates the general description of the journey in the three preceding verses from the first wilderness story recounted in verses 18 through 32. Compare verse 17 with verse 33, which separates the first story from the second. In both there is a mention of traveling "for the space of many days" and of pitching tents. Nephi may have used these verses to indicate that these two incidents were separated by a period of time.

The first episode, generally known as the broken bow incident, is one of the most fascinating in the Book of Mormon. Nephi wrote that his brothers' bows had already lost their spring when disaster struck: he broke his fine steel bow. The entire family, including Lehi, began to murmur. Nephi made a bow out of wood and went to his father for instructions about where to hunt. Lehi inquired of the Lord, was chastened, and was told to look to the Liahona. The family then learned about the true nature of their compass and were astonished by a new writing that appeared on it. The Liahona directed Nephi to the top of a mountain, where he was able to find wild animals for food.

Some familiar with archery have noted that the change from a composite steel bow to a simple wooden bow would have been difficult for Nephi, and he could have been justly proud of his accomplishment.[4] The fact that Nephi made new arrows along with his new bow makes sense, since the wooden bow would not have had the strength of the steel one. It would have been almost impossible to continue to use the same metal arrows with the wooden bow.[5]

This story indicates that hunger was probably a serious problem throughout the eight years in the wilderness. This brings to mind another scriptural story of hunger in the wilderness, this one from the book of Exodus.[6] Compare the two accounts:

And it came to pass that we did return without food to our families, and being much fatigued because of their journey, *they did suffer much for the want of food.* And it came to pass that *Laman and Lemuel and the sons of Ishmael did begin to murmur exceedingly,* because of their sufferings and afflictions in the wilderness; and also my father began to murmur against the Lord his God; yea, and they were all exceedingly sorrowful, even that *they did murmur against the Lord.* (1 Ne. 16:19-20, emphasis added.)

And the whole congregation of the children of Israel *murmured against Moses and Aaron* in the wilderness: And the children of Israel said unto them, . . . ye have brought us forth into this wilderness, to kill this assembly with *hunger.* And Moses said, . . . the Lord heareth your murmurings which ye murmur against him: and what are ye? *Your murmurings are not against us, but against the Lord.* (Ex. 16:2-3, 8, emphasis added.)

In both cases the unusual word *murmur* is used. Forms of the Hebrew root *lwn* (translated "to murmur" in the King James Version) occur eighteen times in the Old Testament.[7] In all of these occurrences, the subject of the verb is "the children of Israel," and all but one of them are connected with the Exodus.[8] The situation is similar in the Book of Mormon. The word appears thirty-three times; of these, nineteen are used in the first eighteen chapters of 1 Nephi in describing Lehi's family in the wilderness.[9] The disproportionate use of such a peculiar word during the Book of Mormon wilderness experience corresponds to a similarly disproportionate use of the word in the Old Testament. This may suggest that the version of the Exodus on the brass plates and that of our Bible are similar, and thus that Nephi's choice of vocabulary was greatly influenced by the words used in the Exodus account. Joseph Smith's translation of this passage was accurate enough to preserve such a correspondence. Also worthy of note is the mention in both texts of the fact that this murmuring had been directed against the Lord himself, rather than against his prophets. The similarity continues in the miraculous way the problem was solved. For Israel, the paradigmatic miracle — manna from heaven — was the solution. For the group in the Book of Mormon, the answer to their problem appears to have been no less wonderful. When the family saw that Nephi had obtained food, "how great was their joy! And it came to pass that they did humble themselves before the Lord, and did give thanks unto him." (1 Ne. 16:32.)

Finally, this story indicates quite a bit about the character of Nephi as opposed to that of Laman, Lemuel, and the sons of Ishmael. On the one hand, the murmurers allowed their circumstances to rule over them. On the other, Nephi was strengthened by the experience: he learned how to make a bow, and he gained confidence in his use of the Liahona and his relationship with the Lord. Nephi also demonstrated his humility and his respect for patriarchal authority by going to his father to ask for directions. This respect for authority is a principal theme of the second incident.

Ishmael, the father of half of the colony, died. (1 Ne. 16:34.) Possibly taking advantage of the grief that accompanied this death, Laman began to sow the seeds of rebellion, planting sinister ideas about the motives of Nephi, their younger brother. His accusation that Nephi "has thought to make himself a king and a ruler over us" is perhaps indicative of jealousy and a short memory, for he had heard from an angel the declaration that the Lord had chosen Nephi to lead the group. (1 Ne. 3:29.)

The uprising was squelched quickly. Nephi wrote that the Lord himself spoke to the group and severely chastised them. He also noted that the Lord again saved the group from starvation, blessing them with food. Apparently the Liahona had ceased to work again, no doubt because of the would-be revolt. (1 Ne. 16:39.)

The Land of Bountiful

After wading through so much affliction, the group must have been truly happy to reach the land named, appropriately, Bountiful. Perhaps some of them even thought this was the much-awaited land of promise. After "many days" Nephi received a divine summons to ascend a mountain, where he received the assignment to build a ship to cross the ocean. Responding in a way that seems to typify his character, he did not express doubt about whether he could build the boat, but rather asked where he could find the raw materials he needed to make the necessary tools. (1 Ne. 17:7-10.)

Nephi informs us that the group had not been allowed to "make much fire" while in the wilderness. (1 Ne. 17:12.) Commentators have usually explained that this was to avoid contact with unfriendly groups.[10] An additional reason was to provide an opportunity for the Lord to prove to the travelers that he was the one who led them. We find similar passages in Exodus:

I will . . . be your light in the wilderness; and I will prepare the way before you, if it so be that ye shall keep my commandments; wherefore, inasmuch as ye shall keep my commandments *ye shall be led towards the promised land; and ye shall know that it is by me that ye are led.* Yea, and the Lord said also that: After ye have arrived in the promised land, *ye shall know that I, the Lord, am God; and that I, the Lord, did deliver you from destruction; yea, that I did bring you out of the land of Jerusalem.* (1 Ne. 17:13-14, emphasis added.)[11]

The Lord went before them by day in a pillar of a cloud, to lead them the way; and by night in a pillar of fire, to give them light; to go by day and night. (Ex. 13:21.)

I will take you to me for a people, and I will be to you a God: *and ye shall know that I am the Lord your God, which bringeth you out from under the burdens of the Egyptians.* (Ex. 6:7-8, emphasis added.)

The similarity of the texts is interesting, but their differences are enlightening as well. In Exodus the concept of a people chosen of God is emphasized, while in the Book of Mormon the idea of a people choosing God through obedience to his commandments is featured.

Returning from the mountain, Nephi made tools and was about to begin building the boat as the Lord had commanded him. His brothers, as was their habit, began to murmur. They were skeptical of Nephi's ability to build a seaworthy craft and of his claim that he had been instructed of the Lord. While the first doubt may have been justifiable,[12] the second demonstrates their spiritual immaturity and poor memories. Had not they themselves also seen an angel and even heard the Lord's voice on more than one occasion? After eight years of listening to Laman and Lemuel's murmuring in the desert, and now hearing them once again, Nephi must have known that the prophetic dreams he and his father had received, in which his brothers did not partake of the fruit of the tree of life, would assuredly be fulfilled. Nephi's feeling of resignation about his brothers was ironically misinterpreted by them as an indication that they had finally triumphed over him. They "rejoiced" in their perceived victory, repeating the accusations Nephi and his father had most likely endured since the group left Jerusalem: they listed for Nephi the afflictions they had suffered (forgetting that he had also suffered them) and declared their belief that "the people who were in the land of Jerusalem were a righteous people." (1 Ne. 17:22.) Nephi responded by recounting the history of the Exodus, touching on many of the ideas he would later use in writing the story of his own wilderness journey.[13] This recapitulation of the Exodus may have been a memorized recitation that was part of the learning of his father mentioned by Nephi at the start of his record.[14] (1 Ne. 1:1.) Perhaps Laman and Lemuel had also learned such recitations as children, for as Nephi talked to them, he at first used the phrase "ye also know" when recounting the basics of the story. As he began explaining the events in more detail, this phrase was discontinued. Laman and Lemuel did not appreciate the true significance of the story, their spiritual understanding not having matured beyond that of their childhood.

One point that Nephi seems to emphasize in his retelling of the Exodus is the fact that "the Lord esteemeth all flesh in one" and that people are "chosen" only if they are righteous. Perhaps Nephi had seen how the perversion of the "chosen people" idea had contributed to the downfall of his people in Jerusalem, and he may have worried that his brothers' belief that "the people who were in the land of Jerusalem were a righteous people" (1 Ne. 17:22) was a sign that they were falling into the same trap.

Near the end of his retelling of the Exodus, Nephi drew a clear parallel between the two wilderness experiences, comparing his brothers to the murmuring children of Israel: "Wherefore, he did bring them out of the land of Egypt. And he did straiten them in the wilderness with his rod; for they hardened their hearts, *even as ye have*; and the Lord straitened them because of their iniquity." (1 Ne. 17:40-41, emphasis added.)

If his brothers were "like unto" the children of Israel, then Nephi must be compared to Moses; one passage from this sermon suggests this idea. Nephi proclaimed the power the Lord had invested in him in a way that brings to mind Moses' power over the Red Sea:

I said unto them: If God had commanded me to do all things I could do them. If he should command me that I should say unto this water, be thou earth, it should be earth: and if I should say it, it would be done. (1 Ne. 17:50.)	But lift thou up thy rod, and stretch out thine hand over the sea, and divide it: and the children of Israel shall go on dry ground through the midst of the sea. (Ex. 14:16.)

After Nephi had finished recounting the story of the Exodus to his brothers and showing them the parallels with their own experience, he was so filled with the Spirit of the Lord that Laman and Lemuel were afraid to touch him "for the space of many days." (1 Ne. 17:52.) Even after this he was prompted by the Lord to deliver a "shock" to them. Perhaps the Lord felt that this was needed, since they had not responded to an angelic visitation or even to his own voice. That Nephi was the one to administer this shock might have been intended to show them once more that he had been chosen to lead the group. The demonstration was apparently a bit too effective, as Laman and Lemuel mistakenly took it as a sign of Nephi's divinity and fell before him in fearful adoration.

The effects of the shock lasted long enough for Nephi to use his brothers' new-found cooperative spirit to finish the construction of the boat. During this time Nephi was privileged with frequent instruction from on high: "I, Nephi, did go into the mount oft, and I did pray oft unto the Lord; wherefore the Lord showed unto me great things." (1 Ne. 18:3.) Mountaintops are the preeminent meeting place for God and his children.[15] "At a time when Moses was caught up into an exceedingly high mountain" (Moses 1:1) he had a vision in which he saw the entire world along with its creation and all of its inhabitants. (Moses 1:1-10.) Perhaps Nephi also was privileged to receive such a vision.

Revelry Among the Travelers

The ship having been completed, the family loaded the supplies they would have needed for the long trip, boarded, and set off for "the promised land." They had been at sea "for the space of many days" when Laman, Lemuel, and the sons of Ishmael, perhaps initially to relieve the boredom of life at sea, began "to make themselves merry." (1 Ne. 18:9.) Nephi's description of this party leads one to compare it to the golden calf incident in the book of Exodus:

After we had been driven forth before the wind for the space of many days, behold, my brethren and the sons of Ishmael and also their wives began to *make themselves merry*, insomuch that they *began to dance, and to sing*, and to speak with much rudeness, yea, even that *they did forget by what power they had been brought thither*: yea, they were lifted up unto *exceeding rudeness*. (1 Ne. 18:9, emphasis added.)

[Aaron] had made . . . a molten calf: and they said *These be thy gods, O Israel, which brought thee up out of the land of Egypt*. (Ex. 32:4.) The people sat down to eat and to drink, and *rose up to play*. (Ex. 32:6.)
And when Joshua heard the noise of the people as they shouted, he said unto Moses, There is a noise of war in the camp. And he said, It is not the voice of them that shout for mastery, neither is it the voice of them that cry for being overcome: but *the noise of them that sing* do I hear. And it came to pass, as soon as he came nigh unto the camp, that he saw the calf, and *the dancing*. (Ex. 32:18-19.)
And . . . Moses saw that *the people were naked*. (Ex. 32:25, emphasis added.)

The singing, dancing, and nakedness in the case of the golden calf were apparently part of the ritual connected with the idol. Could the mention in the Book of Mormon of the "much rudeness" and the "exceeding rudeness" possibly be a euphemism employed by Nephi to express the same type of activity described in the book of Exodus — "Moses saw that the people were naked"? Also very interesting is Nephi's statement that "they did forget by what power they had been brought thither," which was the root of the problem. Compare this to the statement in Exodus referring to the molten calf: "These be thy gods, O Israel, which brought thee up out of the land of Egypt."

Nephi understood the dangers of such behavior and attempted to dissuade his brothers from continuing. Apparently the memory of the shock Nephi had administered had faded. Laman and Lemuel, keenly aware that Nephi was their younger brother, once again were angered by his efforts to lead them. Their old accusation that he desired to be a ruler over them again surfaced. The rebellion that had been threatened so many times while in the wilderness now took place; Nephi was bound and treated "with much harshness." (1 Ne. 18:11.) Laman, Lemuel, and the sons of Ishmael, emboldened by their own rudeness and crazed by their new power over their brother, threatened anyone who opposed them. In response to the mutiny, the Liahona now ceased to function and a tremendous storm began to drive the ship back. One can envision the seriousness of the situation: Lehi and Sariah, both now old, were near death; Jacob and Joseph, the children born in the wilderness, were crying; the wind was howling; and even the fine ship they had built was not strong enough to save the family from the wrath of a justifiably angry God. Finally, after four days of what must have been a terrifying experience, Laman and Lemuel were frightened into releasing their brother.

Nephi did not complain and murmur, although he had ample reason to do so; rather he responded to this crisis as he had to all previous ones: he went before God in humble prayer. He was able to use the Liahona once again and bring the family safely to the promised land. Nephi explained that the new land was blessed with fertile soil, all kinds of wild animals, and metals. (1 Ne. 18:24-25.)

Conclusions

These three chapters, while providing a description of the journey from the old promised land to the new one, also give valuable insights into the personalities of the individuals making the trip. Laman and Lemuel wandered farther away from the strait and narrow path and ceased to hold to the rod of iron (to use the symbols of the tree of Lehi's dream.) In contrast, Nephi grew stronger in his faith and confidence before the Lord. Lehi seems to have aged considerably, perhaps because of his harsh experiences in the wilderness. He must have been content, however, knowing that the responsibilities of leadership were being assumed by someone as reliable and trustworthy as Nephi.

We have also noted the intriguing parallels with the Exodus account. Finally, it is sadly ironic that Jerusalem, the promised land the Israelites had struggled so hard to obtain, had become at the time of Lehi analogous to the land of Egypt at the time of the Exodus. Lehi, a man of God, and his family were no longer safe there, and were forced to seek a *new* promised land.

NOTES

1. Principal among these is Hugh Nibley, *Lehi in the Desert and the World of the Jaredites* (Salt Lake City: Bookcraft, 1952); *Since Cumorah* (Salt Lake City: Deseret Book Company, 1967); *An Approach to the Book of Mormon*, 2nd ed. (Salt Lake City; Deseret Book Company, 1978). Also interesting is Lynn M. Hilton and Hope Hilton, *In Search of Lehi's Trail* (Salt Lake City: Deseret Book Company, 1976), which attempts to establish the route Lehi and his family took and offers ethnographic parallels.

2. For a suggestion as to the location of this valley, see Hilton, pp. 63-68.

3. Lehi's description of the valley as "firm and steadfast" (1 Ne. 2:10), and the fact that the family was not prohibited from building fires there (1 Ne. 7:22) as they later were, leads one to believe that it was a relatively safe place.

4. Nibley, *Lehi in the Desert*, p. 68.

5. "Nephi's Arrows Create Solid Bulls-eye," *Insights: An Ancient Window* (Provo, Utah: F.A.R.M.S., October 1984).

6. While preparing this paper I found numerous similarities between 1 Nephi and Exodus. Only after I had already discovered them was I shown a copy of George S. Tate's work "The Typology of the Exodus Pattern in the Book of Mormon, " in Neal E. Lambert, ed., *Literature of Belief*, Brigham Young University Religious Studies Monograph Series, vol. 5 (Provo, Utah:

Religious Studies Center, 1981), pp. 245-62. I was pleased to see noted there many of the same parallels I had found.

7. Forms of the Hebrew *rgn* are translated three times "to murmur." Of these, two (Deut. 1:27; Ps. 106:25) refer to the Exodus, the exception being Isa. 29:24.

8. Exodus 15:24; 16:2, 7, 8, 9, 12; 17:3, and Numbers 14:2, 27 (3), 29, 36; 16:11, 41; 17:5, 10 all deal with the Exodus. The one exception is Joshua 19:8.

9. The fourteen remaining instances are distributed somewhat evenly throughout the Book of Mormon: 2 Nephi: 5 occurrences; Mosiah: 3; Alma: 5; 3 Nephi: 1.

10. Nibley, *Lehi in the Desert*, pp. 72-77.

11. Nibley has also noted that the wording of this Book of Mormon passage is reminiscent of the Exodus: *An Approach to the Book of Mormon*, p. 107. It should also be pointed out that the Book of Mormon wording "I, the Lord, am God" is perhaps closer to the intent of the Hebrew *'anî yhwh 'elōhēkem* than the King James "I am the Lord your God."

12. Nibley, *Lehi in the Desert*, p. 38.

13. In addition to the article by George S. Tate mentioned above, see "Nephi and the Exodus," *Ensign*, April 1987, p. 64.

14. S. Kent Brown, "Approaches to the Pentateuch," *Studies in Scripture, Vol. 3: The Old Testament*, 2:18.

15. See Mircea Eliade, *Patterns in Comparative Religion*, (New York: Meridian, 1958), pp. 99-102; Richard J. Clifford, *The Cosmic Mountain in Canaan and the Old Testament* (Cambridge: Harvard University Press, 1972).

7

NEPHI ON THE DESTINY OF ISRAEL
(1 Nephi 19-22)

ROBERT L. MILLET

After having arrived in the promised land, Nephi received a commandment of the Lord to begin a record of his people. This record, which we know as the "large plates of Nephi," was begun in approximately 590 B.C. some ten years after the family's departure from Jerusalem. "Upon the plates which I made," Nephi wrote, "I did engraven the record of my father, and also our journeyings in the wilderness, and the prophecies of my father, and also many of mine own prophecies have I engraven upon them." Further, the large plates contained a genealogy of the family of Lehi, taken, no doubt, from the brass plates. (1 Ne. 19:1-2; cf. 1 Ne. 5:12, 16.) For the benefit of his readers, Nephi distinguished between the large plates and the small — the latter being those from which we are now reading, and which he was commanded to begin some twenty years later, in 570 B.C. (2 Ne. 5:28-33.) The small plates — known sometimes as the spiritual record — would detail more of the prophecies and oracles of the servants of the Lord, while the large plates — known as a more secular record — would cover such matters as the journeys of the people, the reigns of the kings, the wars, and the genealogies. (See 1 Ne. 19:3-6.) It is in this setting — a discussion of the roles of the

Robert L. Millet is associate professor of ancient scripture and New Testament area coordinator at Brigham Young University.

small and large plates—that Nephi unfolded a number of important prophecies of the coming of the Savior and the ultimate destiny of the house of Israel.

Prophecies of the Messiah from the Brass Plates

There is no specific reference in the Book of Mormon as to the origins of the brass plates. Nephi explained that "Laban also was a descendant of Joseph, wherefore he and his fathers had kept the records [the brass plates]." (1 Ne. 5:16.) Exactly how long before the time of Laban the brass records were begun is unknown. The record was probably kept in the tribe of Ephraim of Joseph, and thus Laban may well have been of the tribe of Ephraim. (See Gen. 48:5, 13-20; 1 Chr. 5:1-2.) In suggesting how it was that the families of Ephraim and Manasseh (of which Lehi and Ishmael were descendants) came to settle in Jerusalem, Sidney B. Sperry has written: "The Northern Kingdom of Israel fell to the Assyrians when its capital of Samaria capitulated to Sargon II in 722 B.C. The forebears of Laban may have fled to Jerusalem to prevent the sacred records from falling into alien hands. Lehi's grandfather or great-grandfather may have left his northern home for Jerusalem in order to prevent his children from intermarrying and making religious compromises with the foreigners brought into the land by the Assyrians." Brother Sperry then asked the following question: "What happened to the keeping of sacred records when the Israelites became sharply divided on political grounds—so much so that the two nations were enemies?" He then suggested an answer:

> The prophets in both nations probably paid little attention to the political lines of division, but it is improbable that all of them had their words recorded in the scriptures of both nations. From the time of the division until the fall of the Northern Kingdom in 722 B.C., the Brass Plates may well have been the official scripture of the Ten Tribes. It is probable that some prophets wrote on these plates whose writings may not have been recorded on the records kept in Judah. Were Zenos, Zenock, Neum, and Ezias (1 Nephi 19:10; Helaman 8:20) among them? They were all Hebrew prophets known

to the Nephites, but their names do not appear in our current Old Testament. It is also possible that the writings of some prophets in Judah were not placed on the Brass Plates during the period under consideration, but of this we have no way of knowing.[1]

The fact that Lehi's genealogy could be traced back to Joseph — specifically Manasseh (Alma 10:3) — may also imply that the record had its origins in the Northern Kingdom, rather than in Judah in the South. (1 Ne. 3:3, 12; 5:14-16.) In one of the prophecies of Zenos are found these words: "And *as for those who are at Jerusalem* . . ." (1 Ne. 19:13; emphasis added), perhaps suggesting that Zenos was speaking from somewhere other than Jerusalem. Further, note Mormon's words concerning the prophets Zenos and Zenock: "Behold, I say unto you, Yea, many have testified of these things [signs surrounding the death of Christ] . . . and were slain because they testified of these things. Yea, the prophet Zenos did testify of these things, and also Zenock spake concerning these things, because *they testified particularly concerning us, who are the remnant of their seed.*" (3 Ne. 10:15-16; emphasis added.) This passage seems to suggest the possibility that Zenos and Zenock were both of the tribe of Joseph.

The non-biblical prophets mentioned in the Book of Mormon (whose prophecies we suppose were drawn from the brass plates) are named as Zenos, Zenock, Neum, and Ezias. Other than the fact that they lived "since the days of Abraham" (Hel. 8:19), we know very little about them. Of Ezias we know only that he prophesied of the coming of the Messiah. (Hel. 8:19-20.) Neum spoke prophetically of the crucifixion of the Son of Man. (1 Ne. 19:10.) Zenock bore repeated witness of the Savior: that redemption would come only in and through the atoning sacrifice and death of Christ; that the Savior would be lifted up by wicked men; and that the anger of the Father was kindled against those who do not recognize and acknowledge the cost of the Lord's atonement. (See 1 Ne. 19:10; Alma 33:15-17; Hel. 8:18-20; 3 Ne. 10:16.)

We have more information from and about the prophet Zenos than any of the non-biblical prophets of the brass plates. Nephi and Jacob quoted Zenos extensively, and Alma used the words of Zenos on worship and prayer in speaking to the Zoramites. (1 Ne. 19, 22;

Jacob 5; Alma 33:3-11.) "I do not think I overstate the matter," said Elder Bruce R. McConkie, "when I say that next to Isaiah himself... there was not a greater prophet in all Israel than Zenos. And our knowledge of his inspired writings is limited to the quotations and paraphrasing summaries found in the Book of Mormon."[2]

One of the marvels of the Restoration is the divine perspective that has come through the Prophet Joseph Smith concerning Christ's eternal gospel, the realization that Christian prophets have taught Christian doctrines and administered Christian ordinances since the days of Adam. (See Alma 39:17-19; D&C 20:25-26.) Elder McConkie observed that "what interests us more than the books included on the brass plates is the tone and tenor and general approach to the gospel and to salvation that they set forth. *They are gospel oriented and speak of Christ and the various Christian concepts which the world falsely assumes to have originated with Jesus and the early apostles.*"[3] Whereas the biblical prophecies of the Christ are missing or at best veiled, the prophets of the brass plates are bold in testifying of the coming of Jesus Christ and are quite specific as to his ministry.

Nephi delivered a poignant message when he observed that "the things which some men esteem to be of great worth, both to the body and soul, others set at naught and trample under their feet." His illustration is the manner in which the Messiah-Savior would be received in the meridian of time. The people would "set him at naught," Nephi prophesied, "and hearken not to the voice of his counsels." Further, because of the iniquities of the people of the first century, they would "scourge him, and he suffereth it; and they smite him, and he suffereth it. Yea, they spit upon him, and he suffereth it, because of his loving kindness and his long-suffering towards the children of men." And then, in speaking of the Lord Jesus, who is the "God of our fathers," the "God of Abraham, and of Isaac, and the God of Jacob," Nephi explained that he would yield himself to wicked men, "to be lifted up, according to the words of Zenock, and to be crucified, according to words of Neum, and to be buried in a sepulchre, according to the words of Zenos, which he [Zenos] spake concerning the three days of darkness, which should be a sign given of his death." (1 Ne. 19:7, 9-10.) The prophetic particulars and messianic details found on the brass plates are indeed remarkable.

Zenos on the Scattering and Gathering of Israel

Nephi referred a number of times to the words of "the prophet," meaning, it would appear, the words of Zenos. He cited Zenos's prophecies of the cataclysms associated. with the death of Christ — thunderings, lightnings, tempests, fire, smoke, vapor of darkness, and earthquakes — and noted that such calamities will cause the kings of the earth to exclaim: "The God of nature suffers." (1 Ne. 19:11-12; cf. 3 Ne. 8; Moses 7:55-56.)

It was not, however, the earth alone that was to be unsettled because of the murder of the Lord of all life. Those who put him to death — those who had spurned the miracles and signs and wonders, those physical evidences of his divine Sonship — these, because they had "turn[ed] their hearts aside" from the Holy One (1 Ne. 19:14), would be scattered and smitten by the nations of the earth. As to this central Book of Mormon doctrine — the doctrine of the scattering and gathering of Israel — Nephi is unexcelled in his clarity and breadth of expression. Elder Bruce R. McConkie noted: "Our Israelite forebears were scattered because they rejected the gospel, defiled the priesthood, forsook the church, and departed from the kingdom. They were scattered because they turned from the Lord, worshipped false gods, and walked in all the ways of the heathen nations. They were scattered because they . . . rejected the Lord Jehovah, who is the Lord Jesus, of whom all their prophets testified. Israel was scattered for apostasy."[4] In short, a people is scattered when they reject the true Messiah and the true church.

On the other hand, a branch of Israel is gathered when the people accept the true Messiah and become part of the true fold and church of God. (See 2 Ne. 9:2; 25:14.) That gathering is twofold: first spiritual and secondly temporal. People are gathered, first, when they join the true church and, secondly, when they gather to that appropriate location wherein the Saints of God in their area congregate. In short, as Elder McConkie said, "the gathering of Israel consists in believing and accepting and living in harmony with all that the Lord once offered his ancient chosen people . . . It consists of believing the gospel, joining the Church, and coming into the kingdom . . . And it may also consist of assembling to an appointed place or land of worship."[5]

President Spencer W. Kimball stated: "The gathering of Israel consists of joining the true church and their coming to a knowledge of the true God. . . . Any person, therefore, who has accepted the restored gospel, and who now seeks to worship the Lord in his own tongue and with the Saints in the nations where he lives, has complied with the law of the gathering of Israel and is heir to all of the blessings promised the Saints in these last days."[6] Thus Nephi, in speaking specifically of the Jews, and, by extension, of all the house of Israel, said: "When that day cometh, saith the prophet [Zenos], that they no more turn aside their hearts against the Holy One of Israel, then will he remember the covenants which he made to their fathers. Yea," Nephi continued, "then will he remember the isles of the sea; yea, and all the people who are of the house of Israel, will I gather in, saith the Lord, according to the words of the prophet Zenos, from the four quarters of the earth." This final gathering, to be commenced in the dispensation of the fulness of times, is to continue through the Millennium, that day when "all the earth shall see the salvation of the Lord." (1 Ne. 19:15-17.)

Nephi Quotes Isaiah on the Gathering of Israel

Because the gathering of Israel is primarily a "restoration to the knowledge of Christ" (Morm. 9:36), and because Isaiah was a superb witness of the Lord Jesus Christ (2 Ne. 11:2-4)[7], Nephi next turns his attention to the writings of Isaiah. "I did read many things unto [my people]," Nephi explained, "which were written in the books of Moses; but that I might more fully persuade them to believe in the Lord their Redeemer I did read unto them that which was written by the prophet Isaiah; for I did liken all scriptures unto us, that it might be for our profit and learning." (1 Ne. 19:23.) Isaiah's message, written in the first instance to Israel of the eighth century before Christ, has saving relevance for all the house of Israel in any age. "There are many things," Jacob later pointed out, "which have been spoken by Isaiah which may be likened unto you, because ye are of the house of Israel." (2 Ne. 6:5.)

Isaiah, who is also called by Nephi "the prophet," had a panoramic perspective of the destiny of Israel. His was the vision that despite Israel's immaturity and wicked wanderings; despite her infidelity to

Jehovah; and despite her disloyalty to the principles of the everlasting covenant, yet the hand of Israel's God was extended still, and that divine assistance was ever available to his chosen people. In the words of Isaiah (Nephi quoted from what we know as Isaiah 48), Israel has been obstinate, a people whose neck is "an iron sinew" and whose brow is like brass. She has been "a transgressor from the womb," a rebellious nation from the time of her mortal inception. "Nevertheless," the Lord explained to Israel, "for my name's sake will I defer mine anger, and for my praise will I refrain from thee, that I cut thee not off." ·The Lord Jehovah had placed his name and the promise of his power upon the nation of Israel. They were his people; they were to become his peculiar treasure. He had given that name and power to none other, and had no intention of his holy name being forgotten, ignored, or profaned by the surrounding nations. "I will not suffer my name to be polluted," he said, "and I will not give my glory unto another." (1 Ne. 20:4, 8-9, 11.)

Isaiah affirmed that Jehovah was a God of power, and that the destiny of nations was in his hands. Though the Jews would fall to the powerful kingdom to the east — the Babylonians — the Lord would yet "do his pleasure on Babylon, and his arm shall come upon the Chaldeans." When Israel had paid the penalty of her sins, when she had been refined in the furnace of affliction, then the divine directive would be forthcoming: "Go ye forth of Babylon, flee ye from the Chaldeans" for "the Lord hath redeemed his servant Jacob." (See 1 Ne. 20:10, 14, 20.)

Isaiah stressed (in Isaiah 49) that the house of Israel has a mission to the world. It is "a light thing," meaning it is simply not enough, for Israelites to build and strengthen one another (as important as that is); they are to be "a light to the Gentiles," an ensign or standard to the nations, a refuge from the storms of ignorance and confusion and sin. In the last days, in the dispensation of the fulness of times, a light is to break forth unto those who sit in darkness; that light is the fulness of the gospel. (See 1 Ne. 21:6; D&C 45:28.) In the final dispensation of grace, however, the order of presentation of the gospel is to be reversed: the first — Israel — shall be last, and the last — the Gentiles — shall be first. (See Matt. 20:16.) That is, the fulness of the gospel is to be delivered first to a special servant of the Lord, Joseph Smith, Jr. (1 Ne. 21:8; cf. 2 Ne. 3:11; 3 Ne. 21:11), a man living in a great Gentile nation. Then the Gentiles — cultural Gentiles (see 1 Ne. 13:4; 15:13; 22:7; D&C 109:60) — shall take the gospel to the house of Israel — the Lamanites and the Jews. Through this means, the work of the Father — the work of gathering — is to commence in the last days; Israel shall "come from far; and lo, . . . from the north and from the west." Jehovah can no more forget his people in their scattered state than a mother could forget her sucking child. Indeed, the Lord cannot forget Israel, for he has graven them upon the palms of his hands. Jesus Christ cannot forget his people, for he will suffer and die for them. To dramatize the miracle of gathering and to demonstrate the great numbers of scattered Israel that will be restored to their Lord and to their homelands, the Lord spoke to Israel through Isaiah: "The children whom thou shalt have, after thou hast lost the first, shall again in thine ears say: The place is too strait for me; give place to me that I may dwell." (1 Ne. 21:15-16, 20.)

Two of the most difficult verses in all of Isaiah's writings come in chapter 49: "Thus saith the Lord God: Behold, I will lift up mine hand to the Gentiles, and set up my standard to the people; and they shall bring thy sons in their arms, and thy daughters shall be carried upon their shoulders. And kings shall be thy nursing fathers, and their queens thy nursing mothers; they shall bow down to thee with their face towards the earth, and lick up the dust of thy feet; and thou shalt know that I am the Lord; for they shall not be ashamed that wait for me." (1 Ne. 21:22-23.) We find Nephi's prophetic commentary on these verses in 1 Nephi 22:7-14.

According to Nephi, Isaiah was speaking of the establishment of the ensign to the nations, the restoration of the everlasting gospel in the last days. Such would come in a day following the persecution and scattering of the Lamanites — the native Americans — and would take place in that great Gentile nation we know as the United States of America ("upon the face of this land"). It is through Joseph Smith and the Latter-day Saints — cultural Gentiles (see D&C 109:60) — that the message of the gospel of Jesus Christ would go to the house of Israel — the Lamanites and the Jews — in the last days. The Lord thereby treats his covenant people to a royal banquet, to a "feast of fat things," a "supper of the house of the Lord" (D&C 58:8-9); it is a dispensational era wherein men and women of faith may receive and partake of the bread of life and the living waters available only through the church and kingdom of God. The presentation of the message of the Restoration — the delivery of that voice which speaks from the dust — "is likened unto [the house of Israel in the last days] being nourished by the Gentiles and being carried in their arms and upon their shoulders." Such a missionary effort results in "making known of the covenants of the Father of heaven unto Abraham, saying: In thy seed shall all the kindreds of the earth be blessed." (1 Ne. 22:8-9.) That is, by means of the glorious work brought to pass through Joseph Smith and thereafter set in motion by the Saints, the "promises made to the fathers" are to be fully realized. (See Abr. 2:8-10; D&C 2; 110.)

The passage "Kings shall be thy nursing fathers, and their queens thy nursing mothers; they shall bow down to thee with their face towards the earth, and lick up the dust of thy feet," is given meaning later by Jacob, the brother of Nephi. Jacob explained that the ultimate fulfillment of this prophecy is millennial and pertains to the final destruction of the enemies of the covenant people of God: "And blessed are the Gentiles," he wrote, "they of whom the prophet [Isaiah] has written; for behold, if it so be that they shall repent and fight not against Zion, and do not unite themselves to that great and abominable church, they shall be saved . . . . Wherefore, they that fight against Zion and the covenant people of the Lord shall lick up the dust of their feet; and the people of the Lord shall not be ashamed. For the people of the Lord are they who wait for him; for they still wait for the coming of the Messiah." (2 Ne. 6:12-13; cf. 10:7-9.)

Regarding those who afflict Israel in the last days, the Lord warned through Isaiah: "I will feed them that oppress thee with their own flesh; they shall be drunken with their own blood as with sweet wine; and all flesh shall know that I, the Lord, am thy Savior and thy Redeemer, the Mighty One of Jacob." (1 Ne. 21:26.) Nephi's commentary upon this verse is insightful. Having learned through conversion of their own identity and their place in the royal family, Israel is restored to the knowledge of their Lord and God and also to the lands of their inheritance: they shall know that the Lord is their Savior and their Redeemer, the Mighty One of Israel. Further, those nations and elements and organizations that comprise the whore of all the earth — any institution or individual that fights against the church of the Lamb (2 Ne. 10:16) — shall eventually factionalize themselves into ruin and decay through internal strife: "The blood of that great and abominable church, which is the whore of all the earth, shall turn upon their own heads; for they shall war among themselves, and the sword of their own hands shall fall upon their own heads, and they shall be drunken with their own blood." (1 Ne. 22:13.)

Nephi, Malachi, and Zenos on the Millennium

In the midst of his prophetic commentary on the writings of Isaiah, Nephi said: "For behold, saith the prophet, the time cometh speedily that Satan shall have no more power over the hearts of the children of men; for the day soon cometh that all the proud and they who do wickedly shall be as stubble; and the day cometh that they must be burned." (1 Ne. 22:15.) These words are unmistakably similar to those of Malachi, the Old Testament prophet in about 500-400 B.C. Note Malachi's prophecy of the Second Coming: "For, behold, the day cometh, that shall burn as an oven; and *all the proud, yea, and all that do wickedly, shall be stubble: and the day that cometh shall burn them up*, saith the Lord of hosts." (Mal. 4:1; emphasis added.) Later we find Nephi discussing the wicked, "in fine, all those who belong to the kingdom of the devil." These are they "who need fear, and tremble, and quake; they are those who must be brought low in the dust; they are those who must be consumed as stubble; and this is according to the words of the prophet. And the time cometh speedily that the righteous must be led up as calves of the stall, and the Holy One of Israel must reign in dominion, and might, and power, and great glory." (1 Ne. 22:23-24.) A number of years later Nephi prophesied concerning the coming of the Savior to the Americas (note how he likened the destruction of the wicked in the meridian of time to the destruction to come at the end of the world): "All those who are proud, and that do wickedly, the day that cometh shall burn them up, saith the Lord of Hosts, for they shall be as stubble." The righteous, on the other hand, "are they which shall not perish. But the Son of righteousness shall appear unto them; and he shall heal them, and they shall have peace with him." (2 Ne. 26:4, 8-9.) Again, the similarity to Malachi's prophecy is notable: "But *unto you that fear my name shall the Sun of righteousness arise with healing in his wings; and ye shall go forth, and grow up as calves of the stall.*" (Mal. 4:2, emphasis added.) Inasmuch as Nephi's oracle was uttered over one hundred years before the time of Malachi, how do we explain the similarity of language? Elder Bruce R. McConkie taught:

> Our understanding of the prophetic word will be greatly expanded if we know how one prophet quotes another, usually without acknowledging his source.
>
> Either Isaiah or Micah copied the prophetic words of the other relative to the mountain of the Lord's house being established in the last days with all nations flowing thereto. Their ministries overlapped, but we assume that the lesser Micah copied from the greater Isaiah and then appended some words of his own about the Millennial Era.
>
> Some unnamed Old Testament prophet, who obviously was Zenos, as the Book of Mormon testifies, spoke of the day when the wicked would be destroyed as stubble; when the righteous would be "led up as calves of the stall"; when Christ should "rise from the dead, with healing in his wings"; and when the Holy One of Israel would then reign on earth.
>
> Malachi, who lived more than two hundred years after Nephi, uses these very expressions in his prophetic writings. *Can we do other than conclude that both Nephi and Malachi had before them the writings of Zenos?* . . .
>
> Once the Lord has revealed his doctrine in precise language to a chosen prophet, there is no reason why he should inspire another prophet to choose the same words in presenting the same doctrine on a subsequent occasion. It is much easier and simpler to quote that which has already been given in perfection. We are all commanded — including the prophets among us — to search the scriptures and thereby learn what other prophets have presented.[8]

Nephi next taught that the Lord will recompense righteousness.

He will ultimately remove wickedness from the face of the earth. In the words of Nephi, the God of Israel "will not suffer that the wicked shall destroy the righteous." Rather, he will, at the time of his second coming, "cause a great division among the people," a division between the believing and the ungodly. "And the wicked will he destroy; and he will spare his people, yea, even if it so be that he must destroy the wicked by fire" (2 Ne. 30:10; cf. D&C 63:54), by the brightness of his glory.[9] Those who will not receive the Lord Jesus; those who will not hear his voice or the voice of his servants; those who revel in priestcraft and idolatry—these shall be cut off from among the covenant people, separated from those who cherish the words of eternal life. (See 1 Ne. 22:20-23; cf. 3 Ne. 21:11; Deut. 18:19; Acts 3:23; D&C 1:14.)

During the thousand years of peace, the missionary force of the Church of Jesus Christ will intensify, and "the work of the Father" will commence once again. (See 2 Ne. 30:7-15; 3 Ne. 20:17-22; 21:25-29.) The Master will gather "his children from the four quarters of the earth . . . and there shall be one fold and one shepherd; and [Christ] shall feed his sheep, and in him they shall find pasture." The great Millennium, brought in with power, will be maintained by the faithfulness of the people on earth: "Because of the righteousness of his people, Satan has no power; wherefore, he cannot be loosed for the space of many years; for he hath no power over the hearts of the people, for they dwell in righteousness, and the Holy One of Israel reigneth." (1 Ne. 22:25-26.)

Conclusion

Nephi's glimpse of the future—based upon his own seeric experience and the inspired utterances of his prophetic colleagues Zenos and Isaiah—point toward the glorious realization of "the promises made to the fathers." These peerless oracles assure the descendants of Jacob that the God of ancient Abraham is also the God of modern Israel; that the day will soon dawn wherein Zion shall once again evidence her strength and put on her beautiful garments: she will enjoy the authority and power of the holy priesthood. Israel will loose herself from the bands of her neck—be restored to the God of

Israel and enjoy the revelations of heaven reserved for those who aspire to become Jehovah's peculiar treasure. (See Isa. 52:1-2; D&C 113:7-10.)

The prophecies from the brass plates, like those found in other sacred collections, detail pages from Israel's book of possibilities. The house of Israel can be great only as she is good. Nephi therefore bore testimony that "the things which have been written upon the plates of brass are true; and they testify that a man must be obedient to the commandments of God." He brings to an end his first book with the ever-present but necessary call to continued faithfulness: "Wherefore, if ye shall be obedient to the commandments, and endure to the end, ye shall be saved at the last day." (1 Ne. 22:30-31.)

NOTES

1. *Answers to Book of Mormon Questions* (Salt Lake City: Bookcraft, 1967), pp. 43-44.

2. "The Doctrinal Restoration," in *The Joseph Smith Translation: The Restoration of Plain and Precious Things*, eds. Monte S. Nyman and Robert L. Millet (Provo, Utah: Religious Studies Center, Brigham Young University, 1985), p. 17.

3. "The Doctrinal Restoration," p. 17; emphasis added.

4. Bruce R. McConkie, *A New Witness for the Articles of Faith* (Salt Lake City: Deseret Book Company, 1985), p. 515.

5. Ibid.

6. *The Teachings of Spencer W. Kimball*, ed. Edward L. Kimball (Salt Lake City: Bookcraft, 1982), p. 439.

7. One Latter-day Saint writer has indicated that of the 425 verses from Isaiah quoted in the Book of Mormon, 391 of them deal with the attributes or mission of the Messiah. (See Monte S. Nyman, *Great Are the Words of Isaiah* [Salt Lake City: Bookcraft, 1980], p. 7.)

8. "The Doctrinal Restoration," pp. 17-18, emphasis added; see also *A New Witness for the Articles of Faith*, p. 402.

9. See *A New Witness for the Articles of Faith*, pp. 562-63.

8

CREATION, FALL, AND ATONEMENT
(2 Nephi 1, 2)

LaMar E. Garrard

When Joseph Smith lost the first 116 pages of manuscript, upon which was written his translation from the abridgment of the large plates of Nephi, he was forbidden by the Lord to retranslate from this same record in order to replace the lost manuscript. Rather, the Lord instructed him to translate from another record, the small plates of Nephi, which covered the same period of time down to the reign of King Benjamin. (D&C 10:1-50.) Evidently the Lord had always intended that our generation would ultimately receive the translation from the small plates of Nephi,[1] for he explained to Joseph that they "do throw *greater views upon my gospel;* therefore, it is *wisdom in me* that you should translate the first part of the engravings of Nephi." (D&C 10:45, emphasis added.) The first two chapters of 2 Nephi in our present Book of Mormon are part of the translation from these small plates of Nephi, which the Lord in his wisdom intended that our generation should have.

In the first chapter of 2 Nephi, Lehi reminded his sons how merciful God had been to save them from the destruction of Jerusalem by leading them to a land of promise. He told them that their land was "a land of promise, a land which is choice above all other lands," a land of liberty reserved for him and his seed and "those who should

---

LaMar E. Garrard is professor of Church history and doctrine at Brigham Young University.

be led out of other countries by the hand of the Lord." (2 Ne. 1:5.) However, he gave a solemn warning to his sons as well as to their posterity who would inhabit that land: "If the day shall come that they will reject the Holy One of Israel, the true Messiah, their Redeemer and their God, behold, the judgments of him that is just shall rest upon them." (2 Ne. 1:10.)

Not only was Lehi warning his sons, but it seems he was also warning the modern generation. (D&C 10:49-51; 2 Ne. 1:5-7.) In the very next chapter Lehi gave a great doctrinal discourse on the purpose of life, the creation of the earth, the fall of man, and the atonement of Christ. These things that Lehi taught contradict many false teachings and philosophies prevalent in our generation. Accepting these false ideas and philosophies can lead us to lose faith in the validity of the word of God as found in the scriptures. This in turn leads to a disregard for the commandments of God, which come by revelation. Hence, it seems that the Lord wanted this great discourse in chapter 2 to follow the warning given in chapter 1. As modern readers *carefully* and *prayerfully* read these two chapters and gain a testimony of them through the power of the Holy Ghost, they are warned and fortified against the false teachings and theories, proposed in our modern day that would lead to the breaking of God's commandments.

The Creation

There is a tendency for people in our generation to discount the "special creation" account of the origin of our heaven and earth as related in the Bible. The modern trend is to accept a "naturalistic" or "mechanistic" view of the origin of our solar system, including our earth and all things upon it.[2] Such a view proposes that these things came into existence by chance — by the strict operation of "natural law" rather than by God's purposes being fulfilled as a result of his wisdom and power. This mechanistic view looks upon natural law as eternal or self-existent and as determining absolutely what happens to physical matter over a given time. There is no allowance for a divine or supernatural power of any kind over physical matter.[3] Such a view leaves no room for a God who has all knowledge and who thinks and plans (no divine purpose in the universe);[4] for a sovereign God who is all powerful[5] and who is the author of natural law (a God who has control or power directly over physical matter);[6] or for miracles or divine intervention (God cannot change or revoke natural law).[7] This "mechanistic" view also eliminates the spiritual realm in the universe wherein spirit matter (with "intelligence") can influence or control physical or other spirit matter. This assumes that the spirit matter does not exist;[8] people, animals, and plants do not have spirits;[9] there is no such thing as a God with a spirit;[10] and there is no influence whatsoever from God to the spirits of people[11] or to anything else in the universe.[12] Obviously, this view also eliminates revelation, so there can be no such thing as commandments from God. Such a view relegates man (and other "living" creatures) to a position of being mere physical machines with no agency or freedom to act by themselves.[13] They can only be acted upon, since all actions or events are determined completely by preceding physical events and subsequent operation of natural law.

A proponent of this mechanistic viewpoint was the renowned philosopher and logician Bertrand Russell. He claimed that this view emerged as a result of the growth of the scientific outlook of the eighteenth century: "Out of the work of the great men of the seventeenth century a new outlook on the world was developed. . . . I think there were three ingredients in the scientific outlook of the eighteenth century that were specially important: (1) Statements of fact should be based on observation, not on unsupported authority. (2) The inanimate world is a self-acting, self-perpetuating system, in which all changes conform to natural laws. (3) The earth is not the center of the universe, and probably Man is not its purpose (if any); moreover, 'purpose' is a concept which is scientifically useless. These items make up what is called the 'mechanistic outlook' which clergymen denounce."[14]

In contrast to this mechanistic outlook, Lehi declared that he had gained knowledge from sources (Russell's "unsupported authority") other than by observation through the natural senses. These sources were the scriptures and personal revelation. (2 Ne. 1:4, 6; 2:17.) From these sources he declared that there is a God in heaven who—with a definite purpose in mind—created both the heavens and the earth, including people and all other living things: "My sons, I speak unto you these things for *your profit and learning;* for *there is a God*, and he hath *created all things*, both the heavens and the earth, and all things that in them are, both *things to act* and things to be *acted upon*. And to *bring about his eternal purposes in the end of man*, after he had created our first parents, and the beasts of the field and the fowls of the air, and in fine, all things which are created, it must needs be that there was an opposition. . . . Wherefore, the Lord God gave unto man that *he should act for himself*." (2 Ne. 2:14-16; emphasis added.)

Lehi especially wanted his sons to understand that we can act for ourselves, which implies that we have spirits to animate our bodies (a compound being). There is much more to us than just a physical machine with no spirit (one body), subject only to natural law. Such a physical machine would act only according to natural law, for without a spirit it could not act for itself. Lehi elaborated on this theme by telling us that if the universe were strictly physical (one body) rather than physical and spiritual (compound), there would have been no purpose in its creation. His explanation that there must be a spiritual realm as well as a physical one (compound in one) is as follows: "Wherefore all things *must needs be a compound in one;* wherefore, if it should be *one body*, it must needs remain as dead, *having no life* neither death, nor corruption nor incorruption, happiness nor misery, neither sense nor insensibility. Wherefore, it must needs have been created for a thing of naught; wherefore there would have been *no purpose* in the end of its creation. Wherefore, this thing must needs *destroy the wisdom of God and his eternal purposes, and also the power*, and the mercy, and the justice of God." (2 Ne. 2:11-12; emphasis added.)

The Lord has revealed that he created or organized this earth for a *definite purpose:* the earth was created to provide a place where our spirits could come down from our premortal state and obtain physical bodies[15] and grow and progress while being tested or proven to see if we would obey God's commandments while inhabiting these mortal bodies. (Abr. 3:25.) Such an earthly probation could not be possible if we were strictly physical, subject only to natural laws.

The commandments of God (law)[16] come from God by revelation to our spirits[17] and can be either accepted or rejected by those same spirits.[18] If the spirit receives and desires to obey a commandment from God (righteousness), it can direct the body to obey that commandment;[19] and if the spirit refuses to receive and obey that commandment from God (wickedness), it exerts less control over the physical body with its natural influences. (2 Ne. 9:29; Mosiah 3:19.) So, the physical body is influenced by spiritual forces as well as natural forces. This is possible because we are a dual (compound) being composed of *both a spirit and a physical body that interact with each other*, giving us life, sensibility, and agency, or the capability *to act for ourselves* as well as to be acted upon.

Lehi went through a series of hypothetical propositions to demonstrate that if there were no God nor a law given by him to his children (which presupposes a spirit capable of receiving that commandment or law), there could be no wickedness nor its opposite, righteousness. Without righteousness or wickedness, there could be no happiness nor misery and hence no purpose in the creation of the world. Joseph Smith revealed to us that happiness is the object and design of our existence.[20] If we deny that there is a God who has given us his laws, and also deny that we have a spirit that is free to obey or disobey those laws, we are denying the very object and design of our existence. In advocating such a universe where there is no such thing as happiness, we are deceiving ourselves into thinking that we are anything but mechanical extensions of the physical universe, with no control over our destiny. It seems that Lehi was defining existence itself in terms of independence of action with a certain amount of control over our future state:[21] "If ye shall say there is no law, ye shall also say there is no sin. If ye shall say there is no sin, ye shall also say there is no righteousness. And if there be no righteousness there be no happiness. And if there be no righteousness nor happiness there be no punishment nor misery. And if these things are not there is no God. And if there is no God we are not, neither the earth; for there could have been no creation of things, *neither to act* nor to be acted upon; wherefore, all things must have vanished away." (2 Ne. 2:13; emphasis added.)

The Fall of Man

Another great contribution of 2 Nephi 2 is the added knowledge it gives concerning the fall of man; how the transgression of Adam and Eve affected not only them, but all their posterity as well as all other things that were created.

Because of the rise and influence of the mechanistic view previously mentioned, many people in our day look upon the biblical account of the fall as mythological and therefore not to be taken too seriously. However, to the reader of 2 Nephi 2 who has received a witness from the Holy Ghost that the Book of Mormon is true, there is a confirmation that the fall really did occur.[22] This account also throws greater light on other doctrines, such as the origin of man, which are intrinsically associated with the fall.

Many Christians who accept the biblical account of the fall feel that the transgression of Adam and Eve was a terrible sin or disaster that should not have occurred. If only Adam and Eve had not sinned, they claim, the world since that time would have been a much better place to live, without the misery and woe we find in it today. In contrast to this incorrect view, Lehi revealed that the fall was planned by God. There was "divine purpose" involved. Even though Adam and Eve were warned by God of the consequences of partaking of the forbidden fruit, "the Lord God gave unto man that he should act for himself." (2 Ne. 2:16.) The Lord knew that Adam and Eve would exercise that agency and would fall. After the fall, the Lord explained that "all things have been done in the wisdom of him who knoweth all things." (2 Ne. 2:24.)

As mentioned previously, the earth did not come into existence by chance but was created by God through the word of his power to bring about *his eternal purposes*. Besides creating our first parents, he also created "the *beasts of the field* and the *fowls of the air*, and . . . *all things which are created*." (2 Ne. 2:15; emphasis added.) One of the purposes of the creation of the earth was to provide a place where waiting spirits in heaven (the future posterity of Adam and Eve as well as the spirits of the animal world) could come to receive mortal bodies. Bodies of flesh and bone are necessary for happiness in this life as well as in the life hereafter.[23] This *purpose* could not have been fulfilled without the fall. Evidently the transgression of Adam and Eve caused a change in their physical bodies (as well as in the whole physical world),[24] which made possible physical birth (Moses 5:11; 2 Ne. 2:19-25) as well as physical death (Alma 42:2-9; 2 Ne. 2:5). Lehi explained that if Adam and Eve had not fallen, this change would not have taken place, and they never would have had children. Consequently there never would have been a human race: "Behold, if Adam had not transgressed he would not have fallen, but he would have remained in the garden of Eden. And *all things which were created must have remained in the same state in which they were after they were created; and they must have remained forever, and had no end. And they would have had* no *children. . . .* Adam fell that men *might be."* (2 Ne. 2:22, 23, 25; emphasis added.)

Since animals and plants are a part of "all things" that were created,[25] evidently they also—without the fall—would "have remained in the same state in which they were after they were created" and would not have been able to reproduce (and die). Other modern scripture indicates that *all* living organisms (people, animals, and plants) have spirits.[26] These scriptures define life as beginning when the spirit is placed into the physical body.[27] It seems that death involves the removal of that spirit from the physical body so that the body becomes inanimate or lifeless. (Matt. 27:50.) The idea that the fall was necessary to inaugurate reproduction (as well as death) among living organisms, wherein a spirit is placed into the physical body (or taken out), is incompatible with Darwin's theory of organic evolution. Russell points out the logical inconsistencies that result when Christians claim to believe in the Bible—which teaches the fall of man—and at the same time accept theories that rule out the fall of Adam.

> Darwinism has had many effects upon man's outlook on life and the world, in addition to the extrusion of purpose of which I have already spoken. The absence of any sharp line between men and apes is very awkward for theology. When did men get souls? Was the Missing Link capable of sin and therefore worthy of hell? Did Pithecanthropus Erectus have

moral responsibility? Was Homo Pekinienis damned? Did Pilt-
down Man go to heaven? Any answer must be arbitrary.[28]

Since most modern theories of organic evolution still depend
upon chance mutation (which of necessity depends upon the birth
process), the survival of the fittest (which of necessity depends upon
the death process), and millions of years for these processes to have'
been taking place (not just 6,000 years since the fall),[29] it is very
difficult to retain one's belief in the doctrines taught in 2 Nephi 2
(and other modern scripture) and at the same time accept purely
"naturalistic" explanations of the origin of man.

God Is a God of Law and Justice

As mentioned previously, a natural consequence of accepting a
"naturalistic" or "mechanistic" philosophy is to reject the idea of a
moral law in the universe, a law of which God is the author. Since
most of those who advocate this philosophy claim there is no God,
it follows that the concept of sin as the breaking of a commandment
or law of God is illogical. [30] To them, what is morally right or wrong
is *not* determined by God's will but by a consensus of society. To
achieve a better world to live in, they propose that we manipulate
our environment until our behavior coincides with this consensus.

An offshoot of this naturalistic philosophy is advocated by some
who say that there is a God but that there is also an eternal (self-
existing) moral law in the universe that exists independent of God
(*no* God at any time is the author of this law). Some even suggest
that God became God by obeying such a law, which implies that the
law is ultimately the sovereign power in the universe. In such a
universe, it would be more reasonable for people to worship the law
(which incidently has no body, parts, or passions) since it is more
powerful than God and he is subject to it.[31]

In contrast to these views, Lehi again reminds us that the terms
God, law, and *sin* are bi-conditional to each other: to deny that any
one of them exists is to deny that the others exist, and to affirm that
any one of them exists is to affirm that the others exist: "If ye shall
say there is no law, ye shall also say there is no sin. . . . And if these

things are not there is no God. And if there is no God we are not, neither the earth; . . . wherefore, all things must have vanished away." (2 Ne. 2:13.)

Lehi's statement clearly indicates that moral laws in the universe do not exist independent of God: if there is no law, there is no God, and if there is no God, there is no law; for God is *always* the author of law. He further taught that the laws of God are "given unto men" and that people "are instructed sufficiently that they know good from evil." (2 Ne. 2:5.) In still another passage, he stated that not only is God the author of law, but that he will judge us as to how we kept his law and then reward or punish us accordingly: "All men come unto God; wherefore, they stand in the presence of him to be judged of him according to the truth and holiness which is in him. Wherefore, the ends of the law *which the Holy One hath given*, unto the inflicting of the punishment which is affixed . . . " (2 Ne. 2:10; emphasis added.)

The Effects of the Atonement of Christ

Lehi revealed to us that it is possible for Christ to save us from the effects of breaking these very laws He has given us. Because Adam and Eve broke God's law in the garden of Eden, they and all their posterity became subject to spiritual and temporal death: "By the law no flesh is justified; or, by the law men are cut off. Yea, by the temporal law they were cut off; and also, by the spiritual law they perish from that which is good, and become miserable forever." (2 Ne. 2:5.)

As a result of the atonement of Christ, the effects of this broken law (spiritual and temporal death) *will* eventually be overcome by *all* people unconditionally when they are resurrected (overcome temporal death) and are then brought back into the presence of God (overcome spiritual death) to be judged of Christ: "Redemption cometh in and through the Holy Messiah; for he is full of grace and truth. . . . There is no flesh that can dwell in the presence of God, save it be through the merits, and mercy, and grace of the Holy Messiah, who layeth down his life according to the flesh, and taketh it again by the power of the Spirit, that he may bring to pass the resurrection of the dead. . . . And because of the intercession for all,

all men come unto God; wherefore, they stand in the presence of him, to be judged of him according to the truth and holiness which is in him." (2 Ne. 2:6, 8, 10.)

If there had been no atonement, the effect of Adam and Eve's transgression would have been everlasting: Satan would have held us captive to do his will forever. (2 Ne. 9:6-9.) The atonement, however, made it possible for us to be free to follow either God or Satan: "The Messiah cometh in the fulness of time, that he may redeem the children of men from the fall. And *because that they are redeemed from the fall* they have *become free* forever, knowing good from evil; *to act for themselves* and not to be acted upon. . . . Wherefore, men are *free according to the flesh;* and all things are given them which are expedient unto man. And they are free to choose liberty and eternal life, through the great Mediator of all men, or to choose captivity and death, according to the captivity and power of the devil." (2 Ne. 2:26-27; emphasis added.)

Satan was allowed to retain a certain influence or power over the physical world, which includes our physical bodies.[32] Through our fallen flesh, Satan has the power to tempt and try us.[33] But through the power of the atonement, our spirits are innocent when they come into this life and are subject to the influence of God's spirit as long as we do not give in to the flesh:[34] "And now, my sons, I would that ye should look to the great Mediator, and hearken unto his great commandments; and be faithful unto his words, and choose eternal life, according to the *will of his Holy Spirit;* And not choose eternal death, *according to the will of the flesh* and the *evil which is therein, which giveth the spirit of the devil power to captivate,* to bring you down to hell, that he may reign over you in his own kingdom." (2 Ne. 2:28-29; emphasis added.)

The effects of the fall *and* the atonement were to place us in a position were we are subject to two external forces or influences, one from God acting upon our spirits to do good and one from Satan acting upon our flesh to do evil. (Alma 3:26-27; 29:4-5.) The fact that we are subject to these two opposing forces or alternatives (good and evil), and are free to choose between them, makes it possible for us to experience either happiness or misery. When we choose to follow Satan, we become subject to the effects of a broken law, which is spiritual death. This results in misery. However, if we humble ourselves before God and acknowledge to him that we are sorry for breaking *his* laws, repent, are baptized, and develop a faith in Christ's redemptive powers, we are saved from the effects of the broken law by the intercession of Christ. Rather than being punished (spiritual death and misery), we gain *happiness* through the atonement of Christ:

"Behold, he offereth himself a sacrifice for sin, to answer the ends of the law, unto all those who have a broken heart and a contrite spirit; and unto none else can the ends of the law be answered. . . . Wherefore, he is the firstfruits unto God, inasmuch as he shall make intercession for all the children of men; and they that believe in him shall be saved. . . . And . . . men come unto God . . . to be judged of him. . . . Wherefore, the ends of the law which the Holy One hath given, unto the inflicting of the punishment which is affixed, which punishment that is affixed is in opposition to that of the *happiness which is affixed, to answer the ends of the atonement.*" (2 Ne. 2:7, 9-10; emphasis added.)

Happiness, then, would not be possible without the possibility of its alternative, misery. To be physical machines subject only to natural laws, to be slaves of God subject only to his power, or for that matter to be slaves of Lucifer, could not bring happiness: "For it must needs be, that there is an opposition in all things. If not so, . . . righteousness could not be brought to pass, neither wickedness, neither holiness nor misery, neither good nor bad. . . . And if there be no righteousness there be no happiness. And if there be no righteousness nor happiness there be no punishment nor misery. And if these things are not there is no God." (2 Ne. 2:11, 13.)

Besides bringing us the happiness that results from overcoming opposition, our physical bodies also add to our happiness.[35] In fact, gaining a physical but immortal body in the resurrection makes it possible for us to ultimately gain a fulness of joy. (D&C 93:33.) God's *great purpose* or goal was to make it possible for us to gain happiness. That goal could not have been achieved without the fall and the atonement. Lehi summarizes this as follows:

To bring about *his eternal purposes* in the end of man, after he had created our first parents, and the beasts of the field and the fowls of the air . . . it must needs be that there was an opposition; even the forbidden fruit in opposition to the tree of life; . . . Wherefore, the Lord God gave unto man that he should act for himself. Wherefore, man could not act for himself save it should be that he was enticed by the one or the other. . . . And after Adam and Eve had partaken of the forbidden fruit they were driven out of the garden of Eden. . . . And now, behold, if Adam had not transgressed he would not have fallen, but he would have remained in the garden of Eden. And all things which were created must have remained *in the same state* in which they were after they were created; and they must have remained forever, and had no end. And they would have *had no children;* wherefore they would have remained in a state of innocence, having no joy, for they knew no misery; doing no good, for they knew no sin. But behold, *all things have been done in the wisdom of him who knoweth all things.* Adam fell that *men might be;* and men are, that they *might have joy.* (2 Ne. 2:15, 16, 19, 22-25; emphasis added.)

Summary and Conclusions

If the universe were such that there were no God, and natural law was the sovereign power in the universe ("naturalism"), then there would be no commandments of God (God's laws) and we would be mere physical machines with no spirits or freedom to act. In such a universe, there would be no such thing as breaking a commandment of God, and therefore there could have been no fall of man or the possibility of sin. If there were no sin or fall, there would be no need for an atonement and consequently no need for a Christ. Hence, Jesus would not be the Christ. Such are the implications of the naturalistic viewpoint.

God has spoken to our modern generation through the Book of Mormon. The main message of that book (as stated in the title page) is "to the convincing of the Jew and the Gentile that Jesus is the Christ, the Eternal God." The Book of Mormon contains the inspired words of Lehi, who refuted the premises of naturalism, point by point. He stated that there is a God who created this earth and all living things therein, including man. There was a fall of man (which furthered God's purpose), which introduced birth, death, opposition, and sin into this world. There was an atonement provided to remove the effects of the fall, which were spiritual and temporal death. God authors laws for our benefit to lead us to happiness. If we break these laws (sin), there is an atonement provided to wipe away our sins on condition of repentance. Jesus met the requirements necessary for the atonement and is therefore the Christ.

If one carefully and prayerfully reads the Book of Mormon and receives a confirmation through the power of the Holy Ghost that the events and doctrines related in it are true, one avoids accepting false teachings and philosophies that lead to a disregard for God's scripture. Such a disregard would lead to the breaking of God's commandments, which come to us through the scriptures, the prophets, and personal revelation.[36] Hence, by reading and accepting the words contained in the Book of Mormon, we are motivated to keep God's commandments, and our lives are blessed.

NOTES

1. 1 Ne. 9:1-6; W of M 1:6-7; Alma 37:2, 13-14.

2. A more detailed account of the history and rise of naturalism and its implications is given by the author in the following article: "What is Man?," *Hearken O Ye People* (Sandy, Utah: Randall Book Company, 1984), pp. 134-42; hereinafter referred to as "What is Man?"

3. However, Joseph Smith stated and the scriptures reveal that God has all power (Joseph Smith, *Teachings of the Prophet Joseph Smith*, selected by Joseph Fielding Smith [Salt Lake City: Deseret Book Company, 1938], p. 288; D&C 61:1; 93:17; Matt. 28:18) and can command the elements to obey him (D&C 133: 21-24; Hel. 12:6-17; Abr. 2:7; Matt. 21:19-20; John 2:1-11). Sometimes he even delegates that power to mortals. (Moses 1:25; 6:34; 7:13; Jacob 4:6; Hel. 10:4-7, 16; 11:4-17; Ether 12:30.)

4. Joseph Smith stated and the scriptures reveal that God has all knowl-

edge (*Teachings of the Prophet Joseph Smith*, p. 288; D&C 38:2; 88:41; 93:13, 26; Mosiah 4:9; Alma 26:35) and that he makes plans and executes them to fulfill his divine purposes (Abr. 2:8; 3:24; 4:21; 5:1-5; Moses 1:31-39; D&C 3:1-2; 59:21; 101:80; 117:6-7; W of M 1:6-7; *Teachings of the Prophet Joseph Smith*, p. 345).

5. Joseph Smith stated and the scriptures reveal that God is all powerful (see note 3 and also D&C 88:41; 100:1).

6. Joseph Smith stated and the scriptures reveal that with His knowledge and power, God commanded or spoke to the elements with his voice (D&C 29:30-31; 38:3; 88:6-10, 12-13; Moses 1:32) and they obeyed him (Moses 2:6, 9, 11, 14, 20, 24; Abr. 4:7, 9-12, 18) and the solar system was organized or created (Abr. 3:24; Mosiah 4:9; D&C 20:17; Moses 1:33, 35-38). God sustains and upholds the universe (*Teachings of the Prophet Joseph Smith*, p. 345; Col. 1:16-17; Heb. 1:3) as the elements continue obey his voice (D&C 88:12-13, 41) and thereby cause the planets to continue to move in definite orbits (*Teachings of the Prophet Joseph Smith*, pp. 197-98; D&C 88:42-48, Alma 30:44), the sun to rise (Matt. 5:45), the rain and the snow to fall (D&C 117:1), and the flowers and buds to blossom (Moses 2:11-12; Abr. 4:11-12; D&C 117:6-7; *Teachings of the Prophet Joseph Smith*, p. 198). In other words, God is the author of natural law. (D&C 88:13,42; *Teachings of the Prophet Joseph Smith*, pp. 55-56.)

7. God's power was used to stop the earth from rotating for a few hours (Hel. 12:13-15; Josh. 10:12-14; 2 Kgs. 20:8-11), to change water to wine (John 2:1-12), to multiply loaves and fishes (Matt. 14:17-21), to reverse the process of decomposition (John 11:14-44), to cause the rain to cease for a season and then to begin again (Hel. 10:3–11:17), to separate the continents and then later bring them back together again (Gen. 10:25; D&C 133:24), to cause the earth to be broken up into mountains and valleys and then become smooth again (3 Ne. 8:17-18; Moses 7:56; D&C 49:23; 133:22, 40), to move mountains and change the course of rivers (Moses 6:34; 7:13), to move the great oceans to the poles (D&C 133:23), to open up oceans or seas temporarily to provide a passage for people to travel through (Ex. 14:21-31; D&C 133:27), to cover the earth with water and then to uncover it again (Gen. 7:11-8:5), and so on.

8. Besides uncreated physical matter or element (*Teachings of the Prophet Joseph Smith*, pp. 181, 350-52), there exists *uncreated* spirit matter (D&C 131:7-8; *Teachings of the Prophet Joseph Smith*, pp. 158, 207) with the attribute of "intelligence" (*Teachings of the Prophet Joseph Smith*, pp. 352-54).

9. Joseph Smith taught and the scriptures reveal that people, animals,

and plants have spirits (D&C 77:2; 93:23, 33; Moses 3:5, 7, 9, 19; 6:51; Abr. 5:7; *Teachings of the Prophet Joseph Smith*, pp. 352-53.) Our spirits were organized or created from uncreated eternal spirit matter (with the attribute of "intelligence"). See D&C 76:24; 93:21, 23, 29-33; Abr. 3:22; *Teachings of the Prophet Joseph Smith*, pp. 158, 352-54. A more detailed treatment of this subject is given in the following articles written by the author: "What is Man?" pp. 139-149; and "The Origin and Destiny of Man," *Studies in Scripture, Volume 1: The Doctrine and Covenants* (Sandy, Utah: Randall Book Company, 1984), pp. 365-78, hereinafter referred to as "The Origin and Destiny of Man."

10. Since God was once a man (*Teachings of the Prophet Joseph Smith*, pp. 345-46), he has a spirit, but now his spirit is inseparably connected to an immortal, spiritual, resurrected body (which is still a physical body quickened by spirit, not by blood). (D&C 88:27-28; 93:33; 130:22.) Hence God is sometimes referred to as a spiritual personage. (John 4:24; 1 Cor. 15:42-50.)

11. Joseph Smith taught and the scriptures reveal that God speaks to his children (gives revelations) through his Spirit to their spirits. (*Teachings of the Prophet Joseph Smith*, p. 355; D&C 11:10-14; 18:34-36; 84:44-47; 88:11; 93:31-33; Moroni 7:10-19.)

12. The scriptures reveal that the spirit of Christ (D&C 88:6-7; 84:43-45; Moro. 7:16, 18-19) fills the whole universe or immensity of space and is the means of conveying God's commands or law ("the power of God") from his presence (D&C 88:12-13) to physical things such as the sun, moon, stars, and earth (D&C 88:7-10; cf. *Teachings of the Prophet Joseph Smith*, pp. 197-98) and even to living things besides people (D&C 88:13), as all living things have a spirit (Moses 3:5, 7, 9, 19; 6:51; Abr. 5:7; D&C 77:2).

13. A more detailed discussion on this subject is found in "What is Man?" pp. 134-37.

14. Bertrand Russell, *The Impact of Science on Society* (New York: Simon and Schuster, 1953), p. 6, hereinafter referred to as *The Impact of Science on Society*. Russell accepts and advocates the naturalistic view of the world and explains in his book how the discoveries, theories, and methodology of modern science have led to this way of thinking.

15. Abr. 3:24; D&C 49:16-17; 88:19-20, 25; 93:33; *Teachings of the Prophet Joseph Smith*, p. 181.

16. A *law of God* is a *commandment* given by God: the two terms *law* and *commandment* are used synonymously by God. (D&C 20:19-20; 29:30, 34-35; 82:4; 132:12, 54.) Just as a commandment cannot exist by

itself (it must have an originator), neither can a law exist by itself but must have an author: God alludes to himself as a divine King or Ruler (Abr. 3:21; D&C 88:13, 40; 106:6-8) and refers to *his* laws in a possessive sense (D&C 38:21-22; 82:4; 99:5; 132:54; 2 Ne. 9:17). If law existed independent of God, he would be powerless to command or revoke the law as he saw fit (D&C 56:3-6; 75:4-7; *Teachings of the Prophet Joseph Smith*, pp. 194, 256). It should be noted, however, that we are obligated to obey Christ, who acts under the direction of his Father (John 5:19, 30; 8:28; 14:10; 1 Cor. 11:3; 3 Ne. 15:16, 19.) Also, on the basis of certain "principles" that exist independent of God (*Teachings of the Prophet Joseph Smith*, pp. 158, 181, 354, D&C 29:39; 2 Ne. 2:11, 15; Alma 41:10), no doubt God with his infinite wisdom and knowledge is able to formulate laws and give them to man, which if obeyed will raise him to the level of God to enjoy a fulness of joy (*Teachings of the Prophet Joseph Smith*, pp. 49-56, 255, 354; Alma 42:8,16).

17. *Teachings of the Prophet Joseph Smith*, p. 355.

18. D&C 93:31-33; 2 Ne. 10:23-24; Alma 3:26-27.

19. As an example, Christ's spirit obeyed the will of the Father and as a result ruled over his own flesh. (Mosiah 15:1-2, 5-7; see also Rom. 8:10-13.)

20. *Teachings of the Prophet Joseph Smith*, pp. 55, 255.

21. For a further explanation of this subject, see "What is Man," p. 142.

22. The Book of Mormon confirms events related in the Bible and therefore "builds it up." (D&C 10:52, 62.)

23. *Teachings of the Prophet Joseph Smith*, pp. 181, 291-92 (cf. D&C 77:2-3); D&C 49:16-17; 88:17-19, 25-28; 93:33.

24. A more detailed discussion of this subject is found in the following article written by the author: "The Fall of Man," *Principles of the Gospel in Practice* (Salt Lake City: Randall Book Company, 1985), pp. 64-65 (footnotes 81, 82). This article will be referred to hereinafter as "The Fall of Man."

25. 2 Ne. 2:15; Moses 2:11-13, 20-25; Abr. 4:11-13, 20-25.

26. D&C 77:2; Ether 3:15-16; Moses 3:5-8; 6:51.

27. Abr. 5:7-8; Moses 3:7, 9, 19; *Teachings of the Prophet Joseph Smith*, pp. 352-53.

28. *The Impact of Science on Society*, pp. 15-16. Russell also points out that Darwin's work helped bring "naturalism" into full bloom by the dethronement of "purpose." (Pp. 10-12.)

29. Since the earth began its mortal or temporal existence at the time

of the fall, it has been approximately 6,000 years since the earth became mortal. (D&C 77:1, 6-7; 88:25-26.)

30. Korihor, the Anti-Christ, advocated the doctrine of "naturalism." He said there was no God who created and sustains the universe (Alma 30:28, 37-40, 48) and who gives prophecy or revelation (laws) to his children (Alma 30:13-15, 24). Hence, there cannot be any such thing as a breaking of God's laws, so there could be no fall (Alma 30:25) or sin (Alma 30:16-18). Since there is no such thing as breaking God's laws, there is no need for an atonement (Alma 30:17, 26-27) and therefore there is no Christ (Alma 30:12, 22.) He denied that man has a spirit (Alma 30:18) and advocated the doctrine of the survival of the fittest (Alma 30:17). It is interesting that he rejected the witness of the Spirit, the authority of the prophets and scripture (Alma 30:40-46), and demanded in their place physical evidence or a sign. (Alma 30:43-48). He accused the prophets of following foolish traditions (Alma 30:14, 27, 31) and of being guilty of priestcraft (Alma 30:22-23, 27-28.) When people accepted this naturalistic doctrine, he was able to lead away "the hearts of many, causing them to lift up their heads in their wickedness." (Alma 30:18.) He admitted in the end that he had been led away by Satan to preach this naturalistic doctrine. (Alma 30:52-53).

31. Anthon H. Lund explained that God is the author of law and that it is to him that we should pray. He is not impotent, and the laws are subservient to him. See Anthon H. Lund, Conference Report, April 1916, p. 12.

32. "The Fall of Man," pp. 47-56.

33. D&C 29:39-40; 2 Ne. 2:29; 4:17-19, 27; 10:23-24; 3 Ne. 28:36-40.

34. D&C 93:38; Brigham Young, "Faithfulness and Apostasy," *Journal of Discourses* (London: Latter-day Saints' Book Depot, 1854-86) 2:254-57; 9:102-6, 108, 287-88, 305-6; 18:257-59.

35. *Teachings of the Prophet Joseph Smith*, p. 181.

36. See footnote 30.

9

A GREAT DELIVERANCE
(2 Nephi 3-5)

CATHERINE THOMAS

Three main ideas appear in 2 Nephi 3-5: Joseph in Egypt, Nephi's psalm, and the mark of the dark skin. At first glance they seem disparate subjects, but on deeper inspection the reader may see that a major thread of the entire Book of Mormon laces these chapters together, namely, the promise of deliverance, national and personal. In chapter 3 Joseph of Egypt looked down through millennia with his seer's eye and saw the hand of God at work in the preservation and deliverance of his seed. In chapter 4 Nephi received a personal deliverance from the Lord. In chapter 5 the Lamanites rejected the Lord's deliverance and waded through centuries of suffering. Insight into the Redeemer's power, love, and commitment to his children abounds in these chapters.

Deliverance of the Remnant of Jacob

Lehi laid his hands on his son Joseph's head and pronounced a patriarchal blessing that transports the reader to ancient Canaan and Egypt and the times of Joseph, son of Jacob. Lehi's inspired thought concerned the survival of his own seed. In declaring his son's lineage, Lehi recalled his ancestor Joseph of Egypt, with whom a wonderful history lies.

Catherine Thomas is a doctoral student in ancient history at Brigham Young University.

While Joseph was in Egypt, Canaan languished in famine. Having been driven to Egypt by hunger, ten penitent sons of Israel listened to the remarkable account of their younger brother's survival and rise to prominence. Joseph graciously said to them as he revealed his true identity: "Be not grieved, nor angry with yourselves . . . for God did send me before you to preserve life . . . to preserve you a posterity in the earth, and to save your lives by a great deliverance." (Gen. 45:5, 7.) This Joseph was the prototype of the chief gatherers in Israel; this was he who would gather souls, like the corn he gathered into storage, numberless as the sand of the sea; he would "push the people together to the ends of the earth, . . . the ten thousands of Ephraim, and . . . the thousands of Manasseh" (Deut. 33:17); he would also, foreshadowing the Redeemer's deliverance, magnanimously offer life to his own brethren who had rejected him.

When Joseph of Egypt uttered these prophecies that Lehi repeated, he, like Lehi, was near the close of his life; he said to his brethren: "I die, and go unto my fathers; and I go down to my grave with joy. The God of my father Jacob be with you, to deliver you out of affliction in the days of your bondage; for the Lord hath visited me, and I have obtained a promise of the Lord." (JST, Gen. 50:24.) Lehi had, of course, read this promise in the brass plates, and it had become very important to him when he learned that he was a descendant of this Joseph, for the covenants the Lord had made with Joseph of Egypt were very great. (2 Ne. 3:4.) These covenants and prophecies appear in 2 Nephi 3:5-21 and in outline are as follows: Joseph of Egypt's seed would not be completely destroyed, but would be delivered through another of his descendants, Joseph Smith (verses 7-15), by means of the Book of Mormon, which would manifest the Messiah and his covenants with their forefathers, as well as this Israelite branch's true identity. They would be converted and drawn back into the Lord's fold.

It is helpful to see that there is really one main promise here that focuses on Joseph Smith and the Book of Mormon with significant references to Joseph of Egypt and Moses and their roles in the deliverance of this branch of Israel's posterity. These prophecies develop a profile of Joseph Smith and deserve examination.

The first prophecy that concerns Joseph Smith occurs in verses 5 and 6, where the Lord promised that the Messiah would be made manifest to Joseph of Egypt's descendants (Lehi's seed) "in the latter days, in the spirit of power, unto the bringing of them out of darkness unto light—yea, out of hidden darkness and out of captivity unto freedom" through a choice seer. Isaiah described such a condition: "The people that walked in darkness have seen a great light: they that dwell in the land of the shadow of death, upon them hath the light shined" (Isa. 9:2); "Open the blind eyes . . . bring out the prisoners from the prison, and them that sit in darkness out of the prison house" (Isa. 42:7). The prison house or captivity represents the bondage of spiritual ignorance. Joseph Smith, like Moses, would deliver Israel from spiritual bondage (2 Ne. 3:9) through restoration of lost truths. Like Joseph of Egypt, Joseph Smith, his descendant and namesake, would do a saving work. (2 Ne. 3:15.) Pharaoh had named Joseph of Egypt Zaphnath-paaneah, "he who reveals that which is hidden." (Gen. 41:45.) Joseph Smith would disclose many godly mysteries to ancient Joseph's seed, which "by the power of the Lord shall bring my people unto salvation." (2 Ne. 3:15.) The *hidden* darkness may refer to the fact that the true identity of the remnant of Joseph of Egypt in America was unknown for many centuries until the Lord revealed it through Joseph Smith.

"Out of captivity unto freedom" were words that sprang in the hearts of later Book of Mormon prophets too. Joseph of Egypt served as a powerful symbol of deliverance for Captain Moroni, who, in rending his own coat and writing on it the Title of Liberty, recalled Joseph's coat, which his brothers had rent unwittingly in symbol of the rending or scattering of Israel. (Alma 46:23.) Moroni's rent garment signified, as ancient Joseph had prophesied, that a remnant of Joseph's scattered seed would survive. The whole account, then, of Joseph's betrayal and later redemption of his brethren typified that though Israel would be scattered through wickedness, salvation would come to Israel in significant measure from Joseph of Egypt and his seed.

Joseph Smith was only a man, but the Lord promised that he would have the "spirit of power" (2 Ne. 3:5), that "out of weakness he [should] be made strong" (2 Ne. 3:13), and as a mighty one would do mighty wonders (2 Ne. 3:24). Why does the Lord choose the weak things of the earth through which to perform his works? The Lord himself answered: "Lest Israel vaunt themselves against me, saying, Mine own hand hath saved me." (Judg. 7:2.) So great is humanity's need to draw upon the true source of power, that the Lord chooses people who could not possibly succeed on their own resources to demonstrate to all where the power of deliverance really resides. "Yet a man may have great power given him from God," Ammon explained. (Mosiah 8:16.) He went on, remarkably echoing Joseph of Egypt's words about Joseph Smith: "A seer can know of things which are past, and also of things which are to come, and by them shall . . . secret things be made manifest, and *hidden things shall come to light*, and things which are not known shall be made known by them, and also things shall be made known by them which otherwise would not be known. Thus God has provided a means that man, through faith, might work mighty miracles; therefore *he becometh a great benefit to his fellow beings."* (Mosiah 8:17-18; italics added.)

The Doctrine and Covenants details the kinds of power that God gave Joseph Smith: power to translate (1:29), power to lay the foundations of the Church and to bring it out of darkness (1:30), power to preach the gospel (42:6), and priesthood (sealing) power (132:7). Joseph of Egypt said that his namesake would do a work for his brethren that would be of great worth to them. (2 Ne. 3:7.) So great was Joseph Smith's contribution that Elder John Taylor was led to exclaim after his martyrdom: "Joseph Smith, the Prophet and Seer of the Lord, has done more, save Jesus only, for the salvation of men in this world, than any other man that ever lived in it." (D&C 135:3.)

Moses, who Joseph of Egypt prophesied would have judgment in writing and receive the law from the Lord's own finger (2 Ne. 3:17), initiated the record later continued by the seed of Judah. Joseph Smith, fruit of Joseph of Egypt's loins, had a similar stewardship over records in writing the Lord's revelations and translating the Book of Mormon. These two records would "grow together" to the establishment of peace among the latter-day seed of Joseph of Egypt and bring them to the knowledge of the Lord's covenants with their fathers. (2 Ne. 3:12.)[1] The Book of Mormon would come to Joseph of Egypt's posterity as a "cry from the dust" (2 Ne. 3:18-19); over millennia, fathers would cry repentance to their posterity, "even after many generations have gone by them" (2 Ne. 3:20), having power to convince them (2 Ne. 3:11).

Joseph of Egypt referred to a spokesman and scribe for Joseph Smith (2 Ne. 3:17-18), likely Sidney Rigdon (D&C 100:9; 124:103-4). In both Exodus and the Doctrine and Covenants the Lord appointed a revelator and a spokesman.[2] These spokesmen were given to these prophets in their early ministry, but as time went on, the importance of their role seemed to recede as the prophets became mighty in speaking and fully embraced the power of their callings. Exodus 4:10-16, which describes Moses' feelings of weakness, suggests that these spokesmen served at least in part as moral support for the new prophets. One way Joseph Smith was strengthened was in the Lord's appointment of Sidney Rigdon, as D&C 35, a revelation to Elder Rigdon, explains: "I call upon the weak things of the world, those who are unlearned and despised, to thrash the nations by the power of my Spirit. . . . And I have sent forth the fulness of my gospel by the hand of my servant Joseph; and in weakness have I blessed him; and I have given unto him the keys of the mystery of those things which have been sealed. . . . *Wherefore, watch over him that his faith fail not*. . . . And a commandment I give unto thee — that *thou shalt write for him*; and the scriptures shall be given, even as they are in mine own bosom, to the salvation of mine own elect. . . . And *thou shalt preach my gospel and call on the holy prophets to prove his words*, as they shall be given him. (D&C 35:13, 17-20, 23; italics added.)

Having witnessed to the truth of these great prophecies, Lehi commended his youngest son, Joseph, to the boy's elder brother Nephi, left the remainder of his household with a tender father's blessing "according to the feelings of his heart and the Spirit of the Lord which was in him" (2 Ne. 4:12), and went to his own deliverance.

Personal Deliverance

After Lehi was buried, and Nephi remained to bear the burden of leadership, surely the words of Lehi's blessing stirred in his heart and caused him to identify with his ancestor Joseph, who, unlike Nephi, successfully made peace with his abusive brothers. Nephi was cast in the same uncomfortable role as Joseph had been; that is, he had to preach repentance to his elder brothers. We misunderstand both young men if we see them as spoiled little brothers. Nephi exclaimed on one occasion of having rebuked his brothers, "Thus the Spirit of the Lord constraineth me that I should speak." (1 Ne. 7:15.) And again, "I, Nephi, was constrained to speak unto them, according to [the Lord's] word." (2 Ne. 4:14.) But it was not a pleasant task, and it would have been easier and safer to be still.

A psalm is a poem, a song of praise; not a sermon or doctrinal treatise, but an expression of personal religious experience.[3] Nephi's psalm (2 Ne. 4:16-35) employs some of the features characteristic of his Hebrew literary heritage, such as the themes of sorrow in sin, communion with and delight in God, the search for perfection, humility under chastening, and triumph over evil. He framed his feelings in typical Hebrew parallelism, where ideas are repeated with variation or contrasted: "Awake, my soul! No longer droop in sin. Rejoice, O my heart, and give place no more for the enemy of my soul." (2 Ne. 4:28.) But of far more than literary importance is the spiritual insight available in this passage. Though only Nephi's words appear here, the reader may see in them a progression of thought that indicates the presence of the Lord's Spirit; it is, therefore, more of a prayerful dialogue than a soliloquy.

What is the provocation of his prayer? Nephi recorded that his soul delighted in the Lord, but when he desired to rejoice, his heart groaned "because of [his] sins." Close attention to the text reveals what specific sins caused his despair. After his father died, he recorded: "Laman and Lemuel and the sons of Ishmael were angry with me because of the admonitions of the Lord." (2 Ne. 4:13.) It was not so much his brothers' anger against him that he lamented, but the anger of his own soul, a sin that so easily beset him. (2 Ne. 4:18.) Anger at his brothers would seem justifiable; after all, they had tried to kill him. But he found that his own anger interfered with his spiritual peace. In addition, his distress had led him to "slacken [his] strength" (2 Ne. 4:26, 29), perhaps to neglect his responsibilities. Nephi was no stranger to the joy of being that dwells at our core and seeks to be released and expressed; yet fear and guilt seemed to imprison it. He quelled his urge to rejoice. Nevertheless, upon inspired reflection, he began to sense that the disturbance that drew him away from his rest in the Lord might yield to repentance. Was it necessary to let his brothers' unrest lure him from his own inner peace? Was his sorrow, in fact, a yielding to the adversary's temptation to despair? He remembered that God had never abandoned him, but with deep understanding of what it means to be human, had tenderly strengthened and encouraged and loved him. The reader shares Nephi's moment of insight as he suddenly asked a most illuminating question: Why do I embrace this disturbance? Why do I hurt myself? God does not require this of me. Rather, the temptation to despair needs active resistance: "Yea, why should I give way to temptations, that the evil one have place in my heart to destroy my peace and afflict my soul? . . . Awake, my soul! No longer droop in sin. Rejoice, O my heart, and give place no more for the enemy of my soul. Do not anger again because of mine enemies." (2 Ne. 4:27-29.) Nephi realized that he had an alternative to his distress. He cried out, "Oh Lord, wilt thou redeem my soul?" as though to say, "May I dare hope that thou wilt bless me with a personal deliverance?" He prayed to have one fear only: "Wilt thou make me that I may shake at the appearance of sin?" (2 Ne. 4:31.) His prayer implies that the only appropriate fear for one who had found rest in the Lord was the fear that he might foolishly throw it away in sin. Rather, he prayed to be established in the path of the low valley, in the plain road, in that road of submission to the Lord's tutoring, in trusting anticipation of divine solutions that surely come. Then as the Spirit whispered that he might so hope, he declared in joy, "O Lord, I have trusted in thee, and I will trust in thee forever." (2 Ne. 4:34.) He would look for deliverance in no flesh, not even his own. Here he uttered the great truth that delivers each of us from despair, that answers the secret question of the heart: How much can I depend on the Lord? Nephi declared: "Yea, I know that God will give liberally to him that asketh . . . therefore I will lift up my voice unto thee. . . . Behold, my voice shall forever ascend up unto thee, my rock and mine everlasting God." (2 Ne. 4:35.)

This remarkable dialogue demonstrates how inspired prayer works: an outpouring of the deepest needs of the heart, the will to submit, and the consequent sweet infusion of insight and peace that come from an ever-attentive Father. Nephi himself had declared somewhat earlier, "I, Nephi, will show unto you that the tender mercies of the Lord are over all those whom he hath chosen, because of their faith, to make them mighty even unto the power of deliverance." (1 Ne. 1:20.)

The promise of personal deliverance means that divine direction and solutions flow all around the children of God, though they may forget to accept them. Nephi's prayer began with fearful thoughts. But God whispered to him that life is simpler than it appears, because God is in charge of the world and of each of us. We are not responsible for everything. We can keep life simple by casting onto the Lord what we cannot manage alone. As Nephi's life continually demonstrated, God will be supremely helpful when his children remember him. God will deliver them.

Rejection of Deliverance

The Lord's solution to Nephi's present problem with his brothers was geographical separation. He warned Nephi to relocate his family in the wilderness. They founded a new community, named after Nephi, where they carefully observed the law of Moses, kept the precious instruments of the Lord's earlier deliverances, developed their technology, consecrated priests and teachers, crowned their society with the indispensable temple where they observed the sacrifices prescribed by the law of Moses, and, for a time, lived happily. (2 Ne. 5:8-16, 26-27.) This is the first mention in the Book of Mormon of temple building; this temple and later ones became the focal point of the spiritual life of the community: Jacob, King Benjamin, Alma, and Amulek preached their powerful sermons at temples; the resurrected Savior appeared to the Nephites in Bountiful at the temple.

Nephi recorded that it was during this period of spiritual activity, thirty years after their exodus from Jerusalem, that he commenced a second set of plates, the small plates of sacred history. (2 Ne. 5:28-31.) With priesthood, a temple, and sacred records, they had established Zion.

With reference to Nephi's hostile brethren, from whom they had just separated, the Lord said, "Inasmuch as they will not hearken unto thy words they shall be cut off from the presence of the Lord. And behold, they were cut off from his presence." (2 Ne. 5:20.) To be cut off from the Lord's presence in this life means to lose the Holy Ghost. The reader must take care here to understand who was cursing whom when the Lord set the skin of blackness on the Lamanites. The Lamanites cursed *themselves* when they chose to reject the Spirit of the Lord. The Lord, as a result of that choice, set the dark skin upon them to separate them from those who had not rejected the Spirit. (2 Ne. 5:21-23.) The sore cursing was not the dark skin, but the loss of the Holy Ghost, of which the skin coloring was but a mark. The result of losing the Spirit was that the Lamanites became "an idle people, full of mischief and subtlety," "a scourge" to the Nephites, serving as a reminder of the Lord to a people whose prosperity would always be a mixed blessing. (2 Ne. 5:24-25.) The scriptures repeatedly illustrate that the loss of the Spirit in those who have formerly enjoyed it propels them down a path to misery and self-destruction.

What happened to these dark-skinned people? We learn from the scriptures that the Lamanites have two histories. The first history began with Laman and Lemuel and deals with that group who, following the false traditions of their fathers, rebelled against the Lord. These were the people that the Lord marked with a dark skin. The first Lamanite history ended in 3 Nephi 2:15, where the converted Lamanites became white like the Nephites as the dark skin was removed and the Holy Ghost was restored to them. During this period, all the remnant of Joseph were white skinned.

The second history began in 4 Nephi 1:20 when some of Lehi's descendants rejected the Lord's deliverance and left the Church. These dissenters were not pure descendants of Laman and Lemuel, but were of a mixture of lineages: Judah (through Mulek) and Ephraim (through Ishmael) and Manasseh (through Lehi), and of those righteous Nephites present at the Savior's coming. The scripture does not record that the dark skin returned to these dissenters after their apostasy. Therefore, a few hundred years later, the battle of Mormon and Moroni's day was waged not between light and dark races, but between groups who were divergent spiritually. Mormon spoke of these Lamanites about A.D 380: "This people shall be scattered, and *shall become* a dark, a filthy, and a loathsome people, beyond the description of that which ever hath been amongst us, yea, even that which hath been among the Lamanites, and this because of their unbelief and idolatry. . . . They were once a delightsome people, and they had Christ for their shepherd; yea, they were led even by God the Father. . . . But . . . the Lord [will] remember the covenant which he made unto Abraham and unto all the house of Israel." (Morm. 5:15-20; italics added.)

Today, because of this promise to the Lamanites, the skin color of the modern Lamanites has a new significance. That is, it does not signify either a people descended from Laman and Lemuel, or a people in rebellion against God. Rather, that bronze color persists today to identify and set apart the modern remnant of the seed of Joseph for whom wonderful blessings have been reserved, that same group that Joseph of Egypt and all the prophets of the Book of Mormon prayed and sacrificed for, and whose ultimate triumph over darkness they foresaw. Mormon spoke to today's Lamanites: "I speak unto you, ye remnant of the house of Israel. . . . Know ye that ye are of the house of Israel. . . . Know ye that ye must come to the knowledge of your fathers . . . ye are a remnant of the seed of Jacob; therefore ye are numbered among the people of the first covenant." (Morm. 7:1-2, 5, 10.)

The word *fathers* here refers not just to Lehi, but especially to Abraham, Isaac, and Jacob. The blessings and responsibilities that devolve on any branch of Israel devolve on the Lamanites. The "first covenant" is the Lord's covenant with Abraham: "Thy seed . . . shall bear this ministry and Priesthood unto all nations. . . . And in thy seed . . . sh all all the families of the earth be blessed, even with the blessings of the Gospel, which are the blessings of salvation, even of life eternal." (Abr. 2:9-10.) This covenant, renewed by the Lord with successive generations, was the promise of godhood to the house of Israel. Therefore each elder in Israel who, with his bride, enters into the covenant of temple marriage, enters into the ancient covenant of Abraham with the Lord and becomes heir to all the blessings of

Abraham (D&C 132); he becomes as well an heir to the responsibility of carrying the gospel to others. President Spencer W. Kimball issued a prophetic call to these people: "The Lamanites must rise again in dignity and strength to fully join their brethren and sisters of the household of God in carrying forth his work in preparation for that day when the Lord Jesus Christ will return to lead his people, when the millennium will be ushered in, when the earth will be renewed and receive its paradisiacal glory and its lands be united and become one land. For the prophets have said, 'The remnant of the house of Joseph shall be built upon this land; and it shall be a land of their inheritance; and they shall build up a holy city unto the Lord, like unto the Jerusalem of old; and they shall no more be confounded, until the end come when the earth shall pass away.' (Ether 13:8.)"[4]

As Nephi saw in vision the destruction of his seed and the stumbling of the Gentiles, he reaffirmed God's loving involvement with all His children: "Behold, doth he cry unto any, saying: Depart from me? Behold, I say unto you, Nay; but he saith: Come unto me all ye ends of the earth, buy milk and honey, without money and without price.... All men are privileged the one like unto the other, and none are forbidden.... He inviteth them all to come unto him and partake of his goodness; and he denieth none that come unto him, black and white, bond and free, male and female; and he remembereth the heathen; and all are alike unto God, both Jew and Gentile." (2 Ne. 26:25, 28, 33.)

Clearly the Lord actively participated in and directed the manifold deliverances performed through Joseph of Egypt, Moses, Lehi, Nephi, and Joseph Smith. He gives deliverance to nations through mighty prophets and to humble souls through the prayer of faith. Throughout history many loving fathers have carefully tended and nurtured the children of Israel. By countless prayers and tears and sacrifices, through generation on generation from Joseph of Egypt's day to ours, has that promise been renewed of a great deliverance, indeed, "security forever." (2 Ne. 3:2.)

NOTES

1. These covenants are treated in the discussion of 2 Nephi 5.

2. Elder Bruce R. McConkie suggested a new interpretation of 2 Nephi 3:17-18. See *A New Witness for the Articles of Faith* (Salt Lake City: Deseret Book Company, 1986), pp. 425-26.

3. *New Bible Dictionary*, ed. J. D. Douglas, 2nd ed. (Wheaton, Illinois: Tyndale House Publishers, 1982), p. 992.

4. *Ensign*, December 1975, p. 7.

10

REDEMPTION THROUGH THE HOLY MESSIAH
(2 Nephi 6-10)

ROBERT L. MILLET

Jacob, son of Lehi, preceded his powerful discussion of the atonement of Christ by a brief encounter with the writings of Isaiah, a statement of "things which are, and which are to come." (2 Ne. 6:4; cf. Jacob 4:13.) Having been asked by Nephi to read the words of Isaiah to his people, Jacob stressed that "the words which I shall read are they which Isaiah spake concerning all the house of Israel; wherefore, they may be likened unto you, for ye are of the house of Israel." (2 Ne. 6:5.)

After quoting Isaiah 49:22-26 regarding the establishment of the ensign in the last days and the manner in which the gospel banquet is to be served by the Gentiles to the Lamanites and the Jews in the final dispensation, Jacob provided appropriate commentary on these otherwise difficult passages. The meaning of these verses from Isaiah are discussed elsewhere in this book.[1]

Jacob then quoted Isaiah 50:1; 52:1-2. Without undertaking a verse-by-verse commentary, we simply acknowledge that Isaiah's message is directed toward the promise of an eventual return of the scattered remnants of Israel. Although Israel has "sold herself" through repeated transgression; although she has rejected her God and his everlasting covenant; although the people of the covenant

Robert L. Millet is associate professor of ancient scripture and New Testament area coordinator at Brigham Young University.

have been disloyal to the royal within them, yet the decree is sure: Jehovah has not and will not cast them off forever. The Omnipotent One has power to do all things: "O house of Israel, is my hand shortened at all," he asked, "that it cannot redeem, or have I no power to deliver" the exiles to their Lord and to their lands? (2 Ne. 7:1-2.) Through the marvelous work and a wonder of the last days—the restoration of the gospel through the Prophet Joseph Smith—the "Lord shall comfort Zion, he will comfort all her waste places." Because the heavens will have been opened, "a law shall proceed" from God to his people, and, in his words, "I will make my judgment to rest for a light for the people." (2 Ne. 8:3-4; cf. Isa. 2:3.) His promise is fixed and his word is faithful: Israel shall be gathered. Thus, "the redeemed of the Lord shall return" to that Lord, "and come with singing unto Zion," unto the Lord's true Church; "and everlasting joy and holiness shall be upon their heads." (2 Ne. 8:6, 11; cf. 9:2.)

The Doctrine of Redemption from Death

Jacob's understanding of the plan of salvation was grounded in the teachings of his father, based upon what Lehi had learned through revelation and from his study of the brass plates. (See 2 Ne. 2:17.) Further, Jacob himself had enjoyed the ministry and instruction of angels and the revelations of heaven. (See 2 Ne. 2:4; 10:3.) His was a clear conception of and a firm commitment to his Lord and Savior, a quiet but powerful assurance that God had a plan for the redemption and salvation of his children.

The Book of Mormon affirms the antiquity of the doctrine of redemption from death and specifically suggests that the knowledge of the resurrection of Christ and of all people is much older than scholars have supposed. It did not originate with Job (Job 19:25-26), with Ezekiel (Ezek. 37), or during the Babylonian captivity. It was known in the Adamic dispensation that salvation was to be had through the sufferings, death, and resurrection of Jesus Christ. (See Moses 6:51-60.) Enoch likewise "looked and beheld the Son of Man lifted up on the cross, after the manner of men." He further beheld the meridian of time wherein "the saints arose, and were crowned at the right hand of the Son of Man, with crowns of glory." (Moses

7:55-56.) Abraham, the father of the faithful, was also privileged to understand the redemptive labors of the Lord Jesus Christ. "Abram said, Lord God, how wilt thou give me this land [Canaan] for an everlasting inheritance? And the Lord said, Though thou wast dead, yet am I not able to give it thee? And if thou shalt die, yet thou shalt possess it, for the day cometh, that the Son of Man shall live; but how can he live [i.e., have immortality and eternal life] if he be not dead? he must first be quickened [made alive through the resurrection]. And it came to pass," the inspired account continues, "that Abram looked forth and saw the days of the Son of Man, and was glad, and his soul found rest, and he believed in the Lord; and the Lord counted it unto him for righteousness." (JST, Gen. 15:9-12.)

Jacob acknowledged that many of his people had searched the scriptures to better understand these matters, to know of things to come; "wherefore," he added, "I know that ye know that our flesh must waste away and die; nevertheless, in our bodies we shall see God." (2 Ne. 9:4.) Jacob taught that death has passed upon all men as a vital part of the merciful plan of the great Creator. (2 Ne. 9:6.) From God's perspective, life and death are not opposites but points on an eternal spectrum.

Adam's fall brought death. Christ's suffering and death brought life. Adam is thus the father of mortality, Christ the father of immortality.[2] Having experienced spiritual death—being cut off from the presence of God and dying as to things of righteousness (see Alma 12:16; 40:26; 42:9; Hel. 14:18; D&C 29:41)—Adam and his posterity were in need of a universal life force, an infinite atoning power, to deliver them from the grasp of death and hell and open the door once again to eternal life. Indeed, Christ's atonement is infinite in a number of ways. First, it is infinite in that it circumvents the ever-present mortal commonality—physical death. "Save it should be an infinite atonement," Jacob explained, "this corruption could not put on incorruption." In such an eventuality, "this flesh must have laid down to rot and to crumble to its mother earth, to rise no more." (2 Ne. 9:7.)

Second, the atonement of Christ is infinite in the sense that its influence extends to all of the worlds Christ created. The gospel of

Jesus Christ is "the glad tidings . . . that he came into the world, even Jesus, to be crucified for the world, and to bear the sins of the world, and to sanctify the world, and to cleanse it from all unrighteousness; that *through him all might be saved whom the Father had put into his power and made by him.*" (D&C 76:40-41; emphasis added; cf. Moses 1:32-35.) Joseph Smith, in his poetic version of the Vision of the Glories (D&C 76), wrote of the outreach of our Lord's saving grace. "I heard a great voice, bearing record from heav'n,/ He's the Saviour, and only begotten of God—/ By him, of him, and through him, the worlds were all made,/ Even all that careen in the heavens so broad,/ *Whose inhabitants, too, from the first to the last,/ Are sav'd by the very same Saviour of ours;*/ And, of course, are begotten God's daughters and sons,/ By the very same truths, and the very same pow'rs."[3] In a related way, the atonement is infinite in the sense that it covers all sins (with the exception of murder and the sin against the Holy Ghost), and thus makes redemption possible for all people. (A of F 3.)

Third, the Savior's atonement is infinite in the sense that he is an infinite being. Jesus was able to do for us what we simply could not have done for ourselves. To begin with, his was a sinless offering, an act performed by one who was "in all points tempted like as we are, yet without sin." (Heb. 4:15.) In addition, and perhaps most important, Christ was able to do what he did—to suffer in Gethsemane and on Calvary, as well as to rise from the tomb in glorious immortality—because of who and what he was. Jesus of Nazareth was a man, a son of Mary, from whom he inherited mortality—the capacity to know pain and sorrow, to struggle with the flesh, and, finally, to die. Jesus the Christ was also the son of Elohim, the Eternal Father. From that exalted being Jesus inherited the powers of immortality—the power over death, the capacity to live forever. In the purest sense, the sacrifice of Jesus Christ was a voluntary offering. "Therefore doth my Father love me," Jesus said, "because I lay down my life, that I might take it again. No man taketh it from me, but I lay it down of myself. I have power to lay it down [mortality], and I have power to take it again [immortality]. This commandment have I received of my Father." (John 10:17-18.) Amulek also bore witness of the Messiah;

he testified that Jesus would be "the Son of God, yea, infinite and eternal." (Alma 34:14.)

The Wisdom and Mercy of the Great Plan

Jacob's depth of appreciation and feelings of awe for the Savior knew no bounds. He "felt to sing the song of redeeming love" (Alma 5:26), to lift his voice in praise toward that Lord who has redeemed us. "O the wisdom of God," he exulted, "his mercy and grace! For behold, if the flesh should rise no more our spirits must become subject to that angel who fell from before the presence of the Eternal God, and became the devil, to rise no more. And our spirits must have become like unto him, and we become devils, angels to a devil, to be shut out from the presence of our God, and to remain with the father of lies, in misery, like unto himself."(2 Ne. 9:8-9.)

When the preceding verses are pondered, pertinent theological questions arise: Why would the spirits of men be subject to Satan if there had been no resurrection? Why would they become "devils, angels to a devil"? What if a man had lived a good life, a commendable and noble life—why would such a one be subject to Satan in the world of spirits? The answer to these queries lies in an appreciation for the central role of the resurrection of Christ in the overall plan of life and salvation. Joseph Smith was asked: "What are the fundamental principles of your religion?" He answered: "The fundamental principles of our religion are the testimony of the Apostles and Prophets, concerning Jesus Christ, that He died, was buried, and rose again the third day, and ascended into heaven; and *all other things which pertain to our religion are only appendages to it.*"[4] Simply stated, if Christ did not rise from the grave—as he stated he would do—then he was not the promised Messiah. If Christ has not the power to save the body from death, then he surely has not the power to save the spirit from hell. If he did not break the bands of death in the resurrection, then our hope of deliverance from sin through the atonement is futile and unfounded. "Our spirits, stained with sin," wrote Elder Bruce R. McConkie, "unable to cleanse themselves, would be subject to the author of sin everlastingly; we would be followers of Satan; we would be sons of perdition."[5]

"If Christ be not raised," Paul explained to the Corinthians, "your faith is vain; *ye are yet in your sins.*" (1 Cor. 15:17; emphasis added.) In Jacob's language, if the flesh should rise no more, each of us — guilty of some degree of sin — would have no hope for a union of spirit and body and likewise no hope for repentance and forgiveness; we would thus become like unto the devil: we would be spirits forever and damned beings in eternity.

It should be understood that Jacob's whole spiritual scenario, however, is hypothetical; his system of reasoning is created to produce a deeper appreciation for the glorious fact that our Lord *did* suffer and bleed and die; that he *did* take up his body on the third day; that in a way imcomprehensible to us, the effects of our Lord's rise to newness of life pass upon all mankind; and that he has, in reality, made escape possible from the awful monster of death (the grave) and hell (the abode of the wicked in the world of spirits after death). (See 2 Ne. 9:10-13.) Through the resurrection of Christ and of all people, the sting of death is removed. Through individual repentance and the miracle of forgiveness, the victory of the grave is snatched away by the Lord of the living and the dead. (See 1 Cor. 15:54-56.) Our Master has thereby "abolished death, and . . . brought life and immortality to light through the gospel." (2 Tim. 1:10.)[6]

The Doctrine of Eternal Judgment

As noted earlier, the gospel is the "glad tidings" of the atoning mission of our Lord and the plan whereby all people may take full advantage of that atonement. (D&C 76:40-41.) The "principles of the gospel" are those doctrines and ordinances of salvation the knowledge and application of which make it possible for us to rise above carnality and a sinful state and thus prepare for an eventual inheritance with God. The principles of the gospel are: faith in Jesus Christ, repentance, baptism by immersion for the remission of sins, laying on of hands for the gift of the Holy Ghost, enduring to the end, resurrection, and eternal judgment.[7] (See, for example, 2 Ne. 31; 3 Ne. 27.) The latter two doctrines — resurrection and judgment — are among the major topics of the Book of Mormon prophets.

The Book of Mormon attests to the order of things hereafter: at death we enter the world of spirits and experience a "partial judgment."[8] (See Alma 40:11-14.) Thereafter we are resurrected, judged, and consigned to our eternal reward. Jacob taught that after resurrection, all people "must appear before the judgment-seat of the Holy One of Israel," who is Jesus Christ. "And then cometh the judgment, and then must they be judged according to the holy judgment of God." (2 Ne. 9:15.) This final judgment will take place at the end of the Millennium. Those who have been righteous on earth shall receive a righteous body and inherit the reward of the righteous. Those, on the other hand, who have sowed seeds of wickedness on earth shall reap condemnation and never know or partake of the fruit of the tree of life. The devil and his angels, those who are filthy — including the sons of perdition (see D&C 88:35, 102) — "shall be filthy still" after the resurrection. These "shall go away into everlasting fire, prepared for them; and their torment is as a lake of fire and brimstone, whose flame ascendeth up forever and ever and has no end." (2 Ne. 9:16.)[9]

For the righteous, the final judgment will be a formality; they will already have received their celestial, resurrected bodies and will know of their eternal destiny. These are they who have "believed in the Holy One of Israel, they who have endured the crosses of the world, and despised the shame of it." They stood firm in the midst of the tauntings and enticements echoing from that great and spacious building, but were undeterred from their appointed task. These shall inherit that kingdom promised to them on a conditional basis before the world was. (2 Ne. 9:18.) For the wicked, however, the judgment will be a moment of confrontation, a time of soul-stirring and forthright acknowledgment that the ways of the Lord are just.

The Lord Jehovah is the perfect judge, "for he knoweth all things, and there is not anything save he knows it." (2 Ne. 9:20.) In discussing the inevitability of the final judgment, Jacob implored: "Prepare your souls for that glorious day when justice shall be administered unto the righteous, even the day of judgment, that ye may not shrink with awful fear." (2 Ne. 9:46.) "O then, my beloved brethren, come unto the Lord, the Holy One. Remember that his paths are righteous. Behold, the way for man is narrow, but it lieth in a straight course before him, and the keeper of the gate is the Holy One of Israel; and he employeth no servant there; and there is none other way save it be by the gate; for he cannot be deceived, for the Lord God is his name." (2 Ne. 9:41.) A knowledge of our Lord's mercy, an appreciation for his divine justice, and an awareness of his infinite love also suggest to the soul that he waits at the gate, not only to certify us, but also to welcome us.

Christ Suffered for All

In speaking of the coming of the Messiah, Jacob said "Wherefore, as I said unto you, it must needs be expedient that Christ—for in the last night the angel spake unto me that this should be his name[10]— should come among the Jews, among those who are the more wicked part of the world; and they shall crucify him—for thus it behooveth our God, and there is none other nation on earth that would crucify their God." Jacob further added the detail that "because of priestcrafts and iniquities, they at Jerusalem [would] stiffen their necks against him, that he be crucified." This rejection of the Lord by the Jews would lead to their being "scattered among all nations" until "the day cometh that they shall believe" in Christ. Then has the Lord "covenanted with their fathers [Abraham, Isaac, and Jacob] that they shall be restored in the flesh, upon the earth, unto the lands of their inheritance." (2 Ne. 10:3-7.)

Jacob taught that Jesus would come into the world "that he may save all men if they will hearken unto his voice; for behold, he suffereth the pains of all men, yea, the pains of every living creature, both men, women, and children, who belong to the family of Adam." (2 Ne. 9:21.) This is one of the first places in the Book of Mormon record where the nature of Christ's redemptive suffering is discussed. Because the effects of Adam's fall were universal, the effects of the atonement must be universal. Because every son and daughter of Adam and Eve would be subject to sin and death, so also must the atonement of Christ provide escape from the damning influences of sin and the possible dissolution of death.

In Gethsemane and again on the cross[11] our Savior descended in suffering below all things. (See 2 Cor. 8:9; Eph. 4:8-10; D&C 19:2;

88:6.) In a way incomprehensible to the finite mind, the Infinite One took upon him the effects of the sins of all humanity. He who had been the sinless one now became the great sinner; the Father "made him to be sin for us," even he "who knew no sin." (2 Cor. 5:21; cf. Gal. 3:13; Heb. 2:9.) He who had always walked in the light of his God was in the darkness alone; he who had basked constantly in the glory of his Father's Spirit now knew, for the first time, the painful reality associated with alienation from things divine.[12] An angel explained to King Benjamin: "[Christ] shall suffer temptations, and pain of body, hunger, thirst, and fatigue, even more than man can suffer, except it be unto death; for behold, blood cometh from every pore, so great shall be his anguish for the wickedness and the abominations of his people." (Mosiah 3:7.) In a modern revelation Christ graphically described the bitterness of his suffering: "I command you to repent — repent, lest I smite you by the rod of my mouth, and by my wrath, and by my anger, and your sufferings be sore — how sore you know not, how exquisite you know not, yea, how hard to bear you know not. For behold, I, God, have suffered these things for all, that they might not suffer if they would repent; but if they would not repent they must suffer even as I; which suffering caused myself, even God, the greatest of all, to tremble because of pain, and to bleed at every pore, and to suffer both body and spirit — and would that I might not drink the bitter cup, and shrink — nevertheless, glory be to the Father, and I partook and finished my preparations unto the children of men." (D&C 19:15-19; cf. 18:11.)

"Can we," asked a modern apostle, "even in the depths of disease, tell Him anything at all about suffering? In ways we cannot comprehend, our sicknesses and infirmities were borne by Him [see Alma 7:11-12] even before they were borne by us. The very weight of our combined sins caused Him to descend below all. We have never been, nor will we be, in depths such as he has known. Thus His atonement made perfect His empathy and His mercy and His capacity to succor us, for which we can be everlastingly grateful."[13] Our Savior would undergo all of this, Jacob prophesied about 550 B.C., "that the resurrection might pass upon all men, that all might stand before him at the great and judgment day." (2 Ne. 9:22.)

One of the eternal verities taught clearly and persuasively in the Book of Mormon is that the atonement of Christ is extended toward those who were without gospel law while on earth and had no opportunities to participate in the ordinances of salvation. "Where there is no law given," Jacob explained, "there is no punishment; and where there is no punishment there is no condemnation." This is true because "the atonement satisfieth the demands of his justice upon all those who have not the law given to them, . . . and they are restored to that God who gave them breath, which is the Holy One of Israel." (2 Ne. 9:25-26; cf. Mosiah 3:11; Moro. 8:22.) One of the unconditional benefits of the atonement is the decree that no person in all eternity will be denied a blessing that is beyond his or her control to enjoy; no person will be condemned for not observing a commandment or participating in an ordinance of which he or she was ignorant. God knows all things. He, and he alone, can adjudicate humanity, for he alone knows the thoughts and intents of the human heart. (D&C 6:16.) The divine word is sure: "All who have died without a knowledge of this gospel, who would have received it if they had been permitted to tarry, shall be heirs of the celestial kingdom of God; also all that shall die henceforth without a knowledge of it, who would have received it with all their hearts, shall be heirs of that kingdom." The principle undergirding this doctrine is then stated as follows: "For I, the Lord, will judge all men according to their works, *according to the desire of their hearts.*" (D&C 137:7-9; emphasis added; cf. Alma 41:3.) Elder Dallin H. Oaks illustrated this principle as follows:

> When someone genuinely wanted to do something for my father-in-law but was prevented by circumstances, he would say: "Thank you. I will take the good will for the deed." Similarly, I believe that our Father in heaven will receive the true desires of our hearts as a substitute for actions that are genuinely impossible.
>
> Here we see [a] contrast between the laws of God and the laws of men. It is entirely impractical to grant a *legal* advantage on the basis of an intent not translated into action. "I intended to sign that contract" or "We intended to get married" cannot stand as the equivalent of the act required

by law. If the law were to give effect to intentions in lieu of specific acts, it would open the door for too much abuse, since the laws of man have no reliable means of determining our innermost thoughts.

In contrast, the *law of God* can reward a righteous desire because an omniscient God can discern it. As revealed through the prophet of this dispensation, God "is a discerner of the thoughts and intents of the heart." (D&C 33:1.) If a person refrains from a particular act because he is genuinely unable to perform it, but truly would if he could, our Heavenly Father will know this and can reward that person accordingly.[14]

Jacob's List of Warnings

Having spoken at length of Jesus Christ and the atonement, Jacob then turned his attention to the condemnation of specific sins and uttered a series of woes — harsh warnings to the Saints. First of all, he gave a stern warning to the person who sins against light, who "has all the commandments of God, like unto us, and that transgresseth them, and that wasteth the days of his probation." Of such a one Jacob said: "Awful is his state!" (2 Ne. 9:27.) Those who have access to the light are expected to walk in that light, "for of him unto whom much is given much is required; and he who sins against the greater light shall receive the greater condemnation." (D&C 82:3.) Amulek would likewise counsel the Zoramites some 500 years hence: "I beseech of you that ye do not procrastinate the day of your repentance until the end; for after this day of life, which is given us to prepare for eternity, behold, if we do not improve our time while in this life, then cometh the night of darkness wherein there can be no labor performed." (Alma 34:33; cf. Hel. 13:38.)

Jacob also warned against the worship of riches, promising that those who despise the poor and persecute the meek shall eventually find that their riches will perish with them. (2 Ne. 9:30; cf. Mosiah 4:23.) He also warned against:

1. The spiritually deaf who will not hear the word of the Lord, and the spiritually blind who refuse to see things as they really are, who are described in a modern revelation as "walking in darkness at noon-day." (2 Ne. 9:31-32; D&C 95:6.)

2. "The uncircumcised of heart," those who may appear clean outwardly—whose actions seem to accord with the prescribed patterns of living—but whose hearts are corrupt, whose minds lust after the things of this world. (2 Ne. 9:33; cf. Rom 2:29.)

3. Liars, who shall spend their days after this life in hell and shall thereafter go to the telestial kingdom. (2 Ne. 9:34; D&C 76:103-6.)

4. Murderers, for they are worthy of death themselves and shall inherit the least of the kingdoms of glory hereafter. (2 Ne. 9:35; Gen. 9:6; Rev. 21:8; 22:15; D&C 42:19; 76:103.)

5. The immoral, who "shall suffer the wrath of God on earth," even "the vengeance of eternal fire" when the Savior returns. These shall be "cast down to hell and suffer the wrath of Almighty God" in the world of spirits, and shall eventually come forth to dwell in the telestial kingdom. (2 Ne. 9:36; D&C 76:103-6.)

6. Those who worship idols, who rivet their attention and focus their affections upon anything other than the true and living God, for such persons please and play into the hands of Satan and will eventually find themselves in the hands of a jealous God. (2 Ne. 9:37.)

President Ezra Taft Benson taught that "the two groups in the Book of Mormon that seemed to have the greatest difficulty with pride are the 'learned and the rich.' "[15] It is of the former group—those who are proud because of their learning—that Jacob chose to particularize a wo: "O that cunning plan of the evil one!" Jacob said. "O the vainness, and the frailties, and the foolishness of men! When they are learned they think they are wise, and they hearken not unto the counsel of God, for they set it aside, supposing they know of themselves, wherefore, their wisdom is foolishness and it profiteth them not. And they shall perish." (2 Ne. 9:28.) Whenever any people—particularly members of the household of faith—refuse to acknowledge the true Source of all knowledge and wisdom, but choose instead to worship at the shrine of intellect; or whenever they develop an unhealthy allegiance to the philosophies and theories of men but set at naught or ignore entirely the revealed word—then such persons are on the road to spiritual destruction. For the present they are "ever learning, [but] never able to come to the knowledge of the truth." (2 Tim. 3:7.) One day they shall learn of the evils they have perpetrated among their fellow beings and the irreparable damage they have done to their own souls. President Joseph F. Smith explained:

> Among the Latter-day Saints, the preaching of false doctrines disguised as truths of the gospel, may be expected from people of two classes, and practically from these only; they are:
>
> First — The hopelessly ignorant, whose lack of intelligence is due to their indolence and sloth, who make but feeble effort, if indeed any at all, to better themselves by reading and study; those who are afflicted with a dread disease that may develop into an incurable malady — laziness.
>
> Second — The proud and self-vaunting ones, *who read by the lamp of their own conceit;* who interpret by rules of their own contriving; *who have become a law unto themselves,* and so pose as the sole judges of their own doings. *More dangerously ignorant than the first.*[16]

Jacob's advice is timeless; adopting his perspective will prevent a multitude of sins: "To be learned is good if [we] hearken unto the counsels of God." (2 Ne. 9:29.) In short, the key to a person's spiritual success is the eye: "If your eye be single to my glory," the Lord told the Latter-day Saints, "your whole bodies shall be filled with light, and there shall be no darkness in you; and that body which is filled with light comprehendeth all things." (D&C 88:67.) To use Jacob's simple but pointed language, "to be carnally-minded is death, and to be spiritually-minded is life eternal." (2 Ne. 9:39.)

Conclusion

Jacob, son of Lehi, was a gifted philosopher, a profound theologian, and a mighty preacher of righteousness. He was a sensitive seer who enjoyed the gift of discernment, rejoiced in the spirit of prophecy and revelation with which the Lord had blessed him, and spoke to his people, the Nephites, in terms of their true needs. (See 2 Ne. 9:48.) An underlying theme to all his writings was a call to the members of the Church — the house of Israel — to gather to Christ, to "reconcile yourselves to the will of God, and not to the will of the devil and the flesh." (2 Ne. 10:24.) Further, his was an open invitation (like Isaiah's): "Every one that thirsteth, come ye to the waters," the waters of life available through the gospel of Jesus Christ. "Come," he pleaded, "buy wine and milk without money and without price." (2 Ne. 9:50.) That is, come to salvation, which is free (see 2 Ne. 2:4; cf. Isa. 55:1-2), freely available, knowing full well that "after ye are reconciled unto God, that it is only in and through the grace of God that ye are saved" (2 Ne. 10:24). His desire? That the Saints of the Most High would center their lives and focus their actions upon those things that soothe and sanctify the soul, that they would never labor in secondary causes, in endeavors of doubtful worth or questionable productivity. (See 2 Ne. 9:51.) Jacob's desire for his people, and for all of God's children alike, is the same as that of all of the Lord's anointed servants: "Wherefore, may God raise you from death by the power of the resurrection, and also from everlasting death by the power of the atonement, that ye may be received into the eternal kingdom of God, that ye may praise him through grace divine." (2 Ne. 10:25.)

NOTES

1. See Robert L. Millet, "Nephi on the Destiny of Israel," chapter 7 of this volume.

2. Jacob's language is unmistakably similar to that of the language of God to Adam, as found in Joseph Smith's translation of Genesis: "Therefore I give unto you a commandment," the Lord said to our first father, "to teach these things [the plan of salvation] freely unto your children, saying: That by reason of transgression cometh the fall, which fall bringeth death . . . even so ye must be born again into the kingdom of heaven." (Moses 6:58-59; JST, Gen. 6:61-62.) Note the similarity to Jacob's teachings, based, it would appear, upon the brass plates: "There must needs be a power of resurrection, and the resurrection must needs come unto man by reason of the fall; and the fall came by reason of transgression." (2 Ne. 9:6.) For a more detailed study of the possible ties between the JST and the brass plates, see Robert L. Millet, "The Brass Plates: An Inspired and Expanded Version of the Old

Testament," in *The Old Testament and the Latter-day Saints*, Proceedings of the 1986 Sidney B. Sperry Symposium (Salt Lake City: Randall Book Company, 1986), pp. 415-43).

3. See *Times and Seasons* (February 1, 1843), 4:82-83, emphasis added; see also Bruce R. McConkie, *Mormon Doctrine*, 2nd ed. (Salt Lake City: Bookcraft, 1966), p. 65.

4. *Teachings of the Prophet Joseph Smith*, selected by Joseph Fielding Smith (Salt Lake City: Deseret Book Company, 1938), p. 121; emphasis added.

5. *A New Witness for the Articles of Faith* (Salt Lake City: Deseret Book Company, 1985), p. 130.

6. For an insightful comment on the central importance of the resurrection of Christ, see *Teachings of the Prophet Joseph Smith*, p. 62.

7. "The Doctrines of the Resurrection of the Dead and the Eternal Judgment are necessary to preach among the first principles of the Gospel of Jesus Christ." (*Teachings of the Prophet Joseph Smith*, p. 149.)

8. See Joseph F. Smith, *Gospel Doctrine* (Salt Lake City: Deseret Book Company, 1971), pp. 448-49 .

9. "A man is his own tormenter and his own condemner. Hence the saying, They shall go into the lake that burns with fire and brimstone. The torment of disappointment in the mind of man is as exquisite as a lake burning with fire and brimstone. I say, so is the torment of man." (*Teachings of the Prophet Joseph Smith*, p. 357; cf. pp. 310-11.)

10. It is a remarkable thing to discover that, indeed, this is the first time in the Book of Mormon that the name-title *Christ* is given for the Redeemer. Before this he is known by numerous titles, such as Messiah, Holy One of Israel, Shepherd, Lamb of God, Son of the Eternal Father, Savior, and Lord. It is difficult to know exactly what Jacob had in mind here. Did he mean that this was the first occasion when he came to know that the name of the Holy One of Israel, the Messiah, would be Christ? Did he mean that the angel had simply confirmed in his mind the specific name of the Messiah, something the Nephites already knew? The question is largely one of language: we know the Lord Jehovah as *Jesus Christ*, names that mean literally "the Lord is salvation" and "the Messiah or anointed one," respectively. The exact name by whch Christ was known to other peoples of the past (and of different languages) — including the Nephites — is unknown to us. The complete name-title *Jesus Christ* is given for the first time by Nephi in 2 Nephi 25:19. For a more detailed discussion of this matter, see Theodore M. Burton, *God's Greatest Gift* (Salt Lake City: Deseret Book Company, 1976), pp. 153-55.

11. While Jesus was on the cross, between the sixth and ninth hours (between noon and 3 P.M.), all the agonies of Gethsemane returned. (See James E. Talmage, *Jesus the Christ*, 3rd ed. [Salt Lake City: The Church of Jesus Christ of Latter-day Saints, 1916], p. 661; Bruce R. McConkie, *The Mortal Messiah*, 4 vols. [Salt Lake City: Deseret Book Company, 1979-81], 4:224-25.)

12. President Brigham Young taught that it was the withdrawal of the Father's Spirit that caused Jesus to sweat blood. (See *Journal of Discourses* 3:205-6.)

13. Neal A. Maxwell, *Even As I Am* (Salt Lake City: Deseret Book Company, 1982), pp. 116-17.

14. "The Desires of Our Hearts," in *Brigham Young University 1985-86 Devotional and Fireside Speeches* (Provo, Utah: Brigham Young University Publications, 1986), p. 30.

15. Conference Report, April 1986, p. 6.

16. *Gospel Doctrine*, p. 373; emphasis added.

11

NEPHI AND ISAIAH
(2 Nephi 11-25)

KENT P. JACKSON

In his record of his ministry contained on the small plates, Nephi included sixteen chapters from Isaiah's writings as found on the plates of brass.[1] He wrote: "I do not write anything upon plates save it be that I think it be sacred." (1 Ne. 19:6.) Even though space on the plates was limited, he felt that Isaiah's message was important enough for his descendants and the Gentiles of the latter days that he should quote whole sections of it. His reasons for doing so are clear: "That I might more fully persuade them to believe in the Lord their Redeemer I did read unto them that which was written by the prophet Isaiah." (1 Ne. 19:23.) "My soul delighteth in his words," Nephi wrote, "for he verily saw my Redeemer, even as I have seen him." (2 Ne. 11:2; see also 25:5.)

Jacob explained why Isaiah's words had special value for his people: they concerned "all the house of Israel; wherefore, they may be likened unto you, for ye are of the house of Israel. And there are many things which have been spoken by Isaiah which may be likened unto you, because ye are of the house of Israel." (2 Ne. 6:5.) Nephi wrote more about this process of "likening": "I did liken all scriptures unto us, that it might be for our profit and learning. . . . Hear ye the words of the prophet, which were written unto all the house of Israel, and liken them unto yourselves." (1 Ne. 19:23-24.) To "liken" a

---

Kent P. Jackson is associate professor of ancient scripture and Old Testament area coordinator at Brigham Young University.

passage of scripture to oneself is to apply it to one's own circumstances. As both Nephi and Jacob explained, since Isaiah wrote about the house of Israel (often in rather general terms), others of Israel can use his words with specific application to their own situations. Even today, it is wholly appropriate for us to "liken" Isaiah's words to our own experiences, to draw from the principles he taught and apply them to our lives.

But a word of caution is in order, as one Latter-day Saint commentator has pointed out: "To 'liken' a scripture to a different situation than that in which it originated is not always to learn the original message of that scripture. To correctly interpret a scriptural passage is to learn its original meaning. . . . There is a distinction between the interpretation of a scripture and some personal application of the same scripture to show a principle or lesson."[2] Readers should not assume that every statement of an ancient prophet must have a specific meaning in the latter-day setting. Nephi and Jacob set the correct pattern for interpreting Isaiah: they made wise application of the *principles* contained in Isaiah's words to their own circumstances. We should do likewise. The principles of human and divine behavior that were manifest among the people of Isaiah and Nephi are among us in modern society. As we "liken" Isaiah's words to us and apply their principles to our needs, we will find God-given solutions to problems that we in modern society face, individually and collectively.

Nephi wrote: "Behold, my soul delighteth in proving unto my people the truth of the coming of Christ; for, for this end hath the law of Moses been given; and all things which have been given of God from the beginning of the world, unto man, are the typifying of him." (2 Ne. 11:4.) The law of Moses was given — indeed *all things* were given — to typify Christ. A "type" (something that "typifies") is a symbol or pattern of something else. The law of Moses, which taught justice, mercy, vicarious redemption, and forgiveness, was a "type" of Christ.[3] Through its laws and ordinances, the attributes of Christ and his redemptive mission were taught. In conjunction with this, Nephi rejoiced in the grace, justice, power, mercy, and deliverance of the Lord — divine qualities that are among those most frequently emphasized by Isaiah. He rejoiced in "the covenants of the Lord which he hath made to our fathers" (2 Ne. 11:5), also a topic of considerable interest to Isaiah. God covenanted with the forefathers of the house of Israel that he would deliver and restore their descendants in a distant time. This latter-day redemption and restoration of Israel is one of the major topics of the passages of Isaiah quoted in Nephi's record.

Finally, Nephi understood and rejoiced that Christ's mission included not only what he would do in power and glory as the Lord God of the world, but also what he would do in his mortal ministry: "My soul delighteth in proving unto my people that save Christ should come all men must perish." (2 Ne. 11:6.)

The Ministry and Message of Isaiah

Isaiah, son of Amoz, was born in the first half of the 8th century B.C. His call to prophetic service took place about 740, and his ministry, which was centered in Jerusalem, extended for about fifty years. The period in which Isaiah lived was a troubled time for the Israelites. Approximately two centuries earlier, the once-great empire of David and Solomon had been divided into two kingdoms, Israel in the north (the northern ten tribes) and Judah in the south (the tribes of Judah and Benjamin). In the early years of Isaiah's life, both kingdoms were prosperous, and each enjoyed, for the most part, political independence from the larger powers that surrounded them. But both Israel and Judah fell short of the Lord's standards of faith and righteousness, leading ultimately to their destruction.

Isaiah lived to witness the judgments of God against the two kingdoms. Shortly after his ministry began, the Assyrian empire extended its influence into Palestine. Coming from the area of northern Mesopotamia (northern Iraq of today), the Assyrian kings created large empires through extortion, conquest, and plunder. During Isaiah's ministry, both Israel and Judah became subjected to Assyria. Israel was soon destroyed as a nation, with the fall of Samaria in 721 B.C. Its cities were torn down, many people were killed, and many people were taken away captive and relocated in other areas of the Assyrian empire. (See 2 Kgs. 17.) Throughout this period, Judah barely managed to survive. Isaiah constantly reminded its rulers and people to trust in the Lord, rejecting alliances with other nations; the Assyrian threat would pass. It did, but as Isaiah prophesied, rebellion against Jehovah would not go unpunished. God would raise up a greater threat, Babylon, which would execute his divine judgment against his rebellious people.

In my study of Isaiah I have identified what I believe are his three major themes. Almost everything he wrote fits into one of these categories:

1. *Trust in the saving power of the Lord.* Isaiah taught that God's saving power can be trusted both in temporal and spiritual things. We should trust in God to deliver us, not in man. (See 2 Ne. 12:22; 17:1-16; 18:1-4, 9-15; 20:24-34; 22:2; 24:32.)

2. *Covenant people have social and moral obligations.* Isaiah spoke very often about the responsibility of society to care for the needs of its less fortunate members, particularly the widows and orphans. He condemned the rich who oppressed the poor, and he stressed integrity and other virtues. (See 2 Ne. 12:6-7; 13:13-15; 15:23; 19:17; 20:1-4.)

3. *God's justice will prevail.* Isaiah wrote more about this topic than any other. He emphasized that the just would be vindicated and that the unjust would be punished. With special emphasis on the Lord's coming in glory, Isaiah taught that the Lord's justice will ultimately reward each person with what he or she deserves: the wicked will be destroyed at the Lord's coming, and the righteous will live in millennial peace. (See 2 Ne. 12:4, 10-21; 13:1-8, 10-26; 14:1-6; 15:5-6, 25-30; 17:17-25; 18:6-8; 19:1-21; 20:5-19, 24-27; 21:6-9, 14-16; 23:1-22; 24:1-32.)[4]

Understanding Isaiah

It is no secret that some Latter-day Saints find the writings of Isaiah difficult to understand. More than one individual has read in the Book of Mormon as far as 2 Nephi 11 but has found it discouraging to proceed beyond that point, where thirteen straight chapters of Isaiah are quoted. It is not that Isaiah's doctrine is difficult. His doctrine is simple and straightforward — certainly easier than the very complex doctrinal treatments of Jacob and Nephi that precede and follow the Isaiah section. The presumed difficulty with Isaiah lies in other areas. I believe there are three major factors that cause some readers to find Isaiah challenging:

1. *Lack of familiarity with the setting of Isaiah's day*. This includes cultural, geographical, historical, and political conditions. Even though there is a timeless quality to Isaiah's words (more so than in the writings of any other Old Testament prophet, I believe), still his writings were written in a setting that is very different from our own. Isaiah alluded constantly to the political and economic problems of his day. Large sections of his record can be understood only in part without a knowledge of the history of his time and the social challenges that his people faced. (See, for example, 2 Ne. 17:1–18:10; 20:5-19, 24-34; 23:1-5, 14-22; 24:3-31.) Nephi pointed out how an understanding of Isaiah's world is important for understanding Isaiah's writings. He mentioned that he could understand Isaiah because of his knowledge of "the regions round about" and "the things of the Jews": "My soul delighteth in the words of Isaiah, for I came out from Jerusalem, and mine eyes hath beheld the things of the Jews, and I know that the Jews do understand the things of the prophets, and there is none other people that understand the things which were spoken unto the Jews like unto them, save it be that they are taught after the manner of the things of the Jews. But behold I, Nephi, have not taught my children after the manner of the Jews; but behold, I, of myself, have dwelt at Jerusalem, wherefore I know concerning the regions round about." (2 Ne. 25:5-6.)

According to Nephi, no one can understand Isaiah's words as well as the Jews—meaning here the ancient Israelites—unless they are taught "the things of the Jews." He had an advantage, he said, because he knew those things, he had lived in Jerusalem, and he knew "the regions round about."

2. *Lack of understanding of Isaiah's literary style*. Modern readers are often surprised to learn that the revelations of the Old Testament prophets were written mostly in poetry. Isaiah is no exception. In the ancient Near East, including Israel, when the various deities were perceived as speaking they usually did so in poetic style. To

the ancient hearers and readers, poetry seemed to be the most appropriate means of expressing divine words. It conveyed, in their minds, a dignity, beauty, and reverence that could not be expressed in normal prose style, much as we now use, for the same reasons, an old form of English as the language of prayer.

The most common feature of Hebrew poetry is what is called *parallelism*. In a typical poetic verse from the Bible, a concept is expressed twice, in two parallel phrases. The phrases most often mean approximately the same thing, but different words are used in each. The following example from Isaiah illustrates this (Isa. 2:3-4; 2 Ne. 12:3-4):

And many people shall go and say, Come ye,
And let us go up

To the mountain of the Lord,
To the house of the God of Jacob.

And he will teach us of his ways,
And we will walk in his paths.

For out of Zion shall go forth the law,
And the word of the Lord from Jerusalem.

And he shall judge among the nations,
And shall rebuke many people.

And they shall beat their swords into plow-shares,
And their spears into pruning-hooks.

Nation shall not lift up sword against nation,
Neither shall they learn war any more.

Each of these couplets consists of two phrases. Though they are not always strictly synonymous in meaning, for the most part they are clearly parallel in grammatical structure and message. This kind of parallelism is the basic building block of the poetic style of the Old Testament prophets.[5]

Isaiah's prophecy makes frequent use of *metaphor*, a literary device in which a word or phrase meaning one thing is used to represent something else, suggesting a likeness between them. An example is: "My well-beloved hath a vineyard in a very fruitful hill" (2 Ne. 15:1), the vineyard and its vines being identified in 2 Ne. 15:7 as Israel and Judah. Similarly, the king of Assyria, with his ever-expanding empire, is described graphically in 2 Ne. 18:7-8 as a river flooding over its banks: "the waters of the river, strong and many . . . and he shall come up over all the banks. And he shall pass through Judah; he shall overflow and go over." A great latter-day leader, undoubtedly Joseph Smith, is called a "root" (meaning a shoot that grows off a main stem, underground),[6] and an "ensign" (meaning a banner, or rallying point), to whom the nations will gather. (2 Ne. 21:10.)

A *simile* resembles a metaphor, but it uses words such as *like* or *as:* Israel will be "*as* the sand of the sea" (2 Ne. 20:22), while Babylon will be "*as* when God overthrew Sodom and Gomorrah." (2 Ne. 23:19.) An *allegory* is a metaphor in story form. Isaiah's story of the vineyard in 2 Ne. 15 is an allegory.

3. *Problems with translations.* Another reason why English-speaking Latter-day Saints often find Isaiah difficult is the old language of the King James translation, which was first published in 1611. Even though the English of the current edition has been modernized somewhat since that time, it is still very archaic, making understanding a challenge for most readers. English has changed so much since the 17th century that modern readers often have difficulty both with the grammar and the vocabulary of the King James text. This is especially true in the prophetic books, like Isaiah, because of the richness of vocabulary and the complexity of grammar in poetic writing. The great strengths and beauties of the King James Version are more apparent in the Gospels, and in other prose narratives of the Bible.

Some modern translations do an excellent job of preserving the inspired words of the Bible in the same spirit of dignity, beauty, and reverence that is so apparent in the King James text.[7] As a result, many readers have found that reading Isaiah in a good modern translation eliminates much of the difficulty of understanding it.

Nephi added some additional information about understanding the words of Isaiah. He wrote that though the Jews in Jerusalem could understand Isaiah's writings (2 Ne. 25:5), Nephi's own people found them very difficult. He explained why: "For they know not concerning the manner of prophesying among the Jews." (2 Ne. 25:1.) Nephi had endeavored *not* to teach his people the ways of those from whom he had come, "for their works were works of darkness." (2 Ne. 25:2; see also 25:6.) The New World culture of Nephi and his people was to begin with a clean slate, aside from the much-needed sacred influences of the brass plates. One thing that seems to have been lost in the process was "the manner of prophesying among the Jews." Though Nephi never explained what he meant by that phrase, still he presented his own style as a contrast. While Isaiah's prophecies were "not plain," Nephi prophesied "according to the plainness which hath been with me from the time that I came out from Jerusalem with my father; for behold, my soul delighteth in plainness unto my people, that they may learn." (2 Ne. 25:4.) He wrote "according to my plainness; in the which I know that no man can err." (2 Ne. 25:7.) Whereas Isaiah's words were written in a sophisticated literary form with abundant use of carefully crafted poetic styles and images, Nephi's words are clear and to the point. The "manner of prophesying among the Jews," then, may have had reference to the style in which the Israelite prophets preserved the Lord's word. The Book of Mormon does not continue the writing style of the Hebrew prophets. Nowhere in it (except when Old Testament prophets are quoted) do we have revelation presented in poetic style. The revelations of the Book of Mormon, though unparalleled in their depth, power, and message, are presented in a clear, careful, and "plain" manner, that those who read them "may learn" more effectively. (2 Ne. 25:4.)

Nephi's final qualification for understanding Isaiah is not exceeded in its importance by any other: Isaiah's words, he wrote, "are plain unto all those that are filled with the spirit of prophecy." (2 Ne. 25:4.) We should recall that the spirit of prophecy is the spirit of revelation, which is available to anyone who has the Holy Ghost and the testimony of Jesus. (Rev. 19:10.) I have always been happy that Nephi realized that not all modern readers would have the spirit of prophecy to the fullest degree. He chose to write his own words plainly, so that none would be unable to understand his words and the power of his testimony.

Text and Translation in the Book of Mormon

Roughly half of the verses of Isaiah quoted in the Book of Mormon contain the same wording as in the King James text.[8] Most of the material is identical, word-for-word, to the corresponding passages. Of those verses in which the Book of Mormon text reads differently, only a few are sufficiently dissimilar to present a new meaning for the verse. The lack of substantial difference between the Book of Mormon text and modern texts suggests that Isaiah's record has undergone very little change since 600 B.C. The book of Isaiah appears to have suffered less loss of "plain and precious things" than did other parts of the Old Testament.[9]

But the similarities raise another question also. Critics of the Book of Mormon point out that the words would not be identical if the Prophet Joseph Smith had translated directly from an ancient text. One Latter-day Saint scholar has suggested the following: "When Joseph Smith translated the Isaiah references from the small plates of Nephi, he evidently opened his King James Version of the Bible and compared the impression he had received in translating with the words of the King James scholars. If his translation was essentially the same as that of the King James Version, he apparently quoted the verse from the Bible; then his scribe, Oliver Cowdery, copied it down. However, if Joseph Smith's translation did not agree precisely with that of the King James scholars, he would dictate his own translation to the scribe."[10]

I am comfortable with this interpretation. It seems, for the present, to be the best way to explain the close similarities between Joseph Smith's translation of the Book of Mormon and the King James Version.

An Outline of 2 Nephi 12-24 (Isaiah 2-14)

2 Nephi 12 (Isaiah 2)

1. Introduction
2-3. The Lord's house in the last days

4. Millennial peace

5-9. The Lord's complaint against the idolatry of Israel

10-18. The Lord's judgment against the proud and those who worship the work of men's hands

19-21. The idol worshipers fear the Lord's judgment

22. Stop trusting in man

2 Nephi 13 (Isaiah 3)

1-7. Chaos will come upon Judah

8-9. Judah revels in sin

10. It will be well with the righteous

11-12. Disaster will come upon the wicked

13-15. The Lord's judgment

16-26. Condemnation and judgment on Zion's women

2 Nephi 14 (Isaiah 4)

1. Condemnation and judgment on Zion's women, continued

2-6. Millennial restoration, cleansing, and glory

2 Nephi 15 (Isaiah 5)

1-2. The Lord prepared a vineyard, which brought forth bad fruit

3-4. The Lord's complaint against his vineyard

5-6. The vineyard's punishment

7. Israel and Judah are the Lord's vineyard

8-10. Destruction of cities and farms foretold

11-25b. Condemnation of drunkards, the proud, and the wicked

25c-30. Invasion, capture, and destruction by foreign nations

2 Nephi 16 (Isaiah 6)

1-4. Isaiah's glorious vision of the Lord in His temple

5-7. Isaiah's cleansing

8-13. Isaiah's commission to preach

2 Nephi 17 (Isaiah 7)

1-6. King Ahaz (of Judah) commanded not to fear invasion by Pekah (of Israel) and Rezin (of Syria)

7-9. The invasion will not succeed; Israel and Syria will fall

10-16. The sign of Immanuel given to Ahaz: Judah will be delivered

17-20. The coming invasion by the Assyrians

21-25. The emptiness of the land after the coming of the Assyrians

2 Nephi 18 (Isaiah 8)

1-4. The sign of Maher-shalal-hash-baz given: Judah will be delivered

5-8. Judah will be overpowered by Assyria

9-10. Since God is in control, armaments and strategies will be useless.

11-15. The Lord is a sanctuary to those who revere him, but a stumbling block and a snare to the wicked

16-22. Seek revelation from the Lord

2 Nephi 19 (Isaiah 9)

1-7. The Messiah's coming brings justice, righteousness, and peace

8-21. The Lord's anger and judgment against Israel

2 Nephi 20 (Isaiah 10)

1-4. God's anger against the unjust

5-19. God's judgment on the arrogance of Assyria

20-23. A remnant will return to the Lord

24-34. Zion's deliverance from the power of Assyria

2 Nephi 21 (Isaiah 11)

1-5. The rod and stem of Jesse

6-9. Millennial peace

10-13. The root of Jesse, an ensign for the gathering of Israel, Judah, and the Gentiles

14-16. The defeat of the nations

2 Nephi 22 (Isaiah 12)

1-6. A hymn of praise to the Lord

2 Nephi 23 (Isaiah 13)

1. Introduction: A prophecy of doom against Babylon
2-5. The Lord summons the nations to come against Babylon
6-13. Destruction on the day of the Lord
14-22. The destruciton of Babylon

2 Nephi 24 (Isaiah 14)

1-2. The restoration of Israel
3-23. A taunting prophecy against Babylon and her king
24-27. A prophecy of doom against Assyria
28-31. A prophecy of doom against the Phillistines
32. Refuge will be in Zion

We Rejoice in Christ

In Nephi's inspired discussion that followed the thirteen chapters of Isaiah in his record (2 Ne. 25), he outlined the history of the Jews from his own day into the latter days. They were destroyed as a nation and taken captive by the Babylonians (v. 10). They would return and be restored to their land (v. 11). Christ would come among them, and they would reject and crucify him. He would rise from the dead, bringing salvation to those who believe in him (vv. 12-13). Jerusalem would be destroyed again and the Jews scattered "among all nations" (vv. 14-15). Over the course of "many generations" of scattering and scourging, the Jews will become converted to Christ and accept his atonement. They will "believe in Christ, and worship the Father in his name, with pure hearts and clean hands, and look not forward any more for another Messiah" (v. 16). As Jacob (2 Ne. 6:11; 10:7-8), Nephi (1 Ne. 19:15-16), and Jesus (3 Ne. 20:30-33) taught, it will be in that day, after the Jews accept the gospel, that they will be gathered by the Lord to their promised land and established there in righteousness.[11]

As always, the focus of Nephi's discussion was on Jesus Christ: "There is none other name given under heaven save it be this Jesus Christ, of which I have spoken, whereby man can be saved." (2 Ne. 25:20.)

> For we labor diligently to write, to persuade our children, and also our brethren, to believe in Christ, and to be reconciled to God; for we know that it is by grace that we are saved, after all we can do....
>
> And we talk of Christ, we rejoice in Christ, we preach of Christ, we prophesy of Christ, and we write according to our prophecies, that our children may know to what source they may look for a remission of their sins....
>
> And the words which I have spoken shall stand as a testimony against you; for they are sufficient to teach any man the right way; for the right way is to believe in Christ and deny him not; for by denying him ye also deny the prophets and the law.
>
> And now behold, I say unto you that the right way is to believe in Christ, and deny him not; and Christ is the Holy One of Israel; wherefore ye must bow down before him, and worship him with all your might, mind, and strength, and your whole soul. (2 Ne. 25:23, 26, 28-29.)

Perhaps a personal note would not be inappropriate here. It may not be proper to rank God's prophets in terms of their greatness, since all of them, ancient and modern, have been extraordinarily great men, and each has contributed that portion of the word that the Lord has commissioned him to bring forth. Isaiah certainly was great, as the Lord so designated in the Book of Mormon. (3 Ne. 23:1.) As the most oft-quoted prophet in the New Testament and the Book of Mormon, his testimony of the destiny of Israel and the Lord's delivering power resounds through the centuries. But no prophets were ever greater than Nephi, Mormon, and Joseph Smith. It is primarily from them that we in the last days have received our knowledge of the gospel of Jesus Christ with its saving principles and ordinances. The Book of Mormon and the modern revelations are our primary sources of gospel knowledge; they bless our lives more than any other books.[12]

For the very reasons mentioned by Nephi, we have great cause to rejoice in Christ. It is only through him that we can be reconciled to the Father and obtain a remission of our sins. Similarly, we rejoice also in his prophets—Isaiah, Nephi, Mormon, Joseph Smith, and all others, ancient and modern. They are our teachers, and through their testimonies—which were often uttered and preserved at the cost of tremendous sacrifice—we can know the source of our salvation.

NOTES

1. Altogether, almost one-third of the book of Isaiah is quoted or paraphrased in the Book of Mormon. See Monte S. Nyman, *Great Are the Words of Isaiah* (Salt Lake City: Bookcraft, 1980), p. 283.

2. Nyman, *Great Are the Words of Isaiah*, p. 12.

3. See Kent P. Jackson, "The Law of Moses and the Atonement of Christ," *Studies in Scripture, Vol. 3: The Old Testament—Genesis to 2 Samuel*, ed. Kent P. Jackson and Robert L. Millet (Salt Lake City: Randall Book Company, 1985), especially pp. 169-72.

4. The most comprehensive LDS treatment of the book of Isaiah is Victor L. Ludlow, *Isaiah: Prophet, Seer, and Poet* (Salt Lake City: Deseret Book Company, 1982). Also helpful, especially in showing how Isaiah has been interpreted by leaders of the Church, is Monte S. Nyman, *Great Are the Words of Isaiah*.

5. For a convenient discussion of the different types of parallelism, see Ludlow, *Isaiah: Prophet, Seer, and Poet*, pp. 31-39.

6. See Kent P. Jackson, "Revelation Concerning Isaiah," *Studies in Scripture, Vol. 1: The Doctrine and Covenants*, ed. Robert L. Millet and Kent P. Jackson (Salt Lake City: Randall Book Company, 1984), pp. 330-32, and p. 334, note 7.

7. My own impressions of some popular recent translations may be of use to some readers. When the New English Bible (NEB) was produced, its translators sacrificed doctrinal and linguistic accuracy in their attempt to achieve literary quality. In my view, they failed badly at that as well. The Revised Standard Version (RSV) is a linguistically reliable translation, but its translators failed to retain in it the feeling of reverence and devotion that belongs in any translation of a sacred text. As such it is a defective translation. It lacks spirit. The New King James Version (New KJV) is a recommendable update of the King James translation. It does a good job of modernizing the old vocabulary and grammar of the King James Version without removing from it the spirit of devotion that it contains. Finally, in

my view, the best modern English translation of the Bible is the New International Version (NIV). This recent translation was made by a committee of scholars whose belief in the inspiration of the Bible is apparent throughout their work. It is translated in a beautiful literary style that is at the same time very reliable and accurate linguistically. And it expresses an impressive sense of faith, dignity, devotion, and reverence for the things of God.

8. Nyman, *Great Are the Words of Isaiah*, p. 283.

9. See Robert L. Millet, chapter 7 in this volume.

10. Daniel H. Ludlow, *A Companion to Your Study of the Book of Mormon* (Salt Lake City: Deseret Book Company, 1976), pp. 141-42.

11. See also Bruce R. McConkie, *The Millennial Messiah* (Salt Lake City: Deseret Book Company, 1982), pp . 229-30; and see Robert L. Millet, chapter 10 in this volume.

12. See Marion G. Romney, *Ensign*, January 1981, p. 2; Bruce R. McConkie, "The Doctrinal Restoration," in *The Joseph Smith Translation: The Restoration of Plain and Precious Things*, ed. Monte S. Nyman and Robert L. Millet (Provo, Utah: Brigham Young University Religious Studies Center, 1985), pp. 10-11.

12

TWO WAYS IN THE WORLD: THE WARFARE BETWEEN GOD AND SATAN
(2 Nephi 26-30)

ROBERT J. MATTHEWS

The particular segment of Nephi's writings covered in this discussion must be viewed as only a part of Nephi's larger prophecy and also as heavily influenced by his intense interest in the writings of Isaiah. Nephi used plainness in describing two strong forces at work in the world: the work of God, and the influence of the devil. This is a general theme of all scripture. The scriptures also promise that someday the war will be won, that there will be an eventual triumph of God over the devil—a permanent victory of good over evil, of the Saints over their persecutors, of the kingdom of God over the kingdoms of men and of Lucifer. This is the teaching of Isaiah, Jeremiah, Amos, Ezekiel, and all the prophets. The victory will be centered in Jesus Christ. These particular chapters from Nephi follow the same general pattern. Nephi explained the issue with great clarity.

The Standard Works are replete with warnings and observations that there is a war on the earth (and it has existed from the beginning) between the principles of righteousness emanating from God and the perfomance of evil emanating from the devil. Every righteous principle from God has its counterfeit counterpart put forth by the devil. To understand why that warfare exists, we need at least a brief glimpse of the premortal life.

Robert J. Matthews is professor of ancient scripture and dean of religious education at Brigham Young University.

The War in Heaven

Our earliest indication of the conflict is recorded in the scriptures as the "war in heaven," meaning a war that was waged among the spirit children of God in the premortal life. It began, so far as we know, with the rebellion of Lucifer against God over a difference about how God's spirit children (of whom Lucifer was one) could become like God. (See Moses 4:1-4; Abr. 3:23-28; D&C 76:25-26.) We do not know how long the war lasted, but we do know something of the contending armies and the issues. Each side had a major advocate and many followers. The Father's Firstborn (whom we know as Jesus Christ) defended and supported the Father's plan of salvation. Lucifer (who became the devil) wanted some modifications. Fundamentally the differences were over: (1) the principle of agency, which is always coupled with individual responsibility, and (2) the fact that Godhood (with ultimate perfection) can be obtained only through individual effort and excellence. Jesus stood for the absolute necessity of these principles; Lucifer opposed them. It was recognized that if individuals had their agency and if there existed a need for individual effort, then some would not be saved. Lucifer offered to save all people, but not by requiring individuals to consciously strive for excellence. Since he would save them himself, Lucifer wanted the glory and credit. Jesus defended the Father's plan (the gospel), which requires agency, individual effort, and accountability. He gave the glory to the Father.

The war was severe, and it had eternal consequences. Every kind of sin (with the possible exception of sins involving death) was present in that premortal state, and there were many casualties. Repentance was in order for all who sinned; and forgiveness in that premortal life was available through faith in Jesus Christ and obedience to the plan of salvation. (D&C 93:38.) This was not a war just of words and debate and forensics. It was a war of misdeeds, lies, hatred, pride, jealousy, remorse, envy, cursing, blasphemy, deception, theft, cajoling, slander, anger, and sins of almost every kind that are also known in mortality. The issues were so well defined that co-existence was not possible. Those who wholeheartedly supported Lucifer's rebellion became like him; and after having sinned beyond the possibility of reclamation, they were cast out of heaven and placed (as spirits) upon the earth, never to have the opportunity to be born with a body of flesh and bone. The precise number who thus rebelled we do not know, but the scriptures speak of them as a "third part" of the spirits who were originally scheduled for birth into mortality. (Rev. 12:4; D&C 29:36.) If a "third part" means one-third, then there are half as many evil spirits as the remaining two-thirds who are privileged to come to earth through the birth process and obtain physical bodies. That is, there are half as many spirits who rebelled and were cast out as all the mortals who ever have been born or will be born into this world to the end of the millennium. These rebellious spirits are "the devil and his angels," and also "vessels of wrath." (D&C 29:36-37; 76:33.) They are literally devils, forever miserable, and they are enemies of Christ and of all who align themselves with Christ. They are enemies of the Father's plan, and, with as many mortals as they can influence, do the devil's bidding on this earth.

Among the righteous, led by the Savior in that premortal war, were many notable men and women. The Lord's chief assistant was Michael, who later came to earth as Adam. There were also many men and women who are called "the noble and great ones" (Abr. 3:22-23), who are chosen to become the prophets and apostles and servants of God on this earth. They, with the rest of the two-thirds of the spirits, are born one by one into mortality. During their mortal probation, these spirits with their physical bodies soon find that the war in which they were engaged during the premortal life is raging here upon the earth also. In the process of being born, the memory and knowledge of the premortal life is taken away, and so the natural man and woman know nothing of their situation in relation to this war. However, when they read the revelations of God, they learn in a general manner who they are, where they came from, that they were on the Lord's side in the premortal war, and what their course of action should be in this mortal sphere. If they do not read or believe the revelations, the natural man and woman do not perceive the nature or purpose of their life or their responsibilities, or even that a war exists.

In reality, then, we first became acquainted with the "two ways" in our premortal life, and it was there also that we first became acquainted with Jesus Christ and learned that only in the gospel can we find the knowledge, the tools, and the power to combat the devil's program of defeat and enslavement.

There Can Be No Neutral Position

Just as the consequences of the war in heaven were severe and decisive, so also are the consequences of that war, which is now transferred to earth, equally severe and decisive. Neither conflict was a practice session; both are real, and both are of such a nature that every person is involved and affected. In neither war could there be a neutral ground. Why is that? Because when a task must be performed by a certain time, and the consequences are crucial, so-called neutrality by an able-bodied person is an aid and advantage to the enemy. Neutrality under such circumstances renders comfort and assistance to the opposite side. Such feigned neutrality is twice measured, not only in the help it gives the opposition, but in the lack of help that could have been given had the person chosen a side. Not to take a stand is in effect taking a stand for the opposition.

The same principles and issues are still in operation, and the same contenders now find themselves on a new battleground (earth) fighting an old war. It is made new by its introduction to this world at the fall of Adam and is renewed for each individual as he or she is born into mortality. As each of us grows to maturity and begins to sense the conditions of the world around us, we come to realize that these two major forces are at work in the world, affecting every soul. If we have taken the holy scriptures as our guide, we see more clearly the nature of the conflict and what we as individuals must do about it.

With this introduction we are ready to pursue a segment of Nephi's writings as he warns of the devil's work on the earth and tells of the Lord's plan of salvation and defense for humanity. Among the things that Nephi makes clear is that the Lord works in plainness, in truth, and in goodness for the benefit of the world, whereas the devil deals in deception and cunning, appealing to people's pride and physical appetites until he captures their souls in chains and destruction. This is not a pretty prospect, but it is a fair warning that our enemy is clever and will employ every deceptive and devilish means to accomplish his desires.

In this selected portion of Nephi's prophecy, possibly more than in any other place in the scriptures, particular detail is given about the devil's manner of operation and about how he carefully traps people. It may seem strange that a book of God would contain so much about the devil and his ways, but it is necessary in order that mortals might recognize evil when they see it and know how to prepare against it. The Book of Mormon not only shows us what the gospel of Christ is, but it also shows us what it is not.

Christ's Coming to the Nephites Foretold

In 2 Nephi 26:1-2, Nephi wrote that after the Messiah had risen from the dead, he would appear personally to the Nephites, show them his resurrected body, and give them a law for their guidance. This new law would be necessary because, as Nephi had already explained in chapter 25, Christ would fulfill the law of Moses when he came. (2 Ne. 25:24-30.) The Lord would replace the Mosaic Law with the gospel.

Nephi had seen in a vision the future of the Nephites and knew that extensive wickedness would exist among them and that they would experience wars and destructions. He saw that the Nephites would be informed of the birth and the death of Jesus by various signs, yet they would persist in their wickedness. Great earthquakes and other calamities would eventually slay the more wicked among them, after which Jesus in his glory would appear personally to the righteous who remained. (2 Ne. 26:3-9.)

Nephi did not state categorically that God himself would cause the natural calamities such as earthquakes, floods, and whirlwinds for the express purpose of slaying the wicked, but he definitely implied it, and it is also inherent in the message of his prophecy. For example, in 2 Nephi 26:6, he identified the thunderings, lightnings, and earthquakes as "the fire of the anger of the Lord" against the wicked. And in verse 7, Nephi lamented in "pain and anguish" that his people were so thoroughly destroyed, but he acknowledged that God's "ways are just." Such expressions show that Nephi viewed these "natural" occurrences as God-sent. In 2 Nephi 26:8, Nephi observed that the righteous who hearkened unto the words of the prophets would not be destroyed. These observations by Nephi deal with an interesting spiritual law regulating this mortal earth, showing that the behavior of human beings can affect and influence the so-called "natural" phenomena. The language of the scriptures also suggests that God uses these "natural" occurences to punish or at times to reward his children. These expressions cannot simply be a manner of speaking or a literary device, for they are basic not only to Nephi's warning, but also to the prophecy of Zenos cited in 1 Nephi 19:10-12 and the words of the Lord in 3 Nephi 9-10, wherein the literal fulfillment of these prophecies is reported and the voice of the Lord proclaims that it is he himself who has sent the destructions in consequence of the wickedness of the people.

Stumbling Block and Priestcraft

Nephi wrote that in the last days not only would the descendants of his people need to be taught the gospel and be reclaimed from their apostasy, but that the Jews and the Gentiles would likewise need to be taught and reclaimed. (2 Ne. 26:12-15.) He mentioned also that the record of the Nephites would have been written and sealed up, literally hidden in the ground, for safekeeping. Subsequent verses show that the Nephite record (the Book of Mormon) was to be preserved "untouched" so as to be available for later use as a witness of what the Lord actually said. The Book of Mormon is thus spoken of in contrast to the Bible, which has suffered change at the hands of men.

Nephi explained that the Gentiles in the last days would be lifted up in pride and would "have stumbled, because of the greatness of their stumbling block." As a result they would have "built up many churches," which would lack the power of God. (2 Ne. 26:20.) What the "stumbling block" is, Nephi did not say at that point, but he had used the identical language earlier to explain that the Gentiles would stumble because the Bible had been significantly altered and was thus lacking "many plain and precious parts" that had been "taken out" of it. (See 1 Ne.13:28-35.)

In view of Nephi's earlier prophecy and explanation about plain and precious parts being taken from the Bible, we can ascertain that the Gentiles' great "stumbling block" in the last days would be the lack of knowledge and spiritual understanding because of their imperfect Bible, which is the only scriptural record they have ever had.[1] Part of the doctrinal deficiency of the Bible would be made up through the coming forth of the Book of Mormon, as explained in 1 Nephi 13:35-42. Nephi wrote further about the spiritual contribution of the Book of Mormon in 2 Nephi 26 and 27.

Nephi continued his prophecy in 2 Nephi 26, where he described conditions among the Gentiles of the last days. It is a description of spiritual poverty, because the Gentiles (1) would be "lifted up in the pride of their eyes"; (2) would stumble spiritually, as noted earlier, because of their stumbling block; (3) would preach for religious doctrine ther own ideas gained through their own wisdom and learning; (4) would preach for financial gain; (5) would deny the miracles and power of God; (6) would be filled with envy, malice, and strife; and (7) would support secret combinations from the devil. All this can be classified as priestcraft. (2 Ne. 26:20-31.)

Priestcraft is specifically and categorically condemned by the Lord. Nephi said that priestcraft occurred when "men preach and set themselves up for a light unto the world, that they may get gain and praise of the world; but they seek not the welfare of Zion." (2 Ne. 26:29.)

In contrast to the ways of man and the devil, Nephi said that the Lord "doeth not anything save it be for the benefit of the world . . . even that he layeth down his own life that he may draw all men unto him." (2 Ne. 26:24.) Furthermore, "he doeth that which is good among the children of men; and he doeth nothing save it be plain unto the children of men." (2 Ne. 26:33.) The devil works through priestcraft, whereas the Lord works with charity, which is the love of Christ. (2 Ne. 26:30-31; Moro. 7:45.)

The Lord Is Able to Do His Own Work

Nephi stated that in the last days, there would be universal apostasy from the things of God, both among the Gentiles and also among the Jews, not only in this land but in other lands, "yea, even upon all the lands of the earth." (2 Ne. 27:1.)

Paraphrasing Isaiah 29:7-9, Nephi wrote that conditions in the last days would be as though a hungry and thirsty man dreams that he eats and drinks, but when he awakens from his dream he is still hungry and thirsty; or, in other words, his appetite is unsatisfied. This is indicative of the spiritual hunger people have, and of the inability of manmade religions to save souls. The people stagger, he wrote, in spiritual drunkenness and blindness.

Nephi explained that in the midst of this worldwide confusion and apostasy, the Lord would bring forth a book that was sealed. The book would contain the word of God and a "revelation from God, from the beginning of the world to the ending thereof." (2 Ne. 27:7.) Latter-day Saints are familiar with the details of this prophecy and know of the circumstances wherein Martin Harris took a transcript from the Book of Mormon to Professor Charles Anthon in New York City. (See JS–H 1:63-65.)[2] For the purposes of this particular commentary I have chosen not to retell the account so well chronicled in the other sources, but instead to briefly indicate that the prophecy of the sealed book, the learned man, the unlearned man, the coming forth of the Book of Mormon, and the withholding of the sealed portion until people have more faith, are part of the larger message of the "two ways" and the ongoing conflict between the work of God and the works of wickedness on the earth.

In 2 Nephi 27, we find these words of the Lord condemning the unbelieving attitude so often characteristic of the learning of the world: "The book shall be hid from the eyes of the world" (v. 12); the learned seek to read the book for the wrong reasons, "because of the glory of the world, and to get gain . . . and not for the glory of God" (vv. 15, 16). Then shall the Lord God say to the unlearned man, "The learned shall not read them, for they have rejected them," meaning they have rejected the idea of such a book and also rejected the words of the book (v. 20).

The Lord then repeatedly said that he would show to the world that he "can do his own work" (vv. 20-21) by causing the unlearned man to translate the book by miraculous means. In other words, the

Lord will bring forth his word by faith, and not by the learning of men. The point is unmistakably clear that the Lord did not want the Book of Mormon to come forth by the wisdom of the world. Such would have been contrary to the way God has always worked with the human family. It is by faith and miracles, not by pride, learning, and worldly means, that God brings forth his word. To assure us that God will work only by faith, Nephi quoted the Lord as saying: "I am able to do my own work . . . for behold, I am God; and I am a God of miracles; and I will show unto the world that I am the same yesterday, today, and forever; and I work not among the children of men save it be according to their faith" (vv. 21, 23). "Therefore," said the Lord, "I will proceed to do a marvelous work among this people, yea, a marvelous work and a wonder, for the wisdom of their wise and learned shall perish, and the understanding of their prudent shall be hid" (v. 26). This is a strong rejection by the Lord of the pride and the learning of the world and a bold insistence that the Lord can do his own work his own way. As a result of the coming forth of the Book of Mormon, many who were "blind" shall see, many who were "deaf" shall hear, and many "that erred in spirit shall come to understanding, and they that murmured shall learn doctrine" (vv. 29-35).

We can quickly see that 2 Nephi 27 is saying that the Book of Mormon is one of the Lord's effective weapons to enable us to fight against the work and influence of the devil. If we believe the words of the Book of Mormon, we can more readily detect the false doctrines of the world in every category, be they religious, political, or anything else.

The book is spoken of as being "sealed." Because a portion of the gold plates obtained by Joseph Smith was sealed, we have generally identified that portion as the sealed book spoken of in Isaiah 29 and 2 Nephi 27. However, neither Isaiah nor Nephi clearly differentiate between the sealed and unsealed portions of the book. It may be that the "seal" Nephi was speaking of is that the message of the Book of Mormon (even the unsealed and published part) is "sealed" to anyone without faith, to anyone who trusts in the learning of the world and rejects the revelations of God.

Although the book itself (meaning the gold plates) would be "hid from the world," the message of the book (except the sealed portion) is to go forth to all the world. In order to make the record legally binding, or, in scriptural terminology, in order to "establish his word," the Lord promised to provide three witnesses "besides him to whom the book [would] be delivered." These witnesses would behold the book "by the power of God," and would "testify to the truth of the book and the things therein." (2 Ne. 27:12, 14.) Those familiar with the history of the Church and with the Book of Mormon will recognize the fulfillment of this in the Testimony of Three Witnesses, printed in every copy of the Book of Mormon. (See also D&C 17.)

The law of witnesses is discussed in Deuteronomy 19:15, which states that one witness is not sufficient to completely establish a matter, and that "at the mouth of two witnesses, or at the mouth of three witnesses, shall the matter be established." This principle is renewed in the New Testament by the Savior and the apostles. (John 5:31-39; 8:13-18; 2 Cor. 13:1; 1 Tim. 5:19.) The stipulation that there be witnesses does not mean that the testimony of one witness cannot also be true, but rather that two or three witnesses make the matter legally binding. It is the Lord's way of leaving the unbeliever without excuse.

The Devil's Manner of Operation

In the meantime, the devil continues his warfare against the things of God. Being subtle and crafty, he sees no threat to his kingdom if there are many churches, as long as those churches do not teach the gospel of Jesus Christ. 2 Nephi 28 delineates how well Satan has succeeded in the earth in the last days. Nephi prophesied that there would be many churches, but that their priests would "teach with their learning, and deny the Holy Ghost," and would say that the Lord no longer works by miracles, for "he hath done his work." (2 Ne. 28:3-6.)

Another false teaching will be from those who say, "Eat, drink, and be merry, for tomorrow we die, and if we have sinned, God will smite us a little, and in the end we will be saved." (See 2 Ne. 28:7-8.) Nephi branded this as a false, vain, and foolish doctrine. (2 Ne. 28:9.)

One of the assertions of these chapters is that the conditions described are not isolated or local, but that they are worldwide, universal, and deeply entrenched among all peoples. This is not to say that there are no good people, nor people who desire to do good. But as Nephi observed, the whole of mankind "have all gone astray save it be a few, who are the humble followers of Christ; nevertheless, they are led, that in many instances they do err because they are taught by the precepts of men." (2 Ne. 28:14.)

The tenor of Nephi's prophecy is that the whole world is engulfed in pride, sophistry, worldly learning, false teaching, and wickedness. The apostasy has infiltrated the churches, but also false thinking and false philosophy have penetrated every avenue in human activity: educational institutions, government, families, business, industry, and all else. In the midst of this, the Book of Mormon comes to light, by miraculous means, to guide those who have faith. It is especially effective because, having been hidden in the earth for centuries and translated miraculously, it still contains its original purity and plainness.

Nephi summarized the worldly conditions and the success of the devil with an extensive statement about how the devil works. The devil causes some to fight against the things that are good — even to the extent that he "rages in their hearts" to stir them up to anger. Others he pacifies and lulls away into false security, and they say, "All is well," "Zion prospers," everything is fine. Some he flatters and tells that "there is no hell and no devil," and because they believe it, they fail to see the war, or fail to sense that they have any obligation in the matter. Or they might think they are serving the Lord, when in reality they are too passive, or perhaps too vigorous. This is seduction of the worst and most devilish sort, because it leads otherwise honest souls to think they are serving God when in reality they are not. Joseph Smith wrote that "nothing is a greater injury to the children of men than to be under the influence of a false spirit when they think they have the Spirit of God."[3]

"And thus," said Nephi, "the devil cheateth their souls, and leadeth them away carefully down to hell . . . and thus he whispereth in their ears, until he grasps them with his awful chains, from whence there is no deliverance." (2 Ne. 28:20-22.) Or, as Nephi explained in another place, the devil leads people "by the neck" first "with a flaxen cord, until he bindeth them with his strong cords forever." (2 Ne. 26:22.)

According to Nephi, the danger comes when we put our trust in man or "hearken unto the precepts of men, save their precepts shall be given by the power of the Holy Ghost." (2 Ne. 28:31.) Putting trust in man means trusting in worldly systems, institutions, and philosophies.

It would be difficult to miss the underlying message of 2 Nephi 26-28, that the devil has been highly successful in beguiling humanity; corrupting the scriptures; invading the churches; and causing widespread wickedness, murders, deceptions, and apostasy. At the same time, the Lord, through faith and miracles, has brought forth his scriptures, especially the Book of Mormon, as a beacon to all who love righteousness. The deception of pride, riches, worldly learning, and public acclaim are clearly outlined in this prophecy. Again we see that the mission of the Book of Mormon is not only to tell us what the gospel of Jesus Christ is, but also to detail what the gospel is not.

Three Great Scriptural Witnesses for the Lord

The law of witnesses was referred to earlier in connection with 2 Nephi 27:12-14. This subject is again taken up in 2 Nephi 29 and is applied this time not to individual people who are witnesses, but to the books of scripture that are witnesses for the Lord.

Nephi quoted the Lord as having said to him, "The words of your seed [the Book of Mormon] should proceed forth out of my mouth unto your seed; and . . . unto the ends of the earth, for a standard unto my people, which are of the house of Israel." (2 Ne. 29:2.) In other words, the Book of Mormon is to set the standard, showing the word of God and his particular dealings with the Nephite people and all the house of Israel.

Nephi was told by the Lord that many who think they believe the Bible will not accept the Book of Mormon because they think they already have the complete word of the Lord. To counteract this narrow view, the Lord explained that since there are more nations than one, there are more testimonies than one, and that the testimony of two nations is a witness that the Lord is God. The two witnesses in this case are the Bible as a record of the Jews, and the Book of Mormon as a record of the Nephites. The Lord expressed astonishment and near-disgust that the Gentiles would seemingly cling so dearly to the Bible and yet fail to appreciate the Jews (especially the Jewish prophets) who made the Bible possible. (2 Ne. 29:3-6.)

Since there are more nations than one, and since the Lord remembers all his people, he affirms that all his words are not in just one book (the Bible), for he has spoken and will continue to speak to his people everywhere and command them to write his words. He warns us that he speaks the same words (meaning the same principles) to one nation as to another, and that the world will be judged by the words that are written. (2 Ne. 29:7-11.)

The Lord then showed that there are to be three major written testimonies of Christ to come forth: (1) the Bible (of the Jews), (2) the Book of Mormon (of the Nephites), and (3) the records of the lost tribes of Israel, which we do not yet have. These three records are to be shared by each group so that each will eventually have the records of the others. And when Israel is gathered, the records will also be gathered. (2 Ne. 29: 13-14.) By these three records, the law of witnesses will be honored and the word of God established.

These records do not consist only of single books from each major branch of Israel. Just as the Bible is a collection of many books, and the Book of Mormon is a collection also, likewise the record of the ten lost tribes will probably be a collection of various books. It will tell us, when it is received, about the Savior's visit to the ten tribes after his appearance to the Nephites. However, since Ephraim was the leading tribe among the lost tribes anciently, perhaps our present Doctrine and Covenants should be viewed in perspective as a witness for Jesus Christ among latter-day Ephraim, to be combined someday with the other records of the lost tribes when they come forth.

Among the things to be accomplished by the multiple books of scripture are: (1) to give a multiple witness of Christ; (2) to show that the Lord does speak the same gospel to one people as to another, and (3) to prove that God does honor his covenant that he made with Abraham, promising to remember his seed forever. (2 Ne. 29:14.)

The Eventual Restoration of All the House of Israel

Nephi continued his prophecy by declaring that eventually the Lord's people would not only be gathered but also restored. These are two different conditions. Not only will Israel be gathered geographically from their long dispersion throughout the world, but the gospel will be "declared among them," and they will "be restored unto the knowledge of their fathers, and also to the knowledge of Jesus Christ, which was had among their fathers." This restoration will take place among all the branches of Israel — the Jews, the seed of Nephi, and the lost tribes, even among "all nations, kindreds, tongues, and people." (2 Ne. 30:3-8.)

Nephi explained an important concept that is sometimes overlooked by persons who take undue pride in being part of the covenant race, but who fail to recognize that blessings are based on righteousness. He pointed out that the Israelites should not think they are more righteous than the Gentiles solely on the basis of Israelite lineage. Nor should they suppose that all of the Gentiles will be utterly destroyed. Nephi explained the doctrine this way: "As many of the Gentiles as will repent are the covenant people of the Lord; and as many of the Jews as will not repent shall be cast off; for the Lord covenanteth with none save it be with them that repent and believe in his Son, who is the Holy One of Israel." (2 Ne. 30:1-2.)

This principle is known as "gospel adoption," and by it one who is a Gentile by lineage may be adopted into the house of Israel. John the Baptist understood this principle and taught it to the Jews of his day, saying to them, "God is able of these stones to raise up children unto Abraham." The "stones" obviously has reference to the Gentiles. (JST Matt. 3:36; Luke 3:13.) [4] Paul taught the same thing in Galatians 3:25-29, showing that by accepting the gospel of Christ, the Gentiles become the seed of Abraham. This is a fundamental provision of the covenant made to Abraham, as recorded in Abraham 2:10, that "as many as receive this Gospel shall be called after thy name, and shall be accounted thy seed, and shall rise up and bless thee, as their father."

The other part of the statement cited by Nephi, which says that as "many of the Jews as will not repent shall be cast off," needs some explanation. This principle applies to all who are Israelites by blood lineage. It does not mean only the Jews in Jerusalem and the Holy Land. This is made clear by the fact that Nephi was writing to his people, who were of Joseph's lineage. Paul dealt with this subject also, saying: "They are not all Israel, which are of Israel." (Rom. 9:6.) By this Paul meant that some who are of Israel by lineage are not living up to their spiritual privileges and therefore will not receive the blessings that could have been theirs as sons and daughters of Abraham and of the family of Jacob, even though they are of that blood lineage.

Second Nephi 30 closes with the promise of a complete restoration of the work of God on this earth. An entire separation between the wicked and the righteous will occur. The wicked will be destroyed by fire, and peace will be established throughout the earth. Nephi closed with excerpts from Isaiah 11, showing that in the coming era of peace, the animal kingdom shall lose its enmity, so that even a lion and a lamb shall lie down together in harmony. The portion of the human race that survives the burning will be righteous and will make war no more. Then the whole earth will be full of the knowledge of the Lord, and he will make all things known unto his children. Satan and his followers will be bound, and people will no longer follow the devil. At this point, Christ will have prevailed, the "war" will cease, and peace will reign on earth "for a long time." (2 Ne. 30:10-18.)

We know from other scriptures, chiefly D&C 88:110-116, that this period is the Millennium, and that after the thousand years of peace, there will be another season of wickedness. Then the devil, his influence, and his followers will be banished from this earth forever. However, Nephi in his prophecy chose to close with the millennial period.

NOTES

1. See Robert E. Parsons, "The Great and Abominable Church," chapter 5 in this volume.

2. This event is recorded in Joseph Smith, *History of The Church of Jesus Christ of Latter-day Saints*, 2nd ed. rev. Edited by B. H. Roberts (Salt Lake City: The Church of Jesus Christ of Latter-day Saints, 1932-51), 1:19-20; see also Bruce A. Van Orden, "Joseph Smith's Developmental Years," pp. 379-82, in *Studies in Scripture, Vol. 2: The Pearl of Great Price*, ed. Robert L. Millet and Kent P. Jackson (Salt Lake City: Randall Book Company, 1985).

3. Joseph Smith, *Teachings of the Prophet Joseph Smith*, selected by Joseph Fielding Smith (Salt Lake City: Deseret Book Company, 1938), p. 205.

4. See also *Teachings of the Prophet Joseph Smith*, p. 319.

13

THE PROMISE OF ETERNAL LIFE
(2 Nephi 31-33)

JOSEPH F. MCCONKIE

The scriptures do not contain a systematic or disciplined treatment of the doctrines of salvation. For the most part, we are required to sift and search the holy writ to obtain the mind and will of God, and even then our path is often beset with difficulties. In some instances the language is archaic or ambiguous; the meaning of Bible texts can be obscured by poor translation or the loss of words and phrases from the text. Add to this the necessity of correctly divining whether what we read was meant to be figurative or literal and whether the instruction given was conditioned upon a particular set of circumstances, thus subject to change, or represents an announcement of eternal principle.

The challenges of scriptural study are such that the best of scholars have differed and do differ in their understanding. Indeed, nothing serves to measure spiritual maturity or test spiritual integrity better than scriptural study. All who are serious students of the scriptures find from time to time that they must repent of misunderstanding and improve their views.

Some have responded to such difficulties by avoiding the challenge. They are satisfied to depend on interpretations given by others, particularly if the commentary comes from a prominent person. The

Joseph F. McConkie is associate professor of ancient scripture at Brigham Young University.

thought seems to be that all interpretation and meaningful insights will come from a selected few while the rest of us are to depend on their understanding; and that when we are called upon to speak or teach, we are to confine ourselves primarily to weaving together quotations from those commissioned to understand.

Among the glorious doctrines of the Book of Mormon is the assurance that *all* may know and understand the doctrines of salvation. The requisites for such understanding are faith, sincerity, righteousness, and obedience, matters upon which all have equal claim. Thus the hope of salvation, the promise of eternal life, is extended to all on equal grounds. Nephi and his fellow prophets have, for the most part, written with a plainness that far exceeds the clarity of the Bible. Further, the Book of Mormon contains a number of systematic treatments of doctrinal subjects, something noticeably missing in the scripture of the Old World. In the present instance, for example, Nephi discoursed on baptism in a manner that is without peer in the entirety of the Standard Works. In so doing, he responded to vital questions about this ritual over which the Christian world has contended for centuries. More importantly, in establishing these principles relative to baptism, Nephi established principles that apply with equal force to all ordinances of salvation. Salvation, or eternal life, is Nephi's subject—baptism is but the illustration.

The Savior Is Our Example in All Things

Nephi, to dramatize the importance of baptism, wrote that the Savior had to be baptized to "fulfill all righteousness." (2 Ne. 31:5.) The doctrine is both little understood and marvelously important. In the high spiritual sense there is no righteousness without willing submission to all the ordinances of salvation. No more perfect example could be found than Christ himself. Christ, who was sinless, had to be baptized in order to be considered righteous. To be righteous, as the word is used in its highest spiritual sense, means far more than being sinless, pure, or merely good. Righteousness is not simply the absence of evil or impropriety; it is the active seeking of the mind and will of the Father and compliance with that will once it has been obtained.

In Matthew's account of Jesus' baptism, Christ responded to John's reluctance to baptize him by saying, "Suffer it to be so now: for thus it becometh us to fulfill all righteousness." (Matt. 3:15.) The text is quite literally true. Neither John nor Jesus could have been considered righteous had the baptism not taken place. In the general sense, righteousness was understood to embrace the filling of obligations or the observance of legal requirements. In a more strictly religious sense, it was understood to mean conforming to the will of the Father. Thus we see Christ as the personification of righteousness because his whole nature, his every action, conformed to God's will.[1] The scriptures refer to Christ as the Son of Righteousness (2 Ne. 26:9; 3 Ne. 25:2; Ether 9:22), or even as The Righteous (Moses 7:45, 47). "Righteous," as a name-title for Deity, is intended to convey the idea of unswerving faithfulness in the keeping of covenant promises. Salvation and righteousness are thus inseparably linked. "God's righteousness in his judicial reign means that in covenant faithfulness he saves his people."[2]

Nephi identified four ways in which Christ fulfilled all righteousness through his baptism: (1) he humbled himself before the Father (2 Ne. 31:7); (2) he entered a covenant relationship with the Father, promising obedience in keeping the commandments (2 Ne. 31:7); (3) he opened to himself the gate to the celestial kingdom (2 Ne. 31:9); (4) he set a perfect example for all to follow (2 Ne. 31:10).

None but the righteous can be saved; that is, only those who are willing to enter into and honor the covenants of salvation will be heirs of the kingdom of heaven. Christ is the example; all who obtain salvation must obtain it in the same manner that Christ obtained it. As baptism was required of Christ that he might be an heir of salvation, so it is required of all who seek that blessing. Extending this principle beyond the ordinance of baptism, Joseph Smith taught that "if a man gets a fullness of the priesthood of God he has to get it in the same way that Jesus Christ obtained it, and that was by keeping all the commandments and obeying all the ordinances of the house of the Lord."[3]

The Doctrine of Christ

Christ is our example in all things. He ceases to be that if we excuse him from compliance with the ordinances of salvation or the obligation to keep the commandments. It would hardly be consistent to announce one system of salvation for Christ and another for the rest of humanity, and then to stoutly maintain that Christ's actions are the example to be followed. It is asked: Was it necessary for Christ to receive the gift of the Holy Ghost by the laying on of hands? Was it necessary for him to receive the priesthood in the same manner? Did he comply with temple ordinances? and so forth. In response it could be asked: Did he "fulfill all righteousness" in baptism, or was more required of him? Could he have fulfilled all righteousness by selectively keeping the commandments, or was it necessary, as Joseph Smith taught, for him to keep *all* the commandments? On such matters Nephi was emphatic — there is, he declared, but one path to the divine presence, and only by following that path could Jesus show us the way. (2 Ne. 31:9, 18-19.) "This is something of which uninspired men have no comprehension," stated Elder Bruce R. McConkie:

> Truly, he was the Lord Omnipotent before the world was; truly, he was like unto the Father in the pre-mortal life; truly, he was the Son of God here on earth — and yet, with it all, as with all the spirit children of the same Father, he too was subject to all of the terms and conditions of the Father's plan.
>
> He also was born on earth to undergo a mortal probation, to die, to rise again in immortal glory, to be judged according to his works, and to receive his place of infinite glory in the eternal kingdom of his Everlasting Father. How well Paul said: "Though he were a Son, yet learned he obedience by the things which he suffered; and being made perfect, he became the author [that is, the cause] of eternal salvation unto all them that obey him." (Heb. 5:8-9.)[4]

It was required of Christ as it is required of all people, taught Nephi, that he follow the strait and narrow path. (2 Ne. 31:9.) A *straight* path is one without deviation, whereas a *strait* path, as spoken of in this text, is one that is strict, narrow, and rigorous. Both expressions are appropriate descriptions of the path that leads to the presence of God. In this instance, however, the emphasis is on the strictness with which all who would be saved must comply with the ordinances of salvation. Salvation is found only in willing obedience to the Father, never in neglect, disobedience, or the pursuit of one's own will. As it was, it was necessary for Christ to be obedient in all things to work out his salvation. It is necessary for all others to do the same.

Christ was not baptized for a remission of sins—he neither had nor would commit any. Christ was baptized because baptism is required for entrance into the kingdom of God. "Baptism is a sign to God, to angels and to heaven that we do the will of God," declared Joseph Smith, "and there is no other way beneath the heavens whereby God hath ordained for man to come to Him to be saved, and enter into the Kingdom of God, except faith in Jesus Christ, repentance, and baptism for the remission of sins, and any other course is in vain; then you have the promise of the gift of the Holy Ghost."[5]

With marvelous artistry, Nephi painted a word-picture of the path we must follow to obtain the presence of the Father. He depicted baptism as the gate or place of beginning that opens to a strait and narrow path. At this point he asked, "Is all done?" and responded, "Nay; for ye have not come thus far save it were by the word of Christ with unshaken faith in him, relying wholly upon the merits of him who is mighty to save. Wherefore, ye must press forward with a steadfastness in Christ, having a perfect brightness of hope, and a love of God and of all men. Wherefore, if ye shall press forward, feasting upon the word of Christ, and endure to the end, behold, thus saith the Father: Ye shall have eternal life." (2 Ne. 31:19-20.)

Similarly, those following the strait path in our day who are so living that they have been sealed by the Holy Spirit of promise are assured that it will be said unto them, "Ye shall come forth in the first resurrection," meaning that they will "inherit thrones, kingdoms, principalities, and powers, dominions, all heights and depths" and that when they are out of the world they shall pass those stationed to guard the way and to see that no unclean thing enters the presence of the Lord. They are to receive exaltation and glory, "which glory shall be a fulness and a continuation of the seeds forever and ever." Thus the man and woman so sealed are promised that they will "be gods, because they have no end; therefore shall they be from everlasting to everlasting, because they continue; then shall they be above all, because all things are subject unto them. Then shall they be gods, because they have all power, and the angels are subject unto them." (D&C 132:19-20.)

Commenting on this principle, Joseph Smith said: "After a person has faith in Christ, repents of his sins, and is baptized for the remission of his sins and receives the Holy Ghost, (by the laying on of hands), which is the first Comforter, then let him continue to humble himself before God, hungering and thirsting after righteousness, and living by every word of God, and the Lord will soon say unto him, Son, thou shalt be exalted. When the Lord has thoroughly proved him, and finds that the man is determined to serve Him at all hazards, then the man will find his calling and his election made sure, then it will be his privilege to receive the other Comforter, which the Lord hath promised the Saints."[6]

The "doctrine of Christ" (2 Ne. 31:2, 21) is the plan and system whereby the children of God "fulfill all righteousness" by taking upon themselves the name of Christ in baptism, receiving and obeying the principles and ordinances of the gospel, and then enduring to the end in faith. Paul stated it thus: "One Lord, one faith, one baptism" (Eph. 4:5), while errant Christianity would have it "Many Lords, many faiths, and many baptisms." Yet there cannot be contradictory truths. It is a strait and narrow path that leads to the presence of God; there is but one plan of salvation, one priesthood, and one church. The Lord commanded that we "be one," saying, "If ye are not one ye are not mine." (D&C 38:27.) In his great intercessory prayer, Christ implored the Father to help all who embrace the gospel to become one. "I in them," he prayed, "and thou in me, that they may be made perfect in one." (John 17:21-23.) Without such unity there is no perfection, nor can there be salvation. Thus the most perfect of all teaching devices is the announcement that the Father, Son, and Holy Ghost (three separate and distinct personages) are one God. (2 Ne. 31:21.)

Revelation Is the Doctrine of Christ

Introducing his discourse on the necessity of our fulfilling all righteousness, Nephi stated that the Lord "giveth light unto the understanding." (2 Ne. 31:3.) Joseph Smith expanded this principle by saying, "A person may profit by noticing the first intimation of the spirit of revelation; for instance, when you feel pure intelligence flowing into you, it may give you sudden strokes of ideas, so that by noticing it, you may find it fulfilled the same day or soon; (i.e.) those things that were presented unto your minds by the Spirit of God, will come to pass; and thus by learning the Spirit of God and understanding it, you may grow into the principle of revelation, until you become perfect in Christ Jesus."[7]

Continuing, Nephi assured us that the Lord speaks to his children "according to their language, unto their understanding." (2 Ne. 31:3.) God and his angels, when conversing with mortals, speak according to the language and understanding of those whom they have chosen to address. To Joseph Smith, they spoke in English; to Adam, they spoke the pure Adamic tongue; to the Nephites, they spoke the language of the Nephites; and so on. To each person, they speak according to his or her level of understanding. To do otherwise would be futile. Thus, since the days of Adam when language was "pure and undefiled" (Moses 6:6), we have been without the ability to give full or perfect expression to revelations; an imperfect language imposes its imperfections on the expressions of heavenly messengers. In like manner, imperfections in our understanding, particularly those imperfections born of disobedience or lack of faith, impair our ability to understand the revelations the Lord has given us. Thus some will see a thousand times more than others in a single verse of scripture.

Having taught that those who go down into the waters of baptism are entitled to the "baptism of fire and of the Holy Ghost," Nephi said that they could then "speak with a new tongue, yea, even with the tongue of angels." (2 Ne. 31:13-14.) Returning to that matter in 2 Nephi 32, Nephi asked, "Now, how could ye speak with the tongue of angels save it were by the Holy Ghost?" Then he explained that "angels speak by the power of the Holy Ghost" and thus are able to "speak the words of Christ." (2 Ne. 32:2-3.) That is, they are able to say and do what Christ would say and do under the same circumstances. Men and women, when moved upon by the Holy Ghost, can speak with the same power, authority, and doctrinal purity as angels.

Indeed, angels are merely men or women from the other side of the veil of mortality. The message, power, and authority of angels does not differ from those of the Lord's mortal servants.

The importance of receiving the Holy Ghost cannot be overstated. It is only by the power of the Holy Ghost that we can know or teach the doctrines of the kingdom. For instance, in our day the Lord has said: "If ye receive not the Spirit ye shall not teach" (D&C 42:14), meaning that unless that which we teach is sustained by the power of the Lord's Spirit, no teaching or learning can take place. We may have gone through all the right motions and said all the right words, having the "form of godliness," and yet be without "the power thereof." (JS–H 1:19.) Nephi promised his people that if they would "enter in by the way, and receive the Holy Ghost," it would show them all that they must do to be saved in the kingdom of God. This, he declared, "is the doctrine of Christ" and he added that no more doctrine would be given until Christ should manifest himself to the nation of the Nephites in the flesh. (2 Ne. 32:5-6.) With the coming of Christ, the law of Moses, which the Nephites were then called upon to observe, would be done away. In its stead, the ordinance of the sacrament would be given them, the government of the Church would be reorganized, and twelve apostles would be called to stand at the church's head. Perhaps Christ would also instruct them in the performance of vicarious ordinances for the blessing of the dead.

Exhortation to Prayer

Having spoken of the role of the Holy Ghost in leading us to all truth, Nephi turned his attention to the role of the third member of the Godhead in the matter of prayer. "If ye would hearken unto the Spirit which teacheth a man to pray," he said, "ye would know that ye must pray; for the evil spirit teacheth not a man to pray, but teacheth him that he must not pray." (2 Ne. 32:8.) It has ever been the purpose of the adversary to separate men from association with their God. By contrast, no servant of God has ever argued that the heavens are sealed or that the canon of scripture is full. No servant of God has ever suggested that the honest in heart should not seek divine direction in all things.

Only evil spirits would seek to teach men not to pray. The true servant of the Lord has ever been found testifying of Christ and his gospel and challenging those to whom he speaks to seek a spiritual confirmation of it. "Ask of God," is the challenge of the Lord's servants, for he "giveth to all men liberally, and upbraideth not." (James 1:5.) If one seeks to know the truth of the Book of Mormon, we challenge that person to read it, ponder its teachings, and ask of God with an honest heart if it is true. We know full well that no opponent of the Book of Mormon would ever stand before a congregation and invite them to read it and pray to know of its truthfulness. All manner of argument is used against Joseph Smith and against our testimony that he is a prophet. Yet we never hear of the Prophet's critics inviting others to read the Joseph Smith Story (as he himself told it) and then to pray to know of its truthfulness.

The Holy Ghost will always lead a person *to* prayer and *in* prayer. That is, the Spirit teaches us to pray and also gives us direction in the things for which we should pray. To have the Holy Ghost is to have the promise, "It shall be given you what you shall ask" (D&C 50:30), and the promise that "he that asketh in the Spirit asketh according to the will of God; wherefore it is done even as he asketh" (D&C 46:30). The prayer of the Twelve in 3 Nephi is a classic illustration of this principle. Of this prayer we read: "They did not multiply many words, for it was given unto them what they should pray, and they were filled with desire." (3 Ne. 19:24.)

Nephi also established the proper order of prayer, directing that we "pray unto the Father in the name of Christ," and that we counsel with the Lord in all things. This is not to say that we need be "commanded in all things" (D&C 58:26), but rather that having studied a matter out in our minds and having made the best decisions we can (D&C 9:8) — using correct principles and drawing upon past inspiration — we then seek the Lord's confirmation (Morm. 9:25), or, in Nephi's words, we seek to have the Lord "consecrate" our performance that it may be for the welfare of our souls (2 Ne. 32:9).

The Spirit Sustains the Word of Truth

As he concluded his record, Nephi lamented that he was not "mighty in writing, like unto speaking." (2 Ne. 33:1.) Yet he realized that the Holy Ghost was the source of power with which he had touched the hearts of his people, and that the Holy Ghost would also testify of the truthfulness of what he had written. Surely it is no more difficult for the Holy Ghost to testify of the written word than of the spoken word. The simple words of a humble prophet, spoken some 2,600 years ago and sustained by the power of the Spirit, are sufficient to kindle the fires of faith, while the jangling eloquence of the worldly wise rarely lives beyond their own generation.

As an experienced teacher, Nephi knew that many would harden their hearts against the Holy Spirit so that it could have no place in them, and that they would "cast many things away which are written and esteem them as things of naught." (2 Ne. 33:2.) He knew that the record he had made would be rejected by those who denied the spirit of revelation. He also knew that those who rejected the testimony of the Book of Mormon would do so in the name of loyalty to the Bible. (See 2 Ne. 33:10.) Reviewing his writings, he noted that their purpose was to persuade people to do good, to restore to them a knowledge of their ancient fathers, to encourage belief in and testify of Christ, and to teach people to endure in faith to the end so that they could obtain eternal life. He also noted that his words spoke harshly against sin. Quite properly, Nephi concluded that no one "will be angry at the words which I have written save he shall be of the spirit of the devil." (2 Ne. 32:4-5.)

Thus we see that the truth of all things — that is, all things of eternal importance — will be sustained on the one hand by the quiet whisperings of the Spirit and identified on the other by wrath of the adversary. We will always be able to identify the truths of salvation by the opposition of the Prince of Darkness and the contrasting feelings of comfort and assurance that come only from the Prince of Peace. Light and darkness will never meet.

The Seal of Testimony

It is the pattern of the prophets to teach the doctrines of salvation and then to seal their teachings with a testimony that what they have taught is the gospel. As Nephi concluded an earlier discourse, he said: "I have spoken plainly unto you, that ye cannot misunderstand. And the words which I have spoken shall stand as a testimony against you; for they are sufficient to teach any man the right way; for the right way is to believe in Christ and deny him not; for by denying him ye also deny the prophets and the law." (2 Ne. 25:28.) In the truest sense, unless something has been taught, no testimony has been given. As Nephi concluded his record, which contains teachings about the plan of salvation that are unsurpassed in all the holy writ for plainness and spiritual power, Nephi placed a seal upon his testimony or teachings.

Few prophets have been granted the privilege given Nephi of testifying to all the ends of the earth. His testimony is that all must believe in Christ. He admonished them that if they could not believe what he had written, then they should believe in Christ. If they honestly believed in Christ, they would of necessity come to believe what Nephi had written, for he had written nothing but the words of Christ. Nephi further reasoned that one cannot truly believe in the Bible and not at the same time believe in the Book of Mormon. Brigham Young taught the same principle, saying: "There is not that person on the face of the earth who has had the privilege of learning of the Gospel of Jesus Christ from these two books [the Bible and the Book of Mormon], and can say that one is true, and the other is false. No Latter-day Saint, no man or woman, can say the Book of Mormon is true, and at the same time say that the Bible is untrue. If one be true, both are; and if one be false both are false."[8] To believe the words of one is to believe the words of both. (See Mormon 7:9.)

All who reject his record, Nephi declared, will be called upon to meet him face to face at the judgment bar, where they will know that he was commanded of God to write the things he had written. (See 2 Ne. 33:11.) Moroni concluded the Book of Mormon in like manner, saying: "I soon go to rest in the paradise of God, until my spirit and body shall again reunite, and I am brought forth triumphant through the air, to meet you before the pleasing bar of the great Jehovah, the Eternal Judge of both quick and dead." (Moro. 10:34.) In principle this applies to all the holy prophets since the world began. Each will stand at the pleasing bar of God as a witness against those who rejected the things he was commissioned to preach and teach in the name of the Messiah.

Christ was rejected by a nation professing loyalty to the law of Moses. To those of his day the Savior said: "Do not think that I will accuse you to the Father: there is one that accuseth you, even Moses, in whom ye trust. For had ye believed Moses, ye would have believed me: for he wrote of me. But if ye believe not his writings, how shall ye believe my words?" (John 5:45-47.) Similarly, our testimony of Joseph Smith is rejected by many who profess a loyalty to the Bible and the prophets of ages past. Well might Joseph Smith say of them: "Do not think I will accuse you to the Father; there are others that accuse you, even Moses, Isaiah, and Ezekiel, in whom ye trusted. For had ye believed the prophets of the Bible, ye would have believed me; for they wrote of me."

Nephi understood the destiny of the record he was keeping. He knew that it would yet "spring out of the earth" (Ps. 85:11; Isa. 45:8), carrying the testimony of those whose bodies had long since returned to the dust (see Isa. 29:4; 2 Ne. 27:6). "I speak unto you as the voice of one crying from the dust," he said. "Farewell until that great day shall come." (2 Ne. 33:13.)

Conclusion

The plan of salvation is eternal and applies in like manner to those of all ages. Christ is the perfect model—all desiring salvation must earnestly seek to imitate his example. They must follow the path he marked out. As it was necessary for him to know and live gospel principles, so it is for us. As it was necessary for him to enter in at the gate, to obediently comply with the ordinances and rites of the gospel, so it is with us. As it was necessary for him to have the companionship of the Holy Ghost and seek that knowledge and understanding that comes only from heaven, so it is with us. As his conviction, power, and knowledge enabled him to stand independent of all the powers and influences of the earth, so must ours. Such is the path that Nephi invites us to follow, taking the Holy Spirit as our guide and Christ as our example. Such is the path by which we are to fulfill all righteousness and obtain the promise of eternal life.

NOTES

1. Gerhard Kittel and Gerhard Friedrich, editors; translated by Geoffrey W. Bromiley, *Theological Dictionary of the New Testament Abridged in One Volume* (Grand Rapids, Michigan: William B. Eerdmans Publishing Company, 1985), pp. 169-70.

2. Ibid., p. 171.

3. Joseph Smith, *Teachings of the Prophet Joseph Smith*, selected by Joseph Fielding Smith (Salt Lake City: Deseret Book Company, 1938), p. 308.

4. Bruce R. McConkie, "The Mystery of Godliness" (Brigham Young University, 15 Stake Fireside, January 6, 1985).

5. *Teachings of the Prophet Joseph Smith*, p. 198.

6. Ibid., p. 150.

7. *Teachings of the Prophet Joseph Smith*, p. 151.

8. *Journal of Discourses*, 26 vols. (London: Latter-day Saints' Book Depot, 1854-86), 1:38.

14

JACOB: IN HARMONY WITH GOD
(Jacob 1-3, 7)

CLARK V. JOHNSON

Jacob's discourse at the temple taught the people what they had to do to live righteously. His teachings on wealth, pride, and chastity let the people know how they could bring themselves into harmony with God. In spite of Jacob's efforts, Sherem sought to destroy his work among the people by leading them away from belief in God. He even tried to persuade Jacob himself that his position was ideologically unsound. When these events ocurred, Lehi's family had been gone from Jerusalem for at least fifty-six years.

Jacob's Life and Ministry

When Nephi turned the records over to his younger brother Jacob, fifty-five years had passed since Lehi and his family left Jerusalem. (Jacob 1:1.) Jacob was the elder of two sons born to Sariah and Lehi in the wilderness. (1 Ne. 18:7, 19.) He would have been born sometime between 600 and 590 B.C., and he was between forty-four and fifty-four years of age when Nephi charged him to take care of the plates and to teach the people.

The little that is known of Jacob's youth is revealed by his father in an interview shortly before Lehi's death. He called Jacob to him

Clark V. Johnson is associate professor of Church history and doctrine at Brigham Young University.

and explained, "In thy childhood thou hast suffered afflictions and much sorrow, because of the rudeness of thy brethren." (2 Ne. 2:1.) Young Jacob had suffered in the wilderness when Nephi broke his bow; had seen the rebellion of his elder brothers when they threatened both Nephi and Lehi when they were building the ship; and had been on the ship when Laman, Lemuel, and others bound Nephi and threatened to kill him. (1 Ne. 16-19.)

Even though Jacob had suffered much in his youth, Lehi also noted that because of his righteousness he had seen the Savior and knew of his coming "to bring salvation unto men," whom he had redeemed. (2 Ne. 2:3-4.) Finally, Lehi admonished Jacob to stay with Nephi and to spend his life in the service of God. (2 Ne. 2:3.)

The opening verses of the Book of Jacob indicate that Jacob had heeded his father's counsel: he had followed Nephi, and he had spent his life in God's service. (Jacob 1:1-2.) When Nephi gave the records to Jacob, he charged him to write on them sacred things and to teach the people. (Jacob 1:2-4.)

After the death of Lehi, Jacob's elder brothers plotted the death of Nephi and his followers. Nephi, Jacob, and others fled from their brothers into the wilderness and began a new life. (2 Ne. 5:6-13.)

Life in the desert had been hard, and even after they arrived in the promised land, it continued to be difficult as they sought to build homes, synagogues, and a temple. Jacob attested to these hardships late in life when he wrote, "Our lives passed away like as it were unto us a dream, we being a lonesome and a solemn people, wanderers, cast out from Jerusalem, born in tribulation, in a wilderness, and hated of our brethren, which caused wars and contentions; wherefore, we did mourn out our days." (Jacob 7:26.)

In addition to making Jacob custodian of the plates, Nephi, just prior to his death, appointed someone else to be king over his people. (Jacob 1:9.) Because of their love for Nephi, the people desired to "retain in remembrance his name." (Jacob 1:11.) Therefore, they decided that regardless of the name of the new king, he should be called "second Nephi, third Nephi, and so forth." (Jacob 1:11.) Jacob also noted that the people were known by various names: "Nephites, Jacobites, Josephites, Zoramites, Lamanites, Lemuelites, and Ishmaelites," but henceforth they would be known as Nephites, the followers of Nephi, and Lamanites, the followers of Laman and Lemuel. (Jacob 1:13-14.)[1]

When Nephi gave Jacob custody of the plates, he charged him to write sacred things and to include very little history. The history was kept on "other plates." (Jacob 1:2-4.) Nephi wanted Jacob to write only those things that were "precious," which included "preaching that was sacred" and "revelation." (Jacob 1:4.) Speaking of their revelations, Jacob noted: "Because of faith and great anxiety, it truly had been made manifest unto us concerning our people, what things should happen unto them. And we also had many revelations, and the spirit of much prophecy; wherefore, we knew of Christ and his kingdom, which should come." (Jacob 1:5-6.)

Both Jacob and Joseph were consecrated priests over the people. (2 Ne. 5:26; Jacob 1:17-19.)[2] Their obligation was to teach the people, reminding them of their duty toward God. Ignoring this responsibility would have caused the sins of the people to be answered "upon [their] own heads." (Jacob 1:19.) Therefore, Jacob and Joseph taught their people the "word of God with all diligence." (Jacob 1:19.)[3]

A Temple Discourse

Sometime after the death of Nephi, Jacob went to the temple and there taught his people. There are only four temple discourses recorded in the Book of Mormon.[4] Jacob's discourse covered four topics: wealth, pride, chastity, and purity of heart.

The tone of the sermon shows the burden Jacob felt as he declared to the people assembled at the temple that he was "weighed down" with concern for their welfare. (Jacob 2:3.) He did not want to speak to them on the topics he treated, but he felt compelled to because he had received his "errand from the Lord," and he felt that he needed to "magnify [his] office with soberness" that he might "rid [his] garments" of their sins. (Jacob 1:17; 2:2.)[5] He also felt sorrow in teaching those subjects so boldly because of the delicate feelings of the women and children who were present. (Jacob 2:7.)

Wealth and Pride

Jacob began his discourse by pointing out the fact that many of those present sought wealth by searching for gold, silver, and other precious metals. (Jacob 2:12.) He noted that many of them had been successful in their quest, as he expected them to be, for they lived in a land of promise, full of wealth. He warned them to seek the kingdom of God first, and then their wealth would be a blessing to them, for they would use it wisely. He lamented that they had used their wealth to create factions among themselves. Those who were successful flaunted their wealth in front of the poor; instead, he said, they needed to build the kingdom of God and use their wealth to benefit the poor. Wealth in itself is not evil, but the unwise use of wealth leads men and women to do evil; this was what Jacob objected to. President David O. McKay taught: "Gold does not corrupt man; it is in the motive of acquiring that gold that corruption lies."[6]

Later in the Book of Mormon another prophet, Nephi, admonished his people concerning wealth. This was a time not only of an abundance of spiritual blessings, but also of physical prosperity as the people multiplied and built houses, synagogues, and temples. (Hel. 3:7-9.) During a time of repentance the Lord had blessed his Church, and there was so much prosperity in the Church that "the teachers were themselves astonished beyond measure." (Hel. 3:25.) Unfortunately the people were so prosperous in their spiritual and physical wealth that they were "lifted up in pride" and began to persecute their brethren. (Hel. 3:34.)

Likewise in Jacob's day the improper use of wealth led to pride, and the wealthy "afflicted" and "persecuted" their neighbors. (Jacob 2:20.) Jacob reminded the rich Nephites that God gave them their wealth. He finished his discourse on wealth by reminding them that "one being is as precious in [God's] sight as the other. And all flesh is of the dust; and for the selfsame end hath he created them, that they should keep his commandments and glorify him forever." (Jacob 2:21.)

According to Jacob, pride destroys a person's soul. (Jacob 2:16.) Concerning pride President Ezra Taft Benson has said: "In the scriptures there is no such thing as righteous pride. It is always considered a sin. We are not speaking of a wholesome view of self-worth, which is best established by a close relationship with God. But we are speaking of pride as the universal sin. . . . Essentially, pride is a 'my will' rather than 'thy will' approach to life."[7]

Those who seek the kingdom of God first will obtain hope in Christ, and their hearts will be void of pride; then they will use their wealth to benefit the poor and the sick. (Jacob 2:19.)

Jacob lamented that he could not end his discourse at this point, but he explained that he had to speak to them of "grosser crimes," which meant adultery. (Jacob 2:23.) He referred to the lives of David and Solomon and their abominations in having "many wives and concubines," and he told those assembled that God had led them out of Jerusalem so that He might "raise up . . . a righteous branch from the fruit of the loins of Joseph." (Jacob 2:24-25.)[8] Jacob observed that the Lamanites were more righteous than the Nephites in that their husbands and fathers sought only to love their wives and children, and their children's hearts were not broken like those of the Nephite children, whose hearts were "grieved . . . because of the example" that they had set before them. (Jacob 3:7, 10.) The power of example cannot be overstated; as Jacob pointed out, because of the example of the Nephite fathers, their children had lost confidence in the fathers, and the "sobbings of their hearts ascend up to God." (Jacob 2:35.) Finally, he told them that "many hearts died, pierced with deep wounds" because of their actions. (Jacob 2:35.) These words summed up Jacob's teaching, illustrating that what we do affects others.

Jacob told his people that the "word of the Lord" to them was that a man should have one wife and no concubines. (Jacob 2:27.) Speaking in the name of the Lord, he taught that the Lord "delight[s] in the chastity of women. And whoredoms are an abomination before" him. (Jacob 2:27-28.)[9] While that was the law to the Nephites, the Lord also told them, "If I will, saith the Lord of Hosts, raise up seed unto me, I will command my people; otherwise they shall hearken unto these things." (Jacob 2:30.) The law to the Nephite people was the same as the law to the Latter-day Saints today. One man shall have one wife and one woman shall have one husband unless otherwise commanded.

Jacob encouraged his people to put aside their sins, to become "pure in heart" and to look to God "with firmness of mind, and pray unto him with exceeding faith." (Jacob 3:1.) He admonished those that were not pure in heart that if they did not change, the Lord would lead away the righteous from among them. (Jacob 3:4.) This proved to be a prophetic statement as King Mosiah I led his people, who kept the commandments and followed the prophets, from the land of Nephi to Zarahemla in approximately 280 B.C. (Omni 1:12-13.) Jacob ended his temple discourse encouraging his people to shake themselves loose from the power of sin, and he warned them against "fornication and lasciviousness," for he did not want them to suffer the second death. (Jacob 3:11-12.)[10]

The Antichrist[11]

Nephi had warned his people earlier to beware of priestcraft. He had given them several principles so they could recognize it. He had defined priestcraft as the practice of people who "preach and set themselves up for a light unto the world, that they may get gain and praise of the world; but they seek not the welfare of Zion." (2 Ne. 26:29.) Alma taught that if priestcraft were enforced among the Nephites, "it would prove their entire destruction." (Alma 1:12.)

Near the end of Jacob's life there came among the people a man by the name of Sherem. Sherem was "learned," and "he had a perfect knowledge of the language of the people" in that he had "much power of speech." (Jacob 7:4.) His articulate appeal to the people flattered them away from belief in Christ. (Jacob 7:2, 4.)

Sherem was so successful among the people that he boldly sought an opportunity to speak with Jacob to "shake" him "from the faith." (Jacob 7:5.) When he confronted Jacob, Sherem denounced the coming of Christ. He accused Jacob of perverting "the right way of God," and of not keeping the "law of Moses." (Jacob 7:7.) He argued that Jacob had converted the law of Moses "into the worship of a being which . . . shall come many hundred years hence." (Jacob 7:7.) And he reasoned with Jacob that "no man knoweth . . . of things to come." (Jacob 7:7.)[12]

Jacob noted, "The Lord God poured in his Spirit into my soul, insomuch that I did confound [Sherem] in all his words." (Jacob 7:8.) Jacob asked Sherem, "Deniest thou the Christ who shall come?" Sherem answered, "I know that there is no Christ." Jacob inquired,

"Believest thou the scriptures?" Sherem said, "Yea." Jacob answered, "Then ye do not understand them; for they truly testify of Christ." (Jacob 7:9-11.) Jacob told Sherem that the scriptures testified of Christ and that "none of the prophets have written nor prophesied, save they have spoken concerning this Christ." (Jacob 7:11.) Jacob ended the confrontation with his own special witness: "I have heard and seen; and it also has been made manifest unto me by the power of the Holy Ghost; wherefore, I know if there should be no atonement made all mankind must be lost." (Jacob 7:12.) Jacob had received many revelations of the things of God. As he said: "I truly had seen angels, and they had ministered unto me. And also, I had heard the voice of the Lord speaking unto me in very word, from time to time; wherefore, I could not be shaken." (Jacob 7:5.) Jacob had seen the Savior and beheld his mission in his youth. (2 Ne. 2:3-4.) His personal reply to Sherem reveals the inner strength that comes through belief and the reward of belief by God, who reveals himself to a person. Once that revelation is given, the person comes to *know*, and his "knowledge is perfect in that thing." (Alma 32:34.) Jacob had such revealed knowledge of God, and therefore he could not be shaken. (2 Ne. 2:3-4.)

Sherem's reply to Jacob's testimony is the classic argument used by antichrists to prove their point: "Show me a sign." (Jacob 7:13.) Jacob answered, "What am I that I should tempt God to show thee a sign in the thing which thou knowest to be true?" (Jacob 7:14.) The implication is that Sherem sought a sign for something that he already knew was true. Second, Jacob refused to fall into the trap of seeking for a sign, leaving the matter to the will of the Lord. (Jacob 7:14.)[13]

Following their encounter, Sherem became extremely ill for several days. Finally, he asked that the people be gathered together because he wanted to speak to them before he died. (Jacob 7:16.) After denying his previous teachings, he "confessed the Christ, and the power of the Holy Ghost, and the ministering of angels." (Jacob 7:17.) He explained that he had been deceived by the devil. Also, he said, "I fear lest I have committed the unpardonable sin, for I have lied unto God." He did this by denying the scriptures, which "testify of him." (Jacob 7:19.) Sherem ended his speech to the people with these words: "I greatly fear lest my case shall be awful; but I confess unto God." (Jacob 7:19.)

Sherem had had previous witnesses of the scriptures and of the Christ; therefore, he feared that his crime was greater than it could have been, because he had lied concerning his personal witness. Near the end however, he was forced to admit that he had no alternative than to place his trust in God. It would have been much better if Sherem had placed his trust in God voluntarily, rather than reluctantly when he realized he could do nothing else.

Contrast Sherem's experience with Nephi's, when Nephi was lamenting his personal weaknesses and the temptations he encountered. He said, "My heart groaneth because of my sins; nevertheless, I know in whom I have trusted. My God hath been my support." (2 Ne. 4:17-20.) Next he enumerated the blessings he had received from God and reaffirmed his trust in him. (2 Ne. 4:21-35.) A righteous man who struggled with weakness, Nephi did not fear God but looked to him for strength.

Following Sherem's confession and death, "peace and the love of God was restored again among the people; and they searched the scriptures, and hearkened no more to the words of this wicked man." (Jacob 7:23.)

Conclusion

Clearly Jacob's teachings in the temple serve to warn disciples of Christ in every age. Personal moral cleanliness is the same in all ages when the gospel has been taught on the earth. Seeking first the kingdom of God and then seeking the riches of the earth to contribute to the kingdom places men and women in harmony with God. Their motives remain pure and their concern is for the welfare of others; hence, their time and wealth is used wisely, and their lives are in accordance with the will of God. They walk peacefully through life, meeting trials and catastrophes head on, assured that they know in whom they trust. This harmony allows them to receive revelation from God, so that in spite of the antichrists they meet, they, like Jacob, cannot be shaken from their faith.

NOTES

1. Very early in Nephite history, the term *Nephite* came to refer to those who strove to keep the commandments and follow the Savior. (Alma 3:11.) But during some periods of history, the Lamanites were more righteous than the Nephites. (See, for example, Hel. 6:1.) The distinctions between the Nephites and the Lamanites became even more pronounced after the coming of Jesus to the Nephites. The term *Nephite* bore the connotation of one who was a disciple of Christ, or a follower of righteousness. The term *Lamanite* indicated a follower of unrighteousness. (4 Ne. 1:35-43.)

2. There were no Levites among Lehi's family when they came to the new world. They were descendants of Joseph, hence Jacob and Joseph officiated "by virtue of the Melchizedek priesthood." (Joseph Fielding Smith, *Answers to Gospel Questions,* 5 vols., compiled by Joseph Fielding Smith, Jr. [Salt Lake City: Deseret Book Company, 1957-66], 1:124.)

3. The prophets in our own dispensation have taught that God will hold us responsible for those we might have saved if we had done our duty. (John Taylor, *Journal of Discourses,* 26 vols. (London: Latter-day Saints' Book Depot, 1854-86), 20:23.)

4. Jacob and King Benjamin each taught their people in the temples in the lands of Nephi and Zarahemla. The resurrected Savior taught two discourses to the Nephites in the temple at Bountiful. The temple built by Nephi in the Land of Nephi was patterned after Solomon's temple. (2 Ne. 5:16.)

5. "There are times, when as a reproof, a truth is spoken in love and kindness. It is often more painful to him who imparts it than to those who should receive it." (George Reynolds and Janne M. Sjodahl, *Commentary on the Book of Mormon* (Salt Lake City: Deseret Book Company, 1955), p. 457.

6. David O. McKay, *Treasures of Life,* compiled by Clare Middlemiss (Salt Lake City: Deseret Book Company, 1962), pp. 174-75. See also Mosiah 4:16-26; James 5:1-6; D&C 56:16-20; 104:13-18; 1 Timothy 6:3-12, 17-19.

7. Ezra Taft Benson, Conference Report, April 5 and 6, 1986, p. 5.

8. The Doctrine and Covenants teaches us that David, Solomon, and Moses practiced plural marriage and that their wives were given to them by the Lord through his prophets. The Lord further noted that "in nothing did they sin save in those things which they received not of me." (D&C 132:38-39.) David (2 Sam. 12:7-9) and Solomon (1 Kgs. 11:1-4) took wives beyond those sanctioned by the Lord, and in doing so they were condemned.

9. In the Book of Mormon, whoredoms are synonymous with adultery and fornication.

10. "The only persons who will be completely overcome by [the second death] are the sons of perdition, who go with the devil and his angels into 'outer darkness.' All the rest of mankind, even the wicked, will receive some measure of salvation. . . . All those who are permanently subject to the second death are those who have had the testimony of the Holy Ghost and who have known the truth and then have rejected it and put Christ to open shame." (Joseph Fielding Smith, *Answers to Gospel Questions* 1:76, 78.)

11. For the treatment of Sherem as an antichrist, see Daniel H. Ludlow, *A Companion to Your Study of the Book of Mormon* (Salt Lake City: Deseret Book Company, 1976), p. 62, and the Book of Mormon Student Manual (Salt Lake City: Church Educational System, 1986), pp. 131-32.

12. Sherem's teachings were the same as those of two other antichrists that came later in the book of Mormon, Nehor and Korihor. (Alma 1; 30.) They also sought to overthrow the church during their time and denounced the Christ.

13. Bruce R. McConkie wrote: "Because signs — miracles, gifts of the Spirit — always follow belief in the true gospel, it is inevitable that nonbelievers who are in open rebellion against the truth should attempt to disprove the Lord's work by taunting his ministers with the challenge: Show us a sign. . . . Actually, sign-seeking . . . is an evidence of supreme and gross wickedness on their part." However, ". . . to seek the gifts of the Spirit through faith, humility, and devotion to righteousness is not to be confused with sign-seeking." (*Mormon Doctrine*, pp. 714-15.)

15

Nourished by the Good Word of God
(Jacob 4-6)

Kent P. Jackson

In the fourth chapter of his book, Jacob explained the sense of purpose that motivated him in his record-keeping. Consistent with the purpose of the Book of Mormon in general and the motives of each of its authors, Jacob wrote to bring men and women to the Father through Christ: "Wherefore, beloved brethren, be reconciled unto him through the atonement of Christ, his Only Begotten Son, and ye may obtain a resurrection, according to the power of the resurrection which is in Christ, and be presented as the first-fruits of Christ unto God, having faith, and obtained a good hope of glory in him before he manifesteth himself in the flesh." (Jacob 4:11.) In spite of the difficulty of writing on plates, Jacob knew that his words would endure to bless our lives only when engraved on metal. (Jacob 4:1-2.) And even though Christ's coming was yet hundreds of years in the future, Jacob wanted to ensure that we in later generations would know of his testimony concerning Him.

Jacob's land of nativity was in the wilderness — between his family's homeland, Palestine, and their promised inheritance, America. Thus, he bridged the gap between the old and new promised lands. Like his brother Nephi, his sensitivities were not only toward his own family and his future descendants, but also toward the Jews, the people

Kent P. Jackson is associate professor of ancient scripture and Old Testament area coordinator at Brigham Young University.

from whom they had come. (2 Ne. 33:8.) He lamented the blindness that had come upon the Jews because of their looking "beyond the mark." Because they had rejected the Lord's "plainness," he had cursed them with the confusion of their own choosing. (Jacob 4:14.)

It is within this context that Jacob quoted in his record a lengthy passage from the brass plates: an allegory concerning the house of Israel that was recorded by the prophet Zenos. That Jacob would include this long passage in his record attests to its value for us in the latter days, for whom the Book of Mormon was compiled. Since Jacob 5 — Zenos's allegory of the house of Israel — was prepared and preserved for us by the hand of God, we have both a need and a responsibility to understand it.

The Prophet Zenos

Zenos was an ancient Israelite prophet whose writings were on the brass plates but are not preserved in the biblical texts that have come down to us. Our only knowledge of him comes from the Book of Mormon. Since Nephi and Jacob quoted often from Zenos' writings, we know they viewed his words as extremely important for their people — and also for us today, the readers of their record in modern times. Elder Bruce R. McConkie called Zenos "one of the greatest prophets in Israel."[1]

We have no way of knowing anything about Zenos's life, where he came from, or when he wrote, outside of the fact that he wrote his record before 600 B.C. (See Hel. 8:19.) His allegory of the olive tree in Jacob 5 is the longest chapter in the Book of Mormon. Nephi also paraphrased some of Zenos' writings extensively in 1 Nephi 19, and from those writings he learned much concerning the mission of Christ.[2]

Allegory in the Scriptures

Jacob 5 demonstrates the literary skill that was possessed by many of the prophets in ancient Israel. In the Old Testament they almost always used poetic literary forms to convey their messages with dignity and beauty. Most common among the literary forms used was *metaphor*. Metaphor is a literary device in which a word or set of

words is used in place of another, to suggest a likeness or correspondence between them. The following example illustrates this:
"Jesus is the Good Shepherd," and "Jesus said to Peter, 'Feed my
sheep.' " While Jesus may never have been a shepherd in the literal
sense, through the use of the shepherd/sheep metaphor we can envision him as our leader and the source of our well-being, just as we
know that a shepherd leads his sheep and provides for their needs.
Another literary device, the *allegory*, is an extended metaphor in the
form of a story. The stories told by Jesus, called "parables" in the
King James translation, are allegories.

Metaphorical images in the scriptures generally are not intended
to be mysterious or to confuse or conceal. (See JST, Matt. 13:10-11.)
They are artistic forms that most often are intended to be understood.
Most metaphorical imagery can be interpreted without much difficulty from the information provided in the metaphor itself, or from
the context of the scriptural setting. Usually the images have a logical
and readily apparent meaning. Some others require more study and
prayerful thought.

In addition to the many allegories in the Gospels, others are found
elsewhere in the scriptures. Both in the teachings of Jesus and the
writings of his prophets, metaphorical images and allegories concerning vines, vineyards, and trees are common. (See, for example, Isa.
5:1-7; Jer. 2:21; 24:1-10; Hosea 10:1; John 15:1-5; Rom. 11:16-23; 1
Ne. 10:12; 15:15.) Thus the allegory of Zenos in Jacob 5 fits well
within the context of other scriptural images used to describe the
house of Israel.[3]

Scattering and Gathering

Zenos's allegory of the olive tree concerns the scattering and
gathering of the house of Israel. (Jacob 5:3.) It summarizes Israel's
history and foretells its destiny. Before examining the allegory, it is
important to understand the divinely ordained principles that govern
the history of the Lord's covenant people. Perhaps the most important
point with respect to the scattering and gathering is this: An inheritance of well-being in a promised land is a blessing based on righteous
living. Those who are unrighteous lose their inheritance or live under

a curse rather than a blessing. Moses taught this principle to the Israelites prior to their entrance into the promised land. If you fail to keep the commandments, he taught, "ye shall soon utterly perish from off the land whereunto ye go over Jordan to possess it; ye shall not prolong your days upon it, but shall utterly be destroyed. And the Lord shall scatter you among the nations, and ye shall be left few in number among the heathen, whither the Lord shall lead you." (Deut. 4:26-27.) Similarly, Lehi taught his people soon after they entered their promised land:

> Inasmuch as those whom the Lord God shall bring out of the land of Jerusalem shall keep his commandments, they shall prosper upon the face of this land. . . . But behold, when the time cometh that they shall dwindle in unbelief, after they have received so great blessings from the hand of the Lord, . . . behold, I say, if the day shall come that they will reject the Holy One of Israel, the true Messiah, their Redeemer and their God, behold, the judgments of him that is just shall rest upon them. Yea, he will bring other nations unto them, and he will give unto them power, and he will take away from them the lands of their possessions, and he will cause them to be scattered and smitten. (2 Ne. 1:9-11.)

There should be no mistake about this point. No one has a right to a promised land or any other blessing of the Lord's covenants simply on the basis of lineage. (2 Ne. 30:1-2.) Those who fail to live worthily have no promise from the Lord. (1 Ne. 17:35; D&C 82:10.)

Scriptural history gives several examples of groups of Israelites that forfeited their inheritance in promised lands. As a result of apostasy, the northern ten tribes were deported from Palestine from 735 to 721 B.C. (2 Kgs. 15, 17.) The kingdom of Judah was destroyed, and the Jews were deported from Palestine, in 587 B.C. (2 Kgs. 24-25.) The Jaredites and the Nephites were destroyed from their promised lands. (Ether 15; Morm. 6.)

There is also another reason for the scattering of Israel. In addition to groups such as those which the Lord scattered because of their unrighteousness, he has led others away so he could raise up a righteous people and preserve them from the sins of the world and their consequences. Such a group was that of Lehi. Through these methods of scattering, the Lord spread the blood of Abraham throughout the world.

Just as the scriptures teach of the scattering of Israel, they also teach of the subsequent gathering. As the following passages teach, repentance must take place *before* the Lord will gather and restore his once-chosen people. Jacob wrote concerning the gathering of the Jews: "But behold, thus saith the Lord God: *When the day cometh that they shall believe in me, that I am Christ, then have I covenanted with their fathers that they shall be restored in the flesh, upon the earth, unto the lands of their inheritance.* And it shall come to pass that they shall be gathered in from their long dispersion, from the isles of the sea, and from the four parts of the earth." (2 Ne. 10:7-8; emphasis added.) The resurrected Savior taught his people: "It shall come to pass that the time cometh, *when the fulness of my gospel shall be preached unto them; and they shall believe in me*, that I am Jesus Christ, the Son of God, and shall pray unto the Father in my name.... *Then will the Father gather them together again, and give unto them Jerusalem for the land of their inheritance.*" (3 Ne. 20:30-33; emphasis added.)

These passages demonstrate that the house of Israel must first accept the gospel of Jesus Christ before the gathering taught in the scriptures can take place.

In the early days of the Church, the Saints were instructed to gather together in one place. The Lord's desire for the gathering of his Saints today is different. As he revealed to Joseph Smith, "I have other places which I will appoint unto them, and they shall be called stakes, for the curtains or the strength of Zion." (D&C 101:21.) We are instructed to gather Israel and build Zion wherever we are. President Spencer W. Kimball taught: "*The gathering of Israel consists of joining the true Church and coming to a knowledge of the true God....* Any person, therefore, who has accepted the restored gospel, and who now seeks to worship the Lord in his own tongue and with the Saints in the nations where he lives, has complied with the law of the gathering of Israel and is heir to all of the blessings promised the Saints in these last days." President Kimball taught further: "And so the gathering is taking place. Korea is the gathering place for Koreans, Australia for Australians, Brazil for Brazilians, England for the English."[4]

The Allegory of the Olive Tree

Zenos's allegory of the olive tree is the story of the house of Israel. It is important that we understand it, since we of the house of Israel in modern times play an important role in the fulfillment of the Lord's promises concerning his people. I believe that the Lord wants us to know what this chapter means. The text itself gives us some important keys for understanding: "Behold, thus saith the Lord, I will liken thee, O house of Israel, like unto a tame olive-tree." (Jacob 5:3.) This is the most significant element for interpreting the allegory: *the tame olive tree is the house of Israel.* With this knowledge, other major metaphors in the story can be interpreted easily:

Wild Olive Tree: The Gentiles

The Master: The Lord

The Servant: A prophet, or prophets

Grafting natural branches into the wild trees: Branches of Israel dispersed among Gentiles

Grafting wild branches into the natural tree: Adoption of Gentiles into Israel

Nephi defined grafting as coming "to the knowledge of the true Messiah." (1 Ne. 10:14.) Only in doing so are Gentiles adopted into the house of Israel to receive an inheritance as the children of Abraham. (Gal. 3:27-29.)

Pruning, nourishing, and cultivating: The work of the Lord and his servants to save their people

Natural fruit: Faithful Saints and their righteous works, worthy of eternal life (Jacob 5:61)

Wild fruit: Unfaithful individuals and their unrighteous works

With the meanings of these key images in mind, we can interpret much of the allegory and learn from Zenos's message.[5]

Verses 3-4. The natural tree grew old and began to decay: After receiving their promised land of Palestine, many Israelites fell into apostasy (ca. 1200-1000 B.C.).

Verses 5-6. After pruning and cultivating, there was new natural growth, but the top died: The Lord sent prophets to Israel. Some people responded to their message and were righteous; others were not and fell away. Even the priests and rulers most often were counted among those who rejected the Lord's message (ca. 1000 B.C.–A.D. 30).

Verses 7 and 9. The dead natural branches were burned: The destruction of Israel and Judah, with the death of thousands (ca. 735-587 B.C.).

Verses 8, 13-14. Natural branches were grafted and planted throughout the vineyard: Israelites were taken away from Palestine by the Lord (735-587 B.C.). Verse 8 mentions a branch that was *grafted* elsewhere in the orchard, whereas the branches mentioned in verses 13-14 were *planted* in other areas. (See verses 21, 23, 24, 25.) Perhaps grafting here refers to Israelites joining other nations, while planting may refer to groups such as Lehi's that were led off and relocated. (See 2 Ne. 10:22.)

Verses 7, 9-12. Wild branches were grafted into the natural tree: Gentiles joined remnants of Israel to form the Early Christian Church (ca. A.D. 30-100).[6]

Verse 15. A long time passed. The Lord waited to see the results of his actions described in the previous verses.

Verses 16-18. The wild branches on the natural tree bore good fruit on the strength of the natural roots. This grafting saved the tree. Much good fruit was laid up: The Early Christian Church flourished in righteousness because of the adoption of Gentiles into Israel through baptism and membership in the Church. (See Gal. 3:27-29.) Many faithful saints brought forth righteous works (ca. A.D. 30-100).

Verses 19-22. A natural branch, planted in "a poor spot" of the vineyard and long nourished, brought forth much good fruit: A group of scattered Israelites (see verses 13-14) produced faithful saints with righteous works.

Verse 23. A second natural branch, planted in a spot "poorer than the first" and long nourished, brought forth much good fruit: A second group of scattered Israelites (see verses 13-14) produced faithful saints with righteous works.

Verses 24-25. A third natural branch, planted in the choicest spot of ground (verse 43) and long nourished, brought forth both good and wild fruit: These undoubtedly are Lehi's children in their promised land, among whom were both faithful and unfaithful individuals. The "good fruit" and "wild fruit" may not necessarily refer to Lamanites and Nephites, respectively, nor vice versa. Both righteousness and unrighteousness were found among both groups.

Verses 26-28. The Master pruned and cultivated the branch planted in the choicest spot of ground: Prophets were sent to Lehi's descendants to persuade them to repent.

Verse 29. A long time passed. The passage of time indicates the continued development of the activities described in the previous verses.

Verses 30-32. The natural tree with wild branches (see verses 16-18) now brought forth much fruit of "all sorts." But none of it was good: Apostasy had overcome the Christian Church, leaving errant Christianity in all its varieties (ca. A.D. 100-1820).

Verses 33-37. The wild branches on the natural tree had overpowered the roots, yielding bad fruit: False influences had gained control of Christianity, yielding distorted doctrine and incorrect works (ca. A.D. 100-1820).

Verses 38-39. All three natural branches planted elsewhere in the orchard became corrupt: The Israelites who were led out of Palestine and placed elsewhere became unfaithful.

Verse 40. The third natural branch died when the wild fruit overcame the good fruit: The wicked among Lehi's descendants overpowered the righteous (ca. A.D. 200-421).

Verses 41-42. All of the trees brought forth only corrupt fruit: From the time unrighteousness prevailed among Lehi's descendants, there was a universal, worldwide apostasy (ca. A.D. 421-1820).

Verses 43-45. The Master had cleared the ground and planted the third natural branch in the choicest spot of ground. Because the bad fruit was not removed, it was able to overpower the good fruit: Lehi's people, separated from the rest of the world in a chosen land, brought forth both righteous and unrighteous works. Finally, evil was able to prevail over righteousness, until the entire nation was overcome by sin (ca. A.D. 200-421).

Verses 46-48. Despite the care taken by the Master, the branches had overpowered the roots, and the entire orchard had become corrupt: False influences overcame the pure doctrines and practices of the gospel, and a universal apostasy prevailed (ca. A.D. 421-1820).

Verses 49-51. The Master decided not to destroy the corrupted orchard yet: The time for the destruction of the wicked was not yet. As in the parable of the wheat and the tares, the Lord determined not to destroy the world yet, lest chances for future righteousness be destroyed also. (See D&C 86:4-7.)

Verses 52-56. The natural branches that had been planted elsewhere in the orchard were grafted back into the original natural tree, whose branches in turn were grafted onto the roots of those natural branches that had been placed in other parts of the orchard: Formerly isolated groups of scattered Israel became one with the main body of Saints in a worldwide Church. This includes such groups as Lehi's posterity and the descendants of the scattered tribes of Israel. There is a union of Israel and Gentiles in the Lord's church (ca. A.D. 1820 to the Millennium).

Verses 57-72. The Master and his servants, knowing that the end was drawing near and that it would be their last effort in the orchard, worked vigorously to prune and cultivate the trees: The Lord has sent prophets in the last days, through whom he has worked with his convenant people to help them bring forth works of faith and righteousness. (D&C 24:19; 33:3; 39:17; 43:28.) The covenant people of the house of Israel are The Church of Jesus Christ of Latter-day Saints. Only the "most bitter" are expelled from it (verse 57), while the Lord and his servants patiently work with the rest (ca. A.D. 1820 to the Millennium).

Verses 73-76. Natural fruit began to grow throughout the orchard. Over the course of time the bad branches were removed, and all of the trees brought forth good fruit: The Church will become purified through the work of the Lord and his servants. Consistent acts of faith and righteousness will be performed by the Lord's Saints, who will establish Zion in the world and will be found worthy to stand in the Lord's presence when he comes again (the Millennium).

Verse 77. When bad fruit appears again, good and bad will be

gathered to their appropriate places, and the orchard will be burned:
At the end of the Millennium, when Satan will again obtain power
in men's hearts, the Lord will gather the good to himself, and Satan
and his followers will be banished to their "own place," to suffer
eternal condemnation.[7] Then the earth will be burned to prepare the
celestial glory.

God's Arm of Mercy

Jacob provided only a brief footnote to the magnificent words of
his fellow prophet Zenos. He bore testimony that Zenos's words are
true; they will "surely come to pass." (Jacob 6:1.) How blessed are
they who are found in the Lord's service, he wrote; how cursed are
they who will be "cast out into their own place"; how merciful is
God that he remembers his people — "both roots and branches"; how
patient and long-suffering he is to labor in their behalf "all the day
long," though they are "a stiffnecked and gainsaying people." (Jacob
6:3-4.) His final words on this subject, a plea to those who would
someday read his message, show the depth of his feelings for us:

> I beseech of you in words of soberness that ye would
> repent, and come with full purpose of heart, and cleave unto
> God as he cleaveth unto you. And while his arm of mercy is
> extended towards you in the light of the day, harden not your
> hearts. Yea, today, if ye will hear his voice, harden not your
> hearts; for why will ye die? For behold, after ye have been
> nourished by the good word of God all the day long, will ye
> bring forth evil fruit, that ye must be hewn down and cast
> into the fire? . . . O then, my beloved brethren, repent ye, and
> enter in at the strait gate, and continue in the way which is
> narrow, until ye shall obtain eternal life. (Jacob 6:5-7, 11.)

Notes

1. Bruce R. McConkie, *A New Witness for the Articles of Faith* (Salt
Lake City: Deseret Book Company, 1986), p. 558.

2. See Robert E. Parsons, "The Prophecies of the Prophets," in *Second Annual Book of Mormon Symposium: First Nephi*, ed. Monte S. Nyman (Provo, Ut.: Brigham Young University, Religious Studies Center); and Robert L. Millet, "Nephi on the Destiny of Israel," chapter 7 in this volume.

3. For a discussion of another common metaphor used in scripture to represent the house of Israel, see Kent P. Jackson, "The Marriage of Hosea and Jehovah's Covenant with Israel," in *Isaiah and the Prophets*, ed. Monte S. Nyman (Provo, Ut.: Religious Studies Center, Brigham Young University, 1984), pp. 57-73.

4. Spencer W. Kimball, *The Teachings of Spencer W. Kimball*, edited by Edward L. Kimball (Salt Lake City: Bookcraft, 1984), pp. 439-40; emphasis added.

5. An interesting interpretation of the allegory is provided by Monte S. Nyman, *An Ensign to All People* (Salt Lake City: Deseret Book Company, 1987), pp. 21-36. My interpretation differs from his in some key places, particularly with respect to the point in history with which the allegory begins. In general, however, our interpretations have much in common.

6. Monte Nyman has suggested that this grafting includes the joining of Gentiles into Israel from as early as the eighth century B.C.; *An Ensign to All People*, pp. 26-27.

7. To receive one's "own place" is for the wicked to receive their eternal station. (D&C 88:32.) Note how the wording in D&C 88:114, which describes the banishment of Satan and his followers after the Millennium, parallels that of Jacob 5:77.

16

Scribes and Scriptures
(Enos, Jarom, Omni, and the Words of Mormon)

Victor L. Ludlow

This selection of four small books, each only one chapter long, contains valuable lessons on record-keeping and the role of various Book of Mormon scribes. It also covers three hundred fifty years of history and provides one of scripture's clearest examples of how and why a prophet's prayers are answered.

With these books we come to the end of the small plates of Nephi, and through the Words of Mormon we bridge over to Mormon's abridgment of the large plates of Nephi. The Book of Mormon identifies approximately two dozen individuals whose writings are found in this work of scripture, and one third of them are in these four books.[1] From their brief writings we learn some insights about what they recorded, when some of them wrote their records, and why they sometimes did not write more.

Eight individuals served as scribes in these books, and yet their total writing comprises only seven pages of printed text as now organized into three books. The books of Enos, Jarom, and Omni bridge over three hundred fifty years of Nephite history. In other words, if all the thousand-year history of Lehi's posterity were written so succinctly, the Book of Mormon would be a 20-page pamphlet instead of a 531-page book. The records of Enos begin with the death

---

Victor L. Ludlow is associate professor of ancient scripture and director of Bible research at Brigham Young University.

of his father, Jacob, about 500 B.C. The last scribe, Amaleki, turned the small plates of Nephi over to King Benjamin around 145 B.C. These records remained with the large plates of Nephi and were found centuries later by Mormon, who added a few last comments. These three small books, along with the Words of Mormon, barely highlight the Nephite and Lamanite history for this long period. But some developments are mentioned.

Finally, some fine examples of prayer, divine promises, and the validity of spiritual promptings are found in the ninety verses of these books. Enos demonstrated some positive motivations for prolonged, intensive prayers. His story also illustrates why and how the Lord sometimes answers our prayers. Additional teachings on the faith and role of ancient prophets along with ideas on humility and communication through the Spirit are found in these books.

Enos

Enos was the son of Jacob, who was Nephi's younger brother. The posterity of Jacob maintained these records for over four centuries, from 544 B.C. to almost 130 B.C. It is noteworthy that the important small plates of Nephi were not passed on through Nephi's own descendants but were kept by the posterity of his younger brother.

Enos provides a positive model on how and why one receives answers to prayers. As noted in verse 3, Enos had heard the words of his father, Jacob, about eternal life and joy. Enos now hungered for such joy; he prayed all day and into the night. His petition was not because of any serious sins or for selfish motives, but simply because he hungered after the blessings of the Spirit. His request was not granted after a brief prayer, but only after his soul supplicated the Almighty for many hours. As noted in verses 5 and 10, the voice of the Lord came to him and revealed some marvelous truths.

Enos was among those mortals who have received special divine communication through the Holy Spirit. The Holy Ghost serves the Godhead as a revelator, revealing great, new, and important truths. God, with his infinite knowledge and power, has developed a system of communication far superior to anything mortals have yet developed or even conceived. Through the Holy Spirit, he is able to communicate with his children instantly, individually, and personally. However, his spiritual communication is perceived only by certain sensitive individuals. His voice is neither loud nor disturbing, and one might not hear or sense it unless one were in tune with God's soft, still, small voice. (See 1 Kgs. 19:12-13; 3 Ne. 11:3-5; Hel. 5:29-33.)

God can communicate with many people simultaneously yet individually. He provides a simultaneous, instant, individual communication. Even more impressive is the fact that he communicates not only messages but a verification of the truthfulness of those messages. Enos recognized this, as noted in verse 6, as he said that God could not lie.

The Holy Ghost is unique. Through the Holy Ghost, we receive a message, a validation of that message, and then comfort, direction, and peace. Enos expressed this peace and joy in verses 6, 17, and 27.

Perhaps other lessons can be learned from the example of Enos's prayers. Note that he was alone and away from others and the normal pressures of day-to-day living as he meditated and prayed. Verse 3 notes that he took advantage of his situation while hunting to contemplate deeply on the messages of his father, Jacob. A certain amount of privacy and some undisturbed time for meditation is very valuable as we seek for deep personal communion with our Heavenly Father.

Also, seeds of gospel truth had been planted earlier in Enos' soul, and these were now ready to bear new, fresh fruit. Alma later wrote about this process in chapter 32 of his book, and Moroni included the reading and pondering about the works of God as important preparation for prayer, as one seeks to receive the truthfulness and verification of God's word. (Moro. 10:3-5.)

In summary, the account of Enos and his mighty prayer demonstrates the importance of being taught gospel truths, the value of being alone as one meditates and prays, the necessity of prolonged and intense prayer, and, most important, the clear answers and profound peace that prayer can bring as God communicates with us through the Holy Ghost. Enos gives us a short but important lesson in some valuable characteristics of true, powerful prayer.

Scriptures and Prophets

Some other valuable lessons can be learned from the brief writings of Enos. First he wrote about the power of scriptural records as they preserve God's dealings with his children on earth. Then he stressed some rewards of unifying our faith with that of earlier prophets as we respond to their words.

In verses 13-17, Enos prayed about the Nephites and the Lamanites. He mentioned the desire of the Lamanites to destroy the Nephite holy records and asked God to preserve the records and their truths. Enos knew that God could save the records, and in his faith he asked God to do so. God's response was in the form of a covenant, which promised not only that the records would be protected but that they would also come forth to the Lamanites.

God kept this covenant. Thus the Book of Mormon shares an important characteristic with the Bible in that both have been preserved by God from the distant past to be a blessing to his children in the last days. The ancient civilizations of both the Americas and the Middle East surely had many records, manuscripts, and documents that told of their culture, history, and religion. However, these civilizations were often full of selfishness and wickedness, and they would provide role models only of eternally destructive behavior. Their pagan records have largely been destroyed, along with the negative societies that developed them. On the other hand, many scriptures and positive spiritual records from the prophets have been preserved, providing valuable reminders of God's dealings and covenants with his children.

After Enos was promised that his sacred records would be preserved, God told him that earlier prophets had requested the same thing and that they had also received the same promise. Thus the faith of Enos matched the faith of his noble father, uncle, and grandfather. Likewise, we can seek to have not only the same faith as our righteous progenitors and earlier prophets, but we can also develop the same desires in our hearts so that our requests to God can be unified with theirs.[2]

Unfortunately, Enos also provides some examples of what happens to people who do not respond to the messages of the prophets. Verses

22 and 23 indicate the difficult challenge the prophets faced as they tried to bring people's lives into harmony with the truths of the gospel. Prophets face similar obstacles today; often their greatest opposition comes from the Latter-day Saints who should be the first to respond with simple, devout faith to the the prophetic word. However, repeated words of plainness, harshness, and sharpness are often needed to keep God's children from bringing divine destruction upon themselves. (See Enos 1:23.)

Jarom

Jarom, the son of Enos, wrote about half as much as his father. In verse 2 he justified his limited record by stating that the plates on which he was writing, the small plates of Nephi, were small and that he did not feel that he needed to add to the prophecies and revelations that had been written earlier. Apparently the small plates, which Nephi had prepared about one hundred fifty years earlier, were almost filled, and Jarom felt that enough basic teachings of the gospel and the plan of salvation were already on them. He did recognize, however, a need to continue the family genealogy (verse 1) and to write a few things that might benefit the Lamanites (verse 2).

In verses 3 and 4, Jarom contrasted the hardness of the Lamanites with the attitude of some Nephites who had received communion with the Holy Spirit. He stressed two key qualities that spiritual individuals possessed: they were not proud, and they had faith. Humility and faith remain as necessary attributes today for anyone desiring divine communication.

In addition to giving a brief review of Nephite and Lamanite history, Jarom also mentioned that the Lamanites were much more numerous than the Nephites, but that the Nephites prospered more. The Nephites were settled in fine buildings with good agricultural tools and varied weapons of defense. (Verse 8.) The riches and developed society of Jarom's time seem to contrast with the picture portrayed a generation earlier as Enos described a rural, pastoral way of life among the Nephites.[3]

Jarom also recorded an interesting teaching technique of the prophets in verse 11. He said that the prophets and other spiritual teachers of the people taught them to believe in the coming Messiah "as though he already was." This mental association of anticipating something in the future as though it were already present helped the people remember their weaknesses and repent of their sins at that time. Thus further punishments from God were avoided. (Verse 12.) If society today could anticipate Christ's second coming and the reality of the judgment day and resurrection as though they were all happening now, perhaps more people would return to the gospel paths and avoid further divine punishments.

Omni

The small book of Omni contains the record of five scribes; perhaps it could be called more appropriately the book of Amaleki, since he wrote almost two-thirds of the thirty verses. Omni hesitated to write more because of his unworthiness. Amaron wrote only a few verses at the very end of his life. His brother Chemish seemed to follow the same pattern, but he wrote even less. In fact, his single verse distinguishes him as the Book of Mormon writer with the smallest amount of writing. His son, Abinadom, doubled his father's output to a total of two verses. However, he did provide justification for the limited writing by stating that a record of his time was available on the plates kept by their kings. (This would be the large plates of Nephi.) Also, he knew of no new revelations or prophecies to add to the record.

Amaleki wrote most of the material in the book of Omni. His record provides some valuable historical facts that help link the three major colonies of the Book of Mormon together. In verses 20 through 22 he mentioned some records of the ancient Jaredite civilization and that the lone survivor of that colony, Coriantumr, lived for a time among the people of Zarahemla. In verses 12 through 19, Amaleki briefly summarized how Mosiah and a group of righteous Nephites, including Amaleki himself, left the land of Nephi, wandered through the wilderness, and then discovered the people of Zarahemla.

Although the writings of Amaleki are limited, they do point out some values of written records. He mentioned the engravings on a stone that Mosiah translated, providing an account of Coriantumr and his ancient people, whom the Nephites never got to meet. The danger of not having written records is also stressed in this account, because the people of Zarahemla had corrupted their language and religion mainly because of their lack of written records and scriptures. This episode also verifies the words of Nephi given to his brothers as they sought the brass plates of Laban. He told them that the records were important to preserve both their language and the words of the prophets among their people. (1 Ne. 3:19-20.) So although the writings of the Book of Mormon scribes may have been limited at times, their various records provided a continuous linguistic and spiritual foundation for Nephite society.

The Words of Mormon

The Words of Mormon, which he inscribed at the end of the small plates of Nephi, provide further insights into the various records maintained by the Nephites. Mormon lived five centuries after Amaleki, and he received a vast library of various plates from the earlier generations of Nephites. He sought to abridge these records into one set of plates, the plates of Mormon. He started with the time of Lehi and had completed his abridgment down to the time of King Benjamin, the son of King Mosiah who had discovered the people of Zarahemla. In searching for further records of this period, he discovered the small plates of Nephi, which basically overlapped the whole period of his abridgment to that point. However, the small plates of Nephi contained a more spiritual account of these earlier generations, along with a more complete record of key prophecies, revelations, and teachings. Mormon decided to insert this whole record into his own set of plates, and he wrote a few words at the end of the small plates to bridge the last years of the reign of King Benjamin. (Amaleki had given the small plates to King Benjamin in the middle of King Benjamin's reign. Amaleki sensed that he was about to die and had no one else to whom he could entrust these sacred records.)

Mormon not only provided information about how the small plates of Nephi became a part of his abridgment, but more importantly he gave us valuable insights into why God could use one particular, peculiar commandment to test the faith and obedience of three key prophets.

At the beginning of the Book of Mormon history, Nephi had been commanded to make two separate sets of plates. After starting what would be known as the large plates of Nephi, he was later commanded to make a set of more religious records, known as the small plates of Nephi. (1 Ne. 9:2, 4 and 1:17.) After Nephi's death, the large plates remained with the kings down to the time of Mormon, while the small plates went to Jacob and his posterity until the time of Amaleki, who gave them to King Benjamin. Thus the two sets of plates were back into the possession of one person.

After Mormon had completed his abridgment of five hundred years of Nephite history, he may have been somewhat surprised to find the small plates of Nephi, which largely duplicated his efforts. Instead of keeping only one of the sets of records, Mormon was prompted to include the small plates with his abridgment, without really knowing why. (See verse 7.) He apparently did not know what would happen to his records after they would come into the hands of Joseph Smith.

After Joseph Smith received the plates of Mormon, he had completed the translation of 116 pages of manuscript, which comprised Mormon's abridgment from the time of Lehi down to King Benjamin. After the loss of these pages by Martin Harris, the Lord commanded the Prophet to translate further in the plates of Mormon without retranslating the first portion. However, since the small plates contained a more spiritual account of the same time period, the teachings of greatest value were not lost for the readers of the Book of Mormon.

In order for this more spiritual record to be available, Nephi first had to start the small plates, and Mormon had to include them with his abridgment. We can be thankful today that Mormon had the courage to follow his spiritual promptings so that these valuable teachings are now part of our contemporary scripture.

These scriptures, as stated by Mormon in verse 11, have another important function for us today and in the future. At the great and last day when we each stand before the Lord to be judged, these scriptures of the Book of Mormon, along with the testimony of all the scriptures, will provide the "canon" or measuring rod by which we all will be judged. Thus, although the writers from Enos to Amaleki and Mormon did not provide us with intensive, detailed records of their time, their teachings and witnesses do help us understand how God has worked through his scribes and scriptures.

Notes

1. The chronological order of the scribes of the Book of Mormon records that Joseph Smith translated from the small plates of Nephi is: Nephi, Jacob, Enos, Jarom, Omni, Amaron, Chemish, Abinadom, Amaleki, and Mormon. Mormon's abridgment from the large plates of Nephi includes the records of Benjamin, Mosiah, Alma, Helaman, Shiblon (Alma 63:1, 11, 17), Helaman, Helaman, Nephi, Nephi, Amos, Amos (4 Ne. 1:21), Ammaron, and Mormon. Moroni was the last scribe of the major plates given to Joseph Smith. His abridgment of the Jaredite records included material from numerous earlier recorders and writers. Thus one-third of the known two dozen scribes of the Book of Mormon records are found in these four short books.

2. Compare Enos, verse 18, with the Lord's great intercessory prayer as recorded in John 17.

3. Compare Jarom, verse 8, with Enos, verse 21.

17

THE GREAT CONVERSION
(Mosiah 1-6)

RODNEY TURNER

Nowhere in all scripture are the absolutely indispensible minis-trations of the Holy Spirit so clearly dramatized as in the Book of Mormon. The mission of the Holy Spirit in achieving salvation is second only to that of Jesus Christ. Indeed, their labors are so inter-twined that the one cannot be separated from the other. The first of the four most impressive examples of this fact occurred at the close of King Benjamin's reign.[1] His farewell address concerning the "Lord God Omnipotent" was accompanied by an outpouring of the Holy Spirit that produced the spiritual conversion of virtually his entire people. In order to put this remarkable incident in historical per-spective, it will be necessary to briefly review the major events leading up to it.

The Book of Mormon does not give the details of Nephi's church organization, but we know that he established a "holy order" (2 Ne. 6:2) and consecrated his younger brothers, Jacob and Joseph, "priests and teachers over the land" (2 Ne. 5:26).[2] This order was continued by his successors. (Jarom 1:7.) One of king Benjamin's last official acts was to appoint priests to teach those who, following his address, "had taken upon them the name of Christ." (Mosiah 6:1-3.)

In addition to the law of the gospel, the Nephites observed the

---

Rodney Turner is professor of ancient scripture at Brigham Young University.

moral injunctions and ritual aspects of the law of Moses.[3] (1 Ne. 4:15-16; 2 Ne. 5:10; 25:23-30; Jarom 1:5.) They also built a temple patterned after that of Solomon. (2 Ne. 5:16.) Although the Book of Mormon is not explicit on this point, the Melchizedek Priesthood— together with its most sacred ordinances—was undoubtedly received by worthy people beginning with Lehi and Nephi. (See Alma 13:7-12.)

The generations came and went as unnamed prophets and priests labored to persuade the vacillating populace to honor their covenants with God. This early period presents a mixed picture of material prosperity, faithfulness, apathy, and zealous but fruitless missionary work among the Lamanites. Armed conflict between the Nephites and Lamanites began in the reign of Nephi (Jacob 1:10) and continued in a sporadic but increasingly intense fashion throughout the following centuries. Writing of his people, Jarom ruefully observed that God had "not *as yet* swept them off from the face of the land." (Jarom 1:3; italics added.) According to Amaron, by 280 B.C., "the more wicked part of the Nephites were destroyed." (Omni 1:5.) Warned by the Lord, Mosiah I led an exodus of the righteous—those who "would hearken unto the voice of the Lord"—from the land of Nephi northward to the city of Zarahemla, where they joined the numerically superior "Mulekites." (Omni 1:12; see also 1:19 and Mosiah 1:10; 25:2; Hel. 6:10.)[4]

Mosiah's Nephite remnant had been "led by many preachings and prophesyings." (Omni 1:13.) They were spiritually literate, possessing a knowledge of the teachings of Nephi concerning Christ and the law of the gospel. Such was not the case with the people of Zarahemla. Their original Hebrew language had become so badly corrupted that the Nephites could not understand them. Having neither scriptures nor prophets to guide them, they even denied the existence of God. (Omni 1:17.) Consequently, they had to be taught the Nephite tongue before they could be instructed in even basic religious matters. However, in time, the spiritual disparity between the two groups was resolved.[5]

Mosiah's son Benjamin became king sometime in the early or mid–second century. The early years of his reign were marked by war with invading Lamanites, numerous defections to the enemy, and internal religious dissension arising from false Christs, prophets, preachers, and teachers. (Omni 1:24; W of M 1:12-16.) In combating the latter, Benjamin was assisted by many holy prophets who, speaking with power and authority, sharply rebuked the "stiffneckedness" of the people: "Wherefore, with the help of these, king Benjamin, by laboring with all the might of his body and the faculty of his whole soul . . . did once more establish peace in the land." (W of M 1:18.) This peace, born of spiritual unity, doubtless prepared the way for the great conversion of 124 B.C.

Nephite Scripture

The large plates of Nephi (historical chronicles) were the stewardship of all Nephite kings beginning with Nephi himself. These were automatically passed on by Mosiah I to his son Benjamin. However, the small plates of Nephi (containing the spiritual writings of Nephi and his prophet-successors) were handed down through the family of Nephi's brother Jacob. Amaleki completed these plates and, having no son, gave them to King Benjamin. (Omni 1:25.) For the first time in more than three hundred years, all of the Nephite records were combined. Nephi's two sets of plates and the Lord's two laws— the law of Moses and the law of Christ—both converged in one and the same man.

Upon receiving the small plates of Nephi from Amaleki, Benjamin must have eagerly read them and, in doing so, obtained a greater understanding of the teachings of Nephi and Jacob concerning Christ, the gospel, and the future redemption of Israel. Benjamin's reaction was probably similar to that of Mormon, who found their contents "pleasing . . . because of the prophecies of the coming of Christ." (W of M 1:4.) The small plates also contained Nephi's priceless teachings on the baptism of fire and of the Holy Ghost. (See 2 Ne. 31 and 32.) These teachings may well have prepared Benjamin for the angelic revelation he later recounted to his people.

Like Nephi, Benjamin's three sons, Mosiah, Helorum, and Helaman, were taught to read the modified Egyptian script in which Laban's plates of brass and Nephi's plates of gold were written. (1 Ne. 1:2; Mosiah 1:4.) These records constituted the "standard works" of the church of God among the Nephites. The plates of brass were to the Nephites what the Bible is to Latter-day Saints. They were the scriptural foundation of the revelations of Lehi, Nephi, and all Book of Mormon prophets.

The plates of brass contained the "mysteries" or hidden purposes and commandments of God that were to be handed down from generation to generation, thereby binding the faith of the fathers to the children. Without them, Benjamin told his sons, "Even our fathers would have dwindled in unbelief, and we should have been like unto our brethren, the Lamanites, who know nothing concerning these things, or even do not believe them when they are taught them, because of the traditions of their fathers, which are not correct." (Mosiah 1:5.)

The plates of brass contained the word of the Lord from the beginning of time down to the ministry of Jeremiah. (1 Ne. 5:13.) The plates of Nephi, said Benjamin, "contain the records and the sayings of our fathers from the time they left Jerusalem until now, and they are true." (Mosiah 1:6.) The contents of these three sets of plates provided the scriptural underpinnings of Nephite government and law. The corruption of civil law was always preceded by the rejection of those moral principles upon which such laws were founded. (Hel. 4:22; 5:2.) There is a warning in this for all nations of the world today.

In transferring rule to his son Mosiah, King Benjamin also appointed him custodian of the Nephite treasury of sacred things: the plates of brass, the plates of Nephi, the sword of Laban (which Benjamin himself had wielded in defense of his people—W of M 1:13), and the ball or director (the Liahona—Alma 37:38). In addition, Mosiah was also either given or subsequently obtained the "interpreters"—the Urim and Thummim—with which he translated the twenty-four gold plates comprising the record of the Jaredites. (Mosiah 8:13, 19; 28:11-17.)

After thirty-three years, Mosiah conferred all of these sacred objects upon Alma the younger, the high priest over the church, and the first chief judge over the land of Zarahemla. (Mosiah 28:20; 29:42.) He, in turn, conferred them upon his son Helaman (Alma 37:1-3, 21,

23-24, 38), and so on until Moroni hid up Mormon's abridgment of the large plates of Nephi, together with the small plates, the breastplate, and the interpreters (Ether 4:5; JS–H 1:35). It appears that these were the same interpreters used by the brother of Jared. (D&C 17:1.) How Mosiah came to possess them is unknown.

A Solemn Assembly

Three years before his death, knowing that "he must very soon go the way of all the earth," Benjamin instructed Mosiah to call a solemn convocation of the Nephites and the people of Zarahemla. King Benjamin's purpose was twofold: (1) to announce his own abdication and the selection of Mosiah as his successor, and (2) to bestow another name upon his people.

We are uninformed as to when and by whom the temple in Zarahemla was built. However, in all probability it was erected in the third century B.C. by Mosiah I subsequent to his arrival in Zarahemla and after his appointment as king over those living in that land. (Omni 1:12, 19.) It was to this second Nephite temple that the people gathered to hear King Benjamin.

In doing so, they came prepared to offer "sacrifice and burnt offerings according to the law of Moses." (Mosiah 2:3.) This has led to a current theory that the king chose that particular date because it coincided with an annual religious festival. While not unlikely, Benjamin's instructions to his son Mosiah (Mosiah 1:10), together with his unprecedented message to the people, suggest that Mosaic law and ritual were, at best, of secondary concern.

At present, we cannot determine with any accuracy the extent of the land of Zarahemla, nor its population in 124 B.C. However, the fact that the people were given only a day's notice to gather indicates that no point was more than about fifty miles from the city. And although the population is described as being "a great number, even so many that they did not number them" (Mosiah 2:2), even with their tents, they were accommodated within, or adjacent to, the walls of the temple. Then too, while the hastily built tower did not enable King Benjamin to be heard by everyone, such had been its purpose. Therefore, the people could not have been widely scattered. All this suggests that the combined populations of both Nephites and "Mulekites" was, at most, numbered in the thousands.

Yet it was a vast number who gathered to offer sacrifice, give thanks for their blessings, and hear their king. Unable to be heard by everyone, King Benjamin had his words "written and sent forth among those that were not under the sound of his voice." (Mosiah 2:8.)

King Benjamin's Stewardship

King Benjamin was the embodiment of a king of the Melchizedek order — a truly righteous sovereign who was the greatest of all because he was the servant of all. When purely worldly monarchs are measured against his example, they are all found wanting. But King Benjamin partook of the spirit of Nephi, who, in speaking of his own service to his people, said, "I did for them according to that which was in my power." (2 Ne. 5:18.) Doubtless this spirit characterized most, if not all, of Nephi's successors so that his dynasty was surely among the most righteous in all history.

King Benjamin began his message with a traditional accounting of his stewardship. (See Deut. 17:14-20.) He had honored the law of God, and he had not exalted himself above those he served: "I am like as yourselves, subject to all manner of infirmities in body and mind." (Mosiah 2:11.) He had been accepted by the common consent of the people; consecrated by his father, Mosiah I; and preserved by the "matchless power" of the Lord.

His rule had been both whole-hearted and benevolent. Unlike the tyrants of history who viewed their power as an instrument of self-gratification and self-aggrandizement, Benjamin had not robbed his people of their gold and silver, nor confined them in dungeons, nor permitted slavery — a practice common to Israel and the ancient world. The moral injunctions of the law of Moses had been enforced: murder, adultery, plunder, and theft, together with all other forms of immorality, had been forbidden.

Under the Nephite prophet-kings, as in Moses' time, civil and religious authority were one and the same — the government was essentially a theocratic monarchy. It remained a theocracy even when the monarchy was replaced in 91 B.C. by a system of judges. But following the resignation of Alma the younger as the first chief judge, the theocratic character of Nephite government began to be eroded by the division of civil and religious powers and responsibilities. Between the years 50 and 30 B.C., the two were once more unified, only to be separated thereafter until at least A.D. 34.[6] The moral decline of the Nephites and the instability of their later government is evidenced by the fact that six of their last nine chief judges were murdered. The Book of Mormon teaches that the ideal form of government is theocratic—the kingdom of God. (Mosiah 29:12-13.)

The people had not labored to support their king; he had earned his bread by his own sweat as the Lord had commanded Adam. His son, Mosiah, did likewise. (See Mosiah 6:7.) Consequently, the people were not "laden with taxes." (Mosiah 2:14.) Burdensome, unjust taxation is a form of theft. King Benjamin realized that a government has no more right to steal from its citizens than the citizens have to steal from one another. When *all* labor, *none* are oppressed. Since political morality depends upon personal morality, the strict observance of the moral code by both the ruler and the ruled was the very foundation of his benevolent reign.

Benjamin understood that service to mankind is service to God: "I have only been in the service of God." (Mosiah 2:16.) He knew the meaning of stewardship. He knew that king and commoner, president and people—all are accountable for the talents and opportunities afforded them. All must come to judgment. Would that all of us could say with King Benjamin, "I can answer a clear conscience before God this day." (Mosiah 2:15.)

Jesus said: "Let your light so shine before men, that they may see your good works, and glorify your Father which is in heaven." (Matt. 5:16.) This is precisely what King Benjamin wished to do. He wanted the people's gratitude for his service to be magnified toward the Lord: "If I . . . do merit any thanks from you, O how you ought to thank your heavenly King!" (Mosiah 2:19.)

Mortals are forever "unprofitable servants" because the Lord has done far more for his children than they can ever do for him. (Mosiah 2:20-22; Luke 17:7-10.) You are everlastingly in God's debt, said Benjamin, for his having "granted unto you your lives." (Mosiah 2:23-

24.) Our obedience can never repay this debt for life, because obedience only produces ever more blessings. Thus the debt is like an ever-receding horizon before which looms an ever-higher mountain of divine grace.

King Benjamin was keenly aware of our utter dependence upon the Lord: "Can ye say aught of yourselves? I answer you, Nay. Ye cannot say that ye are even as much as the dust of the earth. . . . And I . . . am no better than ye yourselves are." (Mosiah 2:25-26.) This theme is echoed by Mormon: "O how great is the nothingness of the children of men; yea, even they are less than the dust of the earth." (Hel. 12:7.) In other words, where God's commandments are concerned, people are less obedient than the earth itself.

King Benjamin cited himself as an example of human fragility: "I can no longer be . . . your king; for even at this time, my whole frame doth tremble exceedingly while attempting to speak unto you; but the Lord God doth support me." (Mosiah 2:29-30.) He then announced the inspired selection of Mosiah as their new ruler and expressed his own desire that the people would continue faithful and keep "the commandments of God which [would] be delivered unto [them] by him." (Mosiah 2:31; see also Hel. 4:22.)

The Day of Salvation

Benjamin emphasized a major Book of Mormon doctrine: "*This life* is the time for men to prepare to meet God." (Alma 34:32; italics added.) Those having a knowledge of God's laws, as found in the plates of brass and as made known by the Nephite prophets, were without excuse before the bar of God. If a man willfully violated those commandments, and remained defiant, he would die in his sins "an enemy to God." Divine justice would "awaken his immortal soul to a lively sense of his own guilt, which doth cause him to shrink from the presence of the Lord, and doth fill his breast with guilt, and pain, and anguish, which is like an unquenchable fire, whose flame ascendeth up forever and ever." (Mosiah 2:38.) Being unrepentant, he would be ineligible for mercy. "Therefore his final doom is to endure a never-ending torment." (Mosiah 2:38-39; see also 3:25-27.) The repentant, on the other hand, would be blessed both temporally and spiritually and be received into heaven — "a state of never-ending happiness." (Mosiah 2:41.)

Thus, concerning our eternal destiny, the Book of Mormon seems to speak in extremes: the highest heaven and the lowest hell, salvation with God or damnation with the devil.[7] As Nephi told his errant brethren, "The final state of the souls of men is to dwell in the kingdom of God, or to be cast out." (1 Ne. 15:35; see also Mosiah 2:40-41.) A soul is either saved or lost; there is no middle ground. The modifying doctrine of multiple heavens or degrees of salvation, as revealed to Joseph Smith in 1832, is not found in the Book of Mormon.[8] However, there is no real contradiction between the two viewpoints; the concept of multiple heavens is simply an extension of the principle of heaven itself. While a degree of salvation is to be had in all of the "many mansions" comprising the kingdom of God, the fact remains that there is no salvation outside of that kingdom. And all who are saved *do* repent and accept the Savior — every knee will bow and every tongue confess that Jesus is the Christ. (Philip. 2:10-11; Mosiah 27:31.) Those who refuse to repent during their probationary period — the time between birth and resurrection — are sons of perdition; they *do* suffer the fullness of hell or the second death, even as King Benjamin said. *Never* repenting — even after death — they remain "filthy still." (2 Ne. 9:16; D&C 88:35.)

In this regard, another doctrine that is not explicit in the Book of Mormon is that our "probationary state" includes the spirit state as well as mortality. Consequently, the doctrine of postmortal repentance is also missing; the tenor throughout is that physical death seals the fate of the wicked. Only in the dispensation of the fulness of times have we learned the meaning of 1 Peter 3:18-20 and 4:6. (See also D&C 138.) Although Joseph Smith translated the Book of Mormon, it was not until January 21, 1836 that he learned of the doctrine of salvation for the dead. In a vision of the celestial world, he saw his deceased brother Alvin and "marveled how it was that he had obtained an inheritance in that kingom, seeing that he had departed this life before the Lord had set his hand to gather Israel the second time, and had not been baptized for the remission of sins." (D&C 137:6.) Work for the dead began with the resurrection of

Christ; before that event, the gospel was not taught to them. (Moses 7:38-39, 57.) Therefore, before Christ's ministry to the spirit world, the Book of Mormon doctrine that "this life is the [only] time for men to prepare to meet God" (Alma 34:32) was technically correct. Mercifully, modern revelation has extended the meaning of the phrase "this life."

"Glad tidings of great joy" had been communicated to King Benjamin by an angel of the Lord. (Mosiah 3:3; see also Hel. 13:7.)[9] They were to be shared with Benjamin's people so that they, too, might "be filled with joy." (Mosiah 3:4.) These tidings concerned the then-not-far-distant first coming of "the Lord Omnipotent" to the earth. He was to be called "Jesus Christ, the Son of God, the Father of heaven and earth, the Creator of all things from the beginning; and his mother shall be called Mary." (Mosiah 3:8.)

Centuries before, Nephi had written a brief summary of his own vision of the Messiah's mortal ministry and death (1 Ne. 11:31-33); the extent to which Nephi shared that vision with others is unknown. In any case, he did not describe the atonement's attendant agonies. Consequently, the first—and the most graphic—description in the Book of Mormon of Jesus' sufferings was provided by this angel. He prophesied that the Lord Omnipotent would work "mighty miracles" of every kind and also "suffer temptations, and pain of body, hunger, thirst, and fatigue, even more than man can suffer, except it be unto death; for behold, blood cometh from every pore, so great shall be his anguish for the wickedness and the abominations of his people." (Mosiah 3:7; see also Alma 7:11-12; D&C 19:16-18.)

No one else has understood sin as did the sinless Son of God. He alone had the intelligence—the light and truth—to comprehend all of its ramifications. In doing so, Jesus endured false accusations, rejection, betrayal, scourging, crucifixion, and, above all, the wrath of God. (See D&C 88:106.) But all these things prepared him to judge the world. (See D&C 19:2-3.) For he not only knew its sins and suffered because of them, but he triumphed over them. (See John 16:33.) The cross became a sign of God's victory over humanity's last enemy—death and hell.

The fact that the angel prophesied in detail of the Lord's mortal experiences indicates that Jesus accepted his mission — not blindly, but with an understanding of all it would entail. President Joseph F. Smith wrote: "I believe that our Savior . . . no doubt possessed a foreknowledge of all the vicissitudes through which he would have to pass in the mortal tabernacle. . . . If Christ knew beforehand, so did we. But in coming here, we forgot all, that our agency might be free indeed."[10]

Christ's mission was not in vain; neither was it to be trifled with. Salvation cost heaven dearly; the angel's testimony emphasized that fact. The atonement automatically covered those who "died not knowing the will of God concerning them, or who have ignorantly sinned." (Mosiah 3:11; see also 2 Ne. 9:25-26; Moro. 8:22.) This included those heathen nations who lived and died in ignorance of both gospel and Mosaic law, all little children, and the mentally retarded.

Paul wrote: "All have sinned, and come short of the glory of God." (Rom. 3:23; see also Moses 6:57; Alma 42:6, 9.) Therefore, the atonement covered these groups, not because they did not commit sins, but because they were not legally answerable for them. The demands of justice were met in their behalf by the Savior. Speaking of little children, the angel said: "As in Adam, *or by nature*, they fall, even so the blood of Christ atoneth for *their sins*." (Mosiah 3:16; italics added.) Even if young children were free of all sinful thoughts or acts — which they are not — they would still need the atonement to overcome the physical and spiritual effects of the fall. (See Moses 6:55-57.) So it is with all people.

The Book of Mormon does not teach the doctrine of human depravity, but it does teach that people have a fallen nature, and that they are prone to disobedience and ingratitude. (See 2 Ne. 2:29; Alma 34:9; 42:6, 9; Hel. 12:1-7; Ether 3:2.) Only when human nature is contrasted with the divine nature can we begin to appreciate the extent of the fall, and of our utter dependence upon the Redeemer for both physical and spiritual redemption.

Since all are fallen, all must eventually hear the message of redemption. To this end, ancient prophets declared that message "to every kindred, nation, and tongue." (Mosiah 3:13.) The angel's words suggest that a knowledge of Christ was had by the ancient world on a much wider basis than is commonly assumed. (See 2 Ne. 26:13.) In due time, "none shall be found blameless before God, except it be little children." (Mosiah 3:21.) "Every nation, kindred, tongue, and people" will, in effect, hear the angelic message: "Righteousness and truth will I cause to sweep the earth as with a flood." (Moses 7:62.) All will know of the Savior; none will sin in ignorance; none will have claim upon the atonement except those who receive the fullness of the gospel. (Mosiah 3:20-21.) Upon hearing the angel's message, Benjamin's people were "no more blameless in the sight of God." (Mosiah 3:22.) His words would "stand as a bright testimony" against them "at the judgment day." (Mosiah 3:24.) Their relationship to God had changed forever.

The Law and the Atonement

Retroactive in its spiritual effects, the atonement was as efficacious before as it was after the Savior's death. (See D&C 20:26.) The remission of sins, which was preached from the fall, cannot be isolated from the atonement, which makes such remission possible. But the "stiffneckedness" of ancient Israel gave that people an unjustified sense of spiritual security independent of Christ. Rather than recognizing that the very imposition of the law of carnal commandments was proof of their spiritual immaturity, they believed that the law proved them superior to the rest of God's children. (See 1 Ne. 17:33-34.) The temporary means became, for Israel, the permanent end. (See Mosiah 16:14; Alma 34:14.) They did not understand that "the law of Moses availeth nothing except it were through the atonement of his blood." (Mosiah 3:15; see also 13:28-32.)

The "preparatory gospel" was meant to lead to, not supplant, the fulness of the gospel. As was previously noted, Nephi had introduced the "holy order" and taught the law of the gospel to his people. But with the passage of centuries, the Mosaic law and its associated ordinances seem to have overshadowed the doctrine of Christ. (See 2 Ne. 5:10; Jacob 7:7; Jarom 1:5, 11.) The destruction of the first Nephite nation, and the subsequent amalgamation of the Nephite remnant under Mosiah I with the spiritually illiterate people of Zarahemla

(Omni 1:12, 19), probably intensified this trend. But while the law of Moses ministered to the moral and religious needs of "the natural man," it could not deliver Israel from its carnal state.

The Natural Man

"The natural man is an enemy to God, and has been from the fall of Adam." (Mosiah 3:19.) This statement has been interpreted as referring only to very corrupt, wicked persons. However, the term "natural man" is not descriptive of one's moral character, but of one's spiritual relationship to God. The natural man is every person — from the most noble and virtuous to the most ignoble and depraved — who is still in a fallen, unregenerated condition. It is man without the baptism of fire and the Holy Ghost and, therefore, without the remission of sins. In sum, the natural man is anyone who lacks the sanctifying grace of God.

Such an individual is "an enemy to God" because — *from God's perspective* — he or she is *alien* to the divine nature. (See 2 Ne. 9:39.) To some degree, such a person is akin to the devil, who "knew not the mind of God." (Moses 4:6; see also Isa. 55:8-9.) Because of his mind-set, the natural man is incapable of understanding the deep things of God; "they are foolishness unto him." (1 Cor. 2:14; see also Alma 36:4-5; D&C 67:10-12.) The Prophet Joseph Smith described the natural man when he observed: "It is the *constitutional disposition* of mankind to set up stakes and set bounds to the works and ways of the Almighty."[11] Among the bitterest enemies of both Jesus and Joseph Smith were "men of the cloth." Natural men crucified the Savior of the world. Natural men murdered the Prophet in Carthage. Natural men comprise the enemies of Zion today.

Only through the name of Jesus Christ can the natural man, however "good," become a "saint" — a justified, sanctified heir of the celestial kingdom. (See D&C 88:21-22.) Although Benjamin's people had been "a diligent people in keeping the commandments of the Lord" (Mosiah 1:11), they were still in a carnal, "natural" condition when he addressed them (see Mosiah 4:2). When they heard the angel's message, they realized that their own righteous works were insufficient, that every person is in relative bondage to the flesh until he or she "yields to the enticings of the Holy Spirit, and putteth off the natural man and becometh a saint through the atonement of Christ the Lord." (Mosiah 3:19; see also 27:25-26; Alma 5:54; 3 Ne. 27:20.)

The *Holy* Spirit is the creator of *holy* men and women. It enables them to become "as a child, submissive, meek, humble, patient, full of love, willing to submit to all things which the Lord seeth fit to inflict" upon them. (Mosiah 3:19; see also Alma 13:28; Gal. 5:22.) Of ourselves, we can never forge that divine nature; the natural man is necessarily saved by grace—the power of God—after all he can do. (See 2 Ne. 25:23.) In the late second century B.C., of all humanity, only a remnant of Israel in America[12] understood that the heart of salvation is the merits of the Lord Omnipotent.

The Great Conversion

The words of King Benjamin—quickened by the Holy Spirit— had an electrifying effect upon the vast assemblage. The multitude "had fallen to the earth, for the fear of the Lord had come upon them. And they had viewed themselves in their own *carnal* state, even less than the dust of the earth," and as with one voice they cried out: "O have *mercy*, and apply the atoning blood of Christ that we *may receive forgiveness* of our sins, and our *hearts may be purified;* for we believe in Jesus Christ, the Son of God." (Mosiah 4:1-2; italics added.)

Their fervent prayer was heard. The "Spirit of the Lord"—the Holy Spirit or Holy Ghost—descended upon the unnumbered thousands of men, women, and young people, "and they were filled with joy, having received a remission of their sins, and having peace of conscience, because of the exceeding faith which they had in Jesus Christ." (Mosiah 4:3; see also 4:20; 5:2.) They then testified: "The Spirit of the Lord Omnipotent . . . has wrought a mighty change in us, or in our hearts, that we have no more disposition to do evil, but to do good continually." (Mosiah 5:2; see also 4:11-12; Alma 5:13-14; 13:11-12; 19:33.) They *experienced* the miracle of conversion; they had been baptized by the Holy Ghost and by fire. Their spiritual rebirth was complete.[13]

In being born again, they relied "*wholly* upon the merits of him who is mighty to save." (2 Ne. 31:19; italics added. See also Moro. 6:4.) They realized that, where the miracle of rebirth is concerned, we have no merits of our own — we are beggars at the throne of grace. (Mosiah 4:20.) Benjamin pointed out that it was God's greatness and goodness in *granting* a remission of sins that made the people appreciate their own comparative "nothingness, and ... worthless and fallen state." (Mosiah 4:5; see also 4:11.) His seemingly denigrating words only reflected the angel's conscious employment of the title *Lord God Omnipotent.* This exalted title was calcutated to draw a vivid contrast between God's almighty power and his fallen children's ultimate inability to save themselves.[14]

While the proud may chafe at the thought, time will vindicate King Benjamin's characterization of fallen man. Only those who reach the mountain's peak can appreciate its height above the valley floor. Only those who have been born again can comprehend how totally dependent is humanity upon the Lord. Pride is the child of ignorance; true humility comes only with divine knowledge.

The tendency to lean on the arm of flesh rather than to follow the counsels of an all-knowing, all-wise, God has been the cause of mankind's greatest sufferings and sorrows. To be saved, we must acknowledge the limits of human reason, we must understand that "man doth not comprehend all the things which the Lord can comprehend." (Mosiah 4:9; see also Isa. 55:8-9.) Hence, King Benjamin's admonition to "*retain* in remembrance, the greatness of God, and your own nothingness ... and humble yourselves even in the *depths* of humility." (Mosiah 4:11; italics added.) Recall his earlier rhetorical question: "Of what have ye to boast?" (Mosiah 2:24.) Mortals at their best and brightest are but a pale reflection of their Creator.

Having been baptized by fire and the Holy Ghost, King Benjamin's people entered the strait and narrow way that leads to total sanctification and, eventually, to a fullness of eternal life. (See 2 Ne. 31:17-18.) It remained for them to "press forward with a steadfastness in Christ, having a perfect brightness of hope, and a love of God and of all men." (2 Ne. 31:20.) Only in doing so could they retain the remission of sins and the sanctifying powers of the Holy Spirit. (See Mosiah 4:11-12, 26.)

"The fruit of the Spirit," said the Apostle Paul, "is love, joy, peace, longsuffering, gentleness, faith, meekness, temperance." (Gal. 5:22-23.) Having "sown" the baptism of the Spirit, the people would reap that "fruit." They would live peaceably and be honest with their fellow beings. They would provide for their families. They would teach their children to keep the commandments, to be truthful and sober-minded, and to love and serve one another, rather than to "fight and quarrel . . . and serve the devil." (Mosiah 4:14.)

The prevalent notion that children, being children, should be expected to fight and quarrel was challenged by King Benjamin. Parents are obligated to make a sincere effort to educate their children in the ways of righteousness. To fail to do so is to fail as parents. Lehi told his grandchildren: "If ye are brought up in the way ye should go ye will not depart from it." (2 Ne. 4:5, see also Prov. 22:6.) Still, children have their agency; they cannot be coerced into righteousness. Although Benjamin's people had become truly righteous, yet they were unable to share that righteousness with all of their children. Many of those who were little children at the time of the great conversion later rejected Christ and became "a separate people as to their faith, and remained so ever after, even in their carnal and sinful state." (Mosiah 26:1-4.) Among them, for a time, were Alma and the sons of Mosiah.

Are We Not All Beggars?

King Benjamin's teachings on the meaning and obligation of Christian charity are unequaled in all scripture. They are a natural extension of the angel's words concerning our fundamental unworthiness and need for divine mercy: "Are we not all beggars? Do we not all depend upon the same Being, even God, for all the substance which we have? . . . Even at this time, ye have been calling on his name, and begging for a remission of your sins. And has he suffered that ye have begged in vain? Nay; he has poured out his Spirit upon you. . . . And now, if God . . . on whom you are dependent for your lives . . . doth grant unto you whatsoever ye ask that is right . . . O then, how ye ought to impart of the substance that ye have one to another." (Mosiah 4:19-21.)

A plea for reasonable and available material or spiritual assistance cannot be ignored; it must be met. The issue is not worthiness, but need. We all travel the Jericho road—sometimes as the injured Jew, sometimes as "the good Samaritan." It is for God to be just; it is for his children to be merciful. To judge others as unworthy of our help, and then to withhold it, is to assume a prerogative the Lord has not given us. Everything we have belongs to the Lord. He has *commanded* us to share *his* substance with others. Indeed, it is quite impossible for anyone blessed with the Holy Spirit to do otherwise; God's mercy toward us will inevitably spill over into the lives of others.

Worldly wealth is an illusion. No one *possesses* his or her stewardship; all things, including our very lives, belong to the Lord. (Mosiah 4:22.) To withhold one's substance from the needy or from God's work is to "covet that which *ye have not received.*" (Mosiah 4:25; italics added.) Martin Harris was commanded: "Thou shalt not covet thine own property, but impart it freely to the printing of the Book of Mormon." (D&C 19:26.) Jesus spoke of one man as a "fool" because he considered his material wealth his own and thought that it assured him security "for many years." (Luke 12:13-21.) Jesus asked: "If ye have not been faithful in that which is another man's [meaning God's], who shall give you that which is your own?" (Luke 16:12.) Inheriting the "true riches" of heaven depends upon our faithfulness as stewards over the Lord's wealth on earth.

However, the temporal and spiritual needs of others are not to be met in a reckless manner, but "in wisdom and order; for it is not requisite that a man should run faster than he has strength. . . . He should be diligent, that thereby he might win the prize; therefore, all things must be done in order." (Mosiah 4:27.) King Benjamin's metaphor brings to mind the words of Paul: "Do you not know that in a race all the runners run, but only one gets the prize? Run in such a way as to get the prize." (New International Version, 1 Cor. 9:24.)

It is "the little foxes, that spoil the vines." (Song. 2:15.) Small sins can lead to the loss of great blessings. Therefore, instead of citing examples of large, obvious transgressions, King Benjamin admonished his people to keep their word and to return borrowed things. Sin comes in numerous shapes and sizes. Many things people do with impunity and in a casual, thoughtless, manner are sinful in God's sight. His standards are far higher than many suppose: "The Lord cannot look upon sin with the *least* degree of allowance." (Alma 45:16.) Benjamin's people had received a remission of their sins and been called to a higher level of righteousness than the rest of humanity. Much had been given them; much was required. (See D&C 82:3.) Hence the stern warning: "If ye do not watch *yourselves*, and your *thoughts*, and your *words*, and your *deeds*, and observe the commandments of God . . . unto the end of your lives, ye must perish." (Mosiah 4:30; italics added.)

The State of Grace

King Benjamin's people had received the baptism of fire and had entered the strait and narrow way that leads to eternal life. There could be no turning back. Nor did they wish to turn back; they were prepared to establish an everlasting covenant of obedience with the Lord Omnipotent so that, as they said, "we may not bring upon ourselves a never-ending torment . . . that we may not drink out of the cup of the wrath of God." (Mosiah 5:5.)

Their response was not mere hyperbole; they knew that they *did* risk God's wrath. They had attained that level of grace called sanctification, wherein they were endowed by the Spirit with a measure of the divine nature. (See D&C 20:31-34; He. 3:35; 3 Ne. 27:20; Moro. 10:33.) Having done so, they knew that if they thereafter apostatized and their works proved "evil" at the judgment, justice would claim them. They would be "consigned to an awful view of their own guilt and abominations, which doth cause them to shrink . . . into a state of misery and endless torment, from whence *they can no more return.*" (Mosiah 3:25; italics added. See also 5:5.) In short, they would suffer the second death.

Christ warned all who receive the baptism of fire that should they thereafter deny him, it would have been better for them if they had not known him. (2 Ne. 31:14.) He spoke in a similar vein to his twelve Nephite disciples: "He that endureth not unto the end, the same is he that is also hewn down and cast into the fire, from whence they can *no more return*, because of the justice of the Father." (3 Ne. 27:17; italics added.) Such a fall from grace is irreversible.

The ultimate sin is treason against God. It is the knowing denial of one's testimony of Jesus Christ, and it is called the sin against the Holy Ghost. To commit this unpardonable offense is to fall from grace. The Prophet Joseph Smith said: "If men have received the good word of God, and tasted of the powers of the world to come, if they shall fall away, it is impossible to renew them again, seeing they have crucified the Son of God afresh, and put Him to an open shame; so there is a possibility of falling away; you could not be renewed again, and the power of Elijah cannot seal against this sin, for this is a reserve made in the seals and power of the Priesthood."[15] When consciously and totally denied, the knowledge and power that saves becomes the knowledge and power that damns.

Children of Christ

Having been born again, King Benjamin's people had entered into the grace of Christ. They had been made worthy to receive a name that would distinguish them from "all the people which the Lord God [had] brought out of the land of Jerusalem." (Mosiah 1:11.) No longer would these remnants of Ephraim, Manasseh, and Judah be divided by temporal distinctions; a transcendent name would bind them together as one family: "Now, because of the covenant which ye have made ye shall be called the children of Christ, his sons, and his daughters; for behold, *this day* he hath spiritually begotten you; for ye say that your hearts are changed through faith on his name; therefore, ye are *born of him* and have become his sons and his daughters." (Mosiah 5:7; italics added.) Of those groups—including the lost tribes—who had left Israel's ancient promised land, king Benjamin's people were the first of which we have record to be adopted into the spiritual family of Christ. (See Mosiah 1:11.)[16]

In becoming the sons and daughters of Christ, they took upon themselves both his *name* and his *nature*—the two are indivisible. (See 3 Ne. 27:27.) They were prepared to do so because the Lord had lightened the burden of their fallen condition; they had put off the natural man and become Saints. They stood at the "right hand of God"—the hand of mercy, righteousness, power, and salvation. (See Mosiah 5:9; 26:23-24; Hel. 3:30; Moro. 9:26.) In opposition to them are those found at the "left hand of God"—the hand of justice, uncleanness, and damnation—who either reject the name of Christ, or forfeit it through transgression (See Mosiah 5:10, 12; D&C 19:5; 29:27.) And so, at the judgment, all people will be found either on the right or the left hand of God.[17]

King Benjamin did not simply reiterate doctrines already familiar to his people. Quickened by the Holy Spirit, his message parted the veil and revealed "the mysteries" centered in the redeeming grace of "Christ, the Lord God Omnipotent." (Mosiah 5:15.) His people received that grace; they partook of "the mysteries."

Conclusion

"I told the brethren that the Book of Mormon was the most correct of any book on earth, and the keystone of our religion, and a man would get nearer to God by abiding by its precepts, than by any other book."[18] We are yet to appreciate the full significance of Joseph Smith's statement. The Book of Mormon explains—with unequaled power and plainness—the process by which men and women "get nearer to God." In doing so, it provides the most impressive examples to be found in all scripture of how fallen humanity is saved by grace. The conversion of Benjamin's people teaches us that "the power of God unto salvation" (Rom. 1:16) transcends testimony, doctrines, ordinances, religious activity, and even virtuous living—it is the power inherent in the blood of Christ, as administered by and through the Holy Spirit, to endow God's fallen children with the very nature of God.

The words of the angel concerning that power are as applicable to the Latter-day Saints as they were to the Nephites. The "natural man" is as much "an enemy to God" today as he was in King Benjamin's time. Irrespective of all other considerations, a Latter-day Saint remains in that same "carnal state" in which Benjamin's people found themselves until he or she is born again through the fulness of baptism.

Such a baptism involves more than the physical ordinance. It has three components: baptism in water, baptism of the Holy Ghost, and the baptism of fire. "All three baptisms," said Joseph Smith, "make one."[19] He explained: "The baptism of water, without the baptism of fire and the Holy Ghost attending it, is of no use; they are necessarily and inseparably connected."[20] All three components of baptism are essential if one is to be born again. "For by the water [baptism] ye keep the commandment; by the Spirit [baptism] ye are justified, and by the blood [baptism of fire] ye are sanctified." (Moses 6:60.) It was the baptism of fire — administered by the Holy Ghost — that King Benjamin's people received. (See Mosiah 4:3.)[21] It was this culminating baptism that brought them the remission of sins and "peace of conscience." It was through this baptism that they were "born of God" and thereby acquired his spiritual image in their countenances, even as a child's physical features and mannerisms reflect those of its parents.

Every natural man and woman aspiring to the celestial kingdom — whether living or dead — must experience total baptism before he or she can enter the "strait and narrow path which leads to eternal life." (2 Ne. 31:17-18.) Thus, the ordinance must be completed either in mortality or — as will seemingly be the case with most who have lived — in the spirit world. For baptism is the *only* means by which fallen men and women can be born again, obtain the remission of sins, and, in the resurrection, "become holy, without spot." (Moro. 10:33.)

Can we be baptized without being born again? Of course.[22] Over forty years after the conversion of King Benjamin's people, Alma asked the baptized members of the church of Christ in Zarahemla: "Have ye spiritually been born of God? Have ye received his image in your countenances? Have ye *experienced* this *mighty change* in your hearts?" (Alma 5:14; italics added.) We do not know how those in Alma's audience answered his rhetorical questions, but we know that Benjamin's generation would have responded with a resounding, "Yes!"

If Alma were to pose the same questions to members of the church of Christ in this dispensation, what would be our response? True conversion is a *mighty* change in moral and spiritual nature. Those so sanctified see all things through the eyes of God. They join that host of the redeemed described by Alma: "Now they, after being sanctified by the Holy Ghost, having their garments made white, being pure and spotless before God, could not look upon sin save it were with abhorrence." (Alma 13:12; see also 2 Ne. 4:31.) Do we look upon the moral corruptions, the rampant perversions — the "civilized" sins of our generation — with a like "abhorrence?" A thorough cleansing of hearts and minds must be experienced by the obedient among the Latter-day Saints; an outpouring of spiritual power must prepare the way for the redemption of Zion. For Zion consists of the sanctified — "the pure in heart." (D&C 97:21.) It cannot be redeemed by the unclean and the impure.

Therefore, the individual members of the "army of Israel" must experience a conversion akin to that bestowed upon the ancient Nephites. The Lord's latter-day army must become a fit vessel for the powers of the Melchizedek Priesthood: "First let my army become very great, and let it be *sanctified* before me, that it *may become* fair as the sun, and clear as the moon, and that her banners may be terrible unto all nations; that the kingdoms of this world may be constrained to acknowledge that the kingdom of Zion is in very deed the kingdom of our God and his Christ." (D&C 105:31-32; italics added; see also 1 Ne. 14:14; Alma 13:11-12.)[23] Nothing is so "terrible" as the power of Almighty God; nothing is so compelling as virtue and truth.

The mighty conversion of King Benjamin's people foreshadowed the sanctifying fire of the Holy Spirit that later enveloped others among the Nephites and Lamanites, and that will descend upon every Latter-day Saint who *diligently* keeps the Lord's commandments. This vital Book of Momon doctrine is one of the primary reasons why Joseph Smith said that we would "get nearer to God by abiding by its precepts, than by any other book."

NOTES

1. In addition to King Benjamin's people, the effects of the Holy Spirit were visibly manifest on the Lamanite king Lamoni and his wife (Alma 19:6, 13, 33), on three hundred Lamanites (Hel. 5:43-49), and on little children and the twelve Nephite disciples (3 Ne. 17:24; 19:13-15).

2. Jacob and Joseph were *consecrated* priests and teachers, but *ordained* to the "holy order" or greater priesthood. (2 Ne. 6:2.) Elder Joseph Fielding Smith explained that they were priests and teachers in the sense that they were given "a general assignment to teach, direct, and admonish the people." (Joseph Fielding Smith, *Answers to Gospel Questions,* 5 vols., compiled by Joseph Fielding Smith, Jr. [Salt Lake City: Deseret Book Company, 1957-66], 1:124.) Since there were no known descendants of the priestly tribe of Levi in Lehi's colony, the Nephites officiated in the duties of the Levitical priesthood pertaining to the Mosaic law by virtue of the Melchizedek Priesthood which they held.

3. It is apparent from Nephi's teachings on baptism (2 Ne. 31:15-17) that it was practiced in the days of Nephi. However, the first recorded instance is found in Mosiah 18:13-16. The first explicit account of the baptism of fire and of the Holy Ghost in the Book of Mormon involved King Benjamin's people in 124 B.C. (Mosiah 4:1-3, 11; 5:2, 7.)

4. Nephi had fled to the land of Nephi ("the land of our fathers' first inheritance"—Mosiah 9:1) to escape his vengeful brothers (2 Ne. 5:4-8.) The migration of Mosiah I from that land was to the north, were he encountered the people of Zarahemla, the Jewish colony led by Mulek, the son of King Zedekiah, which had fled Jerusalem about 587 B.C. (Omni 1:14-16.)

5. Although Zarahemla's people had to be taught line upon line about Israel's God and his commandments, a clear understanding of Christ was had by the prophets who wrote the small plates. For example, Amaleki—the last writer on those plates—said: "I would that ye should come unto Christ, who is the Holy One of Israel, and partake of his salvation, and the power of his redemption." (Omni 1:26.)

6. The prophet-judges in this twenty-year period were Helaman II and his son Nephi. (Hel. 2:2; 3:37; 5:1.)

7. The doctrine of exaltation is not explicit in the Book of Mormon. However, it seems to be implied by the doctrine of absolute damnation—the one being the necessary opposition to the other. Consequently, the term *saved,* as found therein, is commonly regarded as a synonym for *exalted.* In any case, since the Nephite prophets taught salvation in the context of baptism and rebirth—both basic to celestial glory—being "saved" would be at least tantamount to salvation in the presence of God the Father.

8. The Book of Mormon is a *selective abridgment* of Nephite scripture. By no means does it contain all the doctrines known to the Nephite prophets. (See Alma 12:9; Ether 4:4-8.) Mormon wrote only the "lesser part" of the

things the risen Christ taught the Nephites; the "greater things," said he, "were engraven upon the plates of Nephi." (3 Ne. 26:7-12.) In all likelihood, at least some of the worthy Nephites and Lamanites received, at various times, those doctrines and ordinances associated with modern temple work.

9. The angel did not identify himself. Since no one was yet resurrected, the angel was probably a translated being. I am tempted to suggest Enoch, but this is sheer conjecture on my part.

10. Joseph F. Smith, *Gospel Doctrine*, 5th ed. (Salt Lake City: Deseret Book Company, 1939), p. 13.

11. Joseph Smith, *Teachings of the Prophet Joseph Smith*, selected by Joseph Fielding Smith (Salt Lake City: Deseret Book Company, 1938), p. 320; italics added.

12. The ministry of Abinadi (Mosiah 11-17) and the establishment of a church of Christ by his only known convert, Alma, antedated Benjamin's address by twenty years or more. Therefore, as of 124 B.C., both of these Nephite groups concurrently enjoyed the fulness of the gospel.

13. Since baptism was an ordinance of the "preparatory gospel," which included the Mosaic law (see D&C 84:27), Benjamin's people had already been baptized in water — and, to a degree, in Spirit as well.

14. Insofar as extant scripture is concerned, this angel was the first to speak of Christ as the Lord God Omnipotent. This title appears nowhere in the standard works other than in chapters 3 and 5 of Mosiah, and in Revelation 19:6.

15. *Teachings of the Prophet Joseph Smith*, p. 339; italics added. See also pp. 357-59; Hebrews 6:4-6; 10:26-27.

16. Although Nephi was undoubtedly born again and clearly understood the doctrine (see 2 Ne. 31-32), there is no account of any mass spiritual baptisms among the Nephites before 124 B.C..

17. The term *exaltation* does not appear in the Book of Mormon; however, exaltation is implicit in being sealed up to Christ.

18. *Teachings of the Prophet Joseph Smith*, p. 360; see also p. 314.

19. Joseph Smith, *The Words of Joseph Smith,* compiled and edited by Andrew F. Ehat and Lyndon W. Cook (Provo, Utah: Brigham Young University Religious Studies Center, 1980), p. 354. Daniel Tyler said that Joseph Smith reconciled the three baptisms mentioned in Matthew 3:11 (water, Spirit, and fire) with Ephesians 4:4-5 ("There is . . . one baptism") when he stated: "There is but one baptism; it takes the baptism of water, of the Holy Ghost, and of fire to constitute one full baptism." Hyrum L. Andrus and Helen Mae Andrus, eds., *They Knew the Prophet* (Salt Lake City: Bookcraft, 1974), p. 51.

20. *Teachings of the Prophet Joseph Smith*, p. 360; see also p. 314.

21. The expression *baptism of the Holy Ghost* is not found in the Standard Works. Instead, the spiritual aspects of baptism are always described as the baptism of fire and of the Holy Ghost. We are born again by water, the Spirit, and the blood of Christ. (See Moses 6:59-60.) These three principles correspond to the three phases of total baptism: baptism in water, the baptism of the Holy Ghost, and the baptism of fire and of the Holy Ghost. They may be received individually over a period of time, or on the same occasion—as was the case with the twelve Nephite disciples. (See 3 Ne. 19:11-13.)

22. See Elder Joseph Fielding Smith, Conference Report, October 10, 1958, pp. 21-22.

23. See *Journal of Discourses*, 26 vols. (London: Latter-day Saints' Book Depot, 1854-86), 15:360-61.

18

ZENIFF AND NOAH
(Mosiah 9-13)

KENT P. JACKSON AND MORGAN W. TANNER

Mosiah 9-13 contains scripture that helps us to understand the salvation that comes through Jesus Christ. Within these passages are accounts of three significant men: two rulers, one good (Zeniff) and the other wicked (Noah); and a great prophet (Abinadi). By studying their examples, we can better learn how we may be happiest in our mortal lives and prepare for the life to come. From these passages, we can also learn the significance of the sacrifice of the Lord.

Zeniff and His People

Mosiah 9 begins a record written by Zeniff, who had departed with a large group from the main body of the Nephites to find and possess the original land of their forefathers' inheritance. Their quest brought them to the area called Lehi-Nephi, where they built their cities. The Lamanites allowed them to possess the area, thinking that they would be able to overthrow the Nephites in Lehi-Nephi in a few years and make them work to support the neighboring Lamanites. After twelve years, the Lamanites surprised Zeniff and his people and attacked them, because they feared that the Nephites would become too strong to be put under their rule. Under the leadership of Zeniff, the Nephites were able to defend themselves. They were preserved

---

Kent P. Jackson is associate professor of ancient scripture and Old Testament area coordinator at Brigham Young University. Morgan W. Tanner is a doctoral student in history at the University of California at Los Angeles.

because they had, up to that time, kept the commandments and remembered the Lord. As Zeniff wrote about his people: "For I and my people did cry mightily to the Lord that he would deliver us out of the hands of our enemies, for we were awakened to a remembrance of the deliverance of our fathers. And God did hear our cries and did answer our prayers; and we did go forth in his might; yea, we did go forth against the Lamanites, and in one day and a night . . . we did slay them even until we had driven them out of our land." (Mosiah 9:17-18.) For twenty-two years after the first attack by the Lamanites, Zeniff and his people had peace in their land. During this time, Zeniff organized guards to keep watch over the land to prevent a surprise attack by the Lamanites. He also "did cause that the men should till the ground, and raise all manner of grain and all manner of fruit. . . . And . . . did cause that the women should spin, and toil, and work, and work all manner of fine linen, yea, and cloth of every kind that [his people] might clothe [their] nakedness; and thus [they] did prosper in the land." (Mosiah 10:4-5.) Zeniff understood how to lead his people so that they could live in peace. As the Lord had promised many times before concerning the land: "This land is consecrated unto him whom [the Lord] shall bring. And if it so be that they shall serve him according to the commandments which he hath given, it shall be a land of liberty unto them; wherefore, they shall never be brought down into captivity." (2 Ne. 1:7.)

Contrast the righteous work of Zeniff and his people with the unrighteous labors of Zeniff's son Noah, which will be discussed below. Zeniff and his people prospered in their righteousness because they remembered the Lord. Noah and his people's momentary prosperity was only a facade of strength, because the Lord did not support them.

The Vanities of Noah and His People

While King Benjamin and Zeniff are fine examples of righteous leadership, King Noah is a prime example of unrighteous leadership in the Book of Mormon. The account relates: "[King Noah] did not keep the commandments of God, but he did walk after the desires of his own heart. . . . And he did cause his people to commit sin, and do that which was abominable in the sight of the Lord. Yea, and they did commit whoredoms and all manner of wickedness. And he laid a tax of one fifth part of all they possessed, a fifth part of their gold and of their silver, and a fifth part of their ziff, and of their copper, and of their brass and their iron; and a fifth part of their fatlings; and also a fifth part of all their grain." (Mosiah 11:2-3.)

The account goes on to tell how King Noah had removed from office all of the priests who had been consecrated by his father, Zeniff. He then consecrated priests who were "lifted up in the pride of their hearts." (Mosiah 11:5.) In other words, King Noah put men in positions of authority who were wicked like himself and who would do the evil deeds that he had in store for the people. The tax Noah imposed was for supporting the "laziness, and . . . idolatry, and . . . whoredoms" of the king and his priests. (Mosiah 11:6.) The people labored to support the iniquity of their rulers. Noah's rule was characterized by disobedience to the Lord's commandments: he did whatever he wanted to do, and he caused his people to sin.

Noah's people were taxed heavily and had to work hard to support the wickedness of their government. (Mosiah 11:3-4, 6.) Yet there is no hint in the record that they saw themselves as oppressed. They shared in the wrongdoing of their leaders: "They also became idolatrous, because they were deceived by the vain and flattering words of the king and priests; for they did speak flattering things unto them." (Mosiah 11:7.) The wicked government affected the people, who also became wicked.

Unrighteous governments in all ages have maintained power by appealing to the vanity of the people over whom they rule. Two of the most common ways of doing this are: (1) building large buildings and other highly visible monuments that supposedly demonstrate the greatness and prestige of the nation,[1] and (2) being victorious in warfare, demonstrating the supposed superiority of one's forces over those of a foe. Vain people allow themselves to be seduced by such meaningless and shallow displays of presumed glory.

Mosiah 11 shows that Noah and his priests used both of these flattering methods to subject the people by appealing to their vanity. "King Noah built many elegant and spacious buildings; and he ornamented them with fine work of wood, and of all manner of precious things, of gold, and of silver, and of iron, and of brass, and of ziff, and of copper; and he also built him a spacious palace. . . . And he also caused that his workmen should work all manner of fine work within the walls of the temple. . . . And . . . he built a tower near the temple. . . . [and] caused many buildings to be built in the land." (Mosiah 11:8-10, 12-13.) Notice in these verses the great emphasis on the construction of luxurious buildings during King Noah's reign. A contrasting view of such emphasis on material things was presented by President Spencer W. Kimball:

> The Lord has blessed us as a people with a prosperity unequaled in times past. The resources that have been placed in our power are good, and necessary to our work here on the earth. But I am afraid that many of us have been surfeited with flocks and herds and acres and barns and wealth and have begun to worship them as false gods, and they have power over us. Do we have more of these good things than our faith can stand? Many people spend most of their time working in the service of a self-image that includes sufficient money, stocks, bonds, investment portfolios, property, credit cards, furnishings, automobiles, and the like to guarantee carnal security throughout, it is hoped, a long and happy life.
>
> As the Lord himself said in our day, "They seek not the Lord to establish his righteousness, but every man walketh in his own way, and after the image of his own god, whose image is the likeness of the world, and *whose substance is that of an idol*, which waxeth old and shall perish in Babylon, even Babylon the great, which shall fall." (D&C 1:16, italics added.)[2]

Mosiah 11:16-18 tells how the Lamanites invaded Noah's territory. At first they were successful in their raids, but later Noah's forces were able to defeat them. As a result of their victory, Noah's people increased in their vanity: "Because of this great victory they were lifted up in the pride of their hearts; they did boast in their own strength, saying that their fifty could stand against thousands of the Lamanites; and thus they did boast, and did delight in blood, and the shedding of the blood of their brethren, and this because of the wickedness of their king and priests." Their self-flattery because of military victory led them to "delight in . . . the shedding of the blood of their brethren." (Mosiah 11:19.)

President Kimball wrote:

> In spite of our delight in defining ourselves as modern, and our tendency to think we possess a sophistication that no people in the past ever had—in spite of these things, we are, on the whole, an idolatrous people—a condition most repugnant to the Lord.
>
> We are a warlike people, easily distracted from our assignment of preparing for the coming of the Lord. When enemies rise up, we commit vast resources to the fabrication of gods of stone and steel—ships, planes, missiles, fortifications—and depend on them for protection and deliverance. When threatened, we become anti-enemy instead of pro-kingdom of God; we train a man in the art of war and call him a patriot, thus, in the manner of Satan's counterfeit of true patriotism, perverting the Savior's teaching: "Love your enemies, bless them that curse you, do good to them that hate you, and pray for them which despitefully use you, and persecute you; that ye may be the children of your Father which is in heaven." (Matt. 5:44-45.) . . .
>
> What are we to fear when the Lord is with us? Can we not take the Lord at his word and exercise a particle of faith in him? Our assignment is affirmative: to forsake the things of the world as ends in themselves; to leave off idolatry and press forward in faith; to carry the gospel to our enemies, that they might no longer be our enemies.[3]

Sin and Bondage

In the period of the Nephites' vain glory following their military defeat of the Lamanites, the prophet Abinadi began to preach among them. Through him the Lord offered Noah's people a clear choice of actions with two sure options: (1) they must repent, or (2) they must be taken into bondage. Notice how clearly and unmistakably these choices are spelled out in the following verses:

234

Thus saith the Lord—Wo be unto this people, for I have seen their abominations, and their wickedness, and their whoredoms; and *except they repent* I will visit them in mine anger. And *except they repent* and turn to the Lord their God, behold, I will deliver them into the hands of their enemies; yea, and they shall be brought into bondage; and they shall be afflicted by the hand of their enemies.... And it shall come to pass that *except this people repent* and turn unto the Lord their God, they shall be brought into bondage; and none shall deliver them, except it be the Lord the Almighty God.... And *except they repent* in sackcloth and ashes, and cry mightily to the Lord their God, I will not hear their prayers, neither will I deliver them out of their afflictions. (Mosiah 11:20, 21, 23, 25; italics added.)

The word of the Lord through Abinadi is as valid for us today as it was for Noah's society. People of all nations must repent or suffer spiritual and temporal bondage.[4]

The people of Noah refused to repent, and Abinadi was rejected—not only by Noah and his priests, but by the people as well. As the account states: "The eyes of the people were blinded; therefore they hardened their hearts against the words of Abinadi, and they sought from that time forward to take him. And king Noah hardened his heart against the word of the Lord, and he did not repent of his evil doings." (Mosiah 11:29.)

Two years passed before Abinadi returned. But this time he had a different message from the Lord: "My people ... have hardened their hearts against my words; *they have repented not* of their evil doings; therefore, *I will visit them* in my anger, yea, *in my fierce anger will I visit them* in their iniquities and abominations. Yea, wo be unto this generation! ... Because of their iniquities, *[they] shall be brought into bondage,* and *shall be smitten* on the cheek; yea, and *shall be driven* by men, and *shall be slain;* and the vultures of the air, and the dogs, yea, and the wild beasts, shall devour their flesh." (Mosiah 12:1-2; italics added.) When Abinadi first came before Noah and his priests, he challenged them to repent or be taken into bondage. Now he simply affirmed that their punishment of bondage (and other things) would in fact take place, saying, "It shall come to pass."

Other examples in the scriptures also teach us that eventually it is simply too late to avert disaster by repentance, and the prophesied punishment from the Lord is sure. In Helaman 13-16 is the account of the Lamanite prophet Samuel, whom the Lord had sent to prophesy against the Nephites. He declared to them: "Behold, your days of probation are past; ye have procrastinated the day of your salvation until it is everlastingly too late, and your destruction is made sure." (Hel. 13:38.) Similarly Mormon witnessed a time among his people when "the day of grace was passed with them, both temporally and spiritually," and their destruction was assured. (Morm. 2:15.) King Noah and his people were now under the same condemnation: It was "everlastingly too late" for them.

When Abinadi appeared before King Noah and his priests, he chastised them for failing in their callings as priests and teachers of the people—for neither understanding nor living the principles of righteousness themselves: "Are you priests, and pretend to teach this people, and to understand the spirit of prophesying, and yet desire to know of me what these things mean? I say unto you, wo be unto you for perverting the ways of the Lord! For if ye understand these things ye have not taught them; therefore, ye have perverted the ways of the Lord. Ye have not applied your hearts to understanding; therefore, ye have not been wise. Therefore, what teach ye this people?" (Mosiah 12:25-27.) After teaching King Noah and the priests about the law of Moses, he continued to condemn their actions. King Noah and his priests had not kept the commandments of the Lord, neither had they taught the commandments to their people. Abinadi knew that they were not doing what they should because, as he explained to them: "If ye had [kept the commandments and taught them to the people], the Lord would not have caused me to come forth and to prophesy evil concerning this people." (Mosiah 12:37; 13:25-26.)

Many years earlier, Jacob had written against the evil of which Abinadi was speaking, making reference to his calling among his own people: "We did magnify our office unto the Lord, taking upon us the responsibility, answering the sins of the people upon our own heads if we did not teach them the word of God with all diligence; wherefore, by laboring with our might their blood might not come upon our garments; otherwise their blood would come upon our garments, and we would not be found spotless at the last day." (Jacob 1:19.) Because Noah and his priests failed to teach righteous principles to their people, they led a whole generation into sin.

Through the Redemption of God

Abinadi taught Noah and his priests about the law of Moses and the mission of Jesus Christ. After reciting to them the Ten Commandments (Mosiah 12:34-36; 13:12-24), he discussed with them the nature of the law of Moses. King Noah and his priests believed that they would be saved because they had the law of Moses and (as they said) were keeping it. Abinadi used this opportunity to teach them of the true meaning of the law of sacrifice. He said: "Ye have said that salvation cometh by the law of Moses. I say unto you that it is expedient that ye should keep the law of Moses as yet; but I say unto you, that the time shall come when it shall no more be expedient to keep the law of Moses." (Mosiah 13:27.) Abinadi and faithful Nephites understood well that the law of Moses was not sufficient to save someone, because salvation comes only through the atonement of Jesus Christ. Yet the Nephites lived under the law of Moses—even though they had the gospel—and were commanded to observe the law until the coming of Christ among them.

The law was not sufficent. (Mosiah 13:28.) More was needed, namely the atonement, "which God himself shall make for the sins and iniquities of his people." Without the atonement, all people would "unavoidably perish." Amulek taught: "It is expedient that an atonement should be made; for according to the great plan of the Eternal God there must be an atonement made, or else all mankind must unavoidably perish; yea, all are hardened; yea, all are fallen and are lost, and must perish except it be through the atonement which it is expedient should be made." (Alma 34:9.) But the Israelites needed the strict law of Moses "to keep them in remembrance of God and their duty towards him" because they were "a stiffnecked people." (Mosiah 13:29-30.)

The law of Moses was a type of the gospel of Christ (Mosiah 13:31); it taught, through symbols, the principles of the atonement. This is particularly true of animal sacrifices, which were types of the atoning sacrifice of the Lord Jesus Christ. The sacrifices of the law taught that through the vicarious sacrifice of one who was innocent — the sacrificial animal symbolizing Christ — the sins of the repentant were removed. In the law of Moses there were several kinds of sacrifices; yet there was one central focus, as was revealed in the days of Adam: "This thing is a similitude of the sacrifice of the Only Begotten of the Father, which is full of grace and truth." (Moses 5:7.) Jesus' atoning sacrifice was the theme that undergirded the law of Moses. Sacrifice as a means of worship was symbolic of the atonement, and the sacrifices were meant to teach the principles upon which the atonement was based. Sadly, through most of the history of Israel, apostasy had removed that understanding from the worship of most Israelites.

Since the Law was something temporary that pointed to a greater reality, its "fulfillment" could come only when the greater thing to which it pointed came into existence. In one sense, the law was a great prophecy of which Jesus was the fulfillment. When Jesus came and fulfilled the work for which the Father had sent him, then all of the things that pointed to his coming were fulfilled — not simply in that they no longer existed, but in that the realities they had foreshadowed had come true. Abinadi said that all things pertaining to the law of Moses "were types of things to come." (Mosiah 13:31.)

Many Israelites (and Noah and his priests) could not understand the law "because of the hardness of their hearts." (Mosiah 13:32.) They were spiritually unprepared to understand and accept the higher law of the atonement. They had falsely attributed salvation to the sacrifies of the law of Moses and had lost the symbol of Christ's atoning sacrifice. They did not understand that the sacrifices of the law of Moses were not able to bring about redemption, and that it would be accomplished through the sacrifice of the Only Begotten of the Father. Abinadi explained that "God himself should come down among the children of men." (Mosiah 13:34.) In the next two chapters of the book of Mosiah, Abinadi expounded on this theme with great power.[5]

238

Conclusion

Zeniff and his people were examples of those who seek happiness and security in the things of heaven. They learned that to prosper in the land, they would have to obey the commandments of the Lord. King Noah and his priests, only one generation later, were examples of those who seek happiness and security in the things of the world. They tried to gratify their vanity with the construction of luxurious buildings and to find security without the protection of God. Yet Abinadi taught them of the evil of both their behavior and their outlook. How truly Alma taught: "Wickedness never was happiness." (Alma 41:10.) True happiness and true security can come only from Christ, through whom alone is salvation.

Notes

1. The great Bible scholar George E. Mendenhall called this, half jokingly, "the *edifice* complex." (Personal communication to Kent P. Jackson.)

2. Spencer W. Kimball, "The False Gods We Worship," *Ensign*, June 1976, pp. 4-5.

3. Ibid., p. 6.

4. For a discussion of the fulfillment of Abinadi's prophecy of bondage, see Monte S. Nyman, "Bondage and Deliverance," chapter 20 in this volume.

5. For a detailed discussion of the rest of Abinadi's sermon on this subject to Noah and his priests, see Rodney Turner, "Two Prophets: Abinadi and Alma," chapter 19 in this volume.

19

TWO PROPHETS: ABINADI AND ALMA
(Mosiah 14-18)

RODNEY TURNER

We are introduced to two prophets in chapters 14 through 18 of Mosiah—Abinadi, and Alma the elder. Although their lives touched but briefly, their labors are bound together forever. Abinadi brought the light of the gospel of redemption through Jesus Christ to a people in darkness. Alma carried that light into the lives of others and established anew the church of God. Each played a critical role in the Lord's work in ancient times; each speaks to the Saints in these last days. Each merits our attention.

The Ministry and Message of Abinadi

Abinadi is the John the Baptist of the Book of Mormon. Like John, he was a lone prophet who briefly ministered to a people committed to the law of Moses, who knew little of the Messiah to come and nothing of his actual divinity. Like John, Abinadi preached repentance, warned of the impending judgments of God, and testified of the Messiah to come. Both prophets were opposed by the religious leaders of their day; both were victims of priestcraft—the ultimate hypocrisy. Both denounced the immoral conduct of their respective kings and died violent deaths at their hands. Both Abinadi and John

---

Rodney Turner is professor of ancient scripture at Brigham Young University.

served as transitional prophets, linking together the old and the new covenants — the law of Moses and the law of Christ. In doing so, they functioned as "Eliases," preparing the way for the first coming of the Messiah.

We know nothing of Abinadi's personal life. How old was he when he began his ministry? How did he come to be a prophet? Did he have a wife and children? Did someone weep for him when he died? We can answer none of these questions. However, we do know that Abinadi was a Nephite who, depending on his birthdate, was born either in the land of Zarahemla or the land of Nephi. If the former was the case, he was a member of the Zeniff expedition that left Zarahemla during the early period of King Benjamin's reign (about 200 B.C.) to repossess the "land of their inheritance." (Omni 1:27.)

Zeniff and "a considerable number" of Nephites obtained Lamanite permission to resettle the lands of Lehi-Nephi and Shilom. (Omni 1:29; Mosiah 9:6-8.) Appointed king by his people, Zeniff reigned over that southern colony during Benjamin's concurrent reign over the land of Zarahemla. (Mosiah 7:9.)[1] According to precedent, Zeniff consecrated worthy men to serve as priests.[2] But his son and successor, Noah, was a corrupt ruler who replaced his father's priests with his own immoral supporters — the elder Alma being one of them. (Mosiah 11:5, 10-14; 17:1-2.)[3] Idolatry and gross immorality characterized Noah's Solomon-like reign, and his people succumbed to his example. (Mosiah 7:24-25; 11:1-15.)[4]

It was following a boastful Nephite victory over the Lamanites about the year 150 B.C. that Abinadi, one of King Noah's subjects, came among the people preaching repentance and warning of possible future defeat and bondage. His message only angered the defiant king: "Who is Abinadi, that I and my people should be judged by him, or who is the Lord, that shall bring upon my people such great affliction?" (Mosiah 11:27.) His life sought by king and people alike, the rejected prophet withdrew. Returning in disguise two years later, Abinadi delivered a dire prophecy: failure to repent would mean war, painful bondage, drought, insect infestation, famine, pestilence, and death. King Noah would suffer death by fire (the same fate he was to inflict on Abinadi — see Mosiah 12:2-7.) Noah's people accused

Abinadi of being a false prophet and, as such, subject to the penalty of death. (See Deut. 18:20.) Their arguments were typical of those who reject the prophets: (1) "he pretendeth the Lord hath spoken it"; (2) "we are guiltless, and thou, O king, hast not sinned"; and (3) "we are strong." (Mosiah 12:12-15.)

Imprisoned, Abinadi was finally brought before Noah and his priestly judicial council for final judgment. Their efforts to entrap him were to no avail: "He answered them boldly, and withstood all their questions . . . and did confound them in all their words." (Mosiah 12:19.) Undoubtedly inspired, one of the priests — was it Alma himself? — asked for an explanation of Isaiah 52:7-10, which speaks of Christ and his latter-day Zion. *This passage, together with Isaiah 53, constitutes the scriptural foundation of Abinadi's message.*

Abinadi answered: "Are you priests, and pretend to teach this people, and to understand the spirit of prophesying, and yet desire to know of me what these things mean?" (Mosiah 12:25.) When he asked the priests what they taught their people, they responded, "We teach the law of Moses." In a stinging rebuke, Abinadi then asked: "If ye teach the law of Moses why do ye not keep it?" (Mosiah 12:29; see also Rom. 2:17-23.) As evidence of their hypocrisy, he cited their worship of riches, and their "whoredoms."

Abinadi acknowledged that the Mosaic law *led* to salvation if they kept "the commandments of God" — meaning the decalogue. Beginning to read it, he was interrupted by King Noah: "Away with this fellow, and slay him; for what have we to do with him, for he is mad." (Mosiah 13:1.) The *ad hominem* attack is the final recourse of those who cannot endure the truth. But Abinadi was not mad; he was a *holy* prophet who had been baptized with the Holy Ghost and with fire; he was filled with the Spirit. Like Moses on Sinai, "his face shone with exceeding luster," and they "durst not lay their hands on him." (Mosiah 13:5; see also Ex. 34:29.) Transfigured with glory, he told his cowed audience: "I perceive that it cuts you to your hearts because I tell you the truth concerning your iniquities. Yea, and my words fill you with wonder and amazement, and with anger. . . . But this much I tell you, what you do with me, after this, shall be as a type and a shadow [a portent] of things which are to come." (Mosiah 13:7-10.)

Beginning at the second commandment, Abinadi concluded the decalogue and asked, "Have ye taught this people that they should observe to do all these things for to keep these commandments? I say unto you, Nay." (Mosiah 13:25-26.) Having exposed their duplicity about the law, he then revealed the limitations of the law itself. It was at this point that Abinadi became a transitional prophet, binding the lesser to the greater law, and Moses to Christ: "Salvation doth not come by the law *alone;* and were it not for the atonement, which God himself shall make for the sins and iniquities of his people, that they must unavoidably perish, *notwithstanding the law of Moses."* (Mosiah 13:28; italics added.) In other words, the ultimate efficacy of Israel's works depended upon the works of Christ. Religious works, without faith in the Redeemer, were dead. But until the redemption was accomplished, a "stiffnecked" Israel required a "strict law" of performances "to keep them in remembrance of God." (Mosiah 13:29-30.) However, Israel—unlike Moses and the prophets—failed to understand the divine purpose behind the carnal covenant. Doing so, they made it an end in itself.

Only God could redeem his people. Therefore, "God himself"—the Messiah—was to come among men "in mighty power" and, in due course, be "oppressed and afflicted." (Mosiah 13:34-35; see also 15:1.) In support of his own testimony, Abinadi quoted Isaiah's prophetic summary of the Redeemer's birth, earthly ministry, suffering, and atoning sacrifice.

Chapters 14-16 of Mosiah constitute Abinadi's commentary on Isaiah's prophecy of the promised Messiah (Isaiah 53), the main points of which are:

1. The witness of the prophets concerning the Lord's Servant (the Messiah) had been ignored.

2. The Servant would grow up in God's presence, but in the midst of a spiritually impoverished people.

3. The Servant would be considered as of no worth.

4. The Servant's grief for the blindness and sins of those who despised and rejected him would be God-imposed.

5. Seemingly cursed by God, the Servant would endure the punishment that was rightly due mankind.

6. The Servant's atoning wounds would heal the human family, which had strayed from God.

7. Denied legal protection and justice, the Servant would be mocked and scourged and would go silently to his death like a lamb to the slaughter.

8. What constitutes the Servant's posterity? Who can identify it?

9. Innocent of any crime or deceit, the Servant would be buried in a rich man's tomb.

10. Through his sacrificial death, the Servant would create immortality, claim his spiritual posterity, share the riches of heaven with the righteous, and reign with the Gods.

Nowhere else in all scripture is the mission of the Son of God summarized more completely or with more beauty, simplicity, and power.

Parenthetically, it should be noted that although most biblical scholars reject the prophet Isaiah's authorship of chapter 53 and assign chapters 40 to 56 to an anonymous scribe (known as "deutero-Isaiah"), chapter 54 was quoted by the risen Christ with the comment "Great are the words of Isaiah." (3 Ne. 23:1.) There is but *one* Isaiah. Little wonder that his magnificent prophecy concerning the Messiah's then-future mission was chosen by Abinadi as his primary text.

God Himself Will Come To Earth

The central message of Abinadi to King Noah was essentially the same message an angel of the Lord was to deliver to King Benjamin over twenty years later: "God himself" — "the Lord Omnipotent" — was to come to earth as the Redeemer of mankind. (See Mosiah 3:5; 15:1.) That message would eventually unite three groups: Alma's church, King Limhi's people, and the combined Nephite-Mulekite nation under King Mosiah II.

The doctrine of a divine redeemer had been taught by all of the ancient prophets, beginning with Adam. (See Moses 5:6-12.) It figured prominently in the contents of the plates of brass. (See 1 Ne. 19:10-13.) It fills the pages of the Book of Mormon. Although the Redeemer was known to the Nephite prophets by different titles (God of Jacob, Holy One of Israel, Great Creator, Lamb of God, Messiah, Christ, and so on), in every instance, they were referring to one and the same person. Noah and his priests were either unaware of, or had rejected, the doctrine of a redeeming God; otherwise they would not have seized upon Abinadi's testimony as justification for his execution. (See Mosiah 7:27-28; 17:8.)

Abinadi's teachings in Mosiah 15:1-5 have been cited as an argument for trinitarianism in the Book of Mormon. However, Joseph Smith did not recognize any such doctrine therein. Just eleven days before his death he said: "I have always declared God to be a distinct personage, Jesus Christ a separate and distinct personage from God the Father, and that the Holy Ghost was a distinct personage and a Spirit."[5] The fact that tritheism was what Joseph Smith, its translator, taught, suggests that tritheism is what the Book of Mormon ("the most correct of any book on earth"[6]) teaches as well. There is no "evolutionary development" in the Book of Mormon, nor in Joseph Smith's subsequent teachings, on the nature of the Godhead.

Father, Son, and Holy Ghost constitute the *one* God. (2 Ne. 31:21; Alma 11:44; D&C 20:28.) This "one God" is not a triune god—three in one—but three individual personages bound together by the common bonds of light, truth, and eternal priesthood. Indeed, in the ultimate sense, the "one God" is the sum of *all* the Gods that were, are, and ever will be. In the abstract, the "one God" may be defined as all of the attributes and powers of the Father, Son, and Holy Spirit.

Abinadi, like Isaiah, was concerned with the redemptive mission of "God himself"—that individual deity who embodied the natures of both the Father and the Son—Jesus Christ. Just as a child has a legal right to the surname of its parent, so did the Only Begotten— who was "conceived by the power of God" in spirit and in flesh— have a legal right to the divine name *Father.* (See Mosiah 15:3; Ether 3:14; John 10:36.) Literally possessing his Father's name and powers, the Son was worthy and able to act as the Father's divine surrogate. To this end, he became the Only Begotten Son in the flesh when he was conceived by Mary, a mortal woman.

Begotten of an immortal Father and a mortal mother, Jesus possessed *two natures* (one divine, one human) and, therefore, *two wills* (that of the Father, and that of the Son). He could manifest either nature "at will." The Son, by definition, is one who does not possess the fulness of the power and glory of the Father. (See D&C 93:14-17.) As Son, Jesus was less than, and subject to, his Father. (See John 14:28.) As his flesh was to be subject to his spirit, so was the Son to be subject to the Father. The atonement required the subjection and sacrifice of the fleshly will of the "Son" to the spiritual will of the "Father". This same sacrifice is required of us all; humanity must yield to divinity. The *Son* willed to let the cup pass; the *Father* willed that it should be drunk to its dregs. Abinadi described Jesus' submission as "the will of the Son being swallowed up in the will of the Father." (Mosiah 15:7; see also Luke 22:42; 3 Ne. 11:11.) In a sense, it was not the Son *as* Son, but the Father *in* the Son who atoned. That is, Jesus not only did the will of his Father *in heaven*, but the will of the Father *in himself*. The Father and the Son—being "one God"—came to earth in the person of Jesus of Nazareth. "God himself"—in perfect unity—atoned for the sins of the world.

Abinadi's description of the ministry, rejection, sufferings, trial, and crucifixion of Jesus (Mosiah 15:5-7) is a virtual paraphrase of Isaiah's own prophecy. It is also similar to the words of the angel who was to appear to King Benjamin over twenty years later. (See Mosiah 3:5-10.) When these prophecies are added to those of Nephi (1 Ne. 11:3-33) and Zenock, Neum, and Zenos (1 Ne. 19:8-13), it is obvious that the ancient scriptures from which our present Old Testament was derived were replete with plain and precious teachings concerning the coming of the Redeemer. It is little wonder that Jews and Christians alike err in their attempts to interpret the Bible.

The Atonement

Abinadi stressed the indispensable role of the Redeemer, and, by implication, the inadequacy of the law of Moses, in declaring another Book of Mormon doctrine: the hopelessly lost state of humanity as a result of the fall. "All mankind must have perished"—both physically and spiritually—were it not for the Redeemer. (See 1 Ne. 10:6; 2 Ne. 9:6-9; Mosiah 15:19; 16:4, 6; Alma 34:9; 42:6.)[7]

The atonement was made necessary by the absolute truth that God is inescapably a God of justice. (See Alma 42:13, 22.) Were this not the case, the atonement would have been unnecessary; Jesus' plea would have been granted: he could have let "the cup" pass. Judaism assumes that God, being God, can simply forgive people at will; a spiritual Savior or mediator between God and his children is unnecessary. This is a major reason why Christ is rejected by the Jews. From their standpoint, where salvation is concerned, Jesus Christ is an irrelevance.

However, Isaiah and Abinadi knew better. Said Isaiah: "He was wounded for our transgressions, he was bruised for our iniquities. . . . The Lord hath laid on him the iniquities of us all. . . . For the transgressions of my people was he stricken. . . . Thou shalt make his soul an offering for sin. . . . [He] made intercession for the trangressors." (Mosiah 14:5-12.) And Abinadi echoed Isaiah: "Thus God breaketh the bands of death, . . . standing betwixt them and justice; . . . taken upon himself their iniquity and their transgressions, having redeemed them, and satisfied the demands of justice." (Mosiah 15:8-9.) Plainly, the atonement testifies to the justice, as well as the mercy, of God.

Responding to Isaiah's question, "Who shall declare [reveal] his generation," Abinadi asked Noah's court: "Now what say ye? And who shall be his seed?" (Mosiah 15:10.) Answering his own rhetorical question, Abinadi identified the posterity of Christ as the "heirs of the kingdom of God" — the faithful prophets, and those who believed their testimonies and looked to the Redeemer for salvation. In all scripture, only King Benjamin's people — having obtained a remission of their sins — are explicitly spoken of as "the children of Christ, his sons, and his daughters." (Mosiah 5:7.)[8] They exemplified what is meant by "the seed of Christ." It is not enough to be a child of God; all mankind are *children* of God by virtue of spirit birth. But only those who enter into a valid covenant with Christ and are born again through the complete ordinance of baptism become his sons and daughters. (See Mosiah 27:25; 3 Ne. 9:17; Ether 3:14 ; Moro. 7:48; D&C 25:1.) Consequently, although Christ atoned for the sins of *all* mankind, his sacrifice is efficacious only for those who come unto him with a broken heart and a contrite spirit. (See 2 Ne. 2:7; 9:21.)

Over and over again, the inspiration of the Book of Mormon bursts forth as themes large and small weave themselves into a sacred scriptural tapestry. Recall that in Mosiah 12:20-24 a priest had asked Abinadi the meaning of Isaiah 52:7-10. Having expounded the messianic prophecy in Isaiah 53, Abinadi then identified "him that bringeth good tidings." He explained that he is not one man, but many. He is the composite "Elias" of all ages who prepares the way for the Lord's coming. He is the prophets who were, who are, and who will yet be. He is a peacemaker, bringing the message of reconciliation between God and His children. Therefore, he is every soul, every missionary, every prince of peace who bears witness to the nations of *the* Prince of Peace. The combined message of glad tidings published from the beginning of time will culminate in the coming of "the founder of peace, yea, even the Lord, who has redeemed his people; yea, him who has granted salvation unto his people." (Mosiah 15:18.)

Abinadi looked down the corridors of time and prophesied: "The time shall come that the salvation of the Lord shall be declared to every nation, kindred, tongue, and people." (Mosiah 15:28; see D&C 133:37.) An angel of the Lord was to utter the same prophecy to King Benjamin some two decades later. (See Mosiah 3:20.) The gospel message must "sweep the earth as with a flood" (Moses 7:62) before the climactic judgments of God bring this present world order to an end.

Abinadi returned to Isaiah's prophecy, as quoted by the unidentified priest of king Noah. (See Mosiah 12:21-24.) Having explained the meaning of Isaiah 52:7, he quoted verses 8 through 10 as follows: "Yea, Lord, thy watchmen shall lift up their voice; with the voice together shall they sing; for they shall see eye to eye, when the Lord shall bring again Zion. Break forth into joy, sing together, ye waste places of Jerusalem; for the Lord hath comforted his people, he hath redeemed Jerusalem. The Lord hath made bare his holy arm in the eyes of all the nations; and all the ends of the earth shall see the salvation of our God." (Mosiah 15:29-31.)

This passage was also quoted by the risen Christ to the assembled multitude in Bountiful. (See 3 Ne. 16:18-20.) It concerns the consummation of God's work prior to Christ's millennial reign. The Zion of Joseph in America will first be redeemed, unity will prevail therein, and the Lord's servants will "see eye to eye." Jerusalem will likewise be delivered from her oppressors by the power of God, and all the world will behold the glorious coming of the Lord.

The Resurrection

Humanity's "last enemy" — physical death (the grave), and spiritual death (hell) — can be vanquished only by "God himself." Christ alone could rob the grave of its "victory" and death of its "sting." (Mosiah 16:7-8.)[9] Hence Jesus' words to the distraught Martha: "*I* am the resurrection, and the life." (John 11:25.) "The Son," said Abinadi, "reigneth, and hath power over the dead; therefore, he bringeth to pass the resurrection of the dead." (Mosiah 15:20.)

The Father had commanded Jesus to lay down his life and then take it up again. (See John 10:17-18.) But God gives no commandment without providing a way for its fulfillment; Jesus was provided with that way. He acquired the keys and powers of immortality, of dominion over death, when he was conceived by Mary as the Only Begotten of the Father in the flesh.

However, Jesus could not break the bands of death until he, himself, was bound by them. Therefore, he became "subject even unto death" so that he might conquer death. Having conquered that last enemy for himself,[10] the Redeemer was prepared to break the bands of death for all others. While the atonement conquers spiritual death on conditions of repentance, the resurrection conquers physical death unconditionally as an act of pure grace. This is because we are punished for our own sins — not for Adam's transgression, which imposed physical death on the human race.

The universal resurrection is divided into a first resurrection (of the just, or unto life), and a second resurrection (of the unjust, or unto damnation). (See John 5:29; D&C 76:15-17.) According to modern revelation, the first resurrection includes both the celestial and terrestrial kingdoms. The second resurrection includes the telestial kingdom and the kingdom without glory (a realm of darkness — the final habitation of sons of perdition). The first resurrection began with Christ and spans a period of more than three thousand years.

The second resurrection occurs after Christ's millennial reign at the "end of the earth." (See D&C 38:5; 76:16-17; 88:29-32, 97-101.)

Abinadi's statements on the resurrection should be interpreted in the light of the foregoing. He spoke of "*a* first resurrection" as being "*the* first resurrection" — meaning, first in *point of time*. (See Mosiah 15:21; Alma 40:16-18.) It was to begin with Jesus and to include three classes of the dead: (1) the righteous who had kept the commandments of God, (2) little children, and (3) those who had lived and died in ignorance of the plan of salvation. All three classes were to have "eternal life."

We must understand that each prophet speaks according to his own understanding; his knowlege of a given doctrine may be greater or less than that of another prophet living at another time. But whether prophet or layman, all learn the things of God line upon line. For example, Abinadi assumed — according to Alma's account — that those who died in ignorance of the gospel came forth with the Saints at the time of Jesus' resurrection. (Mosiah 15:24.) And it was Alma's understanding that all who lived up to the time of Christ, both righteous and wicked, were to come forth "before the resurrection of those who die and after the resurrection of Christ." (Alma 40:19.) Revelation to the Prophet Joseph Smith indicates that both of these views must be qualified. The only persons known to have been resurrected with Christ were the Saints — heirs of the celestial kingdom. (See 3 Ne. 23:9; Matt. 27:52.) The terrestrial dead, which includes those who die in ignorance of the gospel law, will not be resurrected until the *second* coming of Christ. (See D&C 45:54; 88:99.)[11]

As there is a first resurrection, so there is a second — both as to time and to quality. Woe to those who come forth in the second resurrection! Having knowingly and wilfully rebelled against God, they die in their sins. (See Mosiah 15:26; John 8:24.) That is, they carry with them the full measure of their guilt and reprobate natures into death. Moroni testified that such "cannot be saved in the kingdom of God." (Moro. 10:26.) Like Noah and his priests, they have "known the commandments of God, and would not keep them." (Mosiah 15:26.) In cutting themselves off from God, they cut themselves off from his atoning sacrifice. Justice, untempered by mercy, lays claim to them, and they suffer the wrath of God in hell before being resurrected into a telestial heaven. (See D&C 76:82-85.) Alma spoke of their spirits as being in "outer darkness," while the righteous were in "paradise." (See Alma 40:12-13.)

The Judgment

In the Book of Mormon, the resurrection is almost always mentioned in connection with the judgment. Abinadi said: "Even this mortal shall put on immortality, and this corruption shall put on incorruption, and shall be brought to stand before the bar of God, to be judged of him according to their works whether they be good or whether they be evil." (Mosiah 16:10.) Everyone must be resurrected because everyone must answer for the deeds done in the body. (See 1 Ne. 15:32; Alma 5:15.) As every nation, kindred, tongue, and people must *hear* the truth in the last days, so must every nation, kindred, tongue, and people *acknowlege* that truth at the last judgment. They "shall see eye to eye and shall confess before God that his judgments are just." (Mosiah 16:1; see also Alma 12:15.) They will find the truth, as it exists in God, to be irresistible. The ten thousand times ten thousand lies, excuses, rationalizations, and evasions that served the unrepentant so well in mortality will have been left behind in the grave. All masks will be stripped away. All will stand naked and defenseless before the all-seeing eye of the Almighty.

Speaking of those who refuse to repent, Alma said: "Our words will condemn us, yea, all our works will condemn us; we shall not be found spotless; and our thoughts will also condemn us; and in this awful state we shall not dare to look up to our God; and we would fain be glad if we could command the rocks and the mountains to fall upon us to hide us from his presence. But this cannot be; *we must come forth* and stand before him in his glory . . . and acknowledge to our everlasting shame that all his judgments are just." (Alma 12:14-15; italics added.) The hell of hells is to stand in the presence of God's holiness having a vivid awareness of one's own filthiness. (See Morm. 9:4-5.)

As before stated, the Book of Mormon reduces the issue of salvation to its most basic level. We must repent and acknowledge the sovereignty of God, or we must suffer the second death, wherein we are sealed to the devil and his fate. (See 1 Ne. 14:7.) This is true doctrine. However, in the wisdom of the Lord, a vital qualification of this doctrine was omitted from the Book of Mormon as we have it: prior to resurrection, one who dies in his sins may, upon soul-deep repentance, escape the second death and be saved![12]

Amulek noted: "After this day of life, which is given us to prepare for eternity, behold, if we do not improve our time while in this life, then cometh the night of darkness wherein there can be no labor performed." (Alma 34:33; see also 3 Ne. 27:33.) However, this statement is sometimes misinterpreted. The "night of darkness" is not death, but *resurrection*. (See Alma 41:5.) The "day of this life" or, in other words, the "probationary state" or "preparatory state" in which we prepare for eternity (Alma 42:10) includes the postmortal sojourn in the spirit world. Were this not the case, there would be no purpose in preaching the gospel to the dead or in performing ordinances for them. Unlike water baptism, faith and repentance cannot be "performed" vicariously; only the immortal spirit can exercise faith unto salvation. Eternal life depends upon eternal obedience.

Latter-day Saints commonly equate eternal life with exaltation in the celestial kingdom. However, the concept of multiple heavens or conditions of salvation, as revealed to Joseph Smith in Doctrine and Covenants 76, is not found in the Book of Mormon. Instead, it speaks in terms of absolutes: one is either saved in the presence of God or damned with the devil and his angels. (See Mosiah 16:10-11.) Consequently, in the Book of Mormon, eternal life is in opposition to eternal death. (See 1 Ne. 14:7; 2 Ne. 1:13; 2:27-29; 10:23.) However, eternal life is actually subdivided into "many mansions" or degrees of glory. This being the case, eternal life is tantamount to salvation as such. That is, every soul resurrected into any state of immortal glory enjoys a degree of eternal life. (See D&C 29:26-29; 88:21-24.) A *fullness* of eternal life *is* exaltation and the "continuation of the lives." (D&C 132:22.) Any state of salvation less than this is a state of damnation or death insofar as spirit progeny or dominion is concerned. (See D&C 131:1-4; 132:25.) However, the issue for Abinadi was not exaltation per se, but *salvation*.[13]

Those resurrected persons of whom Abinadi speaks in Mosiah 16:2-5 are never redeemed from their fallen state. "They were commanded to repent," said Abinadi, "and yet *they would not repent.*" (Mosiah 16:12; italics added.) They remain carnal and everlastingly "filthy still." (See 2 Ne. 9:16; Alma 34:35; D&C 88:32-35.) Cain is representative of that class of souls. Like Lucifer, they are absolute enemies of God and all that he represents. The devil has "all power" over them; they suffer the fullness of the second death. (See 2 Ne. 1:22.) To put the fear of God into them, Abinadi implied that Noah and his priests were prime candidates for such a fate.

Abinadi ended his defense as he had begun it: by testifying that the law of Moses was but "a shadow of those things which are to come," and by admonishing Noah's priests to teach "that redemption cometh through Christ the Lord, who is the very Eternal Father." (Mosiah 16:14-15.)

Nephi pointed out: "When a man speaketh by the power of the Holy Ghost the power of the Holy Ghost carrieth it *unto* the hearts of the children of men. But behold, there are many that harden their hearts against the Holy Spirit, that it hath no place in them." (2 Ne. 33:1-2; italics added.) King Noah and his priests verified his words. The Holy Spirit had carried the inspired words of Abinadi *unto* their hearts, but it could not carry those words *into* their hearts. Agency makes truth resistable. The Prophet Joseph Smith observed: "Men who have no principle of righteousness in themselves, and whose hearts are full of iniquity, and have no desire for the principles of truth, do not understand the word of truth when they hear it. The devil taketh away the word of truth out of their hearts, because there is no desire for righteousness in them."[14]

Death of Abinadi

Like many a prophet before him, and many after him, Abinadi sealed his testimony with his very life. Filled with rage, Noah ordered his immediate execution. However, Noah seems to have been dissuaded from that course by the pleadings of one of his young priests, Alma. Returned to prison, Abinadi languished for three days while Noah and his council searched for a justifiable reason for killing him.

Obviously, no such reason existed; otherwise such a search would have been unnecessary. But they finally "found" a charge they felt they could live with: Abinadi, like Jesus, was guilty of blasphemy in saying that "God himself should come down among the children of men." (Mosiah 17:8.) Pride and self-righteousness carried the day. The law, as they interpreted it and lived it, was all-sufficient; a Redeemer was not needed.

Offered his life if he would retract all that he had said—especially about the sins of Noah and his people—Abinadi pointed out that he could not deny his words because they were true, and because they had been spoken under the influence of the Spirit of Truth. Indeed, Abinadi had knowingly sacrificed his life so that they *could* be spoken under that influence. The prophet prepared to seal his testimony with his blood, saying: "If ye slay me ye will shed innocent blood, and this shall also stand as a testimony against you at the last day." (Mosiah 17:10, 20.)

Momentarily frightened by the threat of God's judgments, the king thought to release Abinadi, but his destructive pride won out when his priests shouted, "He has reviled the king." (Mosiah 17:12.) Abinadi's death by burning[15] foretold a similar fate for a number of Lamanite converts at the hands of the descendants of Noah's priests, the Amulonites. (See Alma 25:4-12.) King Noah also died by fire—as Abinadi foretold—at the hands of some of his own people. (See Mosiah 12:3; 19:20.)

Alma

Of the apparently twenty-five priests comprising King Noah's council, Alma, a descendant of Nephi, was the sole defender and the only known convert of the martyred Abinadi.[16] Cast out, he was obliged to flee for his life. While in hiding "for many days," he wrote "all the words which Abinadi had spoken." (Mosiah 17:4.)[17] It was a period of the profoundest anguish and soul-searching as the young priest "repented of his sins and iniquities" and sought the Lord's forgiveness. It came. At the risk of his life, Alma then secretly went about teaching Abinadi's doctrines to "as many as would hear." (Mosiah 18:1, 3.)

Unable to remain in the city of Nephi, he eventually hid away in a wilderness area named for an earlier Nephite king, Mormon. There his converts came to hear the first principles of salvation: faith, repentance, and redemption through Christ. "After many days" — and undoubtedly by prearrangement — all the souls that Alma had won gathered to the waters of Mormon. Their desire was to be "the fold of God . . . to be called his people." They were willing to "bear one another's burdens . . . to mourn with those that mourn[ed] . . . and comfort those that [stood] in need of comfort . . . to stand as witnesses of God at all times and in all things, and in all places." (Mosiah 18:8-9.) They wanted to be numbered with "those of the first resurrection" — the resurrection of which Abinadi had spoken. In sum, they were prepared to be true followers of Christ. They were ready for baptism.

Baptism constituted the visible witness of their commitment and covenant with the Lord, and the means whereby they could receive "his Spirit more abundantly." The more abundant Spirit is the gift of the Holy Ghost, a gift that can be received only by covenant. Beginning with Helam, whom he joined in the ordinance, and "having authority from the Almighty God" (Mosiah 18:13),[18] Alma proceeded to baptize 204 men and women.[19] These souls constituted the nucleus of the *second* Nephite church — "the church of God, or the Church of Christ" — to be established by the Nephites up to that time. (Mosiah 18:17.)[20] It was, in fact, a *restored* church. Alma had received "power and authority from God"[21] to establish the church in his day, and he was acknowledged by the Nephites as its founder and first presiding high priest. (Mosiah 23:16; 29:47; Alma 5:3; 3 Ne. 5:12.) Thus the first *specific* Book of Mormon reference to a church as an *organized* body of believers in Christ is in connection with events in the land of Nephi about 145 B.C.

Alma ordained one priest to every fifty members of the church. (Mosiah 18:18.) While these priests may have assisted in the ritual requirements — "the performances and ordinances" (2 Ne. 25:30) — of the Mosaic law, they were primarily engaged in instructing the people about the kingdom of God, being commanded to teach nothing except the things that Alma taught or that could be found in the writings of the holy prophets. (See Mosiah 18:19; 25:21.) They had been redeemed; their lives were to reflect that fact. Unity was to be the watchword in all things: "They should look forward with one eye, having one faith and one baptism, having their hearts knit together in unity and in love one towards another." (Mosiah 18:21.) Priests and people alike were to labor for their own material needs in a spirit of mutual caring—the burdens of the needy were to be lifted by the people of their own free will.

In effect, Alma sought to create a Zion society, and he was successful in doing so: "They did walk uprightly before God, imparting to one another both temporally and spiritually according to their needs and their wants." (Mosiah 18:29; see also D&C 51:3.) In this and other instances, the Book of Mormon is designed to prepare the hearts and minds of the Latter-day Saints for the institution of the law of consecration and stewardship—the only law upon which Zion can be founded. (See D&C 105:3-5.) (In this regard, the failure of the Saints in the Prophet Joseph's day to live that law is a major reason for the indictment of the Church in Doctrine and Covenants 84:54-59.)

In spirit and substance, the conversion of Alma's people is very similar to the great conversion that later occurred among King Benjamin's people. These two events prepared the way for the future establishment of Alma's church among the people of the prophet-king, Mosiah, in the land of Zarahemla, and for many significant things that were to occur thereafter. Upon his arrival in Zarahemla in 121 B.C., Alma was authorized by King Mosiah to form branches of the church throughout all the land of Zarahemla and "to ordain priests and teachers over every church." (Mosiah 25:19-22.)[22]

Conclusion

Marvelous are the ways of the Lord! He raised up Isaiah to bear testimony of the redemptive mission of Jesus Christ. He raised up Abinadi to confirm and seal that testimony upon a microcosm of apostate Israel. He raised up Alma to carry Abinadi's message to a small colony of believers who constituted the nucleus of a restored church of Christ. Thereafter, branches were established throughout all the Nephite lands, and missionaries were successful, for the first time in history, in bringing salvation to literally thousands of Lamanites. In turn, Lamanite prophets were raised up to Nephites and Lamanites alike. Thus, when the risen Redeemer appeared, he was greeted by worthy descendants from every branch of Lehi's family! And it all began when the lone Abinadi testified of the Redeemer before a corrupt council of priests and touched the heart and mind of one of them.

NOTES

1. See Omni 1:27-30. The account of this colony of Nephites in their ancient land of Nephi is found in Mosiah 7-22. Zeniff reigned for about thirty-five years (c. 195-160 B.C.).

2. Before leaving Zarahemla, Zeniff very likely had been ordained a high priest of the Melchizedek order.

3. Zeniff undoubtedly restored the temple originally built by Nephi in the sixth century B.C. (2 Ne. 5:16.) King Noah seems to have remodeled this same temple on a grand scale, making it far more elaborate and costly than it previously had been. (Mosiah 11:10.) Like Herod the Great, who remodeled the second temple (that of Zerubbabel; see Ezra 3), Noah's project was doubtless more a matter of personal vanity than genuine piety.

4. Zeniff's group left Zarahemla many years before King Benjamin delivered his discourse on Christ in 124 B.C. (Omni 1:27-30.) The extent to which Zeniff and his people understood the relationship of the law of Moses to Christ is conjectural. In any event, Noah and his priests seem to have been totally ignorant of that relationship, being steeped in idolatry and immorality. (Mosiah 11:6; 12:27-32; 13:28.) Hence the need for the prophet Abinadi to declare essentially the same message to Noah and, more especially, to Alma that Benjamin delivered to his people.

5. Joseph Smith, *Teachings of the Prophet Joseph Smith*, selected by Joseph Fielding Smith (Salt Lake City: Deseret BookCompany, 1938), p. 370; see also D&C 130:22.

6. *Teachings of the Prophet Joseph Smith*, p. 194.

7. See writer's article herein, "The Great Conversion," which discusses the fallen state of the human family and the meaning of the statement "The natural man is an enemy to God."

8. See the writer's article "The Great Conversion" herein.

9. The Apostle Paul also spoke with the tongue — or in the language — of the angels. (See 2 Ne. 32:2-3.) That is why he, too, used the same moving expressions in testifying of the risen Lord. (See also Hosea 13:14.) Critics claim that Abinadi's reference to the grave's victory and death's sting is an anachronism. They do not realize that the language of scripture is the universal language of the Holy Spirit. It has been "spoken" by servants of God from eternity so as to bind all inspired scripture into one harmonious body of truth. Indeed, certain words and phrases constitute deliberate links in a revelatory chain. These links, when followed, lead to a deeper, more accurate understanding of a given doctrine or principle.

10. See 1 Cor. 15:26; *Teachings of the Prophet Joseph Smith* p. 297.

11. Elder Joseph Fielding Smith wrote: "It is evident Alma's understanding of the extent of the resurrection at the time the Savior came forth was limited, therefore he stated only his opinion." (Joseph Fielding Smith, *Answers to Gospel Questions*, 5 vols., compiled by Joseph Fielding Smith, Jr. (Salt Lake City: Deseret Book Company, 1957-66), 1:36.

12. While such are "saved," they have forfeited the opportunity to be saved, much less exalted, in the celestial kingdom. They are heirs only of the telestial kingdom. Procrastination is the thief of exaltation.

13. Doctrine and Covenants 76:72 consigns those who "died without law," or in other words those who died "in their ignorance," to the terrestrial kingdom. According to Abinadi, they have eternal life.

14. *Teachings of the Prophet Joseph Smith*, p. 96.

15. Under the law of Moses, the condemned could suffer death by stoning, burning, or hanging.

16. Although the actual number is not given, it is implied by the fact that Noah's priests later captured and bigamously married twenty-four Lamanite women. (See Mosiah 20:1-5; 23:33.)

17. There is no textual evidence Alma ever conversed privately with Abinadi, or that he was ordained to the Melchizedek priesthood by him. However, Abinadi's initial testimony may have been heard by Alma and served to prepare him for the prophet's final witness two years later.

18. The source of Alma's authority is not given. He may have been ordained by Abinadi, by an angel, or by some unknown person. His authority to establish the church seems independent of any earlier ordination to the priesthood.

19. The joint baptism of Alma and Helam is without precedent in all

scripture. Alma must have felt impressed to share in the first baptism and thereby set the example for all who were to follow. There is no other account of Alma's being baptized. The baptisms performed by Alma are the first recorded in the Book of Mormon.

20. I believe that the phrase "after their transgression" refers to the apostasy in the time of Mosiah I, which led to the destruction of the first Nephite nation (Jarom 1:10; Omni 1:12), rather than that of King Noah and his supporters as described in Zeniff's record (Mosiah 9-22). In any case, had there been a functioning church of Christ in the land of Zarahemla, there would have been no need for Alma to organize a second church, nor for Mosiah to grant Alma permission to set up branches throughout that land. In addressing the Nephites in Zarahemla, Alma said: "We were brought into this land, and here we *began* to establish *the* church of God throughout this land *also.*" (Alma 5:5; italics added.) Though it had many branches, at any given time there was but one authorized church of God. (Mosiah 25:22.)

21. Lacking such authority, King Limhi made no attempt to organize a church or to perform baptisms. (Mosiah 21:33-34.)

22. The priesthood callings cited in the Book of Mormon are teacher, priest, elder, high priest, and, in effect, presiding high priest. Prophets are frequently mentioned. The gift of seership is also cited in connection with Joseph Smith (2 Ne. 3:6-14) and Mosiah II (Mosiah 8:13-17; 28:16).

20

BONDAGE AND DELIVERANCE
(Mosiah 7-8, 19-24)

MONTE S. NYMAN

These chapters from the book of Mosiah constitute a historical section of the Book of Mormon where readers frequently become confused. An understanding of Mosiah 7-8, 19-24 is difficult because the chapters do not follow a chronological sequence. Reading them in chronological order will help the reader follow the story. This chapter will cover the following points: (1) a brief discussion of Zeniff's colony as it fell into Lamanite bondage; (2) the discovery of Limhi and his people by Ammon and a group of men from Zarahemla; (3) a discussion of the principles behind bondage and deliverance; (4) an account of the deliverance of Limhi's people; and (5) an account of the deliverance of Alma's people.

There is a central theme that runs throughout all of these chapters. The theme is bondage. It had been prophesied by the prophet Abinadi, first conditionally (Mosiah 11:20-21) and then unconditionally (Mosiah 12:2), that the Nephites living in the land of Lehi-Nephi would be brought into bondage under the Lamanites. These chapters show much of the fulfillment of this prophecy.

Monte S. Nyman is professor of ancient scripture and associate dean of religious education at Brigham Young University.

Zeniff's Colony in Bondage

Alma responded to the message of Abinadi, and through his efforts several hundred of the Nephites were baptized at the waters of Mormon. After Alma and his converts had fled the land of Nephi (Mosiah 18), the Nephite king, Noah, searched in vain for them and then experienced a division and contention among the remainder of his people. Gideon, an enemy of King Noah, threatened to slay him. After an encounter, the king fled to a nearby tower and was pursued by Gideon. However, the king saw an approaching Lamanite army and used that as an excuse to persuade Gideon to spare his life. The king then commanded his people to flee from the Lamanites, and he led the exodus. They were overtaken by the Lamanites when again the king showed his cowardliness by commanding the men to leave their women and children and flee for their lives. Many refused to do so and caused their fair daughters to plead for the group's lives, resulting in their being in bondage to the Lamanites. They agreed to deliver up King Noah to the Lamanites, to deliver half of all their property and their precious things, and thus they would pay tribute to the Lamanite king each year. (Mosiah 19:1-15.) It will be seen in other sections of the Book of Mormon that the prophecy was also fulfilled at various times with every other group of the Nephites who lived in the Lamanite lands at the time of Abinadi's prophecy. (Alma's people: Mosiah 23:25–24:15; the descendants of Amulon: Alma 25:1-12.)

Limhi, son of Noah and a just man, was appointed by the people to succeed his father as leader of the Nephites who were in bondage. This appointment came following Gideon's secret excursion into the wilderness to find King Noah. He found, however, a body of men returning who had turned against the king and were determined to return to the aid of their wives and children whom they had deserted. King Noah had commanded them not to return, resulting in his being put to death by fire, further fulfilling Abinadi's prophecy. (Mosiah 12:3; 17:15-19.) The priests of Noah were also about to be put to death, but they fled. Under Limhi as king, in this condition of bondage, the Nephites lived peacefully for two years. (Mosiah 19:16-29.)

Following the abduction of twenty-four of the Lamanite daughters by the wicked priests of Noah, the Lamanites came to battle against the Nephites. In the ensuing conflict, the king of the Lamanites was wounded and left for dead. After dressing the king's wounds, the Nephites, thanks to Gideon, determined that it had been the priests of Noah who had captured the Lamanite daughters and convinced the king of this. The king in turn convinced his Lamanite people that the Nephites had not stolen their daughters, so the Lamanites returned in peace to their own lands. (Mosiah 20.)

As the Lamanites further persecuted the Nephites in bondage, also fulfilling another part of Abinadi's prophecy (Mosiah 12:5), the Nephites rose up in rebellion but were beaten down. Many were slain. The cries of the many widows in the land inspired a second and a third futile attempt. (Mosiah 21:1-12.) These attempts humbled the entire group. The group cried "mightily to God; yea, even all the day long did they cry unto their God that he would deliver them out of their afflictions." (Mosiah 21:13-14.) However, the Lord was slow to hear their cry because of their iniquities. He did "soften the hearts of the Lamanites" in that they "began to ease their burdens; yet the Lord did not see fit to deliver them out of bondage . . . [but] they began to prosper by degrees." (Mosiah 21:15-16.)

It seems obvious that the Nephites' prospering by degrees would be in preparation for their future deliverance. They were not at that time ready for the trek required for their escape. Because of the wars there was "a great number of women, more than there was of men; therefore king Limhi commanded that every man should impart to the support of the widows and their children, that they might not perish with hunger." (Mosiah 21:17.) In other words, the Nephites needed to be taught a "welfare system" before they were able to be delivered.

As the Nephites began to prosper, Ammon, a man sent by King Mosiah from Zarahemla, was taken by King Limhi's guards and cast into prison. The chronology now goes back to chapter 7.

The Discovery of Limhi's People

With permission of King Mosiah, Ammon had led a group of sixteen strong men from the land of Zarahemla in search of the people of Zeniff, who had previously departed. (Omni 1:27-30.) After wandering for forty days, they met King Limhi and his guards. After being imprisoned for two days, Ammon and his brethren were brought before the king, and each party's identity was made known. Limhi rejoiced to learn about the people of Zarahemla, and Ammon was thankful to have found the people for whom he had been searching. (Mosiah 7:1-16.)

King Limhi looked upon Ammon and his brethren as an answer to their prayers for deliverance. He called his people together and informed them of Ammon's arrival, suggesting that their time of deliverance was near, for which they should rejoice and trust in the Lord. In a great speech delivered at this time, Limhi gave them and us many principles to learn about bondage and deliverance.

Following King Limhi's address, he invited Ammon to speak to his people and then dismissed the multitude. He then conversed privately with Ammon about the plates that forty-three of his men had found when searching for the land of Zarahemla. Although this discussion fits here chronologically, it will be reserved for the conclusion of this chapter.

The Principles of Bondage and Deliverance

In Limhi's speech, he identified three reasons why the people of Zeniff had fallen into bondage to the Lamanites. The first was that Zeniff, their king, was overzealous to inherit the land of his fathers, "therefore being deceived by the cunning and craftiness of king Laman." (Mosiah 7:21.) To be overzealous means to go beyond what is necessary. A proper balance between lethargic and overzealous could be compared to Alma's admonition to Shiblon about teaching: "Use boldness, but not overbearance." (Alma 38:12.) Either extreme, idleness or fanaticism, subjects a person or people to those who seek power and dominion.

The second cause of bondage listed by King Limhi was transgression. (Mosiah 7:25.) As Joseph Smith taught: "The moment we revolt at anything which comes from God, the devil takes power."[1] Sin dulls the spiritual and mental senses, thus making captivity easier.

Limhi's third cause of bondage was the Nephites' slaying of the prophet Abinadi because he had taught them the truth about God. (Mosiah 7:26-28.) One of the signs of apostasy is a loss of knowledge of God. This is attested to by the Zoramites (Alma 31:15) and could be seen in the religions of Joseph Smith's day (JS–H 1:25-26). Joseph Smith taught: "It is the first principle of the Gospel to know for a certainty the Character of God, and to know that we may converse with him as one man converses with another."[2] Without this communication with God, people are led into the bondage of the philosphies of the world. Through these philosophies, they symbolically slay the prophets, as Nephi said: "The very God of Israel do men trample under their feet; I say, trample under their feet but I would speak in other words — they set him at naught, and hearken not to the voice of his counsels." (1 Ne. 19:7.)

While other things may lead into bondage, these three causes outlined by King Limhi are typical reasons for any time period.

King Limhi also identified for his subjects three results of bondage. These three results were apparently all drawn from their scriptures, the plates of brass, since he was quoting the Lord. Abbreviated, the results are:

1. The people do not prosper, and their activities are stumbling blocks. (Mosiah 7:29.)

2. If the Lord's people sow filthiness, they will reap chaff; the effect is poison. (Mosiah 7:30.)

3. If the Lord's people sow filthiness, they will reap the east wind and destruction. (Mosiah 7:31.)

The last result needs a little explanation. In Palestine, from which the plates of brass came, the east wind brings in the hot temperatures from the desert, resulting in drought and famine. In contrast, the winds from the west bring in the rains from the Mediterranean Sea, resulting in good crops.

These words of the Lord were applied by Limhi to his people. (Mosiah 7:32.) They could likewise be applied to our day; a close observation of our society would undoubtedly reveal that such things are happening to individuals and to large groups.

Upon learning that Ammon had come from the land of Zarahemla, Limhi rejoiced and recognized the hand of the Lord in Ammon's being there. (Mosiah 7:14, 18.) He admonished his people to trust in the God of Abraham, Isaac, and Jacob, and he reminded them of previous deliverances God had performed. (Mosiah 7:19.) Later, either Mormon or Alma was more definite in declaring that "none could deliver them but the Lord their God, yea, even the God of Abraham and Isaac and of Jacob." (Mosiah 23:23.) After stating the causes and the results, Limhi gave three steps they could follow to be delivered from bondage. These steps were (Mosiah 7:33):

1. Turn to the Lord with full purpose of heart.
2. Trust in the Lord.
3. Serve the Lord with diligence of mind.

After they had done these things, the Lord, according to his own will, would deliver them. This formula is exemplified in the experiences of Limhi and Alma's people. In crying mightily to God, they had turned to him. However, they were apparently lacking in sufficient purpose of heart and in their trust in God. Also, they did not seem to be serving the Lord diligently enough, or perhaps they had not served him long enough, for the Lord was slow to answer their prayers because of their iniquities, as previously mentioned. (Compare D&C 101:6-7.) Furthermore, the Lord was preparing them for his own due time of deliverance, which was fast approaching.

The Deliverance of Limhi's People

King Limhi considered Ammon and his brethren to be a godsend. The king had previously sent a small group of men to find the land of Zarahemla, but they had failed in their attempt and become lost. However, they had found the remains of a people and records left from a previous civilization. Limhi rejoiced further in learning of King Mosiah's ability to translate those records once they had arrived at Zarahemla. (Mosiah 21:23-31.)

Since the arrival of Ammon and his brethren, King Limhi and his people had covenanted to serve God and keep his commandments, wanting to be baptized like Alma's people. But none in the land had authority to perform this ordinance, and Ammon considered himself unworthy. (Mosiah 21:32-34.) Ammon's reasons for feeling unworthy are not specified. Perhaps Mosiah chose Ammon and his companions after Mosiah had been teased to the point of weariness. (Mosiah 7:1.) Though they felt themselves unworthy to baptize, they were indeed capable of leading the people back to Zarahemla. The Lord uses people according to their abilities. Another possibility is that Ammon was worthy but the Lord inspired him to decline lest the captive Nephites lose their incentive to return following their baptism. While these possibilities cannot be positively ascertained, it is evident that Limhi's people were now turning to the Lord with full purpose of heart and putting their trust in him. Their trust is exemplified in their devoted study to obtain deliverance from bondage. (Mosiah 21:36.) The Lord has instructed us to study things out in our minds as part of the revelatory process. (D&C 9:8.) Once more Gideon, the stalwart defender of righteousness, entered the picture. His study resulted in a plan to pay a tribute of wine to the Lamanites and to escape through a secret pass while they were drunken. The plan worked, and the people of Limhi were delivered from bondage by the hand of the Lord. (Mosiah 22.)

The Deliverance of Alma's People

In an editorial comment, Mormon discussed the bondage into which Alma's people fell after they had prospered in the land of Helam. Mormon depicted their patience and faith, and he declared that those who trusted in the Lord would be lifted up at the last day, as had happened to Alma's people. He taught that Alma's people had fallen into bondage, a fulfillment of Abinadi's prophecy to another part of the people, and that none could deliver them but the God of Abraham, Isaac, and Jacob. (Mosiah 23:21-24.) Although Mormon's declaration is similar to King Limhi's formula, we will follow Limhi's formula to show how and when Alma's people were delivered.

As Alma's people were tilling their lands in Helam, an army of the Lamanites approached them. In fright they fled to Alma, who admonished them to remember the Lord that they might be delivered. This fits Limhi's instructions to trust in the Lord. The people cried unto the Lord that he would soften the hearts of the Lamanites, in harmony with Limhi's formula for turning to the Lord with full purpose of heart. That Alma's people did this is evident, as the Lord softened the hearts of the Lamanites. (Mosiah 23:25-29.)

266

The Lamanite army had pursued King Limhi's people but had become lost. They then found the priests of Noah who had stolen the Lamanite daughters. (See Mosiah 20.) These priests were accompanying the Lamanite army, and Amulon, their leader, was placed in command of the Lamanite people in the land of Helam, under the jurisdiction of the Lamanite king. Thus he was also over Alma's people (Mosiah 23:30-39), bringing about their bondage.

The priests of Amulon were commissioned to teach the Nephite language to the Lamanites. (Mosiah 24:1-7.) One cannot help but wonder if the Lord's hand was not involved in this assignment. While they did not teach the law of Moses or the words of Abinadi (they were not qualified anyway), did they not prepare the way for the future Nephite missionaries, the sons of Mosiah, to proclaim the gospel among the Lamanites? Such seems very plausible to me.

Since Amulon knew that Alma had once been a priest of Noah and had believed the words of Abinadi, he began to put burdens on Alma's people and placed taskmasters over them. As Alma had previously admonished his people to do, they turned to God and began to pray mightily. Amulon commanded them to stop such praying and placed guards over them to prevent it. Alma's people then secretly poured out their hearts to the Lord and put their trust in him. The Lord rewarded that trust with an acknowledgment of their covenant to him (they had served him as they had covenanted) and his covenant to deliver them from their bondage. He promised to ease their burdens insomuch that they could not feel them. This would be a witness to them and to others that the Lord does visit his people in their afflictions. The Lord fulfilled his promise and strengthened them to bear their burdens. They submitted cheerfully and with patience to the will of the Lord. (Mosiah 24:9-15.)

The people had served the Lord as well as turned to him in trust. But the due time of the Lord had not yet come. Perhaps the Lord was blessing his people physically in preparation for an extremely strenuous twelve-day flight to the land of Zarahemla. The terrain was undoubtedly rough, and the Lamanites would have been in hot pursuit. Without this physical blessing, would Alma's people, including their women and children, have been able to endure as well as to outrun the Lamanite army? Probably not without the Lord's help. The Lord caused a deep sleep to come upon the Lamanites and all their taskmasters, evidently to give the Nephites a head start. He further promised to halt the Lamanites in the valley where the Nephites had pitched camp. (Mosiah 24:16-23.) The people had complied with the Lord's formula, and the Lord delivered his people.

Conclusion

One of the purposes of the Book of Mormon is to warn us of situations and experiences among the Nephites so that we may not have to experience similar situations and experiences. This is certainly a reason we should understand the Lord's promises to the Nephites about bondage. There are many kinds of bondage in addition to physical bondage. A person may be bound by intellectual pursuits, financial extensions, social customs, or many other things. The formula is the same for deliverance from these conditions, and there is none but the God of Abraham, Isaac, and Jacob who can and will deliver his people. (Mosiah 7:19; 23:23.) Yet more important is the admonition to prevent such bondage in our lives. The Book of Mormon suggests some ways we can do that.

Ammon informed King Limhi that Mosiah, the king of Zarahemla, was a prophet, seer, and revelator who could know of things that are past and also of things that are to come. He also had an instrument that enabled him to translate records in an unknown language, such as the records found by the expedition of forty-three men. These we know were the Jaredite records. Like the Nephites, the Jaredites had fallen into bondage, and certainly their unabridged account would have given inspired directions for the Nephites to follow to avoid a similar fate. In modern times we also have a prophet, seer, and revelator, Joseph Smith, who translated the Book of Mormon from an unknown language, reformed Egyptian, with a Urim and Thummim. (Morm. 9:32-33.) We can learn from the Book of Mormon just as the Nephites learned from the Jaredite records. Our challenge is to study and follow the teachings of the Book of Mormon that will keep us from bondage or deliver us from bondage in our day.

NOTES

1. *Teachings of the Prophet Joseph Smith*, selected by Joseph Fielding Smith (Salt Lake City: Deseret Book Company, 1938), p. 181.

2. Ibid., p. 345.

21

The Kingdom of God and the Kingdoms of Men
(Mosiah 25-29)

Kay P. Edwards

The 25th through the 29th chapters of Mosiah are rich with both historical and spiritual insight. The threads of divergent stories about the simultaneous events in the lives of the people of Zarahemla and the two splinter groups from Zeniff's people in Nephi-Lehi — those under King Limhi, and the people led by Alma — come together again as these three groups were united at Zarahemla about 120 B.C.

In Mosiah 25 is recorded an event whose significance can easily be overlooked. It is tucked into the record of the excitement of reunion and homecoming as the people with King Limhi and those with Alma were rejoined with King Mosiah's people at Zarahemla. This event is the coming together of the records of three great migrations from the Old World — the Nephites and Mulekites from the land of Jerusalem, and the Jaredites from the land of Babel. King Limhi had brought with him the gold plates on which the Jaredites had kept the record of their people.

The Book of Mormon account of God's power in preserving these three peoples, and in bringing them across the seemingly impassable ocean that separated the New World from the Old, provides readers today with information about the Lord's people that might otherwise

Kay P. Edwards is professor of family sciences at Brigham Young University.

be unknown. That the records of these three great migrations would come into the possession of a single lineage of record keepers and be preserved until the time of Joseph Smith is a marvel.

Alma Preaches Repentance and Faith

Around time of this great reunion, all the people gathered at Zarahemla to join forces. They called themselves Nephites and were numbered together under the leadership of King Mosiah. (Mosiah 25:13.) Mosiah, who was a prophet, seer, and revelator (Mosiah 8:13-16) as well as king to the Nephites, recognized Alma's spiritual strength. He asked him to speak to the people (Mosiah 25:14-15) and then ordained him high priest and gave him responsibility for administering the church (Mosiah 25:19; 26:7).

Alma used this first opportunity to teach the newly combined Nephites about faith and repentance. In our day, these two principles have again been underscored as the first principles of the same gospel Alma preached. (See A of F 4.)

Repentance denotes a change of mind—a turning away from the sin to which men and women are naturally inclined, and a turning of the heart and will toward God. The repentant person renounces sin and engages in righteous service to God and man. To gain the forgiveness sought through repentance, as Elder Bruce R. McConkie has said, "a person must have a conviction of guilt, a godly sorrow for sin, and a contrite spirit. He must desire to be relieved of the burden of sin, have a fixed determination to forsake his evil ways, be willing to confess his sins, and forgive those who have trespassed against him; he must accept the cleansing power of the blood of Christ as such is offered through the waters of baptism and the conferral of the Holy Ghost."[1]

Faith is not knowledge, but a hope for things that are not seen, but that are true. (Alma 32:21; Heb. 11:1.) As noted in the *Lectures on Faith*, it "is the moving cause of all action . . . in all intelligent beings."[2] To produce salvation, faith must be centered in Jesus Christ. However, Jesus Christ had not yet been born on the earth when Alma exhorted these Nephite people to exercise faith in Him. They were being asked to have hope for the fulfillment of His promise that He would come to earth and that when He did, the way would be made available for them to receive eternal life. Alma's preaching to the people was effective, and when he had finished, King Limhi and all his people expressed a desire to take the next step and be baptized into the church of God. (Mosiah 25:17.)

The Church of God

The church of God is "the organized body of believers who have taken upon themselves the name of Jesus Christ by baptism and confirmation. To be the true church it must be the Lord's church, and must have his laws, his name, and be governed by him through representatives whom he has appointed."[3]

As Elder McConkie has said, this church of God is "a kingdom; it is God's kingdom, the kingdom of God on earth, and as such is designed to prepare men for an inheritance in the kingdom of God in heaven, which is the celestial kingdom. Our Lord Jesus Christ is the Eternal King; his representative on earth is the President of the church."[4]

The church of God is *one* church. (Mosiah 25:22.) However, because its members are numerous and live in geographically diverse places, it is necessary to establish local congregations for the teaching and governance of the people. Each of the Nephite congregations was referred to as a church in Mosiah 25:21, but they were all being taught the word of God from the mouth of Alma, through the priests and teachers appointed to administer the affairs of the church in their area. Just as today, when the members of the Church of Jesus Christ are taught the word of God from the mouth of the prophet through the bishop and stake president appointed to administer the affairs of the church in their area, these people received a single message. In their case, as is true today, nothing was preached except repentance and faith in God. And in their case, as is true today, "the Lord did pour out his Spirit upon them, and they were blessed, and prospered in the land." (Mosiah 25:24.)

The church offices referred to in Mosiah 25:19-21 are those of priest and teacher. This may create some confusion for members of The Church of Jesus Christ of Latter-day Saints because of their familiarity with Church organization today. However, if we had the same task Mormon had, which was to distill centuries of detailed record-keeping down to the essentials necessary to teach his message, we also would have looked for terms that could meaningfully encompass all the disparate titles with which we are familiar. We too would probably have chosen "priests and teachers." However, additional reasons exist for such a designation.

Elder McConkie has noted: "In general terms a *priest* is a minister." A true priest must hold the priesthood, but the "designation . . . has no reference to any particular office in the priesthood."[5] President Joseph Fielding Smith has said that it was common practice among the Nephites to "consecrate priests and teachers, give them administrative responsibility, and send them out to preach, teach, and baptize. . . . These priests and teachers held the Melchizedek Priesthood."[6]

"Book of Mormon prophets gave the title *priest* to officers in [our] dispensation known as *high priests*," according to Elder McConkie. "They were priests of the Melchizedek Priesthood." The Aaronic Priesthood did not exist among the Nephites when Alma lived, "there being none of the lineage empowered in pre-meridian times to hold that priesthood," so there was no need to differentiate between priests of the lesser or greater priesthood.[7]

Anyone appointed to serve as an instructor in the organizations of the church, men or women, are called *teachers*. However, as Elder McConkie has said, "Among the Nephites, brethren holding the Melchizedek Priesthood were selected, consecrated *teachers*, and given teaching and administrative powers and responsibilities. . . . They had jurisdiction over the churches [congregations] and, along with the priests, were 'to preach and to teach the word of God.' (Alma 23:4.) They had power to baptize. (Alma 15:13.)"[8] These men were not receiving an office in the lesser priesthood for there was no Aaronic Priesthood among the Nephites from the time they left Jerusalem until Christ's ministry among them.[9]

Unbelievers and Evildoers

When King Mosiah granted power to Alma to establish the church among the Nephites and gave him authority over it, he was separating church government from state government. Until this time, King Mosiah had held both secular and ecclesiastical authority over the Nephites and Mulekites. Many of those who had been children at the time King Benjamin made his great address to the people had now grown to adulthood and were unbelievers. They refused Alma's teachings on repentance and faith and would not accept baptism into the church of God. Although the unbelievers were relatively few in number, they had a strong influence on many members of the church, causing them to commit sin. It became necessary for the church to reprove these erring members. When Alma appealed to King Mosiah for assistance in judging the unrepentant members, King Mosiah told him that this was a matter for church administration and not a matter of secular government. These people were guilty of violating God's law, not the laws of the land. In his concern to resolve the matter appropriately, Alma "poured out his whole soul to God" in prayer. (Mosiah 26:14.) In response he received a revelation from God that provided the pattern for rendering judgment in the church:

> He that will not hear my voice, the same shall ye not receive into my church, for him I will not receive at the last day. Therefore I say unto you, Go; and whosoever transgresseth against me, him shall ye judge according to the sins which he has committed; and if he confess his sins before thee and me, and repenteth in the sincerity of his heart, him shall ye forgive, and I will forgive him also. Yea, and as often as my people repent will I forgive them their trespasses against me. And ye shall also forgive one another your trespasses; for verily I say unto you, he that forgiveth not his neighbor's trespasses when he says that he repents, the same hath brought himself under condemnation. Now I say unto you, Go; and whosoever will not repent of his sins the same shall not be numbered among my people; and this shall be observed from this time forward. (Mosiah 26:28-32.)

In this dispensation, through the Prophet Joseph Smith, the Lord again outlined the law of his church and the rendering of judgments for the breaking of his laws. (D&C 42.) The actions to be taken by Church administrators in rectifying specific sins have been spelled out, while those committing sins involving a violation of the laws of the land are dealt with by civil authorities according to the laws of the land.

A Miraculous Conversion

To be born again is a prerequisite to receiving the gift of eternal life. (John 3:3.) This rebirth is spiritual; it is patterned after the natural birth that brings us into this world. Spiritual birth, as Elder McConkie has put it, "is to die as pertaining to worldliness and carnality and to become a new creature by the power of the Spirit. It is to begin a new life, a life in which we bridle our passions and control our appetites, a life of righteousness, a spiritual life."[10] This second birth requires two baptisms — the baptism of water as a visible sign, and the baptism of the Spirit, which only the reborn child of God can know and testify of.[11] Elder McConkie said this:

> Those who are born again not only live a new life, but they also have a new father. Their new life is one of righteousness, and their new father is God. They become the sons of God; or, more particularly, they become the sons and daughters of Jesus Christ. They bear, ever thereafter, the name of their new parent; that is, they take upon themselves the name of Christ and become Christians, not only in word but in very deed. They become by adoption the seed or offspring of Christ, the children in his family, the members of his household, which is the perfect household of perfect faith. . . . They also become joint-heirs with him of the fulness of the glory of the Father, thus becoming by adoption the sons of God the Father.[12]

Although it is necessary for each man and woman to experience this rebirth if he or she is to inherit eternal life,[13] it is not necessary, nor is it likely, that each will have a conversion experience as dramatic as that recorded about Alma and the sons of Mosiah. As with Paul on the road to Damascus (Acts 9:3-9), the unique combination of gross wickedness in their sins against the church and the prayers of the church members coupled with the faithful prayers of a father, Alma (and most likely also of Mosiah), was justification for miraculous intervention. An important lesson can be learned from this account.

When a man or woman enters the waters of baptism, he or she manifests a willingness to help bear the burdens of other church members and to mourn with and comfort them as they have need. (Mosiah 18:8-9.) Mosiah 27:14 provides an example of this shared responsibility in action. The prayers of the members of the church for a person have power and meaning and are heard by our Father. More important, the prayers of a faithful parent for a wayward child will be heard and honored by the Lord. He will not violate the agency of the child to choose between good and evil, but He will provide opportunity for repentance and welcome the former sinner back into the fold.

Elder McConkie has said: "Those who are born of the Spirit thereby . . . overcome the world. They die as to carnality and evil; they live as to spirituality and godliness. And it all comes to pass because they have faith in Christ."[14] The subsequent lives of these five young men bear testimony to the totality of the rebirth they experienced. Henceforth, their whole souls were focused on preaching and teaching the gospel of Jesus Christ and strengthening his church.

For the sons of Mosiah, this new commitment was made manifest in their efforts to undo the grievous harm they had done to the church, and in their decision to give up their worldly status as potential heirs of the king to undertake a mission to the Lamanites. (Mosiah 28:1-9.) This decision became the catalyst for a radical change in the secular government of the Nephites.

Government and Its Forms

Government structure can take a variety of forms. Three are pertinent to King Mosiah's discourse on government in Mosiah 29.

A *theocracy* is "government of a state by immediate divine guidance or by officials regarded as divinely guided."[15] This is the prototype government instituted by God, with Jesus Christ at the head and his chosen servants exercising authority under his direction in administering the affairs of his kingdom on earth. Other governmental forms can best be evaluated relative to this prototype.

An *autocracy* is "government in which one person possesses

unlimited power."[16] In this type of government, the concentration of power and authority is retained in one individual, just as in a theocracy, but that individual is no longer divine, but a mortal man or woman. Kingship is an example of this kind of government.

A *democracy* is "government by the people; government in which the supreme power is vested in the people and exercised by them directly or indirectly through a system of representation usually involving periodically held free elections."[17] King Mosiah's instructions to his people that they choose "by the voice of this people, judges" (Mosiah 29:25) introduced a form of democracy into Nephite society.

When Ammon, Aaron, Omner, and Himni (Mosiah 27:34) refused the crown (Mosiah 28:10) and chose to go back to the land of Nephi-Lehi to teach the Lamanites the gospel, they bypassed the traditional assumption that kingship in Nephite society was held by the previous king's eldest son. King Mosiah realized that the appointment of anyone other than his eldest son to the position of king would open the door to contention among his people. It was also possible that the son to whom the kingdom rightly belonged by the laws of primogeniture[18] might change his mind at some future time and the resulting conflict could lead the people into wars and contentions that would destroy not only their society but also the souls of many of the Nephite people. (Mosiah 29:6-9.)

With this in mind, King Mosiah proposed to his people the idea that their welfare might be better assured by making a major change in their government structure — from kingship to a form of democracy. He suggested that this new governmental system be implemented by placing judges chosen by the people at the head of the government. (Mosiah 29:10-11.) He recognized that it is better that men and women be judged by God because He is always just, and that the judgments of human beings are frequently not just. (Mosiah 29:12.) But he felt that choosing wise leaders to serve in these positions was better protection for the people than to take a chance that an unjust king might be given power over them. (Mosiah 29:13-17.)

If the people could be assured that those who held the kingship would be just men, men who would establish and uphold the laws of God, and men who would judge the people according to the commandments of God, it would be desirable to retain the autocratic form of government. (Mosiah 29:13.) The prototype for a righteous king is provided in the Book of Mormon — King Benjamin. However, there was no assurance that those on whom the king's mantle fell would always be righteous. The gross wickedness of King Noah is also recorded in the Book of Mormon as an example of what happens when an unrighteous individual obtains power over the people. (Mosiah 29:18.)

The absolute power wielded by a king can be destructive even to a man who was initially righteous, as the stories of King Saul and King David amply substantiate. (1 Sam. 9-15; 2 Sam.; 1 Kgs. 1-2:11.) To rid the people of an unrighteous king would require much social unrest and even civil war, and to refuse to obey his unrighteous laws would lead to destruction. King Mosiah wanted to spare his people this possibility. (Mosiah 29:21-23.)

The Voice of the People (Judges)

In putting before the people his recommendation that they choose judges to rule over them after his death, King Mosiah was introducing the notion of democracy into Nephite society. His argument was that the voice of the people, as a whole, rarely desires things that are unrighteous or evil, even though some proportion of the people may have unrighteous desires. But he warned the Nephites that they would be destroyed by the judgments of God if the time ever came that the majority of the people chose iniquity over righteousness. (Mosiah 29:27.) He also proposed a system of review and judgment to exercise restraint over the judges and any propensity they might have not to judge according to the law. (Mosiah 29:28-29.)

A cursory reading of Mosiah 29 may raise questions about existing world governments. Confusion can easily arise among members of the worldwide Church of Jesus Christ of Latter-day Saints about their relationship to civil law and the alternative forms that government can take. Mosiah 29 is not a treatise about the superiority of democracy over kingship, but a discussion of fundamental principles of government that should be protected in any form of government.

While many nations are founded on just and righteous principles, there are some whose systems are different from those associated with God's kingdom and the gospel of Jesus Christ. What is the Saints' responsibility when their civil authority comes into conflict with the gospel and the authority of God? Elder Bruce R. McConkie pointed out that religion must be free from any earthly power and subject only to the powers of heaven if it is to have saving power.[19] Thus, governments that inhibit freedom of religion, freedom of worship, and the freedom to choose one's own course curtail and even prevent the choice-making that leads us to salvation.[20]

However, the 12th Article of Faith, enunciated by the Prophet Joseph Smith, states: "We believe in being subject to kings, presidents, rulers, and magistrates, in obeying, honoring, and sustaining the law."

Numerous illustrations in both the Old and New Testaments indicate that the Lord does not always require submission to evil secular power. However, New Testament guidelines give direction on how to function relative to secular authority. Long before the time of Jesus and Peter, divinely established theocracies had ceased to exist. Both Jesus and Peter were subject to secular powers that used religion for their own purposes, or looked upon it as a necessary evil, or viewed it as pious nonsense. Jesus was fully aware of the domination of Rome and the political subservience of the Jews when he said: "Render . . . unto Caesar the things which are Caesar's; and unto God the things that are God's." (Matt. 22:17-21.)

Peter's counsel to the Saints in his day was: "Submit yourselves to every ordinance of man for the Lord's sake; whether it be to the king, as supreme; or unto governors, as unto them that are sent by him for the punishment of evildoers, and for the praise of them that do well." Such a course, Peter said, "is the will of God." Hence these words of counsel: "Honour all men. Love the brotherhood. Fear God. Honour the king." (1 Pet. 2:13-17.)

Elder McConkie has pointed out:

> *Subjection to secular power does not constitute a divine approval of the system of government involved.* . . . Subjection to government is not an endorsement or approval of the governmental system involved. The Lord's counsel . . . is obedience and subjection. . . . Rebellion would bring civil penalties that well might preclude true worship itself. . . .

279

Paul is of one mind with his fellow apostle in counseling the saints "to be subject to principalities and powers, to obey magistrates, to be ready to every good work, to speak evil of no man, to be no brawlers, but gentle, shewing all meekness unto all men." (Titus 3:1-2.) . . . He exhorts that "supplications, prayers, intercession, and giving of thanks, be made for all men; for kings, and for all that are in authority." Why? "That we may lead a quiet and peaceable life in all godliness and honesty." *That is, so that we may be free to live our religion and work out our salvation.* "For this is good and acceptable in the sight of God our Saviour." (1 Timothy 2:1-3.)[21]

Elder McConkie suggested that Paul used the forced obedience to secular authority as a type for obedience to the higher ecclesiastical power held by the church.[22] Through compelled obedience to governments, temporal blessings are gained; should we not then give willing obedience to God from whom we gain eternal life?[23]

Elder James E. Talmage, in 1899, gave this counsel to the Saints for dealing with conflicts between religion and state:

It is the duty of the saints to submit themselves to the laws of their country. Nevertheless, they should use every proper method, as citizens or subjects of their several governments, to secure for themselves and for all men the boon of freedom in religious service. It is not required of them to suffer without protest imposition by lawless persecutors, or through the operation of unjust laws; but their protests should be offered in legal and proper order. The saints have practically demonstrated their acceptance of the doctrine that it is better to suffer evil than to do wrong by purely human opposition to unjust authority. And if by thus submitting themselves to the laws of the land, in the event of such laws being unjust and subversive of human freedom, the people be prevented from doing the work appointed them of God, they are not to be held accountable for the failure to act under the higher law.[24]

It is not the form secular government may take that is at issue. Obviously it has and can have many varieties of form, each effective in a given set of circumstances. The issue is the laws that are created and enforced by a particular form of government. For Church members around the world, the issue is how their actions will be circumscribed and judged under the law. Can they live the principles of the gospel and be free to work out their salvation? King Mosiah stated these three requirements of laws: that they have been handed down by the fathers, that they are correct, and that they have been given by the hand of the Lord. (Mosiah 29:25.) These principles provide the people in any society a standard for evaluating the laws of their secular government.

The Book of Mormon provides a unified set of principles to guide the actions of Church members worldwide, whatever the form of secular government under which they live. It clearly differentiates between our roles as citizens of the land and as believers in the restored gospel, and it amplifies the Savior's counsel to "render . . . unto Caesar the things which are Caesar's; and unto God the things that are God's." (Matt. 22:21.)

Notes

1. Bruce R. McConkie, *Mormon Doctrine*, 2nd ed. (Salt Lake City: Bookcraft, 1966), p. 630.

2. Joseph Smith, *Lectures on Faith*, 1:10.

3. Bible Dictionary, p. 645.

4. Bruce R. McConkie, *A New Witness for the Articles of Faith* (Salt Lake City: Deseret Book Company, 1985), p. 335.

5. McConkie, *Mormon Doctrine*, p. 598.

6. Joseph Fielding Smith, *Doctrines of Salvation*, 3 vols. (Salt Lake City: Bookcraft, 1956), 3:87.

7. McConkie, *Mormon Doctrine*, p. 599.

8. Ibid., p. 776.

9. Ibid.

10. McConkie, *A New Witness for the Articles of Faith*, p. 282.

11. Ibid., p. 283.

12. Ibid., p. 284.

13. For a fuller treatise of this concept, see Kay P. Edwards, "The Early

Judean Ministry," *Studies in Scripture, Vol. 5: The Gospels*, Kent P. Jackson and Robert L. Millet, eds. (Salt Lake City: Deseret Book Company, 1986), pp. 192-95.

14. McConkie, *A New Witness for the Articles of Faith*, p. 289.

15. *Webster's Seventh New Collegiate Dictionary* (Springfield, Mass.: G & C Merriam Co., 1970), p. 915.

16. Ibid., p. 59.

17. Ibid., p. 219.

18. The superior or exclusive right possessed by the eldest son, and particularly his right to succeed to the estate of his ancestor, in right of his seniority by birth, to the exclusion of younger sons. See *Black's Law Dictionary*, 5th ed. (St. Paul, Minn.: West Publishing Co., 1969), p. 1072.

19. McConkie, *A New Witness for the Articles of Faith*, p. 683.

20. Ibid.

21. Ibid., p. 687; italics added.

22. A type is an actual historical reality that points beyond itself to a greater and more powerful reality. See Robert L. Millet, "Lessons in the Wilderness," *Studies in Scripture, Vol. 3: The Old Testament—Genesis to 2 Samuel* (Sandy, Utah: Randall Book, 1985), pp. 197-98.

23. McConkie, *A New Witness for the Articles of Faith*, p. 688.

24. James E. Talmage, *The Articles of Faith* (Salt Lake City: The Church of Jesus Christ of Latter-day Saints, 1973), pp. 422-23.

22

Challenges to the Reign of the Judges
(Alma 1-4)

Mae Blanch

When King Mosiah's eldest son, Aaron, and his three brothers after him refused to accept the throne, Mosiah honored his sons' decision to spend their time in missionary labors rather than to govern the Nephites after their father's death. Faced with the necessity of providing for an orderly transfer of power, Mosiah turned to the Lord and was inspired to set up a new form of government called the reign of judges. Alma the Younger was elected by the people to be the first chief judge of the land. The first four chapters of Alma record the events that challenged this new form of government during Alma's reign.

The exact nature of this system is not given in the Book of Mormon, but there are enough allusions to it to allow some conclusions to be drawn about the kind of government it provided.[1] Perhaps its most important characteristic is that it was government founded on law, law instituted by King Mosiah under the inspiration of the Lord. (Alma 1:1.) By acknowledging the law, the people committed themselves to obey it and to accept the penalties set for disobedience. (Alma 1:14.) Evidently, Nephite law had its foundation in the Mosaic law since lying, stealing, robbing, and murder were forbidden, and the penalty for murder was death. (Alma 1:17-18.)

Mae Blanch is professor of English at Brigham Young University.

One aspect of this divinely inspired law was a guarantee of freedom of conscience. A person could be punished for lying, but no one could be punished for his or her beliefs, no matter how far from the truth they might be. (Alma 1:17.) Thus when the wicked who were opposed to the church and the true gospel that Alma preached began a campaign to win souls away from the truth, they presented their doctrine as their true beliefs, although in most cases they presented lies calculated to deceive the people and to bring these false teachers wealth and power. When the people were righteous, government under the reign of the judges was just and fair, allowing the people to live in peace and security. When some of them began to be wicked, the law could still control them. (Alma 1:32-33.) But when the majority of the people were wicked, then government itself became wicked. Elder George Q. Cannon noted this fact in connection with the government of the United States:

> While the people are pure, while they are upright, while they are willing to observe law, the best results must follow the establishment and maintenance of a government like this; but, on the other hand, if the people become corrupt, if they give way to passion, if they disregard law, if they trample upon constitutional obligations, then a republican form of government like ours becomes the worst tyranny upon the face of the earth. An autocracy is a government of one man, and if he be a tyrant, it is the tyranny of one man; but *the tyranny and irresponsibility of a mob is one of the most grievous despotisms which can exist upon the face of the earth.*[2]

During the first eight years of the reign of the judges, the majority of the people were righteous; therefore, Alma as chief judge was able to deal with the problems that arose and maintain the form of government Mosiah had instituted.

Nehor, the First Challenge to the New Government

During the first year of Alma's reign as chief judge, a man named Nehor began preaching false doctrine to the Nephites, and many of them believed him. (Alma 1:5.) He is described as "a man who was large, and was noted for his much strength." (Alma 1:2.) Perhaps because of his imposing stature or perhaps because the doctrine he taught was appealing, Nehor was successful enough in converting others that he began to establish a church. (Alma 1:6.) The doctrine that won the hearts of his followers was a subtle perversion of the truth. Nehor taught that all people would be saved, no matter what they did. There was no need to fear God; since the Lord had made all people and had also redeemed them, all would have eternal life. (Alma 1:4.) Such doctrine made sin not a matter for repentance, but, according to Nehor, a matter for rejoicing. (Alma 1:4.) Since the Nephites who listened to Nehor already knew that the Lord had indeed made all people and redeemed all people, that they would not be judged for their sins was an easy lie to accept. And since this part of Nehor's teaching suited them, they were willing to go along with his other pronouncement that priests and teachers ought to be supported by the people. Indeed, they gave him enough money that "he began to be lifted up in the pride of his heart, and to wear very costly apparel." (Alma 1:6.)

Nehor might well have continued his wicked proselyting since under the law no one could be condemned for preaching his or her beliefs, but he met one of the servants of God, Gideon. This was the same man who had opposed the wicked reign of King Noah. It was Gideon who chased King Noah to a high tower and would have killed him if a Lamanite army had not been discovered marching upon the Nephites. When Noah and his priests deserted their women and children in their flight into the wilderness to save themselves from the Lamanites, Gideon and his men went after them but did not find them. Later when Gideon was serving as King Limhi's captain, he saved his people from the Lamanites' vengeance when they were accused of kidnapping the daughters of the Lamanites. Gideon placed the blame where it belonged, on the wicked priests of King Noah. Finally, it was Gideon who conceived the plan of getting the Lamanite guards drunk so that Limhi and his people could escape their captivity and join their kindred in Zarahemla. Gideon was qualified to be a defender of the faith in the confrontation with Nehor. When Gideon challenged Nehor with "the words of God," the enraged Nehor smote Gideon with his sword until he killed the good old man. (Alma 1:7-9.) Nehor's rage can be understood when we consider what he would lose if Gideon succeeded in exposing his false teachings. He would lose his wealth and his popularity with his followers, which was the source of his power.

But Nehor had not reckoned on the response of the people who witnessed the murder of Gideon. They seized him and brought him to Alma for judgment. (Alma 1:10.) Although Nehor "pleaded for himself with much boldness " (v. 11), Alma condemned him for both the slaying of Gideon and his practice of priestcraft. Alma warned against this practice, saying that "were priestcraft to be enforced among this people it would prove their entire destruction" (v. 12).

How priestcraft would bring destruction upon the people is suggested by Nephi, who had also condemned priestcraft, saying that the Lord "commandeth that there shall be no priestcrafts; for, behold, priestcrafts are that men preach and set themselves up for a light unto the world, that they may get gain and praise of the world; but they seek not the welfare of Zion." (2 Ne. 26:29.) Nephi's use of the phrase "a light unto the world" recalls the use of this phrase in the scriptures to describe Christ, who is "the light of the world." We might say then that the practitioners of priestcraft set themselves up as rivals to the Lord, that they are guilty not only of lying, but also of a kind of blasphemy in attempting to usurp the power of God in establishing the terms of salvation for humanity. Elder Bruce R. McConkie said: "Priesthood and priestcraft are two opposites; one is of God, the other of the devil. . . . Apostasy is born of priestcrafts . . . for those who engage in them follow vain things, teach false doctrines, love riches, and aspire to personal honors."[3] The first chapter of Alma depicts the Nephite apostasy born of priestcraft.

After Nehor was executed for his crime, the priestcraft he had introduced continued to spread because of the wickedness of some of the people. (Alma 1:16.) Those who did not belong to the church of God began to persecute those who did for their righteousness, for their humility, for their lack of pride, and because they did not pay their priests and teachers. Such persecution had its effect. Although the church forbade its members to retaliate, to persecute those who did not belong to the church, or to fight among themselves, many ignored this law. They "began to be proud, and began to contend warmly with their adversaries, even unto blows; yea, they would smite one another with their fists." (Alma 1:22.) Consequently, many church members were excommunicated and many apostatized.

But as often happens when the righteous undergo trials, those who remained faithful, who "bore with patience the persecution" (Alma 1:25), who maintained equality between teacher of the gospel and learner, who cared for the poor and the sick among them, and who were not proud or given to the wearing of "costly apparel" — those faithful were blessed. They had peace despite the persecutions and, because of their steadfast obedience to God, "began to be exceedingly rich, having abundance of all things whatsoever they stood in need." (Alma 1:29.)

It is interesting that the righteous achieved this happy state even though their society was not without evil. Satan was active in their world as he is in ours, and the wicked were guilty of sorceries, idolatry, idleness, babblings, envyings, strife, wearing costly apparel, pride, persecuting, lying, thieving, robbing, whoredoms, murdering, and "all manner of wickedness." (Alma 1:32.) But because there was a righteous core of people, the laws against such wickedness were enforced and the guilty were punished. Therefore the wicked became "more still" and peace was maintained until the fifth year of the reign of the judges. (Alma 1:33.)

Amlici: A Different Kind of Challenge

At the beginning of the fifth year, another threat to the reign of the judges arose in the form of Amlici, a follower of Nehor. Since the wicked were subdued by the exercise of the just law that Mosiah had established and Alma executed, Amlici, who is described as "a very cunning man, yea, a wise man as to the wisdom of the world," found a way to circumvent the laws. He sought to change the form of government, to make himself king. As king, he could control the law as King Noah had in his reign. The people of the church of God were, therefore, alarmed at the possibility that Amlici might succeed in making himself king. (Alma 2:1-3.)

But once again the law protected them against evil. No change in government was possible without the vote of a majority of the people. Amlici could not become king unless the voice of the people gave consent. The righteous Nephites realized that if Amlici became king, he would destroy the church and deprive them of their freedom to worship God. Mormon recorded the concern and excitement over this issue: "The people assembled themselves together throughout all the land, every man according to his mind, whether it were for or against Amlici, in separate bodies, having much dispute and wonderful contentions one with another." (Alma 2:5.) Notice that although the government in power was opposed to Amlici's proposal, indeed, that it was fighting for its very life, it made no attempt to manipulate or contravene the law, but, rather, scrupulously observed it. The principle of observing and honoring law duly instituted by the people seems to be an earmark of those who would follow God. And rule by the majority, when the majority are righteous, can be trusted. In this instance, Amlici's plan to become king of the Nephites was indeed crushed by the voice of the people. They rejected him; he was lawfully defeated by a majority vote.

The resistance of the wicked to the rule of law is illustrated by Amlici's response to this rejection. He incited his followers to make him king and began a rebellion against the Nephites who remained loyal to the reign of the judges. His followers took the name of Amlicites to honor him and to distinguish themselves from the righteous Nephites. They followed the usual path of the rebellious: they cut themselves off from God's people and fought against them with all their power.

The civil war that ensued resulted in the extensive slaughter of both armies, but since the Nephites were fighting a just war, God strengthened them, and the Amlicites began to flee before them. Although war is always evil, some circumstances exist under which it is justified. Elder Bruce R. McConkie commented on this:

> Self-defense is as justifiable where war is concerned as where one man seeks the life of another, with the obvious conclusion that (from the standpoint of those called upon to engage in armed conflict) some wars are righteous and others are unrighteous. Righteous men are entitled, expected, and obligated to defend themselves; they must engage in battle

when there is no other way to preserve their rights and freedoms and to protect their families, homes, land, and the truths
of salvation which they have espoused.

In many wars, perhaps most, both sides are equally at fault
and neither is justified. But there have been and yet will be
wars in which the balances of eternal justice will show that
one side had the favor of Deity and the other did not.[4]

The Nephites had attempted to resolve the conflict with Amlici
and his followers through a peaceful vote, but the Amlicites refused
to accept the verdict of the people and began the war. Since the
Nephites had no choice but to defend themselves, "their rights and
freedoms, and to protect their families, homes, land, and the truths
of salvation which they [had] espoused," their war was indeed a
righteous war, and the Lord favored their cause.

But this did not mean that the Nephites escaped the sorrows and
desolation of war. Thousands of them died in battle, many of their
wives and children were slain, and even their flocks and herds and
fields of grain were destroyed. And when they defeated the Amlicites,
who fled before the Nephite armies, they were subjected to even
greater losses when the Amlicites joined forces with the Lamanites
and returned "as numerous almost, as it were, as the sands of the
sea" (Alma 2:27) to destroy them.

It must have seemed to the Nephites when their enemies returned
in such formidable strength that they had little chance of victory,
but they "prayed mightily" to the Lord (Alma 2:28), and their prayers
were answered. Exerting all their efforts, the Nephite armies fought
valiantly, and the Lamanites and Amlicites began to fall before them.
Their foes were "met on every hand, and slain and driven, until they
were scattered on the west, and on the north, until they had reached
the wilderness . . . which was infested by wild and ravenous beasts."
(Alma 2:37.) So many were slain on both sides of the conflict that
they could not be numbered. The Nephites buried their dead, but
the Lamanites (the Amlicites now numbered among them) fled, leaving their dead to the wild beasts and the vultures. However, the
Nephites cast the Lamanite dead into the river Sidon, and their bones
were washed out to the depths of the sea.

Being favored of the Lord did not mean that the Nephites had an easy victory. Even Alma, who slew Amlici with his sword, cried to the Lord in the midst of the battle to preserve his life so that he might preserve his people. (Alma 2:30.) Clearly, the Nephites had to do all they were capable of, and then the Lord did what they could not. He strengthened the weaker Nephite army so that they won the battle against far superior numbers; he strengthened Alma so that he could destroy the probably younger and stronger Amlici, the evil directing force of the whole conflict.

An interesting detail that Mormon recorded about the conflict is that the Amlicites marked their foreheads with red to distinguish themselves from the Nephites. (Alma 3:4.) This may have been in imitation of the Lamanites who had marked themselves for battle, and it had the practical purpose of distinguishing the Amlicites from the Nephites so that the Lamanites would not mistakenly kill their new allies. But Mormon pointed out that by so doing, the Amlicites were fulfilling the word of God, who had marked the Lamanites who openly rebelled against him, and also those Nephites who allied themselves with the Lamanites. The Lord had said to the Nephites, "I will set a mark upon him that fighteth against thee and thy seed." (Alma 3:16.) The fact that the Amlicites chose to mark themselves emphasizes that it is through the misuse of agency that evil-doers receive God's curse. They choose to be so marked by their rebellion against God. As Mormon says, "For every man receiveth wages of him whom he listeth to obey, and this according to the words of the spirit of prophecy; therefore let it be according to the truth." (Alma 3:27.)

The challenge of Amlici and his followers had been met and defeated during this tumultuous fifth year of the reign of the judges. Although the Nephite losses numbered in the tens of thousands, they were able to drive the Lamanites out of their land and begin the slow work of rebuilding their society in peace.

The sixth year of the reign of the judges brought peace, but because of the devastation of their land, the loss of their flocks and herds, and the death of loved ones, all of the Nephites "had cause to mourn; and they believed that it was the judgments of God sent upon them because of their wickedness and their abominations; therefore they were awakened to a remembrance of their duty." (Alma 4:3.) This spiritual awakening brought renewed efforts to establish the church of God more fully. Alma himself baptized many. Mormon records that in the seventh year of the reign of the judges, "there were about three thousand five hundred souls that united themselves to the church of God." (Alma 4:5.) Thus two years passed in righteousness, bringing peace and prosperity to the Nephites. But in the eighth year the cycle so frequently seen in Book of Mormon history began its downward course.

Over and over again in the account of the Nephites, we see that the people go through a period of wickedness, war, and destruction, followed by repentance and righteousness, which bring peace and prosperity, which in turn are followed by pride, apostasy, wickedness, war, and destruction. The test of prosperity is one that the Nephites, and many other of God's children, seem unable to meet. Wealth nearly always produces pride, which is the beginning of all other sins: the love of money and the vain things of this world, contentions among the members of the church as well as the nonmembers, envyings, strife, malice, persecution, and inequity of all kinds.

Interestingly enough, an early visible sign of this drift into inequity is what the Book of Mormon prophets refer to as the wearing of costly apparel. This trait, which is seen in the behavior of both men and women, is always associated with pride and wickedness. Jacob rebuked his people for this sin when he called them to repentance, clearly associating it with pride: "The hand of providence hath smiled upon you most pleasingly, that you have obtained many riches; and because some of you have obtained more abundantly than that of your brethren ye are lifted up in the pride of your hearts, and wear stiff necks and high heads because of the costliness of your apparel, and persecute your brethren because ye suppose that ye are better than they." (Jacob 2:13.) Nehor, he who introduced priestcraft to the Nephites, followed this same pattern: "He began to be lifted up in the pride of his heart, and to wear very costly apparel." (Alma 1:6.) In fact, Mormon distinguished between the wicked "wearing costly apparel" (Alma 1:32) and the people of the church of God who "did not wear costly apparel, yet they were neat and comely"

(Alma 1:27). Thus when the rebellion against God began in the eighth year of the reign of judges, "the people of the church began to wax proud, because of their exceeding riches, and their fine silks, and their fine-twined linen, and because of their many flocks and herds, and their gold and their silver, and all manner of precious things, which they had obtained by their industry; and in all these things were they lifted up in the pride of their eyes, for they began to wear very costly apparel." (Alma 4:6.)

An analysis of the attitudes that lead to and are involved with this habit indicates why it is associated with wickedness. First, it promotes idleness and vanity. One who spends many hours coveting, shopping, spending, and adorning oneself becomes increasingly self-absorbed and uninterested in anything requiring that attention to be diverted from self. Accumulation and adornment become the prime concern. This practice is also a way of displaying wealth in a prideful manner, a manifestation of what has been called the "conspicuous consumption" of the rich, which leads to despising the poor as some-how inferior, a separation of people into "us" and "those kind of people." And when money and possessions become the chief marks of distinction in society, then the pursuit of money becomes the only action worthwhile. And if this pursuit requires the sacrifice of honesty, integrity, compassion, and all the other virtues, then so be it, for the love of money is indeed the root of all evil. Thus the wearing of costly apparel involves the soul as much as the body.

The unrighteous pride of the people in the church increased "even to exceed the pride of those who did not belong to the church of God." (Alma 4:9.) Their iniquity served as a spur to the wickedness of the unbelievers until the whole society was well on its way to destruction. The suffering of the poor increased even though those few who had remained humble and faithful did their best to help those in need. Persecution of the believers was common; they en-dured "all manner of afflictions, for Christ's sake" (Alma 4:13), but still looked forward to his coming. Alma, who was not only chief judge but also the high priest of the church, looked on with sorrow as his people sank deeper into evil.

Undoubtedly he searched for a way to save them. He prayed to know what the Lord would have him do, and "the Spirit of the Lord did not fail him." (Alma 4:15.) Alma recognized that when people are wicked, even divinely inspired law will not control them. They must have a change of heart. To teach this message, he chose Nephihah, a wise man approved by the voice of the people, to replace him as chief judge. Nephihah was given power through the voice of the people to enact and enforce laws, according to the laws that already existed, to control the wicked and punish their crimes. But Alma took the action that was needed most. He left his office so that he might go directly to the people to "preach the word of God unto them, to stir them up in remembrance of their duty, and that he might pull down, by the word of God, all the pride and craftiness and all the contentions which were among his people, seeing no way that he might reclaim them save it were in bearing down in pure testimony against them." (Alma 4:19.) Thus at the beginning of the ninth year of the reign of judges, Alma met the greatest challenge yet encountered by his government—the increasing wickedness of his people—with "the testimony of the word, according to the spirit of revelation and prophecy." (Alma 4:20.) This is, without doubt, the only effective answer for the world's problems in any age.

Notes

1. An excellent discussion of the nature of government under the reign of the judges can be found in Richard L. Bushman's "The Book of Mormon and the American Revolution," *Brigham Young University Studies*, vol. 17, no. 1 (Autumn 1976), pp. 3-20.

2. George Q. Cannon in *Journal of Discourses*, 26 vols. (London: Latter-day Saints' Book Depot, 1854-86), 22:136; italics added.

3. Bruce R. McConkie, *Mormon Doctrine*, 2nd ed. (Salt Lake City: Book-craft, 1966), p. 593.

4. Ibid., p. 826.

23

Alma's "Pure Testimony"
(Alma 5-8)

Andrew C. Skinner

In the year 83 B.C. the Old World branch of the house of Israel (Judah) was living out the last few years of a tenuous autonomy in Palestine.[1] Both political and religious rule were held by one Alexander Jannaeus, who was a relative of the Maccabees. He was king and high priest. It is one of the fascinating twists of history that about this same time a New World branch of the house of Israel (the people of Nephi) also saw political and religious authority concentrated in the hands of one person, Alma the Younger. He was both chief judge and high priest.

But here the parallel ends, for while Jannaeus's Aaronic priestly office was, by this time, a hollow shell of titular significance only, Alma operated under the vital and divinely sanctioned power of the higher priesthood (Alma 4:20), having "charge concerning *all* the affairs of the church" (Mosiah 29:42; italics added). This office had been conferred on him by his father, Alma the Elder, in a manner similar to the pattern established by the ancient patriarchs from Adam on down. (Alma 5:3; D&C 107:40-41.) That Alma's administration of all the affairs of the Church (see Alma 6:1, for example) was a right associated with the keys of presidency and also in perfect harmony with the unchanging order of heaven is confirmed in a modern rev-

Andrew Skinner is an instructor of history at Metropolitan State College, Denver, Colorado.

elation on priesthood: "The Melchizedek Priesthood holds the right of presidency, and has power and authority over all the offices in the church in all ages of the world, to administer in spiritual things. The Presidency of the High Priesthood, after the order of Melchizedek, have a right to officiate in all the offices in the church." (D&C 107:8-9.)

There can be little doubt that Alma bore a tremendous, perhaps overwhelming, responsibility as both president of the church and chief judge of the Nephite nation. In the course of executing his duties, his burden was added upon as he saw, firsthand, the wickedness arising in the church; saw the great inequalities, class distinctions, and selfish activities that were and are contrary to the order of Zion and the will of God. (Moses 7:18.)

Like Enos of earlier days, Alma's great desire was for the welfare of his people, that they might return to the Lord. In order to devote himself completely to the goal of spiritually reclaiming the people of Nephi, Alma appointed another in his stead as chief judge and "confined himself wholly to the high priesthood of the holy order of God, to the testimony of the word," all of which came by the spirit of revelation and prophecy. (Alma 4:20.) As we learn, "this he did that he himself might go forth among his people, or among the people of Nephi, that he might preach the word of God unto them, to stir them up in remembrance of their duty, and that he might pull down, by the word of God, all the pride and craftiness and all the contentions which were among his people, seeing no way that he might reclaim them save it were in bearing down in pure testimony against them." (Alma 4:19.)

Elements of "Pure Testimony"

With the chief judgeship left securely in the hands of a wise man, Alma began to carry out his mission to "bear down in pure testimony" to the members of the church, first in the city of Zarahemla. Surely his witness, delivered to the congregation and quoted in the fifth chapter of the book of Alma, constitutes one of the most profound and prophetic sermons in the history of the Lord's people. From it we come to understand the elements and function of pure testimony.

Some might agree that pure testimony is declaration of unconditional truth, unadulterated and uncorrupted by worldly, extraneous, or superfluous matters. But Alma helps us to see that it is even more focused than that. The word *pure* derives from the Latin *purus*, which not only has the meaning of "clear, plain and absolute" (especially in law) but also "clean, cleansing and purifying."[2]

The doctrine of Christ is plain, clear, and absolute, and his mission cleansing or purifying in its effect. Hence, at the heart of all pure testimony is the Savior, his mission and atonement, his redeeming love, his invitation to come and partake of all good things, and the doctrine of repentance. Speaking specifically of the latter days, but applicable to all past generations, the Prophet Joseph Smith said: "The fundamental principles of our religion are the testimony of the Apostles and Prophets, concerning Jesus Christ, that He died, was buried, and rose again the third day, and ascended into heaven; and all other things which pertain to our religion are only appendages to it."[3]

In giving his discourse, Alma bore a powerful testimony of the Lord Jesus Christ—his promised advent, his role as redeemer and judge, and his love for all humanity. His testimony is both personal and authoritative. Early on, it refers to the words of two of the prophets Joseph Smith must have had in mind (Alma the Elder and Abinadi). This testimony was delivered not only in Zarahemla, but in Gideon, Melek, and Ammonihah as well. It "breathes a spirit of love, tolerance, and charity for all,"[4] which is to be expected since those are qualities most fully and deeply associated with the Savior. This testimony was commanded by God to be delivered (Alma 5:44) and was received by revelation (Alma 4:20; 5:46-47), thus corroborating the words of John: "The testimony of Jesus is the spirit of prophecy" (Rev. 19:10). Alma's testimony illuminates the practical application of the doctrines associated with rebirth and provides a kind of spiritual checklist (an inventory of behavioral objectives, if you will) by which the people then and we today can measure our spiritual stature. In addition, Alma's testimony demonstrates his consummate skill as a teacher.

Spiritual Rebirth

To the church at Zarahemla, Alma began his pure testimony by speaking in some detail about change—mighty change—the kind of change that is known as spiritual rebirth. Others preceding Alma taught that change is central to the doctrine of Christ's atonement. Such change moves us from a natural, earthly, and estranged status to one of reconciliation with divine law. "For the natural man is an enemy to God, and has been from the fall of Adam, and will be, forever and ever, unless he yields to the enticings of the Holy Spirit, and putteth off the natural man and becometh a saint through the atonement of Christ the Lord." (Mosiah 3:19.) Thus, to become a saint in the truest sense, one must change from an inferior natural state to a superior spiritual state; one must be spiritually born of God.

It is significant that the Lord has stated unequivocally in every dispensation that his children must be born again (Moses 6:59; John 3:5; D&C 5:16) to be fit for his kingdom. As part of his pure testimony, Alma also reiterated (to his brethren in Gideon) this commandment: "Ye must repent, and be born again, for the Spirit saith if ye are not born again ye cannot inherit the kingdom of heaven." (Alma 7:14.) But more than simply parrot a requirement for exaltation, Alma illuminated the doctrine and set forth the process by which all may experience a mighty change and become spiritually born of God.

A careful reading of Alma's testimony teaches that dynamic and complete spiritual rebirth is contingent upon several conditions. One of these is baptism.

The process of spiritual rebirth actually begins *prior* to baptism. Jesus taught that one cannot even *see* the kingdom without being born again. (John 3:3.) When people gain a testimony that will lead them to baptism, they have started on the path of redemption and spiritual rebirth. In other words, they have *seen* the kingdom of God. When those persons are baptized, they become candidates to be born of the Spirit and enter the kingdom. (John 3:5.) The Prophet Joseph Smith said, "Being born again, comes by the Spirit of God through ordinances."[5]

It is clear that Alma's discourse was addressed to those who were already members of the church through baptism. No doubt there were some in the congregation who were not yet baptized. But these were invited to participate in that basic ordinance so they could receive every blessing of the Lord's chosen, including complete spiritual rebirth. Alma said: "I speak by way of command unto you that belong to the church; and unto those who do not belong to the church I speak by way of invitation, saying: Come and be baptized unto repentance, that ye also may be partakers of the fruit of the tree of life." (Alma 5:62.) Also, in recounting the example of others gone before who experienced a mighty change and thus were born again (the very fathers of the present audience, in fact), Alma explained that they were first baptized by his father, Alma the Elder, who established a church in the land of Mormon. (Alma 5:3-12.)

Alma's pure testimony further intimates that simply being baptized does not guarantee immediate spiritual rebirth. On this matter Elder Bruce R. McConkie stated: "Mere compliance with the formality of the ordinance of baptism does not mean that a person has been born again. No one can be born again without baptism but the immersion in water and the laying on of hands to confer the Holy Ghost do not of themselves guarantee that a person has been or will be born again. The new birth takes place only for those who actually enjoy the gift or companionship of the Holy Ghost, only for those who are fully converted, who have given themselves without restraint to the Lord."[6]

Obviously, the people of the Church of Zarahemla had not given themselves without restraint to the Lord immediately after baptism. Otherwise Alma would not have needed to try so mightily to "stir them up in remembrance of their duty" (Alma 4:19) by recounting the example of their fathers who had been baptized but were only afterward "awakened . . . out of a deep sleep . . . unto God," their souls having been illuminated by the light of the everlasting word (Alma 5:7). That which had changed the earlier saints was knowledge as well as their putting into operation the great activating principle of faith. Alma, no doubt, had the same hope for his current audience.

This brings us to another requisite for spiritual rebirth—faith. Powerful faith and spiritual rebirth are twins. The latter cannot exist without the former. There is no rebirth, no mighty change of heart or exalting spiritual activity without faith. The Prophet Joseph Smith taught: "If men were duly to consider themselves, and turn their thoughts and reflections to the operations of their own minds, they would readily discover that it is faith, and faith only, which is the moving cause of all action in them."[7]

Alma the Younger taught this principle using the example of his own father: "According to his faith there was a mighty change wrought in his heart. Behold I say unto you that this is all true. And behold, he preached the word unto your fathers, and a mighty change was also wrought in their hearts, and they humbled themselves and put their trust in the true and living God. And behold, they were faithful until the end; therefore they were saved." (Alma 5:12-13.)

Through faith Alma the Elder experienced a mighty change that carried over to those he, in turn, taught. Viewed in this context, the summary statement of Joseph Smith from the first Lecture on Faith takes on even deeper significance: "Faith . . . is the first governing principle which has power, dominion, and authority over all things; by it they exist, by it they are upheld, by it they are changed, or by it they remain, agreeable to the will of God. Without it there is no power, and without power there could be no creation nor existence."[8]

Though it is perhaps self-evident, one feels compelled to point out that it is *not* simple "faith" to which both Almas, the Prophet Joseph, and others refer. Rather, it is to faith in the Lord Jesus Christ, in his example, his mission, and his concern for us individually. We see that Alma well understood this when he asked: "Do ye exercise faith in the redemption of him who created you? Do you look forward with an eye of faith, and view this mortal body raised in immortality, and this corruption raised in incorruption . . . ?" (Alma 5:15.)

Alma here implied too that we must have an understanding of the being in whom we are placing our faith. Likewise, Joseph Smith said that in order for any rational and intelligent being to exercise faith in God unto life and salvation (which can come only by spiritual rebirth), that being must have a *correct* idea of God's character, perfections, and attributes. Such an understanding can come only through the continued acquisition of true knowledge, which the Holy Ghost bestows. People may read books about Jesus, or may memorize dates and places about him. But unless the Holy Ghost is the real teacher, such information has a hollow ring. Though the New Testament quotes the testimony of Paul as "no man can say Jesus is Lord but by the Holy Ghost," Joseph Smith clarified and reinforced the importance of the role of the Holy Ghost. He said that 1 Corinthians 12:3 should read: "No man can *know* that Jesus is the Lord, but by the Holy Ghost."[9]

Faith, then, is a necessary part of being born again. It must be found in a person's life both before and after baptism. The Holy Ghost may testify of the Savior and bring a change of heart before baptism, but the exercise of faith in that witness leads one to the saving ordinances. The continuing operation of faith in one's life after baptism then brings about the mighty change and complete spiritual rebirth.

A Spiritual Checklist

After having discussed faith as the activating principle that leads to a mighty change of heart, and after having given examples of it, Alma the Younger went on to discuss other requisites for spiritual rebirth. He spoke pointedly to the brethren before him at Zarahemla, asking them several profound questions that would serve well as a standard and a guide directing any and all to that newness of life available as a result of the rejuvenating and redeeming power of the Savior. These questions constitute what we might call a kind of spiritual checklist, an evaluation to help us determine where we stand in regard to rebirth.

The first three questions, comprising verse 14 of chapter 5, are both an introduction and a summary to all that follows: "Behold, I ask of you, my brethren of the church, have ye spiritually been born of God? Have ye received his image in your countenances? Have ye experienced this mighty change in your hearts?"

Alma then continued with other essential questions bearing on the condition of spiritual rebirth. He asked (paraphrasing his words):

Do you exercise faith in the redemption of Him who created you?

Do you look forward with an eye of faith to the resurrection and judgment?

Can you imagine that you hear the voice of the Lord blessing you and praising your righteous efforts?

Do you imagine that you can lie to or fool an omniscient Savior?

Can you imagine the guilt you will feel at the judgment if you have defied or ignored the commandments?

Can you look to God with a pure heart and clean hands?

If you have ever experienced a change of heart, do you feel that same way now?

Have you been sufficiently humble?

Have you walked blameless before God?

Are you stripped of pride?

Are you stripped of envy?

Do you mock others or treat them with disrespect?

In all of this, Alma really seems to be asking about the demonstration of Christlike qualities, Christlike behavior in our lives. That is why all of his points hark back to verse 14: "Have ye received *his* image in your countenances?"

His Image in Your Countenances

Nowhere is there set forth so succinctly, and in such unmistakable language, the way to judge whether or not we have been born again. We may know by asking two simple questions: Is Christ's image reflected in our countenance? Have we experienced a mighty change of heart?

An "image" is not just an outward visual impression but also a vivid representation, a graphic display, or a total likeness of something. It is a person or thing very much like another, a copy or counterpart. Likewise, *countenance* does not simply mean a facial expression or visual appearance. The word comes from an old French term originally denoting "behavior," "demeanor," or "conduct." In earlier times the word *countenance* was used with these meanings in mind.

Therefore, to receive Christ's image in one's countenance means to acquire the Savior's likeness in behavior, to be a copy or reflection of the Master's life. This is not possible without a mighty change in one's pattern of living. It requires, too, a change in feelings, attitudes, desires, and spiritual commitment. This involves the heart. Reynolds and Sjodahl have said: "The heart is said to be the seat of spiritual light; the source whence springs our love and our devotion, our likes and dislikes, our joys and our sorrows, and our loyalty and fidelity."[10]

According to Alma, the mighty change of heart must be "experienced." Perhaps that is why the concept of spiritual rebirth, "being born again," is considered by some to be difficult to talk about. In fact, it was never intended to be merely "understood" intellectually or in a passive sense. It must be personally experienced. Alma wanted his audience to be active participants. Those who experienced it, said Alma, have "felt to sing the song of redeeming love." (Alma 5:9, 26.) Other scripture confirms that it was so in ancient times as well. (Ps. 147:1-7.) Alma hoped that his people would retain this blessed and favored state (Alma 5:26); for only by remaining "steadfast and immovable, *always* abounding in good works" can celestial glory be guaranteed (Mosiah 5:15; italics added).

As an integral part of his pure testimony, Alma also taught that being born again involved a transcendent and glorious cleansing made available by the Savior's atonement. (See Alma 5:21, 22, 27, and 54.) Such a cleansing, said Alma, is available to all (Alma 5:33) and has been from the foundation of the world. No better explanation of the workings of this sanctification can be presented than the one given to our first father and confirmed by many prophets, Alma being not the least of them.

The Lord told Adam:

> By reason of transgression cometh the fall, which fall bringeth death, and inasmuch as ye were born into the world by water, and blood, and the spirit, which I have made, and so became of dust a living soul, even so ye must be born again into the kingdom of heaven, of water, and of the Spirit, and be cleansed by blood, even the blood of mine Only Begotten; that ye might be sanctified from all sin, and enjoy the words of eternal life in this world, and eternal life in the world to come, even immortal glory; for by the water ye keep the commandment; by the Spirit ye are justified, and by the blood ye are sanctified. (Moses 6:59-60.)

Fruits of Pure Testimony

After Alma delivered his message in Zarahemla, he met with a good measure of success. Several in the church evidently repented and again were set on the strait and narrow path. (Alma 7:4.) Others outside the church also repented, were baptized, and were received into the church. (Alma 6:2.) Alma then went about establishing the proper priesthood order of God by ordaining priests and elders to preside and watch over the kingdom. (Alma 6:1, 4.) The people were also commanded to do some missionary work and some reclaiming of lost souls on their own. (Alma 6:6.) Such were the fruits of Alma's pure testimony.

Yet Alma's testimony was not universally accepted in Zarahemla. Some in the church did not repent, those "who were lifted up in the pride of their hearts." These were excommunicated. (Alma 6:3.) Such were the fruits of pride.[11]

It was Alma's hope that the people in Gideon, where he traveled next to continue his mission, were not so lifted up in pride, so vain, so floundering in disbelief as were his brethren in Zarahemla. (Alma 7:3, 6, 18.) For, said he, there were many things to come, the most important of which was the advent of the Redeemer. (Alma 7:7.) It was fortunate for the people of Gideon that they were found walking in the paths of righteousness. (Alma 7:18-20.) Such an atmosphere fostered the Spirit, and Alma continued with his pure testimony by bearing a powerful and prophetic witness of the mission of the Savior.[12]

He went on to prophesy, in words characteristic of Isaiah's Messianic testimony, of the sufferings, afflictions, and temptations of Jesus—that which is called in 1 Nephi the condescension of God. (1 Ne. 11:16.) Alma's whole intention was, undoubtedly, to engender in his brethren greater faith, devotion, and love for one who, though omnipotent, submitted to *all* the trials of mortality so He could completely understand His people.[13] As Alma said: "He will take upon him their infirmities, that his bowels may be filled with mercy, according to the flesh, that he may know according to the flesh how to succor his people according to their infirmities." (Alma 7:12.)

Alma's pure testimony of the Savior to the people of Gideon is one of the greatest treatises on the atonement found in the Book of Mormon, and only by several readings can one begin to feel the intensity with which it must have been delivered. The prophet, in effect, told his audience that he knew for himself of the "power" of the Savior's deliverance, which is his ability to loose the bands of death, and to take upon himself the sins of his people and blot out their transgressions. (Alma 7:13.) Alma then defined "his people," the Savior's spiritual family, as those who display faith in the Lamb of God by repentance, baptism, and the keeping of God's commandments thenceforth. (Alma 7:14-16.)

The scriptural record tells us that before Alma left he established the order of the church just as he had done in Zarahemla. (Alma 8:1.) However, in Gideon, because of the people's uprightness, he was also able to pronounce upon the people a blessing that the Lord would help them keep themselves spotless, that they would be able to sit down with the ancient prophets, and that the peace of God would rest upon them and upon their houses, lands, flocks, families, and all they possessed. (Alma 7:25-27.) He encouraged them and left some specific objectives (as he had done in Zarahemla) — qualities that are found in those who remain truly converted. He challenged them to be humble, submissive, gentle, patient, long-suffering, temperate in all things, diligent in keeping the commandments, importuning as well as grateful, faithful, hopeful, and charitable. (Alma 7:23-24.) He also taught them many other things that — not surprisingly — cannot be written. (Alma 8:1.)

Lessons in Missionary Work

After his vigorous labors in Zarahemla and Gideon, Alma returned to his own home in Zarahemla and rested from his labors. (Alma 8:1.) Wise counsel given in the latter days for the benefit of both the Lord's servants and the work states: "Do not run faster or labor more than you have strength." (D&C 10:4.) Alma's action is an excellent example of this principle.

After a time, Alma departed for the land of Melek to teach the people there "according to the holy order of God." He was very successful and baptized many throughout the land. (Alma 8:4-5.) Alma next came to Ammonihah, where Satan's influence caused the people to harden their hearts against Alma's pure testimony. The prophet's labors provide a model for *all* missionaries who may have been called to work under difficult circumstances or who meet with little success:

"Nevertheless Alma labored much in the spirit, wrestling with God in mighty prayer, that he would pour out his Spirit upon the people who were in the city; that he would also grant that he might baptize them unto repentance." (Alma 8:10.)

The animosity of the people caused Alma to leave Ammonihah in sorrow and anguish of soul. However, an angel of the Lord comforted him and commanded him to return to the city, where he found Amulek. The latter not only recognized Alma's authority, but he also took in the prophet and helped him in a truly Christlike manner. (Compare Alma 8:26 with Luke 10:30-37 and Matt. 25:34-40.) In return for his temporal sustenance, Alma fed Amulek with spiritual meat. He thus repented and joined Alma as his missionary companion. Both were filled with the Holy Ghost and with great power: "They had power given unto them, insomuch that they could not be confined in dungeons; neither was it possible that any man could slay them; nevertheless they did not exercise their power until they were bound in bands and cast into prison. Now, this was done that the Lord might show forth his power in them." (Alma 8:31.) Once again we are reminded that with God nothing is impossible. (Luke 1:37.)

Conclusion

Alma's pure testimony proved a great blessing in the lives of the people. Many in the church returned to righteous ways and were "reclaimed" as God intended. Others originally outside the scope of the church experienced its saving and exalting ordinances. In every place where pure testimony was heard, save for Ammonihah, the church was set in order according to the priesthood.

Alma's pure testimony presents many important teachings — on pride, on repentance, on faith, and on Christlike living. It contains some of the exact images and language also found among the scriptural records of Old World prophets and apostles. This pure testimony constitutes the great discourse on spiritual rebirth. In an age or time when it seems almost a mark of Christian status in some circles to declare that one is born again, Alma's inspired instruction on the true nature of this doctrine ought to engender in us special gratitude.

Alma's pure testimony was Christ-centered and thus was intended for all people, "both old and young, both bond and free, . . . the aged, and also the middle aged, and the rising generation." (Alma 5:49.) Alma invited all to listen. However, after all is said and done, the most important thing about the words of Alma's pure testimony is that they are all true. As Alma said: "I do know of myself that they are true." (Alma 5:46.)

Notes

1. In 63 B.C., autonomy would end when the Roman Pompey annexed Judea as part of the Roman province of Syria.

2. John C. Traupman, *The New College Latin and English Dictionary* (New York: Amsco School Publications, 1966).

3. Joseph Smith, *Teachings of the Prophet Joseph Smith*, selected by Joseph Fielding Smith (Salt Lake City: Deseret Book Company, 1938), p. 121.

4. Sidney B. Sperry, *Book of Mormon Compendium* (Salt Lake City: Bookcraft, 1968), p. 330.

5. *Teachings of the Prophet Joseph Smith*, p. 162.

6. Bruce R. McConkie, *Mormon Doctrine*, 2nd ed. (Salt Lake City: Bookcraft, 1966), p. 101.

7. *Lectures on Faith* (Salt Lake City: Deseret Book Company, 1985), 1:24.

8. Ibid., 1:10.

9. *Teachings of the Prophet Joseph Smith*, p. 223; italics added.

10. George Reynolds and Janne M. Sjodahl, *Commentary on the Book of Mormon*, 7 vols. (Salt Lake City: Deseret Book Company, 1972), 3:78.

11. For a powerful discourse on pride, see President Ezra Taft Benson, "Cleansing the Inner Vessel," *Ensign*, May 1986, pp. 6-7.

12. For a discussion of the paternity of Christ, as mentioned in Alma 7:10, see Bryant S. Hinckley, *Sermons and Missionary Services of Melvin J. Ballard* (Salt Lake City: Deseret Book Company, 1949), pp. 166-67; Joseph F. Smith, "Father in Heaven Is Literally the Father of Jesus Christ," *The Box Elder News*, January 28, 1915, in James R. Clark, comp., *Messages of the First Presidency of The Church of Jesus Christ of Latter-day Saints*, 6 vols. (Salt Lake City: Bookcraft, 1965-75), 4:327-32. See also Kent P. Jackson, "The Tree of Life and the Ministry of Christ," chapter 4 in this volume.

13. See the discussion in *Mormon Doctrine*, p. 155.

24

The Plan of Redemption — Taught and Rejected
(Alma 9-16)

Larry E. Dahl

The events recorded in Alma 9-16 took place over four or five years, about 82-78 B.C. Chapters 9-14 report the teachings of Alma and Amulek in the city of Ammonihah, and the people's responses to those teachings in the tenth year of the reign of the judges, about 82 B.C. Chapter 15 tells of Alma and Amulek leaving Ammonihah (they were "commanded to depart out of that city" [verse 1]), and going to Sidom, then to Alma's home in Zarahemla. Chapter 16 reports a war with the Lamanites, the destruction of Ammonihah, and a subsequent three-year period of peace and righteousness "in all the region round about, among all the people of the Nephites." (Alma 16:15.)

After stepping down from his position as chief judge, Alma devoted his efforts full-time to preaching the gospel and strengthening the church. His travels brought him to the city of Ammonihah, which was inhabited by Nephites who had rejected the gospel.

At the very time Alma was sent to preach to them, they were plotting to "destroy the liberty" of other Nephites. (Alma 8:17.) They rejected Alma and his message. They "withstood all his words, and reviled him, and spit upon him, and caused that he should be cast out of their city." (Alma 8:13.) "Weighed down with sorrow" (Alma

---

Larry E. Dahl is associate professor of Church history and doctrine and director of Doctrine and Covenants research at Brigham Young University.

6:14), Alma started for the city of Aaron. However, an angel[1] appeared to him and told him to return and preach again in Ammonihah, warning the people that "except they repent the Lord God will destroy them." (Alma 8:16.) "He returned speedily." (Alma 8:18.) On entering the city, he met Amulek, who had also been visited by an angel. The angel told Amulek to return to his house and there receive and provide for a prophet of God. Alma "tarried many days with Amulek before he began to preach unto the people" (Alma 8:27), during which time Amulek was prepared by Alma and by an angel (Alma 10:10) to be a second witness with Alma of the truth of God to the people of Ammonihah.[2]

The People of Ammonihah and Their Response to Alma and Amulek

The beliefs of the people of Ammonihah were "after the order and faith of Nehor" (Alma 14:16), or "of the profession of Nehor" (Alma 15:15). Nehor was the man who introduced priestcraft[3] among the Nephites. (Alma 1:1-16.) He declared that "every priest and teacher ought to become popular; and they ought not to labor with their hands, but that they ought to be supported by the people." (Alma 1:3.) He taught that all people would be saved, therefore there was no need for repentance or for fear and trembling over their sins. (Alma 1:4; 15:15.) Hence, it is not surprising that Zeezrom, a follower of Nehor, challenged Amulek's explanation that God will not (cannot) save people "in their sins." (Alma 11:32-41.) It seems natural also that Zeezrom would think that Amulek, as a preacher, was really interested only in money, and therefore offered him six onties of silver if he would deny the existence of God. (Alma 11:22.)[4] Nor is it surprising that their whole legal system was corrupted, when the "sole purpose" of the lawyers and judges was "to get gain," and "therefore, they did stir up the people to riotings, and all manner of disturbances and wickedness, that they might have more employ, that they might get money according to the suits which were brought before them; therefore they did stir up the people against Alma and Amulek." (Alma 11:20.)[5]

Not all the people of Ammonihah were irretrievably caught up in priestcraft and other false doctrine. Amulek was converted with the help of Alma and an angel. And that there were other basically good people in the city is clear from Amulek's statement that "if it were not for the prayers of the righteous, who are now in the land, that ye would even now be visited with utter destruction." (Alma 10:22.) After the preaching of Alma and Amulek, "many of them did believe . . . and began to repent, and to search the scriptures. But the more part of them were desirous that they might destroy Alma and Amulek." (Alma 14:1-2.) Those who believed were cast out of the city,[6] and their wives and children were burned alive, along with their scriptures and other records. Alma and Amulek had preached that the *wicked* would be cast into a lake of fire and brimstone. (Alma 14:14.) In response, the people of Ammonihah were making sure that *believers* were the ones to so suffer. Amulek, recoiling at the scene, suggested to Alma that they exercise the power of God to save the women and children from the flames. The same idea had occurred to Alma, but he had been constrained by the Spirit. They were reluctant witnesses of a hard but essential truth: God permits the wicked to inflict suffering upon the righteous "that the judgments which he shall exercise upon them in his wrath may be just; and the blood of the innocent shall stand as a witness against them, yea, and cry mightily against them at the last day." (Alma 14:11.)[7] This burning of innocent people is a vivid reminder that agency is critical in the plan of salvation.

Amulek wondered out loud if he and Alma would also be burned, but Alma assured him, "Our work is not finished; therefore they burn us not." (Alma 14:13.) Bound and taunted for not having power to save the believers from fire, and answering nothing, Alma and Amulek were stripped and cast into prison. There, for many days, "lawyers, and judges, and priests, and teachers, who were of the profession of Nehor" questioned them, mocked them, smote them, spat on them, and withheld food from them. (Alma 14:14-22.) Finally, one day the city's chief judge led a host of lawyers and teachers to the prison. The judge smote the prisoners and said: "If ye have the power of God deliver yourselves from these bands, and then we will believe that the Lord will destroy this people according to your words."[8]

(Alma 14:24.) Following the judge's example, "they all went forth and smote them, saying the same words, even until the last." (Alma 14:25.) Alma had had enough! Putting his faith on the line, he cried: "O Lord, give us strength according to our faith which is in Christ, even unto deliverance." (Alma 14:26.) Heavenly strength came. They broke their bands. The prison walls fell, killing all those inside except Alma and Amulek. The citizenry came running to learn the cause of the great noise. Rather than bringing them to believe, as they had claimed such a thing would do, the remarkable deliverance of Alma and Amulek struck them with great fear, and they fled. (Alma 14:29.) Alma and Amulek departed for Sidom, leaving the unrepentant people of Ammonihah to their inevitable end — destruction.

The Message That Was Taught and Rejected

Repent or be spiritually damned and temporally destroyed! That was the message the angel told Alma to deliver as he commanded him to return to Ammonihah after his rejection. (Alma 8:16.) Both Alma and Amulek obeyed the commandment. (Alma 9:12, 18, 24; 10:23, 27.) But that was not the only message. They also taught gospel doctrines that establish why repentance is needed and why the warning of damnation and destruction was not an idle threat. They taught of "one Eternal God," or, in modern terminology, Godhead, consisting of "God the Father," "Christ the Son," and "the Holy Ghost." (Alma 11:26-33, 38, 44.) Amulek explained that the Son is "the very Eternal Father of heaven and of earth" (11:39), or the *creator* of heaven and earth, and that he is also the Redeemer of the world, who would come to save his people *from* their sins, not *in* their sins. They taught of the fall of man through Adam's partaking of the fruit of the tree of knowledge (Alma 12:22), and of the importance of this probationary state in preparing to meet God (Alma 12:21-27). They taught "the plan of redemption" — that mankind can be redeemed from the fall and from individual sin through repentance, made possible "through the blood of the Lamb." (Alma 9:26; 11:34-42; 13:11.) As part of the plan of redemption, they taught the other first principles and ordinances of the gospel — faith, baptism, and the necessity of being "led by the Holy Spirit." (Alma 9:27; 13:28.) They taught that

God holds his children strictly accountable for the light and knowledge available to them, emphasizing specifically that the people of Ammonihah, apostate Nephites, had received much light and many blessings, and that if they did not repent, it would be more tolerable for the Lamanites than for them in the day of judgment. (Alma 9:15-25; 12:9-11, 28-37.)

Alma taught plainly that our opportunities and accountabilities are not restricted to earth-life considerations. Many of God's children were "called and prepared from the foundation of the world according to the foreknowledge of God, on account of their exceeding faith and good works; in the first place being left to choose good or evil; therefore they having chosen good, and exercising exceedingly great faith, are called with a holy calling." (Alma 13:3.)[9] Those who continue to choose good in this second place, or earth life, are "ordained priests, after his holy order, which was after the order of his Son, to teach these things unto the people." (Alma 13:1.) Through faith, repentance, and righteousness, they are "sanctified, and their garments [are] washed white through the blood of the Lamb." (Alma 3:11.) "Now they, after being sanctified by the Holy Ghost, having their garments made white, being pure and spotless before God, could not look upon sin save it were with abhorrence; and there were many, exceedingly great many, who were made pure and entered into the rest of the Lord their God." (Alma 13:12.)[10] Alma yearned for the people of Ammonihah to receive this great blessing. (Alma 13:27-29.)

Others, who in that "first place" were on the "same standing with their brethren" (Alma 13:5),[11] but who did not respond as fully to the truth, did not come to this earth with the same opportunities and responsibilities as their brethren. Still others chose well in "the first place," and were foreordained to important earthly opportunities, but here on earth they "reject the Spirit of God on account of the hardness of their hearts and blindness of their minds." (Alma 13:4.)[12]

Into which group did the Ammonihahites fit? It seems they had come through favored lineage and had received special blessings. Evidently they chose well in the "first place" and therefore came to earth with more than ordinary responsibility. But they were rejecting their opportunities in this second place. Eventually such rejection will catch up to us. In the day of judgment "our words . . . our works . . . our thoughts" will condemn us "if we have hardened our hearts against the word" of God. (Alma 12:13-14.) A sentence of death will be passed upon the unrepentant, who will "have a bright recollection of all [their] guilt." (Alma 11:43.) That same judgment day will bring "eternal life, and salvation" to "those who believe on his name." (Alma 11:40.) Associated with the judgment is a resurrection of the body, "restored to its perfect frame" (Alma 11:44), "their spirits uniting with their bodies, never to be divided; thus the whole becoming spiritual and immortal, that they can no more see corruption" (Alma 11:45).

Another part of the message of Alma and Amulek was the need for prayer and humility "that [we] may not be tempted above that which [we] can bear." (Alma 13:28.)[13]

A rather complete curriculum! God, creation, the fall, the atonement, agency, revelation, the plan of redemption, foreordination, sanctification, judgment, resurrection. And the people of Ammonihah rejected it all. The order of Nehor was more appealing to them. It required no repentance, and it permitted them — even encouraged them — to seek after riches and the honors of men. Mormon's later editorial comment applies here: "And thus we can plainly discern, that after a people have been once enlightened by the Spirit of God, and have had great knowledge of things pertaining to righteousness, and then have fallen away into sin and transgression, they become more hardened, and thus their state becomes worse than though they had never known these things." (Alma 24:30.)

Amulek, the Second Witness

Amulek was a resident of Ammonihah who did not live up to his potential. He said of himself: "I am also a man of *no small reputation* among all those who know me; yea, and behold, I have acquired *much riches* by the hand of my industry." (Alma 10:4; emphasis added.) Undoubtedly, that life-style contributed to his earlier insensitivity to the Spirit of the Lord. He later acknowledged, "I did harden my heart, for I was called many times and I would not hear; therefore

I knew concerning these things, yet I would not know; therefore I went on rebelling against God, in the wickedness of my heart." (Alma 10:6.)[14] Then the angel came. And the angel's coming raises the question of what Amulek did to deserve such a blessing. Perhaps this is an example of the principle of foreordination spoken of in Alma 13. Evidently Amulek, along with the likes of Alma (Mosiah 27) and Paul (Acts 9), was a choice spirit, a "chosen vessel," who was "called and prepared from the foundation of the world according to the foreknowledge of God, on account of [his] exceeding faith and good works" in the "first place," or in the premortal life. (Alma 13:3.) Such pre-earth faithfulness and foreordination may have justified his receiving an angel even though he was temporarily off course here in mortality. Amulek could have rejected the angel's message,[15] but he chose to obey. He returned to his house, received Alma, spent "many days" being tutored by Alma and an angel (Alma 8:27; 10:10), then accompanied Alma in preaching to the people of Ammonihah. He was the second witness demanded by the Ammonihahites. (Alma 9:2, 6.)

Amulek's decision involved much more than a preaching mission. It was also a rejection of his former life. It was, in fact, a double rejection, a reciprocal rejection—"Amulek having forsaken all his gold, and silver, and his precious things, which were in the land of Ammonihah, for the word of God, he being rejected by those who were once his friends and also by his father and his kindred." (Alma 15:16.) Was he rejected by his wife and children[16] as well as by his friends and his father? After leaving Ammonihah and preaching at Sidom, Amulek went with Alma to Zarahemla. "Alma . . . took him to his own house, and did administer unto him in his tribulations, and strengthened him in the Lord." (Alma 15:18.) There is no mention of any family being with him. If indeed the "kindred" who rejected him included his own wife and children, it is no wonder he was suffering "tribulations" and needed the strengthening influence of a loving friend. Choosing God does not ensure against pain. It may even bring pain. And sometimes, even though a person repents and is forgiven, there are inevitable, natural consequences of previous behavior that must be borne. But in God there is also power and peace. Anyone who has experienced both the world and God can empathize with Amulek. They can rejoice with him in his decision for truth, and sorrow with him in his tribulations.

Based in Zarahemla, Amulek continued as a preaching companion to Alma "throughout all the land" for the next three years. (Alma 16:12-15.) "The establishment of the church became general throughout the land," righteousness prevailed, and "the Lord did pour out his Spirit on all the face of the land." (Alma 16:15-16.) Subsequently Amulek went with Alma and others (Alma 31:32) on a mission to the Zoramites, to whom he preached a powerful sermon (Alma 34) about the atonement, justice and mercy, faith and prayer, and the grave danger of procrastinating repentance. Nothing more is said about Amulek's activities. However, he is quoted later by Helaman (Hel. 5:10) and Aminadab (Hel. 5:41), and he is referred to by Moroni as one who had faith sufficient to cause prison walls to tumble. (Ether 12:13.) We are left to wonder how and with whom he spent his later years.

Zeezrom

Zeezrom was one of a group of clever lawyers in the city of Ammonihah who challenged Alma and Amulek. These lawyers intended "that by their cunning devices they might catch them in their words, that they might find witness against them, that they might deliver them to their judges that they might be judged according to the law, and that they might be slain or cast into prison." (Alma 10:13.) Zeezrom "was the foremost to accuse Amulek and Alma, he being one of the most expert among them . . . a man who was expert in the devices of the devil, that he might destroy that which was good." (Alma 10:31; 11:21.) His first tactic was to offer Amulek six onties of silver if he would deny the existence of God. Amulek rebuked him, calling him a "child of hell" who knew of God but loved lucre more. (Alma 11:23-24.) Undaunted, Zeezrom then attempted to have Amulek cross or contradict himself in his terms and ideas. Amulek remained consistent and clear, chastising Zeezrom for his dishonesty. Then Amulek bore witness of the Son of God as Creator and Redeemer, of a future judgment and resurrection when all will be "arraigned before the bar of Christ the Son, and God the Father, and the Holy Spirit" to be judged of their works, having "a bright recollection of all [their] guilt." (Alma 11:39-46.) "Zeezrom . . . began to tremble under a consciousness of his guilt." (Alma 12:1.) After Alma added his testimony, reminding Zeezrom that his thoughts had been perceived through the Spirit and that he had fallen under the influence of the devil, "Zeezrom began to tremble more exceedingly." (Alma 12:7.) He was now convinced that Alma and Amulek had the power of God with them. He turned from heckler to honest investigator and "began to inquire of them diligently, that he might know more concerning the kingdom of God." (Alma 12:8.) Alma then expounded the plan of redemption as recorded in the rest of Alma 12 and 13. Evidently Zeezrom was among the "many" who believed, were cast out of the city, and went to Sidom. (Alma 14:1, 7; 15:1.) After Alma and Amulek were delivered from prison in Ammonihah, they too went to Sidom. There they found Zeezrom "sick . . . with a burning fever, which was caused by the great tribulations of his mind on account of his wickedness." (Alma 15:3.) Zeezrom was now a guilt-ridden, repentant soul. He asked to be healed. "Alma cried unto the Lord, saying: O Lord our God, have mercy on this man, and heal him according to his faith which is in Christ." (Alma 15:10.) "Zeezrom leaped upon his feet, and began to walk. . . . And Alma baptized Zeezrom unto the Lord; and he began from that time forth to preach unto the people." (Alma 15:11-12.)

Zeezrom had experienced a striking metamorphosis from arrogant critic to missionary,[17] through stages including shocked wonderment, honest inquiry, repentant belief, godly sorrow, forgiveness and healing, and baptism. The love and power of God, the atonement of Jesus Christ, and honest hearts make such a journey possible. And Zeezrom is not the only traveler. Many have trod and many will yet tread that same path, reaping peace and happiness in the process.

Conclusion

Alma and Amulek had testified clearly and repeatedly that if the people of Ammonihah did not repent they would be destroyed. (Alma 9:12, 18, 24; 10:20-23.) In spite of God's power being demonstrated in the deliverance of Alma and Amulek, the people of Ammonihah "yet remained a hard-hearted and a stiffnecked people; and they repented not of their sins, ascribing all the power of Alma and Amulek to the devil." (Alma 15:15.) In the eleventh year of the reign of the judges, the year following the warnings of destruction, a Lamanite army "destroyed the people who were in the city of Ammonihah, . . . yea, every living soul of the Ammonihahites was destroyed, and also their great city. . . . Behold, in one day it was left desolate; and the carcasses were mangled by dogs and wild beasts of the wilderness." (Alma 16:1-10; note also 9:4-5.)

"People did not go in to possess the land of Ammonihah for many years. And it was called Desolation of Nehors; for they were of the profession of Nehor, who were slain; and their lands remained desolate." (Alma 16:11.) A sad ending for a once proud and affluent city! It could have been otherwise had they listened to God's servants.

Many lessons can be drawn from Alma 9 through 16. Perhaps the central lesson is that there is a God in heaven to whom people on earth are accountable. He loves us. He has implemented a "plan of redemption" whereby we can "be lifted up at the last day and enter into his rest." (Alma 12:33; 13:29.) Through his Spirit he reaches out to all: the righteous exemplified in these chapters by Alma and the Ammonihahite believers; the temporarily distracted but decent people like Amulek; and even enemies to the cause of truth, whether they will repent as did Zeezrom, or reject the invitation as did most of the people of Ammonihah. And everyone is accountable for how they respond to that Spirit. Those who hearken are blessed with more and more light until they know the mysteries of God in full. Those who harden their hearts against the whisperings of the Spirit of God receive less and less light, until they know nothing of his mysteries. (Alma 12:9-10.) Agency is critical to the plan. It even allows the wicked to inflict suffering upon themselves and others. But justice, as well as mercy, is an attribute of God. In the end, before the bar of God, all people will be judged and rewarded according to their thoughts, their words, and their deeds. The righteous will enter into eternal rest; the wicked will be ashamed. The wicked will "not dare to look up to . . . God; and [they] would fain be glad if [they] could command the rocks and the mountains to fall upon [them] to hide [them] from his presence." (Alma 12:14.)

Perhaps all could benefit from a careful reading of Alma 9-16, then pondering these questions:

1. How often have I been "called" and "would not hear"? (Alma 10:6.) Am I hard of hearing, or am I sometimes simply hard of hearkening?

2. What decisions did I make in "the first place" that led to my opportunities here? To what was I foreordained? How well am I honoring that expectation?

3. Do I understand that choosing God does not necessarily shield one from pain and suffering here in mortality?

4. To what degree am I motivated by the fact that through exceeding faith, repentance, and righteousness, a person can be sanctified "through the blood of the Lamb" while yet on earth? (Alma 13:10-12.)

5. To what extent do I understand the mysteries of God? Can I be trusted with them? (Alma 12:9-11.)

6. Why did Alma give up his position as chief judge, leave his home, and preach to a hostile people? Why did Amulek forsake his riches and suffer estrangement from his family and friends? Would I do that?

7. Just what are my thoughts as I anticipate being "arraigned before the bar of Christ the Son, and God the Father, and the Holy Spirit"? (Alma 11:44.)

As we ponder these questions, it may be helpful to imagine Alma speaking to us as he did to the Ammonihahites: "I wish from the inmost part of my heart, yea, with great anxiety even unto pain, that ye would hearken unto my words, and cast off your sins, and not procrastinate the day of your repentance; but that ye would humble yourselves before the Lord, and call on his holy name, and watch and pray continually, that ye may not be tempted above that which ye can bear, and thus be led by the Holy Spirit, becoming humble, meek, submissive, patient, full of love and all long-suffering; having faith on the Lord; having a hope that ye shall receive eternal life; having the love of God always in your hearts, that ye may be lifted up at the last day and enter into his rest." (Alma 13:27-29.)

Notes

1. This was the same angel who appeared to Alma when Alma was converted. See Mosiah 27; Alma 8:15.
2. See Alma 9:2-6 and 10:12. The people of the city challenged the validity of Alma's testimony because it was the word of only "one man." Amulek provided a second witness.
3. "Priestcrafts are that men preach and set themselves up for a light unto the world, that they may get gain and praise of the world; but they seek not the welfare of Zion." (2 Ne. 26:29.)
4. An onti of silver was equivalent to seven days' wages for a judge. Therefore six onties equaled forty-two days' pay. (Alma 11:3-19.)
5. The Ammonihahite focus upon money discussed in these chapters also make this an appropriate place to include an explanation of their monetary system. The following chart shows the relative values of their currency:

GOLD	SILVER	MEASURE/GRAIN	DAY'S WAGE
	leah	.125	
	shiblum	.25	
	shiblon	.5	
senine	senum	1.000	1,000
antion		1.5	
seon	amnor	2.0	
shum	ezrom	4.0	
limnah	onti	7.0	

For additional information about the Nephite monetary system and its comparison to other ancient systems see "Weights and Measures in the Time of Mosiah II" (Provo, Ut.: Foundation for Ancient Research and Mormon Studies, 1983); Paul R. Jesclard, "A Comparison of the Nephite Monetary System with the Egyptian System of Measure," *Society for Early Historic Archaeology Newsletter* 134 (October 1973); and Richard P. Smith, "The Nephite Monetary System," *Improvement Era* 57 (May 1954), p. 416.
6. These men went to the city of Sidom, where Alma and Amulek later brought the sad news of what had happened to their wives and children. (See Alma 15:1-2.)
7. This principle is taught repeatedly in the scriptures: Alma 60:13; D&C 103:3; 101:78, 93.
8. This is a popular but false notion of many unbelieving people. Compare Luke 16:27-31, D&C 5:7, and Ether 4:8.

9. For a brief interpretive discussion of pre-earth agency, faith, and works, and their relationship to earthly opportunities, see Bruce R. McConkie, *The Mortal Messiah*, Book 1, (Salt Lake City: Deseret Book Company, 1979), pp. 22-26. The last part of Alma 13:3 seems to say that pre-earth blessings of agency, growth, and foreordination were made possible through the retroactive power of the atonement.

10. The principle of entering into the rest of the Lord is referred to at least ten times by Alma in his preaching to the Ammonihahites: Alma 12:34, 34, 36, 37; 13:6, 12, 13, 16, 29; 16:17. With his explanation in 13:11-12, 29, it seems clear that Alma uses the expression to mean that one has qualified for exaltation while yet here in mortality. One can know that he or she has so qualified, and then may have the privilege of the Second Comforter. See D&C 84:19-25; 131:5-6; 2 Pet. 1:1-10, 17-19; Joseph Smith, *Teachings of the Prophet Joseph Smith*, selected by Joseph Fielding Smith (Salt Lake City: Deseret Book Company, 1938), pp. 149-50.

Speaking of another level of entering into the rest of the Lord, President Joseph F. Smith said: "What does it mean? To my mind, it means entering into the knowledge and love of God, having faith in his purpose and in his plan, to such an extent that we know we are right, and that we are not hunting for something else, we are not disturbed by every wind of doctrine." (*Gospel Doctrine*, 5th ed. [Salt Lake City: Deseret Book Company, 1939], p. 58; see also p. 126.)

Both these levels of entering into the rest of the Lord are preliminary to entering into God's eternal rest, into his kingdom and presence, to go no more out.

11. "Same standing" at least means having the same resources and opportunities to choose and progress. There does not appear to be consensus among LDS authors about whether "same standing" includes same capacity and inclination to respond positively to light and truth.

12. President Harold B. Lee spoke of this situation in discussing D&C 121:34, 35. He said: "This suggests that even though we have our free agency here, there are many who were foreordained before the world was, to a greater state than they have prepared themselves for here. Even though they might have been among the noble and great, from among whom the Father declared he would make his chosen leaders, they may fail of that calling here in mortality. Then the Lord poses this question: 'and why are they not chosen?' (D&C 121:34.) Two answers were given—First, 'Because their hearts are set so much upon the things of this world . . . ' And second, they 'aspire to the honors of men.' " (D&C 121:35.) (*Conference Report*, October 1973, p. 7.) Priestcraft again!

13. Often 1 Corinthians 10:13 is quoted to suggest that God will somehow snatch us from any and all circumstances and not permit us to be tempted beyond our ability to withstand. Alma seems to be saying that we have a responsibility in this matter—a responsibility to earnestly strive through prayer and humility to avoid circumstances that may bring overpowering temptations.

14. Others share Amulek's reluctance to listen. President Joseph F. Smith has said: "I believe there are tens of thousands of people who have heard the truth and have been pricked in their hearts, but they are seeking every refuge they possibly can to hide themselves from their convictions of the truth." (*Gospel Doctrine*, pp. 360-61.)

Every person born on this earth is given the Light of Christ, which will lead them to the truth if they hearken to its promptings. Rejecting those promptings brings condemnation. (See D&C 84:45-53; 93:30-32.)

15. Even though a person may qualify for certain earthly opportunities because of pre-earth faithfulness and foreordination, it is no guarantee that he or she will choose good here on earth, either before or after the truth is clearly made known to that person. Perhaps the Ammonihahites are a prime example. Another case in point is that of Laman and Lemuel. (See 1 Ne. 7:16-20; 16:37-38; 17:45-55; 18:8-22; 2 Ne. 5:1-7.)

16. Alma 10:11 indicates that "women" and "children" were part of his "house."

17. Interestingly, Zeezrom's teacher Alma, and later the Apostle Paul, also persecuted the church before they were converted and became powerful missionaries. (See Mosiah 27 and Acts 9.) Most powerful missionaries, however, did not persecute the Church before their conversion. The key is that once a person is converted, he or she feels a strong desire to bring repentance to others.

25

"Show Forth Good Examples in Me"
(Alma 17-23)

Camille Fronk

In his writings of Christ, Nephi taught that "all things which have been given of God from the beginning of the world, unto man, are the typifying of him." (2 Ne. 11:4.) According to Alma, "all things" include ordinances (Alma 13:16), the law of Moses (Alma 25:15), and individuals ordained to teach God's commandments to the human family (Alma 13:1-2). In other words, everything that God has created has been designed to help us understand, appreciate, and recognize the Son of God and his atonement. (Moses 6:63.) As we take the sacrament, we are reminded of his atoning sacrifice. Through baptism, we may better understand Christ's gift of the resurrection and a new life. When we witness obedience and Christlike service in others, we are seeing a type of the Savior in them. Through Christlike actions of others, we come to know the reality of the Savior. Seeing Christ in the lives of others was the message that Annique Juqant attached to her helium balloon: "Live so that those who know you but don't know Him, will want to know Him because they know you."[1]

In describing the manner in which the Savior taught his message, Elder Bruce R. McConkie wrote: "He uses ordinances, rites, acts, and performances; he uses similarities, resemblances, and similitudes so that whatever is done will remind all who are aware of it of a greater

---

Camille Fronk is a seminary instructor in the Salt Lake Valley.

and more important reality. . . . To liken one thing to another is one of the best teaching procedures."[2] There are numerous people and events in scripture that typify Jesus Christ and his mission, providing for us a "shadow of things to come." (Col. 2:17.) Typification of Christ is rich and abundant in chapters 17-23 of Alma. Through the story line, the teachings, and the typology we can know the Savior better and know how we can better serve him. A brief review of the preceding chapters in Alma is first needed to put these people and events in their historical context.

Historical Context up to 90 B.C.

Ammon, Aaron, Omner, and Himni, the four sons of King Mosiah, exemplified Christlike conduct after they experienced the mighty change in their hearts. Previously, these four young men, along with Alma the Younger, had been a "great hinderment to the prosperity of the church of God." (Mosiah 27:9.) In their wicked and rebellious state, they caused dissension among the people, led many to commit iniquity, and tried to bring about the destruction of the church. (Alma 27:8-10.) While engaged in such activities, in answer to the prayers of Alma the Elder and others, these young men saw an angel of the Lord who called them to repentance. Although the road back was painful, they did repent and were "changed from their carnal and fallen state, to a state of righteousness, being redeemed of God." (Alma 27:25.)

Consequently, Ammon, Aaron, Omner, and Himni, along with others who had similar desires, made a request to their father, King Mosiah, to go to the Land of Nephi to teach their brothers the Lamanites. They hoped to lead the Lamanites to believe in God, for "the very thoughts that any soul should endure endless torment did cause them to quake and tremble." (Alma 28:3.) Grateful for the miracle of forgiveness in their own lives, these young men yearned to share with others the joys that come from forgiveness.

The sons of Mosiah were successful on their mission because they diligently searched the scriptures, fasted, and prayed. (Alma 17:2-3.) Departing for their mission, these young men prayed that they would have a portion of the Lord's Spirit to go with them. (Alma

17:9.) As a result, the Lord blessed them with the gifts of prophecy and revelation. (Alma 17:3.) This in turn enabled them to teach with power and authority and become instruments in the hands of the Lord to bring salvation to many souls. (Alma 17:3, 11.) Among the first instructions they received through the Holy Spirit was to "show forth good examples unto them in me" (Alma 17:11), an invitation to reflect the attributes of the Savior.

Exemplifying Christ Through Service

From the time of their request to serve a mission, the four sons of Mosiah began to typify the mission of Jesus Christ. (Mosiah 29:1-3.) They were Christlike when they sacrificed their right as heirs to the Nephite throne in order to teach the gospel to a hardened and idolatrous people. (Alma 17:6, 14.) In so doing, they suffered many afflictions so the Lamanites might be brought to repentance. (Alma 17:5.) Jesus stood before the Father of our spirits in the premortal existence and made a similar request: "Here am I, send me." (Abr. 3:27.) He gave up a position of power to come down to a fallen world where he would suffer many afflictions to bring us salvation. (John 1:1-5; Isa. 53:3-5.)

As Ammon's mission began, he was captured, bound with cords, and brought before the local Lamanite ruler, Lamoni. Lamoni looked kindly upon Ammon and offered him his daughter to marry. The scriptures do not explain why Lamoni acted so favorably toward a Nephite. His initial trust in Ammon may be an indication of Lamoni's goodness and kindness, of Ammon's impressive countenance, or of both. Ammon turned down the invitation to royalty, preferring to be a servant. The perpetual and perfect servant Jesus washed his disciples' feet on the eve of his crucifixion (John 13:14-15), exemplifying what he taught: "He that is greatest among you shall be your servant." (Matt. 23:11.) Positions of power and authority are not pursued by those who want to be Christlike. Rather, they want to serve unselfishly in a way that may never receive public acclaim. Such service has a profound influence on others because it is performed from the heart and testifies of the Savior.

Not only did Ammon's service to Lamoni typify the Savior, but his Christlike actions brought countless Lamanites to a change of heart and a new life. He won the hearts of many Lamanites three days after he began tending the king's flocks near the water of Sebus. When wicked Lamanites scattered the flocks, Ammon's fellow servants were terrified, fearing the same fatal consequences that other unsuccessful servants had received. (Alma 17:26-28.) Ammon, on the other hand, rejoiced because he recognized an opportunity to demonstrate the power of the Lord. As a shepherd, Ammon taught the other servants to gather the sheep, himself leading the way. (John 10:11; 1 Ne. 22:25; D&C 33:6.) When the flock had been gathered, Ammon protected them first with a sling, then with the sword. (Alma 17:36-38.)

Ammon was so successful in reflecting divine power that Lamoni believed Ammon was God, or "the Great Spirit." There had been sufficient evidence to convince Lamoni that Ammon possessed these godlike qualities and was more than a man. To Lamoni and his servants, Ammon appeared to be as righteous (Alma 18:17) and as omniscient (Alma 18:18) as the Great Spirit.[3] When Ammon continued to obey Lamoni's commands even after the excitement at the waters of Sebus, Lamoni exclaimed: "Surely there has not been any servant among all my servants that has been so faithful as this man." (Alma 18:10.) None but Jesus Christ, however, has remembered all the Father's "commandments to execute them." (Alma 18:10.) It is evident that Lamoni's courtiers were convinced that Ammon was the person he typified when they addressed him as "Rabbanah," meaning powerful or great king. (Alma 18:13.) The title is nearly identical to "Rabboni," meaning master, which was uttered by Mary Magdalene to the resurrected Lord. (John 20:16.)

Lamoni had always been taught, through Lamanite tradition, that anything he did was right. (Alma 18:5.)[4] Yet as soon as he believed he might soon stand before the Great Spirit, he experienced immediate feelings of guilt for having killed some of his servants. How did Lamoni know his actions were wrong if he had never been taught right and wrong? The answer lies in the Light of Christ, which is given to every person. (Moro. 7:16-18; D&C 93:2.) President Marion G. Romney stated: "No person is, nor can he be, justified in rejecting these teachings and commandments, which have been revealed by the Lord, on the basis that he does not know they are true, because everything the Lord does or says has within itself the evidence of its own authenticity, and every person is divinely endowed with the means to discover that evidence and know for himself that it is true."[5]

While no one had taught Lamoni the seriousness of such a wrong-doing, his "conscience" was obviously still alert and responding to Ammon's Christlike example.

It took a series of explanations to convince Lamoni that Ammon was not the Lord. First, Ammon flatly declared, "I am not." (Alma 18:19.) Next, Ammon taught Lamoni who God was and about his attributes. (Alma 18:24-32.) He explained his own calling from God and the gifts of the Spirit that helped him accomplish the Lord's work. (Alma 18:33-35.) Finally, Ammon taught Lamoni the gospel from the scriptures, specifically explaining the creation, the fall, and the atonement. (Alma 18:38-39.) Elder Bruce R. McConkie called these "the three pillars of eternity" and the "greatest events that have ever occurred in all eternity." He explained: "If we can gain an understanding of them, then the whole eternal scheme of things will fall into place, and we will be in a position to work out our own salvation. . . . These three are the foundations upon which all things rest. Without any one of them all things would lose their purpose and meaning and the plans and designs of Deity would come to naught."[6]

Ammon was obviously successful at teaching these truths clearly because immediately afterward Lamoni pleaded with the Lord and not Ammon for mercy. (Alma 18:41.) Once Lamoni understood his position before the Lord, his comatose state typified the death of the natural man in preparation for being born again as a man of Christ. Spiritual rebirth begins when one correctly identifies the Redeemer and the need for his mercy.

Lamoni's Conversion

While Lamoni's body took on the appearance of death for three days, his spirit was very much alive and actively learning. Parallel ordeals of the same length of time are found throughout scripture. A few years earlier, Alma the Younger was unable to speak or move during the three days of his spiritual awakening. (Mosiah 27:18-25.)

Paul received his sight after being blind three days, and he was born again. (Acts 9:8-9.) Christ used Jonah's three-days' experience in the belly of a great fish to teach His death and resurrection to the Pharisees. (Matt. 12:40.) Each of these incidents points to the death and resurrection of the Messiah, whose body was in the tomb for three days while his spirit was in the spirit world. But one major difference separates the Savior from these who typify him—the sinless Christ was the Teacher during his three-days' experience, whereas Lamoni, Alma, and Paul were students, being taught the principles of salvation and experiencing the pains of repentance. Christ's three days were not painful nor were they days of darkness, because he is "the light [that] shineth in darkness," the very light of the world. (John 1:5; 8:12.)

The ensuing debate between the queen and the servants over Lamoni's condition and the subsequent dialogue between Ammon and the queen, including the queen's reaction to Ammon, can be compared to the incident when Jesus raised his friend Lazarus from the dead. Martha, Lazarus's sister, did not have the faith to understand what Jesus was teaching when he told her, "Thy brother shall rise again." (John 11:23.) Not until she saw her brother walk out of the tomb did she realize that he was not referring to rising *after* the resurrection. Lamoni's wife, on the other hand, established her beliefs after hearing only the testimony of Ammon and her servants. When Ammon told her that her husband would arise the next day, she responded, "I believe that it shall be according as thou hast said." (Alma 19:9.) It is not surprising that Ammon blessed her for her great faith. (Alma 19:10.)[7]

Lamoni's wife is one of two women in this story who aided in the Lord's work among their people. When Lamoni's entire household had fallen into an unconscious state, a servant named Abish helped in the conversion of many other Lamanites in the land of Ishmael. She had been converted to the Lord many years before as a result of a vision of her father. (Alma 19:16.) One might wonder what she thought during those years. Would she have been confused or frustrated due to her isolated conversion, not knowing what she should do to bring others to the same knowledge? Visions are not idly given by the Lord but reserved for specific purposes. One of the Lord's purposes for visions is "preparing men for salvation."[8] The case of Abish cannot be seen as an exception, for she was prepared to help her people come to a knowledge of salvation. When she witnessed the condition of the king's court, she recognized the power of God and knew what she must do. Her testimony as a Lamanite strengthened the testimony of Ammon, a Nephite foreigner, and satisfied the law of witnesses. (D&C 6:28.)

Being missionary minded, Abish called many in the city to come and see the condition of the king's household, hoping that they too would recognize the power of God and desire to learn of him. (Alma 19:17-18.) One observer was a brother to one of the men who scattered Lamoni's flocks and had been killed by Ammon. He recognized Ammon, now apparently defenseless, and tried to kill him. Instead the man fell dead in the attempt, proving to all those present that Ammon could not be killed. (Alma 19:22.) Unlike Lamoni, Ammon's attempted murderer did not rise again in three days. He was not born again. He had not received the mighty change in his heart. He was truly dead.

The other observers became frightened because they did not understand this great power that aided Ammon. The Lamanites' inability to understand spiritual things caused them to make many incorrect conclusions about Ammon. (See 1 Cor. 2:14.) Some said he was a "monster." (Alma 19:26.)[9] Others thought, as Lamoni had originally surmised, that Ammon was the Great Spirit. (Alma 19:25.) Other spectators believed that the Nephites had been favored by the Great Spirit all along and had now sent Ammon to punish them for their iniquities. (Alma 19:27.) This basic belief in a godlike figure was apparently strengthened by the Lamanites' long observations of the prosperous Nephites. Through their example, seen from afar, the Nephites bore witness of Christ and prepared a people to receive the truth.

When Lamoni, his queen, his household, and Ammon regained consciousness, they taught the spectators the words of Ammon, and many were changed in their hearts that "they had no more desire to do evil." (Alma 19:30, 33.) Never before had such a change come upon his people, and all had been initiated by a visit from a Nephite. Lamoni as king could have been jealous of Ammon and his ability to garner such obedience and respect among the Lamanite people. But there is no sign of such a feeling, only love and compassion for Ammon. Later Lamoni forbade Ammon to serve him and asked him to preach to his people instead. (Alma 21:19, 23.) It is rare to see one of such authority and position as Lamoni be as accepting and teachable before one so traditionally inferior.

Although a great many of the people believed on Ammon and Lamoni's words and were spiritually reborn, many were still hard-hearted and would not listen, even after seeing these great miracles. (Alma 19:32.) In the face of One even greater, there were many who turned away. (John 12:37.) More than anyone else, Jesus knew what it meant to be rejected.

Ammon as a Type of Christ

In retrospect, one recognizes that the temptations placed before Ammon were the same as those that would later be offered to Christ in a more enticing manner. Ammon was presented gifts that would satisfy the carnal appetite. As Lamoni offered Ammon his daughter in marriage and a life of ease (Alma 17:24), so Satan made his tempting offer of turning stones to bread to the fasting Christ. (Matt. 4:2-4.) Ammon could have ruled among the Lamanites, taking advantage of their ignorance when they thought him to be God. (Alma 18:21.) Similarly, Christ was presented with the chance to use his power to gain instant popularity and worldly glory. (Matt. 4:5-7.) Finally, just as the king of the Lamanites promised Ammon worldly riches (Alma 20:23), so did Satan offer the wealth of all the earth if Christ would worship him. (Matt. 4:8-10.) Like the Savior, Ammon did not give in to these worldly pleasures. Both the Savior and Ammon had greater missions to accomplish.

Ammon's encounter with the king of the Lamanites on his way to free his friends from prison marked at least the fourth time his life could have been taken. It gives us occasion to see just how serious the Lord is about keeping his promises. (D&C 82:10.) When Mosiah's sons first asked their father for permission to go as missionaries to the lands of the Lamanites, the Lord promised King Mosiah that He would deliver the young men "out of the hands of the Lamanites." (Mosiah 28:7.) The infallible, protective power of the Lord accompanied these young missionaries while they served among the Lamanites. They did not walk alone. (D&C 84:88.)

When the Lord informed Ammon that some of his fellow missionaries were imprisoned in the land of Middoni, Ammon immediately responded and with Lamoni's help was able to free them. (Alma 20:2-4.)

Ammon's humility as a servant never changed throughout the course of events. Position, notoriety, and scheming tricks to manipulate others were not desires or concerns for him. He seemed to always remember that he was the instrument in the Master's hand, not the source of conversion and power. He was there to assist and be the Lord's servant in whatever capacity he was asked. Such sincerity, testimony, and genuine compassion cannot be feigned — it comes from God.

Teaching the Hardened People of Jerusalem

Further similarities with Christ can be seen in the events that led Aaron and his friends to imprisonment. "It was their lot to have fallen into the hands of a more hardened and a more stiffnecked people" who had no desire to hear the truths of the gospel. (Alma 20:30.) The name of the city in which they resided carried the same name as the city of those who rejected Christ during his mortal ministry — Jerusalem. (Alma 21:1-3.) The city was made up of Amalekites, Amulonites, and Lamanites. They taught that God would save all people (Alma 21:6), the same thing that Satan preached in the premortal existence (Moses 4:1).[10]

When Aaron taught the residents of Jerusalem about the atonement of Christ from the scriptures, they became angry, mocked him, and refused to listen to him. They left him with no alternative but to leave their synagogues. Similarly, many people were angry at Jesus' testimony and thrust him out of their synagogue and city. (Luke 4:28-29.) The descriptions of the demeaning and insulting treatment of the Savior in the Gospel accounts are among the most poignant and graphic. The Roman soldiers, the chief priests, the scribes, the Pharisees, the common people, even one of the thieves who was crucified beside him jeered at him, spat on him, hit him, and spoke blasphemously against him. (Matt. 27:29-31, 39-44; Luke 22:63-65; 23:35-39.) Aaron's unjust and demeaning treatment as a representative of the Lord is not unique or surprising. Christ's servants have always been and will always be persecuted and mistreated as long as followers of the adversary exist. (Matt. 5:10-12; John 15:18-20.)

With the exception of one Amalekite, none of the Nephite descendants were converted in the land of Nephi amid all the missionary success of the four sons of Mosiah. (Alma 23:14.) The Amulonite and Amalekite examples provide another evidence of Mormon's teaching that those who have known the truth and then fall away are more hardened and less receptive to the truth than those who have never known it. (Alma 24:30.) When a member of the Church in Illinois promised to never cause the Church any harm if he were to leave it, the Prophet Joseph Smith replied: "You don't know what you would do. . . . Before you joined the Church you stood on neutral ground. When the gospel was preached good and evil were set before you. You could choose either or neither. There were two opposite masters inviting you to serve them. When you joined this Church you enlisted to serve God. When you did that you left the neutral ground, and you never can get back on to it. Should you forsake the Master you enlisted to serve, it will be by the instigation of the evil one, and you will follow his dictation and be his servant."[11]

The Lamanites could be objective about the gospel when Ammon and his brothers first taught it, their neutral standing allowing them to recognize the truth. It was not the same with the dissenting Nephites. They had chosen to leave the teachings of God and would not be anxious to admit such a mistake when their fellow Nephites retaught them these piercing truths. (1 Ne. 16:2.)

The King over All the Lamanites

Aaron was prompted by the Spirit to leave the land of Middoni and go to the land of Nephi, where the king of the Lamanites, Lamoni's father, lived. When Aaron requested to be the king's servant, the king asked Aaron to teach him the gospel. The king's heart had obviously been softened and prepared since his encounter with Ammon and Lamoni. Like his brother Ammon, Aaron explained the creation of the earth, the fall of Adam, and the atonement of Christ. (Alma 22:12-14.) When the king heard these doctrines taught in clarity and by the Spirit, he fell to the earth, being overcome with joy and the glory of God. (Alma 22:18; 19:6.) Typifying the death of the natural man in this unconscious state, the king soon regained consciousness as one who was centered in Christ. Once he had experienced spiritual rebirth, the king ministered to his household with the power of the Spirit, which brought about their conversion. (Alma 22:23.)

A comparison of what the king was willing to sacrifice as he progressed in his gospel knowledge is an interesting study of the value of truth. After Ammon and Lamoni left him to free Ammon's brother and friends in prison, the king's understanding of the gospel included only the knowledge that Ammon had more power than he. At this point the king was willing to sacrifice half of his kingdom to secure his physical life in the face of Ammon's power. (Alma 20:23.) When Aaron told him about eternal life, the king was willing to relinquish *all* of his kingdom and *all* of his possessions to obtain it. (Alma 22:15.) Finally, when he learned that the atonement covered him only if he were humble, repentant, prayerful, and hopeful, he was willing to give away all his sins. (Alma 22:18.) By contrast, when Jesus asked the rich, young ruler to sell all he owned and give it to the needy, he would not answer as the king of the Lamanites had responded. (Luke 18:18-30.) The Lamanite king's willingness to sacrifice indicated a strong desire for a gift that meant more to him than his sinful life and all of his possessions. (D&C 14:7.)

Having received a change of heart, the king made a proclamation that no one should harm these missionaries, but that they should be allowed to preach the word of God in every part of the land. (Alma 23:1-3.) Due to the king's sanction of their work, there were no obstructions; and the missionaries were able to witness tremendous success among the Lamanite people. (Alma 23:4-5.) Possibilities in missionary work when the truth is first accepted by a nation's ruler are evident in this story. The gospel is generally accepted by the poor and consequently humble people of the world. Less frequently do the wealthy and prestigious citizens of a nation embrace the gospel. When leaders accept the gospel of Christ, it appears that the doors of their nation open so that the people may at least hear the message. There would be little fear of persecution for those who received it, and potentially many more who would experience the testifying influence of the Spirit.

Conclusion

The impact of daily instruction in the gospel was evident among the Lamanites who had been converted. (Alma 21:23.) Prophecy reveals that the same characteristics will exist during the millennium. The converted Lamanites kept the commandments with zeal. (Alma 21:23; 1 Ne. 22:26.) They believed what was taught in the scriptures. (Alma 23:5.) Once converted, they never did fall away (Alma 23:6), and they became a peaceful people. (Alma 23:7.) They received a new name. (Alma 23:16-17; Rev. 2:17.) The curse or effects of the fall was removed, leaving them no longer cut off from the presence of the Lord. (Alma 23:18.)

The experience of these Lamanite people, who were taught by Mosiah's sons and the Spirit of the Lord, show that it is not necessary to wait until the millennial reign to enjoy a peaceful and blessed society. The Lamanite people began to enjoy a life of love and unity when they experienced the mighty change in their hearts and were born again. The fact that the Amulonites, Amalekites, and many Lamanites never did receive the message of salvation preached to them shows that this condition does not depend on the conversion of every person. Rebellious influence need not lessen the joy experienced by those who soften and change their hearts and receive the gifts of the Spirit. (Mosiah 2:41; D&C 35:24.)

Like Lamoni, those converted to Jesus Christ and his gospel feel no envy but only love for God's children. They will learn from those who may appear inferior and are not jealous when those of lesser rank are more loved. Compare King Lamoni's reaction to Ammon when the people viewed Ammon with greater respect than Lamoni (Alma 18:13-14; 21:19-22) and King Saul's jealousy when David was more loved by the people than he (1 Sam. 18:14-16, 28-29). Those who are converted to Christ are not threatened by another's talents and abilities because they are interested in something of intrinsic value, a knowledge of the truth.

Those who are truly converted live the greatest commandments in their correct order, giving such people proper perspective to their lives. Christ taught us to first love the Lord our God and then to love our neighbor as ourselves. (Matt. 22:36-40.) No amount of praise and honor would affect Ammon's desire to continually serve. Those who are born again have no desire to relax and enjoy recognition or a worldly reward. On the contrary, sincere converts are motivated to become better servants and instruments in the hands of the Lord. (Alma 17:11.)

Ofttimes viewed as "more than a man" (Alma 18:2), a person who has experienced the mighty change reflects the influence of the Spirit in his or her countenance. (Alma 5:14.) As in the case of Ammon before King Lamoni, such an appearance may be misinterpreted by those who have not experienced it. Those who receive and correctly identify this new countenance are living in such a way as to warrant the companionship of the Holy Ghost. (Alma 17:2-3; 21:23.)

Those who experience the mighty change in their hearts are converted by hearing the word of God when it is accompanied by a witness of the Holy Ghost. Some Book of Mormon readers may conclude that it was the miraculous show of power that gave Lamoni's people and the sons of Mosiah their testimonies. We misunderstand the faith of these people and the power of the word of God if that is what we conclude. Alma the Younger and Lamoni had similar miraculous spiritual awakenings. Alma bore witness that it was the Holy Spirit who gave him his testimony, not the angel. (Alma 5:45-46.) Those born of God do not require miracles for conversion but respond to the teachings of the Spirit. (Alma 19:35-36.)

Finally, those who are spiritually reborn have great faith in Christ. (Ether 12:15.) Once they understand the gospel plan, converts know to whom they must turn for mercy and forgiveness. Notice the initial exclamations made by those who repented and were born again. When Lamoni regained consciousness, he stood and bore witness of the Savior (Alma 19:13), as did his queen (Alma 19:29). Many people have an intense desire to bear witness of Christ once they have experienced the blessings of his atonement. This witness may be given in words, but as has been illustrated in these chapters of the Book of Mormon, people witness Christ's reality frequently and powerfully by their lives. They take the Lord's request to heart: "Show forth good examples unto them in me." (Alma 17:11.)

Notes

1. Annique Juqant is a young woman from Seoul, Korea, who participated in the Young Women worldwide balloon lift in October of 1986. See "Rising Hopes," *The New Era* (March 1987), p. 22.

2. Bruce R. McConkie, *The Promised Messiah* (Salt Lake City, Utah: Deseret Book Company, 1978), p. 377.

3. The pharaoh recognized Joseph's power of discerning thoughts as well as his loyalty and obedience. See Gen. 41:16, 38. Belshazzar had similar feelings about Daniel. (See Dan. 2:30.)

4. This same absence-of-sin philosophy existed during many periods of Nephite history. See Alma 30:17; Mormon 8:31; 2 Nephi 28:8; Alma 1:4.

5. *Conference Reports*, April 6, 1976, pp. 120-21.

6. Bruce R. McConkie, "The Three Pillars of Eternity," BYU Devotional, Feb. 17, 1981.

7. Christ praised a Canaanite woman for her great faith and immediately healed her daughter as a result of it. (See Matt. 15:21-28.)

8. Bruce R. McConkie, *Mormon Doctrine*, 2nd ed. (Salt Lake City: Bookcraft, 1966), p. 824.

9. People did not understand Enoch; they called him a "wild man." (See Moses 6:37-39.)

10. Nehor taught the same thing. (See Alma 1:4.)

11. *Juvenile Instructor* 27:492.

26

The Lamanite Converts
Firm in the Faith of Christ
(Alma 24-29)

Kent P. Jackson and Darrell L. Matthews

When the sons of Mosiah went on their extended missionary journeys (Alma 17–26), they encountered strong opposition from some of the Lamanites. Their worst opposition, however, came from groups of apostate Nephites. These apostates were in two main groups, the Amalekites and the Amulonites; they are most often mentioned together in the record. While not all Lamanites accepted their message, still the sons of Mosiah enjoyed enormous success among them, converting thousands. The histories of the Nephite apostates and the Lamanite converts stand in clear contrast to each other. From the record of their activities we learn much about life—how the choices we make can lead either to our well-being or to our sorrow.

Amalekites and Amulonites

The Amalekites are first mentioned in Alma 21, where we are told that Aaron, one of Mosiah's sons, went to the land of Jerusalem to preach the gospel to the Lamanites. We learn from Alma 21:2 that the Lamanites, Amalekites, and Amulonites had built the city of Jerusalem. We are also informed that although the Lamanites were a hardened and wicked people, the Amalekites and the Amulonites

---

Kent P. Jackson is associate professor of ancient scripture and Old Testament area coordinator at Brigham Young University. Darrell L. Matthews is a doctoral student in ancient Near Eastern studies at Johns Hopkins University.

were worse. (Alma 21:3.) Because of their extreme wickedness, these two groups "did cause the Lamanites that they should harden their hearts, that they should wax strong in wickedness and their abominations." (Alma 21:3.) Aaron preached to the Amalekites in their places of worship, and as he did so these apostates contended with him.

The Amalekites and the Amulonites were followers of the order of Nehor, who had been a Nephite dissenter. We learn of some of their beliefs in Alma 21-22. They did not believe it possible to know the future. (Alma 21:8.) They believed that God would save all people from their sins. (Alma 21:6.) They also believed and taught that there was a God, which enabled them to receive permission from the Lamanite king to build sanctuaries for their worship. (Alma 22:7.) We later learn that through the preaching of the sons of Mosiah, the Lamanites of seven lands were converted; but of all of these only one Amalekite and no Amulonites were brought back to the truth. (Alma 23:14.) While many of the Lamanites were accepting the true gospel, the Amalekites and Amulonites hardened their hearts even more. Soon after the conversion of the Lamanites, the Amalekites and Amulonites began stirring up all the people who had not been converted to the truth, causing them to fight against the converts. Further on in the book of Alma we are informed that because "the Amalekites were of a more wicked and murderous disposition than the Lamanites were, . . . [the king] appointed chief captains over the Lamanites. And they were all Amalekites and Zoramites." (Alma 43:6.)

We do not know the exact origins of the Amalekites, but the origin of the Amulonites is given in the Book of Mormon. The Amulonites first began to be a separate people in the days of Alma the Elder. While Alma was a priest of the wicked King Noah, there was another priest of the king whose name was Amulon. We are told in Mosiah that some of the exiled priests of the king kidnapped some of the daughters of the Lamanites, because they were ashamed and afraid to return to their wives and families. (Mosiah 20:3-5.) The leader of this group was Amulon. These people were later found by the Lamanites, who had compassion on these priests and their families because of their Lamanite wives. (Mosiah 23:34.) This group then joined the Lamanites. (Mosiah 23:35.) When the people of Alma were discovered by the Lamanites and the followers of Amulon, the Amulonites were given authority over Alma's people. (Mosiah 23:35-39.) Soon after this, the Amulonites began to persecute them and forbade them to pray, under penalty of death. (Mosiah 24.) Shortly thereafter the people of Alma escaped from the control of the Amulonites.

The next we hear about the Amulonites is when the sons of Mosiah began their missionary journeys among the Lamanites. While thousands of the Lamanites converted to the gospel, none of the Amulonites repented of their false and evil traditions. Instead, they encouraged those who had not accepted the truth to persecute those who had.

Ammonites

Soon after the large group of Lamanites had accepted the truths taught to them by the sons of Mosiah and had repented of their sins, they chose for themselves a name to distinguish them from those Lamanites who had not converted to the truth. The name they adopted was Anti-Nephi-Lehies. The precise meaning of the name Anti-Nephi-Lehies is not known, but it appears that the Lamanite converts chose it because they desired a name that would identify them as descendants of Lehi who were not descendants of Nephi. Later the people began to be called "Ammonites," after the leader of the Nephite missionaries who had converted them. (Alma 27:26.) Still later, their children referred to themselves as "Nephites." (Alma 53:16.) According to the Book of Mormon record, these people remained faithful to the gospel and "never did fall away." (Alma 23:6.)

Alma 24-29 describes events that were turning points for both the Lamanites and the Nephites. After the great conversions among the Lamanites, those who had not accepted the truth, led by the Amulonites and Amalekites, came against the converts to destroy them. The Anti-Nephi-Lehies, because of their wicked and murderous past, were afraid to take up arms to defend themselves. They had repented of their sins and feared that, as they put it, "perhaps, if we should stain our swords again they can no more be washed bright through the blood of the Son of our great God, which shall be shed for the atonement of our sins." (Alma 24:13.) At this point King Anti-Nephi-Lehi delivered a powerful and moving discourse, thanking God for his mercy in forgiving them and releasing them from the bondage of sin. He exhorted the people to submit to the will of the Lord. He told them that because of their past sins, it would be better for them to die than to take up arms again. The king concluded his speech by saying: "And now, my brethren, if our brethren seek to destroy us, behold, we will hide away our swords, yea, even we will bury them deep in the earth, that they may be kept bright, as a testimony that we have never used them, at the last day; and if our brethren destroy us, behold, we shall go to our God and shall be saved." (Alma 24:16.) At the conclusion of this speech all the people did as the king advised them, burying their weapons deep in the earth. (Alma 24:17.)

There is no question about the fact that the Book of Mormon holds in extremely high regard these people who, on the grounds of conscience and covenants, refused to bear arms — even in what might normally be considered justifiable self-defense. (See also Alma 24:16-27; 27:2-3, 23-24, 27-30.) The Book of Mormon also teaches that military action in self-defense is justifiable. (See, for example, Alma 48:14-16, 23-25; 53:10-17. See also D&C 98:33-48.) Mormon, reflecting on the example of the Anti-Nephi-Lehies, wrote: "Thus we see that, when these Lamanites were brought to believe and to know the truth, they were firm, and would suffer even unto death rather than commit sin; and thus we see that they buried their . . . weapons of war, for peace." (Alma 24:19.)

When the Lamanites had finished their preparations for war, they came against their kinsmen. As they approached, the righteous people went out to meet them and prostrated themselves on the earth as they called upon their God. The Lamanites fell upon them while they were praying and killed one thousand and five people without any resistance. At this point some of the Lamanites realized that these people were not going to defend themselves, and they stopped their killing. "And there were many whose hearts had swollen in them for those of their brethren who had fallen under the sword, for they repented of the things which they had done. . . . And it came to pass that the people of God were joined that day by more than the number who had been slain." (Alma 24:24, 26.) All of these Lamanites who joined the people of God were descendants of Laman and Lemuel. There were no Amalekites or Amulonites among them. (Alma 24:29.) The slaughter of their brethren only angered the other Lamanites more, and soon they began to fight against the Nephites—first in the city of Ammonihah, and then in different parts of the Nephite territories. In these battles the majority of the people who were slain by the Nephites were the descendants of Amulon and his followers. When the Lamanites saw that they could not overpower the Nephites they returned to their homes, and many of them joined the Anti-Nephi-Lehies. (Alma 25:13.) These converts also buried their weapons of war, as the others had already done. (Alma 25:14.)

The Anti-Nephi-Lehies obeyed the law of Moses, believing that it was a type of Christ's coming. (Alma 25:15.) Obeying the law strengthened their faith in Christ: "They did keep the law of Moses; . . . for it was not all fulfilled. But notwithstanding the law of Moses, they did look forward to the coming of Christ, considering that the law of Moses was a type of his coming, and believing that they must keep those outward performances until the time that he should be revealed unto them. Now they did not suppose that salvation came by the law of Moses; but the law of Moses did serve to strengthen their faith in Christ; and thus they did retain a hope through faith, unto eternal salvation, relying upon the spirit of prophecy, which spake of those things to come." (Alma 25:15-16.)

This is one of the finest statements in the scriptures about the role of the law of Moses as a "type," a symbol or pattern, of the mission of Christ. The faithful Book of Mormon people observed the law of Moses while looking forward to the coming of Christ and while living gospel principles and ordinances. They knew that salvation did not come by the law of Moses but through Christ; yet the law strengthened their faith in Christ and taught them of him through the spirit of prophecy.

Conversion Brings Joy

Alma 26 contains the report given by Ammon and his brothers after their fourteen-year mission among the Lamanites. Ammon and his brothers rejoiced in the happiness that they had received in the service of others: "How great reason have we to rejoice; for could we have supposed when we started from the land of Zarahemla that God would have granted unto us such great blessings? And now, I ask, what great blessings has he bestowed upon us? Can ye tell?" (Alma 26:1-2.) He continued by glorying in the happiness that had been brought to their converts: "Our brethren, the Lamanites, were in darkness, yea, even in the darkest abyss, but behold, how many of them are brought to behold the marvelous light of God! And this is the blessing which hath been bestowed upon us, that we have been made instruments in the hands of God to bring about this great work." (Alma 26:3.) From this scripture we learn that it is a blessing to be an instrument in God's hands to bring the gospel to others. (See also D&C 18:15-16.) The important lesson to be learned from this is that after all of the success that Ammon and his brothers had on their missions, they attributed it all to the Lord. Ammon continued: "I do not boast in my own strength, nor in my own wisdom; but behold, my joy is full, yea, my heart is brim with joy, and I will rejoice in my God. Yea, I know that I am nothing; as to my strength I am weak; therefore I will not boast of myself, but I will boast of my God, for in his strength I can do all things; yea, behold, many mighty miracles we have wrought in this land, for which we will praise his name forever." (Alma 26:11-12.) Here we learn a very important lesson: When we work with the strength of the Lord, all things are possible. If we obey the commandments and follow the teachings of the Church, God will bless us in our righteous desires. Because of their desire and obedience, the sons of Mosiah were blessed with success in their missions. When they gloried in the many miracles they had seen, they did not glory in their own strength; they gloried in the miraculous deeds of God. Of the many miracles that occurred during the missions of the sons of Mosiah, the greatest was the conversion of thousands of souls to the truth.

Ammon recalled the attitude of their fellow Nephites before the sons of Mosiah preached the gospel to their enemies: "Do ye remember, my brethren, that we said unto our brethren in the land of Zarahemla, we go up to the land of Nephi, to preach unto our brethren, the Lamanites, and they laughed us to scorn? For they said unto us: Do ye suppose that ye can bring the Lamanites to the knowledge of the truth? Do ye suppose that ye can convince the Lamanites of the incorrectness of the traditions of their fathers, as stiffnecked a people as they are; whose hearts delight in the shedding of blood; whose days have been spent in the grossest iniquity; whose ways have been the ways of a transgressor from the beginning? Now my brethren, ye remember that this was their language." (Alma 26:23-24.)

It is important for us as Latter-day Saints to remember that we have the responsibility to share the gospel with all the world. This does not include only the nations that we consider to be friendly toward us; it includes all nations. We should never wish evil upon people; we should desire to take the gospel message to them, "with the intent that perhaps we might save some few of their souls." (Alma 26:26.)

President Spencer W. Kimball taught: "What are we to fear when the Lord is with us? Can we not take the Lord at his word and exercise a particle of faith in him? Our assignment is affirmative: . . . to carry the gospel to our enemies, that they might no longer be our enemies."[1] The success of Ammon and his brothers is an effective witness to the power of God's love for all people. And it bears testimony to us today of the gospel's capacity to remove hatred and prejudice from our hearts. Ammon concluded his rejoicing with these words: "Now my brethren, we see that God is mindful of every people, whatsoever land they may be in; yea, he numbereth his people, and his bowels of mercy are over all the earth. Now this is my joy, . . . and I will give thanks unto my God forever." (Alma 26:37.)

Lamanite Converts Join with the Nephites

After the Lamanites had returned from their wars against the Nephites, the Amalekites began to stir them up again. (Alma 27:2.) Keeping the covenant that they had made, the Anti-Nephi-Lehies again refused to take up arms; thus many of them were killed. Upon seeing this, Ammon and his brethren invited the king to gather his people together and take them to the land of Zarahemla to escape destruction from their enemies. (Alma 27:4-5.) The king expressed his fears that the Nephites would not accept them because of the murders they had committed. (Alma 27:6.) He said that if they went, they would submit themselves to being the Nephites' slaves, to right the wrongs they had done to them in the past. Ammon assured him that slavery was contrary to Nephite law. He stated his intention to inquire of the Lord and asked the king if he would go if the Lord told them to do so. To this the king agreed. In response to Ammon's prayer, the Lord told him to take the people out of that land, promising that if they did this they would be preserved. (Alma 27:12.) Obeying the word of the Lord, the people gathered their flocks and herds and left for the land of the Nephites. When they reached the wilderness, they camped while Ammon and his brothers went ahead to see if their people would accept the Anti-Nephi-Lehies into their lands. When they arrived at Zarahemla, they went before the chief judge and explained the situation to him. Soon "the voice of the people came, saying: Behold, we will give up the land of Jershon, which is on the east by the sea, which joins the land Bountiful, which is on the south of the land Bountiful; and this land Jershon is the land we will give unto our brethren for an inheritance." (Alma 27:22.) They continued by promising to supply an army to protect the land of Jershon so that the Anti-Nephi-Lehies would not have to break their covenant not to take up weapons of war. The only condition placed upon the followers of Ammon was that they would be required to give part of their earnings and food to help maintain the Nephite army. With this news, Ammon returned to his people and informed them of the decision of the Nephites. They then continued their journey and soon were settled in the land of Jershon and were "numbered among the people who were of the church of God." (Alma 27:27.) It is then noted that these people "were also distinguished for their zeal towards God, and also towards men; for they were perfectly honest and upright in all things; and they were firm in the faith of Christ, even unto the end." (Alma 27:27.)

Following the settlement of the Ammonites in the land of Jershon, the Lamanites again came against them in battle, a battle "as never had been known among all the people in the land from the time Lehi left Jerusalem; yea, and tens of thousands of the Lamanites were slain and scattered abroad." (Alma 28:2.) Many Nephites were killed also, but ultimately "the Lamanites were driven and scattered, and the people of Nephi returned again to their land." (Alma 28:3.) In spite of the great losses among the Nephites, the Nephites continued to protect the Ammonites, and they never complained or blamed the Ammonites for the battles that followed. They supported the Ammonites in their covenant not to take up arms again.

According to Our Desires and God's Wisdom

At the end of the account of the mission of the sons of Mosiah to the Lamanites and their relocation among the Nephites, Alma added a brief commentary on some of the gospel principles involved in the events that had transpired. He lamented the fact that he could not preach repentance with even greater power, but he strove to be content with the calling the Lord had given him. (Alma 29:1-3.) He wrote further: "I know that he granteth unto men according to their desire, whether it be unto death or unto life; yea, I know that he allotteth unto men, yea, decreeth unto them decrees which are unalterable, according to their wills, whether they be unto salvation or unto destruction." (Alma 29:4.) Because we have agency, we control our final destiny. With this agency, we are accountable for our decisions, whether we do good or evil, and choose between happiness and sorrow, since these are the inevitable consequences of those choices. President Ezra Taft Benson has taught: "We are free to choose, but we are not free to alter the consequences of those choices."[2] Those who are not accountable and do not know good from evil are blameless, "but he that knoweth good and evil, to him it is given according to his desires, whether he desireth good or evil, life or death, joy or remorse of conscience." (Alma 29:5.)

Alma also taught that God grants gospel knowledge to his children according to his divine wisdom. "The Lord doth grant unto all nations, of their own nation and tongue, to teach his word, yea, in wisdom, all that he seeth fit that they should have." (Alma 29:8.) The Lord gives to all nations that portion of his word that they are prepared to receive. Those who do not harden their hearts against the portion of the word of the Lord that they are given receive "the greater portion of the word," until they know the mysteries of God "in full." (Alma 12:10.) On the other hand, those who do harden their hearts against the word of the Lord receive the "lesser portion of the word until they know nothing concerning his mysteries; and then they are taken captive by the devil, and led by his will down to destruction." (Alma 12:11.) Ammon promised that those who repent, exercise faith, bring forth good works, and pray continually will know the mysteries of God. Moreover, they will bring "thousands of souls" to repentance. (Alma 26:22.) Mormon applied this same principle to those who were the most wicked in the account that we have been discussing, the Amalekites and Amulonites, who were apostates from the Nephites and had once had the gospel: "Thus we can plainly discern, that after a people have been once enlightened by the Spirit of God, and have had great knowledge of things pertaining to righteousness, and then have fallen away into sin and transgression, they become more hardened, and thus their state becomes worse than though they had never known these things." (Alma 24:30.)

Conclusion

From these chapters of Alma we can learn some valuable lessons. First, we should do all possible to avoid sin. The Ammonites were willing to face death rather than break their oath and chance becoming wicked once again. While few will ever be asked to make such a choice, all people are faced with critical choices every day. By flirting with sin we risk bringing spiritual death upon ourselves; by avoiding sin we can be granted eternal life. The important lessons learned from these chapters can be summarized by a statement from Mormon: "Thus we see the great call of diligence of men to labor in the vineyards of the Lord; and thus we see the great reason of sorrow, and also of rejoicing—sorrow because of death and destruction among men, and joy because of the light of Christ unto life." (Alma 28:14.)

The record contained in Alma 24 through 29 presents us with stark contrasts, most notably in the behavior of the devout Lamanite converts and the evil apostates from the Nephites. The scriptures teach by means of such contrasts, so that we in the last days can choose to pattern our lives after the righteous examples of those who have gone before.

Notes

1. Spencer W. Kimball, "The False Gods We Worship," *Ensign*, June 1976, p. 6.

2. Ezra Taft Benson, *Come Unto Christ* (Salt Lake City: Deseret Book Company, 1983), p. 40.

Scripture Index

THE OLD TESTAMENT

THE NEW TESTAMENT

THE BOOK OF MORMON

17:10-16	141	24:3-23	142	26:29	152; 180; 286; 318, n. 3
17:17-20	141	24:3-31	135		
17:17-25	134	24:14	77		
17:21-25	141	24:24-27	142	26:30-31	152
18:1-4	141	24:28-31	142	26:33	152
18:1-4, 9-15	134	24:32	134, 142	27	154
18:5-8	141	25:1	138	27:1	153
18:6-8	134	25:2	138	27:4, 8-9	83
18:7-8	137	25:4	138	27:6	173
18:9-10	141	25:5	131, 138	27:7	153
18:11-15	141	25:5-6	135	27:12	153
18:16-22	141	25:6	19, 138	27:12, 14	155
19:1-7	141	25:7	138	27:12-14	157
19:1-21	134	25:10	142	27:15, 16	153
19:8-21	141	25:11	142	27:20	153
19:17	134	25:12-13	142	27:20-21	153
20:1-4	134, 141	25:14-15	142	27:21, 23	154
20:5-19	141	25:16	142	27:26	154
20:5-19, 24-27	134	25:19	36, 129, n. 10	27:29-35	154
				28:3-6	155
20:5-19, 24-34	135	25:20	142	28:7-8	155
		25:21	5	28:8	334, n. 4
20:20-23	141	25:23	218	28:9	155
20:22	137	25:23, 26	29	28:14	156
20:24-34	134, 141	25:23, 26, 28-29	142	28:20-22	157
21:1-5	141			28:31	157
21:6-9	141	25:23-30	206	29:2	157
21:6-9, 14-16	134	25:24-30	150	29:3-6	158
		25:28	172	29:7-11	158
21:10	137	25:30	255	29:13-14	158
21:10-13	141	26:1-2	150	29:14	159
21:14-16	141	26:3-9	150	30:1-2	159, 188
22:1-6	141	26:6	150	30:3-8	159
22:2	134	26:7	150	30:7-15	84
23:1	142	26:8	151	30:10	84
23:1-5, 14-22	135	26:9	164	30:10-18	160
		26:12-15	151	31	120, 207
23:1-22	134	26:13	216	31–32	228, n. 16
23:2-5	142	26:20	151	31:2, 21	167
23:6-13	142	26:20-31	152	31:3	168
23:14-22	142	26:22	157	31:5	163
23:19	137	26:24	152	31:7	164
24:1-2	142	26:25, 28, 33	113	31:9	164, 165
24:1-32	134			31:9, 18-19	165

THE DOCTRINE AND COVENANTS

THE PEARL OF GREAT PRICE

Subject Index

Aaron: preaches unsuccessfully in Jerusalem, 329-30; teaches Lamanite king, 330-31

Abinadi: first mission of, 234-35, 241; prophesies bondage for Noah's people, 235; chastises wicked priests, 236, 242; likened to John the Baptist, 240-41; historical background of, 241; quotes prophecies of Isaiah, 243-44, 247-48; death of, 253-54

Abish, 326-27

Abraham, blessings of, promised to Lamanites, 112-13

Adam, priesthood organization of, 45

Adultery, Jacob decries, 179

Agency: depends on atonement, 95; war in heaven over, 147; does not preclude consequences, 343

Allegory, 137, 186-87

Alma the elder: conversion of, 254; baptizes many and establishes church, 255-56; authority of, 258 n. 18; people of, in bondage to Lamanites, 266-67; worries and prays over unbelievers, 274

Alma the younger: receives sacred objects, 208; conversion of, 275; resigns judgment seat to preach, 292-93, 295; as chief judge and high priest, 294-95; bears testimony of Christ, 296, 303-4; discusses requisites for spiritual rebirth, 300-

301; fruits of labors of, 302-3; further missionary labors of, 304-5; imprisonment and deliverance of, 309-10

Altar of stones, 23

Amaleki, 201-2

Amalekites, 335-37

Amlici: seeks to become king, 287; incites followers to begin civil war, 288; defeated by majority vote, 288

Amlicites, 288-90

Ammon: discovers people of Limhi, 262-63; declines to baptize Limhi's people, 265-66

Ammon, son of Mosiah: humility of, 323, 329; serves, teaches, and converts Lamoni, 323-25; enemy attempts to kill, 327; as type of Christ, 328-29; joy of, in conversion of Lamanites, 340-42

Ammonihah: Alma leaves, and returns to, 305, 308; wickedness of people in, 307-8; conversion of some in, 309; burning of believers in, 309; destruction of, 316

Ammonites, 337-39, 341-43

Amulek: meets and succors Alma, 305, 308; Zeezrom offers money to, 308, 314; imprisonment and deliverance of, 309-10; abandons former life to join Alma, 312-13; serves as Alma's missionary companion, 313-14

Amulon, 267, 336

Children, rearing, in righteousness, 220

Church: devil sets up, in opposition to God's kingdom, 45; established by Nephi, 205; established by Alma the elder, 255; scattered congregations of, 272; of God, definition of, 272; priests and teachers in, 272-73; separation of, from secular government, 273-74; proper relation of, to government, 278-81; persecution of members of, 286-87, 292; excommunication of unrighteous from, 303; Alma establishes, at Gideon, 304

Columbus, Christopher, 46-47

Condescension: of God the Father, 38-40; of Jesus Christ, 40-41

Conversion: of King Benjamin's followers, 218-19; involves mighty change, 225; prototypes of, 332-34

Costly apparel, wearing of, 291-92

Countenance, receiving Christ's image in, 301-2

Covenants of God with Joseph of Egypt, 104

Cowdery, Oliver, describes translation work, 16

Creation: tendency to discount scriptural accounts of, 87; mechanistic view of, 87-88; purpose in, 89-90, 91-92

Darwin, Charles, 92

Dead, salvation for, 213-14, 252

Dead Sea Scrolls, 49, 53

Death: redemption from, 116-18; introduced by fall of Adam, 117; physical, Christ conquered, 249; second, 253

Democracy: definition of, 277; Mosiah II proposes to Nephites, 277-78; danger of, if people are unrighteous, 284

Egyptian influence in Judah, 18

Enos: as model of prayer, 197-98; prays for preservation of records, 199

Eusebius on corruption of Bible texts, 52

Evolution, organic, theories of, 92-93

Exaltation: qualifying for, 166-67; differentiated from salvation, 252

Exodus of Israel: Lehites' experience likened to, 64-65, 66-69; Nephi recounts story of, 67-68

Ezias, 75

Ezra, 48

Faith: definition of, 271-72; essential to spiritual rebirth, 298-99

Fall of Adam: Lehi's teachings concerning, 91-92; necessary to plan of salvation, 92, 97; physical and spiritual effects of, 215

Father, Jesus Christ as, 245-46

Foreordination, 319 n. 12

Future, Nephi's vision of, 44-45

Gathering of Israel: Nephi quotes Isaiah on, 77-82; repentance must precede, 189

Gentiles: Nephi sees, in vision, 46-47; gospel to be restored among, 79-80; stumbling block of, 151-52; adoption of, into Israel, 159-60

Gideon: threatens to slay King Noah, 261; blames Noah's priests for abductions, 262; proposes getting Lamanites drunk, 266; slain by Nehor, 285

God: drawing near to, through reading Book of Mormon, 6-7; glory of, having eye single to, 13-14; condescension of, 38-40; love of, symbolized by tree of life, 39; as author of law, 93-94, 100-101 n. 16; omnipotence of, 98 n. 3, 99 n. 7;

238; observed among Nephites, 205-6; was to lead to, not supplant, full gospel, 216; Abinadi's discussion of, 237-38, 242-43; Abinadi declares inadequacy of, 246-47; observed among Ammonites, 339

Law: is bi-conditional with God, 93-94; effects of broken, overcome by Christ, 94; being subject to secular, 279-81; Nephite government founded on, 283-84

Learning, worldly, 126-27; 153-54

Lee, Harold B., 319 n. 12

Lehi: Nephi abridges record of, 17; family of, lived at Jerusalem, 19-20; sees vision of Jerusalem's destruction, 20; testified of coming of Messiah, 21; is warned in dream to flee into wilderness, 21; possible route of, in wilderness, 22-23; sons of, 24-25; sees vision of tree of life, 35; doctrinal discourse given by, 87; on creation, 88-90; on fall of Adam, 91-92; on law and sin, 93-94; on atonement of Christ, 94-97; gives patriarchal blessing to Joseph, 103; words of, to Jacob, 176

Lemuel, valley of, 61, 71 n. 2-3

Liahona: appearance and functioning of, 61-62; as type of Christ, 62; directed Nephi in finding food, 63

Limhi: becomes king of Nephite colony, 261; Ammon discovers people of, 262-63

Literary devices in Isaiah's writings, 135-37

Lucifer, rebellion of, 147-48

Lund, Anthon H., 102 n. 30

Malachi, prophecies of, about millennium, 82-84

Marvelous work and a wonder, 12, 154

Mary, mother of Christ, 38-39

McConkie, Bruce R.: on condescension of God, 38, 41; on church of devil, 55; on Christian concepts in brass plates, 76; on prophet Zenos, 76; on gathering of Israel, 77; on scattering of Israel, 77; on prophets quoting one another, 83; on being subject to Satan, 119; on Christ's mortal obedience, 165; on seeking signs, 184 n. 13; on repentance, 271; on kingdom of God on earth, 272; on priests and teachers in Book of Mormon, 273; on spiritual rebirth, 275, 276; on subjection to government, 279-80; on self-defense in war, 288-89; on baptism, 298; on Savior's teaching methods, 321-22; on three pillars of eternity, 325

McKay, David O., 178

Mechanistic view of creation, 87-88, 97

Meditation, 198

Metaphor, 137, 186-87

Michael, 148

Mighty change of heart, 299, 302

Millennium: Nephi writes of, 58-59; prophecies concerning, 82-84; Nephi prophesies concerning, 160

Missionary work: Abinadi prophesies of, 248; of sons of Mosiah among Lamanites, 322-23, 331; sanctioned by Lamanite king, 331-32; sons of Mosiah rejoice in, 340-42

Monetary system, explanation of, 318 n. 5

Mormon, abridgment task of, 202

Moroni: appearance of, to Joseph Smith, 11-12; counsel given by, to Joseph Smith, 12-14

Moses, 27, 68

Mosiah I leads expedition to Zarahemla, 206

Mosiah II: receives sacred objects from Benjamin, 208; ability of, to translate records, 268; becomes leader of various Nephite groups,

271; separates church from secular government, 273-74; sons of, are converted, 276; sons of, refuse kingship, 277; sons of, go on mission to Lamanites, 322-23; conversion of sons of, 322; God promises to protect sons of, 329

Murmuring, 24, 64

Naturalism, 92-93, 97, 102 n. 30

Natural disasters, 150-51

Natural man as enemy to God, 217, 297

Nebuchadnezzar, 19

Nehor: false doctrines taught by, 284-85; slays Gideon, 285; trial and execution of, 286; order of, followed in Ammonihah, 308; order of, followed by apostate groups, 336

Nephi: greatness of, 24-25; describes purpose of writings, 29; small plates of, 34; sees Lehi's vision and interpretation, 35; sees future events in vision, 44-45; relates broken bow incident, 63-65; character of, demonstrated by incidents described, 65-66, 70; is commanded to build ship, 65-66; quotes Isaiah, 78; quotes Zenos on millennium, 82-84; likened to Joseph of Egypt, 108; psalm of, 108-10; God warns, to flee from brothers, 110; emphasizes belief in Christ, 142-43; seals writings with testimony, 171-73; gives records to Jacob, 175-77

Nephihah, 293

Nephites: Nephi foresees destruction of, 150-51; people become known as, 176-77; theocratic government of, 210-11; spiritual awakening among, following war, 290-91; converted Lamanites join with, 342-43

Neum, 75

Neutrality, impossibility of, 149

Nibley, Hugh, on corruption of Bible texts, 52-53

Noah, King: wickedness of, 231-32; elegant buildings constructed for, 232-33; vanity of people of, 233-34; hardens heart against Abinadi's message, 235; death of, 254, 261; commands people to flee from Lamanites, 261

Oaks, Dallin H., 124-25

Obedience: perfect, of Christ, 164-66; necessary to salvation, 165-66

Olive tree, allegory of, 187-94

Omni, book of, 201-2

Opposition, need for, 96-97

Ordinances, Christ's subjection to, 165

Parallelism, 136

Parents: goodly, described in scriptures, 17-18; responsibilities of, toward children, 220

Persecution: of church members, 286-87, 292; of believers in Ammonihah, 309

Petersen, Mark E., 49

Plural marriage, 183 n. 8

Prayer: inspired, of Nephi, 110; evil spirits teach people to avoid, 169; Nephi's exhortations regarding, 169-70; role of Holy Ghost in, 170; Enos as model of, 197-98; Amulon forbids, 267

Premortal life: war in, 147-49; faithfulness in, 311

Pride: as result of wealth, 178; accompanying wealth, 291-92

Priestcraft: condemnation of, 152; destructive nature of, 180; introduced by Nehor, 286, 308

Priesthood, callings in, mentioned in Book of Mormon, 259 n. 22

Book of Mormon

Part 2

Alma 30 to Moroni

CONTENTS

Contents

PREFACE

Nothing bears a stronger testimony to the mission of the Prophet Joseph Smith than the Book of Mormon. Its detailed historical narrative, intricate and consistent geographical presentation, and profound description of human nature demonstrate beyond doubt that no uninspired person could have produced such a book. More importantly, its unparalleled description of the doctrine of God and its uncompromising testimony to the mission of Jesus Christ shout from the housetops that the Book of Mormon is true—the work of the Lord—and that Joseph Smith, through whom God brought it forth, was the Lord's servant.

We Latter-day Saints gratefully acknowledge the Book of Mormon as the keystone of our religion, revealed by the Lord to provide a sure foundation of our faith. In the Church we accept not only the truthfulness of its doctrine, but also the historicity of the events it describes. Those who choose to do otherwise not only deny the Lord's witness concerning it (see D&C 17:6) but also forfeit the blessings that attend those who read it, love it, and abide by the doctrine and precepts to which it bears testimony.

Studies in Scripture, Vol. 8: Alma 30 to Moroni was written to accompany one's personal study of the Book of Mormon. The authors and the editor acknowledge that there is no substitute for carefully searching the scriptures themselves, and we encourage all to do so. The Studies in Scripture series is presented as a resource to help readers in that effort.

This volume emphasizes the teachings of the Book of Mormon. The authors have stressed the messages contained in the sermons and writings of its prophets. At the same time, they have discussed Book of Mormon history in order to clarify the narrative and emphasize the lessons that are taught through historical events. Since the primary purpose of the Book of Mormon itself is to teach and bear testimony of the gospel of Jesus Christ, our purpose in this volume has been to do likewise. Thus we have considered external evidences of the Book of Mormon, as well as contextual and comparative studies, to be of lesser value for this work.

Each of the contributors is responsible for his or her own conclusions. This book is a private endeavor and not a production of either Brigham Young University or The Church of Jesus Christ of Latter-day Saints. Although the writers and the editor have sought to be in harmony with the teachings of the scriptures and the leaders of the Church, the reader should not regard this work as a primary source for gospel understanding but should turn instead to the scriptures and the words of modern prophets for authoritative doctrinal statements.

I express my appreciation to the management and staff of Deseret Book Company, to my assistant Charles J. Baldwin, and to the contributors to this volume, whose knowledge and spiritual sensitivities are apparent throughout its pages. I am also most thankful for the expert assistance of my colleagues Robert E. Parsons, Rex C. Reeve, Jr., and Robert L. Millet, whose wisdom and advice have added much to this book.

KENT P. JACKSON

1

KORIHOR THE ANTI-CHRIST
(Alma 30)

LaMar Garrard

After the people of Anti-Nephi-Lehi left their homeland among the Lamanites, they were allowed to live among the Nephites in the land of Jershon, where they were called the people of Ammon. Later came a great battle between the Lamanites and the Nephites in which the Lamanites were defeated. After this great battle was a period of peace throughout the land. Then appeared a man named Korihor, who came into the land of Zarahemla and preached against the prophecies of the coming of Christ. He also went to the land of Jershon and preached among the people of Ammon. However, these people took him before their high priest, who commanded him to be carried out of the land. Korihor then went to the land of Gideon to preach and was eventually brought before Giddonah, the high priest there. When Giddonah saw the hardness of Korihor's heart, he had him brought before Alma, the chief judge and governor over the land. Alma 30 discusses what Korihor taught in Zarahemla, Jershon, and Gideon; his trial before Alma; and his downfall.

The writer of this account is Mormon, who called Korihor an anti-Christ. Alma 30 is part of an abridgment made by Mormon—under the direction and inspiration of the Lord—from a larger, more detailed account by earlier prophets. In vision Nephi saw that this record would eventually come forth in the latter days for the benefit of our modern generation. (1 Ne. 13:32-36.) Keeping this in mind,

LaMar E. Garrard is professor of Church history and doctrine at Brigham Young University.

why would the Lord direct Mormon to devote an entire chapter to the details of the teachings and final destiny of Korihor when so many other things were written on the original plates? As we compare the teachings of this man and the beliefs of those today who advocate the philosophy of naturalism, we see a striking similarity. I believe that the Lord foresaw the adverse effects of naturalism on our modern world and therefore purposely directed Mormon to include the teachings of Korihor in his record. Those who read and accept the Book of Mormon are thereby warned against accepting the philosophical assumptions of naturalism. What one believes about the universe is important because it affects one's behavior, for "as [a man] thinketh in his heart, so is he." (Prov. 23:7.)

The Rise of Naturalism

E. A. Burtt, in his book *The Metaphysical Foundations of Modern Physical Science,* traces cosmological thinking from medieval to modern times. He points out that the naturalistic viewpoint has made great inroads into the thinking of many of our modern generation. Even though we may not all be philosophers or scientists, still the philosophies of those around us affect our thinking even though we may not realize it. Burtt explains that sometimes we accept a philosophical position without being aware of its implications and hence it produces a subtle and pervasive control over our thinking.

> How curious, after all, is the way in which we moderns think about our world! And it is so novel, too. The cosmology underlying our mental processes is but three centuries old— a mere infant in the history of thought—and yet we cling to it with the same embarrassed zeal with which a young father fondles his new-born baby. Like him, we are ignorant enough of its precise nature; like him, we nevertheless take it piously to be ours and allow it a subtly pervasive and unhindered control over our thinking.[1]

Bertrand Russell was a renowned mathematician and philosopher who advocated the naturalistic viewpoint. He claimed that as science has arisen in the past 300 years and has become so pragmatically successful in our lives, it has become a dominant factor in determining the beliefs of educated people: "As a result of the new control over the environment which scientific knowledge has conferred, a new philosophy is growing up, involving a changed conception of man's place in the universe."[2] He went on to explain that it is our personal acceptance of the premises on which the scientific method was based that has changed our way of thinking about the world around us:

> Out of the work of the great men of the seventeenth century a new outlook on the world was developed, and it was this outlook, not specific arguments, which brought about the decay of the belief in portents, witchcraft, demoniacal possession, and so forth. I think there were three ingredients in the scientific outlook of the eighteenth century that were specially important.
>
> (1) Statements of fact should be based on observation, not on unsupported authority.
>
> (2) The inanimate world is a self-acting, self-perpetuating system, in which all changes conform to natural laws.
>
> (3) The earth is not the center of the universe, and probably Man is not its purpose (if any); moreover, "purpose" is a concept which is scientifically useless.[3]

We advocate the philosophy of naturalism (whether we realize it or not) when we no longer regard these statements as restricted outlooks to be taken only in scientific endeavors but shift to the following positions: knowledge cannot be gained by any other means than by the use of the natural senses, the universe is really an inanimate self-acting and self-perpetuating system, and there is no real purpose in the existence of the universe.[4] This chapter will compare these fundamental assumptions of naturalism with Korihor's teachings to show the similarity between the two. The implications of accepting these assumptions will then be examined.

Methods of Gaining Knowledge

Science has become successful in predicting, controlling, and explaining many natural events by making the restriction that in any scientific endeavor all conclusions must be based upon public, repeatable observations using the natural senses. This has proved advantageous for the progress of science, but if we allow this restriction to become part of our personal epistemology or method of gaining knowledge of the world around us, it automatically eliminates any knowledge coming to us from God through the living prophets, the scriptures, or personal revelation.

Korihor took the naturalistic viewpoint. He advocated that what the prophets say and have said (their recorded words, or scriptures) are foolish traditions (Russell's unsupported authority), since we cannot know of anything that does not come through the natural senses (things we cannot see): "O ye that are bound down under a foolish and a vain hope, why do ye yoke yourselves with such foolish things? Why do ye look for a Christ? For *no man can know of anything which is to come.* Behold, these things which ye call prophecies, which ye say are handed down by holy prophets, behold, *they are foolish traditions of your fathers.* How do ye know of their surety? Behold, *ye cannot know of things which ye do not see."* (Alma 30:13-15; emphasis added.)

Because of Korihor's position that we cannot know anything of the world around us except through empirical observation, he claimed we cannot know that there is a God, "a being who never has been seen or known, who never was nor ever will be." (Alma 30:28.) When Alma confronted him directly and asked him if he believed in a God, he answered no (Alma 30:38) and went on to explain that he would believe in God only if he were given a sign, some empirical evidence: "If thou wilt show me a sign, that I may be convinced that there is a God, yea, show unto me that he hath power, and then will I be convinced of the truth of thy words." (Alma 30:43.) Later he took more of an agnostic rather than an atheistic position, but he still maintained his position that knowledge of such things comes only by empirical observation: "I do not deny the existence of a God, but I do not believe that there is a God . . . and except ye show me a sign, I will not believe." (Alma 30:48.)

Alma, on the other hand, held that we can obtain knowledge from God by revelation as well as through the natural senses. By not hardening our hearts, we can receive revelation to our spirits that confirms to us that the words of the prophets and the scriptures are true.[5] Alma rebuked Korihor, saying that he was resisting the promptings of the Holy Spirit; otherwise he would accept the words of the prophets and the scriptures and believe in God:

> And now what evidence have ye that there is no God, or that Christ cometh not? I say unto you that ye have none, save it be your word only. But, behold, I have all things as a testimony that these things are true; and ye also have all things as a testimony unto you that they are true; and will ye deny them? Believest thou that these things are true?
>
> Behold, I know that thou believest, but thou art possessed with a lying spirit, and *ye have put off the Spirit of God* that it may have no place in you. . . .
>
> Will ye say, Show unto me a sign, when ye have *the testimony of all these thy brethren,* and also *all the holy prophets?* The *scriptures* are laid before thee, yea, and all things denote there is a God. . . . And yet do ye go about, leading away the hearts of this people, testifying unto them there is no God? And yet will ye deny against all these witnesses? And he said: Yea, I will deny, except ye shall show me a sign.
>
> And now it came to pass that Alma said unto him: Behold, I am grieved because of the hardness of your heart, yea, that *ye will still resist the spirit of the truth,* that thy soul may be destroyed. (Alma 30:40-42, 44-46; emphasis added.)

The Nature of the Universe

Russell's second point was that science has become pragmatically successful by assuming that the world around us is a self-acting, self-perpetuating system in which all changes conform to natural laws. Russell explains that before the rise of modern physics, it was thought that all motion resulted from the action of living beings with souls:

> Before Galileo it had been thought that a lifeless body will not move of itself, and if it is in motion it will gradually come to rest. Only living beings, it was thought, could move without help of some external agency. Aristotle thought that the heavenly bodies were pushed by Gods. Here on earth, animals can set themselves in motion and can cause motion in dead

matter. . . . Everything depends upon impulsion from the souls of living beings.

So long as this view prevailed, physics as an independent science was impossible, since the physical world was thought to be not causally self-contained. But Galileo and Newton between them proved that all the movements of the planets, and of dead matter on the earth, proceed according to the law of physics, and once started, will continue indefinitely. There is no need of mind in this process.[6]

At a later date the philosopher and mathematician Descartes "held that not only dead matter, but the bodies of animals also, are wholly governed by the laws of physics."[7] The French freethinkers and the eighteenth-century materialists took the next step by saying that all causes are material in nature, and that mental occurrences are inoperative by-products. We will see, however, that if we accept these views as part of our personal cosmology, certain implications result that are contrary to the words of the prophets and the scriptures.

Belief in a self-acting, self-perpetuating system in which all changes conform to natural law eliminates a belief that God has any power to direct or control matter.[8] Such a position is that of naturalism. Instead of believing that God is the author of all natural law and therefore ultimately controls all phenomena in the physical universe (theism), the naturalist believes that self-existing "Law" is the sovereign power in the universe and ultimately controls all phenomena.[9] According to this view, all causation is material (according to natural law) rather than mental (originating in the mind of God or some other living creature).

Burtt points out that the shift from theism (in medieval times) to naturalism (in modern times) was gradual. In the early history of science, many scientists held theistic views.[10] Their religious beliefs led them to conclude that God controls all matter by his power and that he commands this matter to behave in certain ways. To them God was sovereign and therefore the author of all natural laws. As scientists, they attempted to discover these laws by gathering facts empirically in an attempt to induce from them certain regularities in nature. Once these regularities (natural laws) were found, the scientists could better predict, control, and explain the phenomena in the universe around them. However, to them God was not just a super scientist or super engineer who discovered and worked with self-existing natural laws; rather, he was the Great Creator, who authored the laws they were attempting to discover. Thus, a description of how matter behaves would also be a description of the handiwork of God. This was the position of Alma when rebutting the position of Korihor: "Will ye say, Show unto me a sign, when ye have the testimony of all these thy brethren, and also all the holy prophets? The scriptures are laid before thee, yea, and all things denote there is a God; yea, even the earth, and all things that are upon the face of it, yea, and *its motion,* yea, and also all *the planets which move in their regular form do witness that there is a Supreme Creator."* (Alma 30:44; emphasis added.)

If God had no power to command and direct matter, then Alma would not have given God credit for the orderly motion of the earth and other heavenly bodies. Alma's position is substantiated by the word of the Lord in modern revelation wherein the regular motion of the heavenly bodies is attributed to God's commands (law), which reach all matter through the Spirit of Christ:[11]

> Which truth shineth. This is the light of Christ. . . . Which light proceedeth forth from the presence of God to fill the immensity of space—the light which is in all things, which giveth life to all things, which is *the law by which all things are governed,* even the power of God who sitteth upon his throne. . . . And again, verily I say unto you, *he hath given a law unto all things, by which they move in their times and their seasons;* and their courses are fixed, even the courses of the heavens and the earth. . . . The earth rolls upon her wings, and the sun giveth his light by day, and the moon giveth her light by night, and the stars also give their light, as they roll upon their wings in their glory, in the midst of the power of God. . . . Behold, all these are kingdoms, and any man who hath seen any or the least of these hath seen God moving in his majesty and power. (D&C 88:7, 12-13, 42-43, 45, 47; emphasis added.)

The Nature of Humanity

In Russell's second statement, he not only advocated a self-acting and self-perpetuating universe, but also one that was inanimate. A universe that was self-acting and self-perpetuating, where all changes result from the operation of natural law, would of necessity be one where man was merely a physical machine. Such a machine would be controlled completely by natural law, leaving no room for a spirit within the physical body to interact with the body and influence its actions. Some early scientists such as Johannes Muller believed that humans were composed of more than a mere body that was a physical machine. However, some of Muller's own students made a pact among themselves to promote the idea that people's actions were the result of no forces other than the operation of natural law. They were eventually successful in promoting that view, which has now become a traditional way of thinking for many of our modern scientists,[12] especially in the field of behavioristic psychology.[13]

Coming back to Korihor, we find that his views pertaining to humanity were consistent with these naturalistic views. Korihor implied that people had no spirits when he said that "when a man was dead, that was the end thereof." (Alma 30:18.) Furthermore, in such a mechanical universe as that advocated by Korihor, there could be no place for such things as God's law given by his prophets. Consequently, Korihor taught that the words of the prophets were not from God but were mere traditions of men. We also find Korihor teaching that even if people did not live according to the words of the prophets, they still would not "offend some unknown being, who they say is God." (Alma 30:28.)

The Effects of Korihor's Naturalistic Doctrine

In such a naturalistic universe as that advocated by Korihor, where there were no laws of God to break, there could be no sin nor spiritual death that results from sin. Instead of being motivated in their behavior by a fear or love of God, people's actions would be motivated by a survival of the fittest, both physically and mentally, which was no crime. Holding such naturalistic views would influence people to believe that they were not accountable to a higher power for their actions. As a result, they would be led away into sin. Mormon comments on Korihor's teachings and their effect on the people of his day as follows: "Many more such things did he say unto them, telling them that . . . every man fared in this life according to the management of the creature; therefore every man prospered according to his genius, and that every man conquered according to his strength; and whatsoever a man did was no crime. And thus he did preach unto them, leading away the hearts of many, causing them to lift up their heads in their wickedness, yea, leading away many women, and also men, to commit whoredoms." (Alma 30:17-18.)

Since Korihor's universe held no room for a God, God's laws, or certain effects resulting from the breaking of these laws, to be consistent he would have to deny the fall of man which came as the result of the transgression of Adam and Eve. The scriptures describe how the transgression of a commandment of God in the Garden of Eden by our first parents affected not only them but all their posterity by causing them to become mortals subject to spiritual and temporal death. (Alma 42:2-14.) It seems that Korihor was denying the fall when he said: "Ye say that this people is a guilty and a fallen people, because of the transgression of a parent. Behold, I say that a child is not guilty because of its parents." (Alma 30:25.)

Ancient as well as modern scriptures teach that an atonement was needed to provide a remission of personal sins (on conditions of repentance) as well as to overcome the effects of the fall of Adam and Eve. (2 Ne. 9:1-13; Alma 42:12-16.) Again to be consistent with his other naturalistic views, Korihor would have had to deny a need for an atonement and of course a need for Christ to perform the atonement. Concerning the atonement, he said "that there could be no atonement made for the sins of men." (Alma 30:17.) He also stated that to "look forward and say ye see a remission of your sins . . . is the effect of a frenzied mind; and this derangement of your minds comes because of the traditions of your fathers, which lead you away into a belief of things which are not so." (Alma 30:16.) Since Korihor did not believe in sin or a need for an atonement to overcome the effects of sin, he claimed that the idea of a Christ slain for the sins of the world was a foolish tradition of the Nephites used by their priests to keep them in bondage: "Ye . . . say that Christ shall come. But behold, I say that ye do not know that there shall be a Christ. And *ye say also that he shall be slain for the sins of the world—*

and thus *ye lead away this people after the foolish traditions of your fathers*, and according to your own desires; and ye keep them down, even as it were in bondage, that ye may glut yourselves with the labors of their hands." (Alma 30:26-27; emphasis added.)

Consequently, he taught the people "that there should be no Christ" (Alma 30:12) and that to look forward to the coming of Christ was to yoke themselves "under a foolish and a vain hope" (Alma 30:13).

Why Korihor Was an Anti-Christ

It is now easy to see why Mormon labeled Korihor an Anti-Christ: Korihor was denying the truth of those doctrines that made it necessary that Jesus was (and is) the Christ. The role of Christ is two-fold.[14] First, he is the Lord God of this world. He attained to this position in premortal life. (Abr. 3:19-21; D&C 38:1-3.) As the Lord God, his word is law to the physical elements, and by his word or power he created or organized this world and continues to sustain and uphold it. He also gives his word (or law) to people on earth, and they have a spirit within them with the capacity to receive and obey his word (or law) or to reject it. Even though each person has a physical body subject to natural law, the spirit within that body can control the body's outward behavior.[15]

Christ's second role is that of Savior or Redeemer. Because Jesus was born the Son of God and performed the atonement during his mortal ministry, he gained power to overcome the effect of people's breaking the very laws he gave in his role as the Lord God. (2 Ne. 2:10.) Hence, he gained power to overcome the effects of the fall as well as to overcome the effects of individual sin, if the person sincerely repents and strives to live the gospel. The purpose of creation was to give people joy, which comes when they overcome spiritual and temporal death through the atonement of Christ.[16] Korihor denied all this (Alma 30:22, 35), as do the "naturalists" of our day who hold similar viewpoints.[17]

In his final confrontation with Alma, Korihor exclaimed he would never believe in God unless he received a physical sign as a manifestation of God's power. Finally, the Lord allowed Alma to give him a sign, but it was to his condemnation: Korihor was struck dumb by the power of God. Korihor then confessed that his doctrines were false and were authored by the devil:

> Now when Alma had said these words, Korihor was struck dumb, that he could not have utterance, according to the words of Alma. . . . And Korihor put forth his hand and wrote, saying: I know that I am dumb, for I cannot speak; and I know that nothing save it were the power of God could bring this upon me; yea, and I also knew that there was a God. But behold, *the devil hath deceived me*; for he appeared unto me in the form of an angel, and said unto me: Go and reclaim this people, for they have all gone astray after an unknown God. And he said unto me: *There is no God; yea, and he taught me that which I should say. And I have taught his words*; and I taught them because they were pleasing unto the carnal mind; and I taught them, even until I had much success, insomuch that I verily believed that they were true; and for this cause I withstood the truth, even until I have brought this great curse upon me. (Alma 30:50, 52-53; emphasis added.)

Summary and Conclusions

If we accept the Book of Mormon as the word of God, the account of Korihor teaches us that the beliefs associated with the philosophy of naturalism are anti-Christ in nature. Science itself should not be anti-Christ, for its methodology should restrict scientists to making statements only about things that can be observed through the natural senses. Some scientists have taken theistic views while others have taken naturalistic views about the nature of the universe, but both groups have acted as philosophers, making statements that go beyond what can be confirmed publicly through the natural senses. According to C. S. Lewis, what is behind the things science observes cannot (and should not) be answered by the scientist if he or she is speaking as a scientist. Lewis comments on the role of science in solving the question of whether God created the universe and continues to uphold it, or whether it is merely an inanimate, self-perpetuating system with no God involved:

Wherever there have been thinking men both views turn up. And note this too. You cannot find out which view is the right one by science in the ordinary sense. Science works by experiments. It watches how things behave. Every scientific statement in the long run, however complicated it looks, really means something like, "I pointed the telescope to such and such a part of the sky at 2:20 A.M. on January 15th and saw so-and-so," or, "I put some of this stuff in a pot and heated it to such-and-such a temperature and it did so-and-so." Do not think I am saying anything against science: I am only saying what its job is. And the more scientific a man is, the more (I believe) he would agree with me that this is the job of science — and a very useful and necessary job it is too. But why anything comes to be there at all, and whether there is anything behind the things science observes — something of a different kind — this is not a scientific question. If there is "Something Behind," then either it will have to remain altogether unknown to men or *else make itself known in some different way.* The statement that there is any such thing, and the statement that there is no such thing, are neither of them statements that science can make. And real scientists do not usually make them.[18]

C. S. Lewis makes a good point. As a result of scientists using the methodology of science in the last few centuries, an enormous amount of valuable knowledge has been gained about the world around us, knowledge that can be confirmed by empirical observation. However, God has given us revelation through his prophets and through scripture, which reveal to us many things about the universe that cannot be observed in a scientific way. Sometimes what the philosophers say about our universe disagrees with what God has revealed. However, God will confirm to us that the knowledge he has given to us by the prophets and the scriptures is true. That confirmation can come to our spirits through the Holy Ghost if we sincerely ask for it.[19] God has said that part of our test here is to see if we will seek the truth through the power of the Holy Ghost: "Ye shall live by every word which proceedeth forth out of the mouth of God. For he will give unto the faithful line upon line, precept upon precept; and I will try you and prove you herewith." (D&C 98: 11-12.)

Consequently, if we seek and gain a confirmation through the power of the Holy Ghost that the Book of Mormon is true, we can use the contents of that book as a guide in detecting the beliefs of our modern generation that are anti-Christ in nature. It is our responsibility to not "put off the Spirit of God" (Alma 30:42) as did Korihor so that we may not "be seduced by evil spirits, or doctrines of devils, or the commandments of men; for some are of men, and others of devils." (D&C 46:7.)

NOTES

1. Edwin Arthur Burtt, *The Metaphysical Foundations of Modern Physical Science* (London: Routledge & Kegan Paul Ltd., 1950).

2. Bertrand Russell, *The Impact of Science on Society* (New York: Simon and Schuster, 1953), pp. 1-2.

3. *The Impact of Science on Society*, p. 6.

4. Russell held the extreme position of naturalism by advocating all three of these assumptions as being true. There are various other positions that are not quite so extreme. However, advocating any one of these assumptions as being true results in holding a position that is still not in accordance with the words of the scriptures and the prophets. For example, a "deist" believes that God created the universe to begin with but then withdrew, and that since then the universe has run by itself according to natural law. In such a universe there could be no miracles or revelations because there would be no divine intervention after the creation.

5. Alma 5:45-48. Joseph Smith stated that revelation comes "to our spirits precisely as though we had no bodies at all." (Joseph Smith, *Teachings of the Prophet Joseph Smith*, selected by Joseph Fielding Smith [Salt Lake City: Deseret Book Company, 1938], p. 355.) See also D&C 6:14-17, 22-24; 18:1-5; 29:7; Moroni 10:4-5.

6. *The Impact of Science on Society*, pp. 9-10.

7. *The Impact of Science on Society*, p. 10.

8. The Prophet Joseph Smith and the scriptures indicate that when God commands the elements, they obey his will. (Abr. 2:7; Moses 1:25; Hel.

12:7-17; D&C 133:23; *Teachings of the Prophet Joseph Smith*, pp. 197-98.) This earth had its origin first as a plan in the mind of God. (Abr. 3:24; 5:1-3.) He then spoke to or commanded the elements (D&C 38:3) by means of his spirit (D&C 29:30-32), and they obeyed him (Abr. 4:9-11, 18, 21, 25). They continue to obey him and are thus governed (D&C 88:7-13) or upheld by his power (*Teachings of the Prophet Joseph Smith*, pp. 55-56, 345.) In other words, what we *describe* the elements as doing (natural law) is nothing more than what God has *prescribed* them to do. Furthermore, God tells us that it is offensive to him to not acknowledge his hand in all things. (D&C 59:21.) A more detailed discussion on this subject is given by the author in "Creation, Fall, and Atonement," *Studies in Scripture, Vol. 7: 1 Nephi to Alma 29*, ed. Kent P. Jackson (Salt Lake City: Deseret Book Company, 1987), pp. 87-90, 98-100.

9. A more detailed discussion on the shift from theism to naturalism is given by the author in "What Is Man?" *Hearken O Ye People* (Sandy, Utah: Randall Book Company, 1984), pp. 134-42.

10. As an example, Burtt points out that both Robert Boyle and Isaac Newton held theistic beliefs. See *The Metaphysical Foundations of Modern Physical Science*, pp. 289-90.

11. Joseph Smith also gave God credit for the movement of the heavenly bodies when he said that "God set the sun, the moon, and the stars in the heavens, and gave them their laws, conditions and bounds, which they cannot pass, except by His commandments; they all move in perfect harmony in their sphere and order." (*Teachings of the Prophet Joseph Smith*, pp. 197-98.)

12. Edwin G. Boring, *A History of Experimental Psychology* (New York City: Appleton-Century-Crofts, 1957), p. 708.

13. A more detailed discussion of the naturalistic views on humanity is given by the author in "What Is Man?" pp. 133-39.

14. A more detailed discussion of the two roles of Christ is given by the author in "Jesus Is the Christ," *Studies in Scripture, Vol. 5: The Gospels*, ed. Kent B. Jackson and Robert L. Millet (Salt Lake City: Deseret Book Company, 1986), pp. 323-40.

15. As an example, Christ's spirit ruled over his body at all times. (Mosiah 15:5-7.)

16. 2 Nephi 2:10-13, 25; Alma 42:16; D&C 101:35-38; *Teachings of the Prophet Joseph Smith*, p. 255. A more detailed discussion on the subject of the joy that comes from overcoming spiritual and temporal death is given by the author in "The Fall of Man," *Principles of the Gospel in Practice* (Salt Lake City: Randall Book Co., 1985), pp. 48-58.

14

17. It should be recalled that the naturalist denies that there is "purpose" in the universe. Burtt summarizes Russell's naturalistic beliefs on this subject as follows: "To Russell, man is but the chance and temporary product of a blind and purposeless nature, an irrelevant spectator of her doings, almost an alien intruder on her domain. No high place in a cosmic teleology is his; his ideals, his hopes, his mystic raptures, are but the creations of his own errant and enthusiastic imagination, without standing or application to a real world interpreted mechanically in terms of space, time, and unconscious, though eternal atoms. His mother earth is but a speck in the boundlessness of space, his place even on the earth but insignificant and precarious, in a word, he is at the mercy of brute forces that unknowingly happened to throw him into being, and promise ere long just as unknowingly to snuff out the candle of his little day. Himself and all that is dear to him will in course of time become 'buried in a universe of ruins.' " (*The Metaphysical Foundations of Modern Physical Science*, p. 10.)

18. C. S. Lewis, *Mere Christianity* (New York: Macmillan, 1960), p. 32, emphasis added.

19. Moroni 10:4-5; D&C 6:14-17, 22-24; 18:1-4; James 1:5-6; Matt. 7: 7-11.

2

A FAITH UNTO SALVATION
(Alma 31-33)

RODNEY TURNER

The religion of the ancient Zoramites in the Book of Mormon is paralleled by much of the religion practiced in our modern world: it was false, superficial, undemanding, impotent, and Christless. Consequently, the message of God's prophets to that misguided people is as relevant now as it was over two thousand years ago. While religious illusions may serve us in time, they will fail us in eternity. Only a faith centered in things as they really are and as they really will be can produce the knowledge that saves. Such a faith was the topic of the message delivered to certain Zoramites by the prophet Alma in 74 B.C.

Four False Faiths

Alma's teachings and those of his companion, Amulek (Alma 34), can best be understood in the larger context of certain incorrect doctrines that arose from time to time among the Nephites beginning in the days of Jacob. These erroneous ideas had one thing in common: they denied the future coming of God to the earth in the person of Jesus Christ. The underlying question in them all was the same as it is now: How are we saved? The Book of Mormon describes five variant answers to this question. Four of them are false.

Of these four, the first was advocated by a man named Sherem,

---

Rodney Turner is professor of Church history and doctrine at Brigham Young University.

16

who lived in the sixth century B.C. He taught that the law of Moses was all-sufficient for salvation. (See Jacob 7:7.) Characteristically, Sherem was a learned, eloquent speaker who denied the possibility of prophecy but then proceeded to prophesy himself: "I know that there is no Christ, neither has been, nor ever will be." (Jacob 7:9.) Deceived by the devil, Sherem became Satan's servant and led many souls into apostasy. Struck down by God, and knowing that he was dying, he confessed: "I fear lest I have committed the unpardonable sin, for I have lied unto God; for I denied the Christ, and said that I believed the scriptures; and they truly testify of him." (Jacob 7:19.) The spirit of Sherem—denying prophets and prophecy—is with us today.

The second heresy arose some four hundred years later in 91 B.C. when a man named Nehor taught a pleasing doctrine of universal salvation without the need for repentance: "For the Lord had created all men, and had also redeemed all men; and, in the end, all men should have eternal life." (Alma 1:4; cf. 15:15.) Humanity's redemption required no sacrifice on God's part; he simply willed it. So Nehorism predestined everyone to heaven; hell was no problem.

The spirit of Nehorism is alive and well in many Christian churches where much sermonizing on God's unconditional love can be heard. Because God loves us, they say, sin is not as sinful as once thought. And if there is a hell—which is doubtful—it will be a vast improvement over the old fire-and-brimstone one of eternal burnings. This deceptive attitude was foreseen by Nephi: "There shall also be many which shall say: Eat, drink, and be merry; nevertheless, fear God—he will justify in committing a little sin; yea, lie a little, take the advantage of one because of his words, dig a pit for thy neighbor; there is no harm in this; and do all these things, for tomorrow we die; and if it so be that we are guilty, God will beat us with a few stripes, and at last we shall be saved in the kingdom of God." (2 Ne. 28:8.) In advocating a paid ministry, Nehor introduced priestcraft among the Nephites.[1] Opposed by an aged man named Gideon, a member of Alma's church, Nehor slew him and was executed for his murder. But Nehorism did not die with its founder; it wreaked great havoc among the Nephites for at least twenty more years.

The third, and probably the most charismatic, of the great heretics in the Book of Mormon was the anti-Christ Korihor.[2] He denied the existence of anything beyond the natural order.[3] God, Christ, prophecy, immortality, and judgment were products of false traditions and deranged minds. His advocacy of jungle law ("every man conquered according to his strength; and whatsoever a man did was no crime" — Alma 30:17) promoted rampant immorality among his eager followers. Korihor's descent from theism ("I always knew that there was a God" — Alma 30:52) into professed atheism and its frequent companion, libertinism ("I taught them because they were pleasing unto the carnal mind; and I taught them, even until I had much success, insomuch that I verily believed that they were true" — Alma 30:53) is a classic example of self-delusion. Like Sherem, Korihor demanded a sign and, like Sherem, was struck dumb. Thereafter, while begging food among another group of apostates, the Zoramites, he was trampled to death. Mormon concluded his account of this pathetic anti-Christ by observing: "Thus we see that the devil will not support his children at the last day, but doth speedily drag them down to hell." (Alma 30:60; cf. 2 Ne. 28:21.)

The fourth false faith was advocated by a man named Zoram[4] who, with his followers, had apostatized from Alma's church of Christ. Like Sherem, Nehor, and Korihor, the Zoramites denied that there would ever be an incarnated — flesh and bone — Christ. How could there be? God was "a spirit forever." (Alma 31:15.) They thanked their immaterial God for having "made it known unto us that there shall be no Christ." They were also grateful that God had "elected us that we shall be saved, whilst all around us are elected to be cast by thy wrath down to hell; for the which holiness, O God, we thank thee." (Alma 31:16-17.)

Their weekly group-devotion on the "Rameumptom," a prayer tower that dominated their synagogues, consisted of this single, formalized, self-congratulatory prayer. Having taken care of their spiritual obligations for the week, "they returned to their homes, never speaking of their God again until they had assembled themselves together again to the holy stand." (Alma 31:23.) Their choral exercise in vanity sufficed to appease their God and permitted them to freely indulge themselves. Having been predestined to holiness and salvation, they had no need for daily prayer or obedience to restrictive commandments. The issue of life after death had been fully and happily settled; they could get on with the things of this world. Such is the underlying assumption of every "Sunday religion." It renders God a practical irrelevance. He exists, but he need not be taken too seriously. The false doctrines of Sherem, Nehor, Korihor, and Zoram were both predictive and representative of those apostate religious beliefs — Christian and non-Christian — that shroud the world in spiritual darkness in these latter days.

True Faith

To combat the Zoramite heresy, and knowing that "preaching of the word . . . had had more powerful effect upon the minds of the people than the sword, or anything else, . . . therefore Alma thought it was expedient that they should try the virtue of the word of God." (Alma 31:5.) The battle between truth and error, righteousness and rebellion, was joined.

Spiritual Humility

Bad religion breeds bad societies. The Zoramites created a class system that ostracized their less fortunate brothers and sisters from the very synagogues they had built. But — as has been the case from time immemorial — it was these downtrodden souls who proved most responsive to the message of Alma and his companions.[5] Impoverished "as to things of the world," they are described as "poor in heart" or "lowly in heart." (Alma 32:3-4, 8.) That is, they were disspirited and quite hopeless.[6] Alma "beheld that their afflictions had truly humbled them, and that they were in a preparation to hear the word." (Alma 32:6.)

Spiritual humility — the recognition of one's dependence upon God for all things temporal and spiritual, coupled with a willingness to accept his law — is a precondition for true repentance. Some achieve this humility only after they have been "compelled to be humble" by those "slings and arrows of outrageous fortune" of which Hamlet soliloquized. Some do so only after they have been brought face-to-face with the stark truth about themselves and the God they defied, or never knew.

Some will never learn humility and, therefore, never repent even when they stand before God with a "perfect knowledge" of their guilt and uncleanness.[7] However, God's truth will prove irresistible, and they will acknowledge to their "everlasting shame that all his judgments are just." (Alma 12:15; cf. 2 Ne. 9:13-16.) President Spencer W. Kimball wrote one "disbeliever": "The time will come when there will be a surrender of every person who has ever lived on this earth . . . and it will be an unforced surrender, an unconditional surrender. When will it be for you? . . . It is not *if* you will capitulate to the great truth; it is *when*, for I know that you cannot indefinitely resist the power and pressure of truth."[8]

"Therefore," said Alma, "blessed are they who humble themselves without being compelled to be humble . . . who would humble themselves, let them be in whatsoever circumstances they might." (Alma 32:16, 25.) Such spirits are in tune with the Holy Spirit. "Without compulsory means" (D&C 121:46), the intelligence, virtue, and truth in them draws them to the intelligence, virtue, and truth in God (see D&C 88:40). Perhaps they developed much of this affinity with the divine in their premortal existence, although undoubtedly it can be developed during mortality as well. Elder Bruce R. McConkie referred to this disposition as "the talent for spirituality. Those so endowed find it easy to believe the truth in this life."[9] Needless to say, the sooner genuine humility—"a broken heart and a contrite spirit" (2 Ne. 2:7)—is achieved, the better off one is.

Sign-Seekers

To be "compelled to know" is characteristic of the carnally minded. This disposition results from an empirical or rational mind-set that accepts only what can be perceived through the physical senses or is deemed reasonable. (See Hel. 16:17-18.) But physical experiences and secular knowledge are the common property of the entire, disparate human race without regard to spirituality or moral character. A person may be a gifted artist, scientist, or philosopher, and a scoundrel at the same time. A university degree is not a prerequisite for salvation. Rather, we are saved only as we gain spiritual intelligence—light and truth, the glory of God. (See D&C 93:36.) Such knowledge comes only through faith and its resulting works. Paul wrote: "The natural man receiveth not the things of the Spirit of God: for they are foolishness unto him: neither can he know them, because they are spiritually discerned." (1 Cor. 2:14.) The sign-seeker is the natural man par excellence. For him, if a thing cannot be seen, heard, touched, tasted, or smelled, it does not exist. Thus such people demand "a sign from heaven" before they will acknowledge the reality of "things which are not seen." Alma asked: "Is this faith? Behold, I say unto you, Nay; for if a man knoweth a thing he hath no cause to believe, for he knoweth it." (Alma 32:18.) When certitude is obtained, faith is swallowed up in knowledge, becoming one with it. But, as we shall see, faith is indispensable in acquiring the knowledge that leads to salvation. To demand such knowledge in the absence of faith is to invite disaster. Those who do so will never obtain a fullness of either faith or knowledge.

The sign-seekers, the God-tempters, presume to put the Almighty on trial by challenging him to prove his own existence. Korihor typified them: "Except ye show me a sign, I will not believe." (Alma 30:48.) In their pride, the Korihors of this world set up the preconditions under which they may condescend to believe. But it is all a sham; their insistence on signs is not meant to foster faith but to justify doubt. And the seed of faith will never grow in the soil of doubt. Where there is a will to doubt, a heavenly sign or evidence will be ignored, rejected, or rationalized away. The Lord told young Joseph Smith: "Behold, if they will not believe my words, they would not believe you, my servant Joseph, if it were possible that you should show them all these things [obtained from the hill Cumorah] which I have committed unto you." (D&C 5:7; cf. Luke 16:31.) The rational mind will always reject what the hardened heart is unprepared to accept. That is why signs without faith are a barrier against, not a path to, God.

The last thing sign-seekers should seek is a sign. In insisting upon knowing before believing, they become their own worst enemy. "How much more cursed is he that knoweth the will of God and doeth it not, than he that only believeth, or only hath cause to believe, and falleth into transgression?" (Alma 32:19; cf. D&C 63:7, 11; 82:3.) The principle enunciated by Moroni—"Ye receive no witness until after the trial of your faith" (Ether 12:6)—is a blessing. Knowledge in excess of one's will and wisdom is a formula for disaster in all things. The world's understanding of nuclear energy far exceeds their ability to control it, because that knowledge does not rest upon a commitment to moral law. This condition accounts for the very real likelihood that we will yet be confronted with nuclear war. Power without principle is a scourge in every age.

Just as a wise parent keeps medicine or tools out of a child's reach, so does God withhold divine knowledge from the ill-prepared.[10] In his wisdom and mercy, he has ordained that faith must precede certitude so that, in the very process of exercising faith, the individual develops the spiritual maturity needed to possess divine knowledge in righteousness. Thus capacitated, such knowledge magnifies rather than diminishes one's relationship to God.

For example, the Lord promised the brother of Jared that if he developed sufficient faith he could be shown all things. The brother of Jared did so, "wherefore [Christ] showed him all things, for he could no longer be kept without the veil." (Ether 12:21.) Christ was bound by his own promise; he could not deny the brother of Jared the knowledge his faith had prepared him to receive. This is an eternal principle. Hence the Prophet Joseph Smith's remark: "God hath not revealed anything to Joseph, but what He will make known unto the Twelve, and even the least Saint may know all things *as fast as he is able to bear them.*"[11]

Faith versus Knowledge

In scripture, faith and belief are frequently employed as interchangeable terms.[12] In its broadest sense, faith is belief in the existence, virtue, validity, or efficacy of something or someone, seen or unseen, past, present, or future.[13] It may be a good faith or a bad faith; it may be constructive or destructive. It all depends upon the nature of the person or thing that is its object. However, Alma delimited faith to belief in what is real and deserving of trust—the doctrine of Christ. Hence, he spoke of "things which are not seen, *which are true.*" (Alma 32:21; italics added.)

Alma begged the Zoramites to "exercise a particle of faith, yea, even if you can no more than desire to believe, let this desire work in you." (Alma 32:27.) The "desire to believe" becomes the motivation for the "trial of faith," which eventually produces a "perfect knowledge" or verification of what was, at first, only an unproven possibility. When the desire to believe is combined with effort, faith is born, and when faith is born, saving works follow.

Alma used the example of planting a seed (his own testimony of Christ—Alma 33:1) in the hope of growing a tree, the fruit of which would be everlasting life (Alma 32:27-43). As each step of the "experiment" is verified by observed results, there is no further need to exercise faith in what has become an accomplished fact. For example, when the "seed" germinates, there is no longer need to have faith that it *will* germinate: "Yea, your knowledge is perfect *in that thing*, and your faith is dormant; and this because *you know*, for ye know that the word hath swelled your souls, and ye also know that it hath sprouted up, that your understanding doth begin to be enlightened, and your mind doth begin to expand." (Alma 32:34; italics added.)

While each successfully accomplished phase of the experiment is replaced with certitude or perfect knowledge *of that phase*, faith is still needed in carrying out each *subsequent* phase of the experiment. So initial faith produces initial knowledge, which, in turn, produces more faith, which then leads to even more knowledge, and so on until one's knowledge is perfect or complete pertaining to the *entire* experiment.

This same process was advocated by Jesus when he said: "If any man will do [God's] will, he shall know of the doctrine, whether it be of God, or whether I speak of myself." (John 7:17.) This is simply the scientific method raised to the spiritual plane: we do in order to know. As we live the gospel, we reap an ever greater harvest of faith and knowledge until, like God himself, our faith and our knowledge become perfect in all things. For those who aspire to that divine state, the faith-to-knowledge process must continue into eternity until they obtain "a fulness of truth, yea, even of all truth." (D&C 93:26.) Like Adam and Eve, they will have become as the Gods who forever partake of both the tree of life and the tree of knowledge. Such is that "perfect day" called exaltation. (See D&C 50:24.)

Hope

As faith is not knowledge, but the means to knowledge, so faith is not hope, but the basis of hope: "If ye have faith ye hope for things which are not seen, which are true." (Alma 32:21.)[14] Faith and hope are inseparable; one does not exist without the other. (See Moro. 7:41-42.) Faith in the redemptive power of Christ produces the hope of everlasting life, "the heavenly gift." (Ether 12:8.) Once that hope is realized, it is no longer hoped for; it is possessed. Paul wrote: "We are saved by hope: but hope that is seen [realized] is not hope: for what a man seeth, why doth he yet hope for?" (Rom. 8:24.) However, if the "tree of life" —which grows from a testimony of Christ—never matures, "it is because your ground [soul] is barren, and ye will not nourish the tree." (Alma 32:39.) No matter how fervent one's faith in the beginning, if the person becomes neglectful, apathetic, or rebellious, faith dies. And when faith dies, hope dies with it. But as Alma assured the Zoramites, if, with "an eye of faith,"[15] and with great diligence and patience, we nourish the word, "[we] shall pluck the fruit . . . which is most precious . . . and . . . feast upon this fruit even until [we] are filled, that [we] hunger not, neither shall [we] thirst." (Alma 32:42.)

The Prophetic Witness

Alma's general teachings on faith became increasingly specific as he brought his message to its climax. Driven from their synagogues, the despised Zoramites felt that they could no longer worship God. (See Alma 32:2, 3, 5; 33:2.) Somewhat perplexed by Alma's message, they asked two questions: (1) Should they believe in but one God? and (2) How were they to begin exercising faith?

Alma responded by first quoting two ancient prophets of Israel, Zenos and Zenock. Zenos taught that the real issue was not *where* or *when* one prays—it can be any place, any time—but *how*, and *to whom*, one prays. Zenos stressed that prayers are heard and mercy is extended through the Son of God. Said he: "Thou hast turned thy judgments [the demands of justice] away from me, *because of thy Son."* (Alma 33:11; italics added.) Zenock testified that Israel "will not understand thy mercies which thou hast bestowed upon them *because of thy Son."* (Alma 33:16; italics added; see 34:7.)[16] Moses taught the same doctrine: the brazen serpent symbolized the saving power of the God of Israel.[17] "But few understood the meaning of those things, and this because of the hardness of their hearts." (Alma 33:20.) Nevertheless, every true prophet understood and testified of the Son of God. (See Jacob 7:11; 3 Ne. 20:24.) Their combined testimonies of the promised Messiah constituted the "seed" the Zoramites were to plant in their hearts. "And as it beginneth to swell even so nourish it by your faith. And behold, it will become a tree, springing up in you unto everlasting life." (Alma 33:23.) Where can we worship? Everywhere. When should we worship? Always. Whom should we worship? The only true God.[18]

Conclusion

Prominent among the many truths taught by Alma are the following: God is not an amorphous spirit ruling with arbitrary indifference over human affairs. He responds to our prayers and is profoundly involved in our lives, so much so that he sent his Son into the world to rescue us from endless temporal and spiritual death.

Prayer is not a weekly ritual but a daily necessity. It is not a means of evading our responsibilities; rather, it is an expression of commitment to them. Disdain of others renders prayer a vain, hypocritical exercise in self-delusion. If we would have God hear our cries, we cannot be deaf to the pleas of those around us.

True faith is not centered in ourselves but in the Lord; not in our virtues but in his. We believe in ourselves because we believe in him. Saving faith—unlike the credulity of the Zoramites, ancient and modern—is not a static, lifeless, attitude of self-complacency requiring nothing and giving nothing. Rather, true faith is dynamic and demanding. It is a lifetime process of spiritual growth wherein we work out our salvation "with fear before God." (Alma 34:37; cf. Philip. 2:12.) "Faith precedes the miracle" of revelation. To know—as God knows—the hidden things of time and eternity, we must first become like him. Only as we are transformed through faith are we capacitated to receive the blessings and responsibilities of spiritual knowledge.

Faith in Jesus Christ, the Redeemer of mankind, is the key to salvation and a knowledge of all things. Those who walk the strait and narrow way with "an eye of faith" shall be perfected in all the knowledge of God: "And to them will I reveal all mysteries, yea, all the hidden mysteries of my kingdom from days of old, and for ages to come, will I make known unto them the good pleasure of my will concerning all things pertaining to my kingdom. Yea, even the wonders of eternity shall they know, and things to come will I show them, even the things of many generations." (D&C 76:7-8.) Thus, from the tiny seed of mortal faith in the Son of Man will come an immortal knowledge of God and his unimaginable mysteries. It only remains for us to plant that seed and nourish it with diligence.

NOTES

1. "Priestcrafts are that men preach and set themselves up for a light unto the world, that they may get gain and praise of the world; but they seek not the welfare of Zion." (2 Ne. 26:29.)

2. Korihor is the only person called anti-Christ in the Book of Mormon. (See Alma 30:6, 12.)

3. The contemporary philosophies of naturalism, existentialism, and secular humanism take the same position. See chapter 1 in this volume.

4. Zoram's lineage is not given, but he quite possibly descended from Laban's servant of the same name. (See 1 Ne. 4:35; Alma 30:59; 31:1; 54:23.)

5. Alma was accompanied by his two sons Shiblon and Corianton, three sons of Mosiah (Ammon, Aaron, and Omner), and Amulek and Zeezrom. (See Alma 31:32.)

6. It is commonly assumed that the phrase "poor in spirit" (Matt. 5:3) refers to the humble and spiritually rich. However, as used by Alma and Jesus, the phrase refers to those who are impoverished spiritually.

7. See Joseph Smith, *Teachings of the Prophet Joseph Smith*, selected by Joseph Fielding Smith (Salt Lake City: Deseret Book Company, 1938), p. 358.

8. *Ensign*, September 1978, p. 8. Italics in original.

9. Bruce R. McConkie, *The Millennial Messiah* (Salt Lake City: Deseret Book Company, 1982), p. 234.

10. For the most part, the Lord provides *evidences* rather than *proofs* of spiritual matters. For example, the Book of Mormon does not constitute a proof of its own teachings. Hence, Moroni's admonition to the reader to ask God "if these things are not true." (Moro. 10:4.)

11. *Teachings of the Prophet Joseph Smith*, p. 149; italics added.

12. For example, see 3 Nephi 19:20, 28. The gospel of John consistently uses the word "believe" rather than the word "faith."

13. In the vast majority of instances in scripture, faith is defined in terms of what is real or true; however, a few passages refer to a vain faith, meaning one that is centered in something or someone that is false, nonexistent, or unjustifiable. (See 3 Ne. 1:8; Moro. 7:44; D&C 104:55; 1 Cor. 15:14.)

14. Like the words of Alma, Paul's oft-quoted words in JST Hebrews 11:1 define faith as belief in the existence of unseen or unobtained realities that can be hoped for because of Christ. For example, faith in Christ's atonement is the basis for the hope of a future remission of sins.

15. The "eye of faith" sees eternal verities that lie beyond mortality and the natural order. Lacking that "eye," we are blind to eternal and spiritual realities.

16. Zenos and Zenock were prophets in Israel before 600 B.C. Their writings are on the plates of brass but not in the Old Testament. (See 1 Ne. 19:10, 12, 16; Jacob 5:1; 6:1; Alma 34:7; Hel. 8:19-20; 15:11; and 3 Ne. 10:16.) It is obvious from their testimonies that "plain and precious" truths are missing from the Old Testament as well as the New Testament. The result is the distorted view of the religion of ancient Israel current among biblical scholars. Israel was taught that God's Son was to come to earth and atone for the sins of the world. Her sins are all the more reprehensible because of this knowledge.

17. See Numbers 21:9; 1 Nephi 17:41; 2 Nephi 25:20; Helaman 8:14-15.

18. The Book of Mormon makes it clear that the Son of God (Jehovah, the Holy One of Israel, the Messiah, the Redeemer, Jesus Christ, etc.) is subordinate to his literal Father. However, by "investiture of authority" the Son serves under his Father in a dual capacity and bears a joint title: Father and Son. "And they are one God, yea, the very Eternal Father of heaven and earth." (Mosiah 15:4; cf. Ether 3:14.) It is this "one God" to whom the Zoramites—and all people—are to look for salvation. This "one God" is emphasized throughout holy writ.

3

THE INFINITE ATONEMENT OF GOD
(Alma 34–35)

RODNEY TURNER

A major doctrine of the Book of Mormon is that as a result of Adam's transgression, "all mankind became a lost and fallen people." (Alma 12:22.)[1] The whole world was lost to God, and only God could redeem it from its fallen state. (See 1 Ne. 10:6.) The message with which Amulek climaxed Alma's preceding discourse (Alma 31-33) was that God — in the person of Jesus Christ — would bring about that imperative redemption.

Zoramite Religion

Amulek's audience consisted of Zoramites — a Nephite faction that had apostatized from the church of God and turned to the worship of idols. They believed that God (who was "a spirit forever") had elected them to be saved "whilst all around [them were] elected to be cast by [God's] wrath down to hell." (Alma 31:15-17.) This pre-destinarian doctrine implied that, for all practical purposes, God was independent of all moral considerations: he could forgive sins and save souls — or not — as he chose, without regard to justice, mercy, or any other divine principle. That being the case, a Redeemer was not really needed, and there never would be one.

It was the rejection of the message of the prophets concerning the future coming of a divine Redeemer that was at the heart of the

Rodney Turner is professor of Church history and doctrine at Brigham Young University.

28

Zoramite apostasy. Like much erroneous doctrine, it did not stem from faulty logic but from incorrect premises. Wrong assumptions produce wrong conclusions. The syllogistic argument of the Zoramites—like many theological propositions—was logically valid but materially false.[2]

Although Christ is spoken of in the Book of Mormon as "the Lord God Omnipotent" (Mosiah 5:15), yet he does not function as an absolutely omnipotent being. If he did, the Zoramite argument would have been correct and there would have been no inescapable need for an atoning sacrifice. But the Almighty works in harmony with the various systems of law he has established. (See D&C 88:36-38.) That is why he cannot lie (Ether 3:12), "look upon sin with the least degree of allowance" (Alma 45:16), grant mercy without repentance, or save a sinner in his sins (Alma 11:37; 42:24). Thus, it is more accurate to say that God rules as a *pen*-omnipotent being rather than as an absolute monarch.

Testimony of the Prophets

In whom were the Zoramites to believe—a predestinarian God who arbitrarily saved or damned as he chose, or a God who respected human agency and governed with justice, equity, and mercy? Amulek addressed their dilemma. He reminded them that they were not ignorant of the truth: "These things were taught unto you bountifully before your dissension from among us." (Alma 34:2.) But failing to nourish the "seed" of testimony, they had failed to harvest its intended fruit. Continuing Alma's analogy (Alma 32:28), Amulek invited the Zoramites: "Have so much faith as even to plant the word in your hearts, that ye may try the experiment of its goodness." Only by doing so could they determine "whether the word [the truth] be in the Son of God, or whether there shall be no Christ." (Alma 34:4-5.) Amulek had done this; he knew the answer to that critical question.

To the testimonies of Alma, Zenos, Zenock, and Moses, Amulek added his own: "I do know that Christ shall come." (Alma 34:8.) He *knew* because he had *experienced* a witness from the Lord to that effect. He did not merely rationalize, conjecture, hypothesize, or assume such a being; he knew by direct revelation that there would be a Christ. So certain, so absolute is such knowledge, that any denial of it is the ultimate lie called the sin against the Holy Ghost. The Prophet Joseph Smith said that one guilty of this sin "has got to say that the sun does not shine while he sees it; he has got to deny Jesus Christ when the heavens have been opened to him, and to deny the plan of salvation with his eyes open to the truth of it."[3] While the apostate Zoramites claimed that God had told them that there would be no Christ (Alma 31:16), their unsupported lie was refuted by the Spirit of truth. This Spirit enables the prophets—and those sent by them—to "seal both on earth and in heaven [the spirit world], the unbelieving and rebellious." (D&C 1:8; cf. 2 Ne. 11:3; 27:14; 33:10-15.)

The Nature of Fallen Humanity

Amulek did not mince words; his testimony was categorical and emphatic: "According to the great plan of the Eternal God there must be an atonement made, or else all mankind must unavoidably perish; yea, all are hardened; yea, all àre fallen and are lost, and must perish except it be through the atonement which it is expedient should be made." (Alma 34:9.) Amulek's description of humanity as hardened, fallen, and lost must be understood in context. The Book of Mormon does not teach an Augustinian-like doctrine of human depravity. This now largely rejected concept defined humans as creatures of God who, through willful rebellion, became essentially incapable of any virtuous thought or act.

While rejecting this extreme doctrine, the Book of Mormon does describe mankind as "carnal, sensual, and devilish, by nature." (Alma 42:10; Mosiah 16:3.) That is, because of the Fall, people tend to yield to the undisciplined, unsanctified appetites and passions of the flesh.[4] Just as gravity abets poor physical posture, so does the Fall abet poor moral and spiritual posture. Those who cater to their fleshly appetites become "devilish" because they subject themselves to the will of the devil. (See Mosiah 16:3.)

But Augustine's doctrine of human depravity differs from the Book of Mormon doctrine of the Fall on two important points. First, Augustine viewed mortals as *creatures* of God whose nature was "a mean between the angelic and the bestial."[5] As such, mortals at their best could only aspire to "the company of the angels," who were themselves but creatures of God. Thus humanity's immortal horizon was circumscribed by their literal creaturehood.[6]

Secondly, humanity's depravity was total, their *whole* being—soul and flesh—was in revolt against God: "For the soul, revelling in its own liberty, and scorning to serve God, was itself deprived of the command it had formerly maintained over the body. And because it [the soul] had willfully deserted its superior Lord, it no longer held [controlled] its own inferior servant; neither could it hold the flesh subject, as it would always have been able to do had it remained itself subject to God. . . . And thus, from the bad use of free will, there originated the whole train of evil, which, with its concatenation of miseries, convoys the human race from its depraved origin, as from a corrupt root, on to the destruction of the second death, which has no end, those only being excepted who are freed by the grace of God."[7]

The Book of Mormon does not support this view. It is not the *whole* soul—spirit and flesh—that is corrupt and "an enemy to God" (Mosiah 3:19), but only the person's *fallen mortal nature*—a nature *inherited* through Adam's necessary transgression. Through the atonement of Christ, this *initially corrupt* nature may be overcome, sanctified, and glorified. Therefore, humanity's condemnation is not that as mortals they were born carnal, sensual, and devilish,[8] but that they choose to *remain* so when given the opportunity to repent and overcome that condition. For, contrary to Augustine, the gospel is not designed to restore some people to an acceptable creature state as immortal angels, but to endow all who fully repent with the very nature of God—both in spirit and in flesh. Those who do so achieve a fullness of eternal life.

The Infinite Atonement of Christ

The "great plan of the Eternal God" was formulated in the eternities. It was not a spur-of-the-moment reaction to unforeseen problems arising from Adam's transgression. All was foreordained; all was *planned.* The critical elements in that eternal plan were moral agency, the Fall, the Atonement, the resurrection, and the judgment. Moral agency led to the Fall, and the Fall made the three-fold mission of Christ (atonement, resurrection, and judgment) imperative. The Almighty does not rule by mere fiat, nor does he ignore the moral imbalance in the universe caused by the cumulative sins of mankind.

Yet some who reject the atonement of Christ argue, "How can one mortal die for the sins of all mortals?" The answer is, he cannot. No mortal, however virtuous, can atone for the sins of another, let alone the sins of all mankind. (See Alma 34:11-12.) Why not? Because as a result of Adam's transgression, "*all* mankind became a lost and fallen people." (Alma 12:22; italics added.) If *all* are lost, who can save them? Only an infinite Being—free of the spiritual consequences of the Fall—could do so. Only a God could atone for the sins of the world. Only by God satisfying the righteous demands of divine justice could the truly penitent be saved by divine mercy. (See Alma 34:15-16; 42:13-15, 22-25.) Therefore, "God himself shall come down among the children of men, and shall redeem his people." (Mosiah 15:1.) "God himself atoneth for the sins of the world." (Alma 42:15.)

Lest the idolatrous Zoramites assume that the God called Christ would be a mere mortal, Amulek explained: "It shall not be a *human* sacrifice; but it must be an *infinite* and eternal sacrifice." (Alma 34:10; italics added; cf. 42:15.) In the Book of Mormon, we read of God's infinite goodness, mercy, and grace. (See 2 Ne. 9:7; 25:16.) In other words, all that pertains to God is infinite, even as the adjectives eternal, endless, and everlasting describe his divine nature. (See D&C 19:10-13.) Therefore, the Atonement was an infinite act because it was performed by an infinite Being. The nature of the act reflected the nature of the Actor.

The Prophet Joseph Smith taught that the atonement of Jesus Christ was efficacious not only for mankind on this earth, but for the human family on other earths as well. In his poetic parallel of Doctrine and Covenants 76:23-24, the Prophet wrote of the worlds the Saviour had organized:

> Whose inhabitants, too, from the first to the last,
> Are sav'd by the very same Saviour of ours;
> And, of course, are begotten God's daughters and sons
> By the very same truths and the very same powers.[9]

The Book of Mormon is silent on this doctrine. It treats the Atonement only in terms of Adam's posterity on this earth: "He [Christ] suffereth the pains of all men, yea, the pains of every living creature, both men, women, and children, who belong to the family of Adam." (2 Ne. 9:21.) That Jesus Christ performed an infinite atonement is beyond dispute, but how far-reaching it was pertaining to all the worlds that were, are, and will be is, as yet, unrevealed.[10]

Because of the Fall, the laws and commandments of God save no one. To the contrary, they tend to condemn everyone.[11] Yet with the Lord's help, his laws are livable. The Savior "kept the law of God, and remained without sin, showing thereby that it is in the power of man to keep the law and remain also without sin."[12]

Justice is the essence of law: we reap what we sow. Alma called this principle "the plan of restoration." (Alma 41:2.) And, said he, "restoration is to bring back *again* evil for evil . . . good for that which is good." (Alma 41:13; italics added.) That is, we are personally accountable for how we use the gift of moral agency. In harmony with this principle, Amulek asked: "Now, if a man murdereth, behold will our law, *which is just,* take the life of his brother? I say unto you, Nay. But the law requireth the life of him who hath murdered." (Alma 34:11-12; italics added.)

Speaking of the Mosaic order, Amulek declared Christ to be "the whole meaning of the law, every whit pointing to that great and last sacrifice; and that great and last sacrifice will be the Son of God, yea, infinite and eternal." (Alma 34:14.) Sacrifice began with Adam as an ordinance of the fullness of the gospel and was continued under Moses as an aspect of the "preparatory gospel," which included the Mosaic law. (See Moses 5:5-7; D&C 84:26-27.)

However, "the law of Moses availeth nothing except it were through the atonement of his blood." (Mosiah 3:15; cf. Alma 26:16.) Without Christ, the law was a shadow without substance. More to the point, without Christ humanity stood naked and helpless before the justice of God no matter how faithfully the law might have been observed. It is the Redeemer's atoning sacrifice—an act of infinite mercy—that provides the essential motivation for the faith taught by Alma and Amulek. For in the absence of God's mercy, why should anyone have faith? Life would still be a dead-end street leading to death, hell, and the devil. (See 2 Ne. 9:7-9; Jacob 7:12.) Thus God's mercy justifies human faith. And faith, in turn, begets the hope of eternal life. This hope is justified by the works of divine love that complete the triangle of salvation: faith, hope, and charity. (See Alma 34:27-29; Moro. 7:38-48.)

The Night of Darkness and the Day of Mercy

In the final analysis, people have but two choices: to be saved in the kingdom of God or to be damned in the kingdom of the devil; there is no third alternative. (See 2 Ne. 2:27-29; Alma 41:4.) Whatever the choice, it will be made *this side* of eternity *before* the last judgment. Hence, Amulek's warning: "Now is the time and the day of *your* salvation; . . . *this life* is the time for men to prepare to meet God."[13] (Alma 34:31-32; italics added.) When the sun sets on the day of probation, "then cometh the night of darkness wherein there can be *no labor* performed." (Alma 34:33; italics added; cf. Alma 41:5, 7; 3 Ne. 27:33.) That "night" is the time when "it is everlastingly too late" (Hel. 13:38) to perform the labors of repentance. "For the Spirit of the Lord will not *always* strive with man." (2 Ne. 26:11; italics added.)

Alma was told by an angel that at death the righteous entered "a state of happiness, which is called paradise," while the wicked were consigned to a state of misery or "outer darkness." (Alma 40:12-13.) This black-or-white description of the post-mortal state was something of a generalization. It did not explicitly cover that gray host of spirits who—while not totally bereft of the Spirit of the Lord—were nevertheless unredeemed.[14]

Amulek taught: "That same spirit which doth possess your bodies at the time that ye go out of *this life,* that same spirit will have power to possess your *body* in that eternal world." (Alma 34:34; italics added.) "This life" means "this probationary state" (Alma 42:10), and "that eternal world" is the post-resurrection, *not* the spirit, world. "That same spirit" is one's distilled, fundamental self, stripped of all the transitory, superficial baggage acquired in mortality. It is what the soul really is in its fixed, resurrected state, rather than what it appeared to be at any given moment in its fluid, probationary state.[15] What it really is determines what it really desires. These desires, free of all mitigating entanglements, constitute the soul's own self-judgment. (See Alma 41:3-7.)[16]

The explicit teachings of Alma and Amulek quoted above must, therefore, be understood in the time frame of those who lived *before* the Savior initiated his appointed ministry to the unredeemed in the spirit world. Until that hour there was "a great gulf" (Luke 16:26) between those in "paradise" and those in "outer darkness." The latter were, relatively speaking, "in darkness, and a state of awful, fearful looking for the fiery indignation of the wrath of God upon them." (Alma 40:14.) Some thirty-five hundred years before Alma's day, Enoch learned that the unrepentant who perished in the world-wide Flood would be "in torment" in a "prison" prepared for them by the Lord.[17] (See Moses 7:38-39; cf. 6:29.) There they, and all like them, remained until Jesus personally inaugurated the spirit world dispensation of the gospel. Messengers were commissioned by the then-disembodied Son of God to bring the message of salvation "to those who had died in their sins, without a knowledge of the truth, or in transgression, having rejected the prophets." (D&C 138:32.)[18]

Thanks to the merciful Redeemer, eternity—the "night of darkness wherein there can be no labor performed"—was seemingly held back, and the probationary "day of salvation" extended even to the second resurrection! This post-mortal gospel dispensation enables those who repent after death to come forth from their prison of torment and despair and stand on the right hand of God—the hand of salvation.[19] Thus the gates of hell do not prevail against Christ and his priesthood. The vast majority of mankind will pass through those gates and be saved in the "many mansions" comprising the immortal kingdom of God! (See D&C 76:111.)

But to forever reject Christ is to forever forfeit mercy. In that event, it is "as though there had been no redemption made." (Alma 12:18; cf. verse 32.) Justice exercises total dominion, and mercy stands mute. Such is the fate of those children of perdition who, never repenting, are never redeemed. They are known as the "filthy still"[20] who are sealed up to Satan and suffer the fullness of the second death. (See 2 Ne. 9:15-16; Alma 12:16-17; 34:35.)

The rest of mankind — whatever their sins — will eventually repent: "And after they have *paid the penalty of their transgressions,* and are washed clean, shall receive a reward according to their works, for *they are heirs of salvation.*" (D&C 138:59; italics added; cf. 76:43-44, 88.)[21] And so beginning with the Book of Mormon, God's great plan of happiness for all of his children has been revealed, line upon line, in this, the dispensation of the fullness of times!

Epilogue

Upon completing their mission, Alma, Amulek, and their fellow companions left Antionum and journeyed northward to the land of Jershon — the home of the people of Ammon, the Lamanite converts who had taken the name Anti-Nephi-Lehies. (Alma 23:17.) They were soon joined by those Zoramites who, because they accepted the teachings about Christ, had been driven out by their leaders who sought to perpetuate priestcraft. The people of Ammon fed and clothed the wretched Zoramites and even provided them with inheritances.

Ironically, Alma's mission of peace provoked a war in 74 B.C. Infuriated by the Ammonites' acts of charity, the unbelieving Zoramites not only joined the Lamanites in preparing for war but actually became Lamanites. (Alma 43:4.) Their descent into even greater spiritual darkness bore out an earlier observation by Amulek: "They that will harden their hearts, to them is given the lesser portion of the word until they know nothing concerning his mysteries; and then they are taken captive by the devil, and led by his will down to destruction. Now this is what is meant by the chains of hell." (Alma 12:11.)

Under oath never to take up arms again (Alma 24:18), the people of Ammon temporarily left Jershon to the defending Nephite armies — whom they materially supported — and withdrew to the land of Melek, west of the Sidon river. However, the converted Zoramites remained to support the Nephite armies in defending the land of Jershon. The "chief captains" of the Lamanite armies were Amalekites and Zoramites—fanatical enemies of their own Nephite people. But within the year—and with devastating losses to the Lamanites—the Nephites, led by young general Moroni and "inspired by a better cause" (Alma 43:45), proved victorious.

Meanwhile, Alma and his associates returned to Zarahemla, "having been instruments in the hands of God of bringing many of the Zoramites to repentance." (Alma 35:14.) But during the war, Alma "could not rest." (Alma 43:1.) With his three sons, Helaman, Shiblon, and Corianton, he went forth for the last time to declare the truth. Then, after giving final instructions to his sons, prophesying the eventual destruction of the Nephite nation, and reaffirming America's law of inheritance, "he departed out of the land of Zarahemla, as if to go into the land of Melek. And it came to pass that he was never heard of more." (Alma 45:10-18.) Thus passed from the scene two of the Lord's most faithful witnesses, Alma and Amulek.

Conclusion

The heart of the plan of salvation is the infinite atoning sacrifice of the Son of God. Without him, there is no salvation for anyone. His merits, combined with faith and its ordained works, open the door to an appropriate mansion in the kingdom of God for all who call upon his name either in this world or in the world to come.

The Lord's witnesses, both divine and human, leave humanity without excuse. Nephi wrote: "Wherefore, by the words of three, God hath said, I will establish my word. Nevertheless, God sendeth more witnesses, and *he proveth all his words.*" (2 Ne. 11:3; italics added; cf. D&C 6:28.) To their own testimonies, Alma and Amulek added those of Zenos, Zenock, and Moses. All such prophetic testimonies are quickened, made alive, by the over-arching witness of the Holy Spirit. (See Alma 30:44; 31:34-36; 34:30, 33, 38.) "When a man speaketh by the power of the Holy Ghost the power of the Holy Ghost carrieth it unto the hearts of the children of men. But behold, there are many that harden their hearts against the Holy Spirit, that it hath no place in them." (2 Ne. 33:1-2.)

The sum and substance of the prophet Amulek's discourse on the infinite atonement of the Son of God is, "That ye contend no more against the Holy Ghost, but that ye receive it, and take upon you the name of Christ; that ye humble yourselves even to the dust, and worship God, in whatsoever place ye may be in, in spirit and in truth." (Alma 34:38.) Peace of mind, lasting happiness, and salvation in the presence of God the Father are assured to all who heed this counsel.

NOTES

1. Exactly why one man and woman's transgression led to everyone's transgression is not explicitly revealed in scripture. However, God is just; we are no more accountable to him for someone else's acts in one estate than we are in another. Possibly, the Fall affected all people because all people—exercising their agency—became willing co-partners in Adam's foreordained fall. That is, humanity covenanted to accept the Fall's temporary negative consequences (spiritual and physical death) so as to obtain its ultimate blessings (immortality and eternal life).

2. If the major premise of a syllogism is false, regardless of how valid the reasoning, the conclusion will be materially—that is to say, factually—false. The major premise of the Zoramites (God saves whom he chooses) was false, therefore the conclusion (Christ is unnecessary) was factually incorrect. Logic determines the soundness or validity of one's reasoning, but it cannot, of itself, establish its factual correctness.

3. Joseph Smith, *Teachings of the Prophet Joseph Smith*, selected by Joseph Fielding Smith (Salt Lake City: Deseret Book Company, 1938), p. 358.

4. It is in this sense that mankind is "conceived in sin." (Moses 6:55; cf. Ps. 51:5.) That is, whereas the human spirit—a child of God—was conceived by divine parents in a holy estate, its mortal tabernacle was brought by mortal parents into an unholy, imperfect estate.

5. *The City of God*, chapter 21.

6. While the Book of Mormon also speaks of man as a creature, it is always in the context of his *fallen* physical nature, not of his relationship to God as an immortal spirit or soul. The doctrine that man is the literal spirit offspring of divine parents was apparently made known to Joseph Smith subsequent to the publication of the Book of Mormon.

7. *The City of God*, chapters 13 and 14.

8. Speaking of little children, an angel of the Lord told king Benjamin that "as in Adam, *or by nature*, they fall, even so the blood of Christ atoneth for their sins." (Mosiah 3:16; italics added.)

9. See Bruce R. McConkie, *Mormon Doctrine*, 2nd ed. [Salt Lake City: Bookcraft, 1966], p. 66.

10. It is understood that Christ redeems every earth he has organized under the Father's direction. The question is whether this is literally all existing earths, or only a limited number. Elder Bruce R. McConkie defined the word "infinite" quantitatively as well as qualitatively: "The atonement of Christ, being literally and truly infinite, applies to an infinite number of earths." (Bruce R. McConkie, *Mormon Doctrine*, p. 65.)

11. Only Jesus Christ lived the law of God with perfectness. "For all have sinned, and come short of the glory of God." (Rom. 3:23; cf. 4:15; Gal. 2:16; 3:10-13.)

12. *Lectures on Faith* (Salt Lake City: Deseret Book Company, 1985), no. 5, par. 2.

13. Amulek was addressing a people who knew of Christ and had the opportunity to repent and come unto him. Such are expected to do so and be faithful until the end of "the life of the mortal body." (Mosiah 4:6.)

14. The extent to which Alma and Amulek understood the doctrine of post-mortal repentance and salvation is unknown. Their silence on the matter does not prove that they were unaware of it. The stark dichotomy described by Alma may have been designed to make clear the issue of life and death facing his wayward son Corianton, and all mankind. (See Alma 39:3-8; 42:29-30; 2 Ne. 2:27.) The Lord has deliberately employed some extreme terminology so that "it might work upon the hearts of the children of men, altogether for my name's glory." (D&C 19:7; cf. 43:25.)

15. Alma, the four sons of Mosiah, and the Apostle Paul are examples of people whose conduct at one period of their lives belied their true worth. Indeed, the doctrine of salvation of the dead is predicated upon the assumption that a "mighty change" of heart (Alma 5:14) is possible for some even beyond the grave.

16. The teachings of Alma and Amulek are directed *only* to those having a knowledge of Christ and his commandments. They do not apply to any little children or to any adults who lived and died in ignorance of God's will (without his law). These two classes are automatically redeemed (saved) by virtue of the power of the Atonement. See 2 Nephi 9:25-27; Moroni 8:19-22.

17. All who reject Christ are sent to this "prison." See D&C 76:73-74, 82-85, 106; JST 1 Peter 3:20; 4:6.

18. See also John 5:25; JST 1 Peter 3:18-20; 4:6; D&C 138:20-22, 29-37.

19. See Moses 7:57; Isaiah 42:7; 61:1; D&C 128:22.

20. See 2 Nephi 9:16; Mormon 9:14; D&C 29:44; 88:35.

21. In scripture, salvation is not always synonomous with exaltation. To be saved is one thing; to be exalted, another. There is no "gospel of the second chance." Elder Melvin J. Ballard stated Church doctrine when he said: "In this day any man or woman who has had a good chance to have heard the Gospel to receive it and embrace it and enjoy its blessings and privileges, who lived during their life in absolute indifference to these things, ignoring it, and neglected it, need not hope or anticipate that when they are dead the work can be done for them and they gain Celestial Glory." (*The Three Degrees of Glory* [Salt Lake City: Deseret Book Company, n.d.], p. 23.) In any given case, only God can determine what constitutes a "good chance" to receive and live the gospel. Regardless of their eternal state, all who are saved in any heaven or degree of glory are "heirs of salvation." Those who inherit the telestial kingdom are specifically spoken of as "heirs of salvation." (D&C 76:88.)

4

ALMA'S COUNSEL TO HIS SONS
(Alma 36–38)

Clark V. Johnson

Inherent within the gospel is the divine power given by God to act in his name. God restored this authority to the Prophet Joseph Smith through John the Baptist; Peter, James, and John; and Elijah. (JS–H 1:69; D&C 13; 27:12; 110:16.)[1] Once a man holds the Melchizedek Priesthood and receives in the temple with his wife those covenants and ordinances available, he has the divine right to preside over his family. This means that he may importune the Lord for inspiration and then bless and counsel his family. King Benjamin taught his people: "Ye will not suffer your children that they go hungry, or naked; neither will ye suffer that they transgress the laws of God, and fight and quarrel one with another." (Mosiah 4:14.) In this dispensation the Lord stated, "I have commanded you to bring up your children in light and truth." (D&C 93:40.) He then instructed Frederick G. Williams, Sidney Rigdon, Joseph Smith, Jr., and Newell K. Whitney to go home and teach their families. (D&C 93:41-49.) The scriptures contain several examples of fathers seeking inspiration and instructing their children.

Alma and His Sons

Alma is an example of a father who counseled his sons. He explained to them: "The Spirit of the Lord doth say unto me: Command

Clark V. Johnson is associate professor of Church history and doctrine at Brigham Young University.

thy children to do good." (Alma 39:12.) Under the guidance of the Spirit, Alma approached each of his sons differently as he urged them to keep the commandments, as he taught them the doctrines of the gospel, and as he bore them his testimony.

Alma promised his sons Helaman and Shiblon that if they kept the commandments they would "prosper in the land." (Alma 36:1; 38:1.) Unlike Eli in the Old Testament, who apparently did not discipline his sons sufficiently for their misconduct, Alma confronted Corianton about his lack of diligence in keeping the commandments. (Alma 39:2; 1 Sam. 2:22-25, 27-34.) Whether Alma taught his sons collectively or individually in a personal interview cannot be determined. Yet even though the approach in addressing each son was different, his discussions have one thing in common: They are Christ-centered. (Alma 36; 37:9, 43-47; 38:8-9; 39:15.)

Unlike his brothers Shiblon and Corianton, Helaman did not accompany his father on the mission to the Zoramites. (Alma 31:7.) Alma encouraged his eldest son, Helaman, to place his trust in God. He promised Helaman that God would support him in his trials, troubles, and afflictions. (Alma 31:7; 36:3.) He referred to the scriptures to teach Helaman that God sustains his children if they worship him and keep his commandments. He challenged him to remember the bondage of their ancestors and that God had supported them in their afflictions. He also referred to the enslavement of ancient Israel. Alma reminded Helaman that God had delivered Israel from the Egyptians by allowing them to pass through the Red Sea safely, while destroying Pharaoh's army. (Alma 36:2, 28-29.) The promise to each group was prosperity. Israel did prosper physically in the land, as Abraham, Isaac, and Jacob prospered both physically and spiritually as they achieved eternal life. (D&C 132:28, 36-37.)

Alma concluded his remarks to Helaman by referring to the "shadow" and "type" found within the scriptures. Reminding Helaman of the history of his father Lehi, Alma said, "They tarried in the wilderness, or did not travel a direct course . . . because of their transgressions."[2] (Alma 37:42.) The reason for their wanderings was their lack of faith. The Liahona worked only according to their faith and obedience. Alma taught "that these things are not without a shadow; for as our fathers were slothful to give heed to this compass (now these things were temporal) they did not prosper; even so it is with things which are spiritual." (Alma 37:43.) Thus, the Liahona or "shadow" served the same purpose to Lehi's family that the brazen serpent had served to ancient Israel. (1 Ne. 17:41; Num. 21:4-9.) The Liahona was a "shadow" or "type" that strengthened their faith and led them to Christ.

Alma promised Helaman that the words of Christ "carry us beyond this vale of sorrow [earth life] into a far better land of promise [eternal life]." (Alma 37:45.) Hence, the promised land has a two-fold interpretation. First, it is a physical place to live, where God blesses his children temporally. Second, it has spiritual significance in which God blesses his children with experiences to lead them to eternal life. Alma concluded his interview by admonishing his son not to be slothful because of the easiness of the way, but to "look to God and live." (Alma 37:46-47.)

Shiblon was a faithful missionary and had endured many hardships. During his mission, he was imprisoned and stoned by the Zoramites. (Alma 38:3-4.) Alma commended this faithful son for his "steadiness" and "faithfulness" during a time of persecution. (Alma 38:2.) He also gave special counsel to this son who had brought him "great joy." (Alma 38:3.) Alma cautioned Shiblon to beware of pride, not to boast of his own wisdom, to be diligent and temperate, to use boldness, but not overbearance, to bridle his passions, to refrain from idleness, and to pray. (Alma 38:10-13.) He instructed him to acknowledge the power of God in his prayers, and to remember his own weaknesses, to pray for his brethren, and to "acknowledge [his] unworthiness before God at all times." (Alma 38:14.)

Alma's Testimony

Alma loved his sons and wanted only the best in life for each of them. As he bore his testimony to them he said, "I would not that ye think that I know of myself," for *"if I had not been born of God I should not have known these things."* (Alma 36:4-5; emphasis added.) He continued to explain that he and the sons of Mosiah had sought to destroy the church of God. (Alma 36:6; Mosiah 27:8-10.)

They were stopped by an angel who promised their destruction if they continued, and they fell to the earth in fear. (Alma 36:7-9.) Alma noted that he did not hear the rest of the words spoken by the angel, but he remembered all his sins, and was "tormented with the pains of hell." (Alma 36:11, 13.) He asserted that he did not want to be brought into the presence of God, for he was ashamed, and he knew he was unworthy. It was at this moment that he remembered the teachings of his father "concerning the coming of one Jesus Christ, a Son of God, to atone for the sins of the world." (Alma 36:17.) He said, "I cried within my heart: O Jesus, thou Son of God, have mercy on me, who am in the gall of bitterness." (Alma 36:18.) From that moment on Alma did not remember his sins, but he knew joy, and then he said, "Methought I saw, even as our father Lehi saw, God sitting upon his throne, surrounded with numberless concourses of angels, in the attitude of singing and praising their God; yea, and my soul did long to be there." (Alma 36:22; 1 Ne. 1:8-15; Isa. 6:1-6.) He ended his testimony by pointing out that after this experience he had sought continually to teach the people the truth.

Most people do not gain a testimony by having experiences with angels. Almost all testimonies come through prayer, as did that of Enos. Enos said: "My soul hungered; and I kneeled down before my Maker, and I cried unto him in mighty prayer. . . . There came a voice unto me, saying: Enos, thy sins are forgiven thee, and thou shalt be blessed. And I, Enos, knew that God could not lie; wherefore, my guilt was swept away." (Enos 1:4-6.) Elder Bruce R. McConkie wrote:

> Any accountable person can gain a testimony of the gospel by obedience to that law upon which the receipt of such knowledge is predicated. This is the formula: 1. He must desire to know the truth of the gospel, of the Book of Mormon, of the Church, or of whatever matter is involved. 2. He must study and learn the basic facts relative to the matter involved. "Search the scriptures." (John 5:39). "Search these commandments," (D&C 1:37). 3. He must practice the principles and truths learned, conforming his life to them. "My doctrine is not mine, but his that sent me. If any man will do his will, he shall know of the doctrine, whether it be of God, or whether I speak of myself" (John 7:16-17). 4. He must pray to the

Father in the name of Christ, in faith, and the truth will then be made manifest by revelation "by the power of the Holy Ghost. And by the power of the Holy Ghost ye may know the truth of all things" (Moroni 10:3-5; 1 Corinthians 2).[3]

Many times a testimony comes through fulfilling the challenge Moroni issued to those who have read the Book of Mormon. He promised those who read the book a special witness from the Holy Ghost regarding its veracity. (Moroni 10:4-5.) Testimonies are borne about many things and are expressed in many different ways. Latter-day Saints are expected to receive revelation. Elder McConkie pointed out that "every devoted, obedient, and righteous person on the earth has and does receive revelation from God. Revelation is the natural inheritance of all the faithful. . . . The saints are expected (because they have the gift of the Holy Ghost) to gain personal revelation and guidance rather than to run to the First Presidency or some other church leaders to be told what to do."[4]

When Alma related his witness to Shiblon, he only alluded to his conversion, which he had told in great detail to Helaman, and then, he testified boldly of Jesus Christ. (Alma 38:6-9.) To his son Corianton, Alma testified powerfully, while teaching him the doctrines of the kingdom. (Alma 39-42.)

Alma's Charge to His Sons

During his interviews with his sons, Alma challenged each to keep the commandments, to be an example, and to teach the gospel to the people. (Alma 37:47; 38:15; 42:31.) However, he gave Helaman additional responsibilities.

Alma entrusted Helaman with the sacred records: the plates of brass, the twenty-four plates belonging to the Jaredites, and the records of the Nephites, as well as the interpreters or Urim and Thummim, and the Liahona. (Alma 37:24.)

The records that Alma and his predecessors kept served two purposes. First, they had been used to teach the Nephites and the Lamanites. Alma stated, "Were it not for these things that these records do contain, which are on these plates, Ammon and his brethren could not have convinced so many thousands of the Lamanites of the incorrect tradition of their fathers." These records brought the Lamanites to the knowledge of the Lord and caused them "to rejoice in Jesus Christ their Redeemer." (Alma 37:8-9.) Second, speaking prophetically he said that these records will show God's "power unto future generations." (Alma 37:14, 18-19.)

With the responsibility of keeping the sacred artifacts safe, Helaman was also admonished to write and continue the record. (Alma 37:2, 47.) Likewise, a modern father might entrust to one of his children journals, papers, and diaries belonging to previous generations. From such records may come spiritual witnesses to enrich the lives of living family members as well as future generations.

Conclusions

The Book of Mormon contains several father-son encounters: Father Lehi with Laman, Lemuel, Sam, Nephi, Jacob, and Joseph; Alma the Elder and Mosiah with their sons; and Mormon and Moroni. But none is more soul-searching than the counsel given to Helaman, Shiblon, and Corianton by Alma. Each of these fathers, like Alma, had one thing in mind, the welfare of his children. Alma counseled his sons about physical and spiritual matters. He encouraged them to put their trust in God, to keep his commandments, to pray, to keep records, to be an example, and to teach the gospel to others. And, like the others, he blessed them. Modern-day scripture instructs us · to "set in order" our own homes. (D&C 93:43.) Nothing is more beautiful than Mormon's farewell to his son, Moroni. After instructing his faithful son one final time, Mormon, echoing the desire of every father, wrote, "Behold, my son, I recommend thee unto God." (Moro. 9:22.)

NOTES

1. See also Joseph Smith, *Teachings of the Prophet Joseph Smith*, selected by Joseph Fielding Smith (Salt Lake City: Deseret Book Company, 1938), pp. 158, 323, 337-38.

2. Lehi and his family wandered eight years in the wilderness. (1. Ne. 17:4.)

3. Bruce R. McConkie, *Mormon Doctrine*, 2nd ed. (Salt Lake City: Book-craft, 1966), pp. 786-87.

4. *Mormon Doctrine*, pp. 644-45.

5

THE PATH OF REPENTANCE
(Alma 39)

ROBERT L. MILLET

Alma discovered, to his horror, that his son Corianton had been guilty of sexual sin during his mission to the Zoramites; he had become involved with a harlot named Isabel, a woman of degraded character and morals who had contributed to the downfall of many men. In the words of Alma, Corianton had yielded to moral temptation for several reasons, reasons that should cause the Saints of the twentieth century to take note:

1. He had become haughty, had yielded to feelings of self-sufficiency. He had begun to boast in his own strength (Alma 39:2), to rely less and less on the arm of the Lord and more and more on the arm of flesh. In our day, Corianton might have been heard to say repeatedly, "I can handle it!" Corianton learned through a painful process that no man or woman has sufficient strength to resist the enticements of the father of lies. Alma had pleaded almost a decade earlier with a rebellious people: "Cast off your sins, and [do] not procrastinate the day of your repentance; but *humble yourselves before the Lord*, and *call on his holy name*, and watch and pray continually, that ye may not be tempted above that which ye can bear." (Alma 13:27-28; emphasis added.)

2. Corianton had forsaken his ministry (Alma 39:3), had left his duty station. He was not where he had been assigned to be. One who sings "I'll go where you want me to go, dear Lord," must not then

---

Robert L. Millet is associate professor of ancient scripture at Brigham Young University.

be guilty of desertion, of negligence and waywardness when the assignment comes. "No man," the Savior declared, "having put his hand to the plough, and looking back, is fit for the kingdom of God." (Luke 9:62.)

3. He had begun to associate with the wrong kinds of people; he eventually surrendered to the allurements and pressures to conform to the ways of the worldly. But, Alma scolded, because others gave in to sin was no reason for him to do the same: "This was no excuse for thee, my son. Thou shouldst have tended to the ministry wherewith thou wast entrusted." (Alma 39:3-4.)

The Seriousness of Sexual Transgression

Alma then placed all things in perspective by stressing the seriousness of this immoral practice: he explained that only two sins were greater abominations in the sight of God—the sin against the Holy Ghost, and murder or the shedding of innocent blood. In speaking of the former sin, he taught: "If ye deny the Holy Ghost when it once has had place in you, and ye know that ye deny it, behold, this is a sin which is unpardonable." (Alma 39:6.)

"All manner of sin and blasphemy shall be forgiven unto men," Jesus warned, "but the blasphemy against the Holy Ghost shall not be forgiven unto men, . . . neither in this world, neither in the world to come." (Matt. 12:31-32.) These are they who "know [God's] power, and have been made partakers thereof, and suffered themselves through the power of the devil to be overcome, and to deny the truth and defy [God's] power—they are they who are the sons of perdition, . . . vessels of wrath," enemies to the cause of truth, "having denied the Holy Spirit after having received it, and having denied the Only Begotten Son of the Father, having crucified him unto themselves and put him to an open shame." (D&C 76:31-35.)[1] Joseph Smith declared:

> All sins shall be forgiven, except the sin against the Holy Ghost; for Jesus will save all except the sons of perdition. What must a man do to commit the unpardonable sin? He must receive the Holy Ghost, have the heavens opened unto him, and know God, and then sin against Him. After a man has

sinned against the Holy Ghost, there is no repentance for him. He has got to say that the sun does not shine while he sees it; he has got to deny Jesus Christ when the heavens have been opened unto him, and to deny the plan of salvation with his eyes open to the truth of it; and from that time he begins to be an enemy.[2]

The sin against the Holy Ghost is *unpardonable* because it is not covered by the atoning blood of Christ and because no amount of personal suffering on the part of the sinner can atone for the pernicious deed.

"Whosoever murdereth against the light and knowledge of God, it is not easy for him to obtain forgiveness," Alma warned. (Alma 39:6.) "A murderer," Joseph Smith explained, "one that sheds innocent blood, cannot have forgiveness."[3] Murder is thus referred to as an *unforgivable* sin, a heinous crime against humanity, an offense not covered by the atoning blood of Christ and for which deliverance from hell in the world of spirits is possible only after much personal suffering. "There are sins unto death," wrote Elder Bruce R. McConkie, "meaning spiritual death. There are sins for which there is no forgiveness, neither in this world nor in the world to come. There are sins which utterly and completely preclude the sinner from gaining eternal life. Hence there are sins for which repentance does not operate, sins that the atoning blood of Christ will not wash away, sins for which the sinner must suffer and pay the full penalty personally."[4]

Sexual immorality ranks third in order of serious offenses before God because it, like murder, deals with life. One who tampers with virtue prematurely or inappropriately—outside of marriage—tampers with the powers of life. Elder Boyd K. Packer has taught: "There was provided in our bodies—and this is sacred—a power of creation, a light, so to speak, that has the power to kindle other lights. This gift was to be used only within the sacred bonds of marriage. Through the exercise of this power of creation, a mortal body may be conceived, a spirit enter into it, and a new soul born into this life." Further, this power "is a gift from God our Father. In the righteous exercise of it as in nothing else, we may come close to him." On the other hand, "God has declared in unmistakable language that misery and sorrow will follow the violation of the laws of chastity.... Crowning glory awaits you if you live worthily. The loss of the crown may well be punishment enough. Often, very often, we are punished as much by our sins as we are for them."[5]

A Pattern for Repentance

It would appear that much of Corianton's problem was borne of doctrinal ignorance and misunderstanding, particularly concerning the appropriateness of justice and punishment for sin. (See Alma 41:1; 42:1.) It is fitting, then, that Alma should instruct his son about repentance and point the way back to the path of peace and happiness.

First, having stressed the seriousness of the offense, Alma sought now to ensure that Corianton was experiencing godly sorrow for sin, the kind of sorrow that is an essential element of true repentance. In short, Alma desired that his son experience appropriate guilt—no more than is requisite, but surely no less than is needful to bring about change. Alma observed: "I would to God that ye had not been guilty of so great a crime. I would not dwell upon your crimes, to harrow up your soul, if it were not for your good." (Alma 39:7; compare 2 Cor. 7:10.) Alma later remarked: "And now, my son, I desire that ye should let these things trouble you no more, and only let your sins trouble you, with that trouble which shall bring you down unto repentance." (Alma 42:29.) Alma knew only too well the awful agony associated with grievous sin; on the other hand, he understood as few others do how intense pain could be turned to consummate joy, how suffering could make saints out of sinners. Appropriate guilt can and does have a sanctifying effect: it alerts the offender to the spiritual chasm between himself and his Maker and motivates him thereafter to a godly walk and conduct.

"Now my son," Alma continued, "I would that ye should repent and forsake your sins, and go no more after the lusts of your eyes, but cross yourself in all these things." (Alma 39:9.) For Corianton to "cross himself" was for him to turn away from evil inclinations, to deny himself of worldly lusts, to work at cross purposes from the natural man, to forsake worldly paths, and to chart and navigate a course of righteousness. (See 3 Ne. 12:30.) "As well as establishing

51

worthy goals, charting the course prevents one from living an unplanned, haphazard life — a tumbleweed existence."[6] Those desirous of keeping themselves from sinful practices must often change associations, places, and attitudes toward life. Corianton was specifically advised to lean upon his older brothers — Helaman and Shiblon — for support, to look to their example and seek their counsel. "Ye stand in need to be nourished by your brothers," Alma said. (Alma 39:10.)

Because Corianton's abominable deeds rang so loudly in the ears of the Zoramites, the words of the Nephite missionaries did not have the spiritual appeal they might otherwise have had. "How great iniquity ye brought upon the Zoramites," Alma chastened the errant son, "for when they saw your conduct they would not believe in my words." (Alma 39:11.) It was thus incumbent upon Corianton — a major part of his repentance and a key to forgiveness — to make restitution where possible. "Turn to the Lord with all your mind, might, and strength; that ye lead away the hearts of no more to do wickedly; but rather return unto them, and acknowledge your faults and that wrong which ye have done." (Alma 39:13.) President Joseph F. Smith asked: "Does repentance consist of sorrow for wrong doing?" "Yes," he answered, "but is this all? By no means."

> True repentance only is acceptable to God, nothing short of it will answer the purpose. Then what is true repentance? True repentance is not only sorrow for sins, and humble penitence and contrition before God, but it involves the necessity of turning away from them, a discontinuance of all evil practices and deeds, a thorough reformation of life, a vital change from evil to good, from vice to virtue, from darkness to light. Not only so, but to make restitution, so far as it is possible, for all the wrongs we have done, to pay our debts, and restore to God and man their rights — that which is due to them from us. This is true repentance, and the exercise of the will and all the powers of body and mind is demanded, to complete this glorious work of repentance; then God will accept it.[7]

Indeed, Corianton learned, as do we all, that repentance consists of a major realignment of priorities, a turn from the fleeting, and an acceptance of the permanent. "Seek not after riches nor the vain things of this world," a tender father thus counseled, "for behold, you cannot carry them with you." (Alma 39:14.)

No discussion of repentance would be complete without a focus upon the power and saving grace available through the redemptive work of Jesus Christ. And thus it is that Alma set forth in plain and unmistakable language the significance of the timeless and eternal sacrifice available through the blood of him who is man's Advocate with the Father. Alma's testimony (see Alma 39:17-18) is in harmony with that of John the Revelator: Jesus Christ is the Lamb slain from the foundation of the world (Rev. 13:8). The Book of Mormon provides a restoration of a vital and precious truth, a verity largely absent from the biblical record: the knowledge that Christian prophets have taught Christian doctrine and administered Christian ordinances since the beginning of time. Our Lord's atonement reaches from creation's dawn to millennial splendor; the children of God from Eden to Armaggedon can have their sins remitted in the name of the Holy One of Israel. That is, the atonement applies to "not only those who believed after he came in the meridian of time, in the flesh, but all those from the beginning, even as many as were before he came, who believed in the words of the holy prophets, . . . as well as those who should come after, who should believe in the gifts and callings of God by the Holy Ghost." (D&C 20:26-27.)

The Return of the Prodigal

Corianton's sin was abhorrent to God and the people of God. It hindered the work of the Lord among the Zoramites and caused deep pain and sorrow for those who knew and loved him. But it was not an unpardonable nor an unforgivable sin. Though it is true that the Holy One cannot look upon sin with the least degree of allowance, it is also true that "he that repents and does the commandments of the Lord shall be forgiven." (D&C 1:31-32; see also Alma 45:16.) God the Father is anxious for the return of his children to the path of righteousness and peace, perhaps infinitely more so than we can now perceive. Elder Orson F. Whitney held out this hope for the parents of wandering or wayward children:

> You parents of the wilful and the wayward: Don't give

them up. Don't cast them off. They are not utterly lost. The shepherd will find his sheep. They were his before they were yours—long before he entrusted them to your care; and you cannot begin to love them as he loves them. They have but strayed in ignorance from the Path of Right, and God is merciful to ignorance. Only the fulness of knowledge brings the fulness of accountability. Our Heavenly Father is far more merciful, infinitely more charitable, than even the best of his servants, and the Everlasting Gospel is mightier in power to save than our narrow finite minds can comprehend.[8]

President J. Reuben Clark observed: "I feel that [the Lord] will give that punishment which is the very least that our transgression will justify. . . . I believe that when it comes to making the rewards for our good conduct, he will give the maximum that it is possible to give."[9]

Alma was not only a concerned father; he was a prophet of God and the president of the Church. His was the gift of discernment and the spirit of prophecy and revelation. He was thus able to judge whether Corianton's repentance was genuine and when his heart was right before God. Knowing these things, it is touching to read these words of Alma to his son: "And now, O my son, ye are called of God to preach the word unto this people. And now, my son, go thy way, declare the word with truth and soberness, that thou mayest bring souls unto repentance, that the great plan of mercy may have claim upon them. And may God grant unto you even according to my words. Amen." (Alma 42:31.) We have every reason to believe that Corianton's repentance was complete, that he "crossed himself" and forsook sinful practices, places, and people, and that he qualified to return to the ministry and to full fellowship among the household of faith. We read of Corianton's labors a year or so later: "Thus ended the nineteenth year of the reign of the judges over the people of Nephi. Yea, and there was continual peace among them, and exceedingly great prosperity in the church because of their heed and diligence which they gave unto *the word of God, which was declared unto them by* Helaman, and Shiblon, and *Corianton*, and Ammon and his brethren, yea, and by all those who had been ordained by the holy order of God." (Alma 49:29-30, emphasis added.)[10] Truly salvation is free (2 Ne. 2:4), freely available, and the Lord's hand is extended to all, such that "whosoever will come may come and partake of the waters of life freely" (Alma 42:27; cf. Isa. 55:1-2).

NOTES

1. There is a sense in which those who have "shed innocent blood" are guilty of the sin against the Holy Ghost. That person who becomes a son of perdition crucifies Christ anew. (Compare Heb. 6:4-6.) "He gets the spirit of the devil—the same spirit that they had who crucified the Lord of Life—the same spirit that sins against the Holy Ghost." (*Teachings of the Prophet Joseph Smith*, selected by Joseph Fielding Smith [Salt Lake City: Deseret Book Company, 1976], p. 358.) "The blasphemy against the Holy Ghost, which shall not be forgiven in the world nor out of the world, is in that *ye commit murder wherein ye shed innocent blood*, and *assent unto my death*." (D&C 132:27; emphasis added.) See also Bruce R. McConkie, *Doctrinal New Testament Commentary*, 3 vols. (Salt Lake City: Bookcraft, 1965-73), 3:116, 345; *The Mortal Messiah: From Bethlehem to Calvary*, 4 vols. (Salt Lake City: Deseret Book Company, 1979-81), 2:216; *A New Witness for the Articles of Faith* (Salt Lake City: Deseret Book Company, 1985), p. 233.

2. *Teachings of the Prophet Joseph Smith*, p. 358.

3. Ibid., p. 339.

4. *A New Witness for the Articles of Faith*, p. 231.

5. Boyd K. Packer, *Conference Report*, April 1972, pp. 136-38.

6. Spencer W. Kimball, *The Miracle of Forgiveness* (Salt Lake City: Bookcraft, 1969), pp. 233-34.

7. Joseph F. Smith, *Gospel Doctrine* (Salt Lake City: Deseret Book Company, 1971), pp. 100-101.

8. *Conference Report*, April 1929, p. 110.

9. From "As Ye Sow . . . ," Address at Brigham Young University, May 3, 1955.

10. Later in the story we read of Corianton busily engaged in the work of the Lord. (See Alma 63:10.)

6

JUSTICE, MERCY, AND THE LIFE BEYOND
(Alma 40–42)

ROBERT L. MILLET

It is in the context of a serious father-and-son discussion — counsel by Alma to his errant son, Corianton — that we are able to read some of the deepest and most profound doctrine in the Book of Mormon. Because life is at best tenuous; because death is an ever-present reality; and because all men and women must eventually put off this mortal coil and engage a new existence that is, for the most part, strange and unknown, a theological discussion of life after life is welcomed and appreciated. The prophet Alma, recognizing that resurrection — the inseparable union of spirit and body — did not immediately follow death, inquired of the Lord about the state of the soul between death and the resurrection. An angel, a citizen himself of the world of spirits, taught Alma about the nature of the afterworld. And it is through Alma's explanation of these things to his son that we become privy to sacred and solemn matters.

Between Death and Resurrection

Before discussing the doctrine of resurrection and the law of restoration — the principle that all people will be raised to that level of glory commensurate with the lives they lived in mortality — Alma turned his attention to a discussion of the postmortal spirit world, a matter he had "inquired diligently of the Lord to know." (Alma 40:9.)

Robert L. Millet is associate professor of ancient scripture at Brigham Young University.

He explained that, according to what he had been taught by an angel, "the spirits of all men, as soon as they are departed from this mortal body, yea, the spirits[1] of all men, whether they be good or evil, are taken home to that God who gave them life." (Alma 40:11.) "Then shall the dust return to the earth as it was," said the Preacher, "and the spirit shall return unto God who gave it." (Eccl. 12:7.) Both of these scriptural preachers were speaking in broadest terms and should not be interpreted to mean that the spirit—at the time of death—goes into the immediate presence of the Lord. President Brigham Young explained that to speak of the spirit returning to the God who gave it means that "when the spirits leave their bodies they are in the presence of our Father and God" in the sense that they "are prepared then to see, hear and understand spiritual things."[2] To go into the "presence" of God is not necessarily to be "placed within a few yards or rods, or within a short distance of his person."[3] President George Q. Cannon explained: "Alma, when he says that 'the spirits of all men, as soon as they are departed from this mortal body, . . . are taken home to that God who gave them life,' has the idea, doubtless, in his mind that our God is omnipresent—not in His own personality but through His minister, the Holy Spirit. He does not intend to convey the idea that they are immediately ushered into the personal presence of God. He evidently uses that phrase in a qualified sense."[4]

The transition from time into eternity is immediate. As the physical self breathes its last breath, the spirit self passes through a veil separating this world from the next. At this point the spirit experiences what might be called a "partial judgment."[5] Those who have been true and faithful to their trust in mortality, Alma explained, are received into *paradise*, "a state of rest, a state of peace, where they shall rest from all their troubles and from all care, and sorrow." (Alma 40:12.) As I have written elsewhere, "those things which burdened the obedient—the worldly cares and struggles, the vicissitudes of life—are shed with the physical body. Paradise is a place where the spirit is free to think and act with a renewed capacity and with the vigor and enthusiasm which characterized one in his prime. Though a person does not rest per se from the work associated with the plan of salvation . . . , at the same time he is delivered from those cares and worries associated with a fallen world and a corrupt body."[6]

Those, on the other hand, who have been wicked on earth—who gave themselves up to the lusts and lasciviousness of the flesh—shall be received into that portion of the spirit world called *hell* or *outer darkness*,[7] a place of "weeping, and wailing, and gnashing of teeth, and this because of their own iniquity, being led captive by the will of the devil." (Alma 40:13.) Joseph Smith explained: "The great misery of departed spirits in the world of spirits, where they go after death, is to know that they come short of the glory that others enjoy and that they might have enjoyed themselves, and they are their own accusers."[8] On another occasion the Prophet taught: "A man is his own tormenter and his own condemner. Hence the saying, They shall go into the lake that burns with fire and brimstone. The torment of disappointment in the mind of man is as exquisite as a lake burning with fire and brimstone. I say, so is the torment of man."[9] Hell or outer darkness is both a place—a part of the world of spirits where suffering and sorrow and repentance take place—and a state—a condition of the mind associated with remorseful realization. The righteous remain in paradise and the wicked in hell until the time of their resurrection. (Alma 40:14.)[10]

The Doctrine of Resurrection

No doctrine provides a more powerful assurance and comfort to the bereaved than the doctrine of resurrection—the verity that all who have taken physical bodies through birth shall survive death, shall receive those bodies again in the resurrection. Resurrection is a doctrine as old as the world: it is not a creation of the first-century Christians, nor a belief spawned by the Jews in Babylonian captivity. It was taught to Adam, discussed by Enoch, and testified of by Abraham. Any people through the ages who have gained the understanding of the ministry of the Messiah, who have come to know by revelation of the coming of Jesus Christ, have likewise gained the understanding that Christ would break the bands of death and open the door for all others to be likewise raised from death to life in glorious immortality. It was just so with the Nephites. Alma, the noble patriarch, sought to inform and inspire his son on this fundamental principle of the Christian religion.[11]

"The soul shall be restored to the body," Alma explained, "and the body to the soul; yea, and every limb and joint shall be restored to its body; yea, even a hair of the head shall not be lost; but all things shall be restored to their proper and perfect frame." (Alma 40:23; cf. 11:43.)[12] Joseph Smith provided additional insight into the nature of the resurrection when he said: "As concerning the resurrection, I will merely say that all men will come from the grave as they lie down, whether old or young; there will not be 'added unto their stature one cubit,' neither taken from it; all will be raised by the power of God, having spirit in their bodies, and not blood."[13]

A prophetic successor, Joseph F. Smith, observed: "The body will come forth as it is laid to rest, for there is no growth or development in the grave. As it is laid down, so will it arise, and changes to perfection will come by the law of restitution. But the spirit will continue to expand and develop, and the body, after the resurrection will develop to the full stature of man."[14]

Alma's discussion of the first resurrection (Alma 40:16-20) is slightly difficult to follow. At first it appears that Alma was suggesting that the first resurrection consists of the resurrection of all persons— righteous and wicked—who had lived before Christ. (See Alma 40:16.) Abinadi had clearly stated, however, that the first resurrection would be made up of "the prophets, and all those that have believed in their words, or all those that have kept the commandments of God." (Mosiah 15:22.) That is to say, from Abinadi's and Alma's chronological perspective, the first resurrection would be made up of the righteous dead—"an innumerable company of the spirits of the just" (D&C 138:12)—from Adam to Christ. From our perspective in the final dispensation, with information revealed to Joseph Smith, we know that the first resurrection will resume at the time of the Second Coming; the Savior will bring with him the hosts of the righteous from the meridian of time to the time of his coming. Finally Alma did give his opinion on the matter—an opinion that is in fact accurate and appropriate—that "the souls and the bodies are reunited, *of the righteous*, at the resurrection of Christ, and his ascension into heaven." (Alma 40:20; emphasis added.)[15]

The Lord has stated in a modern revelation that "the resurrection from the dead is the redemption of the soul." (D&C 88:16.) Death is not the end. The grave shall not have won the victory. The prophetic promise is sure. Joseph Smith declared: "All your losses will be made up to you in the resurrection, provided you continue faithful. By the vision of the Almighty I have seen it."[16]

The Doctrine of Restoration

The resurrection, Alma explained, is but a part of a larger system of restoration: not only shall spirit and body be inseparably united, but all things shall hereafter be restored to the way they were here. In short, our station and reward hereafter shall be directly related to the manner in which we managed our time and spiritual resources while in this life. It is thus ludicrous to suppose that one could hope for a glorious resurrection and transcendent reward hereafter when his or her thoughts and actions in this life were shoddy and superficial. What was to Paul the Law of the Harvest ("whatsoever a man soweth, that shall he also reap" — Gal. 6:7) was to Alma the Law of Restoration. "The plan of restoration," he observed, "is requisite with the justice of God; for it is requisite that all things should be restored to their proper order." Further, "it is requisite with the justice of God that men should be judged according to their works; and if their works were good in this life, and the desires of their hearts were good, that they should also, at the last day, be restored unto that which is good," what we would know as exaltation in the highest heaven. "And if their works are evil they shall be restored unto them for evil." (Alma 41:2-4.)

Wickedness here never was and never will be happiness here or hereafter. Carnality here never was and never will be spirituality here or hereafter. Charting a course contrary to God and his plan in this life can never lead to spiritual union and joy with him in the life to come. (See Alma 41:10-11.) Moroni focused the attention of his readers upon the stark reality of the Law of Restoration in these words: "Do ye suppose that ye shall dwell with [God] under a consciousness of your guilt? Do ye suppose that ye could be happy to dwell with that holy Being, when your souls are racked with a consciousness of guilt that ye have ever abused his laws? Behold, I say unto you that ye would be more miserable to dwell with a holy and just God, under a consciousness of your filthiness before him, than ye would to dwell with the damned souls in hell." (Morm. 9:3-4.) A modern revelation thus stated that "they who are not sanctified through the law which I have given unto you, even the law of Christ, must inherit another kingdom, even that of a terrestrial kingdom, or that of a telestial kingdom."

> For he who is not able to abide the law of a celestial kingdom cannot abide a celestial glory. And he who cannot abide the law of a terrestrial kingdom cannot abide a terrestrial glory. And he who cannot abide the law of a telestial kingdom cannot abide a telestial glory; therefore he is not meet for a kingdom of glory. Therefore he must abide a kingdom which is not a kingdom of glory.
>
> They who are of a celestial spirit [in mortality] shall receive [in the resurrection] the same body which was a natural body; even ye shall receive your bodies, and your glory shall be that glory by which your bodies are quickened. Ye who are quickened by a portion of the celestial glory shall then receive of the same, even a fulness. And they who are quickened by a portion of the terrestrial glory shall then receive of the same, even a fulness. And also they who are quickened by a portion of the telestial glory shall then receive of the same, even a fulness. (D&C 88:21-24, 28-31.)

In summary, "that which ye do send out [the life we live, the deeds we do] shall return unto you again, and be restored; therefore, the word restoration more fully condemneth the sinner, and justifieth him not at all." (Alma 41:15.)

Justice and Mercy: The Delicate Balance

To demonstrate the necessity and timelessness of justice and to show that there are always consequences for our transgressions, Alma recounted the story of the fall of Adam and Eve. The fall brought on the justice of God and resulted in physical and spiritual death, both of which were necessary in the eternal plan of the Father. "Now behold," Alma continued, "it was not expedient that man should be reclaimed from this . . . death, for that would destroy the great plan of happiness." (Alma 42:8.) Jacob had noted earlier that "death hath passed upon all men, to fulfil the merciful plan of the great Creator." (2 Ne. 9:6.) It was necessary for the justice of a God to be meted out in order for the mercy of a God to be extended; as the fall is the father of the atonement, so justice paves the way for mercy. (See Alma 42:1-13.)

The balance of justice and mercy is achieved only in and through a God, only in and through a being in whom there is a perfect balance, through him who is both infinitely just and merciful. The balance is achieved only by him who is sinless and upon whom justice has no claim, through him who has no need of pardoning mercy. Elder Boyd K. Packer beautifully illustrated the role of Christ as Mediator in the following parable:

> There was once a man who wanted something very much. It seemed more important than anything else in his life. In order for him to have his desire, he incurred a great debt.
>
> He had been warned about going into that much debt, and particularly about his creditor. But it seemed so important for him to do what he wanted to do and to have what he wanted right now. He was sure he could pay for it later.
>
> So he signed a contract. He would pay it off some time along the way. He didn't worry too much about it, for the due date seemed such a long time away. He had what he wanted now, and that was what seemed important.
>
> The creditor was always somewhere in the back of his mind, and he made token payments now and again, thinking somehow that the day of reckoning really would never come.
>
> But as it always does, the day came, and the contract fell due. The debt had not been fully paid. His creditor appeared and demanded payment in full.
>
> Only then did he realize that his creditor not only had the power to repossess all that he owned, but the power to cast him into prison as well.

"I cannot pay you, for I have not the power to do so," he confessed.

"Then," said the creditor, "we will exercise the contract, take your possessions, and you shall go to prison. You agreed to that. It was your choice. You signed the contract, and now it must be enforced."

"Can you not extend the time or forgive the debt?" the debtor begged. "Arrange some way for me to keep what I have and not go to prison. Surely you believe in mercy? Will you not show mercy?"

The creditor replied, "Mercy is always so one-sided. It would serve only you. If I show mercy to you, it will leave me unpaid. It is justice I demand. Do you believe in justice?"

"I believed in justice when I signed the contract," the debtor said. "It was on my side then, for I thought it would protect me. I did not need mercy then, nor think I should need it ever. Justice, I thought, would serve both of us equally as well."

"It is justice that demands that you pay the contract or suffer the penalty," the creditor replied. "That is the law. You have agreed to it and that is the way it must be. Mercy cannot rob justice."

There they were: One meting out justice, the other pleading for mercy. Neither could prevail except at the expense of the other.

"If you do not forgive the debt there will be no mercy," the debtor pleaded.

"If I do, there will be no justice," was the reply.

Both laws, it seemed, could not be served. They are two eternal ideals that appear to contradict one another. Is there no way for justice to be fully served, and mercy also?

There is a way! The law of justice *can* be fully satisfied and mercy *can* be fully extended—but it takes someone else. And so it happened this time.

The debtor had a friend. He came to help. He knew the debtor well. He knew him to be shortsighted. He thought him foolish to have gotten himself into such a predicament. Nevertheless, he wanted to help because he loved him. He stepped between them, faced the creditor, and made this offer:

"I will pay the debt if you will free the debtor from his

contract so that he may keep his possessions and not go to prison."

As the creditor was pondering the offer, the mediator added, "You demanded justice. Though he cannot pay you, I will do so. You will have been justly dealt with and can ask no more. It would not be just."

And so the creditor agreed.

The mediator turned then to the debtor. "If I pay your debt, will you accept me as your creditor?"

"Oh yes, yes," cried the debtor. "You save me from prison and show mercy to me."

"Then," said the benefactor, "you will pay the debt to me and I will set the terms. It will not be easy, but it will be possible. I will provide a way. You need not go to prison."

And so it was that the creditor was paid in full. He had been justly dealt with. No contract had been broken.

The debtor, in turn, had been extended mercy. Both laws stood fulfilled. Because there was a mediator, justice had claimed its full share, and mercy was fully satisfied.[17]

The scriptures affirm that "there is one God, and one mediator between God and men, the man Christ Jesus." (1 Tim. 2:5.) Mercy comes because of the atonement. Mercy is extended to the penitent. (Alma 42:23.) Those who accept Christ as their Benefactor and pay the appropriate price of repentance are delivered from the demands of justice and come to know that freedom and peace available only through him who is the Way, the Truth, and the Life. (John 8:31-32.)

Can God Cease to Be God?

In seeking to dramatize the absolute necessity for God's justice to be meted out where appropriate, Alma spoke to Corianton of a most unusual hypothetical situation. "According to justice," he said, "the plan of redemption could not be brought about, only on conditions of repentance of men in this probationary state, yea, this preparatory state; for except it were for these conditions, mercy could not take effect except it should destroy the work of justice. Now the work of justice could not be destroyed; if so, *God would cease to be God*." Alma explained further that "there is a law given, and a punishment affixed, and a repentance granted; which repentance, mercy claimeth; otherwise, justice claimeth the creature and exe-cuteth the law, and the law inflicteth the punishment; if not so, the works of justice would be destroyed, and *God would cease to be God."* (Alma 42:13, 22, emphasis added; see also v. 25.) Some have taken these verses to mean that it is indeed possible for God to cease to be God; that if he should, by some bizarre means, fail to function in perfectness, he would be unseated and removed from his place of preeminence; that the forces in the universe would demand his ab-dication from the heavenly throne. Such ideas are to some quite stimulating. They are, nonetheless, erroneous and misleading.

Joseph Smith taught and the scriptures boldly and repeatedly attest to the fact that God is omnipotent, omniscient, and, by the power of his Holy Spirit, omnipresent. The Prophet taught that "God is the *only supreme governor and independent being* in whom all fulness and perfection dwell; . . . without beginning of days or end of life; and that in him every good gift and every good principle dwell; and that he is the Father of lights; *in him the principle of faith dwells independently*, and he is the object in whom the faith of all other rational and accountable beings center for life and salvation."[18] Joseph Smith also stated:

> It is . . . necessary, in order to the exercise of faith in God unto life and salvation, that men should have the idea of the existence of the attribute justice in him; for without the idea of the existence of the attribute justice in the Deity, men could not have confidence sufficient to place themselves under his guidance and direction; for they would be filled with fear and doubt lest the judge of all the earth would not do right, and thus fear or doubt, existing in the mind, would preclude the possibility of the exercise of faith in him for life and salvation. But when the idea of the existence of the attribute justice in the Deity is fairly planted in the mind, it leaves no room for doubt to get into the heart, and the mind is enabled to cast itself upon the Almighty without fear and without doubt, and with the most unshaken confidence, believing that the Judge of all the earth will do right.[19]

The fact of the matter is that God will not nor cannot cease to be God. His title, his status, and his exalted position are forever fixed and immutable. Exalted beings simply do not apostatize! They do not slip! It is contrary to their divine nature to lie or cheat or be impartial. God is not dependent on others for his Godhood, nor can he be impeached. Nor need the Saints of God spend a particle of a second worrying and fretting about the Almighty falling from grace. For members of the Church to do so, in fact—as the Prophet has suggested—is to err in doctrine as to the true nature of God and thus fall short of that dynamic faith which leads to life and salvation. Alma's hypothetical case is just that—purely hypothetical. He is arguing toward the impossible to demonstrate the logical certainty of his position—that mercy cannot rob justice. It is as if Alma had said: "To suppose that one can break the laws of God with impunity; to suppose that one can live a life of sin and have the atonement of Christ—the mercy of the Lord—rob justice of its due, is to suppose that which *cannot* be. It is as absurd as to suppose that God could cease to be God!" Truly, Alma explained, "*God ceaseth not to be God*, and mercy claimeth the penitent, and mercy cometh because of the atonement.... For behold, justice exerciseth all his demands, and also mercy claimeth all which is her own; and thus, none but the truly penitent are saved." (Alma 42:23-24; emphasis added.)

NOTES

1. Alma repeatedly used the word *soul* to refer to the spirit (see vv. 7, 9, 11, 14, 15, 17, 18, 21, 23). This, of course, is a different usage from the more specific definition of soul (the spirit and the body) contained in D&C 88:15; see also 2 Nephi 9:13.

2. *Journal of Discourses*, 26 vols. (London: Latter-day Saints' Book Depot, 1854-86), 3:368.

3. Orson Pratt, ibid., 16:365.

4. George Q. Cannon, *Gospel Truth*, 2 vols. in one, comp. Jerreld L. Newquist (Salt Lake City: Deseret Book Company, 1987), p. 58.

5. This expression is used by Joseph F. Smith (see *Gospel Doctrine* [Salt Lake City: Deseret Book Company, 1971], pp. 448-49) and is probably

what Alma was describing in Alma 40:15 as an initial consignment to happiness or misery before the actual resurrection.

6. Robert L. Millet and Joseph Fielding McConkie, *The Life Beyond* (Salt Lake City: Bookcraft, 1986), p. 18. For a discussion of the Savior's statement to the thief on the cross, "To day shalt thou be with me in paradise" (Luke 23:43), see *The Life Beyond*, pp. 19-20, 168.

7. With but few exceptions, *outer darkness* refers to hell, the place of suffering and sadness and confrontation in the spirit world. (See Alma 34:33; 40:13-14; 41:7; D&C 38:5; 138:22, 30, 57; Isa. 49:9.) "So complete is the darkness prevailing in the minds of these spirits, so wholly has gospel light been shut out of their consciences, that they know little or nothing of the plan of salvation, and have little hope within themselves of advancement and progression through the saving grace of Christ." (Bruce R. McConkie, *Mormon Doctrine*, 2nd. ed. [Salt Lake City: Bookcraft, 1966], pp. 551-52.)

8. Joseph Smith, *Teachings of the Prophet Joseph Smith*, selected by Joseph Fielding Smith (Salt Lake City: Deseret Book Company, 1938), pp. 310-11.

9. Ibid., p. 357.

10. The entire spirit world, and not just that portion designated as hell, is appropriately called a "spirit prison." (See D&C 45:17; 138:15, 18, 50; Moses 7:55-57; *Teachings of the Prophet Joseph Smith*, p. 310; Orson Pratt, *Journal of Discourses*, 1:289-90; Brigham Young, *Journal of Discourses*, 3:95; Bruce R. McConkie, *Ensign*, August 1976, p. 11.) Paradise will be vacated and its residents released to a glorious resurrection at the second coming of Christ. Hell comes to an end at the time of the second resurrection, at the end of the Millennium.

11. Joseph Smith explained that "the fundamental principles of our religion are the testimony of the Apostles and Prophets, concerning Jesus Christ, that He died, was buried, and rose again the third day, and ascended into heaven; and all other things which pertain to our religion are only appendages to it." (*Teachings of the Prophet Joseph Smith*, p. 121; cf. 1 Cor. 15:1-4.)

12. Joseph Smith distinguished between the fundamental and nonfundamental elements of the body. "There is no fundamental principle," he taught, "belonging to a human system that ever goes into another in this world or in the world to come; I care not what the theories of men are. We have the testimony that God will raise us up, and he has the power to do it. If anyone supposes that any part of our bodies, that is, the fundamental parts thereof, ever goes into another body, he is mistaken." (*History of the*

Church of Jesus Christ of Latter-day Saints, 2nd ed. rev., edited by B. H. Roberts [Salt Lake City: The Church of Jesus Christ of Latter-day Saints, 1932-51], 5:339.)

13. *Teachings of the Prophet Joseph Smith*, pp. 199-200.

14. *Improvement Era*, June 1904, pp. 623-24; see also *Gospel Doctrine*, pp. 23, 447-48. President Smith's son, Joseph Fielding Smith, commented on these words as follows: "President Smith was in full accord with Amulek and Alma. He taught that the body will be restored as stated in Alma 11:42-45 and 40:22-23. While he expresses the thought that the body will come forth as it was laid down, he also expresses the thought that it will take time to adjust the body from the condition of imperfections. This, of course, is reasonable, but at the same time the length of time to make these adjustments will not cover any appreciable extent of time.

"President Smith never intended to convey the thought that it would require weeks or months of time in order for the defects to be removed. These changes will come naturally, of course, but *almost instantly*. We cannot look upon it in any other way." (Joseph Fielding Smith, *Doctrines of Salvation*, 3 vols., comp. Bruce R. McConkie [Salt Lake City: Bookcraft, 1954-56], 2:293-94.)

15. "It is evident Alma's understanding of the extent of the resurrection at the time the Savior came forth from the dead was limited, therefore he stated only his opinion." (Joseph Fielding Smith, *Answers to Gospel Questions*, 5 vols., compiled by Joseph Fielding Smith, Jr. [Salt Lake City: Deseret Book Company, 1957-66], 1:36; see also *Doctrines of Salvation*, 2:300.)

16. *Teachings of the Prophet Joseph Smith*, p. 296.

17. *Conference Report*, April 1977, pp. 79-80.

18. *Lectures on Faith* (Salt Lake City: Deseret Book Company, 1985), 2:2.

19. Ibid., 4:13. In a limited meaning of the phrase, therefore, God *can* cease to be God in the mind of mortals, but never in an absolute sense. That is to say, if people do not understand that God Almighty possesses all attributes in perfection, they cannot exercise saving faith in him—he ceases to be God to them!

7

INSPIRED BY A BETTER CAUSE
(Alma 43–51)

H. DEAN GARRETT

Mormon, as the compiler of the Book of Mormon, was faced with the challenge of determining what to include in his abridged record. In making his decisions, he was guided by two factors. The first was the charge given him by the Lord to write those things "which have been commanded." (3 Ne. 26:12.) The second influence was Mormon's understanding of the times and the conditions under which the records would come forth in the last days. Thus directed, Mormon deliberately selected those events and discourses from the original plates that best met the needs his future book would serve.

His account of the record of Alma is a good illustration of Mormon's methodology. In the first part of this book, he dedicated considerable space to the missionary labors of Alma and the four sons of Mosiah. However, in recording the events of their missions, he announced that he was changing his emphasis: "Now we shall say no more concerning their preaching, except that they preached the word, and the truth, according to the spirit of prophecy and revelation; and they preached after the holy order of God by which they were called. And now I return to an account of the wars between the Nephites and the Lamanites in the eighteenth year of the reign of the judges." (Alma 43:2-3.)

This was a curious decision for Mormon to make. If the Book of Mormon was intended to be used by a church greatly involved in

H. Dean Garrett is assistant professor of Church history and doctrine at Brigham Young University.

missionary work, would it not be more beneficial for the readers of the book to be instructed in the missionary experiences of Alma and the sons of Mosiah? Why write about the wars of the Nephites?

An analysis of the composition of the Book of Mormon might lead us to an answer to such questions. Sixty-four percent of the history covered from 1 Nephi to Mormon 6, comprising 220 pages, is found in Alma 1 to 3 Nephi 10, surely an inordinate amount of space for a diminutive amount of history.[1] A unique historical pattern is found in this section of the Book of Mormon. In Alma 1-42, Mormon emphasized priestcraft, materialism, social-economic inequality, and other social problems. This period is followed in Alma 43-63 by a period of war and civil disruptions. This dissension led to a corruption of civil government (as described in the book of Helaman) and to the eventual collapse of the government (see 3 Nephi 1-10). At this point, the Savior visited the people.

A similar pattern of social problems, priestcrafts, materialism, wars, government corruption, and disrupted life is prophesied for the last days leading to the Savior's second coming. (D&C 45:16-48; D&C 87; Mormon 8:26-41.) As indicated, Mormon and his successor, Moroni, saw our day (see Mormon 8:27-31) and took from the history and prophecies of the Nephites those events that would best help the readers of their record in the day in which it would come forth. Since Mormon knew of the wars and chaos that would characterize the last days, he abbreviated his account of the missionary efforts of Alma and the sons of Mosiah and emphasized the challenges created by war and social turmoil, along with the reaction of the righteous to those challenges.

Motivations for War

A study of the Nephite-Lamanite wars provides helpful insights into the motivations of people or nations at war. In Alma 43, Mormon related how the Zoramites joined the Lamanites (under Zerahemnah) and an apostate group of Nephites called Amalekites to war against the Nephites. Because the Amalekites and Zoramites were "of a more wicked and murderous disposition than the Lamanites," Zerahemnah placed them as "chief captains" over his armies. (Alma 43:6.) In doing this, the Lamanite leader wished to "preserve their hatred towards the Nephites" and to "stir up the Lamanites to anger against the Nephites." His personal design was to "usurp great power over them [the Lamanites], and also that he might gain power over the Nephites by bringing them into bondage." (Alma 43:7-8.) It appears that Zerahemnah's motivation for going to war was his hatred of the Nephites and his thirst for power.

On the other hand, the Nephites entered this war with a far different attitude. It was their desire to "support their lands and their houses, and their wives, and their children, that they might preserve them from the hands of their enemies; and also that they might preserve their rights and their privileges, yea, and also their liberty, that they might worship God according to their desires." (Alma 43:9.) Because of the Lamanites' hatred toward them and because of the evil desires of their apostate allies, the Nephites knew they would suffer much death and an insufferable bondage if they fell prey to their enemies.

The major motivation of each of these groups determined the approach each took in preparing for war and in actually fighting. The Lamanites gathered themselves with anger, while the Nephites responded with resolve and preparation.

The leader of the Nephites, Moroni, "had prepared his people with breastplates and with arm-shields, yea, and also shields to defend their heads, and also they were dressed with thick clothing." (Alma 43:19.) The Lamanites, on the other hand, had their weapons of war, but they were naked, except for a "skin which was girded about their loins." (Alma 43:20.) The Nephites also prepared for battle by spying on the foe and by seeking direction from the prophet Alma.

The motivation that people have for going to war often dictates the manner in which the conflict is pursued. Even though the Lamanites were not prepared to battle a more physically prepared foe, nevertheless they "did fight exceedingly; yea, never had the Lamanites been known to fight with such exceedingly great strength and courage, no, not even from the beginning. And they were inspired by the Zoramites and the Amalekites, who were their chief captains and leaders, and by Zerahemnah, who was their chief captain, or their chief leader and commander; yea, they did fight like dragons." (Alma 43:43-44.) The Nephites, however, were inspired by a greater cause. They "were not fighting for monarchy nor power but they were fighting for their homes and their liberties, their wives and their children, and their all, yea, for their rites of worship and their church." (Alma 43:45.)

The Nephites were fighting for a higher cause — "their duty which they owed to their God." (Alma 43:46.) They were fighting under a God-given mandate that declared: "Inasmuch as ye are not guilty of the first offense, neither the second, ye shall not suffer yourselves to be slain by the hands of your enemies." And again, the Lord said: "Ye shall defend your families even unto bloodshed. Therefore for this cause were the Nephites contending with the Lamanites, to defend themselves, and their families, and their lands, their country, and their rights, and their religions." (Alma 43:46-47.) This motivation produced a faith in the Nephites that allowed them to fight with valor, for when they began to fear and were about to flee the fierceness of the Lamanites, a reminder of their cause from Moroni allowed them to turn on the Lamanites with power. (See Alma 43:48-50.) On the other hand, when the Lamanites saw the power of the Nephites, they were filled with fear and "were struck with terror." (Alma 43:53.)

The account of this war clarified an important concept: there might be a justifiable reason for going to war. That reason should not include the motivation to gain power, nor control, nor should it be out of anger or hatred. The Lord simply stated that if the Nephites were not guilty of the first or second offense, they should not allow themselves to be slain by their enemies. (Alma 43:46.) This same counsel was given to the early saints through the Prophet Joseph Smith. In the Doctrine and Covenants, section 98, the Lord gave this command: "Now, I speak unto you concerning your families — if men will smite you, or your families, once, and ye bear it patiently and revile not against them, neither seek revenge, ye shall be rewarded; but if ye bear it not patiently, it shall be accounted unto you as being meted out as a just measure unto you." (D&C 98:23-24.) The Lord further instructed the saints that if they bore these attacks the third and fourth times, their rewards would be increased. However, if their enemies escaped the vengeance of God, then a warning voice should be raised that if the enemy came against them again, the Lord would have "delivered thine enemy into thine hands." (D&C 98:29.) If the saints spared the enemy, they would be blessed, but if "thou rewardest him according to his works thou art justified; if he has sought thy life, and thy life is endangered by him, thine enemy is in thine hands and thou art justified." (D&C 98:31.)

The Lord applied this same law to nations, with the injunction that "if any nation, tongue, or people should proclaim war against them, they should first lift a standard of peace unto that people, nation, or tongue." (D&C 98:34.) If that people or nation did not accept the standard of peace, then the same procedures would be followed the second and third time. After this procedure was followed, the Lord would "justify them in going out to battle against that nation, tongue, or people. And I, the Lord, would fight their battles." (D&C 98:36-37.) This law of war was given to Nephi, Joseph, Jacob, Abraham, "and all mine ancient prophets and apostles." (D&C 98:32.)

The Lord commanded his people to "renounce war and proclaim peace" (D&C 98:16), but he does give a nation the right to go to war. President David O. McKay suggested the following righteous reasons for war:

> I still say that there are conditions when entrance into war is justifiable, and when a Christian nation may, without violation of principles, take up arms against an opposing force. Such a condition, however, is not a real or fancied insult given by one nation to another. When this occurs proper reparation may be made by mutual understanding, apology or by arbitration. Neither is there justifiable cause found in a desire or even a need for territorial expansion. The taking of territory implies the subjugation of the weak to the strong—the application of the jungle law. Nor is war justified in an attempt to enforce a new order of government, or even to impel others to a particular form of worship, however better the government or eternally true the principles of the enforced religion may be.[2]

An example of this philosophy is found in the Book of Mormon when Mormon, the abridger, was acting as the military leader for the

Nephites. After great victories over the Lamanites, the Nephites began to "boast in their own strength, and began to swear before the heavens that they would avenge themselves of the blood of their brethren who had been slain by their enemies. And they did swear by the heavens, and also by the throne of God, that they would go up to battle against their enemies, and would cut them off from the face of the land." (Morm. 3:9-10.)

This attitude did not reflect the "law of war" as defined by the Lord. Thus Mormon "did utterly refuse from this time forth to be a commander and a leader of this people, because of their wickedness and abomination" (Morm. 3:11), even though Mormon had led the Nephites in battle many times. Furthermore, "when they had sworn by all that had been forbidden them by our Lord and Savior Jesus Christ, that they would go up unto their enemies to battle, and avenge themselves of the blood of their brethren, behold the voice of the Lord came unto me, saying: Vengeance is mine, and I will repay; and because this people repented not after I had delivered them, behold, they shall be cut off from the face of the earth." (Morm. 3:14-15.)

A message to the people of the latter days from the war period of the Book of Mormon would be that if there must be war, then it must be entered for the right reasons and under proper circumstances if people desire the blessings of God. Writing to Zerahemnah, Captain Moroni made this interesting observation: "Ye see that God will support, and keep, and preserve us, so long as we are faithful unto him, and unto our faith, and our religion; and never will the Lord suffer that we shall be destroyed except we should fall into transgression and deny our faith." (Alma 44:4.)

In a day when prophecies note that there will be wars and rumors of wars (JS–M 1:28-29), there are some who question their role in supporting a government that is preparing for war. As nations prepare from time to time to go to war, what should be an individual's role? Must one support the government? Is one morally responsible to take sides? Mormon pointed out in the Book of Alma that perhaps the side is not as important to one's personal salvation as the motivation.

The Fight for Liberty

Mormon continued the account of the wars of the Nephites by interjecting a prophecy of Alma. Alma, before his final departure, told his son Helaman that the Nephites would dwindle in unbelief until a final destruction of his people took place. (See Alma 45:10-16.) As Helaman and his brethren tried to organize the people, "there arose a dissension among them, and they would not give heed to the words of Helaman and his brethren." (Alma 45:23.) This reaction to the attempts of Helaman to establish righteousness laid a foundation for internal dissent. Those who would not give heed to "Helaman and his brethren were gathered together against their brethren." (Alma 46:1.) This dissension allowed a man by the name of Amalickiah to create a movement to make him king over the Nephites. There were many in the church who accepted the flatteries of Amalickiah and therefore broke away from the Church. "And thus were the affairs of the people of Nephi exceedingly precarious and dangerous, notwithstanding their great victory which they had had over the Lamanites, and their great rejoicings which they had had because of their deliverance by the hand of the Lord." (Alma 46:7.) It does not take long for a people who are full of pride to "forget the Lord their God" and "be led away by the evil one." (Alma 46:8.) One wicked individual can cause great wickedness to take place among such a people. (See Alma 46:9.)

On the other hand, one righteous person can make a difference in such a setting. Captain Moroni reacted to this situation by making a banner (the Title of Liberty) on which he wrote this reminder: "In memory of our God, our religion, and freedom, and our peace, our wives, and our children." (Alma 46:12.) He prayed fervently to the Lord for "the blessings of liberty to rest upon his brethren, so long as there should a band of Christians remain to possess the land." (Alma 46:13.) This became such an important time for Moroni that he challenged all his supporters to "enter into a covenant that they will maintain their rights, and their religion, that the Lord God may bless them." (Alma 46:20.)

The battle that followed forced Amalickiah and his people into the wilderness. The Amalickiahites who were taken captive were given the option of joining the people of Moroni by entering into the covenant with them. Those Amalickiahites who "would not enter into a covenant to support the cause of freedom, that they might maintain a free government, he caused to be put to death; and there were but few who denied the covenant of freedom." (Alma 46:35.)

The Amalickiahites who had fled joined forces with the Lamanites; and, through treachery and murder, Amalickiah became the king of the Lamanites. It was still his design to control the Nephites, and thus a great battle ensued. The righteous Nephites turned to God in preparation for this war. Mormon observed that the wicked Nephites "became more hardened and impenitent, and more wild, wicked and ferocious than the Lamanites." (Alma 47:36.) This battle for the Nephite nation, which lead to much dissension among the Nephites, was due to their own wickedness. Mormon stated: "For it has been their quarrelings and their contentions, yea, their murderings, and their plunderings, their idolatry, their whoredoms, and their abominations, which were among themselves, which brought upon them their wars and their destructions." (Alma 50:21.) No matter who the leader was, this wickedness caused some to seek an overthrow of freedom, to replace the government with a monarchy. Thus they had the kingmen trying to seize power, and the ensuing battle between the kingmen and the freemen took place. (See Alma 50-51.)

This dissension so weakened the Nephites that "while Moroni was thus breaking down the wars and contentions among his own people, and subjecting them to peace and civilization" (Alma 51:22), the Lamanites again attacked and tried to overpower the Nephites. Mormon showed, by his account, that wickedness brought dissent, and dissent brought the threat of destruction from outside forces. The only way that the Nephites could stay free was to stay righteous.

Edmund Burke echoed these same feelings when he stated:

> Men are qualified for civil liberty in exact proportion to their disposition to put moral chains upon their own appetites, in proportion as their love to justice is above their rapacity, in proportion as their soundness and sobriety of understanding is above their vanity and presumption, in proportion as they are more disposed to listen to the counsels of the wise and good, in preference to the flattery of knaves. Society cannot exist, unless a controlling power upon will and appetite be placed somewhere; and the less of it there is within, the more

there must be without. It is ordained in the eternal constitution of things, that men of intemperate minds cannot be free. Their passions forge their fetters.[3]

The Individual and War

Can righteousness be maintained and happiness be found in an atmosphere of wars and rumors of war? Can righteous people remain righteous under such circumstances? Mormon gave us insights into the answers to these questions by describing how the Nephites struggled through this period. He made this intriguing observation about the Nephites who were preparing for war: "And those who were faithful in keeping the commandments of the Lord were delivered at all times, whilst thousands of their wicked brethren have been consigned to bondage, or to perish by the sword, or to dwindle in unbelief, and mingle with the Lamanites. But behold there never was a happier time among the people of Nephi, since the days of Nephi, than in the days of Moroni." (Alma 50:22-23.)

Yet the challenges and struggles that come with war come to the individual. Can a righteous, peaceful individual maintain those qualities in an atmosphere of hatred, along with an environment where life is not respected nor God revered? The answer to this question is also found in this section of the Book of Mormon. We are given the example of Captain Moroni. He did not want to shed blood, but he loved peace and desired to keep the commandments. Yet he spent most of his adult life in war. His profession appeared to be that of a military leader. He took good men into battle, and he had to watch many of them suffer and die.

Even with this life-style, he still remained righteous. Mormon gave this description of him: "If all men had been, and were, and ever would be, like unto Moroni, behold, the very powers of hell would have been shaken forever; yea, the devil would never have power over the hearts of the children of men." (Alma 48:17.)

Moroni remained righteous, strong, and powerful even in an environment where death, suffering, pain, and hatred became the norm. The question can then be asked, "Can a Latter-day Saint be righteous in a military environment?" The answer, based on Moroni's experience, is yes.

Conclusion

The Book of Mormon was designed to prepare its readers to survive the problems of the latter days. Book of Mormon prophets stated that this book would be brought forth when there would be wars and other social problems. Elder Marion G. Romney made this observation: "Latter-day Saints know that this earth will never again, during its telestial existence, be free from civil disturbance and war."[4] This being true, if people of these latter days have any hope, it will be founded in righteousness. We must be careful that we do not follow the pattern of the Book of Mormon people who had more faith in their own armaments than they had in God. A modern-day general, Omar N. Bradley, once warned: "We have grasped the mystery of the atom and rejected the Sermon on the Mount. . . . Ours is a world of nuclear giants and ethical infants. We know more about war than we know about peace, more about killing than we know about living."[5]

In our society today, we find that we are well prepared for war. In our preparation, however, we have lost the spiritual strength to prevent it.

President Dwight D. Eisenhower observed: "Every gun made, every warship launched, every rocket fired signifies, in the final sense, a theft from those who hunger and are not fed, those who are cold and are not clothed. This world in arms is not spending money alone. It is spending the sweat of its laborers, the genius of its scientists, the hopes of its children. . . . This is not a way of life at all, in any true sense. Under the cloud of threatening war, it is humanity hanging from a cross of iron."[6]

The cry in these days is for righteousness. If there is to be hope for a peaceful future, it will be because people repent and serve the Lord. The First Presidency, in a Christmas message to the world, made this plea:

> We are dismayed by the growing tensions among the nations, and the unrestricted building of arsenals of war,

including huge and threatening nuclear weaponry. Nuclear war, when unleashed on a scale for which the nations are preparing, spares no living thing within the perimeter of its initial destructive force, and sears and maims and kills wherever its pervasive cloud reaches.

While recognizing the need for strength to repel any aggressor, we are enjoined by the word of God to "renounce war and proclaim peace." We call upon the heads of nations to sit down and reason together in good faith to resolve their differences. If men of good will can bring themselves to do so, they may save the world from a holocaust, the depth and breadth of which can scarcely be imagined. We are confident that when there is enough of a desire for peace and a will to bring it about, it is not beyond the possibility of attainment.[7]

It is the duty of every Latter-day Saint to live righteously enough to be an influence for peace. However, if the time comes that they have to fight "for their homes and their liberties, their wives and their children, and their all, yea, for their rites of worship and their church" (Alma 43:45), then they must be prepared to respond in righteousness and with purity of heart.

NOTES

1. See H. Dean Garrett, "The Book of Mormon on War," *A Symposium on the Book of Mormon* (Salt Lake City: Church Education System, 1986), pp. 47-53, for a more thorough discussion of this concept.

2. *Conference Report*, April 1942, p. 72.

3. *The Works of the Right Honorable Edmund Burke* (Boston: Little, Brown, and Company, 1889), pp. 51-52.

4. "Peace in This World," *Improvement Era*, June 1967, p. 77.

5. Cited in Louis Fischer, *The Life of Mahatma Ghandi* (New York: Harper & Brothers, Publishers, 1950), p. 349.

6. *Peace with Justice, Selected Addresses of Dwight D. Eisenhower* (New York: Columbia University Press, 1961) pp. 37-38.

7. "From the First Presidency," *Church News*, 20 Dec. 1980, p. 3.

8

RIGHTEOUS OATHS, REPROOF, AND RECONCILIATION
(Alma 52–63)

SPENCER J. CONDIE

The concluding chapters of the book of Alma are not only an exciting account of ingenious military strategies but also a spiritual saga in which humble followers of Christ encounter in exquisite detail "an opposition in all things." (2 Ne. 2:11.) This is the a story of a people with deep, abiding faith despite unrestrained wickedness in the world in which they lived. These chapters reassure us that there are still promises to keep, notwithstanding the fact that others may engage in deception, intrigue, and even murder to gain greater power. This is the unusual story of larger-than-life military leaders who loved their troops more than themselves and who loved liberty more than life.

One of the great lessons of the Nephite-Lamanite war, and perhaps all wars, was that "many had become *hardened*, because of the exceedingly great length of the war; and many were *softened* because of their afflictions, insomuch that they did humble themselves before God, even in the depth of humility." (Alma 62:41; emphasis added.)

Alma's successor as chief judge, Nephihah, died, and his son Pahoran "was appointed chief judge and governor over the people." (Alma 50:37-40.) Citizens who have inherited a long, traditional, constitutionally based form of government take for granted the smooth transition of leadership from one leader to another. But in

---

Spencer J. Condie is professor of ancient scripture at Brigham Young University.

many societies, even today, the death of a ruler or the transition from a military rule to a more civilian form of government sometimes creates a leadership vacuum filled only after revolution and bloodshed. Unless the transition is considered legitimate by the opposition, political turmoil will likely result.

Such was the political climate in 67 B.C. Notwithstanding the ever present external threat of Lamanite invasions, the Nephites became divided among themselves, and a revolutionary movement of so-called "king-men" sought to alter the laws of the land in order to remove the duly appointed Pahoran from the judgment seat. (Alma 51:2-5.)

The matter was put to a vote, and "the voice of the people came in favor of the freemen, and Pahoran retained the judgment-seat" (Alma 51:7). But order in the land of Zarahemla was short-lived, because the dreaded king of the Lamanites, Amalickiah, "had gathered together a wonderfully great army" (Alma 51:11) and quickly took possession of the heavily fortified cities of Nephihah, Lehi, Morianton, Omner, Gid, and Mulek (Alma 51:25-27). But the fearless leader of one of the Nephite armies, Teancum, successfully resisted the forces of Amalickiah and bravely stole into the Lamanite camp at night and thrust a javelin into the Lamanite leader's heart. (Alma 51:33-34.) Shortly thereafter, the king's equally bloodthirsty brother, Ammoron, was appointed to be a king over the Lamanites.

Teancum concluded that it would be impossible to attack the Lamanites in their fortified cities, so the chief captains of the Nephite armies held a council of war and developed a plan to "decoy the Lamanites out of their strongholds." (Alma 52:17-21.) Teancum led a token force near the seashore while Moroni led his forces into the wilderness. The Lamanites pursued Teancum in vain while Moroni marched back to take the city of Mulek. (Alma 52:22-26.)

In the meantime, Captain Lehi marched against the weary Lamanites with a fresh Nephite army that joined forces with Moroni's army. A furious battle ensued. Jacob, the head of the Lamanites, was slain, and Moroni himself was wounded. The chief captains of the Lamanites "came forth and threw down their weapons," but those who would not surrender voluntarily were taken as prisoners. (Alma

52:27-40.) The Nephites used these prisoners of war to dig trenches around the city of Bountiful and to build a "breastwork of timbers" around the ditches to fortify the city.

Just as the tides of fortune seemed to be turning in a favorable direction, while Moroni was away from Zarahemla, the Lamanites had caused great dissensions among the Nephites and had taken possession of several cities on the west sea, south. (Alma 53:8-9.)

The Nephite armies had regained the city of Mulek and fortified the land of Bountiful. In the process they were now confronted with the simultaneous problems of regaining their other lost cities, dealing with the dissension and intrigue between the king-men and freemen back at headquarters, watching over an ever-increasing number of prisoners of war, and protecting the Ammonites who had taken an oath never again to fight. Who could assume responsibility for leading and defending this people amidst such apparently insurmountable problems?

A Profile of Captain Moroni

The record describes Moroni as "a strong and a mighty man," "a man of a perfect understanding," "a man that did not delight in bloodshed," "a man whose soul did joy in the liberty and the freedom of his country." (Alma 48:11.) "If all men had been, and were, and ever would be, like unto Moroni, behold, the very powers of hell would have been shaken forever; yea, the devil would never have power over the hearts of the children of men." (Alma 48:17.)

Moroni had been appointed chief captain only two years previously at the age of twenty-five. (Alma 43:17.) He was a very astute strategist and tactician and was absolutely fearless, a style of leadership involving considerable risks as he, himself, was wounded in battle. (Alma 52:35.) In describing the desirable qualities of a great leader, Hugh Nibley cites Moroni's character traits as the epitome of the consummate leader. Said Nibley: "Leaders are movers and shakers, original, inventive, unpredictable, imaginative, full of surprises that discomfit the enemy in war and the main office in peace."[1]

Yes, indeed, Moroni was righteous, intelligent, creative, and courageous. But what of his communication skills? May it be said of

Captain Moroni that he was seldom, if ever, misunderstood. A case in point is the letter he wrote to Ammoron in response to an offer to exchange prisoners. The Lamanites had not only taken captive Nephite soldiers, but their wives and children as well. Thus, it was an enticing offer to exchange prisoners. But Moroni would agree only on his own terms: a Nephite family for each Lamanite prisoner. (Alma 54:11.)

To underscore the intensity of his feelings about Ammoron's aggressive attempts to take the Nephite lands through bloodshed, Moroni wrote: "I would tell you concerning that awful hell that awaits to receive such murderers as thou and thy brother have been" (Alma 54:7), and "it supposeth me that thou art a child of hell" (Alma 54:11). Then, just in case Ammoron did not catch the full flavor of his message, Moroni added the afterthought: "Behold, I am in my anger." (Alma 54:13.)

Here was the right man, in the right place, at the right time! Moroni's integrity would not allow him to bargain cheaply the lives of the Nephite families in question, especially without an assurance from Ammoron that he would no longer seek to destroy the Nephites (Alma 54:13), and so Moroni refused Ammoron's offer to exchange prisoners (Alma 55:1-2).

Never one to shrink from his duty to free the Nephite prisoners of war, Moroni identified a Lamanite convert within his own ranks whom he sent by night to the city of Gid, where the Lamanites were guarding numerous Nephite prisoners. This courier, whose name was Laman, took with him a few other men and some bottles of strong wine. Upon reaching the Lamanite camp, the Nephite platoon indicated that they had just escaped from the Nephite camp. The Lamanites were only too happy to welcome them and to drink their specially prepared wine. (Alma 55:4-13.)

As soon as the Lamanite guards had had their fill of wine and had sunk into a drunken slumber, Laman's platoon returned to report to Captain Moroni. Moroni's troops returned to the city of Gid and quietly armed the Nephite prisoners while the Lamanites slept. In the morning the Lamanites awakened to discover that they were surrounded. Perhaps with tongue in cheek, the chronicler of these events wrote: "In these circumstances they found that it was not expedient that they should fight with the Nephites." (Alma 55:23.)

Again we are reminded that Moroni "did not delight in murder or bloodshed, but he delighted in the saving of his people from destruction." (Alma 55:19.) So it was that the Lamanite prisoners' lives were spared, and they were subsequently put to work fortifying the city of Gid. (Alma 55:25.)

As mentioned previously, protracted war can either harden or soften a people, coarsen or refine them, create cynicism or build faith. As for the Nephites, they "were not slow to remember the Lord their God in this their time of affliction." (Alma 55:31.)

Promises to Keep

As internal dissensions among the Nephites added fuel to the already raging fires of war with the Lamanites, the need for additional valiant Nephite warriors became critical. And so it was that the faithful people of Ammon, Lamanite converts who had been the beneficiaries of Nephite protection for several years, felt such an acute sense of obligation to assist in the war effort that they were about to break the oath they had taken never to bear arms and shed the blood of another. (See Alma 24.) "But behold, as they were about to take their weapons of war, they were overpowered by the persuasions of Helaman and his brethren, for they were about to break the oath which they had made." (Alma 53:14.)

Long before the age of notarized signatures, of quintuplicate copies of contracts with countless qualifications and exceptions, there was a time when a verbal oath had all the pulling power necessary to bind someone to his word. The commitment to oaths among the people of the Book of Mormon is everywhere evident, from the reciprocal promises between Nephi and Zoram (1 Ne. 4:33-37) to the refusal of Zerahemnah, the Lamanite leader, to take an oath "which we know that we shall break" (Alma 44:8), to the people of Morianton who, "upon their covenanting to keep the peace," were once again allowed to return to their lands (Alma 50:36).

Whether made by the righteous or the wicked, an oath was a sacred promise to be kept inviolate under any and all circumstances.

Few examples of broken oaths are recorded in the entire Book of Mormon, and these breaches occurred under very unusual mitigating circumstances. (See Mosiah 19:20–20:24.)

Hugh Nibley has provided enlightening evidence of the great binding power of oaths in the ancient Arab world.[2] Henry Sumner Maine, in his classic treatise on Ancient Law, also cites examples of binding verbal oaths from Roman Law and more recent Anglo-Saxon jurisprudence.[3] Indeed, our own contemporary courtroom oath "to swear the truth, the whole truth, and nothing but the truth" is not to be taken lightly (as indicted perjurers have painfully discovered).

How could the Nephites resolve their current dilemma? They had a critical shortage of troops and were encumbered by an obligation to protect the faithful Ammonites who had taken an oath not to bear arms. The Ammonites "had many sons, who had not entered into a covenant that they would not take their weapons of war to defend themselves against their enemies. . . . And they entered into a covenant to fight for the liberty of the Nephites." (Alma 53:16–17.)

Two Thousand Heroic Mothers

There are about two thousand mothers whose names remain unknown but whose faithful stripling sons helped to alter the course of Nephite history. Helaman was selected to lead them and described his young "sons" as being "exceedingly valiant for courage, and also for strength and activity . . . men who were true at all times in whatsoever thing they were entrusted. Yea, they were men of truth and soberness, for they had been taught to keep the commandments of God and to walk uprightly before him." (Alma 53:20–21.) Helaman further shared the observation that "they had been taught by their mothers, that if they did not doubt, God would deliver them. And they rehearsed unto me the words of their mothers, saying: We do not doubt our mothers knew it." (Alma 53:47-48.)

The age of these young warriors is not stated, but Helaman once referred to them as "men" (Alma 53:20), sometimes as "striplings" (Alma 53:22; 56:57), other times as his "little sons" (Alma 56:30 and 56:39), but most frequently as "my sons" (Alma 56:10, 27, 44, 46, 57:22). Regardless of the young men's ages, their parents' permission to leave home was certainly not given without sacrifice. Their numbers began with an even two thousand but eventually increased to two thousand and sixty. (Alma 57:6.)

Just as the mothers reared sons of great faith and courage, the fathers sacrificed in delivering provisions to their sons. (Alma 56:27.) Though the Ammonite fathers would not bear arms, they gave "a large portion of their substance" in support of the Nephite armies. (Alma 43:13.)

Helaman and his "little sons" were under the command of Antipus, who ordered them to divert the attention of the Lamanites by marching to a neighboring city near the seashore. As the Lamanites began to pursue the stripling warriors, Antipus's troops marched in hot pursuit of the Lamanites. Just as the weary troops "were about to fall into the hands of the Lamanites," Helaman's little army came to the rescue, surrounding the enemy. As the dust settled, the Nephites were clearly victorious, and the Lamanites were taken prisoner. (Alma 56:30-54.)

With typical paternalistic concern, Helaman surveyed his army and was overjoyed to discover that not a single one of his stripling soldiers had "fallen to the earth." (Alma 56:56.)

Shortly thereafter, Helaman's army received, in addition to fresh provisions, sixty more Ammonite sons to strengthen their numbers. (Alma 57:6.) Through a fortuitous set of circumstances, the supply line to the Lamanites was interrupted by the Nephites, and for want of food the Lamanites surrendered the city of Cumeni. Now the troops of Helaman were overburdened with an excessive number of prisoners to guard, and they were ultimately compelled to slay many of those who persisted in fighting, while the other prisoners were escorted by a contingent of Helaman's troops back to the land of Zarahemla. (Alma 57:7-16.)

Meanwhile, Ammoron's army had received new provisions, and "a numerous army of men" had engaged the remaining stripling soldiers in a desperate battle. In the moment of greatest despair, those who had escorted the prisoners to Zarahemla returned to the battlefield and successfully drove the Lamanites back to the city of Manti. This time, the census of wounded revealed that two hundred of

Helaman's army "had fainted because of the loss of blood; nevertheless, according to the goodness of God . . . there was not one soul of them who did perish," notwithstanding the fact that, without exception, every stripling had been wounded. (Alma 57:25.) Referring once again to their unshakable faith, Helaman described his sons as "young, and their minds are firm, and they do put their trust in God continually." (Alma 57:27.)

The joy of previous victories was short lived, however. Helaman wrote in an epistle to Moroni that their supply line had been most unreliable for several months, and that they "were about to perish for the want of food." (Alma 58:7.) But in their hour of affliction, Helaman wrote that "we did pour out our souls in prayer to God, that he would strengthen us and deliver us out of the hands of our enemies . . . and it came to pass that the Lord our God did visit us with assurances that he would deliver us." (Alma 58:10-11.)

Although greatly outnumbered by the Lamanites, Helaman again employed a strategy of dividing and conquering. One of the Nephite captains, Gid, led his troops into the wilderness on the right, while Teomner and his troops entered the wilderness on the left.

As the Lamanites attacked Helaman's army, the armies of Gid and Teomner cut off the Lamanite spies, hurried to the Lamanite-occupied city of Manti, and overwhelmed the guards who had been left behind. Helaman led his troops in the direction of Zarahemla, and while the Lamanites slept, the striplings changed course and continued marching toward the city of Manti, thus taking possession of it before the Lamanites returned. (Alma 58:16-29.)

After recounting their successes in a letter to Moroni, Helaman then broached the subject of an unreliable supply line, suspecting "that there is some faction in the government, that they do not send more men to our assistance," adding with typical faith: "We trust God will deliver us." (Alma 58:36-37.)

Reproof and Reconciliation

Upon receiving Helaman's request for aid, Moroni, ever the great advocate for his army, "immediately sent an epistle to Pahoran," asking for reinforcements. (Alma 59.) When the city of Nephihah was lost because the expected help never arrived, Moroni sent another epistle to Pahoran, expressing his anger with the seeming indifference of the government. (Alma 60.)

The 121st section of the Doctrine and Covenants contains some of the greatest counsel in holy writ regarding the proper exercise of authority. The Lord revealed to the Prophet Joseph Smith that "no power or influence can or ought to be maintained by virtue of the priesthood, only by persuasion, by long-suffering, by gentleness and meekness, and by love unfeigned; by kindness, and pure knowledge. . . . Reproving betimes with sharpness, when moved upon by the Holy Ghost." (D&C 121:41-43.)

Some readers may be surprised at the sharpness of Moroni's epistle to Pahoran, the leader of the land. It may be well to examine Moroni's letter within the context in which it was written. Moroni had served as chief captain of the Nephite armies for more than a dozen years, and he was weary of war. Secondly, he was writing as an advocate for Helaman and his army. Thirdly, he told Pahoran that they would not complain if their afflictions had been confined to "hunger, thirst, and fatigue" (Alma 60:3), but his greatest concern was the unnecessary "slaughter among our people" (Alma 60:5).

Congruent with the Lord's counsel to be patient and long-suffering, Moroni had suffered various afflictions for over twelve years. But now his emotions were brimming with anger, and he did, indeed, reprove Pahoran with sharpness. There is one crucial element that Moroni overlooked: pure knowledge. That is to say, before reproving with sharpness it is well to have all the facts straight. The suspicions of Helaman and Moroni about the intrigue and dissension on the home front were all well founded; however, Moroni's aspersions against Pahoran were not grounded in truth.

Nevertheless, the magnanimous, charitable Pahoran received Moroni's scorching letter in the spirit in which it should have been written and accepted it with joy and a forgiving heart.

Another important element of the Lord's counsel on exercising power and authority involves "reproving *betimes* with sharpness." Many English-speaking people assume that the meaning of this archaic word, *betimes,* means "frequently" or "sometimes," but this is not the case. *Betimes* means literally "before it is too late." It is significant in this context that Pahoran responds to Moroni's letter by saying, "I do joy in receiving your epistle, for *I was somewhat worried concerning what we should do*, whether it should be just in us to go against our brethren." (Alma 61:19; emphasis added.)

One gathers the impression that Pahoran, perhaps like the great high priest Eli of old, knew full well that remedial action should be taken but lacked the motivation to follow through until the message was sent in an unmistakable fashion that could not be misunderstood. Not until he received Moroni's sharp message did Pahoran make the firm resolve to clean house on the home front in order to be unified against the Lamanite armies.

Even while castigating Pahoran in his letter, Moroni nonetheless addressed the loftier side of Pahoran's character as he challenged him to "come out and show unto me a true spirit of freedom." (Alma 60:25.) Moroni's sharp epistle was the catalyst in overcoming Pahoran's indecisiveness.

Strength Through Unity

After Moroni received Pahoran's gracious reply, "his heart did take courage." He began to march toward the land of Gideon, and "thousands did flock unto his standard, and did take up their swords in the defence of their freedom." (Alma 62:1-5.) As Moroni and Pahoran united their forces, "they became exceedingly strong" and successfully rooted out the king-men, the internal dissenters who would have toppled the government from within. After being placed on trial in accordance with the laws of the land, "those king-men, whosoever would not take up arms in the defence of their country, but would fight against it, were put to death." (Alma 62:6-9.)

As Pahoran and Moroni's troops engaged the Lamanites in battle, they influenced the defeated Lamanites "to enter into a covenant that they would no more take up their weapons of war against the Nephites." (Alma 62:16.) Underscoring the binding power of verbal promises, those who made this covenant were sent to live with the Ammonites in peace.

A series of dramatic, successive victories occurred as the ranks of Moroni and Pahoran were joined by the armies of Lehi and Teancum. Filled with exceeding anger toward Ammoron, Teancum stealthily cast a javelin into Ammoron's heart just as he had done with Ammoron's brother, Amalickiah. But this time he was pursued and slain. (Alma 62:35-36.) A mighty warrior had fallen.

With the demise of Ammoron, the Nephites were able to drive the Lamanites from the land, and peace was at least temporarily restored. Pahoran returned to his rightful place in the chief judgment-seat. Helaman began again "to preach unto the people the word of God," and the church was reestablished throughout the land. (Alma 62:44-46.) Captain Moroni relinquished his military command to his son, Moronihah, and retired in peace. (Alma 62:43.)

And the Nephite people "did pray unto the Lord their God continually, insomuch that the Lord did bless them, according to his word, so that they did wax strong and prosper in the land." (Alma 62:51.)

An Exceedingly Curious Man

Two years following the death of Helaman and the year following Moroni's death, "an exceedingly curious man" by the name of Hagoth built and launched a large ship "into the west sea, by the narrow neck which led into the land northward." (Alma 63:5.) John L. Sorenson builds a rather persuasive case for locating this launching point at the Gulf of Tehuantepec in Mesoamerica. His careful reasoning is well worth consideration.[4]

After taking several provisions and people with him, Hagoth returned the next year to build other ships and to take "many more people" and provisions with him to the land northward. "And it came to pass that they were never heard of more." (Alma 63:7-8.)

Students of Polynesian cultural history have sought to examine a possible link between Hagoth's voyages and the origins of the peoples of the South Pacific. R. Lanier Britsch has concluded that any such relationship "is not clear,"[5] and Sorenson contends that available anthropological information neither confirms nor refutes it.[6] Still, Church leaders have taught from time to time that Polynesians are descendants of Lehi, through Hagoth's voyages or other such travels of the Nephites and Lamanites.[7]

NOTES

1. Hugh Nibley, *Brigham Young Univeristy Summer Commencement Address*, August 19, 1983.

2. Hugh Nibley, *Lehi in the Desert and the World of the Jaredites* (Salt Lake City: Bookcraft, 1952), pp. 117-18, 196.

3. Sir Henry Sumner Maine, *Ancient Law* (New York: H. Holt and Co., 1885).

4. John L. Sorenson, *An Ancient American Setting for the Book of Mormon* (Salt Lake City: Deseret Book Company, and Provo, Utah: Foundation for Ancient Research and Mormon Studies, 1985) pp. 265-68.

5. R. Lanier Britsch, "Maori Traditions and the Mormon Church," *New Era*, June 1981, pp. 38-46.

6. Sorenson, *An Ancient American Setting*, p. 269.

7. See W. A. Cole and E. W. Jensen, *Israel in the Pacific* (Salt Lake City: Genealogical Society of Utah, 1961), p. 388; *Conference Report*, April 1962, p. 112; *Church News*, May 10, 1958, p. 2.

9

THEIR OWN WORST ENEMIES
(Helaman 1–6)

Daniel C. Peterson

Chapters 1-6 of Helaman cover fully thirty years and offer us a fairly good glimpse into how Mormon the editor worked. This section of the Book of Mormon is largely an example of what is often termed "annalistic" writing. "Annals," a type of historical record-keeping with many Near Eastern parallels, feature a narrative of events listed year by year. This is precisely what we find in these chapters. With only a single exception, every one of the thirty years extending from the fortieth year of the judges up to the sixty-ninth (from 52 to 23 B.C) is explicitly mentioned in these chapters. Sometimes, it is true, the year is cited very briefly, with only the most perfunctory indication of the state of the Nephites or of some event that occurred. Consider, for example, Helaman 3:1-2: In these verses, Mormon tells us very briefly that 49 B.C was characterized by a small problem with pride which was settled in that same year, and that the years 48 and 47 saw little or no contention. Likewise, Helaman 3:32-33 chronicles very briefly the years 43-40 B.C, which saw the Nephites decline from "peace and exceedingly great joy" to a cancerously growing pride, and Helaman 4:1-10 carries us from 38 to 31 B.C.[1]

We know already from the title page of the Book of Mormon that it is "an abridgment of the record of the people of Nephi," and we know that it was Mormon himself who was responsible for most of the condensation. It is possible, almost, to picture him at his task:

Daniel C. Peterson is assistant professor of Arabic at Brigham Young University.

He sits at a sort of writing table, surrounded by centuries of the records of his people. (Perhaps, given his central role in the violent events of his time, he does most of his writing in stolen moments in a military commander's field tent.) As he reads through the chronicles that have come to him, he knows he can include only a small portion in his abridgment. Therefore, under the inspiration of the Lord, he chooses what he thinks important and interesting, making occasional comments on the material he selects. However, he is too honest, too conscientious and thorough, to simply leave whole periods out of the record. Thus, for example, when he comes to his sources for the years 43-40 B.C., he finds a host of events and details that he cannot put into his book. But he can draw a lesson from them, and in this case the moral he distills from his source-chronicles is the evil of pride.

Rarely did Mormon go into an event or a sermon in great detail. Much of the record briefly summarizes what must have been a vast archive of source materials. (This is, of course, one of the frustrations of those who would read the Book of Mormon as an archaeological guidebook or as a geographical manual — such historical, archaeological, and geographical details as exist in it are there incidentally and sketchily. Mormon was serious about his assignment.)

Sedition and Invasion

Two spectacular events dominate the first chapter of the book of Helaman — a succession crisis accompanied by an assassination, and a successful but short-lived Lamanite seizure of the central Nephite lands. However, neither of these events proved as significant in the long term as the rise of a terrorist group that came to be called the "Gadianton robbers."

In 52 B.C., the great chief judge Pahoran I, who had presided over the Nephites during the recent period of wars, was dead. He left behind him a number of sons, among whom three — Pahoran, Paanchi, and Pacumeni — offered themselves as candidates to succeed their father. Each had his supporters, but Pahoran was chosen to occupy the judgment seat. Pacumeni gave up his claims and fell in behind the leadership of his brother, but Paanchi and his faction refused to reconcile themselves to their defeat. Instead, they began to plot a *coup d'état*. This was, of course, something that the government could not tolerate, and Paanchi was arrested and condemned to death. (And, although the record does not explicitly say so, it is likely that he was, in fact, executed.)

Furious over the failure of their attempt at sedition, a group of Paanchi's partisans dispatched an assassin, one Kishkumen, to eliminate their triumphant rival. Pahoran II, whose reign can have lasted at the most only a few months, was murdered as he sat upon the judgment seat, apparently while giving audience.[2]

Successful, Kishkumen escaped and returned to those who had sent him. The conspirators then swore an oath of silence. Intriguingly, the Nephite record tells us that it was a religious oath, "swearing by their everlasting Maker." (Hel. 1:11.) This seems odd to those of us unaccustomed to thinking of murder as a religious act. But the very word *assassin* was given to us by a religious sect of the medieval Near East who bore it as a name. The "Assassins" carried out daring murders for many years from mixed religious and political motives.[3] And it would seem, from the story of Cain and Abel as recorded in the book of Moses, that such "religious" oaths go back to the very beginning of human history. (See Moses 5:29.) Indeed, the Book of Mormon declares that the origin of such murderous conspiracies can be traced back to Lucifer through Cain, "who was a murderer from the beginning." (Ether 8:15; cf. Hel. 6:26-30.) Following their strange, quasi-religious meeting, the successful conspirators dispersed to their various ordinary pursuits, blending into Nephite society in such a way that the government could find only some of them. So religiously—if we may use that word—did they keep their oaths, that many of the group, including Kishkumen himself, remained at large.

In that same year, Pacumeni, the last of the three sons of Pahoran the First who had contested the judgment seat, was chosen to govern the Nephite nation. His reign was destined, however, to be just as short as that of his assassinated brother. The king of the Lamanites, perhaps sensing that the turmoil at the heart of the Nephite govenment offered him a major opportunity for success, chose the year 51 B.C. for a major invasion. It may be remembered that this king, named

Tubaloth, was not really a Lamanite. Rather, he was the son of Ammoron, the brother and successor of the notoriously unscrupulous Nephite adventurer, Amalickiah.[4] Tubaloth had chosen yet another dissenter from the Nephites, by the name of Coriantumr, to lead his warriors. It was certainly a common practice of those who would lead the Lamanites into battle against the Nephites to choose apostates as their assistants. (See, for an example of this, Alma 43:6-7.) These apostates could be counted upon to feel a powerful hatred for the Nephites, which made them very useful to the great manipulators who appear with such appalling frequency in the pages of the Book of Mormon.

Tubaloth's apparent guess that the Nephites' contentions had given him an opening was quite correct. Security in the Nephite heartland was almost nonexistent, owing to the breakdown in the government. Moronihah, the supreme commander of the Nephite armies, evidently faced with a shortage of troops, had chosen to place those that were available to him on the perimeter of Nephite territory. That is, they were stationed all about the lands of the Nephites, on the borders. Under the circumstances, this was the reasonable thing to do. But it also had its risks, since, as in the case of the notorious Maginot line in World War II, any invader who could get past the initial resistance at the border would find few obstacles from that point on.

And that is precisely what happened. Coriantumr launched a kind of *blitzkrieg*, piercing the Nephite border defenses, and seized the capital city of Zarahemla. The conquest was quick and, for the moment, total. Pacumeni, the chief judge, was killed. Perhaps somewhat astonished himself at the scope of his victory, Coriantumr then marched toward the other chief Nephite city, Bountiful. En route, he mopped up what disorganized opposition he encountered—the Nephites having been taken so completely by surprise that they did not even have time to mobilize a challenge to him.

But Coriantumr would not reach Bountiful. As Hugh Nibley points out, his drive "had been successful because it was completely unexpected; and it had been unexpected because it was utterly foolish."[5] It was utterly foolish because, having penetrated the Nephite defense

on the circumference and seized the center of the land, Coriantumr
was now, by the very nature of his own success, surrounded. Moronihah and his loyal subordinate officer, Lehi, caught the Lamanite
intruders from before and behind, and, following a bloody battle in
which Coriantumr was killed, left them no alternative but surrender.
It was a humiliating defeat.

The Nephites must surely have breathed a massive sigh of relief
at this point. If so, they were premature. For the remnants of the
conspiracy that had killed Pahoran II were still at large, and, having
previously tasted success, were apparently little disposed to go into
retirement. While Coriantumr's daring invasion had been spectacular,
it was to have little if any lasting effect; the future belonged, rather,
in a very real sense, to the conspiracy that had begun the year before.

Gadianton

In the aftermath of the Lamanite invasion of 51 B.C., the Nephite
government began to reconstitute itself. With all of the politically
active sons of Pahoran I now dead, the choice of the people fell upon
Helaman, the son of Helaman, to lead them. There was another,
though, who wanted to rule. One Gadianton, who, like so many of
the great agitators in the Book of Mormon, "was exceedingly expert
in many words" (Hel. 2:4), at this point insinuated himself into the
leadership of the old Paanchist conspiracy. If they would put him on
the judgment seat, he said, he would reward them with power and
authority.[6] They agreed to make the attempt. And, although they
would never be successful in Gadianton's lifetime, so complete was
his control over them and so completely were they identified with
him that ever afterward they were known among the Nephites as
"Gadianton's robbers."

Kishkumen, therefore, their tried and tested instrument in the
case of Pahoran II, was dispatched to assassinate Helaman. But the
new chief judge had not forgotten about the seditionists still on the
loose among his people, and he had inaugurated a partially successful
plan to infiltrate their organization. As Kishkumen proceeded toward
the judgment seat to reprise his earlier triumph, he was stabbed to
death by one of Helaman's operatives, who then ran to the chief judge

to alert him to the developing situation. (The smooth way in which Kishkumen is taken care of—in total silence; see Hel. 2:9—makes us suspect that this "servant" of Helaman's was more than an ordinary domestic helper or government office-worker. Indeed, he may well have been the ancient equivalent of a professional intelligence specialist.[7])

Helaman's men were, however, unable to apprehend the wily Gadianton and his partisans. When Kishkumen did not return within the expected time, Gadianton did not wait around to be caught. Instead, he and his followers escaped from the city into the wilderness, where they and their successors would operate frequently in the next several centuries—offering a textbook illustration of guerrilla warfare.[8] They did not fade away. "More of this Gadianton shall be spoken hereafter," wrote Mormon. "And behold, in the end of this book [by which he meant the Book of Mormon as a whole] ye shall see that this Gadianton did prove the overthrow, yea, almost the entire destruction of the people of Nephi." (Hel. 2:12-13.)

A Season of Emigration to the North

Helaman 3 records that many people left the land of Zarahemla in 46 B.C. and made their way into the land to the north. (In this northward emigration, they were following the precedent that had been set a decade earlier by Hagoth and his people. See Alma 63:4-10.) They traveled a great distance to a region of "large bodies of water and many rivers." (Hel. 3:4.)[9] This area had previously sustained a large population that the Nephites identified with the earlier people known as the Jaredites (see Ether 1:1), and it had (in a situation we today can well imagine) been stripped of its timber.[10] Thus, given the fact that they could not rely upon wood for their construction materials, these colonists resorted to working with cement, although they also imported wood from the south and attempted, as a long-term solution to the problem, to reforest the land. (Hel. 3:7-10.)

Meanwhile, back in the central Nephite lands, the affairs of the people alternately prospered and decayed. In 43 B.C., for example, peace had been established and the church was flourishing. Referring to this time, Mormon noted that such blessings were—and always had been—open to all. "Thus," he wrote, "we may see that the Lord is merciful unto all who will, in the sincerity of their hearts, call upon his holy name. Yea, thus we see that the gate of heaven is open unto all, even to those who will believe on the name of Jesus Christ, who is the Son of God. Yea, we see that whosoever will may lay hold upon the word of God, which is quick and powerful, which shall divide asunder all the cunning and the snares and the wiles of the devil, and lead the man of Christ in a straight and narrow course across that everlasting gulf of misery which is prepared to engulf the wicked—and land their souls, yea, their immortal souls, at the right hand of God in the kingdom of heaven, to sit down with Abraham, and Isaac, and with Jacob, and with all our holy fathers, to go no more out." (Hel. 3:27-30.) There was never any need in Nephite history—and there is none in our own time—for the suffering and misery that inevitably accompany wickedness. Yet we are prey to the same temptations as our ancestors. One of the hopes of the scriptural writers who so frankly recorded the sins and errors of their own times was that we of a latter day might profit from their experiences, and, in many cases, avoid repeating them. (See, for example, Morm. 9:31 and Ps. 78:5-8.)

How are we to avoid falling into the same snares as did many of those before us? In his entry for 41 B.C., Mormon gave us a large portion of the answer to that question. In that year, class distinctions began again to appear within the church, and some members of the church gave themselves over to pride and arrogance, and to mistreating the more humble among their brothers and sisters. But amidst all the pain and despite all the discomfort that must have attended this situation, these humble saints remained faithful to God and to their covenants. We are told that "they did fast and pray oft, and did wax stronger and stronger in their humility, and firmer and firmer in the faith of Christ, unto the filling their souls with joy and consolation, yea, even to the purifying and the sanctification of their hearts, which sanctification cometh because of their yielding their hearts unto God." (Hel. 3:35.) Thus, in the face of adversity and perhaps even pain, the Lord's true saints drew yet closer to him, through fasting, prayer, and humble obedience. His true saints do so today, as well.

"Except the Lord Keep the City . . . "

For the year 38 B.C., Mormon's abridgment refers briefly to the rise of contention within the church, which became so severe that it eventually resulted in violence and bloodshed. "And the rebellious part were slain and driven out of the land, and they did go unto the king of the Lamanites. And it came to pass that they did endeavor to stir up the Lamanites to war against the Nephites." (Hel. 4:2-3.)

However, the Lamanites had been beaten too many times in the memory of many still living to be very enthusiastic about yet another assault on the Nephites; they were, in fact, "exceedingly afraid." (Hel. 4:3.) The great war narrated in the Book of Alma had ended in utter Lamanite defeat only a little more than two decades earlier, and the spectacular campaign led by Coriantumr had concluded disastrously just thirteen years before. And both of these military catastrophes had been set in motion by dissenters from the Nephites, who often seemed more than willing to fight their erstwhile brethren down to the last drop of Lamanite blood. Thus, the Lamanites did not respond favorably to the incitements of this particular group of dissenters.

But yet another wave of apostates arrived in Lamanite territory in the following year, and, with them fanning the flames kindled by the earlier group, the resistance of the Lamanites began to weaken. Finally, in 35 B.C., the Lamanites again launched an invasion of Nephite territory. By the next year, they had taken Zarahemla, the Nephite capital. Moronihah and his armies attempted a counterattack, but by 31 B.C. they had managed to recover only half of their original possessions.

It is at this point that Mormon, himself a great military commander, interrupted his narrative to offer some observations on the reasons behind the Nephites' inability to respond effectively to this invasion. It is highly interesting, however, that his remarks not only do not center on military strategy and tactical considerations, but indeed do not raise such issues at all. Rather, he wrote, the cause of the Nephites' weakness was their wickedness — a wickedness that extended even into the church of God. "And it was because of the pride of their hearts, because of their exceeding riches, yea, it was because of their oppression to the poor, withholding their food from the hungry, withholding their clothing from the naked, and smiting their humble brethren upon the cheek, making a mock of that which was sacred, denying the spirit of prophecy and of revelation, murdering, plundering, lying, stealing, committing adultery, rising up in great contentions, and deserting away into the land of Nephi, among the Lamanites — and because of this their great wickedness, and their boastings in their own strength, they were *left* in their own strength." (Hel. 4:12-13, emphasis added.)[11]

Mormon, of course, was sufficiently astute as a military strategist to know what it would mean for the Nephites to be left to merely their own strength. They had been vastly outnumbered by the Lamanites for many generations. If it came to a struggle of numbers, there could be only one outcome. Even the contemporary Nephites, wicked as they were, could see the disastrous implications of their course: "And they saw that they had become weak, like unto their brethren, the Lamanites, and that the Spirit of the Lord did no more preserve them; and they saw that the Lamanites were exceedingly more numerous than they, and except they should cleave unto the Lord their God they must unavoidably perish. For behold, they saw that the strength of the Lamanites was as great as their strength, even man for man." (Hel. 4:24-26.)

The greatness of Mormon, as well as of Moroni, consisted at least partially of the fact that, competent as the Nephites were, they continued to recognize that the Lord is the ultimate arbiter of human affairs. And they never became so obsessed with military tactics and technology as to forget that it is a nation's moral and spiritual resources that will most surely and fundamentally determine its fate. "Except the Lord keep the city," wrote the Psalmist, "the watchman waketh but in vain." (Ps. 127:1.)[12]

Roots, Not Branches

Nephi, son of Helaman, knew, fully as well as would the later chronicler Mormon, that the fundamental problem of the Nephites at this period was spiritual rather than military.[13] For this reason, he decided to devote all his energies to a spiritual solution. In that same year, 30 B.C., he resigned the judgment seat and, with his brother Lehi, undertook full-time preaching of the gospel.

The task was urgent if the Nephites were to be saved from themselves. "For as their laws and their governments were established by the voice of the people, and they who chose evil were more numerous than they who chose good, therefore they were ripening for destruction, for the laws had become corrupted." (Hel. 5:2.) This was precisely the situation King Mosiah II had foreseen as a frightening but remote possibility six decades earlier, when he abolished the monarchy and established the Nephite system of judges. The laws of the Nephites, he had said, were correct and divinely given. Further, he had said, placing the direction of the nation in the hands of a more representative form of government would tend to ensure the continuation of those laws in their correct form, since the majority of the people were unlikely to choose evil over good. But, he had continued, "if the time comes that the voice of the people doth choose iniquity, then is the time that the judgments of God will come upon you." (Mosiah 29:25-27.) And now, probably within the lifetimes of some who had heard him give that historic address, his fears had been realized.[14]

The two brothers, Nephi and Lehi, began their missionary tour at the city of Bountiful and went through a number of the settlements still under Nephite rule. Finally, they entered the territories that had been under Lamanite control since the war of four years earlier. There, in occupied Zarahemla, they preached with such power that they were able to win over many of the Nephite dissenters who had stirred up that war in the first place. But their success did not end with that. They were also able to convert fully eight thousand of the Lamanites who had settled in the former Nephite lands.

Perhaps heartened by this almost unprecedented success, Nephi and Lehi crossed over into Lamanite country itself, into the old land of Nephi. There, however, the reception was rather more chilly. They were captured by a Lamanite army and were almost immediately cast into prison under sentence of death. (After all, they were Nephites, hereditary enemies of the Lamanites — and very prominent ones at that.)

But when their keepers came to fetch them for execution, the Lord intervened. "Nephi and Lehi were encircled about as if by fire, even insomuch that they durst not lay their hands upon them." (Hel. 5:23.) Encouraged by this, the brothers began to preach to their would-be killers — accompanied by earthquakes, a preternatural "cloud of darkness," and a voice from heaven. Quite evidently, the Lord was working here in a major way, for purposes important to him. And, indeed, his intervention in this instance would be of major historical importance, as succeeding chapters of Helaman make clear.[15]

In the face of this supernatural display, the Lamanites were immobilized. Fortunately, one of the apostate Nephites was nearby. Such apostates could be the most bitter and implacable of enemies to the truths of God, but they were also capable — as in the case of this man, one Aminadab — of dredging up from deep in their memories the childhood teachings that would allow them to receive the gospel and teach it to others.[16] Aminadab was able to answer the now earnest inquiries of the Lamanites, and to explain to them how they could be delivered from the cloud of darkness that had engulfed them.

Calling upon the Lord, the newly humbled Lamanites were delivered — and not only so, but they were visited by angels and commended by the heavenly voice. This powerful experience created an instant missionary force of three hundred eager converts. Within a short time, "the more part of the Lamanites were convinced of them." (Hel. 5:50.)

The Tables Turned

Nephi and Lehi had apparently had little success preaching among the Nephites, but they had triumphed spectacularly with the Lamanites and their sympathizers. There ensued now a period that explodes the oversimplified view of the Book of Mormon held by some who do not know it well. For them, the book is a long but uncomplicated tale of white-hatted Nephites and black-hatted Lamanite villains. Certainly, however, for the period under discussion here nothing could be further from the truth.

Helaman 6 describes a time when the Lamanites were righteous, and the Nephites wicked. The Lamanites even sent missionaries among their former enemies and were able, at least temporarily, to bring many of them to the truth and to repentance. And their prosperity was not simply spiritual. With many Nephites and Lamanites converted to the Lord, peace was established, barriers to free trade fell, and — as a predictable consequence — the entire land became prosperous. (Hel. 6:7-9.)[17]

Wealth, however, carries with it major risks to the spiritual well-being of those who possess it. It can, in fact, come to possess *them*. Sometimes, oddly, those who have more than enough of worldly goods can become more obsessed with them than those who must struggle just to make ends meet. So it was with the Nephites at this time. "They began to set their hearts upon their riches." (Hel. 6:17.) They resurrected the old conspiratorial oaths and plans of Gadianton's band. The Lamanites were horrified at this new outbreak of Gadiantonism and made every effort to eradicate it. The Nephites, on the other hand, took to the new possibilities for organized evil with notable enthusiasm. By 24 B.C., their government was firmly in the hands of a revolutionary sect that had taken its immediate beginning in the political turmoil of a quarter of a century earlier.

Chapters 1-6 of Helaman end, thus, on a rather depressing note. From the gospel of Christ, the Nephites had turned to a set of practices and doctrines originating with his archenemy. Of these, Mormon wrote, "They were put into the heart of Gadianton by that same being who did entice our first parents to partake of the forbidden fruit — yea, that same being who did plot with Cain, that if he would murder his brother Abel it should not be known unto the world. And he did plot with Cain and his followers from that time forth." (Hel. 6:26-27; cf. Moses 5:29-33, 47-51.)

Nevertheless, Mormon did not leave us without hope. Under the inspiration of the Lord he gave us important keys for avoiding, individually and as a society, the fate of the Nephites, and he stressed to us that the Lord's blessing and help is available freely, and to all.

Surely the counsel of Helaman to his sons, Nephi and Lehi, was preserved on the golden plates because of its continuing relevance to our day: "My sons," said Helaman, "remember, remember that it is upon the rock of our Redeemer, who is Christ, the Son of God, that ye must build your foundation; that when the devil shall send forth his mighty winds, yea, his shafts in the whirlwind, yea, when all his hail and his mighty storm shall beat upon you, it shall have no power over you to drag you down to the gulf of misery and endless wo, because of the rock upon which ye are built, which is a sure foundation, a foundation whereon if men build they cannot fall." (Hel. 5:12.)

NOTES

1. Probably the best example of what we are discussing here is 4 Nephi 1:6. This verse has been greatly ridiculed by some critics of the Book of Mormon, but it is, in fact, an exceptionally good illustration of the annalist, Mormon, at work. Manifestly, he was summarizing other chronicles that he had before him. However, so little was happening in this period that even the conscientious Mormon began to omit annual accounts. It is apparently difficult even for inspired authors to make good and happy times live up to our taste for the sensational and the horrific. "May you live in interesting times!" is, in fact, an old Chinese curse. And Leo Tolstoy began his great novel *Anna Karenina* with the marvelous line: "Happy families are all alike; every unhappy family is unhappy in its own way." As a glance at the headlines of supermarket tabloids or five minutes listening to gossip will show, we fallen humans tend to find negative news much more interesting than positive.

2. This would, of course, be a time when the chief judge would be easily accessible to a would-be assassin. (One thinks of the similar murder of Saudi Arabia's King Faisal in 1975.) It would also make for a memorable public "statement," if such were the motive of Kishkumen's handlers.

3. The Assassins offer, in fact, a remarkably close parallel to the "secret combinations" of the Nephite and Jaredite traditions. Similar groups are also attested in ancient Mesoamerica. See, on the latter, John L. Sorenson, *An Ancient American Setting for the Book of Mormon* (Salt Lake City: Deseret

Book Company, and Provo, Utah: Foundation for Ancient Research and Mormon Studies, 1985), pp. 300-309.

4. On Amalickiah's rise to power and his subsequent career, see Alma 46-49, 51.

5. Hugh W. Nibley, *Since Cumorah* (Salt Lake City: Deseret Book Company, 1967), p. 367. Hitler's attack on the Soviet Union was likewise an initial triumph but foolish and disastrous in the long term—as Napoleon could have predicted from personal experience.

6. One cannot fail to be reminded of the takeover of an already-existing conspiratorial group in the Weimar Republic—the National Socialist German Workers' Party—by an ambitious young ex-corporal named Adolf Hitler. If anyone could be said to be "exceedingly expert in many words," it is he. Yet the pattern holds with remarkable consistency wherever such conspiracies arise: Lenin, Mussolini, and Castro also come to mind. All were leaders of revolutionary organizations; all were given to seemingly endless speeches.

7. This would not be anachronistic. We need only mention the *Ping-fa* ("The Art of War"), written about 400 B.C. by the Chinese military thinker, Sun-tzu. Its discussion of intelligence-gathering techniques shows that they are very ancient indeed.

8. On the Gadianton bands as guerrillas, see Ray C. Hillam, "The Gadianton Robbers and Protracted War," *Brigham Young University Studies* 15 (Winter 1975): 215-24. The present author is (sporadically) working on a lengthy study of the Gadianton organizations that will discuss this and several other aspects of their activities.

9. According to a model of Book of Mormon geography that is widely accepted among students of the subject, and which the present writer, too, finds plausible, this area may well have been the Valley of Mexico. See Sorenson, *Ancient American Setting*, pp. 266-67. It would seem, at any event, that the colonization of Teotihuacán occurred during the same period as the Nephite-Lamanite migrations to the north that are recorded in this and adjacent portions of the Book of Mormon. See David A. Palmer, *In Search of Cumorah* (Bountiful: Horizon Publishers, 1981), pp. 188-91. A variant of the Sorenson model (Palmer, *Cumorah*, p. 186) suggests the area of modern Veracruz as a possible site.

10. In conversation with Prof. John L. Sorenson on this point, he suggests that if the area is, in fact, to be identified with the Valley of Mexico, it is probably too far north to have actually been part of historic Jaredite territory. However, Nephite knowledge of northern geography beyond a certain point seems to have been vague at best. Certainly they *thought* this area to have been in formerly Jaredite country.

11. Mormon was to face the same mindset in his own day, and with even more calamitous results. See Mormon 4:8; 5:2, 6.

12. A challenging modern counterpart to this ancient principle may be found in the notable essay by President Spencer W. Kimball, entitled "The False Gods We Worship," in the *Ensign* for June 1976.

13. Nephi's spiritual sensitivity, with that of his brother, Lehi, probably owed much to the teaching of their father, Helaman. Hel. 5:6-7 speaks volumes of his desire to instill in them a sense of heritage and of the models they were to emulate. See also Hel. 5:8-12.

14. Mosiah's comments had been recalled a decade later by Amulek, speaking to the people of Ammonihah. (See Alma 10:19.) The similarity between the wording of this passage and that of Helaman 5:2 is striking.

15. For much of the remainder of the Book of Helaman, it is the Lamanites and not the Nephites who were the righteous followers of the Lord. This was, of course, the period of Samuel the Lamanite.

16. One recalls also the dissenters at Zarahemla. (See above, and Hel. 5:17.) This thought can be of comfort to parents who have watched their children reject their teachings and drift from or rebel against the Church. Gospel seeds once planted can bear fruit even many years later.

17. The principle underlying this situation is put in modern terms by the Nobel laureate economist Paul A. Samuelson, in his famous textbook, *Economics*, 8th ed. (New York: McGraw-Hill, 1970), p. 668: "There is essentially only one argument for free or freer trade, but it is an exceedingly powerful one, namely: *Unhampered trade promotes a mutually profitable international division of labor, greatly enhances the potential real national product of all countries, and makes possible higher standards of living all over the globe.*" (Emphasis in the original.) That the Book of Mormon so well depicts the operation of an economic law that was not generally recognized in Joseph Smith's time — and perhaps is not yet, even today — is a good illustration of its plausibility as authentic historiographical material.

10

GOD'S WAYS OR MAN'S: THE ULTIMATE CHOICE
(Helaman 7–12)

REX C. REEVE, JR.

The struggle between good and evil in the pre-earth life has continued on this earth since the days of Adam. Men and women in each generation have again been faced with the opportunity to choose good over evil. The Lord in his wisdom has provided a plan whereby each individual can be instructed sufficiently. Then all are free to choose according to the desires of their heart, either the path leading to eternal life or the path leading to eternal misery. They are not free, however, to choose the results. They must receive the consequences unalterably decreed of God that are attached to the path of their choice.

In the plan of the Lord, sufficient knowledge is revealed so that both paths, with their consequences, are clearly defined. Men and women are then invited to come unto Christ and partake of the rewards prepared for the righteous. The Book of Mormon is unequaled in all literature in outlining both paths and their consequences and then inviting and leading people to Christ if they desire to follow him. Joseph Smith said, "I told the brethren that the Book of Mormon was the most correct of any book on earth, and the keystone of our religion, and a man would get nearer to God by abiding by its precepts, than by any other book."[1] After someone has read and understood the Book of Mormon, he or she has been in-

Rex C. Reeve, Jr., is assistant professor of ancient scripture at Brigham Young University.

structed sufficiently to know good from evil. The final judgment, with reward or punishment, will hinge on the person's choices based on knowledge received from this book. The Book of Mormon is a book of contrasts: Nephi versus Laman, Jacob versus Sherem, Alma versus Korihor. As the Book of Mormon defines these contrasts, it shows clearly the rewards for good and the punishments for evil. The plan and the path leading in both directions with immediate and long-range consequences are clearly defined.

In abridging the records from the large plates of Nephi, Mormon included a classic example of the contrast between good and evil in Helaman 7-12. These chapters paint the picture of the wickedness of the Nephites contrasted with the righteousness of Nephi. On the one hand Mormon was moved to decry forcefully the terrible disobedience of the natural man. (Hel. 12.) On the other hand he included the great blessings and powers the Lord gave to Nephi because of his personal righteousness and his consistent obedience.

In Helaman 7-12 Mormon abridged the record of Nephi, the son of Helaman. The events of this portion of the Book of Mormon took place shortly before the birth of the Savior, between 23 B.C. and 7 B.C. The condition among the Nephites was one of wickedness. Gadianton robbers filled the judgment seats and were using the powers of government to further their purposes. They condemned the righteous because of their righteousness and let the wicked go unpunished because of their money. (Hel. 7:4-5.) This great iniquity was a cause of sorrow to Nephi; he wished that he could have lived in the days of father Lehi and Nephi when they first came out of Jerusalem. Then he could have had joy because of the righteousness of his brethren. Yet he realized that he was called to his own day and was destined to experience sorrow his whole life because of his people. (Hel. 7:6-9.)

The wicked would not soften their hearts even after Nephi's preaching, his miracles, and his prophecies about the murder of the chief judge. The leaders of his people were angry when he spoke plainly about their corruption, their secret works, and their impending destruction. In the hardness of their hearts they even rejected the testimony and doctrine of Christ that had been given by Abraham,

Moses, Zenos, Zenock, Ezias, Isaiah, Jeremiah, Lehi, and Nephi. (Hel. 8-9.)

About 20 B.C contention led to war among all the people of Nephi. The Gadianton robbers carried on their secret works, and it seemed that all the people would be destroyed. (Hel. 11:1-2.) In the second year of the war, Nephi pleaded with the Lord to send a famine to motivate the people to repentance rather than let them all die in war. (Hel. 11:4.)

According to Nephi's words, the Lord sent a famine; there was no rain and hence no yield of crops. The war ceased, but the death of thousands among the Nephites and the Lamanites continued because of the famine. (Hel. 11:4-5.) Faced with total destruction, the people began to remember the Lord and pleaded with Nephi to turn away God's wrath. (Hel. 11:7-8.) Seeing their repentance and their humility, Nephi asked the Lord to send rain and again bless the lands to be productive. Even though famine, pestilence, and death forced their repentance and humility, the Lord answered Nephi's prayers and sent rain. (Hel. 11:10-17.)

For some, the return to the Lord was permanent, and with thankfulness they remained faithful and steadfast. For others — a few at first, but the numbers steadily increased — repentance was short lived, and the memory of the goodness of the Lord was soon forgotten. Among those who dissented from their spiritual commitments, wickedness soon replaced righteousness. The secret plans of Gadianton were again sought out, and within a few years robbing, plundering, and murders returned and the people were again heading for destruction. (Hel. 11:24-37.)

The Unsteadiness of the Natural Man

The burden of abridging the records of this unstable and fickle period of Nephite history prompted Mormon to leave the history and make some general observations about humanity in this fallen state: "And thus we can behold how false, and also the unsteadiness of the hearts of the children of men." (Hel. 12:1.) "False" means being disloyal, unfaithful, or not being what one purports to be. "Unsteady" refers to being changeable, inconsistent, erratic in habits, purpose, or behavior.

Mormon continued by noting: "Yea, we can see that the Lord in his great infinite goodness doth bless and prosper those who put their trust in him." (Hel. 12:1.) This was the original promise of the Lord to every group he brought to the promised land: If they would keep his commandments they would be blessed and prosper. (Ether 2:7-9; 1 Ne. 2:20.) Mormon then wrote: "Yea, and we may see at the very time when he doth prosper his people . . . yea, then is the time that they do harden their hearts, and do forget the Lord their God, and do trample under their feet the Holy One." (Hel. 12:2.) To trample God under their feet means to set aside his counsels and to be disobedient to his commands. (See 1 Ne. 19:7.)

Mormon's next observation is, "And thus we see that except the Lord doth chasten his people with many afflictions, yea, except he doth visit them with death and with terror, and with famine and with all manner of pestilence, they will not remember him." (Hel. 12:3) The experience of Nephi and his people with the famine provided ample evidence of the truth of Mormon's observation. Mormon continued by describing in plain terms the almost universal weaknesses in fallen humanity that are so offensive to the Lord.

Fallen men and women are (Hel. 12:4-6):

1. Foolish
2. Vain
3. Evil and devilish
4. Quick to do iniquity
5. Slow to do good
6. Quick to hearken to the words of the evil one
7. Quick to set their hearts on the vain things of the world
8. Quick to be lifted up in pride
9. Quick to boast
10. Slow to remember the Lord their God
11. Slow to give ear to God's counsels
12. Slow to walk in wisdom's paths
13. Not desirous that the Lord their God, who created them, should rule and reign over them

14. Eager to set aside God's counsel

15. Not desirous that God should be their guide

With the tendencies of fallen people to reject the Lord and not have him be their guide, Mormon declared that they are less than the dust of the earth. At least the dust obeys the voice of God when he commands it to move. At the voice of the Lord the hills and mountains quake and are broken up. By the power of his voice the whole earth shakes and the rocks tremble. In response to a divinely given command the earth actually stops in its rotation, thus lengthening the hours of the day. (Hel. 12:7-15.)[2] The elements gladly obey the voice of the Lord, but people willingly choose to disobey.

People have the freedom to disobey the Lord, but if they do, they must accept the consequences of disobedience. The Lord has the power to curse people or to cut them off from his presence forever because of their sins. Mormon lamented the fate of those who are accursed of the Lord, for they cannot be saved and shall be consigned to a state of endless misery or everlasting damnation. Though Mormon strongly decried the wicked and inconsistent tendencies of humanity, in a spirit of sweetness he reminded us that repentance has been provided that they may be saved. (Hel. 12:20-26.) In his mercy God has provided the opportunity for all to repent and change. (Hel. 12:22.) For those who will do so and obey the voice of the Lord, the fallen tendencies of disobedience and sin may be overcome. Mormon prayed that people would be brought to repentance and bring forth good works so they could receive the blessings of the Lord, because through the law of justice all will be "restored unto grace for grace, according to their works." (Hel. 12:24.)

The Spiritual Consistency of Nephi

In stark contrast to the wickedness and disobedience Mormon had been reporting, he chose to include in his record a few verses about Nephi. At a time when Nephi was "much cast down because of the wickedness of the people . . . a voice came unto him saying: Blessed art thou, Nephi, for those things which thou hast done." (Hel. 10:3-4.) Almost point for point Mormon showed how Nephi exhibited the exact opposite of the fallen tendencies of most others. By faithful obedience Nephi found favor with the Lord and was given power and great blessings.

The Lord's word continued: "For I have beheld how thou hast with unwearyingness declared the word, which I have given unto thee, unto this people." (Hel. 10:4.) The Lord had been watching, was aware of Nephi as an individual, and knew what he had done. How important it was for Nephi to know that his efforts were known and appreciated. Those lonely years when he quietly withstood temptation or when he stood firm against the tide of sin and wickedness among his people were not in vain. An effective tool of Satan in deceiving people is to make them think that they are alone and that no one knows or cares. For those who will listen, the Lord answers Satan's deceit simply by saying "I have beheld." The thing the Lord beheld that pleased him so was Nephi's consistency. The Lord used the word "unwearyingness" at least twice to describe how Nephi had declared the word. This is in contrast to the observation of Mormon about the unsteadiness of the hearts of others. A sign of spiritual maturity is the tendency to be consistent and steadfast in righteousness or in service.

The Lord continued to tell Nephi why he was pleased with him: "And thou hast not feared them, and hast not sought thine own life, but hast sought my will, and to keep my commandments." (Hel. 10:4.) Nephi did not fear those who opposed the will of the Lord; he did not yield to their demands that he join them; and he did not compromise his standards for fear of losing the favor of the world. This kind of spiritual courage, that displaces the fear of men, is another essential element in gaining favor with the Lord.

In contrast to Mormon's words that the natural man does not desire that God should be his guide or rule over him, Nephi was singled out for his willingness to do the will of the Lord, even ahead of his own will and desires. Putting God's will first in one's life is essential to pleasing the Lord. The first principle of the gospel is faith in the Lord Jesus Christ. Faith can be defined as coming to know the true Christ while never having seen him, or coming to know the true Christ well enough (not having seen him) that one desires to do things the Lord's way. The natural result of a successful effort to come to know Christ is the desire to do his will and keep his commandments. (See John 14:15, 23; 1 John 5:3.)

The Lord said to Nephi: "Because thou hast done this with such unwearyingness, behold, I will bless thee forever." (Hel. 10:5.) What does it mean to have the Lord say he will bless someone forever? Could there be a better promise given to anyone? From the Book of Mormon and from other modern revelations we know that eternal life—exaltation in the celestial kingdom—is the blessing the Lord provides forever (in the eternities) for his faithful children. From Mormon's account we learn that Nephi had done two basic things to bring such a treasured reward: First, he had not sought to do his own will, but rather the will of God. (Hel. 10:4.) Nephi brought his own will and desires into complete harmony with those of the Lord. Second, Nephi had unwearyingly labored to deliver the word of the Lord to the people. He had proven that he could be trusted to always fill his assignment, and he demonstrated a consistent concern for the welfare of his people.

In addition to the blessings of the eternities, Nephi was promised blessings and power in this life: "And I will make thee mighty in word and in deed, in faith and in works; yea, even that all things shall be done unto thee according to thy word, for thou shalt not ask that which is contrary to my will. . . . Ye shall have power over this people, and shall smite the earth with famine, and with pestilence." (Hel. 10:5-6.) Nephi was given power to have anything he desired: he could control the elements, he could have power over the people, and no one could stand against him. By diligent obedience he had gained the confidence of the Lord. God knew that Nephi could be trusted with this power and that he would not ask for anything contrary to the will of heaven.

The Lord continued by saying, "I give unto you power, that whatsoever ye shall seal on earth shall be sealed in heaven; and whatsoever ye shall loose on earth shall be loosed in heaven." (Hel. 10:7; cf. Matt. 16:16-19.) In addition to his other powers and blessings, Nephi was given power to perform acts in this life that would be valid and binding after death and recognized in heaven. For those of his people who would listen and respond, Nephi had the power to seal upon them the blessings of an eternal family and eternal increase.

Nephi continued to prove faithful to the trust and confidence of the Lord. He was instructed to declare to the people that the Lord God, who is almighty, was displeased with them and would destroy them if they did not repent. (Hel. 10:11.) The next verse recorded by Mormon seems to sum up the attitude and commitment of Nephi that was so appreciated by God. "When the Lord had spoken these words unto Nephi, he did stop and did not go unto his own house, but did return unto the multitudes who were scattered about upon the face of the land, and began to declare unto them the word of the Lord." (Hel. 10:12.) Even when faced with the difficult task of bringing his people to repentance, Nephi obeyed immediately. He demonstrated what it really means to have an eye single to the glory of God, to have one's own will swallowed up in the will of the Lord. It would have been natural to want to return to the comfort and security of his own home and family, but on this occasion Nephi did not return to his house until after he had accomplished with exactness the desires of the Lord.

Conclusion

Fallen humanity is an enemy to God. The natural man is quick to do wrong, and slow and unsteady in his obedience to the will of the Lord. The Lord, in order to reclaim his disobedient children, must chasten them with afflictions, suffering, and even natural disasters.

Each person is faced with the choice between good and evil as part of the plan of life. The Book of Mormon outlines the choices available and clearly defines the consequences. In these chapters Mormon gave examples of both extremes. The Nephite people were wicked, and only war, famine, and death could command their attention long enough to bring them to even a temporary state of repentance. Because of their choice to pursue their own desires and follow the wickedness of the world, they were in danger of being cursed forever. In contrast, Mormon included the account of Nephi, which shows that faithfulness is possible even when the majority of the people choose to disobey the Lord.

What Nephi did to gain such great favor and blessings from the Lord could be repeated by anyone in any generation. No insurmountable task is required to please the Lord; steady obedience brings the approval and blessings of heaven. The obedience and blessings of Nephi follow a pattern that is consistent throughout the Book of Mormon and that all true disciples of Christ must follow to gain the same blessings. Nephi, when faced with the choice between convenience and inconvenience, between good and evil, sought for and obtained the things of God. He rejected the allurements of his world and increased his effort to build his faith and be constant in his obedience to the Lord. He sought the welfare of his people and subjected his own desires to those of God.

Nephi was given the assurance that his efforts were pleasing to God and was thus given the right to use the Lord's power for the benefit of his people. He was given the sealing power of the priesthood, the power to bind and loose on earth and in heaven. Finally, he was given the assurance that his consistent obedience had prepared him for the blessings of the Lord throughout the eternities. He had successfully met the challenges of mortality and received the assurance that his salvation was secure. His soul was at rest. And his example is before us.

NOTES

1. Joseph Smith, *History of The Church of Jesus Christ of Latter-day Saints*, 2nd ed. rev., edited by B. H. Roberts (Salt Lake City: The Church of Jesus Christ of Latter-day Saints, 1932-51), 4:461.

2. Mormon explained that it is the earth that revolves around the sun, and not vice versa. (Hel. 12:14-15.)

11

SAMUEL THE LAMANITE
(Helaman 13–16)

MAE BLANCH

As the time of the Savior's birth approached, the Nephite people became increasingly wicked. Following a brief period of repentance after the Lord chastised the people with a famine, they rapidly fell back into their sinful ways. Mormon recorded, "In the eighty and second year they began again to forget the Lord their God. And in the eighty and third year they began to wax strong in iniquity. And in the eighty and fourth year they did not mend their ways. And it came to pass in the eighty and fifth year they did wax stronger and stronger in their pride, and in their wickedness; and thus they were ripening again for destruction." (Hel. 11:36-37.) But the Lord never destroys a people without giving them every chance to return to him. As he had done many times before, he sent a prophet to plead for their repentance and to warn them of the inevitable consequences if they refused to hear his message.

We know little about Samuel except that he was a Lamanite, that he came to Zarahemla to preach the word of God, that he was rejected and cast out by the people and was returning to his own country when he received revelation from the Lord that he should go back to the city and "prophesy unto the people whatsoever things should come into his heart." (Hel. 13:3.) Perhaps the fact that he was a Lamanite — from a people estranged from the Lord and the Nephites until some of them had been converted — would make his message from the Lord more impressive. But such was not the case. When he

---

Mae Blanch is professor of English literature at Brigham Young University.

116

returned to the city, the wicked Nephites would not let him enter, and he was forced to mount the wall surrounding Zarahemla to tell them what the Lord would have them know. Through Samuel's voice the Lord warned the Nephites of what would befall them unless they repented. Samuel recounted the ways in which they had offended the Lord, warned them of the immediate and long-range consequences of their sins, prophesied of the birth and death of the Lord Jesus whose mission made repentance possible, gave them an account of the faithful Lamanites as an example of true repentance, and made clear the choice the Lord was giving them. The account of Samuel closes with a brief description of the reaction of the people who heard him.

The Sins of the Nephites

The great sin of the people in Zarahemla was that they substituted love of riches for love of God. Samuel told them that they were "cursed because of [their] riches" and that the wealth itself was cursed because they had not heard and obeyed the commandments of God, who gave them the riches. Their materialism was summed up by Samuel: "Ye do not remember the Lord your God in the things with which he hath blessed you, but ye do always remember your riches." (Hel. 13:21-22.) And their materialism brought the usual train of sins: pride, boasting, ostentatious life-style ("great swelling"), envy, strife, malice, persecution, murder, and "all manner of iniquities." If we read current news accounts of crimes committed for the sake of riches, we recognize that, as Ecclesiastes says, there is nothing new under the sun. (Eccl. 1:9-10.)

With such sins on their conscience, the Nephites further offended God by rejecting his prophets. They not only cast them out of their cities, but they also mocked and stoned them, even killing them and doing "all manner of iniquity unto them, even as they did of old." (Hel. 13:24.) But they deceived themselves with the boast that had they lived in earlier days they would not have slain the prophets or cast them out. They maintained that their present action was justified since the prophets like Samuel whom they rejected were false prophets. Samuel pointed out their hypocrisy when he described those they accepted: "Behold, if a man shall come among you and shall say: Do this, and there is no iniquity; do that and ye shall not suffer; yea, he will say: Walk after the pride of your own hearts; yea, walk after the pride of your eyes, and do whatsoever your heart desireth—and if a man shall come among you and say this, ye will receive him, and say that he is a prophet." (Hel. 13:27.) The Nephites then were not willing to take the first step of repentance: to acknowledge their sins. Instead they quieted conscience with the soothing and false counsel of "foolish and blind guides." (Hel. 13:29.)

The Consequences of Unrepented Sin

As Samuel stood on the wall of the city, the Lord "put into his heart" many prophetic warnings of what would befall the wicked who failed to repent. The prophecies deal with immediate consequences and the long-range destruction that would wipe the Nephites from the earth. The first consequence of their sins, which evidently had taken place already, was the withdrawal of the Lord's Spirit. Since the people were unwilling to listen to Samuel, they gave evidence that they had already lost the Spirit of the Lord. Now the Lord warned them that he would "suffer them no longer." (Hel. 13:8.) Nevertheless, immediately after the warning that he would "visit them in [his] fierce anger," the Lord promised mercy to those who would repent. (Hel. 13:10-11.) That there were some righteous individuals in the city was the only thing that saved it from immediate destruction. But when the time came that they would cast out the faithful, the city would be destroyed. The curse placed on the land was an ironically appropriate punishment for the sins of the people. Since they worshipped riches rather than God, the Lord cursed the land so that "whoso shall hide up treasures in the earth shall find them again no more . . . save he be a righteous man and shall hide it up unto the Lord." (Hel. 13:18.) The evil was not in the riches, but in the hearts of those who loved them more than they loved God. Therefore, they would lose the thing they had set their hearts on. Allied to this loss would be the loss of wealth and goods, which would become "slippery"; nothing could be kept safe. "Behold, we lay a tool here and on the morrow it is gone; and behold, our swords are taken from us in the day we have sought them for battle." (Hel. 13:34.) It is not surprising that in a society where wealth is more important than God, stealing should be raised to a fine art. Theft, fraud, deception, loss of treasure buried to keep it safe would bring the people to poverty—the loss of their false god.

It is interesting to note that the first warning from Samuel concerned the "heavy destruction" that would come upon the people when 400 years should pass. We know from the account in 3 Nephi that the wicked then alive would be entirely destroyed at the coming of the Savior, just a few short years away. But Samuel's warning seems to refer to the final battles of the Nephites, when they were destroyed by the Lamanites. We know that the Nephite people had been greatly blessed by the Lord throughout their history, that they had witnessed many miracles and had been taught the true gospel by many great prophets. Yet despite this evidence of God's love, they would fall into evil ways and bring destruction on themselves. Samuel must have seen that this pattern would be repeated until they would finally destroy their whole civilization.

Samuel Prophesies of Christ

Perhaps to give hope to those who may have been turned toward repentance, Samuel prophesied of the coming of the Savior in specific detail. He set an exact time: five years would pass and "then cometh the Son of God to redeem all those who shall believe on his name." (Hel. 14:2.) He told the people that there would be two days with no darkness, although they should see the rising and setting of the sun, but "the night shall not be darkened" on the night before the Savior would be born. There would also be a new star and other "signs and wonders in heaven." (Hel. 14:3-6.) How appropriate that the signs accompanying the birth of the "light of the world" should be wonders appearing in the light of heaven. The fulfillment of Samuel's prophecies is recorded in the first chapter of 3 Nephi. Samuel also told the Nephites the meaning of Christ's birth. "And it shall come to pass that whosoever shall believe on the Son of God, the same shall have everlasting life." (Hel. 14:8.)

Samuel spoke of the Savior's death, its meaning for mankind, and the signs that would accompany it. He taught that Christ "surely must die that salvation may come." (Hel. 14:15.) His death would be necessary to bring about the resurrection—overcoming physical death—which would bring man back into the presence of God. It would overcome the first spiritual death when Adam and Eve were cast out of God's presence for disobedience. Finally, "it bringeth to pass the condition of repentance, that whosoever repenteth" shall not be cast out of the presence of God a second time, thus suffering a second spiritual death, "cut off again as to things pertaining to righteousness." (Hel. 14:18.) Mortals will now have a choice: "He hath given unto you that ye might know good from evil, and he hath given unto you that ye might choose life or death; and ye can do good and be restored unto that which is good, or have that which is good restored unto you; or ye can do evil, and have that which is evil restored unto you." (Hel. 14:31.)[1] Thus the death of the Savior makes repentance and the resulting forgiveness possible; without Christ's sacrifice we would not have that choice.

Despite the necessity of Christ's death, Samuel warned the Nephites that it would be accompanied by terrifying signs. As light was the sign of his birth, so darkness would be the sign of his death: "In that day that he shall suffer death the sun shall be darkened and refuse to give his light unto you; and also the moon and the stars; and there shall be no light upon the face of this land, even from the time that he shall suffer death, for the space of three days, to the time that he shall rise again from the dead." (Hel. 14:20.) Light would be extinguished from the earth and the whole world of nature would be in turmoil. There would be tempests with thunder and lightnings, earthquakes so severe that mountains would become valleys and valleys mountains; many cities and highways would be destroyed. All of these violent signs would be given, said Samuel, "to the intent that there should be no cause for unbelief among the children of men." (Hel. 14:28.) The fulfillment of these prophecies about the death of Christ is found in 3 Nephi 8. If the people of Zarahemla had only accepted Christ and looked forward to his coming, they could have avoided the destruction of which Samuel had been sent to warn them.

The Lamanite Example of True Repentance

Perhaps in an effort to shame the Nephites into repenting, Samuel reminded them that "they have been a chosen people of the Lord; yea, the people of Nephi hath he loved, and also hath he chastened them; yea, in the days of their iniquities hath he chastened them because he loveth them." On the other hand, the Lamanites had been rejected for the evil committed "because of the iniquity of the tradition of their fathers." (Hel. 15:3-4.) But once they had been converted by righteous Nephites, they had proved more faithful than the Nephites. The example of the Lamanites follows the steps of repentance outlined by President Spencer W. Kimball:

1. Sorrow for sin.
2. Abandonment of sin.
3. Confession of sin.
4. Restitution for sin.
5. Doing the will of the Lord.[2]

Once converted, the Lamanites experienced such sorrow for their killing of the Nephites that their hearts were changed. They gave a clear sign of abandoning their sin by burying their weapons of war. Their fear that they might again be tempted to slay another human being is indicated by their willingness to "be trodden down and slain by their enemies" rather than "lift their swords against them, and this because of their faith in Christ." (Hel. 15:9.) Such action clearly confesses that their former action against those they considered enemies was sinful. They could not restore the lives they had taken, but they would give their own lives rather than commit further sin. Samuel further testified that the Lamanites were now doing the will of God: "The more part of them are in the path of their duty, and they do walk circumspectly before God, and they do observe to keep his commandments and his statutes and his judgments according to the law of Moses." (Hel. 15:5.) Not only did they follow the will of God in their daily lives, but they also sought "with unwearied diligence" and much success to convert the rest of the Lamanites. Samuel said, "There are many who do add to their numbers daily." (Hel. 15:6.) The prophet could rightfully point to the Lamanites as an example of true repentance for the Nephites, since they believed in "the holy scriptures, yea, the prophecies of the holy prophets, which are written, which leadeth them to faith on the Lord, and unto repentance, which faith and repentance bringeth a change of heart unto them." (Hel. 15:7.) Their contrast to the Nephites is reflected in Samuel's prophecy on their eventual fate. Unlike the Nephites, they would not be destroyed, but their days would be prolonged. They would suffer "afflictions," they would be "driven to and fro upon the face of the earth, and be hunted, and . . . smitten and scattered abroad, having no place for refuge," yet the Lord would show them mercy. (Hel. 15:12.) Yet their descendants would "be brought to the true knowledge . . . of their Redeemer, and . . . be numbered among his sheep." (Hel. 15:13.) Through Samuel, the Lord offered the same opportunity to the Nephites; if they would repent as the Lamanites had done, they too would be saved.

The Result of Samuel's Message

The great power of Samuel's sermon brought some of the Nephites to repentance. They sought out Nephi to confess their sins and be baptized. But most of the crowd attacked Samuel, throwing stones or shooting arrows at him in their anger at the truth. When Samuel was protected from their missiles by the Spirit of the Lord, many more of the Nephites recognized him as a prophet, believed his words, and also went to be baptized by Nephi. Nephi was likewise prophesying of the same things Samuel had foreseen, and thus those who believed Samuel were once again part of the Lord's people.

But the greater part of those who heard Samuel rejected his warning, rationalizing that the power that protected him from their attack was of the devil. When they called on their captains to seize him, Samuel "did cast himself down from the wall, and did flee out of their lands, yea, even unto his own country, and began to preach and to prophesy among his own people." (Hel. 16:7.) Samuel had followed the Lord's instructions, and some souls had been saved. The rest had assured their own destruction by rejecting God, who had lovingly sent Samuel in a last effort to reclaim them.

Their way of dealing with Samuel's prophecies when they began to be fulfilled is characteristic of those who have ears but will not hear. They "began to depend upon their own strength and upon their own wisdom, saying: Some things they may have guessed right, among so many; but behold, we know that all these great and marvelous works cannot come to pass." (Hel. 16:15-16.) They reasoned themselves into total disbelief, saying that if Christ should come, and if he were the Son of God, he would surely show himself to them as well as to those in Jerusalem, never realizing that had they believed, they would indeed have been privileged to see the Savior, that he would indeed visit his followers in their land.

To explain the courage and persistence of Samuel in bringing God's plea to their hostile ears, they "imagine[d] up in their hearts" a plot conceived by Samuel to keep them in ignorance by trying to convince them of "a wicked tradition," handed down by their fathers, of a "great and marvelous thing" which would happen in a distant land. They could have no firsthand knowledge of such a miracle, but those who maintained that it was so, did so to keep them in ignorance. Since the wicked Nephites would have to depend on the believers to teach them, they would be kept as servants to Samuel and those who taught what he taught. The lack of reason in such an explanation evidently did not trouble them, "for Satan did stir them up to do iniquity continually; yea, he did go about spreading rumors and contentions upon all the face of the land, that he might harden the hearts of the people against that which was good and against that which should come." (Hel. 16:22.)

Speaking the Word of the Lord

With our knowledge of the fulfillment of Samuel's prophecies, we might wonder how the people of Zarahemla could have been so blind to the truth. But Samuel's experience might be considered a typical one for the Lord's prophets. Elder Richard L. Evans once spoke of the general public reaction to the words of a prophet of God:

> We find ourselves often quoting the words of the prophets, and, lest there be some doubt as to what a prophet is, we submit that it is one who, under the appointment and inspiration of the Lord God, speaks truth as the spirit moves him,

regardless of what the world is thinking and regardless of what men would like to hear.

And, therefore, a prophet is seldom popular, and the cost of being a prophet is always great, for he may be called upon to say those things which are not pleasing, . . . and he may find himself fighting against a tide of mass-misconception, and, as history records, be stoned, crucified, banished, ridiculed, shunned, or rejected. For the truth is not pleasing unto all men, and time has proved that majorities are not always right. . . .

It is not important that a prophet should say those things with which you and I are in full accord. But it is important that you and I should bring ourselves into full accord with those things which a prophet speaks by virtue of his office and calling.[3]

Samuel fits this description. He spoke the word of the Lord to a people, the majority of whom were unwilling to hear him. But their unwillingness did not change the truth of his words or the fate that would fall upon them because they rejected him. The book of Helaman ends with his account, just one year before the birth of the Savior, which would mark the beginning of the fulfillment of all his prophecies.

NOTES

1. The principle of choice in salvation has been emphasized by many prophets. Moses so taught the children of Israel when they were wandering in the wilderness. (See Deuteronomy 30:15-20.) Lehi in his last sermon to his sons before his death made the same declaration. (See 2 Nephi 2:26-29.)

2. Spencer W. Kimball, "Be Ye Clean," *Brigham Young University Speeches of the Year* (Provo, 4 May 1954), pp. 8-9.

3. Richard L. Evans, *Improvement Era*, November 1939, p. 672.

12

A JUST AND A TRUE RECORD
(3 Nephi 1–5)

TERRENCE L. SZINK

Chapters one through five of 3 Nephi, covering twenty-five years of Nephite history, are primarily historical narrative, written by Mormon using the records he had at his disposal. Perhaps the most significant event in these chapters is the manifestation of the signs accompanying the birth of Christ, which Samuel the Lamanite had prophesied. In addition, there is a repetition of the cyclical pattern of righteousness-prosperity-pride-fall-repentance-righteousness, which seems to be a major theme of the Book of Mormon. In this cycle the Gadianton robbers play a major role, threatening the very existence of Nephite society. Finally, Mormon wrote directly to latter-day readers about his work as the compiler of the Book of Mormon and testified of that work.

The Fate of Nephi, the Son of Helaman

Third Nephi begins with an interesting statement about Nephi the son of Helaman. Mormon wrote that he "departed out of the land, and whither he went, no man knoweth" (3 Ne. 1:3) and that he "did not return to the land of Zarahemla, and could nowhere be found in all the land" (3 Ne. 2:9). This is reminiscent of a similar passage about Nephi's great-grandfather Alma the younger: "He departed out of the land of Zarahemla . . . and it came to pass that he was never heard of

Terrence L. Szink is a doctoral student in ancient Near Eastern studies at the University of California at Los Angeles.

more; as to his death or burial we know not of." (Alma 45:18.)[1] In Alma's day the church members speculated that he might have been "taken up" by the Lord as was Moses. Although there is no similar declaration in the Book of Mormon about Nephi the son of Helaman, he was certainly a candidate for translation considering the type of life he led and the power of God with which he was endowed.[2] Whatever his fate, he entrusted the records and the responsibilities that accompanied them to his son and namesake.

The First Christmas in the New World

In the Old World the events surrounding the birth of Christ were taking place. These would be recorded by the writers of the Gospels and come to be known as the Christmas story. This story has become, along with the accounts of Christ's death and resurrection, one of the best-known episodes in his life. No less dramatic were the happenings on the American continents.[3]

Several years had passed since Samuel the Lamanite had stood upon the walls of Zarahemla and foretold what would happen as the birth of the Savior drew near. Ironically, while the prophecies were "fulfilled more fully" the people began to doubt them even more. (3 Ne. 1:4-6.) Finally, in a way reminiscent of evil Haman's actions in the book of Esther, the wicked set a day for the death of the believers if the sign accompanying the birth of Jesus (a day, a night, and a day that should appear as one day) were not fulfilled. Nephi, sorrowed by the wickedness of the people, went before the Lord in behalf of his band of believers. We are told he prayed all day. As the evening approached, he heard the voice of the Lord: "Lift up your head and be of good cheer; for behold, the time is at hand, and on this night shall the sign be given, and on the morrow come I into the world, to show unto the world that I will fulfill all that which I have caused to be spoken by the mouth of my holy prophets." (3 Ne. 1:13.)

The mood here is similar to that of the angelic proclamation of "good tidings of great joy" to the shepherds in Judea, and rightly so, for those Nephites who had believed in the words of the prophets would be spared. That night the sign was given, and there was astonishment throughout all the land. The unbelievers saw that their plan to destroy the people of God had failed; now realizing that all which the prophets had said was true and seeing their own murderous nature, they began to fear. When the sun rose in the morning, Satan began trying to deceive the people, but so overwhelming was the power of this sign that for the time being "the more part of the people did believe, and were converted unto the Lord." (3 Ne. 1:22.) Though the conversion may have been genuine at that time, it did not last long. The passing of only three years found most of the people "hard in their hearts, and blind in their minds, and [they] began to disbelieve all which they had heard and seen." (3 Ne. 2:1.)

This slide toward general apostasy had been seen in a small group who believed that since Christ had been born it was no longer necessary to obey the law of Moses. They were most likely a sincere group of believers who had simply misunderstood the scriptures, for they "soon became converted, and were convinced of the error which they were in . . . and did confess their faults." (3 Ne. 1:25.) The law of Moses was indeed fulfilled in Christ, but not until after his death and resurrection.[4] When the resurrected Christ later appeared to the Nephites, he told them: "One jot nor one tittle hath not passed away from the law, but in me it hath all been fulfilled." (3 Ne. 12:18.) The old law would be fulfilled only when the higher law of the gospel was given in its place. (3 Ne. 12:19.)

During the first two years after the manifestation of the sign, many Nephites and Lamanites dissented and went into the wilderness to join the Gadianton robbers. These robbers hid in the mountains in caves and secret places; they were responsible for much violence among the Nephites.

The number of people who disbelieved the signs and the coming of Christ increased to such an extent that dissenters seemingly no longer felt the need to flee to the Gadianton robbers but remained with the Nephites and Lamanites. On the surface it is difficult to see how the people could fall so quickly after being converted.[5] As mentioned above, this conversion was the result of an outward sign and required no work on the part of the people. They had seen the sign but, for the most part, they did not sustain their faith. Thus Satan was able to blind their minds and harden their hearts until they "began to wax strong in wickedness and abominations." (3 Ne. 2:3.) It should also be recalled that before the sign of the night without darkness they had doubted the other signs even as they had begun to multiply. It is ironic, however, that although they did not believe the sign, "the Nephites began to reckon their time from this period when the sign was given, or from the coming of Christ." (3 Ne. 2:8.) They had previously marked time from when Lehi and his family had left Jerusalem and later from the start of the reign of the judges.[6] This is perhaps analogous to the situation in the western world where time is also calculated from the birth of Christ and yet a great number of people do not believe in Jesus as the Son of God.

The Gadianton Threat

No doubt strengthened by the number of dissenters that had joined them and encouraged by the weakening of society that usually attends any apostasy, the Gadianton robbers grew ever bolder.[7] They now began attacking entire cities successfully. To defend themselves against this threat, the converted Lamanites joined with the Nephites and were "numbered among" them. (3 Ne. 2:15-16.) This new combined army was able to achieve some success over the robbers, but this was short lived because of the general wickedness of the Nephites—for where there is corruption there is also weakness. The Lord's promise to Nephi about his descendants seems to apply in this case: "If it so be that they [the Nephites] rebel against me, they [the Lamanites, or in this case the Gadianton robbers] shall be a scourge unto thy seed, to stir them up in the ways of remembrance." (1 Ne. 2:24.)

The Nephite society was on the brink of annihilation, or as Mormon put it, "the sword of destruction did hang over them." (3 Ne. 2:19.)

At this point in the record, Mormon inserted a most unusual document—a letter written by Giddianhi, the leader of the Gadianton robbers, to Lachoneus, the governor of the Nephites. This text is interesting because it is one of the few places in the Book of Mormon that provides a glimpse of the so-called "traditions of the fathers" that characterized the groups that opposed the Nephite nation. Another example of the presentation of the alternative tradition is the letter of Ammoron, a Lamanite king, to captain Moroni, written forty-seven years earlier and recorded in Alma 54. A comparison between the two is informative. In both letters there is a request for the surrender of the Nephites (Alma 54:18; 3 Ne. 3:6-7), although in the case of Giddianhi, it is more an invitation to Lachoneus to turn the people over to him and join with him in oppressing them. Both opponents claim that they have been wronged and that they have been unjustly deprived of their "rights of government." (Alma 54:17-18; 3 Ne. 3:10.) Both letters contain a rejection of God (Alma 54:21-22; 3 Ne. 3:2); and finally, both threaten destruction (Alma 54:20; 3 Ne. 3:3-4).

The differences in the letters demonstrate that in the case of the Gadianton robbers, the Nephites were confronted with an enemy much more sophisticated and dangerous than any previous. Giddianhi's letter mentions oaths and describes his organization as a "secret society" whose works are of "ancient date." (3 Ne. 3:9.) Ancient indeed! Mormon explained that although the Gadianton robbers did not obtain their secret oaths from the twenty-four gold plates of the Jaredites, which had been discovered by an expedition sent by Limhi, they were the same oaths that secret societies have used since the foundation of the earth, for "they were put into the heart of Gadianton by that same being who did entice our first parents to partake of the forbidden fruit." (Hel. 6:26.) The oaths and plans that served as the foundation for this society were hidden up whenever the group was in danger of extinction due to the righteousness of the Nephite nation. (Hel. 11:25.) When the wickedness again allowed the robbers to operate effectively, the old plans and oaths were sought out and the Gadianton robbers returned. (Hel. 11:26.) The oaths were the glue that held the evil society together, the penalty for betrayal being death. This generated a devotion to corruption not found among any previous enemy of the Nephites. An example of this commitment is the fact that even after they were defeated by the Nephites and given a chance at freedom if they would promise to cease murdering, there were some who remained loyal to the Gadianton cause. (3 Ne. 5:5.)

Another difference in the letters is the sophisticated tone of Giddianhi's message. He continually complimented Lachoneus, referring to him as "most noble," praised his "firmness" and his "noble spirit in the field of battle." He claimed to be motivated by a feeling for the welfare of the Nephite leader. All this was intended to entice Lachoneus into selling his people out and joining with the robbers, and it is in striking contrast to the direct boldness of Ammoron's letter. Giddianhi was a "smooth operator," a man who, although apparently well educated, was entirely without conscience and not to be trusted under any circumstance.

A final difference is in the titles of the two leaders. Ammoron was the "king" of the Lamanites, while Giddianhi was the "governor of the secret society of Gadianton." We can in no way be sure that the term "governor" designated in this case an elected official of a democratic society. Yet it does serve to remind us that the Gadianton robbers began as a quasi-political organization (Hel. 2:1-5), and in the mind of its leader still was one. He claimed he was merely trying to recoup the rights of his people.

After examining Giddianhi's letter, it is clear why the Gadianton organization was so dangerous and, in fact, according to Mormon, ultimately "did prove the overthrow, yea, almost the entire destruction of the people of Nephi." (Hel. 2:13.) They were a sophisticated and murderous group who were after both political and economic power.[8] It is not difficult to see parallels to the Gadianton robbers in our day. Perhaps the most obvious examples are the rich and powerful drug trafficking organizations that threaten to destroy our society. They use many of the same tactics and have the same goals as the Gadianton robbers.[9]

As captain Moroni had done before him, Lachoneus showed true courage in his response to Giddianhi's letter. Realizing that his people were in grave danger, he sent a proclamation to all the people and told them to build strong fortifications and gather themselves together with all their animals and provisions. Furthermore, he understood that military preparations were not enough, warning his people: "As the Lord liveth, except ye repent of all your iniquities, and cry unto the Lord, ye will in nowise be delivered out of the hands of those Gadianton robbers." (3 Ne. 3:15.)

As part of the preparations, a "great prophet" who "had the spirit of revelation" named Gidgiddoni was appointed chief captain over the Nephite armies. (3 Ne. 3:19.)[10] Although the people had faith in Gidgiddoni as a prophet, they misunderstood his role in leading them. They assumed he could lead them in a successful offensive battle against the Gadianton robbers; however, he explained that the Lord would not help them launch a first-strike attack against their enemies but would only help them defend themselves.[11]

By the end of the seventeenth year (from the time of the sign of the birth of Christ), the defensive preparations were near completion. Not only had the people gathered themselves together, but perhaps more importantly "they did repent of all their sins; and they did put up their prayers unto the Lord their God, that he would deliver them in the time that their enemies should come down against them to battle." (3 Ne. 3:25.)

Almost a year passed before the armies of robbers descended from the mountains to attack the Nephites and dispossess them of their lands and property. They must have been greatly surprised to find that the Nephites had assembled in a strong defensive position and that the land had been stripped of everything. The weakness of the Gadianton robbers was now exposed: "There was no way that they could subsist save it were to plunder and rob and murder." (3 Ne. 4:5.) They were literally a parasite whose host was no longer providing food.

Giddianhi decided to attack the Nephites despite their great numbers and strong position. The description Mormon gave of the robbers as they approached is unusually detailed and graphic: "They were girded about after the manner of robbers; and they had a lamb-skin about their loins, and they were dyed in blood, and their heads were shorn, and they had headplates upon them; and great and terrible was the appearance of the armies of Giddianhi, because of their armor, and because of their being dyed in blood." (3 Ne. 4:7.)

As this army of robbers advanced, the Nephites fell to the earth in prayer, which caused the robbers to assume incorrectly that they had fallen because of fear. What followed was a horrific battle in which more life was lost than at any time since Lehi had left Jerusalem. (3 Ne. 4:11.) The robbers were beaten and Giddianhi was killed.

At least two and a half years passed before the robbers, led by a man named Zemnarihah, appeared again. This time instead of a direct attack, they tried to lay siege, but the Nephites had stored enough food to last seven years (3 Ne. 4:4) while the robbers had to rely on game hunted in the wilderness. Soon the robbers were "about to perish with hunger" and were losing large numbers of men to the Nephites who were "continually marching out by day and by night, and falling upon their armies." (3 Ne. 4:20-21.)

Zemnarihah saw that continuing the siege was useless and decided to withdraw and take his people north. Gidgiddoni knew of the robber's plan and did not want them to escape, perhaps fearing that they would only wait until they had regained strength and return. He also knew of their weakness because of lack of food and sent his troops out at night to cut off all ways of retreat and surround the robbers. Seeing their predicament, many of the robbers surrendered; those who did not were killed by the Nephites. The fate of the leader Zemnarihah is interesting: "Their leader, Zemnarihah, was taken and hanged upon a tree, yea, even upon the top thereof until he was dead. And when they had hanged him until he was dead they did fell the tree to the earth, and did cry with a loud voice, saying: May the Lord preserve his people in righteousness and in holiness of heart, that they may cause to be felled to the earth all who shall seek to slay them because of power and secret combinations, even as this man hath been felled to the earth." (3 Ne. 4:28-29.)

This ritual is similar in underlying thought to Egyptian oaths called execration texts. In such texts, the Egyptians of the Middle Kingdom ritually cursed their enemies by writing their names on bowls or figures of clay and then smashing them. As they broke the bowls or figures they believed they were destroying the power of those whose names were inscribed thereon. The following is an example of a text written on such a bowl: "All men, all people, all folk, all males, all eunuchs, all women, and all officials, who may rebel, who may plot, who may fight, who may talk of fighting, or who may talk of rebelling, and every rebel who talks of rebelling—in this entire land."[12]

Note that there is a subtle difference in the two rituals—the Egyptians directly cursed the enemy, while in the Book of Mormon the people asked that they might be strengthened through their righteousness in order that they may destroy the enemy.

The victory over the Gadianton robbers was celebrated joyously. The people praised God for their deliverance, for they realized that he had been the one who had saved them: "'Their hearts were swollen with joy, unto the gushing out of many tears, because of the great goodness of God in delivering them out of the hands of their enemies; and they knew it was because of their repentance and their humility that they had been delivered from an everlasting destruction." (3 Ne. 4:33.)

This passage contains the principle Lachoneus was trying to teach his people and the message Mormon wanted to convey to us when he wrote this section of the Book of Mormon: The only way to combat the kind of wickedness the Gadianton robbers represented is with the strength obtained through personal and collective righteousness. To overcome the evil power of secret oaths we must make sacred covenants with God and abide by them. For example, above I mentioned my belief that traffickers in illegal drugs represent a modern-day example of the Gadianton robbers. The *demand* for these drugs must be cut off just as the Nephites cut off the food supply of the army of the robbers. This can be done through obedience to the word of God.

The triumph over the robbers was complete; not one escaped. All who were not killed were cast into prison, where the word of God was taught to them. Some converted and covenanted to cease murdering; however, as noted above, some chose to remain loyal to the Gadianton philosophy. These were punished according to the law.

Significantly, Mormon wrote that at this time "there was not a living soul among all the people of the Nephites who did doubt in the least the words of all the holy prophets who had spoken; for they knew that it must needs be that they must be fulfilled." (3 Ne. 5:1.)

This statement implied that any dissenters subsequent to this period would be in willful rebellion against God. The people of the

Nephite nation remained together for another three years after the victory over the Gadianton robbers. Apparently they lived off the provisions they had stored.[13] This small period of time must have been a golden era, for the people had forsaken their sins and "did serve God with all diligence day and night." (3 Ne. 5:3.)

Mormon and His Book

At this point Mormon interrupted the narrative and inserted an explanation about the sources he was working with and a testimony of his work. These few verses are fascinating because in them Mormon stepped back from his role as editor and discussed that role with the reader. Evidently the three years following the defeat of the Gadianton robbers was a period of great literary activity. With no wars to fight and a large supply of food, the people had time to write about the experiences through which they had just passed. Perhaps these experiences, which Mormon described as "great and marvelous" (3 Ne. 5:8), included the "many signs which had been given" (3 Ne. 5:2) both preceding the birth of Christ (3 Ne. 1:4) and since that time. At any rate, Mormon wrote that his book does not contain "even a hundredth part" of all that happened. He did indicate that "there are records which do contain all the proceedings of this people." (3 Ne. 5:8-9.) He also mentioned a "shorter but true account" written by Nephi. Mormon was here referring to Nephi the son of Nephi, since at this point his remarks seem to be confined to the twenty-five years following the manifestation of the sign of the birth of Christ. This "shorter but true account" given by Nephi the son of Nephi was recorded on the large plates of Nephi and served as the basis for the Book of Mormon's version of what happened during the twenty-five years. (3 Ne. 5:9-11.)

The discussion about his sources led Mormon to testify about his record; this testimony can be best understood when compared to Nephi's statement at the beginning of the small plates. The two have many points in common: the writer or editor (a) declared that he made the plates with his own hand (1 Ne. 1:3; 3 Ne. 5:11), (b) gave a short autobiographical statement (1 Ne. 1:1; 3 Ne. 5:12-13), (c) briefly stated the source of his information—Nephi wrote "I make it according to my knowledge" (1 Ne. 1:3), while Mormon wrote: "Therefore I do make my record from the accounts which have been given by those who were before me, until the commencement of my day; and then I do make a record of the things which I have seen with mine own eyes" (3 Ne. 5:16-17), (d) testified of his record—Nephi wrote, "I know that the record which I make is true" (1 Ne. 1:3); Mormon testified in almost the same language "I know the record which I make to be a just and a true record" (3 Ne. 5:18), and (e) mentioned his language (1 Ne. 1:2; 3 Ne. 5:18).[14] So many similarities cannot be attributed to mere chance; I believe that these two prophets employed what was a specific Nephite formula for giving testimony. It is difficult to say whether the formula was a literary device or had formed part of the Nephite legal system.

It is interesting that this was the first time in the Book of Mormon, as Mormon compiled it, that he identified himself by name, for though his name appears in the Words of Mormon, that book was written on the small plates of Nephi.[15] One might have expected Mormon to introduce himself and testify at the beginning of the record, as did Nephi in the small plates of Nephi; perhaps such an introduction and testimony were found in the first part of the book of Lehi, which constituted the 116 pages of manuscript lost by Martin Harris.

Mormon finished his small personal insertion into the text with a short prophecy regarding Israel. He began by declaring that he was a "pure descendant of Lehi" (3 Ne. 5:20), implying that careful genealogy was kept among the Nephites. Third Nephi 5:21 is a statement of what the Lord had done for Israel in the past. This verse is a wonderful example of parallelism, a poetic device used often in the Old Testament.[16] The following arrangement illustrates the poetic structure:

Surely he hath blessed	the house	of Jacob
and hath been merciful unto	the seed	of Joseph.

Notice how each unit in the first half of the verse is balanced by a similar unit in the second half. The opening statement is followed by an elaboration and the prophecy concerning each group. The seed of Joseph, a subgroup of the house of Jacob, will again be brought "to the knowledge of the Lord their God." (3 Ne. 5:23.) This must have been especially meaningful for Mormon because the seed of Joseph included the descendants of Lehi. The last three verses of 3 Nephi 5 pertain to the house of Jacob as a whole. Its members will again be made aware of the covenant they have made and will come to a knowledge of Jesus Christ. Then they shall be "gathered in from the four quarters of the earth unto their own lands." (3 Ne. 5:26.)

Conclusion

These five chapters demonstrate how splendidly complex the Book of Mormon is. They contain history, prophecy, poetry, drama, and a touch of mystery (what happened to Nephi?). More importantly, their editor, Mormon, constructed them as he did the Book of Mormon as a whole, so that they teach us valuable lessons. We can learn about the significance of the Spirit's help in gaining a strong testimony, the dangers of evil organizations, and, most importantly, the power of righteousness over evil.

NOTES

I would like to thank Todd Compton, Dale Baldwin, and Dick Walker for their valuable assistance in the preparation of this chapter.

1. Nephi and Alma in fact led very similar lives. Among other things both were judges (Nephi—Helaman 3:37; Alma—Mosiah 29:42-44), both gave up their judgeship to devote more time to service in the church (Nephi—Helaman 5:1-4; Alma—Alma 4:20), both were thrown into prison because of their preachings but were miraculously delivered (Nephi—Helaman 5:21-44; Alma—Alma 14:22-28), both were granted great power (Nephi—Helaman 10:5-10; Alma—Alma 8:31), and, finally, weary with the wickedness of their people, both wished for something different than the circumstances in which they found themselves: Nephi wanted to live in the days when Lehi and his family left Jerusalem (Helaman 7:7), and Alma wanted to speak with the voice of an angel (Alma 29:1-3).

2. Other Book of Mormon commentators have also suggested that Nephi may have been translated. See Joseph Fielding Smith, *Doctrines of*

Salvation, 3 vols., compiled by Bruce R. McConkie (Salt Lake City: Bookcraft, 1954-56), 2:107, 110; Sidney B. Sperry, *The Book of Mormon Testifies,* 3rd ed. (Salt Lake City: Bookcraft, 1952), p. 285; Brian Best, "Nephi, Lehi, and Samuel the Lamanite," *Ensign* (December 1977), p. 51. Daniel Ludlow notes the similarities between Nephi and Alma but does not speculate regarding the fate of Nephi. (*A Companion to Your Study of the Book of Mormon* (Salt Lake City: Deseret Book Company, 1976), pp. 252-53.

3. Sidney Sperry included verses 4-21 of the first chapter of 3 Nephi in what he entitled "the American Gospel," maintaining that it serves as a prologue to Christ's teachings in the Nephite record in the same way the story of the birth of the Savior is an introduction to the New Testament Gospels. (*The Book of Mormon Testifies,* p. 286.)

4. See Ludlow, *A Companion to Your Study of the Book of Mormon,* pp. 253-54.

5. See Sperry, *The Book of Mormon Testifies,* p. 286.

6. For an interesting discussion of the Nephite reckoning of time see John L. Sorenson, *An Ancient American Setting for the Book of Mormon* (Salt Lake City: Deseret Book Company, and Provo, Utah: Foundation for Ancient Research and Mormon Studies, 1985), pp. 270-76.

7. Hugh Nibley has written insightfully on the problem of the Gadianton robbers. For an interesting evaluation of this society see "The Way of the Wicked," *An Approach to the Book of Mormon,* 2nd ed. (Salt Lake City: Deseret Book Company, 1978), pp. 317-36; "Good People and Bad People," *Since Cumorah* (Salt Lake City: Deseret Book Company, 1967), pp. 373-409.

8. Sorenson sees control of trade as both a primary motive and fundamental tactic of the Gadianton robbers; *An Ancient American Setting for the Book of Mormon,* pp. 300-309.

9. Recent articles in *Time* (March 14, 1988) document the seriousness of the problems caused by drug traffickers. According to the article, among other things "70% of all local crimes (in Detroit) are drug related" (p. 21), and 67% of a rising number of murders in Washington, D.C., are due to local drug wars (p. 22). According to Ed Koch, mayor of New York, "the political aim of the drug traffickers is to make addicts of all of us." (P. 20.) Attorney General Edwin Meese said about the efforts by some countries in helping the U.S. stop the supply of drugs, "They are less than fully successful because of intimidation, bribery and corruption." (P. 18.) And finally, Sterling Johnson, a special narcotics prosecutor in New York City, suggests, "Every American better just pray each night that we don't lose [the war on drugs]." (P. 20.)

10. See J. Lindblom, *Prophecy in Ancient Israel* (Philadelphia: Fortress, 1962), p. 75, for a discussion of Old Testament prophets involved in military activities.

11. See Ludlow, *A Companion to Your Study of the Book of Mormon*, pp. 254-56, for an explanation of the Lord's counsel regarding the waging of offensive war.

12. John A. Wilson, "Egyptian Rituals and Incantations," in *Ancient Near Eastern Texts Relating to the Old Testament*, ed. James B. Pritchard, 3rd ed. (Princeton: Princeton University Press, 1969), p. 329.

13. Not only had the provisions lasted seven years (year 18 to year 25) just as Mormon had said (3 Ne. 4:4), but there were some left over (3 Ne. 6:2).

14. D. Kelly Ogden has also noted some of these characteristics in "Answering the Lord's Call," *Studies in Scripture, Vol. 7: 1 Nephi to Alma 29*, ed. Kent P. Jackson (Salt Lake City: Deseret Book Company, 1987), pp. 17-18.

15. See Sperry, *The Book of Mormon Testifies*, pp. 166-67; Victor L. Ludlow, "Scribes and Scriptures," *Studies in Scripture, Vol. 7: 1 Nephi to Alma 29*, p. 202.

16. For a brief examination of parallelism in the Bible see N.K. Gottwald, "Parallelism," *Interpreters Dictionary of the Bible* (Nashville: Abingdon, 1962), pp. 830-34.

13

THE DOWNFALL OF THE NEPHITE NATION: LESSONS FOR OUR TIME
(3 Nephi 6–10)

GARY LEE WALKER

During the twenty-five years that passed after the birth of Jesus Christ in Bethlehem, both the Nephites and the Lamanites were greatly troubled by the Gadianton robbers. By A.D. 13, this band of thieves and murderers "had become so numerous, and did slay so many of the people, and did lay waste so many cities, and did spread so much death and carnage throughout the land, that it became expedient that all the people, both the Nephites and the Lamanites, should take up arms against them." (3 Ne. 2:11.) Amid this great crisis, "the converted Lamanites" joined the Nephite nation.

The next eight years were times of wars and great trials for the Nephites. Lachoneus, the righteous governor of the land, gathered his people into the central areas of Zarahemla and Bountiful and appointed Gidgiddoni, a great military and spiritual leader, to guide the Nephite army. (3 Ne. 3:13-19.) Hearkening to the counsel of their inspired leaders, the Nephite people repented "of all their sins; and they did put up their prayers unto the Lord their God, that he would deliver them in the time that their enemies should come down against them to battle." (3 Ne. 3:25.)

The faith of the righteous was rewarded, for all the Gadianton robbers were either captured or slain by the Nephite armies. (3 Ne. 5:4-6.) Thus, the Nephites "put an end to all those wicked, and secret,

---

Gary Lee Walker is a doctoral student in history at Brigham Young University.

and abominable combinations, in the which there was so much wickedness, and so many murders committed." (3 Ne. 5:6.)

The years between A.D. 26 and A.D. 29 saw the Nephites prosper and again become an industrious people. Demonstrating that they were true Saints, the Nephites preached the word of God to the incarcerated robbers and gave them the opportunity to "repent of their sins and enter into a covenant that they would murder no more." (3 Ne. 5:4.) The repentant prisoners were mercifully allowed to work on their own lands so that they might provide for themselves and live peacefully with the Nephites. (3 Ne. 6:3.) Law and order was established because "they had formed their laws according to equity and justice." (3 Ne. 6:4.) Building programs ensued that included the establishment of new cities and the repair of many old ones. (3 Ne. 6:7.) Transportation improved by way of new roads and highways that were "cast up" (3 Ne. 6:8), suggesting that the latter were major construction projects that provided significant routes to important centers throughout the land.

Pride: A Tool of Satan

Within three short years, however, the great wealth and prosperity enjoyed by the people became a burden with which they could not cope, and pride began to enter into the hearts of the rich and the powerful. (3 Ne. 6:10-11.) Many years before, the prophet Jacob had warned: "Wo unto the rich, who are rich as to the things of the world. For because they are rich they despise the poor, and they persecute the meek, and their hearts are upon their treasures; wherefore, their treasure is their god. And behold, their treasure shall perish with them also." (2 Ne. 9:30, 42.) The words of Jacob would find part of their fulfillment in the punishments that were soon to be meted out to the proud and boastful Nephites.

The record states that class distinctions developed and that learning became more important to the rich than humility. (3 Ne. 6:12-13.) The resulting feelings of inequality caused not only class distinctions but an emergence of church factions, "insomuch that the church began to be broken up" (3 Ne. 6:14) in A.D. 30. With the exception of a small group of faithful, steadfast Lamanites (3 Ne.

6:14), a general apostasy from the church resulted from the insidious pride of the people. This self-exaltation blinded the multitude from the truth as taught by the Lord's servants and provided the key for Satan to again have "great power, unto the stirring up of the people to do all manner of iniquity, and to the puffing them up with pride, tempting them to seek for power, and authority, and riches, and the vain things of the world." (3 Ne. 6:15.) With this power, the Evil One was given unlimited license to lead the Nephites to "a state of awful wickedness." (3 Ne. 6:17.)

More condemnation was brought upon the heads of the Nephites because they rejected the teachings of the brass plates and the servants of the Lord. "Now they did not sin ignorantly, for they knew the will of God concerning them, for it had been taught unto them; therefore they did wilfully rebel against God." (3 Ne. 6:18.) The high and mighty of the land joined in numerous conspiracies and had the inspired prophets murdered, which was not only an offense against God but also against the laws of the land. (3 Ne. 6:21-24.) These servants of the Lord had both warned the people of their sins and testified of the death and resurrection of Jesus Christ, which was shortly to take place. (3 Ne. 6:20.) Pride and wealth had closed the eyes and ears of the haughty Nephites and had opened the gate for Satan to seduce them into doing his bidding. Secret combinations were formed again, and covenants were made to destroy the people of God and the established government of the land. (3 Ne. 6:27-30.)

The Fruits of Rejecting God's Servants

As the wickedness of the people increased and those who had made covenants in the secret orders gained more power, the government collapsed and the chief judge was murdered. The resulting chaos brought the Nephite society into disorganization. (3 Ne. 7:1-2.) With no centralized government, the people turned to a tribal organization. Mormon recorded that they separated "one from another into tribes, every man according to his family and his kindred and friends; . . . and every tribe did appoint a chief or a leader over them; and thus they became tribes and leaders of tribes." (3 Ne. 7:2-3.)[1] Although a greater stability would be restored after the appearance of the resurrected Lord, it is interesting to note that this "tribal" organization would again prevail after the final collapse of the government around A.D. 400. One thousand years later, when the Americas were "discovered" by the Europeans, a tribal organization would still exist among the descendants of these people.

The secret combinations, now in full power, managed to elevate a leader called Jacob to the position of king. He is described by Mormon as "one of the chiefest who had given his voice against the prophets who testified of Jesus." (3 Ne. 7:10.) Although a disjointed social structure now existed in the land (3 Ne. 7:14), the various groups were united against the secret combination that terrorized them (3 Ne. 7:11). This is not to say that these tribal units were righteous, for we are told that "their hearts were turned from the Lord their God, and they did stone the prophets and did cast them out from among them." (3 Ne. 7:14.)

This period in Nephite history was a time of terror, anarchy, and bloodshed. Into this maelstrom came one of the greatest prophets of all time. Nephi, son of Nephi and grandson of Helaman (3 Ne. 1:2-3), had been given custodianship of the records by his father in A.D. 1. Greatly blessed and endowed with many spiritual gifts, this great Nephite prophet bore a final witness to the wicked of his generation. His ministrations and preachings were attended by great miracles that he performed in the name of the Lord. (3 Ne. 7:15-26.) The wicked recognized the power and authority of this great prophet, but, as is tragically true in all generations, the truth only made the wicked angry. Thus, they rejected the word of the Lord from his authorized servant. (3 Ne. 7:18, 20.) Nephi labored for three years among his people, crying repentance and baptizing those who would heed his words. By A.D. 33, he apparently experienced some success, for he ordained "men unto this ministry, that all such as should come unto them should be baptized with water." (3 Ne. 7:23-25.) The number of converts would have been relatively small, however, when one considers the destruction that would shortly befall this wicked generation.

Hundreds of years earlier, Nephi, son of Lehi, was given a vision of the great calamities that would befall the Nephite nation in A.D.

34. (1 Ne. 12:2-5.) Forty years before the crucifixion of the Messiah, Samuel the Lamanite enumerated in glorious prophecy the exact nature of the events that would accompany the voluntary death of the Savior on the cross at Golgotha, outside Jerusalem. (Hel. 14:20-28.) As A.D. 34 dawned, the people were now ripe in iniquity for the judgments of God.

On the other side of the world, at the appointed hour, the Master hung on the cross and voluntarily gave up his life with the words: "Father, into thy hands I commend my spirit." (Luke 23:46.) As the veil of the temple was torn asunder by a great earthquake, the American continent also experienced great calamities — storms, tempests, earthquakes, thunders, and lightnings "as never had been known in all the land." (3 Ne. 8:5-7.) The severity of these natural calamities cannot be overemphasized. Mormon wrote that they continued for three hours (3 Ne. 8:19), an incredible span of time when one considers the damage done to many great cities by earthquakes lasting only a few seconds.[2]

Through the violence and destructive powers of these elements, controlled and used by the Lord to fulfill His purposes,[3] "the face of the whole earth became deformed." (3 Ne. 8:17.) The destruction was devastating: great cities were destroyed by fire or covered by the sea or with earth; plain areas, once level and smooth, were rippled and disfigured and covered with rocks and boulders thrown up from the bowels of the earth; great chasms swallowed entire towns and their populations; buildings were leveled; people were carried away in great whirlwinds, never to be seen again. (3 Ne. 8:8-18.) Jacobugath, the center of government of king Jacob and the secret combinations, was burned with fire "because of their sins and their wickedness, which was above all the wickedness of the whole earth, because of their secret murders and combinations; for it was they that did destroy the peace of [the] people and the government of the land." (3 Ne. 9:9.)

After the three hours of destruction had passed, a thick darkness fell over the land, "insomuch that the inhabitants thereof who had not fallen could feel the vapor of darkness." (3 Ne. 8:20.) As terrible as the natural calamities had been, the ensuing darkness must have been equally horrifying if not more so, for it lasted for three days. (3 Ne. 8:23.) During this time, the darkness was so oppressive that no light shone from the sky and no fire could be kindled. (3 Ne. 8:21-22.) Recognizing their sins and the evils that they had allowed to consume their lives, the survivors howled and lamented. (3 Ne. 8:23-25.) We are not told how many of the Nephites perished, but the number must have been great when one considers the magnitude of the natural disasters unleashed by the Lord. Mormon wrote: "It was the more righteous part of the people who were saved, and it was they who received the prophets and stoned them not; and it was they who had not shed the blood of the saints, who were spared." (3 Ne. 10:12.)

The Voice of the Lord to a Stricken People

As the remaining Nephites lamented their tragic state in the oppressive darkness, the voice of the Lord was heard throughout the land, dispelling the spiritual darkness that had so long engulfed the nation. (3 Ne. 9:1.) The extent of the destruction was revealed to the survivors. The Messiah stated that he had caused the deaths of the wicked. His purpose, he said, was "to hide their wickedness and abominations from before my face, that the blood of the prophets and the saints should not come up any more unto me against them." (3 Ne. 9:8.) After promising eternal life to all who would repent and follow him, Jesus declared his divinity and announced that the preparatory law of Moses was now "fulfilled." (3 Ne. 9:14-17; 15:5.) The new requirement of a broken heart and a contrite spirit was declared. (3 Ne. 9:20.) After Jesus attested to his resurrection, silence fell over the land. (3 Ne. 9:22; 10:1.)

The words of the Master had a tremendous impact on the multitude, for "they did cease lamenting and howling for the loss of their kindred which had been slain." (3 Ne. 10:2.) Although there would be more tears and lamentation (3 Ne. 10:8), hope was surely beginning to return to the stricken people. Later, the voice of the Lord again spoke to the Nephites, telling them how many times he had warned them and had tried to save them from the calamities, if only they would have heeded his words spoken by his servants. (3 Ne.

10:4-7; compare D&C 43:24-25.) During this period, there were great noises because the earth was in constant commotion. (3 Ne. 10:9.) As the elements and the earth returned to normal, the people found joy in their survival and in the words spoken by the Lord. (3 Ne. 10:10.)

Mormon concludes his words by testifying that the events of the past three days had been foretold by many prophets, including Zenos and Zenock, whose records are still lost to us. (3 Ne. 10:15-17.) He revealed that the Nephites and Lamanites were descendants of the ancient Israelite prophets, which may help account for the extensive quoting of their words in the Book of Mormon.[4] He ended his account by announcing the greatest event recorded in the Book of Mormon: the appearance of Jesus Christ to the righteous remnants of the Nephites and the Lamanites.

Lessons for Our Time

President Ezra Taft Benson has stated that the Book of Mormon "was written for our day."[5] He has counseled us to ask ourselves while studying these scriptures: "Why did the Lord inspire Mormon (or Moroni or Alma) to include that in his record?"[6] Asking this question can bring great insight as one reads the Nephite history recorded in 3 Nephi 6-10. Although there are many lessons to be learned by carefully studying these chapters, the striking parallels between the ancient Nephite nation and our generation are significant.

The period of Nephite history under consideration took place just a few short years before the death and resurrection of the Lord Jesus Christ. Our present generation is living in the twilight years before his glorious second coming. The condition of our time is very similar to that of the Nephite nation prior to A.D. 34. They were greatly blessed with learning, and many acquired great wealth and position. Paul, speaking of our time, said that people would be "ever learning, and never able to come to the knowledge of the truth" (2 Tim. 3:7), referring to the gospel plan. These words equally apply to the Nephites before A.D. 34. Their pride and self-aggrandizement blinded them to the teachings of the servants of the Lord. Their achievements in learning caused them to forsake righteousness. How strikingly poignant are the words of Mormon as he described the sorry state of his people who "had turned from their righteousness, like the dog to his vomit, or like the sow to her wallowing in the mire." (3 Ne. 7:8.)

The pride and self-exaltation of the Nephites created an atmosphere of contention that resulted in class distinctions and church factions. Satan was given power to control the minds and actions of the wicked Nephites. Today, he again is exhibiting great strength in disrupting societies and world peace. The earth abounds with false religions, false philosophies, and church factions. Moroni, in speaking of our time, said it would be "a day when the power of God shall be denied, and churches become defiled and be lifted up in the pride of their hearts; yea, even in a day when leaders of churches and teachers shall rise in the pride of their hearts, even to the envying of them who belong to their churches." (Morm. 8:28.) He continued on to prophesy that there would be "churches built up that shall say: Come unto me, and for your money you shall be forgiven of your sins." (Morm. 8:32.) The Nephites allowed wickedness to corrupt and destroy their churches and society. Can we not learn from their bad example and avoid disputations and controversies that might cause contention in our churches, communities, and families?

As the apostasy in the land rapidly increased, the Nephites again entered into forbidden covenants and secret combinations. Prophets and authorized ministers were killed, and Satan ruled supreme. Again, the parallels to our day are obvious. Speaking of our time, the Lord said that "iniquity shall abound" (JS–M 1:30) and that "the whole earth shall be in commotion" (D&C 45:26). Our day witnesses political unrest, terrorist activities, destruction of life and property, wars and riots, and political movements that are committed to the overthrow of righteous institutions. Does not this sound like Nephi's description of his day (compare 3 Ne. 6-7)? As we contemplate these tragic occurrences of our time, we need only to study 3 Nephi 8-9 to ascertain the fate that awaits the wicked of our generation if they continue on their present course.

Moroni, by the gift of prophecy, foresaw our day and wrote in vivid detail about the conditions that would prevail in it. (See Morm. 8:26-40.) In vision, he saw our time plagued by the very problems mentioned in the preceding paragraph. The Doctrine and Covenants explicitly describes the events of the last days and the signs and wonders that will be displayed and recognized by the righteous prior to the Second Coming. The Nephites also had been given prophecy and signs that told of the death and resurrection of the Lord. (3 Ne. 8:3-4.) If the signs had been heeded instead of doubted, many thousands more of the Nephites would have been saved from the destructions and calamities that accompanied the death of the Savior on the cross.

Elder Bruce R. McConkie, in speaking about the details of the events recorded in 3 Nephi 8-10, wrote: "No single historical event in the whole Book of Mormon account is recorded in so great detail or at such extended length as the fulfillment of the signs signifying that Jesus had been lifted up upon the cross and had voluntarily laid down his life for the world."[7]

The Lord desired that these events be testified of in our generation; this is one of the purposes of the coming forth of the Book of Mormon in our time. We can benefit from the careful reading of the tragic events that befell the major portion of the Nephite nation. Surely these things are a pattern of what is yet to come at the Second Coming. The Lord has preserved these accounts for our generation to learn from and to serve as a warning to the wicked of the world. In the Lord's preface to the Doctrine and Covenants, he said: "The voice of the Lord is unto all men, and there is none to escape; and there is no eye that shall not see, neither ear that shall not hear, neither heart that shall not be penetrated. . . . And the voice of warning shall be unto all people." (D&C 1:2, 4.)

The voice of the Lord can be found within the pages of the Book of Mormon. It is for our day. The catastrophic events that befell the wicked Nephites at the time of the death and resurrection of Jesus Christ are a pattern of occurrences yet to come. Our goal is to prayerfully search the Book of Mormon and study the lessons contained therein, that we may be warned and prepared.

NOTES

1. See Daniel H. Ludlow, *A Companion to Your Study of the Book of Mormon* (Salt Lake City: Deseret Book Company, 1976), p. 258.

2. See *Book of Mormon (Religion 121-122) Student Manual*, 2nd ed. (Salt Lake City: The Church of Jesus Christ of Latter-day Saints, 1979), pp. 390-91 for some interesting facts about the destructive force of modern-day earthquakes.

3. Bruce R. McConkie, *Mormon Doctrine*, 2nd ed. (Salt Lake City: Bookcraft, 1966), pp. 211-12. Also see *Conference Report*, April 1977, pp. 4-5 for President Spencer W. Kimball's remarks on the Lord's use of the weather to discipline his people.

4. Ludlow, *Companion*, pp. 244, 260.

5. *Ensign*, Nov. 1986, p. 6.

6. Ibid.

7. Bruce R. McConkie, *The Promised Messiah: The First Coming of Christ* (Salt Lake City: Deseret Book Company, 1978), p. 542.

14

THE APPEARANCE OF CHRIST TO THE PEOPLE OF NEPHI
(3 Nephi 11–14)

S. Brent Farley

"I am the light and the life of the world." (3 Ne. 9:18.) The apex of the Book of Mormon is revealed in the personal appearance of Jesus Christ to the more righteous part of Lehi's descendants, who had witnessed the sweet and the bitter in the years preceding this grand event. A night with no darkness had heralded the day of the Savior's birth. Numerous conversions were countered by rampant apostasy. Civil war raged as the Gadianton robbers threatened destruction. Murderous villians took the lives of prophets, while others like Nephi stood with such power that none could disbelieve their words. Finally, God himself rained destruction upon rampant wickedness as city after city was destroyed in the Americas. As the devil laughed in his darkened kingdom, the Savior revealed his word and his will to those who remained upon the earth, saved from destruction by their righteousness.

Soon after the holocaust, a great multitude of people was gathered, marveling about the great changes that had occurred in the earth's surface. Significantly, they were gathered near the temple in Bountiful, a land whose name signifies a plenteous bestowal of gifts. As they were discussing the mission of Christ, "they heard a voice as if it came out of heaven," a small or quiet voice that "did pierce them to the very soul, and did cause their hearts to burn." (3 Ne. 11:3.)

S. Brent Farley is an instructor at the LDS Institute of Religion at Utah State University.

A solemn awe overshadowed them as they cast their eyes around, not understanding the communication. A second time the voice came. A second time they did not understand. As they attuned themselves in deep concentration, they were prepared by the Father for the introduction of his Son. When the voice came the third time, they listened with more than their physical ears, for they were able to decipher the sound as they gazed intently toward heaven, whence the voice came. "Behold my Beloved Son, in whom I am well pleased, in whom I have glorified my name — hear ye him." (3 Ne. 11:7.)

The very reading of such a glorious account brings peace to the heart; but how much more so when we read that "they saw a Man descending out of heaven; and he was clothed in a white robe; and he came down and stood in the midst of them." (3 Ne. 11:8.) None dared to speak; eyes were fixed upon this being they thought to be an angel. But what a glorious thrill must have surged through their souls as they heard the words, "Behold, I am Jesus Christ, whom the prophets testified shall come into the world." (3 Ne. 11:10.) Before them stood a God; a premortal brother; a perfect man now clothed with a resurrected, immortal body of flesh and bone. He had paid the awful price of the sins of all humanity in the garden of Gethsemane and upon the cross. He was, under the Father, the very creator of the earth upon which he now stood. He was, in the sight of the gathered multitude, the one being in all eternity who could open to them the gates of heaven if they so believed.

Who could possibly comprehend the emotions of those who gazed at their Savior? But imagine further their feelings at his invitation: "Arise and come forth unto me, that ye may thrust your hands into my side, and also that ye may feel the prints of the nails in my hands and in my feet, that ye may know that I am the God of Israel, and the God of the whole earth, and have been slain for the sins of the world." (3 Ne. 11:14.) Obediently and with solemn reverence they went forth "and thrust their hands into his side, and did feel the prints of the nails in his hands and in his feet; and this they did do, going forth *one by one* until they had *all* gone forth, and did see with their eyes and did feel with their hands, and did know of a surety and did bear record, that it was he, of whom it was written by the prophets, that should come." (3 Ne. 11:15, emphasis added.) The prints of the nails in his hands and his feet! Little children had felt; the aged touched; the sick and the lame reached out to his hands; not one soul was left out. All had come to Christ, one at a time, and gained the sure witness of his divinity. In unity they cried out: "Hosanna! Blessed be the name of the Most High God!" (3 Ne. 11:17.) Then they fell again to their knees in worship.

Authority and Ordinances

What would the Lord do next? How long would he stay? Would he have any more to say to his people? If so, what would have greatest priority? He called Nephi from the congregation. Nephi was the prophet, the mouthpiece of the Lord; he would stand as the representative of Christ upon that continent when Jesus again ascended into heaven. He would speak to the church, as directed by the Lord. Then the Twelve were called forth. As with the old world, so with the new: The Church of Jesus Christ would be directed by a prophet at the head of the church and a quorum of twelve other leaders. (3 Ne. 11:18-22.)

Primary emphasis was placed upon baptism. In just twenty-two verses containing the opening remarks of the Savior, the word *baptism* (or one of its forms) occurs nineteen times. (3 Ne. 11:22–12:2.) Without valid baptism by one having authority from the Lord, we could not return to dwell with the Father and the Son in heaven. Baptism is, in the literal and eternal sense, a unifying ordinance between God and his people. Hence, the principle of unity as exemplified in the Godhead was connected with the instructions regarding baptism: "After this manner shall ye baptize in my name; for behold, verily I say unto you, that the Father, and the Son, and the Holy Ghost are one." (3 Ne. 11:27.) Given the new church organization (no longer under the law of Moses), all were to be baptized as an entrance into the Lord's newly formed church.[1]

In the beginning of chapter 12, the Twelve were commissioned and presented to the multitude "to be your servants" (verse 1); they were given power and authority from God to unify his children in harmony with gospel principles and ordinances. If the people accepted the Lord's representatives as ministers of the gospel and complied with their preaching, God himself would baptize them "with fire and with the Holy Ghost." (3 Ne. 12:1.) Believing God's servants was tantamount to believing God.

The Beatitudes

The resurrected Christ next gave to the disciples the unifying course of instruction that he had given to his disciples in Judea, now known as the Sermon on the Mount. This beautiful discourse provides a pattern by which one can follow the example of the Savior and strive for perfection. The prelude is referred to as the Beatitudes.

1. "Blessed are the poor in spirit who come unto me, for theirs is the kingdom of heaven." (3 Ne. 12:3.) In one sense, to be "poor in spirit" is to realize that we are nothing in mortality without a Savior. Without an atoning sacrifice, none could leave mortality to return to the presence of God. In fact, all would die only to become angels to the devil, to remain in misery forever. (2 Ne. 9:8-9.) How destitute and poor indeed!

Being "poor in spirit" is not to feel continuous hopelessness because of our fallen state; it is to feel continuous dependence upon the Savior. We realize the difference between God and his mortal children, appreciate the condescending love of the Savior, and humbly seek to unify ourselves with God. We never attribute greatness to ourselves but seek to emulate the example of the Atoning One to the best of our mortal ability, ever aware of the need to overcome weakness and resist temptation.

2. "Blessed are all they that mourn." (3 Ne. 12:4.) Who would not mourn at the hopeless prospect of our fallen state? But they shall be comforted. Our lost and fallen state may be overcome. A Savior was provided whereby all will be resurrected and all may be saved in the kingdom of God. What great comfort! A Savior atoned for the sins of all who would accept him. Thus all may become blessed and happy if they so choose.

When the humble Saints mourn over trial and difficulty, they are promised comfort. They are given the peace that comes from Christ, wherein their hearts are not to be troubled or afraid. (John 14:27.)

They are given "the Comforter, which is the Holy Ghost" to teach them and guide them. (John 14:26.) When death, trial, or tragedy strikes, their hearts are softened and comforted by the Spirit of Truth, which whispers peace and opens the perspective of eternal joy. If one sins, the mourning is a godly sorrow that brings repentance, forgiveness, and the comfort of restored peace. (2 Cor. 7:10; Mosiah 4:3.)

3. "And blessed are the meek, for they shall inherit the earth." (3 Ne. 12:5.) Elder Bruce R. McConkie explained: "In the scriptural sense the meek are the God-fearing and the righteous. . . . [They] are those who keep the commandments and are fit persons to associate with Him in whom meekness was perfected."[2] To be meek is to be mild and gentle. It does not imply weakness, for the prime example of meekness calmed the angry waves, cast out devils, and performed mighty miracles. To be meek is to be humble. It is a characteristic of strength.

4. "And blessed are all they who do hunger and thirst after righteousness, for they shall be filled with the Holy Ghost." (3 Ne. 12:6.) The closer we grow to God, the greater is our desire to improve. This desire is like thirsting for water or hungering for food. It is a critical longing for nourishment and health: it is the longing for the health of the spirit. Those who sup at the table of the Lord become as dependent upon his words for their spirits as they are upon food for their bodies. The satisfaction of that desire for righteousness is fed by the constant companionship of the Holy Ghost. Losing that closeness is akin to the threat of starvation.

5. "And blessed are the merciful, for they shall obtain mercy." (3 Ne. 12:7.) The merciful are those who are "compassionate; tender; unwilling to give pain; not cruel."[3] Such shall receive the blessing of mercy, which "tempers justice, and induces . . . [forgiveness of] trespasses and injuries, and to forbear punishment, or inflict less than law or justice will warrant. In this sense, there is perhaps no word in our language precisely synonymous with *mercy*. That which comes nearest to it is grace."[4]

6. "And blessed are all the pure in heart, for they shall see God." (3 Ne. 12:8.) To be pure is to be free from the taint of unrepented

sins. This, of course, is only possible through the gospel of Jesus Christ. Though none are perfect in this life (except for the Savior), those who are striving to the best of their abilities qualify for the ongoing and renewable quality of purity of heart. Such may obtain closeness to God and see him. This may be symbolic in the sense of recognizing the hand of God in all things and feeling his influence in life, but its apex is literal. This promise has the seal of God, who testified: "It shall come to pass that every soul who forsaketh his sins and cometh unto me, and calleth on my name, and obeyeth my voice, and keepeth my commandments, shall see my face and know that I am." (D&C 93:1.) Elder Bruce R. McConkie testified: "We have the power—and it is our privilege—so to live, that becoming pure in heart, we shall see the face of God while we yet dwell as mortals."[5] It is not a requirement that we see God in this life in order to be saved; it is a possible blessing. However, it is a guaranteed right of all who are pure in heart to see God, whether in this life or the next, or in both.

There follow two more beatitudes (peacemaking and enduring persecution); but what could be a more transcending point than to qualify to do what the Nephite/Lamanite culture was now doing—to see the face of the Lord?

The Higher Plane of the Gospel

Those who follow the path marked by the beatitudes are accounted as "salt" and "light"! (3 Ne. 12:13-16.) Salt has a distinctive property (or savor) that enhances the flavor of foods. Its addition tends to bring out the best of that to which it is added. So would the Saints become the enhancers of those who accept the gospel. The commission to do this had a warning, however. If the savor was lost, then "wherewith shall the earth be salted? The salt shall be thenceforth good for nothing, but to be cast out and to be trodden under foot of men." (3 Ne. 12:13.) Salt does not lose its savor by age, but rather by mixture and contamination. Correspondingly, the gospel does not lose its savor by age, but rather when it is mixed with the philosophies of men and devils. Salt is also a preservative. The gospel was intended to be preserved in purity. Its effects were to preserve the Saints in righteousness that they might attain their celestial destiny. How appropriate was the Lord's analogy!

The Saints, the "salt of the earth," were to be the lights to which people in a darkened world could seek. In the book of Revelation, the church organizations were compared to candlesticks, and the servants in those organizations were compared to stars. (See Rev. 1:20.) Jesus himself had "his countenance . . . as the sun shining in his strength." (JST, Rev. 1:16.) What was the light that would emanate from the mortal servants? It was not the light of their own development, but rather the light of the master they served. "Behold I am the light which ye shall hold up—that which ye have seen me do." (3 Ne. 18:24.) The commission to be a light to the world had two aspects: (1) a missionary charge to guide others to Christ, and (2) a charge to remain faithful and constantly progress until perfect.

The symbolism of light and salt were appropriately placed together in the sacred text. Old Testament sacrificial rituals used salt as a token of gospel covenants. (See Lev. 2:13 and Num. 18:19.) The Lord explained to Joseph Smith: "I have sent mine everlasting *covenant* into the world, to be a *light* to the world, and to be a standard for my people, and for the Gentiles to seek to it, and to be a messenger before my face to prepare the way before me." (D&C 45:9; emphasis added.) Thus salt represents the gospel covenant, which is a light to the world.

The higher plane of Christianity for which the law of Moses served as a schoolmaster was now contrasted with the letter of the Mosiac law. It was well known that killing was condemned and carried an awful penalty; but short of this heinous sin, anger also carried a condemnation that could bring the punishment of hell. Even the manifestation of contempt ("Raca") or belittlement ("thou fool") toward a fellow being carried a punishment so terrible as to merit a sentence in hell. (3 Ne. 12:22.) To come to God required one's best efforts to live in unity with one's brothers and sisters. (3 Ne. 12: 23-26.)

Next to murder in seriousness was adultery, expressly forbidden by God. Jesus also noted the seriousness of lust: "Whosoever looketh on a woman, to lust after her, hath committed adultery already in his heart." (3 Ne. 12:28.) The thoughts precede the actions: "For as he thinketh in his heart, so is he." (Prov. 23:7.) Jesus was teaching accountability for thoughts as well as actions; either of these could cost one's salvation. Controlling the mind and impulses could obliterate the outward commission of serious sin. Knowing that Satan often clothes temptations in attractive apparel, Jesus commanded denial; therein would one take up his cross (3 Ne. 12:29-30), for it would be a battle and a trial to learn to resist the influence of Satan.

What was the ultimate goal the Lord had in mind for those who controlled their thoughts and actions? It was perfection. "Therefore I would that ye should be perfect even as I, or your Father who is in heaven is perfect." (3 Ne. 12:48.) The gospel is a ladder of progression whose top rung sits in eternity, but whose legs are planted firmly upon the earth. The Savior was teaching how to take the steps on this side of the veil. In so doing, his followers would be building a Zion society. They would be striving to be "of one heart and one mind, and [to dwell] in righteousness." (Moses 7:18.)

Attached to that definition of Zion was the injunction that there be "no poor among them." The Savior expressed his will that "ye should do alms unto the poor." (3 Ne. 13:1.) The giving of alms is most often associated with money; the Greek origin, however, suggests "kindness" and "kind acts."[6] Monetary support is only a portion of almsgiving. The Saints were to help the unfortunate; but they were not to do it to build their own reputations. They were to do it to build up the poor and help establish Zion. "Take heed that ye do not your alms before men to be seen of them; otherwise ye have no reward of your Father who is in heaven." (3 Ne. 13:1.)

The Lord's Prayer

As with the giving of alms, so with the offering of personal prayers. The hypocrites prayed in public for public reward, and that was what they received. The Saints were to pray in secret to their Eternal Father, who, hearing in secret, would reward them openly. Vain (or fruitless) repetitions were unnecessary and unhelpful; lengthy prayers (for the sake of expounding) were not approved. (3 Ne. 13:5-8.) The Lord repeated to his American Saints the concise model referred to as "the Lord's prayer." The total prayer could easily be read in less than thirty seconds. The intent was not to encourage short prayers but to make a valid contrast with the "much speaking" and the "vain repetitions" of the hypocrites, who prayed for show. In doing so, the Lord left a basic pattern to guide the secret prayers of the children of his kingdom.

"Our Father who art in heaven, hallowed be thy name." (3 Ne. 13:9.) All prayers were to be directed to the Father of our spirits, the Heavenly Parent from whose presence we came at birth. It was to be a Father/son or Father/daughter relationship between him and his offspring; that attitude and that goal should temper our prayers.

"Thy will be done on earth as it is in heaven." (3 Ne. 13:10.) (The phrase "thy kingdom come" was dropped, the establishment of the church possibly fulfilling that plea). We typically give thanks early in our prayers for the blessings we have received. We then typically (and rightfully) ask for the Lord's help in our daily concerns. Whatever the plea, whether for self or family, for sacred purpose or secular, the guiding principle is that it should all be in harmony with God's will. That is a guiding principle of prayer.

"And forgive us our debts, as we forgive our debtors." (3 Ne. 13:11.) Since "all have sinned, and come short of the glory of God" (Rom. 3:23), then all need the redemptive power gained through repentance and forgiveness. The debts we would most want to be relieved of are our debts to justice when we have sinned. Such relief is available through repentance. And, as we are seeking mercy, we are required as a prerequisite to extend mercy to others. "I, the Lord, will forgive whom I will forgive, but of you it is required to forgive all." (D&C 64:10.) This relieves the one offended of the destructive burden that resentment and anger can cause.[7]

"And lead us not into temptation, but deliver us from evil." (3 Ne. 13:12.) Or, as the Joseph Smith Translation of Matthew 6:14 clarifies, "And suffer us not to be led into temptation." A basic and regular element of our prayers should be a plea for help in avoiding the pitfalls and snares laid by Satan. He is a major adversary to God, and thus to God's children. Temptation is a constant threat, and the devil a constant foe; it is necessary and wise in our prayers to seek guidance to follow the path of the Lord and avoid the crossroads offered by Perdition. Our plea is that in the end we will be delivered from evil forever to dwell with God in his kingdom of glory.

"For thine is the kingdom, and the power, and the glory, forever." (3 Ne. 13:13.) We acknowledge that God's plan is perfect and that his kingdom is the greatest reward for the human race. His is the glory forever, which he is willing to share with those who humbly and diligently seek to do his will on earth. As thoughts precede actions, so do prayers precede progress.

Building upon the Rock of Christ

When harmony exists between prayers and actions, mortal endeavors build eternal rewards "where neither moth nor rust doth corrupt, and where thieves do not break through nor steal." (3 Ne. 13:13.) But it requires the commitment of the heart; if the heart is set on earthly treasures, then the reward will be that of the hypocrites: an earthly reward. When the heart is set upon the things of heaven, then the light of heaven is borne in upon that soul until the fullness of light is attained. No compromise is possible between light and darkness. "Ye cannot serve God and Mammon." (3 Ne. 13:24.) "Mammon" refers to riches. The problem is not that a good person cannot be rich and righteous; the problem is that if the person serves riches, he or she has crowded out the true God for a false one of worldly origin. (3 Ne. 13:19-24.) How many souls have been purchased by Satan through wealth!

After giving special instructions to the Twelve (3 Ne. 13:25-34), Jesus addressed the topic of judgment. In the familiar words of the biblical account, he said, "Judge not, that ye be not judged." (3 Ne. 14:1; Matt. 7:1.) The Joseph Smith Translation adds an important qualification: "Judge not unrighteously, that ye be not judged: but judge righteous judgment." (JST, Matt. 7:1-2.) Life is a series of judgments, but caution is especially needed when we judge our fellow beings. Misjudgment is common because we know not the hearts, minds, and intents of those around us. Jesus asked: "Why beholdest thou the mote that is in thy brother's eye, but considerest not the beam that is in thine own eye?" (3 Ne. 13:3.) The mote referred to a speck or chip, whereas the beam referred to a large wooden beam used in constructing buildings. Before we can judge another and offer help, we must be rid of the impairments to our own vision, which may consist of false information, hypocrisy, sin, or any number of things. Being in tune with the Spirit is the only safe basis for judgment: "He that is spiritual judgeth all things." (1 Cor. 2:15.) Some priesthood leaders (such as bishops and stake presidents) are given a special commission of judgment; they are to judge under the inspired direction of their Master, to whom all judgment is given. (John 5:22.)

The Savior promised that to those who asked would be given; to those who knocked, the door would be opened. (3 Ne. 14:7-8.) What were the qualifications for worthy asking and receiving? The golden rule (3 Ne. 14:12) and the keeping of the commandments (referred to as a strait or narrow gate and a narrow way—verses 13-14). Those who entered therein and remained upon the path of obedience would obtain. Those who led in other directions were "false prophets, who come to you in sheep's clothing, but inwardly they are ravening wolves." (3 Ne. 14:15.)

Their fruits would give them away (3 Ne. 14:16-23), for many of their hearts would be set on mammon, whether of money, of public acclaim, or of Satanic obedience. Their homes would be upon sandy foundations and would fall when the storms came. (3 Ne. 14:26-27.)

Those who brought forth good fruit would be solidly anchored, for they followed the teachings of the Savior. They listened and applied; they progressed along the narrow way as explained in the Sermon on the Mount; they judged righteous judgment and were humble. They sought from the Lord and obtained from his hand. They were the ones who heard the Lord's sayings and did them. They were likened "unto a wise man, who built his house upon a rock." (3 Ne. 14:24-25.) The rock upon which they built was Christ. The Christ now stood before them, teaching eternal truths with eternal rewards. God himself translated heavenly concepts into language appropriate to the understanding of his listeners. His truth was consistent and constant. It was intended for all: for those who were listening first-hand, and for those millions who would later read the account. The scripture produced came directly from the lips of the Savior of the world; he knew whereof he spake. And so do those who follow his teachings, for the Spirit of Truth enters their hearts just as readily as in the days of the Nephite and Lamanite congregation there, in his presence.[8]

NOTES

1. Joseph Fielding Smith, *Answers to Gospel Questions,* (Salt Lake City: Deseret Book Company, 1960), vol 3, pp. 205-6.

2. Bruce R. McConkie, *The Millennial Messiah* (Salt Lake City: Deseret Book Company, 1982), p. 698.

3. Noah Webster, *1828 American Dictionary Of The English Language* (San Francisco: Foundation For American Christian Education, 1985), "merciful."

4. Ibid., "mercy."

5. Bruce R. McConkie, *Conference Report,* Oct. 1977, p. 52.

6. Robert Young, *Young's Analytical Concordance to the Bible* (Grand Rapids: Wm. B. Eerdmans Publishing Companion, 1970), p. 28.

7. Marion D. Hanks, *Conference Report,* Oct. 1973, pp. 15-16.

8. For further information on the Sermon on the Mount, see Robert A. Cloward, "The Sermon on the Mount in the JST and the Book of Mormon," pp. 163-200 in *The Joseph Smith Translation: The Restoration of Plain and Precious Things,* ed. M. S. Nyman and R. L. Millet (Provo, Utah: Religious Studies Center, Brigham Young University, 1985); Catherine Thomas, "The Sermon on the Mount: The Sacrifice of the Human Heart," pp. 236-50 in *Studies in Scripture, Vol. 5: The Gospels,* ed. Kent P. Jackson and Robert L. Millet (Salt Lake City: Deseret Book Company, 1986).

15

CHRIST'S AUTHORITY, HIS OTHER SHEEP, AND THE REDEMPTION OF ISRAEL
(3 Nephi 15-16)

ROBERT J. MATTHEWS

Jesus was speaking to about twenty-five hundred assembled Nephites on his first visit to them after his resurrection. (3 Ne. 17:25.) He had just shown them his glorified body and told them he was the promised Messiah whom the prophets had testified would come. They had examined the marks of the crucifixion in his hands, feet, and side. He selected twelve special disciples and testified to the multitude of their divine calling. (3 Ne. 12.) These twelve were, in fact, apostles, although the record does not specifically so designate them. (See Moroni 2:1-3.)[1]

Jesus then gave the Nephite twelve and multitude instructions similar to the Sermon on the Mount, with some important variations due to the different setting and circumstances of this sermon compared to the one in Palestine. (Compare Matt. 5-7 with 3 Ne. 12-14.)

The Authority of Jesus

That portion of the Savior's instruction that parallels the Sermon on the Mount seems to have a natural ending at the close of 3 Nephi 14, concluding with the parable of the houses built on sand and on rock. However, readers of the New Testament will remember that Matthew 7:28-29 adds a comment that Jesus' hearers in Palestine

Robert J. Matthews is professor of ancient scripture at Brigham Young University.

were "astonished at his doctrine: for he taught them as one having authority, and not as the scribes." The JST records this as: "He taught them as one having authority from God, and not as having authority from the Scribes." (JST Matt. 7:37.) At first glance it appears that this item concerning Jesus' authority is missing in the 3 Nephi account. Its parallel however, is in fact found in the subsequent chapter, in 3 Nephi 15:1-10. The two-verse, one-sentence observation of 28 words in Matthew is in 3 Nephi a ten-verse, thirteen-sentence, 364-word declaration by Jesus. The 3 Nephi expression includes several concepts dealing with Jesus' authority. First Jesus affirmed that the instruction he had just given them contained "the things which I taught [in the Holy Land] before I ascended to my Father" (v. 1). He then explained: "I am he who gave the law" to Moses, and "the law in me is fulfilled" (vv. 3-8). He further established his identity, and thus his authority, by saying that he, Jesus, was the God who covenanted with Israel (v. 5). Earlier, at the beginning of this visit, he had declared to the multitude that he was "the God of Israel, and the God of the whole earth," and had "been slain for the sins of the world." (3 Ne. 11:14.)

Jesus further attested to his authority by saying, "I am the law, and the light. Look unto me . . . and ye shall live," and he promised that unto those who obey him to the end, he would "give eternal life." (3 Ne. 15:9.) The authority theme is continued with Jesus saying: "*I* have given unto you the commandments; therefore keep *my* commandments. And this is the law and the prophets, for they truly testified of *me*" (v. 10, emphasis added).

It would be difficult to miss the point that Jesus in these verses was giving an unqualified statement of his authority and primal position (under the Father) both on earth and in heaven. As noted, this is a much stronger statement than the brief comment by Matthew at the close of the Sermon on the Mount, yet it is parallel to it in its placement at the end of the Sermon.

Other Sheep

The remaining fourteen verses of chapter 15 deal chiefly with a detailed explanation that the Nephites and the Lamanites are the "other sheep" once spoken of by Jesus to the Jews in Palestine, as recorded in John 10:16. Most readers of the Book of Mormon are aware that Jesus visited these "other sheep" in America. However, the Savior was so definitive on this point that it deserves particular attention. The passage in John 10:16 was cited by Jesus in 3 Nephi 15:16-17 as follows: "This much did the Father command me, that I should tell unto them: That other sheep I have which are not of this fold; them also I must bring, and they shall hear my voice; and there shall be one fold, and one shepherd."

Jesus said that the Father had commanded him to teach the Jews about the "other sheep," but when he did so (as explained in this verse), the Jews failed to understand the meaning. It appears that it was not only the multitude of the Jews but even the brethren in the Jewish Church who missed the meaning. This failure came from "stiffneckedness and unbelief." Therefore Jesus was "commanded to say no more of the Father" to the Jews about the subject. (3 Ne. 15:18.)

The Jews thought that the "other sheep" were the Gentiles. (3 Ne. 15:22.) This is suggested also in John 7:35, when the unbelieving Jews said, "Will he go unto the dispersed among the Gentiles, and teach the Gentiles?" This misconception has been a popular inter-pretation by modern biblical scholars also.[2]

It is at this point in Jesus' explanation that the doctrine becomes extremely valuable to our understanding of Jesus' worldwide mission, and also as an aid to the intepretation of scripture. Jesus' words to the Nephites are as follows:

> Verily I say unto you, that ye are they of whom I said: Other sheep I have which are not of this fold; them also I must bring, and they shall hear my voice; and there shall be one fold, and one shepherd. And they [the Jews] understood me not, for they supposed it had been the Gentiles; for they understood not that the Gentiles should be converted through their preaching. And they understood me not that I said they shall hear my voice; and they understood me not that the Gentiles should not at any time hear my voice — that I should not manifest myself unto them save it were by the Holy Ghost. But behold, ye have both heard my voice, and seen me, and

ye are my sheep, and ye are numbered among those whom the Father hath given me. (3 Ne. 15:21-24.)

The crux of the statement is that Jesus will not at any time manifest himself personally nor by his audible voice to a Gentile nation. Such an event is declared to be a blessing reserved for those who are of the house of Israel. The Gentiles are to be converted through the preaching of those who are of Israel, and Jesus will manifest himself to the believing Gentiles through the Holy Ghost. This same concept is referred to in 1 Nephi 10:11, wherein Lehi said that Jesus would "make himself manifest, by the Holy Ghost, unto the Gentiles." This procedure is a provision of, and is in harmony with, the covenant to Abraham, as stated in Abraham 2:9-10, that Abraham's descendants have the responsibility of the ministry and will carry the priesthood and the gospel unto all nations.

Emphasis on the covenant of Abraham, which places a responsibility for the ministry on his literal seed, does not mean that a faithful Gentile has less access to the blessings of heaven than do those of Abraham's seed. Once a Gentile has the gospel and obeys it, all the blessings of eternal life are offered to that person. But in the timetable and economy of the Lord, in the meridian of time and even before, those of literal Israelite lineage had the first opportunity to receive the gospel, and also the responsibility to carry it to the other nations. It is a priority of opportunity, not only in the time of Jesus, but ever since the time of Abraham himself.

The Sheep of Yet Another Fold to Be Visited

In addition to clearly establishing the identity of the Book of Mormon peoples as the "other sheep" of John 10:16, the Savior told of yet other "sheep" of Israel whom he would visit. He had already alluded to this third group in 3 Nephi 15:20 with the words: "The other tribes hath the Father separated from them [the Jews]; and it is because of their [the Jews'] iniquity that they [the Jews] know not of them." In other words, because of their own unbelief the Jews did not know of the Nephites or of the other tribes.

The Savior then told the Nephites about the third group, the so-called "lost tribes," by saying precisely these things about them: (1)

"I have other sheep, which are not of this land [America], neither of the land of Jerusalem, neither in any parts of that land round about whither I have been to minister." (3 Ne. 16:1.) (2) These other sheep had never been visited personally by the Savior, but (3) they were about to receive such a visit. This would probably be similar to his visit to the Nephites. We read: "They of whom I speak are they who have not as yet *heard my voice*; neither have I at any time manifested myself unto them. But I have received a commandment of the Father that I shall go unto them, and that they shall *hear my voice*, and shall be numbered among my sheep, that there may be one fold and one shepherd; therefore I go to *show* myself unto them." (3 Ne. 16:2-3; emphasis added.)

General information concerning the "lost tribes" need not be a mystery. They were captured and led away from the land of Palestine about 735-721 B.C. by the Assyrians. (2 Kgs. 15-17.) They consist primarily of all the tribes of Israel except Judah and Benjamin, which are the Jews. Nephi makes reference to them in his own day, about 130-150 years after the tribes had departed from Palestine: "It appears that the house of Israel, sooner or later, will be scattered upon all the face of the earth, and also among all nations. And behold, there are many who are already lost from the knowledge of those who are at Jerusalem. Yea, the more part of all the tribes have been led away; and they are scattered to and fro upon the isles of the sea; and whither they are none of us knoweth, save that we know that they have been led away." (1 Ne. 22:3-4.)

And Jacob added: "The Lord God has led away from time to time from the house of Israel, according to his will and pleasure. And now behold, the Lord remembereth all them who have been broken off." (2 Ne. 10:22.)

Later Nephi quoted the Lord as saying:

> I shall speak unto the Jews and they shall write it; and I shall also speak unto the Nephites and they shall write it; and I shall also speak unto the other tribes of the house of Israel, which I have led away, and they shall write it; and I shall also speak unto all nations of the earth and they shall write it.
>
> And it shall come to pass that the Jews shall have the words of the Nephites, and the Nephites shall have the words

of the Jews; and the Nephites and the Jews shall have the words of the lost tribes of Israel; and the lost tribes of Israel shall have the words of the Nephites and the Jews. (2 Ne. 29:12-13.)

In 3 Nephi 17:4 Jesus told the Nephites he was ready to visit the "lost tribes of Israel" and to "show" himself unto them, "for they are not lost unto the Father, for he knoweth whither he hath taken them." The Tenth Article of Faith speaks also of the restoration of the ten lost tribes. Furthermore, the keys for gathering them were given to the Prophet Joseph Smith in the Kirtland Temple on April 3, 1836. (D&C 110:11.)

It seems natural to conclude that when we receive the record of the lost tribes, it will contain an account of Jesus' visit, showing his body to them with the same unmistakable evidence as he did to the Nephites, whereby they saw him, touched him, heard him, and knew for a certainty that he is the God of Israel and was slain for the sins of the world and raised from the grave as a resurrected personage.

Ask and Ye Shall Receive

It is very clear in the material we have covered that the Savior revealed much more to the Nephites (and thus to all who read the Book of Mormon) than he did to the Jews, and he was desirous that a record should be kept of this visit. Therefore Jesus commanded the Nephites to write an account of it. A major concept at work in this whole episode is that one must seek for spiritual knowledge. The rule, as given in 3 Nephi 14:7-8, and in many other places, is that knowledge is given to those who ask, seek, and knock. If we do not ask for gospel knowledge, we probably will not receive it. Hence the Lord's instructions were as follows:

> I command you that ye shall write these sayings after I am gone, that if it so be that my people at Jerusalem, they who have seen me and been with me in my ministry, do not ask the Father in my name, that they may receive a knowledge of you by the Holy Ghost, and also of the other tribes whom they know not of, that these sayings which ye shall write shall be kept and shall be manifested unto the Gentiles, that through

the fulness of the Gentiles, the remnant of their seed, who shall be scattered forth upon the face of the earth because of their unbelief, may be brought in, or may be brought to a knowledge of me, their Redeemer. (3 Ne. 16:4.)

The Lord wanted the various groups of scattered Israel to be known, especially in the last days, and if the Jewish New Testament apostles didn't ask, and therefore didn't learn of these groups (and consequently would not include it in the New Testament), the world could, in the last days, receive an awareness of these groups from the Book of Mormon.

Since the New Testament contains only the one brief mention in John 10:16, and since no explanation or further identification is given, then in light of the Savior's instruction in 3 Nephi 16:4 (cited above), we conclude that the New Testament people did not ask and did not receive the information. We are therefore doubly indebted to the Book of Mormon for its singular ability to enlarge our comprehension of the Savior's worldwide mission and personal visits to the various groups of Israel—the Jews, the Nephites, and the lost tribes.

Pattern Prophecies of Isaiah

The Lord continued his instruction by saying that since those peoples who are on a national basis primarily descendants of Israel (the Jews, Lehi's descendants, the other tribes, etc.) will have rejected the gospel, in the "latter day" the truth shall come first to the Gentiles and from them to the house of Israel. (3 Ne. 16:7.) This is a reversal of the order in earlier days.

However (the Lord continued), if the Gentiles do not honor the gospel after having so great a blessing offered to them, and after having scattered the remnants of Israel (the Lamanites) in the Americas, the Lord will then remember the covenants he made with the forebears of present-day Israel (that is, the covenants with Abraham, Isaac, Jacob, Joseph, Moses, Lehi, Nephi, Jacob, Enos, Mormon, etc.) and will put judgments upon the Gentiles and take the fullness of the gospel away from them. He will bring forth his people Israel out of obscurity, out of oppression, and Israel will be gathered and restored to the true Church and fold of God. Israel will then be blessed with the same knowledge and the same promises of salvation that were given to their righteous fathers. (3 Ne. 16:8-16.)

Jesus informed his hearers that at the time of gathering and restoration of Israel, these words of Isaiah would be fulfilled: "Thy watchmen shall lift up the voice; with the voice together shall they sing, for they shall see eye to eye when the Lord shall bring again Zion. Break forth into joy, sing together, ye waste places of Jerusalem; for the Lord hath comforted his people, he hath redeemed Jerusalem. The Lord hath made bare his holy arm in the eyes of all the nations; and all the ends of the earth shall see the salvation of God." (3 Ne. 16:18-20; Isa. 52:8-10.)

There is a lesson to be observed here. Blessings once offered become cursings if they are rejected. The Gentiles will be given great opportunity, but if they "sin against" the gospel and treat it lightly, they will lose it and have to bear the consequences.

The events spoken of in this chapter dealing with the Gentiles and the reclamation and restoration of Israel, whether it be the Jews, the Nephites and Lamanites, or the lost tribes, is a pattern that will be repeated wherever there are Gentiles who do not believe and Israelites who do believe. In the foregoing passage, Isaiah speaks of "Jerusalem," yet Jesus used these verses with reference to the Nephites. Much of Isaiah's prophesying can be termed what I call "pattern prophecies." They can and will be fulfilled at different times and in different places, among the various groups of Israel. Therefore, Nephi wrote, "Hear ye the words of the prophet [Isaiah] . . . and liken them unto yourselves." (1 Ne. 19:23-24; 2 Ne. 11:8.)

"Gentiles" in the Book of Mormon

The Book of Mormon speaks of the Gentiles on the American continent, in contrast to the Nephites and Lamanites, who are Israelites. It is the Gentile who will bring the gospel to the Lamanites. The Book of Mormon will come forth "by way of the Gentile." (See 1 Nephi 15:17; also title page.) The early settlers of North America of European heritage are spoken of as Gentiles. (1 Ne. 13:13-19.) Yet, Latter-day Saints of European descent hold that they are of Israel, particularly descended through Joseph and Ephraim. They learn this through their patriarchal blessings. This merits additional discussion.

Two terms frequently appearing in the scriptures are *Israel* and *Gentile.* These were originally used to designate distinct peoples. Israel meant the literal descendants of Jacob and the twelve sons of Jacob, or house of Israel. The Gentiles, as the word literally means, were "the other people." The word "Gentile" first appears in Genesis 10:4-5 with reference to the descendants of Japheth. Eventually both of these words were enlarged in their scope to include land designations—the land where the Israelites lived, and the land where the Gentiles lived. Still a third meaning eventually developed, so that "Israel" designated those who by covenant accept the true religion, and "Gentiles" meant those who did not. This is evident in Paul's statement, "They are not all Israel, which are of Israel." (Rom. 9:6.) That is, Paul says there is believing Israel and there is blood Israel, and sometimes these two conditions are not found in the same people. Thus a Gentile, one not genealogically of the blood of Israel, may become an Israelite by adoption through his or her belief, baptism, and the action of the Holy Ghost.[3]

America, as is the case with Europe, has been peopled by those who have been without the fullness of the gospel for many centuries, yet they have much of the blood of Israel in their veins. They are not easily identified or recognized as Israelites and therefore are spoken of as Gentiles, in contrast to those of more recognizable Israelite identity such as the Jews and the Lamanites. Hence, the great American nation is spoken of in the Book of Mormon as a Gentile nation, even though we, as Church members, know we have the blood of Israel in us. This condition is described by the Prophet Joseph Smith in D&C 109:58, 60, saying we are "the sons of Jacob" but are "identified with the Gentiles."

It is actually a fact that the membership of the Church is largely of the literal seed of Abraham through Joseph, by blood descent. This is the message of D&C 86:9-10: "Ye are lawful heirs, according to the flesh, ... and the priesthood ... must needs remain through you and your lineage." The same concept is continued in D&C 90:10; 96:7; 98:32; 113:8; 132:30-31.[4]

The Lord is using the descendants of Joseph, through Ephraim and Mannasseh, being drawn out of Gentile society, to bring the gospel to the world in the last days. As Joseph fed his brothers with bread in ancient times and thus was a blessing to them — although for a long time they did not know or recognize him — so in the last days the seed of Joseph, ordained and clothed with the gospel of salvation, has the "bread of life" to nourish the inhabitants of the earth who are in an impoverished spiritual condition.

As it was anciently, so is it now. The recipients have hardly recognized or sensed that their benefactors are the literal descendants of Joseph, fulfilling their responsibility under the covenant of Abraham. That Joseph's seed should have such a mission is the message of an informative textual restoration found in JST Genesis 48:8-11, with Jacob speaking to his son Joseph:

> O my son, [God] hath blessed me in raising thee up to be a servant unto me, in saving my house from death; in delivering my people, thy brethren, from famine which was sore in the land; wherefore the God of thy fathers shall bless thee, and the fruit of thy loins, that they shall be blessed above thy brethren, and above thy father's house; for thou hast prevailed, and thy father's house hath bowed down unto thee, even as it was shown unto thee, before thou wast sold into Egypt by the hands of thy brethren; wherefore thy brethren shall bow down unto thee, from generation to generation, unto the fruit of thy loins for ever; for thou shalt be a light unto my people, to deliver them in the days of their captivity, from bondage; and to bring salvation unto them, when they are altogether bowed down under sin. (JST Gen. 48:8-11.)

The "bondage" spoken of in verse 11 must not be confused with the bondage of Israel in Egypt, for it was Moses (of the tribe of Levi) and not Joseph's seed who led Israel out of that. It is a spiritual bondage of the last days, a universal apostasy, from which Joseph's seed rescues his brothers and sisters in the fullness of times. A careful reading of the passage makes this clear, as does the subsequent chapter of Genesis wherein Joseph, speaking to his brethren, prophesies first of Moses and of Aaron, and then of a latter-day seer named Joseph as found in JST Genesis 50:24-38. This prophecy, which was in the plates of brass, is the basis of Lehi's words in 2 Nephi 3:6-18, and is also restored to us through the Joseph Smith Translation of Genesis by the Prophet Joseph Smith.

NOTES

1. See also the chapter heading to Moroni 2, and Joseph Smith, the "Wentworth Letter," *History of The Church of Jesus Christ of Latter-day Saints*, 2nd ed. rev., edited by B. H. Roberts (Salt Lake City: The Church of Jesus Christ of Latter-day Saints, 1932-51), 4:538.

2. For example, the noted and respected F. F. Bruce approvingly quotes R. A. Knox as saying of John 10:16, "Our Lord evidently refers to the Gentiles who would believe him." (F. F. Bruce, *The Books and the Parchments* [London: Revell Company, 1955], p. 199.) The Reverend J. R. Dummelow in his *Commentary on the Holy Bible* (New York: MacMillan, 1960, p. 792) also interprets the "other sheep" of John 10:16 as the Gentiles and writes, "The Gentiles are also God's children. The gospel is for them also, and Jew and Gentile shall form one Church under one shepherd."

3. Joseph Smith, *Teachings of the Prophet Joseph Smith*, selected by Joseph Fielding Smith (Salt Lake City: Deseret Book Company, 1938), pp. 149-50.

4. Further reading on this subject can be found in Joseph Fielding Smith, "Who are the Gentiles?" *Answers to Gospel Questions*, 5 vols., compiled by Joseph Fielding Smith, Jr. (Salt Lake City: Deseret Book Company, 1957-66), 1:138-41; Bruce R. McConkie, "Gentiles," *Mormon Doctrine*, 2nd ed. (Salt Lake City: Bookcraft, 1966); and Bruce R. McConkie, *A New Witness for the Articles of Faith* (Salt Lake City: Deseret Book Company, 1985), pp. 518, 529-30.

16

THEOPHANY
(3 Nephi 17–19)

CATHERINE THOMAS

Only after 1830 could one who sought God turn to a book to read about the true nature and post-resurrection ministry of the living, corporeal, resurrected Son of God. But when Joseph Smith entered the grove in 1820, the world had lain more than 1,600 years in ignorance of the nature of God. About A.D. 180 Irenaeus, Bishop of Lyons, France, wrote: "The Father of all is at a vast distance from those affections and passions which operate among men. He is a simple, uncompounded Being, without diverse members, and altogether like, and equal to Himself, since He is wholly understanding, and wholly spirit, and wholly thought, and wholly intelligence, and wholly reason, and wholly hearing, and wholly seeing, and wholly light, and the whole source of all that is good."[1]

A few years after Irenaeus, Origen (ca. A.D. 230), a church scholar, described the Father and the Son: "Setting aside all thought of a material body, we say that [Christ] was begotten of the invisible and incorporeal God apart from any bodily feeling, like an act of will proceeding from the mind."[2] Much of the Christian world today repeats creeds that describe a passionless, bodiless God.

The Prophet Joseph had seen more truth in a short interview with the Father and the Son than centuries of theological sophistry could discover. Further truths concerning the nature of God poured into our dark world through the pages of 3 Nephi. Joseph Smith

Catherine Thomas is a doctoral student in ancient history at Brigham Young University.

remarked near the end of his life: "If men do not comprehend the character of God, they do not comprehend themselves."[3] We will examine here several insights from 3 Nephi 17-19 that pertain to the divine nature and its implications for man.

The First Day: God Revealed As a Man

One of the first doctrines to disappear when apostasy conceives in the hearts of mortals is the fact that God is a glorified man. When people repress that doctrine, they forget who they really are and what they may become (cf. the Zoramites, Alma 31:15). One of the first things Joseph Smith learned as the Lord undertook to educate him was that he was created in the literal image of the Father and the Son. Many express outrage at this doctrine, believing that it diminishes God and at the same time presumptuously exalts man. But Joseph Smith did not invent the idea. The Bible plainly speaks of man's creation in the image of God (Gen. 1:26-27); Jacob saw God face to face (Gen. 32:30); God has feet (Ex. 24:10); he has a finger (Ex. 31:18); Moses saw his face (Ex. 33:11) and his back parts (Ex. 33:23) and spoke to God mouth to mouth (Num. 12:8). The "eyes of the Lord" and the "ears of the Lord" occur frequently in the Prophets and in Psalms. In Genesis God walks about in the garden. (Genesis 3:8.)

As apostasy progressed in the intertestamental period, as well as in the post–New Testament period, many theologians found the idea that God has a body and emotions to be an embarrassment.[4] In spite of the fact that both the Old and New Testaments abound in expressions of God's love, joy, sadness, pity, and compassion, theologians of the third and fourth centuries A.D. preferred to envision God as impassible. R.M. Grant writes: "From the writings of early Christians after New Testament times we can discover relatively few references to God's love, though a few writers provide exceptions. In general the themes which were first developed were those related to God's transcendence and his relation to the cosmos."[5] Hilary of Poitiers (ca. A.D. 350) declared that Christ felt the *assault* of suffering but not the *pain* of suffering; it was as if a weapon were to pierce water or fire or air. He allowed that Christ did display thirst and sorrow and hunger, but only for the sake of others, not to satisfy his own needs.[6] Origen and other fathers avoided the themes of Christ's physical suffering in Gethsemane and of the atonement. The writings of even the Apostolic Fathers (second century A.D.) showed a marked weakening of the atonement idea, giving a minor place to the atoning value of his death.[7] These themes of the nebulous and unfeeling nature of God sufficiently distanced God from mortals that they could occupy themselves with irrelevant spiritual debates. Settling for less in God, they could require less of themselves. But in Joseph Smith's day a new generation had come to the earth, and it was ripe for restoration of true doctrine.

With the sweet refreshment of simple truth, 3 Nephi described the appearance of the resurrected Christ: From heaven a Man descended clothed in a white robe. He declared he was the Christ and invited the people to confirm that by coming forward and thrusting their hands into his side and feeling the prints of the nails. (3 Ne. 11:14.) Twenty-five hundred people (3 Ne. 17:25), one by one, saw with their eyes, felt with their hands, and bore record that it was indeed Christ (3 Ne. 11:15).[8] Each person saw and felt the tangible body of the resurrected Christ. The Apostle John declared: "Every spirit that confesseth that Jesus Christ is come in the flesh is of God: and every spirit that confesseth not that Jesus Christ is come in the flesh is not of God: and this is that spirit of antichrist." (1 Jn. 4:2-3.)

God's Response to Man's Desire

As it grew late in the first day of the Savior's visit, and he had finished the teaching tasks of that day, he looked round on the people and declared: "Behold, my time is at hand." (3 Ne. 17:1.) "Go ye unto your homes, and ponder upon the things which I have said, and ask of the Father, in my name, that ye may understand, and prepare your minds[9] for the morrow, and I come unto you again. But now I go unto the Father and . . . unto the lost tribes of Israel." (3 Ne. 17:4.) Emotionally and physically spent, the people were overwhelmed. Yet their eyes held his.

Earlier the Lord taught them: "Blessed are all they who do hunger and thirst after righteousness, for they shall be filled with the Holy

Ghost." (3 Ne. 12:6.) They were not satisfied; they were hungry. They yearned for him. His intent was to go to the bosom of his Father and to visit the Lost Tribes, but the Nephites' desire prevailed with him. He invited them to bring their sick. As many as could crowd near him kissed his feet and bathed them with their tears. (3 Ne. 17:10.) He was compelled by their longing for him. They brought all their children. Then Jesus commanded the multitude to kneel. Groaning "within himself," he prayed; he was standing: "Father, I am troubled because of the wickedness of the people of the house of Israel." (3 Ne. 17:14.) Kneeling, he continued his prayer, uttering things that could not be written; but those of the multitude who heard him bore record (3 Ne. 17:15): "The eye hath never seen, neither hath the ear heard, before, so great and marvelous things as we saw and heard Jesus speak unto the Father; and no tongue can speak, neither can there be written by any man, neither can the hearts of men conceive so great and marvelous things as we both saw and heard Jesus speak; and no one can conceive of the joy which filled our souls at the time we heard him pray for us unto the Father." (3 Ne. 17:16-17.) Jesus arose to find the multitude overcome with joy. His joy was full in theirs. (3 Ne. 17:20.) Weeping, he took the children one by one,[10] blessed them, and prayed to the Father for them. Then he wept again (3 Ne. 17:22): "Behold your little ones." The heavens opened, and angels descended in a fiery element that encircled the children; the angels ministered to them.[11]

Rendering comfort, relief, and healing knowledge belong to eternity. The whole host of heaven serves the cause of the healing and exaltation of God's children. Such simple virtues will continue into the eternities. Whatever Christ models for us is designed to endure in us. Whatever he teaches us he himself practices. Jesus, even though master of all, is servant of all. (Matt. 20:27.)

Bread of Life and the Mind of Christ

The Savior's next act was to institute the sacrament. (3 Ne. 18.) The Nephites ascended in their divine experience. They had witnessed outward manifestations of the Holy Ghost; now Jesus showed them how they could realize the promise of being inwardly filled in

175

their hunger for the divine presence. He blessed bread and wine and instructed them to eat.

The Lord uses the image of "eating," whether fruit or bread or fish or living water, to provide a tangible symbol of obtaining a higher spiritual life, as though one could "eat" to replace one's old self with new cells of more dynamic and gifted life. Adam and Eve ate a new way of life (Gen. 3); the ancient Israelites ate the elements of the Passover and were delivered from spiritual and physical death (Ex. 12); they lived by the manna from heaven in the wilderness (Ex. 16); Lehi ate the fruit of the tree of Christ's love (1 Ne. 8); Jeremiah, Ezekiel, and John ate the words of Christ (Jer. 15:16; Ezek. 3:1; Rev. 10:10); Jesus bade the squeamish Jews to live by eating his flesh and blood (John 6:48-58). In each case, the people "ingested" the Holy Ghost, or obtained access to blessings through Christ. (1 Cor. 2:16.) The scripture records that the disciples and multitude were filled. (3 Ne. 18:4-5.) They were not only physically satisfied from an abundance of food, but also with what bread and wine represent: the spirit and body of Christ through the atonement. (3 Ne. 18:7.) Their physical satisfaction served as a device to teach spiritual satisfaction. In the sacrament covenant we promise to keep the commandments in exchange for the power to keep the commandments. We eat the emblems of the atonement to receive the spirit, the power, and the mind of Christ. The sacrament is not optional; it is the ordinance that unlocks the flow of the Holy Ghost and provides progression along the path of light and fulness.

True Prayer

True prayer is characterized by the presence of the Holy Ghost; that is, the Holy Ghost shows us what we may ask for and what we may obtain power to do: "Wherefore . . . feast upon the words of Christ; for behold, the words of Christ will tell you all things what ye should do. . . . It [the Holy Ghost] will show unto you all things what ye should do." (2 Ne. 32:3, 5.) The words of Christ come not only from the scripture, but through the Holy Ghost as well.

Now that the multitude had eaten the sacrament, they were prepared to receive the mind of Christ through prayer. He is the light;

he has set the example in prayer. (3 Ne. 18:16.) If we do not pray, we are in danger, because without the influence of Christ, we will absorb the influence of Satan. (3 Ne. 18:15, 18.) The Lord taught specifics:

1. (V. 19.) We pray to the Father of our spirits in the name of Christ, who is the Father of our spiritual rebirth. Our first Father holds the power of exaltation (Matt. 20:23; 3 Ne. 27:14-16); our second Father, Christ, holds the power of our spiritual rebirth on the path to our exaltation.

2. (V. 20.) (a) Ask aright, (b) believe, (c) receive: Prayer is *labor* in the spirit. Casually done, it has no power. We strain upward in spirit to grasp the answers we seek. We live for the Holy Ghost so that when we pray, we know what to ask for. Having power in the Holy Ghost, we have assurance that what we pray for will be granted. We believe, that is, we envision the realized blessing and actively receive it. "Believing," as it is used in the scriptures, signifies powerful confidence born of personal righteousness. (Hel. 14:13.)

3. (Vv. 21-23.) We learn that we may draw down the blessings of heaven on our loved ones, on the community of Saints, and on those who come to investigate. Prayer is not optional. We simply cannot move forward on the path of light without the Holy Ghost to illuminate the way.

The light that we must hold up, that must not be veiled in bushels of sin, fear, or pride, is the spirit of Christ that springs in us: "Behold I am the light which ye shall hold up—that which ye have seen me do." (3 Ne. 18:24.) We hold up, not the darkness of our own wills, but the light and love of God as Jesus demonstrated. He calls us to his works—not only sacrament, baptism, and so on, but also mighty miracles.

The image of holding up a light suggests that we hold up Christ's light in a dark world so those who are lost may come and have refuge in Jesus. Christ has given all in total consecration to the cause of saving God's children. We are to do the same in giving ourselves physically ("that ye might feel and see" [3 Ne. 18:25]) as well as spiritually, standing always behind his will rather than trotting ours out to the fore, being blind guides. (D&C 19:38-41.) For us to give less than all is by definition temptation and sin. (3 Ne. 18:25.) In fact, the implication is that if we do not actively and with full purpose of heart pursue the dissemination of Christ's light, we will find ourselves at cross purposes with God's will. Consecration saves us from ourselves.

Though we pray for and nurture those who live at the fringes of gospel commitment, the sacrament is reserved only for those in full fellowship. An unworthy person who takes the sacrament enters into spiritual chaos. If dangerous to the flock, the person shall not be numbered among them; that is, he or she may not be kept on the records of the church. But our responsibility to *minister* to the person continues as long as he or she will be ministered to. We never give up on someone lest Christ should "heal" the person and we be the means of bringing salvation to him or her. (3 Ne. 18:32.)

"And now I go unto the Father, because it is expedient that I should go unto the Father for your sakes." (3 Ne. 18:35.) The Lord made a similar statement to his apostles in Jerusalem: "It is expedient for you that I go away: for if I go not away, the Comforter will not come unto you; but if I depart, I will send him unto you." (John 16:7.) Christ had unveiled his glory to these Nephites. Spiritual realities were visually present with him. But we are here to live by faith, not by sight (2 Cor. 5:7), even though we lived by sight in our premortal home. It is not helpful for us at this stage of our progression to live with external visual heavenly manifestations. That fact underlies our separation from our premortal home. The reason is that *inner* perceptors of truth may not develop in the presence of manifestations. Now that we live on earth, we have even greater need for contact with our Heavenly Father. The Holy Ghost is sent to provide this contact by developing these inner perceptors. When those spiritual senses are developed, then we may reenter the presence of heavenly beings. The Second Comforter, or the physical presence of Christ and the Father, can come when we have developed our inner spiritual senses through the Holy Ghost.

The Savior's last act on this first day was to give his twelve disciples power to bestow the indispensable gift of the Holy Ghost (3 Ne.

18:36-37), that unseen link with the spiritual world. A heavenly cloud veiled his ascension into heaven.

The Second Day: Transfiguration

Through the night the people made known widely the fact that Jesus would return the next day. At the appointed time, Nephi and the rest of the Twelve divided the multitude into twelve groups; each disciple commenced teaching. After prayer, they accurately repeated the very words that Jesus had spoken the day before. (3 Ne. 19:8.) They prayed as Jesus had taught them, which was to pray for the Holy Ghost. Then Nephi baptized the rest of the Twelve, who received the Holy Ghost[12] and the baptism of fire; angels returned to minister again. Jesus appeared in the midst of this heavenly fire, and at his command his disciples began to pray to him, calling him their Lord and God. (3 Ne. 19:18.) Jesus explained in 3 Nephi 19:22 that they prayed to him rather than the Father because Jesus was with them. But the instruction under all other circumstances was to pray to the Father in the name of Jesus Christ. (3 Ne. 19:7.) We want to ask what they prayed to him. We cannot answer fully until we have experienced this kind of prayer ourselves, because the experience is grasped in one's spirit. But one thing we observe is that Jesus — even after his resurrection — continued to set the example in prayer.

Jesus thanked the Father for the giving of the Holy Ghost and prayed that all who heard the words of his disciples would believe them. The Lord encircled them with his love and righteousness, and they entered together into at-one-ment as Jesus prayed for that state of oneness. (3 Ne. 19:23.) It was a joyful fruition of his recent painful atonement.

It is the possession of the fullness that brings people into oneness with each other. As the Father has granted fullness to the Son, so a portion had been granted through the Holy Ghost to the disciples.

Jesus returned from prayer to find the disciples still praying: "It was given unto them what they should pray, and they were filled with desire. And it came pass that Jesus blessed them as they did pray unto him; and his countenance did smile upon them, and the light of his countenance did shine upon them, and behold they were as white as the countenance and also the garments of Jesus; and behold the whiteness thereof did exceed all the whiteness, yea, even there could be nothing upon earth so white as the whiteness thereof. And Jesus said unto them: Pray on; nevertheless they did not cease to pray." (3 Ne. 19:24-26.)

The Holy Ghost performs two of his functions in these passages: he fills those praying with catalytic desire, and he burns out impurities and cleanses them. In this process the disciples were transfigured, being empowered to endure the presence of heavenly elements and beings without being wholly consumed. (D&C 76:118.)

"Father, I thank thee that thou hast purified those whom I have chosen, because of their faith, and I pray for them, and also for them who shall believe on their words, that they may be purified in me, through faith on their words, even as they are purified in me." (3 Ne. 19:28.) We grasp here the meaning of the promise to those disciples who believe the words of the Lord's apostles and prophets. We too can experience this increasing purification and glory of the Lord. The Holy Ghost performs this purification for our entrance into the Lord's presence. We cannot cleanse ourselves. This process is initiated by our desire and effort, but it is consummated by the power of the Lord. (D&C 88:74.)

"Father, I pray not for the world, but for those whom thou hast given me out of the world, because of their faith, that they may be purified in me, that I may be in them as thou, Father, art in me, that we may be one, that I may be glorified in them." (3 Ne. 19:29.) Jesus spoke of being *glorified*. As we understand from D&C 93, *glory* is a manifestation related to light, truth, and intelligence; that is, to fullness. The reception of the fullness causes one to be glorified.

"When Jesus had spoken these words he came again unto his disciples; and behold they did pray steadfastly, without ceasing, unto him; and he did smile upon them again; and behold they were white, even as Jesus." (3 Ne. 19:30.) What does the shining, smiling face of God signify? The smile reflects the joy in God's nature and his giving of that joy to his receptive children. Elder Melvin J. Ballard experienced that divine smile:

As I entered the door, I saw, seated on a raised platform,

the most glorious Being my eyes have ever beheld or that I ever conceived existed in all the eternal worlds. As I approached to be introduced, he arose and stepped towards me with extended arms, and he smiled as he softly spoke my name. If I shall live to be a million years old, I shall never forget that smile. He took me into his arms and kissed me, pressed me to his bosom, and blessed me, until the marrow of my bones seemed to melt! When he had finished, I knelt at his feet, and, as I bathed them with my tears and kisses, I saw the prints of the nails in the feet of the Redeemer of the world. The feeling that I had in the presence of him who hath all things in his hands, to have his love, his affection, and his blessing was such that if I ever can receive that of which I had but a foretaste, I would give all that I am, all that I ever hope to be, to feel what I then felt.[13]

"The multitude did hear and do bear record; and their hearts were open and they did understand in their hearts the words which he prayed . . . [which] cannot be written, neither can they be uttered by man." (3 Ne. 19:33.) God has granted to many the right and power to communicate to others important things pertaining to the mysteries of the kingdom (although even this information is understood by the Holy Ghost). But there is reserved by God that knowledge which is communicated only by God directly to the one whose heart is prepared. This knowledge cannot be communicated to others. Joseph Smith wrote as he viewed the mysteries and works of God: "Which [works and mysteries of God] he commanded us we should not write while we were yet in the Spirit, and are not lawful for man to utter; neither is man capable to make them known, for they are only to be seen and understood by the power of the Holy Spirit, which God bestows on those who love him, and purify themselves before him; to whom he grants this privilege of seeing and knowing for themselves; that through the power and manifestation of the Spirit, while in the flesh, they may be able to bear his presence in the world of glory." (D&C 76:115-118.)

Conclusion

In these chapters we observe how like God man is, how he is organized on the same principles that God is, and how it is man's destiny to develop into a Godly being. Through Christ, we learn that God is a man, that he has a tangible body; we see that he is deeply sensitive, patient, loving, and responsive to the pure desires of his children. He teaches us to study him and be as he is. We observe that coming to the sacrament table hungry in spirit will prepare us to receive the Holy Ghost and the mind of Christ. We begin to understand how intimate a relationship he offers us. We learn that he stands ready to share his fullness as fast as we can put aside the veil of fear and sin. We sense that a stronger envisioning of the spiritual realities around us might draw us closer to a face-to-face view.

NOTES

1. "Adversus Haereses," 10.3. *The Ante-Nicene Fathers* (Grand Rapids: Eerdmans, 1885).

2. "De Principiis," 4.4.1, in G.W. Butterworth, ed., *Origen: On First Principles* (New York: Harper & Row, 1966), pp. 313-14.

3. King Follett Discourse (Willard Richards's account) in *The Words of Joseph Smith*, Andrew F. Ehat and Lyndon W. Cook eds. (Provo, Utah: Religious Studies Center, 1981), p. 340.

4. Edwin Hatch, *The Influence of Greek Ideas and Usages upon the Christian Church* (London: Williams and Norgate, 1914), p. 69; for anthropomorphisms in the Old Testament, see Cecil Roth, "Anthropomorphism," *Encyclopaedia Judaica*, vol. 3 (Jerusalem: Keter Publishing House, 1972), p. 53.

5. Robert M. Grant, *The Early Christian Doctrine of God* (Charlottesville: Univ. Press of Virginia, 1966), pp. 4-5.

6. *De Trinitas*, 10-23.

7. J.N.D. Kelly, *Early Christian Doctrines*, rev. ed. (San Franciso: Harper & Row, 1978), p. 165.

8. The image of 2,500 people going forth one by one arrests our attention. Even if each person had only ten seconds to touch the Lord's body, that adds up to nearly seven hours that he stood patiently and graciously allowed this examination.

9. The Lord reminded us of the place our agency has in our receiving spiritual growth and blessing. We may understand spiritual experience too

passively, *waiting* for something to happen to us. Perhaps we wait too patiently for the arrival of the spiritual blessings we need. We may not realize that many blessings require, initially, acts of will on our part, a labor in the spirit, a setting aside of time: cleansing of selfish purpose from the heart, submission, envisioning the blessing, thanks in anticipation of receiving the blessing. God gave us agency, and it may have more power than we have used.

10. This is the second use of "one by one" and reassures us of the Lord's individual attention to each of his children. Again we calculate how much time the blessing of many hundreds of children individually must have taken. He illustrated what he says later: "I know my sheep, and they are numbered." (3 Ne. 18:31.)

11. Cf. Matt 20:28: "The Son of man came not to be ministered unto, but to minister." *The New Bible Dictionary* notes that the Hebrew term *mesaret* (LXX *leitourgos*) and its correlates normally refer to temple service, or else to the ministration of angels. It refers to service in general, has the special connotation of lowly service, often of a subordinate. In Luke 22:27 Christ appears among the disciples as *ho diakonon*, "one who serves." (J. D. Douglas, ed. *New Bible Dictionary*, 2nd ed. [Wheaton, Illinois: Tyndale House Publishers, 1982].) Ministering suggests the giving of spiritual gifts for relief and comfort.

12. These Nephites had baptism all along, but with the establishment of a new organization of the Church, they all underwent baptism and confirmation for admission into the new order.

13. Bryant S. Hinckley, *Sermons and Missionary Service of Melvin J. Ballard* (Salt Lake City: Deseret Book Company, 1949), pp. 155-56.

17

THE FINAL GATHERING TO CHRIST
(3 Nephi 20–22)

JOSEPH F. MCCONKIE

The instruction given by Christ to the Nephites included a prophetic description of the most singular events of the last days. In teaching of such things, the Savior affirmed that the Father had not forgotten the covenant he had made with his people—the house of Israel—and that his word would be fulfilled, every jot and tittle. Briefly stated, that promise was that they would be gathered in from "the east and from the west, and from the south and from the north," and that they would "be brought to the knowledge of the Lord their God, who hath redeemed them." (3 Ne. 20:13.) This latter-day gathering, Christ testified, would be first spiritual and then temporal. Israel, he said, must return first to their covenants and then to their covenant lands.

The Sword of God's Justice

Christ commanded the Nephites to record the things he said to them. He prophesied that what was written would eventually come forth through the Gentiles [Joseph Smith and the tribe of Ephraim] to the remnant of Israel who had been scattered throughout the earth for faithless rejection of the Messiah. Christ affirmed that in the last days they would be gathered on condition of faithful acceptance of him. That is, through the testimony of the Nephite record they would

Joseph F. McConkie is professor of ancient scripture at Brigham Young University.

obtain a knowledge of their Redeemer and "then" be gathered in, that Christ might fulfill the covenant he had made with "all the people of the house of Israel." (3 Ne. 16:4-5.)

Christ gave the Nephites a prophetic description of the restoration of the fullness of the gospel in the last days, announcing that it would come through the Gentiles. The word *Gentile* is used in this context to emphasize that it would not be the nation of Israel—that nation formed by God—who would bring forth the word of life, but rather those possessing believing blood who had been scattered among Gentile nations. Thus *Gentiles* as used in the Book of Mormon includes faithful descendants of Abraham, Isaac, and Jacob who are not of the tribe of Judah or who are not transplanted Jewish nationals; that is, citizens of the Southern Kingdom. This time of restoration is known to us as the "times of the Gentiles." When the time comes that the Gentiles partake of that same dark spirit known to the tribe of Judah in the meridian of time, they too, the Savior said, would come to know the chastening hand of the Lord and know it in the same measure. Of that day and time the resurrected Christ said, "Then will I remember my covenant which I have made unto my people, O house of Israel, and I will bring my gospel unto them." (See 3 Ne. 16:11, 6-14.) Thus the Savior explained that in the final dispensation the gospel would go first to the Gentiles; after they had rejected it, it would be taken to the Jews.

We learn from the Joseph Smith Translation that Christ foretold these same events to the inner circle of faithful Saints in the Old World. In a private explanation of the parable of the householder, he said that the kingdom of God would be taken from the Jews in the meridian day and given to the Gentiles. He said that in the last days, he would "let again his vineyard unto other husbandmen," also Gentiles, who would "render him the fruits in their seasons." Nevertheless, wicked Gentiles would also be destroyed, he prophesied, "when the Lord should descend out of heaven to reign in his vineyard, which is the earth and the inhabitants thereof." (JST, Matt. 21:47-56.)

This day of vengeance is millennial; it refers to the Second Coming. Christ used the words of Micah to describe it: "The remnant of Jacob shall be among the Gentiles in the midst of many people as a lion among the beasts of the forest, as a young lion among the flocks of sheep: who, if he go through, both treadeth down, and teareth in pieces, and none can deliver." (Micah 5:8; 3 Ne. 20:16; 21:12.) The prophecy has no reference to the Lamanites or any other remnant of Israel waging war against Gentile oppressors. Such is not the Lord's system. At his coming, the wicked will be destroyed and the righteous preserved; those who have rejected his prophets "shall be cut off." Elder Bruce R. McConkie explained: "It shall be with power, as though a young lion went forth rending and tearing in pieces a helpless flock of sheep. And so, if the Gentiles do not repent and believe in Christ after the gospel is restored among them, then, when the Lord comes, they will be destroyed and the triumph of Israel—because they kept the commandments and did receive the gospel—that triumph will be complete."[1]

Christ further emphasized that this final gathering was to be his doing and not that of mortals—a matter of making bare his arm in contrast to the arm of flesh. He said, "I will gather my people together as a man gathereth his sheaves into the floor." He then added to the imagery of the ferocious lion that of a goring bull. Again the prophetic promise is given in the words of Micah: "I will make thine horn iron, and I will make thy hoofs brass: and thou shalt beat in pieces many people: and I will consecrate their gain unto the Lord, and their substance unto the Lord of the whole earth."[2] (Micah 4:13.) Christ's commentary was simple and direct: "And behold, I am he who doeth it." The sword of God's justice, he declared, shall hang over all the nations of the Gentiles, and unless they repent it shall fall upon them. As for the house of Israel—it would be for God to establish his own people. (3 Ne. 20:19-21.)

The New Jerusalem

As to the establishment of his people, the Savior told the Nephites that their land would be the place of a New Jerusalem. The Americas— apparently the whole land—had been promised to the seed of Joseph, for such was the covenant Christ made with Joseph's father, Jacob. Jacob had prophesied that Joseph's branches (Ephraim and

Manasseh) would cross the waters to inherit "the utmost bound of the everlasting hills." (Gen. 49:22, 26; see also Deut. 33:15.) Yet long before that day, Enoch had written of a time when the Lord would gather his elect from the four quarters of the earth, to a place he would prepare, a holy city, wherein his people would ready themselves for his coming, and wherein would be found his tabernacle (the temple). This place was to be "called Zion, a New Jerusalem." (Moses 7:62.) At that time, and again this is clearly millennial, Christ said, "The powers of heaven shall be in the midst of this people; yea, even I will be in the midst of you." (3 Ne. 20:22.)

A little later in this same discourse, Christ again quoted Micah relative to the ravishing lion and the destruction of the unrepentant Gentiles. Again he announced that the rebellious were to be cut off from the house of Israel, while promising that the righteous would be numbered among his church. "And they shall come in unto the covenant and be numbered among this the remnant of Jacob, unto whom I have given this land for their inheritance," he said. (3 Ne. 21:12-22; Micah 5:8-15.) Thus the believing and obedient will be called on to build the New Jerusalem. "And they shall assist my people, the remnant of Jacob, and also as many of the house of Israel as shall come, that they may build a city, which shall be called the New Jerusalem." (3 Ne. 21:23.) All such labors, we learn from the Doctrine and Covenants, are to be accomplished by the authority of the priesthood and under the direction of those holding its keys. (D&C 42:8-9, 30-42; 45:66-71; 52:2, 42-43; 57:1-5; 58:7, 44-58; 84:2-5.) "And then shall they [those who have embraced the restored covenant through baptism] assist my people that they may be gathered in, who are scattered upon all the face of the land, in unto the New Jerusalem." As we shall yet see, the greater part of the gathering will take place after the building of the New Jerusalem, for only then "shall the power of heaven come down among them" and Christ reign personally upon the earth. (See 3 Ne. 21:20-25.)

Thus, this New Jerusalem shall become "a land of peace, a city of refuge, a place of safety for the saints of the Most High God; and the glory of the Lord shall be there, and the terror of the Lord also shall be there, insomuch that the wicked will not come unto it, and it shall be called Zion. And it shall come to pass among the wicked, that every man that will not take his sword against his neighbor must needs flee unto Zion for safety. And there shall be gathered unto it out of every nation under heaven; and it shall be the only people that shall not be at war one with another. And it shall be said among the wicked: Let us not go up to battle against Zion, for the inhabitants of Zion are terrible; wherefore we cannot stand. And it shall come to pass that the righteous shall be gathered out from among all nations, and shall come to Zion, singing with songs of everlasting joy." (D&C 45:66-71.)

All of Israel's Prophets Testified of Christ

Surely the reader of Christ's discourse on the gathering will not overlook how closely he tied the Nephites to their ancient forebears in the Old World. Though they would have their own Zion, their own Jerusalem, their own prophets, and their own scripture, they were to be united with the faithful of all nations and all ages. There is but one Shepherd and one fold—one Christ and one message of salvation. All prophets speak with the same voice. "I am he of whom Moses spake," Christ declared, and thus it follows that to profess Moses is to profess Christ. "Verily I say unto you, yea, and all the prophets from Samuel [the first prophet of the nation of Israel] and those that follow after [and this is everlastingly so], as many as have spoken, have testified of me." (3 Ne. 20:23-24.) We have no greater evidence of the taking of the "plain" and the "precious" from the records of the Old Testament than the expunging of the testimony of its prophets relative to Christ.

Blessings of the Covenant

Joseph Smith's translation of the Abraham papyrus opens to us a flood of knowledge about the covenant God made with our ancient father—knowledge now lost to those whose understanding is limited to the Bible. From the record we learn that Abraham was promised that his seed—his literal descendants—were to hold the priesthood and carry the message of salvation, even the blessings of eternal life, to all nations. (Abr. 2:9, 11.) This right has not been given to those of any other lineage. In our present text, Christ reminds the Nephites that they are the children of the prophets and thus inheritors of the promises made to Abraham. It was because of that covenant that Christ had come to them and sought to turn them from their iniquities. (3 Ne. 20:25-26.)

Amplifying the Abrahamic covenant over that preserved for us in the Bible, the Savior said that he had promised Abraham that through his posterity all the families of the earth would be blessed by the "pouring out of the Holy Ghost," which blessing would make the Gentiles "mighty above all, unto the scattering of . . . [the] house of Israel." The Gentiles, he said, would be a "scourge unto the people of this land," meaning Lehi's descendants in the last days. Nevertheless, after the fullness of the gospel had gone forth among the Gentiles, if they hardened their hearts and returned to their iniquities all these evils would return to them. (3 Ne. 20:27-28.)

The Day of Jewish Conversion

When the day of the Gentile has been fulfilled, that is, when the gospel will be taken from them because of their iniquities, the Savior will remember the covenant he made with those of Judah to return them to their ancient covenant land. Of this yet future day, he said, "The fulness of my gospel shall be preached unto them; and they shall believe in me, that I am Jesus Christ, the Son of God, and shall pray unto the Father in my name." After their conversion to Christ, after that time when their "watchmen" come to see "eye to eye" with their Savior, "then will the Father gather them together again, and give unto them Jerusalem for the land of their inheritance." (3 Ne. 20:29-33.)

Of this matter Elder Bruce R. McConkie wrote: "As all the world knows, many Jews are now gathering to Palestine, where they have their own nation and way of worship, all without reference to a belief in Christ or an acceptance of the laws and ordinances of his everlasting gospel. Is this the latter-day gathering of the Jews of which the scriptures speak? No! It is not; let there be no misunderstanding in any discerning mind on this point. This gathering of the Jews to their homeland, and their organization into a nation and a kingdom, is not the gathering promised by the prophets. It does not fulfill the ancient promises. Those who have thus assembled have not gathered into the true Church and fold of their ancient Messiah. They have not received again the saving truths of that very gospel which blessed Moses their lawgiver, and Elijah their prophet, and Peter, James, and John, whom their fathers rejected."[3]

It will be in this future setting, the Savior explained, that the prophecies of Isaiah relative to Zion putting on her strength (the authority of the priesthood), and loosing herself from the bands of her neck (returning to the Lord and receiving revelation) shall be fulfilled. (See Isaiah 52:1-2; D&C 113:7-10.) This is to be a day in which "my people shall know my name; yea, in that day they shall know that I am he that doth speak." In that day they will rejoice in those who have brought the message of salvation to them and invited them to depart a wicked world to once more worship their God with pure hearts and clean hands and to clothe themselves in white garments, having been washed in the blood of the Lamb. (See 3 Ne. 20:39-42; 2 Ne. 25:16; Ether 13:10-12.)

The Great Prophet of the Restoration

To this point Christ was describing the restoration of the gospel, Israel being clothed again with the priesthood, and the coming of the revelations of heaven, all of which are requisite to the gathering of Israel in the last days. It is natural at this point that some reference be made to the servant-prophet who would represent the Lord in accomplishing such a marvelous work and wonder. This is precisely what Christ did, though he went about it in an unusual way. He quoted four verses from Isaiah that are obviously Messianic—verses descriptive of his mortal ministry, which was now complete. (See 3 Ne. 20:42-45; Isa. 52:12-15.) The context in which Christ used these verses and the manner in which he returned to phrases from them a little later in this discourse make it obvious that he was applying them to the great prophet of the Restoration, who, like himself, was to be a suffering servant. Obviously these verses, like many others—

and this is particularly so in the writings of Isaiah—were intended by the spirit of revelation to embrace multiple fulfillment.[4]

Concluding his prophetic description of the return of those of Judah to their ancient land, Christ testified: "All these things shall surely come, even as the Father hath commanded me. Then shall this covenant which the Father hath covenanted with his people be fulfilled; and then shall Jerusalem be inhabited again with my people, and it shall be the land of their inheritance." (3 Ne. 20:46.)

Jesus then gave his Nephite congregation a sign so they would know when these things—specifically the gathering of Israel and the establishment of Zion—"shall be about to take place." The sign embraced a series of events including the establishment of a free people in the United States of America; the restoration of the gospel; the taking of the gospel to the Lamanites; and the martyrdom of the prophet-servant of the Restoration and his eternal triumph in the kingdom of God. Commenting on this prophecy, Moroni later wrote: "When ye shall receive this record [the Book of Mormon] ye may know that the work of the Father has commenced upon all the face of the land." (3 Ne. 21:1-10; Ether 4:17.)

At this point in the Savior's remarks it becomes evident why he quoted Isaiah's prophecies about a suffering servant to identify the great prophet who would stand at the head of the latter-day gathering of Israel. The prophet was to be "hurt" or "marred," even as the Savior had been "hurt" and "marred" in his mortal ministry by the enemies of truth. How perfect the parallel between Joseph Smith and Jesus Christ—both were hounded and rejected by the religious leaders of their day; both were scorned and accused of being possessed by a devil; indeed, both were accused of blasphemy; and of course both sealed their testimony with their blood as martyrs, having given offense to none but the legions of darkness.

The Magnitude of the Gathering

The greatness of Israel's gathering must match the greatness of its scattering. For thousands of years the children of Abraham have been sifted among the nations of the earth. Even today the scattering of the chosen seed continues. Israel has been scattered for rebellion against their God; for rejecting his prophets; for breaking their covenants; indeed, for crucifying their Messiah. The gathering, which comes in answer to the scattering, must be equally extensive. It must reach to the ends of the earth, center in obedience to the God of heaven, call forth living prophets, and demand acceptance of Jesus as the Christ.

By what voice is scattered Israel to be called back to the covenants and lands of their fathers? Should it not be by the voice of their fathers? A voice from the dust? A voice bearing the testimony common to all the holy prophets since the world began? Ought it not to center in the testimony of Christ? Such was the promise of the Savior—a book to come forth—a book containing the testimony of Christ and the true points of doctrine, a book bringing those of the latter days to the knowledge of their forebears, a book containing the knowledge of the covenants of salvation. Such was the promise of the Savior, a promise with a warning that all who reject the book and its witness "shall be cut off from among the people who are of the covenant." (3 Ne. 21:11.)

"But if they will repent and hearken unto my words," the Savior declared, "and harden not their hearts, I will establish my church among them, and they shall come in unto the covenant and be numbered among this the remnant of Jacob"—having reference to Lehi's seed; for they and as many as shall come to the covenant shall help build the New Jerusalem. "Then shall the power of heaven come down among them" and the Savior be in their midst. (3 Ne. 21:22-25.)

The text then declares that at this time—and it is clearly millennial—the work of the Father shall "commence" in gathering the dispersed of Israel—the tribes that have been lost—back to the land of their inheritance. There is no mistaking the intended meaning. Four times in three verses the Lord said that the labor of gathering Israel will "commence" at this time. (See 3 Ne. 21:26-28.) Having so declared, Jesus then sustained his point by quoting Isaiah 54, with the announcement that this is also the time of its fulfillment. This chapter tells the story of returning Israel using the metaphor of the marriage covenant. "More are the children of the desolate than the children of the married wife, saith the Lord." That is, greater are the numbers of Israel born outside of the covenant than those born within it. "Enlarge the place of thy tent, and let them stretch forth the curtains of thy habitations; spare not, lengthen thy cords and strengthen thy stakes." Make ready for the great numbers who will be gathered, that is, join the Church, during the millennium — so great, in fact, that the number of those who joined before is not even a beginning in comparison. "For thou shalt break forth on the right hand and on the left, and thy seed shall inherit the Gentiles and make the desolate cities to be inhabited." (3 Ne. 22:1-3; Isa. 54:1-3.)

"And all thy children shall be taught of the Lord; and great shall be the peace of thy children. . . . No weapon that is formed against thee shall prosper; and every tongue that shall revile against thee in judgment thou shalt condemn. This is the heritage of the servants of the Lord, and their righteousness is of me, saith the Lord." (3 Ne. 22:13, 17; Isa. 54:13, 17.)

Conclusion

We have no more authoritative or informative source on the latter-day gathering of Israel than the words of Christ recorded in 3 Nephi 20-22. The discourse has not received its proper due among those who have taught and written on the subject. In fact, it has often been the source of doctrinal mischief. As is so often the case where faulty interpretations are concerned, those claiming these teachings of the Savior as their source practice what could be termed theological kidnapping — taking a passage out of context and holding it hostage to sustain some speculative view. Perhaps the greatest error in the interpretation of the Savior's words has been the failure to read them as a unit.

These comments of the Savior certainly affirm that neither he nor his Father has forgotten the covenants made to our ancient progenitors. The promises God made to the posterity of Abraham, Isaac, and Jacob are real! The Abrahamic covenant is not an allegory; it is not a Bible story that is to be spiritualized away. The gathering of Israel will be literal, and it is literal Israel that is to be gathered. The promises given to the seed of Abraham are as real as the dirt and dust upon which he set his feet of flesh and blood, they are as real as the brick and mortar with which the New Jerusalem is to be built, as real as the sweat and tears with which the Jerusalem of old is to be rebuilt.

Yet, as is always the case, a spiritual gathering must precede the physical gathering—a gathering that centers in the restoration of the "fulness of the gospel," the "pouring out of the Holy Ghost," the reestablishing of the "true points" of Christ's doctrine, the believing in his words, the repentance of sin and coming unto the "Beloved Son." "I will establish my church among them," Christ declared, "and they shall come in unto the covenant."

The heart of the gathering is the testimony of Jesus. Those who reject that testimony particularly and specifically as it comes forth in the record of the Nephites and at the hands of the Prophet Joseph Smith are to be cut off from among the Lord's people. One can hardly overstate the importance of the Book of Mormon in this epic drama of Israel's gathering. "What, then, is the power of the Book of Mormon?" Elder McConkie asked. "It will build the New Jerusalem; it will prepare a people for the Second Coming; it will usher in the Millennium—at least it will play such an important part in all of these that its value and power can scarcely be overstated."[5]

NOTES

1. Bruce R. McConkie, *The Mortal Messiah*, 4 vols. (Salt Lake City: Deseret Book Company, 1979-81), 4:334-35. See also *The Millennial Messiah* (Salt Lake City: Deseret Book Company, 1982), pp. 244-48.

2. We are told in the Doctrine and Covenants that returning Israel will bring "their rich treasures" with them. (D&C 133:30.) Traditionally it has been supposed that this means scriptural records. It is, however, quite possible that the text means what it says—that returning Israel will in fact bring rich treasures. When Abraham and Sarah returned after their trial in Egypt to that sacred land promised them, they went "rich in cattle, in silver, and in gold," returning first to Bethel—the house of God—and its altar that they might call upon the name of the Lord. (Gen. 13:2-4.) Similarly, before the children of Israel left Egypt to return to the promised land to rebuild

194

their temple and call upon God, they were directed to obtain from the Egyptians their "jewels of silver, and jewels of gold." (Ex. 11:2.) When the Jews were freed from their captivity in Babylon to return to Palestine to rebuild the Holy City and its temple, the treasure houses of that great nation were opened to them, and they returned laden with silver and gold. (Ezra 7:15-21.) Thus, when Israel returns to claim the blessings of the temple in the last days, should they not return with their rich treasures as their forebears did before them?

3. *The Millennial Messiah*, p. 229.

4. See Joseph Fielding McConkie and Robert L. Millet, *Doctrinal Commentary on the Book of Mormon* (Salt Lake City: Bookcraft, 1987), 1:157.

5. *The Millennial Messiah*, p. 171.

18

TEACHING FROM THE WORDS OF THE PROPHETS
(3 Nephi 23–26)

KENT P. JACKSON

The greatest instructional session recorded in history took place while the resurrected Jesus taught his disciples in the Americas. The Lord God Almighty—who had revealed covenants, laws, and ordinances to his children since the beginning—stood among mortals who had purified themselves and had been found worthy to be in his presence. In this setting Jesus was with individuals who were saints, "holy ones," whose faith had enabled them to escape the cleansing destruction preceding his coming and to enjoy his subsequent visit among them. Thus Jesus could teach them his gospel in its fullness and purity, unconstrained by the presence of the unfaithful.

It is instructive in this context to observe how Jesus taught his disciples.[1] In his sermons he drew freely from the words he had inspired his earlier messengers to write, much more so than he had done in his mortal ministry in Palestine as far as we can tell from the New Testament. He frequently cited passages from the Hebrew scriptures and gave divine commentary to them. He also quoted entire chapters. (3 Ne. 22 = Isa. 54; 3 Ne. 24-25 = Mal. 3-4.)

Great Are the Words

After having quoted the 54th chapter of Isaiah (3 Ne. 22), Jesus gave Isaiah an unprecedented endorsement, calling his words "great"

Kent P. Jackson is associate professor of ancient scripture at Brigham Young University.

and commanding his disciples to search them. (3 Ne. 23:1.)[2] Isaiah's words are great because they touch on "all things" concerning the house of Israel, thus also being of importance to the Gentiles. (3 Ne. 23:2.) Jesus reminded his listeners of the eternal value of such scripture: those who hearken to the Lord's revealed word, repent, and are baptized will be saved. (3 Ne. 23:5.)

As the word of God revealed to prophets is precious, it is important that it be recorded properly, along with the fulfillment of things that God makes known. Jesus, noting the absence of some important information in the Nephite record, commanded that it be included. (3 Ne. 23:6-13.)

The Savior taught from the scriptures, setting the example for all gospel teachers to follow. As Mormon reported, he "expounded all the scriptures in one." (3 Ne. 23:14; see also 24:1; 26:1-2.) To "expound all scriptures in one" perhaps means to bring all the revealed word of God to one focal point, laying stress on that toward which all scripture points—the mission of Jesus Christ.[3] Having done this, Jesus commanded his disciples that they teach to others what he had taught them, thus building a chain of pure doctrinal understanding that would continue into subsequent generations.

As Jesus expounded the scriptures to his American saints, he quoted to them the revelations that now comprise Malachi 3 and 4 in the Old Testament. These chapters contain significant doctrinal material that reveals much concerning the Lord's coming. Perhaps that is why the Lord directed that they be written in the Nephite record, and perhaps it is why Mormon was inspired to include them in his Book of Mormon abridgment for us.

Because of the fragmented nature of the material in Malachi 3 and 4, in which a diverse variety of topics is discussed in short (sometimes unconnected) segments, this section appears to be a collection of utterances—a quote book—and not a continuous prophecy. Perhaps some of the brief quotations may not even be those of Malachi himself. Elder Bruce R. McConkie suggested that Malachi was quoting (specifically in Mal. 4:1-2) from the words of the ancient prophet Zenos, whose writings were contained on the plates of brass but are not found in the Bible as it stands today. (See 1 Ne. 22:15, 24.)[4]

The Day of Christ's Coming

The revelation in 3 Nephi 24:1-2 (Mal. 3:1-2) prophesies of the Lord's messenger who would be sent to prepare the way before His coming in glory. The terminology in this passage seems to refer clearly to the Second Coming, yet the same words are used in the New Testament to describe John the Baptist, the messenger sent to prepare the way before the Lord's coming in mortality. (See Matt. 11:10; Mark 1:2.) The passage was rightly applied to John, who prepared the way for the Lord's first coming, but the ultimate fulfillment of the prophecy will be in the latter days. It tells of the appearance of the Lord "suddenly" in his temple, asking rhetorically who will be able to endure his coming and the cleansing that will accompany it.

The scriptures do not identify the messenger to whom Malachi referred. Many messengers have in fact been involved in preparing the way for Christ, participating in the restoration of the gospel before his coming. Some of these messengers have been mortal and some angelic. Among the heavenly messengers of the Restoration the following could be listed: John the Baptist and Peter, James, and John, who restored priesthood power to Joseph Smith; Elijah, the bearer of priesthood keys, whose coming is the subject of discussion in Malachi's next chapter; and Moroni, the heavenly messenger who set the latter-day work into motion.[5] Perhaps what Malachi envisioned was not an individual but the *collective ministry* of all the messengers who restored doctrine and keys in the last days, each in turn preparing the way for Christ.

The Prophet Joseph Smith was also a great messenger sent to prepare the way for the Lord. As John was sent anciently, Joseph Smith was sent into the world in modern times to establish the Lord's work prior to the Second Coming.[6]

Perhaps an even broader interpretation may be of value. The Lord revealed: "I have sent mine everlasting covenant into the world, to be a light to the world, and to be a standard for my people, and for the Gentiles to seek to it, and to be a messenger before my face to prepare the way before me." (D&C 45:9.) Thus the gospel — restored in the latter days to make the world ready for the Lord — is a messenger sent before him.

As Malachi foretold, when Christ comes he will "purify the sons of Levi," so they will "offer unto the Lord an offering in righteousness." (3 Ne. 24:3.) The descendants of Levi, who still exist among the Jews throughout the world, are rightful heirs to the Priesthood of Aaron. Yet they are now outside of the covenants of the gospel, which are found only in The Church of Jesus Christ of Latter-day Saints, and thus are unable to fill the role to which their family had been chosen by revelation and set apart in ancient times. As part of the restoration of all things, the tribe of Levi once again will fill a priesthood function in the Lord's kingdom — after they become converted, are purified at the Lord's coming, join the Church of Jesus Christ, and are born again of the Spirit. Joseph Smith taught:

> All the ordinances and duties that ever have been required by the priesthood under the direction and commandments of the Almighty, in any of the dispensations, shall all be had in the last dispensation. Therefore all things had under the authority of the priesthood at any former period shall be had again — bringing to pass the restoration spoken of by the mouth of all the holy prophets. Then shall the sons of Levi offer an acceptable sacrifice to the Lord. . . .
>
> We frequently have mention made of the offering of sacrifice by the servants of the Most High in ancient days prior to the Law of Moses, which ordinances will be continued when the priesthood is restored with all its authority, power, and blessings. . . . These sacrifices as well as every ordinance belonging to the priesthood will, when the temple of the Lord shall be built and the sons [of] Levi be purified, be fully restored and attended to — then all their powers, ramifications, and blessings. This ever was and will exist when the powers of the Melchizedek Priesthood are sufficiently manifest. Else how can the restitution of all things spoken of by all the holy prophets be brought to pass? It is not to be understood that the Law of Moses will be established again with all its rites and variety of ceremonies; this had never been spoken of by

the prophets. But those things which existed prior [to] Moses' day, namely sacrifice, will be continued.[7]

From this passage it appears that the Levites will offer animal sacrifice in the Millennium, in restoration of the offerings that were in force before the Law of Moses. From our available information on the subject, it cannot be said whether this will be a lasting, ongoing ordinance or a short-term event to complete this cycle of the restoration of all things and signal that the Levites are again in the covenant and have assumed their rightful priesthood function in the house of Israel.[8] In any case, as Joseph Smith taught, "The Lord will purify the sons of Levi, good or bad, for it is through them that blessings flow to Israel.... And then, and not till then, 'shall the offering of Judah and Jerusalem be pleasant unto the Lord, as in days of old and as in former years' [3 Ne. 24:4]."[9]

In verses 5-7, the Lord directed his anger against individuals and societies who are guilty of sins against God and fellow beings. (3 Ne. 24:5.) "Return unto me," he pleaded, "and I will return unto you." (3 Ne. 24:7.) One matter of concern specified by the Lord is tithing. That Malachi's great passage regarding the payment of tithes (3 Ne. 24:8-12; Mal. 3:8-12) was quoted by the Savior on this occasion highlights its importance. Latter-day Saints who have put the Lord to the test, as he invited (verse 10), can testify to the fulfillment of God's promises. It is not unlikely that the law of tithing was an important part of the Lord's plan for the Nephites, as it is for us today.

Malachi's revelation drew a stark contrast between those who are humble and receptive to the Lord's will and those who are not. Some speak against God, find no value in doing his will, and even question his justice. (3 Ne. 24:13-15.) But those who revere the Lord can rejoice that their righteousness is recorded in God's "book of remembrance." (3 Ne. 24:16.) Their reward is sure: "They shall be mine, saith the Lord of Hosts, in that day when I make up my jewels." (3 Ne. 24:17.) The relevance of this section of Malachi to Jesus' audience seems clear. Those who did not trust the prophetic announcements of his coming—and thus did not prepare—were cut off. Yet those who were faithful enjoyed the Savior's presence, even then. Later Jesus rejoiced that they would not be lost. (3 Ne. 27:30-31.)

With Healing in His Wings

The setting for the fulfillment of 3 Nephi 25:1 (Mal. 4:1) is the destruction of the wicked that will be part of the earth's cleansing preparatory to the Lord's return in glory. When Jesus returns, the earth must be purified. Whether by repentance or by destruction, wickedness of all forms must be removed before Christ will dwell here, for only those who are worthy will be privileged to live in his presence.[10]

Verses 2 and 3 continue the theme of the cleansing that will attend the Second Coming. The Lord foretold the condition of those who "fear [his] name." For them, "the Son of Righteousness [shall] arise with healing in his wings." In the Bible the term "Sun" is used, whereas here in the Book of Mormon the record uses "Son." The translators of the King James Bible correctly recognized the term "Sun of righteousness" as an allusion to the Lord, noting this understanding by the use of the capital letter in the word "Sun." Their interpretation is borne out by the Book of Mormon, where the phrase is personified completely—"Son of Righteousness." (3 Ne. 25:2.)[11] Verse 3 speaks of the righteous treading on the wicked in that day of the Lord's justice. This should be interpreted in the context of the overall destruction of evil and the ultimate victory of good over bad.[12]

The setting in which Jesus quoted this passage helps us understand its relevance to the situation of his listeners. The Savior's visit to the Americas provides a pattern that will be followed on a worldwide scale at his second coming. As Malachi foretold, the day of the Lord's coming is one of destruction for the wicked, while for the righteous it will be a day of unimaginable blessings. (3 Ne. 25:1-2.) What could better describe what the Nephites had gone through and were then experiencing? The "Son of Righteousness" had arisen in their midst, "with healing in his wings."

Verse 4, on face value, appears to be a reminder to observe the Law of Moses, which was in force in Malachi's day but was fulfilled in Christ. Perhaps we can suggest that Malachi's statement makes reference to something else. Joseph Smith, in commenting on this verse, taught: "[The] law revealed to Moses in Horeb *never was revealed to the children of Israel*,"[13] apparently referring to the *higher law* revealed to Moses that Israel did not receive because of rebellion. (See JST Ex. 34:1-2; D&C 84:23-25.) It may be that Malachi's intent, and Jesus' in quoting the verse, was to draw attention to the higher law that Moses obtained but that Israel was unworthy to receive. In that case, the reference to the law received by Moses would not be out of place with the discussion in the following verses concerning Elijah's coming. Jesus' listeners on this occasion were worthy and able to receive the higher law, priesthood, ordinances, and blessings that God revealed to Moses on the mountain but that their Israelite ancestors had forfeited.

The Coming of Elijah

When Moroni appeared to the Prophet Joseph Smith during the night of September 21-22, 1823, he quoted Malachi 4:5-6 (3 Ne. 25:5-6) quite differently than it is recorded in either the Bible or the Book of Mormon: "Behold, I will reveal unto you the Priesthood, by the hand of Elijah the prophet, before the coming of the great and dreadful day of the Lord. And he shall plant in the hearts of the children the promises made to the fathers, and the hearts of the children shall turn to their fathers. If it were not so, the whole earth would be utterly wasted at his coming." (JS–H 1:38-39; see also D&C 2.) This passage, in either version, is one of the most important scriptures of the Restoration, since it foretells the creation of the links of priesthood power that bind and seal both ordinances and generations on earth and in heaven.[14] The prophecy of Elijah's coming was fulfilled on April 3, 1836, as the ancient prophet who held the keys of sealing power appeared to the founding prophet of the last dispensation to restore those keys to the earth. (D&C 110:13-16.)[15]

In the recorded teachings and writings of Joseph Smith, the Prophet taught on the subject of Malachi 4:5-6 more than on any other passage of scripture. Among other things, he taught: "Elijah was the last prophet that held the keys of this priesthood, and who will, before the last dispensation, restore the authority and deliver the keys of this priesthood in order that all the ordinances may be attended to in righteousness. . . . Why send Elijah? Because he holds the keys of the authority to administer in all the ordinances of the priesthood, and without the authority the ordinances could not be administered in righteousness."[16] The priesthood keys restored by Elijah provide the sealing power for all ordinances of the priesthood, making those performed on earth valid in the heavens and enabling worthy couples and families to be sealed together for the eternities. On another occasion the Prophet taught:

> Now the word "turn" here should be translated "bind" or "seal." But what is the object of this important mission, or how is it to be fulfilled? The keys are to be delivered, the spirit of Elijah is to come, the gospel to be established, the Saints of God gathered, Zion built up, and the Saints to come up as saviors on Mount Zion. But how are they to become saviors on Mount Zion? By building their temples, erecting their baptismal fonts, and going forth and receiving all the ordinances, baptisms, confirmations, washings, anointings, ordinations, and sealing powers upon our heads in behalf of all our progenitors who are dead, and redeem them that they may come forth in the first resurrection and be exalted to thrones of glory with us. And herein is the chain that binds the hearts of the fathers to the children, and the children to the fathers, which fulfills the mission of Elijah.[17]

Since ordinances performed on earth are valid in the eternities, it follows, in the Lord's plan, that ordinances can be performed by this power on earth in behalf of those who are already in the spirit world. Thus Elijah's coming makes temple work for the dead possible and provides the welding link between generations.

It is not unlikely that the Savior's visit to the Nephites initiated an era of intense temple activity among them. It is also not unreasonable that he used Malachi's prophecy as a means to stress eternal marriage and the other blessings of Elijah's sealing mission. (See 4 Ne. 1:11.) How appropriate, then, was his quoting of this important passage for their benefit and for the blessing of those in the future who would read their record.

Greater Things

Using the revelations of Malachi as his starting point, Jesus taught his disciples of the future of the world, the earth's regeneration, his coming in glory, and the judgment that all will face, "according to the mercy, and the justice, and the holiness which is in Christ." (3 Ne. 26:5.) Concerning this transcendent instructional session, Mormon wrote: "There cannot be written in this book even a hundredth part of the things which Jesus did truly teach unto the people." (3 Ne. 26:6.)

Mormon included in his account some important information concerning the writing of his record, and in doing so he taught an important gospel principle. He mentioned that a fuller account of Jesus' teaching was contained on the plates of Nephi, from which he had abridged the record that we have in 3 Nephi. (3 Ne. 26:7.) Concerning the latter-day readers of his account, he wrote: "When they shall have received this, which is expedient that they should have first, to try their faith, and if it shall so be that they shall believe these things then shall the greater things be made manifest unto them." (3 Ne. 26:9.) The "greater things" will be made known to us, in the Lord's due time, in accordance with the faith with which we receive what has already been revealed. The corollary is also true: "If it so be that they will not believe these things, then shall the greater things be withheld from them, unto their condemnation." (3 Ne. 26:10.) This principle was taught eloquently by Alma: "He that will harden his heart, the same receiveth the lesser portion of the word; and he that will not harden his heart, to him is given the greater portion of the word until it is given unto him to know the mysteries of God until he know them in full. And they that will harden their hearts, to them is given the lesser portion of the word, until they know nothing concerning his mysteries; and then they are taken captive by the devil, and led by his will down to destruction." (Alma 12:10-11.)

The importance of this principle should not be overlooked by anyone. In the Lord's mercy, he has revealed to us what in his wisdom he knows that we need. (Alma 29:8.) If we feast on—and believe in—what has been revealed already, more will be revealed to us, either through the inspiration of the Holy Spirit or through the revelation of more scripture at a later time. If we do not learn — and thus do not gain faith in — what the Lord has made known to the world already, we are closing the door on wonderful opportunities. It is no wonder, then, that modern prophets have counseled us repeatedly to make scripture study an important part of our lives.[18]

Mormon's account preserves examples of the principle described in the preceding paragraphs. As he was about to write more concerning the Savior's teachings, the Lord forbade him, saying, "I will try the faith of my people." (3 Ne. 26:11.) In the remainder of 3 Nephi 26, prohibitions against writing more are expressed in two other places (verses 16, 18).

Jesus taught his Nephite saints for three days, after which he appeared to them frequently. On these occasions one of the most remarkable occurrences in all of human history took place. As the Savior taught and ministered to the young children of the assembled believers, he so filled them with the Spirit that they said "great and marvelous things" to their parents, even greater than Christ himself had revealed to them! So great were the "marvelous things" the children taught their parents that it was forbidden that anyone should write them. (3 Ne. 26:14, 16.)

Jesus' ministry healed physical as well as spiritual infirmities. He restored the sick to health and cured the lame, the blind, and the deaf; he even raised a man from the dead. (3 Ne. 26:15.) As the Master had set his priesthood organization into operation earlier in his visit, those whom he had chosen administered the blessings of the gospel to others, teaching and baptizing. Those who received baptism "were filled with the Holy Ghost. And many of them saw and heard unspeakable things, which are not lawful to be written." (3 Ne. 26:17-18.)

Mormon summarized the results of Jesus' visit on the lives of the people: they ministered one to another, "they had all things common ... every man dealing justly, one with another" and doing "all things even as Jesus had commanded them." (3 Ne. 26:19-20.)

A Pattern for the Last Days

One reason why the Book of Mormon is so important for our time is that it provides a pattern for the events of the last days. Thus, we would do well to observe what it teaches us. Just as in ancient America, the period preceding Christ's second coming will be characterized by wickedness, wars, and social chaos. (3 Ne. 2-7; JS–M 1:29-30.) At the same time that the Saints will be strengthening Zion in anticipation of the Lord's return (3 Ne. 7:15-26; Moses 7:62), Satan's work will be spreading in the earth (3 Ne. 2-7; JS–M 1:22). Destruction of wickedness will cleanse the earth (3 Ne. 8-10; D&C 29:14-21), and those to whom the Savior will appear will be among "the more righteous" (3 Ne. 10:12; D&C 45:56-57). Members of the Church, who enjoy gospel blessings prior to his coming, will teach the gospel to everyone else, and the whole world will soon be converted. (4 Ne. 1:1-2; Jer. 31:34.) The Lord will be with his people and teach them (3 Ne. 11-27; D&C 101:32-34), and a glorious period of peace and righteousness will follow (4 Ne. 1:1-18; Isa. 11:6-9).

Notes

1. See the discussions in chapters 14-19 in this book.

2. For a discussion of Isaiah in the Book of Mormon, see Kent P. Jackson, "Nephi and Isaiah," in *Studies in Scripture, Vol. 7: 1 Nephi to Alma 29*, ed. Kent P. Jackson (Salt Lake City: Deseret Book Company, 1987), pp. 131-45.

3. See Bruce R. McConkie, *The Mortal Messiah: From Bethlehem to Calvary*, 4 vols. (Salt Lake City: Deseret Book Company, 1979-81), 4:365-68.

4. Bruce R. McConkie, "The Doctrinal Restoration," in *The Joseph Smith Translation: Restoring Plain and Precious Truths*, ed. Monte S. Nyman and Robert L. Millet (Provo, Utah: Religious Studies Center, Brigham Young University, 1985), p. 18.

5. See Kent P. Jackson, "The Appearance of Moroni to Joseph Smith," in *Studies in Scripture, Vol. 2: The Pearl of Great Price*, ed. Robert L. Millet and Kent P. Jackson (Salt Lake City: Randall Books, 1985), p. 341.

6. See Joseph Fielding Smith, *Doctrines of Salvation*, 3 vols., comp. Bruce R. McConkie (Salt Lake City: Bookcraft, 1954-56), 3:10-12; and Bruce R. McConkie, *Mormon Doctrine*, 2nd ed. (Salt Lake City: Bookcraft, 1966), p. 488.

7. Joseph Smith, October 5, 1840, recorded by Robert B. Thompson; Andrew F. Ehat and Lyndon W. Cook, comp. and ed., *The Words of Joseph Smith* (Provo, Utah: Religious Studies Center, 1980), pp. 42-44; see also pp. 50-51, note 1. All quotations from Joseph Smith in this chapter have been edited for spelling and punctuation.

8. See Joseph Fielding Smith, *Doctrines of Salvation* 3:93-94; Bruce R. McConkie, *Mormon Doctrine*, p. 666; *The Mortal Messiah* 1:128.

9. Joseph Smith, March 21, 1841, recorded by Martha Jane Coray; Ehat and Cook, *The Words of Joseph Smith*, p. 66.

10. See Kent P. Jackson, "The Signs of the Times: Be Not Troubled," in *Studies in Scripture, Vol. 1: The Doctrine and Covenants*, ed. Robert L. Millet and Kent P. Jackson (Salt Lake City: Randall Books, 1984), pp. 186-200.

11. The personification of the metaphor "sun" to the explicit "Son" need not be viewed as a scribal matter, regardless of what may have been either in Malachi's original text or on the gold plates of Mormon's abridgment. There is no reason not to assume that the Book of Mormon text here is deliberate and inspired.

12. In conjunction with this, see the interpretation of 3 Ne. 21:12-17 in chapter 17 of this volume.

13. Joseph Smith, August 27, 1843, recorded by Willard Richards; Ehat and Cook, *The Words of Joseph Smith*, p. 244, emphasis added.

14. See Charles R. Harrell, "Turning the Hearts of the Fathers and the Children," in *Studies in Scripture, Vol. 1*, pp. 57-63.

15. See Milton V. Backman, Jr., and Robert L. Millet, "Heavenly Manifestations in the Kirtland Temple," in *Studies in Scripture, Vol. 1*, pp. 426-29.

16. Joseph Smith, October 5, 1840, recorded by Robert B. Thompson; Ehat and Cook, *The Words of Joseph Smith*, p. 43.

17. Joseph Smith, January 21, 1844, recorded by Wilford Woodruff; Ehat and Cook, *The Words of Joseph Smith*, p. 318.

18. For example, see President Ezra Taft Benson, "The Book of Mormon: Keystone of Our Religion," in *Studies in Scripture, Vol. 7*, pp. 1-16.

19
BUILT UPON CHRIST'S GOSPEL
(3 Nephi 27–30)

KENT P. JACKSON AND DARRELL L. MATTHEWS

After the Savior appeared to the Nephites and established his church among them, the twelve disciples went through the land preaching the gospel and baptizing into the church those who repented. While traveling they became aware of disputes among the members of the church concerning the name by which it should be called. In order to obtain from the Lord an answer to the matter, they "united in mighty prayer and fasting." (3 Ne. 27:1.) In response to their prayers, Christ appeared to them and taught them. This visit of Jesus to his disciples is his last recorded visit to them.

The Name of the Church

While the disciples were praying to know by what name the church should be called, "Jesus came and stood in the midst of them, and said unto them: What will ye that I shall give unto you? And they said unto him: Lord, we will that thou wouldst tell us the name whereby we shall call this church; for there are disputations among the people concerning this matter." (3 Ne. 27:2-3; see Isa. 58:9, 11.) In response to this question, Jesus asked why the people should dispute over this issue: "Have they not read the scriptures?" (3 Ne. 27:5.)

The Savior then taught his disciples that those who wish to follow

---

Darrell L. Matthews is a doctoral student in ancient languages at Johns Hopkins University. Kent P. Jackson is associate professor of ancient scripture at Brigham Young University.

him must take upon themselves his name. He gave specific instructions concerning the name of the church: "Therefore ye shall call the church in my name; and ye shall call upon the Father in my name that he will bless the church for my sake. And how be it my church save it be called in my name? For if a church be called in Moses' name then it be Moses' church; or if it be called in the name of a man then it be the church of a man; but if it be called in my name then it is my church, if it so be that they are built upon my gospel." (3 Ne. 27:7-8.) In this explanation of the importance of the name of the church, two major points are emphasized. The first is that the true church must be named after Christ; the second is that it must be "built upon" his gospel. If only the first criterion were mentioned, any church using Christ's name could possibly be the true church. When the second requirement is added, it eliminates all churches that possess Christ's name while not containing his gospel in its fullness. It limits the true church to only one; The Church of Jesus Christ of Latter-day Saints meets both of these requirements. (D&C 115:4; 1:30.)

In addition to these requirements, Christ told the disciples: "If it so be that the church is built upon my gospel then will the Father show forth his own works in it." (3 Ne. 27:10.) From other scriptures we learn that some of the Father's works are spiritual gifts (1 Cor. 12:8-14; D&C 46:10-26), living prophets, service, and love—characteristics found in the Lord's church.

Christ continued by warning the disciples what would happen if the church were not built on his gospel: "But if it be not built upon my gospel, and is built upon the works of men, or upon the works of the devil, verily I say unto you they have joy in their works for a season, and by and by the end cometh, and they are hewn down and cast into the fire, from whence there is no return. For their works do follow them, for it is because of their works that they are hewn down; therefore remember the things that I have told you." (3 Ne. 27:11-12.) People who follow a false or incomplete gospel may have joy in their activities for a time during this life, but when the end comes they will not enjoy an inheritance in the celestial kingdom.

209

Thus the Lord has placed upon us the calling of missionary work, to make the blessings of the fullness of the gospel available for all people.

The Gospel

After Christ taught his disciples about the name and importance of his church, he taught them plainly what the true gospel consists of. In 3 Nephi 27:13-22 the Lord gave us the scriptures' fullest definition of his gospel. Christ taught his disciples: "This is the gospel which I have given unto you—that I came into the world to do the will of my Father, because my Father sent me." (3 Ne. 27:13.) He continued by teaching that his Father had sent him to be lifted up on the cross in order to draw the people of the world to him. "As I have been lifted up by men even so should men be lifted up by the Father, to stand before me, to be judged of their works, whether they be good or whether they be evil." (3 Ne. 27:14.) Jesus affirmed that those who repent and are baptized in his name will be blessed: "If he endureth to the end, behold, him will I hold guiltless before my Father at that day when I shall stand to judge the world. And he that endureth not unto the end, the same is he that is also hewn down and cast into the fire, from whence they can no more return, because of the justice of the Father." (3 Ne. 27:16-17.) This is the gospel of the Father, who "fulfilleth the words which he hath given, and he lieth not, but fulfilleth all his words." (3 Ne. 27:18.) Jesus taught that only those who repent of their sins and endure to the end will be worthy of God's kingdom.

The Savior continued: "Now this is the commandment: Repent, all ye ends of the earth, and come unto me and be baptized in my name, that ye may be sanctified by the reception of the Holy Ghost, that ye may stand spotless before me at the last day." (3 Ne. 27:20.) This statement is at the core of the gospel. Repentance allows Christ's atonement to become an active part in our lives, and those who live with and follow the promptings of the Holy Ghost will have the assurance that they have washed their garments in Christ's blood and will have a place at his right hand. Jesus then concluded: "This is my gospel; and ye know the things that ye must do in my church; for the works which ye have seen me do that shall ye also do; for that which ye have seen me do even that shall ye do; therefore, if ye do these things blessed are ye, for ye shall be lifted up at the last day." (3 Ne. 27:21-22.) These few verses contain the most concise and clear definition of the gospel, given by the Lord himself. It can be summarized as follows: (1) the atonement, (2) faith, (3) repentance, (4) baptism, (5) reception of the Holy Spirit, (6) enduring to the end, and (7) judgment. It is significant that in Christ's own definition the gospel consists essentially of two parts—the atonement of Christ, and the principles and ordinances required of us to make the atonement effective in our lives.

Jesus commanded his disciples to write the things they had been taught, "save it be those which are forbidden." (3 Ne. 27:23.) Because of the disciples' faithfulness in carrying out this command, we today have this beautiful section of scripture.

Results of Living the Gospel

After Jesus had commanded his disciples to write his teachings, he told them that their people would be judged out of their writings: "Write the works of this people, which shall be, even as hath been written, of that which hath been. For behold, out of the books which have been written, and which shall be written, shall this people be judged, for by them shall their works be known unto men." (3 Ne. 27:24-25.) He then taught his disciples that the Father keeps a record of all things and that all the world will be judged from those records. He also told them that they would be the judges of their people: "Ye shall be judges of this people, according to the judgment which I shall give unto you, which shall be just. Therefore, what manner of men ought ye to be? Verily I say unto you, even as I am." (3 Ne. 27:27.) This command is given to us all, to live our lives so we can be like Christ. In this instance, his disciples were specifically commanded to be like their Lord so they would be ready to be the judges of their people, following Jesus' example in judgment. To accomplish this assignment, they would need to become like their Savior, and by so doing their judgment would be just. (Cf. Moro. 7:18-19.)

The final verses of 3 Nephi 27 make clear to us some of the results of obeying or disobeying God's commandments. First Jesus spoke about prayer: "Whatsoever things ye shall ask the Father in my name shall be given unto you. Therefore, ask, and ye shall receive; knock, and it shall be opened unto you; for he that asketh, receiveth; and unto him that knocketh, it shall be opened." (3 Ne. 27:28-29.) Evidently these disciples had reached the point in their worthiness that they would not ask for anything unrighteously; Christ placed no conditions on this statement. Thus whatever they asked would be granted. (See also Nephi's example in Helaman 10:4-10.)

Christ told his listeners some of his joys and sorrows. We learn that he was pleased with those whom he was visiting: "My joy is great, even unto fulness, because of you, and also this generation; yea, and even the Father rejoiceth, and also all the holy angels, because of you and this generation; for none of them are lost." (3 Ne. 27:30.) Readers should pay special attention to the fact that our personal actions can cause Christ, the Father, and angels to rejoice or sorrow. Knowing God's feelings for us and his intense concern for each of us as individuals, we should conduct our lives so as to bring honor and joy to those heavenly beings who care so much for our welfare.

In 3 Nephi 27:30, we find an excellent example of what can be achieved in this mortal life. These people had achieved such righteousness that if they continued in it they would be saved in the Father's kingdom. After expressing his joy about those whom he visited, Christ told of his sorrow concerning the future generations of the Nephites: "It sorroweth me because of the fourth generation from this generation, for they are led away captive by [the devil] even as was the son of perdition; for they will sell me for silver and for gold, and for that which moth doth corrupt and which thieves can break through and steal. And in that day will I visit them, even in turning their works upon their own heads." (3 Ne. 27:32.) The Lord knew that the righteousness achieved by those he visited would not continue in all the later generations. He knew that it would decay as people became proud and materialistic, and he sorrowed for those who would be lost.

The Three Nephites

When Christ finished explaining his gospel to the Nephite disciples, he spoke individually to each of the Twelve: "What is it that ye desire of me, after that I am gone to the Father? And they all spake, save it were three, saying: We desire that after we have lived unto the age of man, that our ministry, wherein thou hast called us, may have an end, that we may speedily come unto thee in thy kingdom." (3 Ne. 28:1-2.) Jesus granted their request and told them that when they had reached the age of seventy-two they would join him in his kingdom.

The Savior then turned to the three who had not yet requested anything of him and asked them again what they desired of him. These three disciples still did not reply, because

> they sorrowed in their hearts, for they durst not speak unto him the thing which they desired. And he said unto them: Behold, I know your thoughts, and ye have desired the thing which John, my beloved, who was with me in my ministry, before that I was lifted up by the Jews, desired of me. [See John 21:21-23; D&C 7.] Therefore, more blessed are ye, for ye shall never taste of death; but ye shall live to behold all the doings of the Father unto the children of men, even until all things shall be fulfilled according to the will of the Father, when I shall come in my glory with the powers of heaven. (3 Ne. 28:5-7.)

The three would not "taste of death." While they continued in their earthly ministry, they would not experience pain of the flesh; the only pain they would feel would be sorrow for the sins of the world. "And all this will I do because of the thing which ye have desired of me, for ye have desired that ye might bring the souls of men unto me, while the world shall stand. And for this cause ye shall have fulness of joy; and ye shall sit down in the kingdom of my Father; yea, your joy shall be full." (3 Ne. 28:9-10.) In Doctrine and Covenants 7, we learn that the Lord told John that his desire was greater than that of the others because he had desired to continue to bring souls unto Christ while the others had wanted to finish their ministry and enter the kingdom of God. Both were righteous desires, but John and the Three Nephites desired a "greater work." (D&C 7:6.) Then "the heavens were opened, and they were caught up into heaven, and saw and heard unspeakable things." (3 Ne. 28:13.) The things which they saw and heard are not recorded because they were commanded not to reveal them to anyone. (3 Ne. 28:14.) This experience was so wonderful that the disciples were not even sure if "they were in the body or out of the body," because they were transfigured so "they could behold the things of God." (3 Ne. 28:15.)

Following this glorious experience, all of the disciples continued their ministries. The nine, when they had reached the age of seventy-two, were received into God's kingdom. The three who had chosen to continue their ministry until Christ's coming in glory remained. Mormon reported that these three "did go forth upon the face of the land, and did minister unto all the people, uniting as many to the church as would believe in their preaching; baptizing them, and as many as were baptized did receive the Holy Ghost." (3 Ne. 28:18.) In later generations, in spite of the works of righteousness that the Three Nephites performed, there were some who hated them. Because of this they were persecuted, but they were delivered by the hand of God. (3 Ne. 28:19-22; 4 Ne. 1:30-37; Morm. 1:13-16.)

Years later the Three Nephites ministered to Mormon. He wrote that they will also minister unto the Gentiles, the Jews, "the scattered tribes of Israel, and unto all nations, kindreds, tongues and people, and shall bring out of them unto Jesus many souls, that their desire may be fulfilled, and also because of the convincing power of God which is in them." (3 Ne. 28:26-29.) Their great righteousness makes it possible for them to show themselves to whomever they desire. Because of this, the work that they will perform before Christ's coming will be "great and marvelous."

At this point in the record, Mormon warned those who would reject the teachings of Jesus and those whom he sends to warn the world: "Wo be unto him that will not hearken unto the words of Jesus, and also to them whom he hath chosen and sent among them; for whoso receiveth not the words of Jesus and the words of those whom he hath sent receiveth not him; and therefore he will not receive them at the last day; and it would be better for them if they had not been born." (3 Ne. 28:34-35.)

Mormon's Counsel to the Gentiles

In the last two chapters of 3 Nephi, Mormon gave inspired counsel to his future readers, particularly the Gentiles. In the Book of Mormon, the term *Gentiles* generally refers to those who are neither Jews nor descendants of Lehi. Thus most Latter-day Saints today are Gentiles according to Book of Mormon terminology. Mormon's message has great relevance for us today; he saw our day and the pitfalls into which many of our time would fall. These last two chapters of 3 Nephi warn us of specific things against which we need to protect ourselves.

Mormon wrote that when the Book of Mormon would come forth, the restoration of scattered Israel would be starting: "When the Lord shall see fit, in his wisdom, that these sayings shall come unto the Gentiles according to his word, then ye may know that the covenant which the Father hath made with the children of Israel, concerning their restoration to the lands of their inheritance, is already beginning to be fulfilled." (3 Ne. 29:1.) The restoration of the house of Israel must of necessity follow the restoration of the gospel, the priesthood, the covenants, and true doctrine. The coming forth of the Book of Mormon played a vital role in this process.

Mormon followed with the assurance that although many would doubt that God could fulfill his promises to his covenant people, he would in reality do just that: "Ye need not imagine in your hearts that the words which have been spoken are vain, for behold, the Lord will remember his covenant which he hath made unto his people of the house of Israel." (3 Ne. 29:3.) Then he gave specific warnings of problems prevalent in our day. We are told that many would spurn the doings of God, "deny the revelations of the Lord, and . . . shall say the Lord no longer worketh by revelation, or by prophecy, or by gifts, or by tongues, or by healings, or by the power of the Holy Ghost." (3 Ne. 29:5-6.) Mormon continued:

> Yea, and wo unto him that shall say at that day, to get gain, that there can be no miracle wrought by Jesus Christ; for he that doeth this shall become like unto the son of perdition, for whom there was no mercy, according to the word of Christ! Yea, and ye need not any longer hiss, nor spurn, nor make game of the Jews, nor any of the remnant of the house of Israel; for behold, the Lord remembereth his covenant unto them, and he will do unto them according to that which he hath sworn. Therefore ye need not suppose that ye can turn

215

the right hand of the Lord unto the left, that he may not execute judgment unto the fulfilling of the covenant which he hath made unto the house of Israel. (3 Ne. 29:7-9.)

These words speak directly to our day. Mormon saw our time and warned us that many would deny revelation and the various gifts of the Holy Ghost; many would say that no miracles can be performed. Among the greatest of the miracles to which he referred would be the restoration of the house of Israel, which takes place in a miraculous fashion in the Church today, in accord with the ancient promises.

For centuries, many have believed that revelation and the gifts of the Spirit were lost from the world with the death of the early apostles and thus are no longer needed. Some believe that God has revealed all that will ever need to be revealed and is no longer active in the affairs of humanity: "He hath done his work." (2 Ne. 28:5-6.) Some who deny the existence of miracles and the gifts of the Spirit are also found within the Church and fail to see the hand of the Lord directing its affairs today. Some, still claiming to be Latter-day Saints, engage in personal or public opposition to doctrines and policies established by the Lord's prophets. This is one manifestation of the lack of faith foreseen by Mormon.

After Mormon had recorded the warnings to the Gentiles, he made a plea for repentance. He urged them to put away their wicked ways and accept the gospel:

> Hearken, O ye Gentiles, and hear the words of Jesus Christ, the Son of the living God, which he hath commanded me that I should speak concerning you, for, behold he commandeth me that I should write, saying: Turn, all ye Gentiles, from your wicked ways; and repent of your evil doings, of your lyings and deceivings, and of your whoredoms, and of your secret abominations, and your idolatries, and of your murders, and your priestcrafts, and your envyings, and your strifes, and from all your wickedness and abominations, and come unto me, and be baptized in my name, that ye may receive a remission of your sins, and be filled with the Holy Ghost, that ye may be numbered with my people who are of the house of Israel. (3 Ne. 30:2.)

In Mormon's plea for repentance he wrote to all the world. Since the problems of our generation, which Mormon saw, exist among some in the Church today, his call for repentance is also to us.

Conclusion

Before Jesus left the people of the American continent, he challenged them to accept his teachings and direct their lives accordingly. "Enter ye in at the strait gate; for strait is the gate, and narrow is the way that leads to life, and few there be that find it; but wide is the gate, and broad the way which leads to death, and many there be that travel therein, until the night cometh, wherein no man can work." (3 Ne. 27:33.) The events recorded in the Book of Mormon serve as a witness to us in the latter days that living by the principles of the gospel leads to temporal and eternal joy: "There was no contention in the land, because of the love of God which did dwell in the hearts of the people. And there were no envyings, nor strifes, nor tumults, nor whoredoms, nor lyings, nor murders, nor any manner of lasciviousness; and surely there could not be a happier people among all the people who had been created by the hand of God." (4 Ne. 1:15-16.) In 4 Nephi we have an example of a people who overcame their sins and obeyed the commandments of the Lord, which brought great joy into their lives. Because of this example we know that it is possible for us also to reach that high state of righteousness.

The Book of Mormon, which witnesses to the results of righteousness, is also a witness that rejection of gospel principles brings sadness and destruction. The final fate of the Nephites testifies to that truth. Since we decide by our actions if we will follow the Lord or not, let us choose to follow the righteous example of those among whom the Savior ministered in the Book of Mormon.

20

THE COURSE OF PEACE AND APOSTASY
(4 Nephi–Mormon 2)

ANDREW C. SKINNER

Nephi's prophecies concerning the condescension of God (1 Ne. 11:16; 2 Ne. 4:26) had been fulfilled to the fullest measure as Christ concluded his post-resurrection sojourn among his New World disciples. (3 Ne. 28:12.) A God had come to earth now on two continents. The pure gospel plan had been taught by its executor, old prophecies had come to pass and new ones been given, miracles had been performed, and people had been changed. The book of 4 Nephi is a testament of the profound effects of the Savior's visit on the lives of the American people.

Fourth Nephi is a record of great righteousness as well as tremendous wickedness. With the first two chapters of Mormon's personal account of his experience, it forms a cohesive unit that constitutes a classic study on the course and structure of apostasy, showing human beings at their best and worst. Perhaps this is the most significant contribution to our theological and spiritual education made by 4 Nephi, Mormon 1, and Mormon 2.

However, 4 Nephi is of singular importance in another distinct but related aspect. Nowhere is Mormon's inspired editorial ability and prophetic mantle better demonstrated or more apparent than in 4 Nephi. It cannot be doubted that Mormon was a *great* prophet. He received a personal visit from the Savior at age fifteen (Mormon 1:15) and, thus, retained from his youth the spirit of prophecy. For, as John

---

Andrew C. Skinner is instructor of history at Metropolitan State College, Denver, Colorado.

218

wrote, "The testimony of Jesus is the spirit of prophecy." (Rev. 19:10.) From Mormon's work of abridgment on the records that make up 4 Nephi, we might well conclude that one of the most important aspects of a true prophet's responsibility involves not just the prediction of the future, but also the presentation of the past in such a way as to reveal and teach the lessons of life needed to be learned for exaltation. Thus, Mormon desired to open up the past and the future to the understanding of generations who would follow. He wrote, for example: "It came to pass that two hundred years had passed away; and the second generation had all passed away save it were a few. And now I, Mormon, would that ye should know that the people had multiplied, insomuch that they were spread upon all the face of the land, and that they had become exceedingly rich, because of their prosperity in Christ." (4 Ne. 1:22-23.)

Here Mormon testified that though he was not an eyewitness, he knew that the source of prosperity in ancient times was Christ, with the implication that it is Christ who can also point the way to well-being in every age.

The actual eyewitnesses to the events recounted in 4 Nephi (those who kept the sacred records before Mormon became their custodian) include Nephi, son of Nephi the disciple of Christ and the person for whom the book was named; Nephi's son and grandson—both named Amos; and Ammaron. We do not know the size of the original records or the amount of information kept by these brethren. But we do know that it was Mormon's inspired and prophetic redaction of all the records that would bring to future generations the essential spiritual lessons of Nephite and Lamanite history in distilled form and, thus, by its very succinctness make those lessons more concentrated, compact, and poignant to us.

In forty-nine short verses we are shown the heights and depths of a civilization's spiritual and moral condition. In forty-nine short verses we are shown the practical workings of the law of the celestial kingdom, the true order of heaven on earth, and the ideal pattern of welfare service. Also, in forty-nine short verses the reader is shown the basest impulses of a telestial society. Also in these verses we are shown the circumstances and atmosphere that will exist during

Christ's millennial reign in stark contrast to Satan's avowed purposes, influence, and workings. And, finally, in these short verses we are taken through almost one-third (approximately 300) of all the years covered by the entire Book of Mormon (approximately 1,000). Truly the magnitude of Mormon's prophetic task and accomplishment is shown clearly here.

Some readers may lament the fact that one of the greatest periods of Nephite civilization — an era of ultimate earthly peace, prosperity, and spirituality — was given such relatively sparse historical treatment. Sidney Sperry observed that "it is unfortunate — at least vexing that the great Golden Era of Nephite history . . . should be so sparingly treated by Mormon, the abridger."[1]

However, it must be remembered, first, that sometimes things were commanded by the Lord not to be discussed in the records. (3 Ne. 26:11, 18.) A similar injunction may have applied to this portion of the abridgment. Second, Mormon's purpose was not the writing of history, nor was it historical embellishment or even enlargement. His abridgment was guided by inspiration and was first and foremost intended to teach the most important truths of the kingdom as they could be culled *from* history. Mormon said at one point:

> I do this for a wise purpose; for thus it whispereth me, according to the workings of the Spirit of the Lord which is in me. And now, I do not know all things; but the Lord knoweth all things which are to come; wherefore, he worketh in me to do according to his will. And my prayer to God is concerning my brethren, that they may once again come to the knowledge of God, yea, the redemption of Christ; that they may once again be a delightsome people. And now I, Mormon, proceed to finish out my record, which I take from the plates of Nephi; and I make it according to the knowledge and the understanding which God has given me. (Words of Mormon 1:7-9.)

It has been noted in commentaries that when originally published, 3 and 4 Nephi were both called "Nephi."[2] In 1879 Elder Orson Pratt added the separate titles, 3 and 4 Nephi, to help distinguish the works from one another. Each has a different emphasis and intent — one being an American Gospel recording the Savior's visit and physical presence, the other recounting the effect of that visit and the eventual decline of an entire culture.

Effect of the Savior's Visit

As 3 Nephi testifies, dramatic physical changes occurred on the American landscape immediately preceding the coming of the resurrected Christ to the New World. (3 Ne. 8.) They were some of the most impressive events ever to occur on the Western Hemisphere. And, yet, as significant as those changes were, even greater changes took place after the Savior finished his visit and departed. These greater changes occurred in the hearts, minds, and souls of the Nephites and Lamanites for one hundred and sixty-seven years after Jesus left.

As 4 Nephi reports, so powerful an effect did the Savior's presence and testimony have on the people that they were all converted to the Lord, joined the one true church that had been formed "in all the lands round about" (a phrase likely indicating the establishment of several branches or units of the Church in various geographic sectors), and began living the celestial law. There were no disputations among the people, justice everywhere prevailed, all earthly possessions were distributed equitably, and distinctions between rich and poor were eradicated. Such a condition recalls a similar circumstance found at the same time in the Old World when, after the Lord's ascension, members of the Church of Jesus Christ also enjoyed the blessings of the gospel, though perhaps to a lesser degree: "With great power gave the apostles witness of the resurrection of the Lord Jesus: and great grace was upon them all. Neither was there any among them that lacked: for as many as were possessors of lands or houses sold them, and brought the prices of the things that were sold, and laid them down at the apostles' feet: and distribution was made unto every man according as he had need." (Acts 4:33-35.)

Of course, the greatest difference between the New and Old World church is that the latter still had to contend with an outside culture in the throes of wickedness, while the former flourished in circumstances where all people were converted to the Lord. (4 Ne. 1:2.) Thus, the Book of Mormon peoples enjoyed their blessed state for a long time. As Mormon wrote: "How blessed were they! For the Lord did bless them in all their doings; yea, even they were blessed and prospered until an hundred and ten years had passed away; and the first generation from Christ had passed away, and there was no contention in all the land." (4 Ne. 1:18.)

Still, eventually the New World church succumbed to the same fate that befell the Old. Satan got hold upon the hearts of men and women (4 Ne. 1:28), and great apostasy ensued. We are left to lament and wonder whether or not the adversary is so powerful as to *always* triumph over good in the hearts of mortals if given enough time. After all, the people of Nephi had lived the Order of Zion for one hundred and sixty-seven years. Why not longer?

If we look at the example of the people of Enoch, we are taught that evil need not always conquer good, that mortals are capable of *continuing* to live in righteousness until they can no longer be withheld from God's abode. Witness the testimony of Moses: "The Lord called his people ZION, because they were of one heart and one mind, and dwelt in righteousness; and there was no poor among them. And Enoch *continued* his preaching in righteousness unto the people of God. . . . And it came to pass that the Lord showed unto Enoch all the inhabitants of the earth; and he beheld, and lo, Zion, *in process of time*, was taken up into heaven. And the Lord said unto Enoch: Behold mine abode forever." (Moses 7:18-19, 21; emphasis added.)

These examples show that in every age or dispensation when the Spirit of the Lord rests mightily upon God's children, and is heeded, the same unifying social and economic order predominates and produces a Zion society. This is confirmed by latter-day history and scripture. The order is called the law of the celestial kingdom. (D&C 105:4-5.) Fourth Nephi shows that it *is* a law of unity: "There were no robbers, nor murderers, neither were there Lamanites, nor any manner of -ites; but they were in *one*, the children of Christ, and heirs to the kingdom of God." (4 Ne. 1:17; emphasis added.)

In modern times the Lord has confirmed the importance of unity as an essential aspect of the law of the celestial kingdom. Said he: "Be one; and if ye are not one ye are not mine." (D&C 38:27.)

The most striking thing about the law of the celestial kingdom as it operated among the Nephites and Lamanites, and others as well, was the economic equality that prevailed. The scriptures use the phrase "all things common" to describe the condition. This was not a system of communal ownership such as has been advocated by nineteenth- and twentieth-century secular political theories. Nor did it mean that each person had exactly the same amount of personal goods. As the Lord explained in latter-day revelation concerning his divine law of economic equality: "You are to be equal, or in other words, you are to have equal claims on the properties, for the benefit of managing the concerns of your stewardships, every man according to his wants and his needs, inasmuch as his wants are just." (D&C 82:17.)

The following instruction may help to further clarify the matter:

> The scriptural phrase "they had all things common" (Acts 4:32; see also Acts 2:44; 3 Nephi 26:19; 4 Nephi 1:3) is used to characterize those who lived the law of consecration in ancient times. Some have speculated that the term *common* suggests a type of communalism or "Christian Communism." This interpretation is in error. The Prophet Joseph Smith taught clearly the true nature of having all things common: "I preached on the stand about one hour on the 2nd chapter of Acts, designing to show the folly of common stock (holding property in common). In Nauvoo every one is steward over his own (property)."[3]
>
> Each stewardship is considered private property, and the residues and surpluses consecrated for the storehouse became the "common property of the whole church" (D&C 82:18). It is referred to as the "common property" because every covenant member of the order had access to it, according to his just "wants" and "needs," including the need to improve his stewardship.[4]

Millennial Conditions Foreshadowed

Conformity to the law of the celestial kingdom (under which all were economically prosperous and without social distinctions) brought the combined Nephite and Lamanite people many blessings, not the least of which was peace in all the land. In fact, of all the varied things Mormon could have chosen to include in the highly abridged record, it is most significant that he chose to repeat the fact that peace pervaded the land. In the initial twenty-three verses of 4 Nephi, Mormon reported no fewer than five times that there were no contentions in the land and that peace abounded.

This peace resulted, directly, in great prosperity as well as the working of mighty miracles. These phenomena were centered in Christ. We learn that "the *Lord* did prosper [the people] exceedingly in the land" (4 Ne. 1:7) and that no miracles were done "save it were in the name of Jesus" (4 Ne. 1:5). Of course, Christ is the Prince of Peace, and when any of God's children at any time live the *gospel* of Christ then the *peace* of Christ is promised. In fact, the Lord said to the Nephites: "The mountains shall depart and the hills be removed, but my kindness shall not depart from thee, neither shall the *covenant of my peace* be removed, saith the Lord that hath mercy on thee." (3 Ne. 22:10; emphasis added.)

The conditions spoken of in 4 Nephi parallel and foreshadow those that will exist during the thousand-year period of Christ's millennial reign, the hallmarks of which are also righteousness, peace, and prosperity. During that future era, just as in bygone times described by Mormon, enmity shall cease (D&C 101:26), and nation will no longer lift up sword against nation (Isa. 2:4).

In other respects, too, the millennium and the celestial-like era described in 4 Nephi will be very much alike. Immediately after the Savior's departure from the American continent, his disciples formed the one true church of Christ in the lands round about, and many were baptized. Eventually all people were converted to the Lord (4 Ne. 1:1-2) and each received the Holy Ghost, which testified personally of the Savior. Regarding missionary activity during the millennium, Elder Bruce R. McConkie has written:

> With the destruction of the wicked and the fall of the great and abominable church (D&C 29:21; 88:94) — events destined to accompany the ushering in of the millennium — the conversion of men to the truths of the gospel will become easy. In due course every living soul on earth will come to

the knowledge of the truth.... This means that when "all things shall be made known unto the children of men" (2 Ne. 30:15-18), they all shall accept the gospel.... This will be the day when the great promise to Israel is fulfilled: "And they shall teach no more every man his neighbour, and every man his brother, saying Know the Lord: for *they shall all know me*, from the least of them unto the greatest of them." (Jer. 31:34.)[5]

Mormon wrote "that the people of Nephi did *wax strong*, and did *multiply* exceedingly fast." (4 Ne. 1:10; emphasis added.) We also gather from the record that all, except for a very small portion, of the second generation born after the coming of Christ to America grew up in the ways of the Lord (4 Ne. 1:18-22.) Concerning the millennium, we read about those same conditions that are to exist again: "They shall *multiply* and *wax strong*, and their children shall grow up without sin unto salvation." (D&C 45:48; emphasis added.) Thus, the people of the great Nephite golden age already had what the righteous of our day yearn to see—a millennial-like existence.

Zion Lost

It is one of the greatest tragedies of human history that what could have been a story with an ending very similar to that of the city of Enoch so quickly and thoroughly turned into one of complete iniquity. The Nephites and Lamanites from A.D. 36 to A.D. 200 possessed every good thing. As Mormon stated, "Surely there could not be a happier people among all the people who had been created by the hand of God." (4 Ne. 1:16.) However, after a time this great happiness was lost forever, and the decay of their civilization was absolute.

Just as spiritual rebirth is a process (see Alma 5), so too is spiritual death. The last half of 4 Nephi as well as Mormon 1 and 2 chronicle the course and structure of the final great Nephite apostasy, whose most striking features seem to be the loss of humility, the loss of unity, and the growth of greed and hardness of heart among the people. We may outline the progress of this spiritual death in a general way.

1. Tremendous prosperity brought unrighteous pride and haughtiness. The people forgot the source of their prosperity. (4 Ne. 1:23-24.)

2. Pride fostered the disintegration of unity among the people, both economically and socially. The law of the celestial kingdom was broken, and Zion was lost. (4 Ne. 1:25-26.)

3. Satan used class differentiation and social stratification as tools not only to foster enmity between groups of people (4 Ne. 1:29), but also to encourage greed (4 Ne. 1:26). People *en masse* began identifying themselves by many different names; there were all manner of "-ites." (4 Ne. 1:36.)

4. People's hearts were hardened; the true church was continually rejected, and sacred things such as the sacrament and other ordinances were trifled with. (4 Ne. 1:26, 34; see also D&C 6:11-12.)

5. Children were purposely taught to hate righteousness (4 Ne. 1:39), which goes against instructions to parents with children in Zion (D&C 68:25-28).

6. Secret oaths and combinations again began to be administered by the devil to combine against all righteousness. (4 Ne. 1:42; see also 3 Ne. 6:28-30.) Secret combinations spread to such an extent that "there were none that were righteous save it were the disciples of Jesus." (4 Ne. 1:46.)

7. Warfare spread over the face of the land. (Morm. 1:8.)

8. Finally, wickedness covered the whole face of the land, and the Lord removed his beloved disciples. Spiritual enlightenment, heavenly gifts, and miracles completely ceased, "the Holy Ghost did not come upon any" (Morm. 1:13-14), and the "day of grace" passed from the people (Morm. 2:15).

Mormon recorded that things eventually became so bad that all life and property were in jeopardy. (Morm. 2:10.) Such a condition produced sorrow and mourning. Yet, it was not sorrowing unto repentance, "but it was rather the sorrowing of the damned, because the Lord would not always suffer them to take happiness in sin." (Morm. 2:13.) Thus, the fate of a nation—indeed, a civilization—was sealed because they would not repent! (See Morm. 2:8.)

The More Sure Word

In the midst of recounting the course of Nephite apostasy and spiritual death, Mormon took time to tell us a little about himself. He recorded that he was a sober child, which we may take to mean one full of reason, self-control, and emotional balance, who was not extreme or frivolous but serious-minded and educated. (Morm. 1:2.) Like Nephi of old, he was large in stature while still a young man. But he was also like Nephi in one other important respect; he, too, was a living witness of the reality of Christ's divinity. As he testified: "I, being fifteen years of age and being somewhat of a sober mind, therefore I was visited of the Lord, and tasted and knew of the goodness of Jesus." (Morm. 1:15.)

In this regard, Mormon is reminiscent of others who had similar experiences. We have already mentioned Nephi, who, being very young, large in stature, and desirous to know the mysteries of God, cried unto the Lord and was visited by him. (1 Ne. 2:16.) The Old Testament prophet Samuel was another young man who was visited by the Lord. (1 Sam. 3:4-21.) In modern times, of course, we have the testimony of Joseph Smith, who, as a teenager, beheld the Father and the Son. (JS–H 1:17.) As these prophets and others of like experience teach us, young people can accomplish great and marvelous things, and the prophetic call does not depend on age, wealth, or circumstances.

Mormon suffered greatly because of the wickedness of his people. However, he was buoyed up and received some comfort in the sure knowledge that he would be lifted up at the last day just as the Savior had promised. (3 Ne. 27:14.) Said Mormon: "Wo is me because of their wickedness; for my heart has been filled with sorrow because of their wickedness, all my days; nevertheless, I know that I shall be lifted up at the last day." (Morm. 2:19.)

Mormon's knowledge was well founded. He had received the Second Comforter (D&C 88:3-4, 67-68) and possessed the more sure word of prophecy, as did other Nephite prophets including Alma (Mosiah 26:20), Enos (Enos 1:27), and the Twelve on the American continent (3 Ne. 28:3). Modern revelation teaches: "The more sure word of prophecy means a man's knowing that he is sealed up unto eternal life, by revelation and the spirit of prophecy, through the power of the Holy Priesthood." (D&C 131:5.) Such was the anchor to Mormon's soul in the face of the worst kind of calamity.

Knowing what he did and having the testimony he did, Mormon endeavored to preach to his people. However, the Lord forbade him from doing so. The people had "wilfully rebelled against their God" and sinned against the light. (Morm. 1:16.) Concerning the final outcome of these willful rebels, only the Lord can say definitively. However, the following statement is instructive and may apply in this situation: "Thus saith the Lord concerning all those who know my power, and have been made partakers thereof, and suffered themselves through the power of the devil to be overcome, and to deny the truth and defy my power—They are they who are the sons of perdition, of whom I say that it had been better for them never to have been born." (D&C 76:31-32.)

Whatever the eternal condition of the people of Nephi might be, we can say with certainty that their rebellion cost them dearly in this life and in the next.

Conclusion

Mormon's abridged record instructs us clearly on the nature and course of apostasy. Humility brought faith in Christ, which brought unity and peace, which then, in turn, brought pride as people forgot the real source of their achievements. Ultimately, hatred, destruction, and bloodshed filled the land while secret combinations raged against all righteousness. Peace was forever lost. Of these things Mormon's words are at once a report, an urging, and a warning. We can and ought to learn from the Nephites that living the law of the celestial kingdom transforms the world spiritually. But how can we live this law in our modern society? How can we even come close to conformity with the Lord's law when the rest of the world seems to be entrenched in sin, greed, avarice, and hatred?

While we may not be able to do everything, we can do something. Witness the words of President Marion G. Romney:

> Full implementation of the united order must, according to the revelation, await the redemption of Zion (See D&C

105:34.) In the meantime — while we are being more perfectly taught and are gaining experience — we should be strictly living the principles of the united order insofar as they are embodied in present Church requirements, such as tithing, fast offerings, welfare projects, storehouses, and other principles and practices. Through these programs we should, as individuals, implement in our own lives the basis of the united order.[6]

We also ought to learn from the Nephites that pride and envy lead to hatred, the breakdown of society, and the loss of peace. Modern prophets have given similar warnings. Elder Marvin J. Ashton said:

> True Christians have no time for contention. Lasting peace cannot be built while we are reviling or hating others. Those who preach hate, ridicule, and untruths cannot be classified as peacemakers. Until they repent they will reap the harvest to which those engaged in the business of hatred are entitled. Feelings of enmity and malice can never be compatible with feelings of peace.
>
> "The wicked are like the troubled sea, when it cannot rest, whose waters cast up mire and dirt. There is no peace, saith my God, to the wicked." (Isa. 57:20-21.)[7]

Mormon's record stands as a witness to his own prophetic calling and testifies of the greatness of the man. From personal experience, Mormon taught us that a witness of the Savior gives one strength and hope, even in the worst circumstances and surroundings. With the Spirit we are strong. Without the Spirit we are "left to ourselves," and we "become weak like unto our [unrighteous] brethren." (Morm. 2:26.) Let us resolve to learn the lessons that Mormon's record teaches.

NOTES

1. Sidney B. Sperry, *Book of Mormon Compendium* (Salt Lake City: Bookcraft, 1968), p. 434.

2. Ibid., for example.

3. Joseph Smith, *History of The Church of Jesus Christ of Latter-day Saints*, 2nd ed. rev., edited by B. H. Roberts (Salt Lake City: The Church of Jesus Christ of Latter-day Saints, 1932-51), 6:37-38.

4. *Doctrine and Covenants Student Manual: Religion 324–325* (Salt Lake City: Church Educational System, 1981), p. 425.

5. Bruce R. McConkie, *Mormon Doctrine*, 2nd ed. (Salt Lake City: Bookcraft, 1966), p. 499.

6. *Ensign*, May 1977, p. 94.

7. *Ensign*, November 1985, p. 69.

21

MORMON AND THE DESTRUCTION OF NEPHITE CIVILIZATION
(Mormon 3–9)

THOMAS W. MACKAY

What Mormon must have felt, after nearly sixty years as general, historian, and prophet, as he helplessly witnessed his nation intent on spiritual suicide and utter annihilation! Although he found the behavior of his people reprehensible, still he had compassion for them. He offered his help, but he was unable to avert the imminent danger. And it was in this society that he had to rear his son and successor, Moroni. Mormon's humanity, his anguish, and his individuality all resound from the pages of the book, especially in that short segment entitled "The Book of Mormon."

Shaping the Historian's Mind

As we analyze Mormon's worldview, we realize from comments he made elsewhere in his abridgment of the historical record that certain people and events affected him deeply. For example, he wrote of king Benjamin in glowing terms, for ideals of industry, compassion, concern for the poor and needy, and a focus on the spiritual needs of people—these all leap out from Mormon's words. Mormon recounted how Alma's unwavering devotion to the gospel developed after he was moved by Abinadi's teachings and how it persisted in the face of adverse circumstances, despite the rebellion of people he

Thomas W. Mackay is professor of Greek and Latin at Brigham Young University.

loved, including one of his sons. Later, the conversion of the younger Alma—who resigned from political leadership to "preach the word of God" (Alma 4:19; cf. Alma 31:5)—and his experiences in teaching the people provided rich materials for the history. These individuals, with Moroni, Helaman, Nephi, and Samuel, also furnished patterns for Mormon's life.

But negative examples also abound in Mormon's account. What a contrast to these leaders Mormon made when he referred to Benjamin's contemporary, king Noah. But the wicked influence of individual apostates and leaders like Amlici, Nehor, Korihor, and Amalickiah pales in comparison to the social havoc wrought by the Gadianton robbers (contemporaneously, as though part of a worldwide phenomenon, robber bands and social deterioration were also a severe problem in the Roman Empire of the third century and again in the fifth century and later). So the prophet and historian noted at Mormon 1:18, 2:8, 28 the persistent presence of the Gadianton bands, answering his comment in Helaman 1-2, when the practice of a secret combination was introduced among the Nephites.[1] For at Helaman 2:12-14 Mormon observed, "More of this Gadianton shall be spoken hereafter. . . . And behold, in the end of this book ye shall see that this Gadianton did prove the overthrow, yea, almost the entire destruction of the people of Nephi. Behold I do not mean the end of the book of Helaman, but I mean the end of the book of Nephi, from which I have taken all the account which I have written." Thus we comprehend how Mormon had clearly seen from prophecy and from the social ills of his own lifetime the nature and origin of the destructive forces among the Nephites. This perspective was later echoed by his son Moroni, who lamented that "they [secret combinations] have caused the destruction of this people of whom I am now speaking [the Jaredite civilization], and also the destruction of the people of Nephi." (Ether 8:21.)

Other interests of Mormon included the military exploits of a man he deeply respected, the namesake of his own son: Moroni.[2] Of this great man Mormon said, "If all men had been and were, and ever would be, like unto Moroni, behold, the very powers of hell would have been shaken forever." (Alma 48:17; see 48:11-16.) This Moroni had delighted in preserving his people, not in shedding blood. Moroni's attitude, augmented by the example of the bravery and faith of Helaman's young warriors, became almost a preoccupation with Mormon.

The visit of the Savior and its effect on people nearly overwhelmed Mormon. And he had a special feeling for the three translated Nephite disciples; he had seen them himself. (3 Ne. 28:26; cf. Morm. 8:11.) In contrast to the three disciples, the response of his contemporary society must have struck Mormon forcibly, for despite his own preaching (Morm. 3:11-5:2), the Nephites refused to repent. Mormon learned how to evaluate society from experience, from abridging the Nephite records, and from heavenly visitants. So he based his historical judgment on the righteousness of the people, not on manifestations of military, political, financial, or cultural success. We discover this interpretation of history everywhere in Mormon's writings.

The first two chapters of Mormon continue the history recounted in 4 Nephi. The account begins with the injunction of the aged prophet Ammaron to the young Mormon, then but "about ten years of age" (Morm. 1:2), that he record the Nephite history of his lifetime. Nevertheless we must recall that this portion of Mormon's writings (Mormon 1-7) and the earlier bridge, "The Words of Mormon," between the small plates of Nephi (1 Nephi to Omni) and Mormon's abridgment of Mosiah from the large plates of Nephi were both made at the end of Mormon's life. Even the three chapters of Mormon's writings and teachings that Moroni inserted (Moroni 7-9) apparently antedate Mormon 7. Mormon's concluding message in Mormon 7 is poignant and direct. It thus reflects the maturity of his development as prophet-historian and offers his conclusion to the whole matter: the spiritual and cultural lessons future generations should learn from the disintegration of a once-flourishing civilization. These lessons are precisely the major motifs of the lengthy account of Nephite history that today bears his name.

An Age of Social Decay

As we pick up the story in Mormon 3, the prophet-historian had been divinely called to succeed the old prophet Ammaron. (Morm.

1:2-4.) Before this time, increasing tensions and conflicts split Nephite society into separate groups, and most people drifted from righteousness. (4 Ne. 1:27-38, 42-46; Morm. 1:7-11, 13-14.) Hence spiritual gifts and manifestations generally ceased (Morm. 1:14; cf. Morm. 9:20), though Mormon himself saw the Lord (Morm. 1:15). But in general the land was cursed; Gadianton robbers abounded; people hid up treasures, never to regain them; magic and witchcraft infected society, just as had been prophesied. (Hel. 13:30-38; 4 Ne. 1:45-46; Morm. 1:17-19; cf. Morm. 2:8, 10.) At fifteen, Mormon became military commander for the Nephites, but he had only limited success. (Morm. 2:1-11, 20-27.) Finally, in A.D. 350[3] a major mutual nonaggression pact was established among the Nephites, Lamanites, and Gadianton robbers. It did not last. Although ten years passed without battle, both Nephites and Lamanites made military preparations. (Morm. 3:1, 4.)

During the cessation of hostilities, the Nephites listened to Mormon only as their military and political leader, not as a prophet. (Morm. 3:1-3.) That was the same condition as twenty years previous, when the people lamented the wars and the degeneration of society, but only because those problems interfered with their own pleasures. Mormon pointedly commented that "their sorrowing was not unto repentance, because of the goodness of God; but it was rather the sorrowing of the damned, because the Lord would not always suffer them to take happiness in sin." (Morm. 2:13.)

In an epistle intended to intimidate his foe,[4] the Lamanite king announced his intention to resume war. In response, the Nephites fortified their cities and gathered "at the land Desolation, to a city which was in the borders, by the narrow pass which led into the land southward" (Morm. 3:5) — ironically, where the Jaredite armies had exterminated each other. In successive years (A.D. 361 and 362; Morm. 3:7-8) the Nephites repulsed the Lamanites, and those defensive victories altered Nephite desires: they wanted to go on the offensive against their enemies and utterly destroy *them*! Both sides were thoroughly infected with the same malady that afflicted the Jaredites and has been recorded of various nations: genocide of the opposition viewed as the only remedy.

In response, Mormon resigned, refusing to lead the offensive. He became "as an idle witness" (Morm. 3:16), as the Lord had commanded him. In the midst of this narrative, Mormon changed his authorial stance and directly addressed his audience, exhorting them to repentance and to an awareness of the impending final judgment. (Morm. 3:17-22.) So he indicated implicitly his disapproval of warfare, particularly for vengeance or for any purpose other than what had motivated Moroni.[5] Defense, not offense, and compassion, not annihilation, should be the motivating forces. He clearly stated this principle in his final words: "Know ye that ye must lay down your weapons of war, and delight no more in the shedding of blood, and take them not again, save it be that God shall command you." (Morm. 7:4.)

In an all-out offensive, the Lamanites assaulted and captured the key city Desolation, only to lose it again the following year. Lusting for each other's blood, both sides became depraved. Nearly a millennium before Mormon recorded the culmination of hostilities between Nephites and Lamanites, Nephi could boldly state that the invading house of Israel was more righteous than the prior inhabitants: "This people had rejected every word of God, and they were ripe in iniquity; and the fulness of the wrath of God was upon them; and the Lord did curse the land against them ... unto their destruction, and he did bless it unto our fathers unto their obtaining power over it." (1 Ne. 17:35.) For Nephi, God "raiseth up a righteous nation, and destroyeth the nations of the wicked." (1 Ne. 17:37.) By contrast, to Mormon "the judgments of God will overtake the wicked; and it is by the wicked that the wicked are punished" (Morm. 4:5), for in his day he could discern no people who would qualify as righteous.

The belligerents fought ghastly battles, slaughtering women and children; but in their campaign of A.D. 367, the Nephites, furious because of the enemy's atrocities, drove out the invading and occupying forces of the Lamanites. (Morm. 4:10-16.) The next attack of the Lamanites, in A.D. 375, marked the point of no return for the genocidal war. (Morm. 4:18.) Overwhelming the pivotal stronghold of Desolation once more, the Lamanites quickly drove forward. Despite a repetition of wartime atrocities against their families, the

Nephites were so utterly terrorized that they fled, leaving all behind. (Morm. 4:19-22.) Under these circumstances, Mormon retrieved the records that Ammaron had deposited, but we may suppose that he had already abridged much of Nephite history from the various records while he was a nonparticipant in the battles from A.D. 362 (Morm. 3:11) to sometime after the Lamanites commenced their offensive in 375 (Morm. 5:1). He completed the abridgment and hid away his source records just before the final battle. (Morm. 6:6.)

Mormon was not deluded. He realized that the Nephites had not changed, yet his compassion led him to accept command once more. As Mormon and his armies swept by cities, they gathered Nephites into their retreating hosts. Many inhabitants would not believe that the Lamanites sought complete extermination of their enemies. However, the Nephite cities were soon obliterated. (Morm. 5:4-5.) Mormon's fuller account of these years on the plates of Nephi must have sickened him, and he summarizes only briefly for his modern audience. During these bleak days following the renewal of war in A.D. 375, the events described in Mormon's epistle to Moroni, recorded in Moroni 9, likely took place, for both there and in Mormon 5:16-18, Mormon lamented the moral, social, and spiritual degeneration of the Nephites. Their failure to repent left them as chaff blown on the wind, or as a storm-tossed ship without a rudder. (Mormon's similes are almost Homeric here [Morm. 5:18].) Then, as he did in Mormon 3, the prophet-historian again addressed his future audience, the Gentiles (Morm. 5:19-24), directing them to repent or to face destruction by "a remnant of the seed of Jacob" (Morm. 5:24).

The Final Battle and Its Aftermath

Mormon's account of the horrifying end of the war is brief—fifteen verses. His epistle to the Lamanite king set the battlefield: Cumorah. (Morm. 6:1-3.) The abundance of water in that region was striking enough to merit mention, perhaps indicating that the Nephites were often not in such terrain. The year was A.D. 384, the seventy-third year of Mormon's life. The entire populace, the full spectrum of age and physical strength, awaited the attack of the imposing Lamanite army (Morm. 6:7-8); as they did so, they experienced "that awful fear of death which fills the breasts of all the wicked" (Morm. 6:7).

In the fierce fighting that ensued, Mormon himself was wounded and left for dead amid his army. (Morm. 6:10.) The battle arrangements of the Nephites called for a general for every ten thousand combatants. Mormon named thirteen Nephite generals, including Mormon and Moroni, and noted "that there were ten more who did fall by the sword." (Morm. 6:15.) Every group of ten thousand was slaughtered, usually with their generals. Of the Nephite multitude, numbering roughly 230,000, that fought at Cumorah—and the Nephite host was dwarfed by "the greatness of their [the Lamanites'] numbers" (Morm. 6:8)—only twenty-four people survived, "and also a few who had escaped into the south countries and a few who had deserted over unto the Lamanites" (Morm. 6:15).[6] We learn from Moroni that those Nephites who escaped "were hunted by the Lamanites, until they were all destroyed." (Morm. 8:2, 7.) Among those slain was his father, Mormon, which left Moroni to a difficult and solitary life for another thirty-five years. (Morm. 8:3-5; Moro. 10:1.) If we may assume that Mormon 8:6 ("four hundred years have passed away since the coming of our Lord") marks the date of Moroni's first record on his father's plates, then Mormon, though aged and wounded, might have survived for a while. Perhaps the twenty-four survivors separated and agreed to rendezvous periodically, but within fifteen years of the battle, Moroni was without family or friend. Curiously, not all the demented fury and blood-lust was directed against the Nephites, for Moroni observed that "the Lamanites are at war one with another; and the whole face of this land is one continual round of murder and bloodshed; and no one knoweth the end of the war." (Morm. 8:8.) That is indeed poetic justice for the victorious nation.

Final Advice from a Dying Prophet, General, and Historian

After briefly recording the outcome of the battle (Morm. 6:1-15), Mormon lamented the insane destruction of his people. They simply refused to repent and to obey God's laws: "O ye fair ones, how could ye have departed from the ways of the Lord! O ye fair ones, how could ye have rejected that Jesus, who stood with open arms to receive you! Behold, if ye had not done this, ye would not have fallen. But behold, ye are fallen, and I mourn your loss." (Morm. 6:17-18.) As he proceeded, he referred to the last judgment, and this thought turned him to address his future audience directly. Whereas Mormon occasionally imbedded comments in his abridgment (as at 3 Ne. 30:1-2) and also composed an entire chapter on his approach to history (Hel. 12), we may view Mormon 7 as his final plea and loving advice to a civilization that would experience many of the same destructive forces that played out on the Americas anciently. This chapter warrants our careful and complete attention.

Speaking to the remnant of the house of Israel (that is, the descendants of the Lehi-Mulekite civilizations and others from among the Gentile nations who would read this record), Mormon proclaimed the following:

1. "Know ye that ye are of the house of Israel." (Morm. 7:2.) A correct sense of identity is essential to proper behavior. Pride in one's heritage and future, as prophesied in the scriptures, includes the blessings promised to Abraham, Isaac, and Jacob. Until you know who you are, you can never reach your potential. In positing this as his first instruction, Mormon combined the insight of the prophet with that of the historian. As long as people are oriented in time, with a historical perspective, they have a sense of identity; and Mormon, as other prophets in the Book of Mormon, always hearkened back to the religious origins of the house of Israel and its prophetic future.

2. "Know ye that ye must come unto repentance, or ye cannot be saved." (Morm. 7:3.) Through his account of Nephite history and through his own efforts with his contemporaries, Mormon always put matters into correct perspective: Put your life in order and be forgiven for sins through the atonement, or else all other accomplishments in life are transitory and vain.

3. "Know ye that ye must lay down your weapons of war, and delight no more in the shedding of blood, and take them not again, save it be that God shall command you." (Morm. 7:4.) This injunction

is stunning. First, it is specific and immediately follows the prophet-historian's call to repentance and his exhortation to understand our true identity. Second, it comes from one who was a military commander for fifty years. Nevertheless, he advocated a position not unlike that of the people of Anti-Nephi-Lehi; and certainly his hero Moroni also used restraint and took a defensive stance unless God directed otherwise. For a world with hundredfold overkill capability, what better message, what more apt charge could be written? This injunction is not the fanatical rambling of a demented, antisocial radical; rather it came from an active politician-general of many years. His historical and prophetic perspective also allowed him to deliver to our generation what we need desperately to know.

4. "Know ye that ye must come to the knowledge of your fathers, and repent of all your sins and iniquities, and believe in Jesus Christ, that he is the Son of God, and that . . . he hath risen again; . . . and he bringeth to pass the resurrection of the dead, whereby man must be raised to stand before his judgment-seat." (Morm. 7:5-6.) In a sense this repeats the first two points and joins to them Mormon's lament to the slain of his people. (Morm. 6:16-22.) We should live so that we will not be ashamed on judgment day; that is, we should repent and be forgiven for past misdeeds, then be inspired to do good in the future. By focusing on the final judgment, Mormon sought to motivate us to view life from an eternal perspective, the very thing the Nephites had lost.

5. "And he hath brought to pass the redemption of the world, whereby he that is found guiltless before him at the judgment day hath it given unto him to dwell in the presence of God in his kingdom . . . in a state of happiness which hath no end." (Morm. 7:7.) With his reaffirmation of the reality of the atonement and of the possibility of endless happiness following the brief period of trial in our mortal existence, Mormon tied back to the most important of the promises to Abraham, Isaac, and Jacob: that the Redeemer of the world would come from their posterity and perform the expiatory sacrifice for all, bringing about a universal resurrection, with individual rewards conditional upon faith, repentance, and obedience.

6. "Therefore repent, and be baptized in the name of Jesus, and

lay hold upon the gospel of Christ, which shall be set before you, not only in this record but also in the record which shall come unto the Gentiles from the Jews, which record shall come from the Gentiles unto you. For behold, this is written for the intent that ye may believe that; and if ye believe that ye will believe this also; and if ye believe this ye will know concerning your fathers, and also the marvelous works which were wrought by the power of God among them." (Morm. 7:8-9.) With the injunction to repent and be baptized, Mormon linked his message to his previous thought. Once acquired, an understanding of the principles of the gospel and of God's concern for his children is best reinforced by continual pondering of the scriptures. Mormon knew well that in our day, two major records, the Bible and the Book of Mormon, would corroborate each other and mutually support the restoration of the true gospel on the earth.

7. "And ye will also know that ye are a remnant of the seed of Jacob; therefore ye are numbered among the people of the first covenant; and if it so be that ye believe in Christ, and are baptized, first with water, then with fire and with the Holy Ghost, following the example of our Savior, according to that which he hath commanded us, it shall be well with you in the day of judgment." (Morm. 7:10.) Mormon now returned to his first injunction — to know and appreciate what it means to belong to the house of Israel. The historical anchor of personal and group identity not only has strong religious implications, but it is also a psychologically sound principle. By including the specific steps to take to abide by the gospel covenant, Mormon unified and summarized his statement: faith in Christ, baptism of water and of spirit, and constant obedience will lead to happiness when we are finally judged, as we will all surely be.

A Son Completes his Father's Work

As he sensed his life was coming to an end, Mormon gave his records to his son Moroni and directed him to complete the book. (Morm. 6:6; 8:1, 3; Moro. 9:24.) How was it not complete? The historical record after the visit of the Savior is extremely brief, by both choice and commandment. (Morm. 5:9; cf. 3 Ne. 26:6-12 [especially 11].) More significantly, when Mormon summarized the Jaredite record that Mosiah had translated, a record preserved for us in Moroni's abridgment under the name of Ether, he said, "This account shall be written hereafter; for behold, it is expedient that all people should know the things which are written in this account." (Mosiah 28:19.) This was one task he marked out for himself that he had not finished, and he perhaps spoke of this with Moroni. At least what Mormon mentioned in his epistle (Moro. 9:23) seems to be contemporary with the last year of the Nephite-Lamanite war, A.D. 384. (Or perhaps Moroni, while reading his father's record, came across the passage quoted above and, with filial devotion, did not want his father's promise to be unfulfilled.)

Moroni did continue his father's record. The trials and difficulties of his solitary existence are poignantly portrayed in Mormon 8:2-11, where even Moroni for some time seemed not to have been visited by the three Nephite disciples, who were translated and who had ministered among the Nephites and Lamanites until the wickedness of the people made it impossible to continue. Moroni dearly wanted his future readers to accept his record without being critical and negative, for he knew of his human weaknesses and failings. (Morm. 8:12-13, 17; cf. Ether 12:23-29, 35-36, 40.) Nevertheless, the record is true. It is divinely inspired. Perhaps he completed his first brief statement at Mormon 8:13 ("I make an end of speaking concerning this people. I am the son of Mormon, and my father was a descendant of Nephi"), for the next verse is almost another colophon that introduces the writer: "I am the same who hideth up this record unto the Lord" (Morm. 8:14). But our verse and chapter divisions are artificial and modern, not ancient, and so it seems that Mormon 8:13-14 is one continuous and unbroken statement. And Moroni's abridgment of Ether (that is, the twenty-four gold plates of the Jaredite record given by Limhi to the seer and king Mosiah, son of Benjamin) was probably accomplished at the same time as Mormon 8-9. However, to judge from Moroni 1:1, some time, perhaps as much as twenty years (Moro. 10:1), passed before Moroni composed the book that bears his name. As his father did, Moroni turned to his future audience and addressed them as though present, a voice crying from the dust. (Morm. 8:13-14.) His description of our days is precise and pointed, for he knew us through the spirit of prophecy. His concern was simple: as a civilization, we are following the same path as the Jaredites and Nephites, so he offered us a strong word of warning.

Just as his father prophesied how the Bible and the Book of Mormon would corroborate each other, Moroni made clear that no desire of personal fame or wealth and no intimidating threat will mar the appearance of the Nephite record in the last days. (Morm. 8:14-22.) But the book will be brought to a civilization where "miracles are done away" (Morm. 8:26) and where there are "secret combinations" (i.e., Gadianton-type groups; Morm. 8:27). Also, the social ills will pervade even the churches; corruption, rampant materialism, selfishness, and pride characterize the people. (Morm. 8:28-41.) Hence, because of social and spiritual problems left unattended, "the sword of vengeance hangeth over you." (Morm. 8:41.)

In the final chapter of Mormon, Moroni wrote with an apocalyptic view to the future. Though his audience was centuries removed, he addressed them directly. His message, echoing his father's warnings, emphasized the reality of the final judgment (Morm. 9:1-6), and Moroni linked together fall, atonement, resurrection, and judgment (Morm. 9:12-14). Disbelief in continuing revelation, miracles, and other religious matters is inconsistent with scriptural accounts of God's dealings with humanity. (Morm. 9:7-18.) For if God, who does not change, did miracles in the past, only a lack of faith can cause miracles to cease. Moroni then cited the Lord's injunction to his Nephite disciples or apostles (Morm. 9:22-25), a passage parallel to Mark 16:15-18.[7] Thus a cessation of miracles marks out the people as needing to change, to accept the gospel, and to look to the judgment. (Morm. 9:26-30.)

In an aside, Moroni referred to the language of the Nephites as "reformed Egyptian," and he also observed that the Nephites knew Hebrew—but in an altered form. (Morm. 9:32-34.) Since Nephite "reformed Egyptian" had been modified "according to our manner of speech," this was probably their primary written language. It was apparently also the primary language of the brass plates: "He [Lehi] having been taught in the language of the Egyptians therefore he could read these engravings." (Mosiah 1:4.) As we noted above, Moroni was a very self-conscious writer. He wanted people to read and to receive his message without worrying about minute details, for this book was to restore the gospel and its covenants to the house of Israel, particularly the latter-day remnant of Lehi's expedition. (Morm. 9:34-37.) He remained in harmony with his father's general scheme and purpose. Moroni dutifully completed what Mormon had undertaken.

NOTES

1. See also Alma 37:27-32 (about the secret combinations among the Jaredites), Helaman 6:17-32, and 4 Nephi 1:42, 46; also Hugh Nibley, *An Approach to the Book of Mormon* (Salt Lake City: Deseret Book, 1957), pp. 315-34 (now reprinted in a third edition [Salt Lake City: Deseret Book Company, and Provo, Utah: Foundation for Ancient Research and Mormon Studies, 1988], pp. 378-99).

2. Hugh Nibley, *Since Cumorah* (Salt Lake: Deseret Book Company, 1967), pp. 330-66.

3. The dating system *Anno Domini* or from the birth of Christ developed very early in Nephite records and accurately records the year as given. However, in the Greco-Roman world it was imposed on the historical narratives and records especially due to the influence of Dionysius Exiguus (sixth century) and the Venerable Bede (early eighth century). Unfortunately historical inaccuracies and lack of precise information apparently led to misplacing the birth of Christ about three to five years late, since Herod died in March, 4 B.C (F. F. Bruce, *New Testament History* [2nd ed.; London: Oliphants, 1977], p. 22), so if we wanted to put Book of Mormon dates in a timeline with traditional dating for the Roman world, we would need to adjust them accordingly. The year of the treaty would perhaps be circa 346/47. (For the date of Christ's birth, see Bruce R. McConkie, *The Mortal Messiah* [Salt Lake City: Deseret Book Company, 1979], 1:349-50, note 2; J. Reuben Clark, *Our Lord of the Gospels* [Salt Lake City: Deseret Book Company, 1954], p. vii; and Jack Finegan, *Handbook of Biblical Chronology* [Princeton: Princeton University Press, 1964], pp. 215-59; for the general problems and source materials for ancient chronology, see Alan E. Samuel,

Greek and Roman Chronology, Handbuch der Altertumswissenschaft, 1.7 [Munich: C.H. Beck'sche Verlagsbuchhandlung, 1972].)

4. Cf. Hugh Nibley, *Lehi in the Desert and the World of the Jaredites* (Salt Lake: Bookcraft, 1952), pp. 229-31.

5. Cf. Nibley, *Since Cumorah*, pp. 330-66 *passim*, but especially pp. 330, 340-41, 344, 348, 351-52.

6. Cf. Hugh Nibley, *Lehi in the Desert and the World of the Jaredites*, pp. 238-42.

7. There is no full parallel in the New Testament for Mormon 9:25 ("Whosoever shall believe in my name, doubting nothing, unto him will I confirm all my words, even unto the ends of the earth") except James 1:5-6. But Mormon 9:22-24 does give us cause to accept the longer ending of Mark as authentic early Christian scripture, despite textual questions based on manuscript tradition.

22

CHRIST AND THE JAREDITES
(Ether 1-4)

KENT P. JACKSON

As the ancient Jaredite civilization came to its dehumanizing end, the prophet Ether completed the record of his people, which he wrote on twenty-four plates of gold. He had been rejected by his people, as had other prophets, and now he saw their demise — living in a cave while he recorded the last days of a once-great society. (Ether 13:13-14.) Ether became a witness that the prophecies of annihilation had come true.[1] Once he had recorded that witness, he hid away the book, trusting it into the hands of God and knowing, we can be sure, that it would be made known to others in the due time of the Lord. (Ether 15:33.)[2]

Years later, a Nephite king named Limhi, son of Noah, sent an expedition of explorers to find the city of Zarahemla from which their ancestors had come. Limhi hoped to reunite his people with their fellow Nephites, from whom his colony had been separated for eighty years. Instead of finding Zarahemla, the explorers found the ruins of an ancient civilization and brought back artifacts to testify to their find. The most noteworthy of the artifacts was a record, written on "twenty-four plates which are filled with engravings, and they are of pure gold." (Mosiah 8:9; see also 8:7-14.) The due time of the Lord had arrived, and Ether's record had been discovered.

Limhi and his people could not read the plates but had an intense desire to know of their contents. Thus when Ammon and his party

---

Kent P. Jackson is associate professor of ancient scripture at Brigham Young University.

arrived from Zarahemla and told Limhi about King Mosiah—a seer who by means of some "interpreters" could make known the content of the record—Limhi "rejoiced exceedingly, and gave thanks to God, saying: Doubtless a great mystery is contained within these plates, and these interpreters were doubtless prepared for the purpose of unfolding all such mysteries to the children of men." (Mosiah 8:19; see also 8:12-14; 21:25-28.) Mosiah did translate the record, by means of "those two stones which were fastened into the two rims of a bow," which had been "prepared from the beginning, and were handed down from generation to generation, for the purpose of interpreting languages." (Mosiah 28:13-14; see also 28:11-18.)

The Nephites, anxious to learn about the nation whose history was on the record, mourned "exceedingly" and were "filled with sorrow" when they heard the tragic story of the Jaredites. Nonetheless, "it gave them much knowledge, in the which they did rejoice." (Mosiah 28:18.) In writing the book of Mosiah, Mormon noted that the Jaredite history would be included later in his record, for "all people should know the things which are written in this account." (Mosiah 28:19.) He died without including it in the Book of Mormon, but his son, Moroni, accomplished the task. "And now I, Moroni, proceed to give an account of those ancient inhabitants who were destroyed by the hand of the Lord upon the face of this north country. And I take mine account from the twenty and four plates which were found by the people of Limhi, which is called the Book of Ether." (Ether 1:1-2.) With these words, Moroni began his abridgment of the twenty-four gold plates of the Jaredite record.

Moroni found, as Mosiah had discovered earlier (Mosiah 28:17), that the Jaredite plates contained a history that extended from the creation of Adam to the time of Ether. He chose to begin his abridgment with the formation of the Jaredite colony at the time of the Tower of Babel, supposing that a record of the earlier period would already be available in the Bible at the time when the Book of Mormon would come forth. (Ether 1:3-4.)[3]

Jared and Mahonri Moriancumer

Moroni's abridgment of Ether's record devotes a third of its total space to the first generation of Jaredite history—the time of Jared and his brother and the successful establishment of their colony in the New World. The account begins at the time of the Tower of Babel, traditionally believed to be in Mesopotamia (modern-day Iraq).[4] Two great leaders are prominent at the beginning of the account—Jared and his brother, who is called in the narrative "the brother of Jared." There is no suggestion in Moroni's abridgment why he is known by this name. Perhaps his name was not recorded on Ether's twenty-four plates, or perhaps he was actually called "the brother of Jared."[5] In 1892, George Reynolds wrote that Joseph Smith had identified the brother of Jared's name as Mahonri Moriancumer.[6] Even though the reference comes from a late second-hand source, it has been accepted widely, and for the sake of convenience it will be used here. The narrative in the first chapter seems to suggest that the leader of the group was Jared. Yet he clearly recognized his brother's tremendous spiritual qualities and often took the initiative to ask him to inquire of the Lord for guidance in their collective mission. (See, for example, Ether 1:34, 36, 38.)

The Travels of the Jaredites

Knowing the intention of the Lord to confound the languages and scatter people over the earth, Jared asked his brother to pray that their language would not be confounded. Then he asked him to inquire about the relocation of their families and friends to another part of the world: "Who knoweth but the Lord will carry us forth into a land which is choice above all the earth? And if it so be, let us be faithful unto the Lord, that we may receive it for our inheritance." (Ether 1:38.) The Lord did, in fact, direct them to a promised land. With their families, their friends, and their friends' families, Jared and Mahonri Moriancumer trusted their future into the hands of God and followed his directions to a new home. With them they took flocks "of every kind," birds, fish, swarms of honeybees, and seeds of every kind. (Ether 2:1-3.) They traveled northward into a valley called "Nimrod," from which the Lord commanded them to travel "into the wilderness, yea into that quarter where there never had man been. And it came to pass that the Lord did go before them, and did talk with them as he stood in a cloud, and gave directions whither they should travel." Their journey included crossing "many waters, being directed continually by the hand of the Lord." (Ether 2:5-6.) It continued until they arrived at the "great sea which divideth the lands," at which point they stopped their journey for four years. It was from this location, which they named Moriancumer (Ether 2:13), that they later sailed across the ocean to their land of promise. The record does not give much specific information about the route of the group's travels from the valley of Nimrod to Moriancumer. Elder George Reynolds suggested: "It is evident that they first traveled northward, but whether they turned east or west is not so apparent. The general idea is that they turned eastward and crossed Central Asia."[7]

A Promised Land

In his discussion of the journeys of the Jaredites, Moroni took the opportunity to interject some profound information about the land of promise to which Jared and his people were traveling. Certainly he was in a unique position to write about the covenants and curses associated with a promised land. He knew the history of his own people and had himself witnessed their destruction. He also knew the final end of the Jaredite civilization, which makes his comments on their beginning most meaningful. He made his point clearly:

> Whoso should possess this land of promise, from that time henceforth and forever, should serve him, the true and only God, or they should be swept off when the fulness of his wrath should come upon them.
>
> And now, we can behold the decrees of God concerning this land, that it is a land of promise; and whatsoever nation shall possess it shall serve God, or they shall be swept off when the fulness of his wrath shall come upon them. And the fulness of his wrath cometh upon them when they are ripened in iniquity. (Ether 2:8-9.)

Those who desire to live in a land of promise must serve the true and only God. Those who fail to do so will be "swept off" when they reach the point of being "ripened in iniquity," that is, when their wickedness reaches the point at which punishment is inevitable.

Moroni was speaking of the Americas, which was the promised

land to the peoples of the Book of Mormon—the Jaredites, the Mulekites, and the Lehites. As he mentioned in verse 10, it was "choice above all other lands." Because the land was so vast, fertile, and rich, both the Nephites and the Jaredites were able to become extremely prosperous within a short time after their arrivals. (1 Ne. 18:24-25; Ether 6:28.) But when Moroni wrote his record, both of those civilizations had already gone to ruin for failing to serve God. He was not writing to them but to us in the latter days, the modern readers of his book.

Since the European discovery of the New World, when people from many lands began colonizing the Americas, they found a land in which God had provided an incredible richness of natural resources. Using those resources, they built, in a relatively short time, a civilization of unprecedented prosperity. Yet Moroni, who saw the world in the last days, gave somber warnings to the people of our time, explaining why the records of these fallen peoples were preserved for our benefit: "This cometh unto you, O ye Gentiles, that ye may know the decrees of God—that ye may repent, and not continue in your iniquities until the fulness come, that ye may not bring down the fulness of the wrath of God upon you as the inhabitants of the land have hitherto done." (Ether 2:11.)

Perhaps Moroni had in mind specifically those modern readers who would live in the land once promised to his own people—America—whose inhabitants now are already, collectively speaking, "ripening in their iniquity." But his warnings are appropriate for all people everywhere, for all nations are ripening in iniquity. He wrote these words so people in all lands could repent and avoid the calamities to which the Jaredites and his own people had subjected themselves.

Not all covenant people share the same promised lands. Palestine was the promised land and gathering place for the Israelites in ancient times; the Americas were the promised land and gathering place for the ancient Jaredites and the children of Lehi. Today each land is the land of promise and the place of gathering for those who live in it,[8] and the warnings and promises that Moroni gave in Ether 2:8-12 apply to all Latter-day Saints in their own nations. We can enjoy the blessings and the promises only if we and our fellow citizens, wherever we may live, "serve the God of the land, who is Jesus Christ." (Ether 2:12.)

Obtaining Light

Having been instructed by the Lord to build boats to convey his people across the waters, the brother of Jared successfully fulfilled the Lord's wishes. Yet God's instructions did not include showing him how light would be provided in the boats. For this he needed to exert his own initiative and make the best use of his God-given intellectual and spiritual resources. The Lord gave the brother of Jared an opportunity to grow. By making it necessary for him to find a way to light the barges, the Lord was challenging him to exercise his *agency*, his *intelligence*, and his *faith.*

The Lord motivated the brother of Jared to exercise his agency by placing on *him* the responsibility to find light for the barges. He had to make a decision himself rather than expecting God to do all that was needed. Mahonri exercised his intelligence by devising a solution that was functionally possible. His solution was, in fact, a good one; but it still required divine approval (which it received). And it still needed a miracle to make it work; only the Lord himself could create the light. Concerning the experience of the brother of Jared, Elder Harold B. Lee wrote: "It was as though the Lord were saying to him, 'Look, I gave you a mind to think with, and I gave you agency to use it. Now you do all you can do to help yourself with this problem; and then, after you've done all you can, I'll step in to help you.' "9 Mahonri's enormous faith was demonstrated when he asked the Lord to touch the stones and provide light. He knew that the Lord would hear his plea, once he had exerted himself as the Lord required: "I know, O Lord, that thou hast all power, and can do whatsoever thou wilt for the benefit of man. . . . O Lord, thou canst do this. We know that thou art able to show forth great power." (Ether 3:4-5.) And the Lord did.

An Encounter with Christ

What followed is one of the greatest events in scriptural history: "The veil was taken from off the eyes of the brother of Jared, and he saw the finger of the Lord; and it was as the finger of a man, like unto flesh and blood." (Ether 3:6.) Seeing the Lord's finger was a startling revelation to him: "I saw the finger of the Lord. . . . I knew not that the Lord had flesh and blood." (Ether 3:8.) In response to Mahonri's faith, Jehovah decided to reveal more to him about the nature of God: "Because of thy faith thou hast seen that I shall take upon me flesh and blood. . . . Sawest thou more than this? And he answered: Nay; Lord, show thyself unto me." (Ether 3:9-10.) The Lord showed himself to the brother of Jared with these words: "Seest thou that ye are created after mine own image? Yea, even all men were created in the beginning after mine own image. Behold, this body, which ye now behold, is the body of my spirit; and man have I created after the body of my spirit; and even as I appear unto thee to be in the spirit will I appear unto my people in the flesh." (Ether 3:15-16.)

Mahonri was speaking with Jehovah, who later was born on earth, received a physical body, and was called Jesus Christ. Like other ancient prophets, he beheld the Lord's spirit body, in the image of which all men were created. (Gen. 1:26; Moses 1:6; Ether 3:15-16.) We cannot tell from the account exactly what the brother of Jared knew about the nature of God prior to this vision. But it appears in verse 8 that he was startled to see what he thought was a body of "flesh and blood." The Lord's comments in verse 16 make it clear that it was a body of spirit that the prophet saw. His misunderstanding shows that a spirit body resembles the flesh-and-blood body with which we are familiar. (D&C 77:2.)

Moroni provided a valuable summary: "Jesus showed himself unto this man in the spirit, even after the manner and in the likeness of the same body even as he showed himself unto the Nephites." (Ether 3:17.)

A most remarkable aspect of this experience is the powerful demonstration of faith on the part of Mahonri Moriancumer. Because he so completely *knew* that God would provide the light, the Lord could not keep him inside the veil that separates the earthly realm from the divine. "Never has man come before me with such exceeding faith as thou hast," said Jehovah. (Ether 3:9.) The prophet showed even greater faith when he requested, "Lord, show thyself unto me."

(Ether 3:10.) He testified that he believed the Lord's words before hearing them, knowing that God cannot lie. (Ether 3:12.) As Moroni reported, "Having this perfect knowledge of God, he could not be kept from within the veil." Indeed, "the Lord could not withhold *anything* from him, for he knew that the Lord could show him *all* things." (Ether 3:20, 26, emphasis added; see also Ether 12:20-21.) As a result of this faith, his exaltation was assured. His ultimate return to the presence of God had been given divine confirmation, and he then was permitted to see God and abide in his presence. (Ether 3:12-13.)[10]

Then came a statement from the Lord that sets the brother of Jared apart from every other person who had ever lived on earth up to that time: "*Never* have I showed myself unto man whom I have created, for *never* has man believed in me as thou hast." (Ether 3:15, emphasis added; see also verse 9.) The uniqueness of Mahonri Moriancumer's faith justified the uniqueness of Jehovah's revelation to him. No one else—including such prophets as Adam, Seth, Enoch, and Noah—had ever experienced in mortality such a manifestation of God, because no one else had ever exercised such faith.

Although the first part of verse 15 is difficult to understand, it is clear that there was something extraordinary about the appearance of the Lord to the brother of Jared, whose faith exceeded that of every other person since the beginning of time. We know from the scriptures that others had seen God, yet the Lord stated to the brother of Jared: "Never have I showed myself unto man."[11] Perhaps the following discussion will explain the Lord's statement.

The brother of Jared was speaking with Jehovah, "the Lord Omnipotent who reigneth, who was, and is from all eternity to all eternity, . . . the Father of heaven and earth, the Creator of all things from the beginning." (Mosiah 3:5, 8; see also Alma 11:39.) Under the direction of God the Father, whom we call Elohim, Jehovah is God of the universe, presiding over all things. Having been endowed by Elohim with infinite power, glory, and authority, Jehovah *is* the Father. He is God who spoke and still speaks to the prophets, who designed and reveals laws for the blessing of his people, and who directs the affairs of mortals on earth.

We know also that Jehovah is the same being who later came into the world as Jesus Christ. He became a being of dual nature: *Father* and *Son, God* and *Man.* (See Mosiah 15.) Prior to his mortal birth, he was the Lord Jehovah (Father, God); while he walked the earth he was the mortal Jesus Christ (Son, Man). Now he sits again on a throne of glory in the heavens. (See Philip. 2:5-11; Col. 1:12-20.)[12]

Concerning Jehovah's work, Elder Joseph Fielding Smith wrote:

> All revelation since the fall has come through Jesus Christ, who is the Jehovah of the Old Testament. In all of the scriptures, where God is mentioned and where he has appeared, it was Jehovah who talked with Abraham, with Noah, Enoch, Moses and all the prophets. He is the God of Israel, the Holy One of Israel; the one who led that nation out of Egyptian bondage, and who gave and fulfilled the Law of Moses. (1 Ne. 19:10; 3 Ne 11:10, 14; 15:2-9.) The Father [that is, Elohim] has never dealt with man directly and personally since the fall, and he has never appeared except to introduce and bear record of the Son.[13]

President Smith also taught: "The Father has honored Christ by placing his name upon him, so that he can minister in and through that name *as though he were the Father;* and thus, so far as power and authority are concerned, *his words and acts become and are those of the Father.*"[14]

Since Jehovah is empowered with the fulness of Elohim and is commissioned to speak in his behalf, he stands in the place of the Father and speaks the Father's words. Thus when he appeared in ancient times he was the Father, filling in every way the role of God. When giving revelation to prophets, he spoke of the mortal mission of Jesus Christ in the third person — that is, with the words of and from the perspective of God the Father, as though Jesus Christ were someone else. This explains Jehovah's discussion of Christ in Moses 1 and in many other scriptures.[15]

It seems from the scriptures that with one exception, in all the recorded manifestations of Jehovah prior to his birth in the flesh, he appeared in his role as God the Father, speaking the words of the Father. The exception is this appearance to the brother of Jared in

Ether 3. He said: "Behold, I am Jesus Christ. I am the Father and the Son. In me shall all mankind have life, and that eternally, even they who shall believe on my name; and they shall become my sons and my daughters. And never have I showed myself unto man whom I have created, for never has man believed in me as thou hast." (Ether 3:14-15.)

It appears that the uniqueness of this situation, brought about because of Mahonri Moriancumer's unparalleled faith, was the fact that Jehovah appeared to him in his role as Jesus — whereas to others he had shown himself as the Father. Never before, as far as we can tell from the scriptures, had Jesus Christ shown himself unto man. And, in fact, nowhere else in the scriptures do we have an example of Jehovah appearing in his role as Jesus until his coming in the flesh. As Moroni reported, "Having this perfect knowledge of God, *he could not be kept from within the veil; therefore he saw Jesus;* and he did minister unto him." (Ether 3:20, emphasis added.) To the brother of Jared the Lord revealed his complete nature: God who would become Man. Perhaps that is a reason why he commanded that the account of the appearance not be known in the world until after his mortal ministry. (Ether 3:21.)

Exercising Faith in the Lord

Mahonri's vision was not over with the appearance of Christ. The Lord "showed unto the brother of Jared *all* the inhabitants of the earth which had been, and also *all* that would be; and he withheld them not from his sight, even unto the ends of the earth." (Ether 4:25, emphasis added; cf. Moses 1:27-28.)[16] The Lord had told him that if he believed he could be shown all things, it would be so. Because he did, God "*could not* withhold *anything* from him, for he knew that the Lord could show him all things." (Ether 3:26, emphasis added.) This was no ordinary man; few people who have ever lived have been greater. Faith is the process of reaching out beyond our knowledge. The more knowledge we possess, the farther we can reach. The faith of Mahonri Moriancumer was so great that *nothing* could be withheld from him. Nowhere in the scriptures do we have an example of more perfect faith.

The sacredness of the event required that the record of it be kept sacred as well. The brother of Jared was commanded to write down what he had experienced and to seal it up, along with two stones that the Lord provided for interpreting such sacred records. (Ether 3:22-23, 27-28; 4:2.) Moroni, the inspired historian of the account, knew that the record was a treasure of inestimable worth, to be preserved to come forth among a righteous generation. Until humanity is worthy of such an endowment of knowledge, the record will remain sealed. (Ether 4:6-7.) To see what Mahonri Moriancumer saw will require the same kind of faith that he had. Likely that level of faith will not be had in the Church sufficiently until the Millennium. (See D&C 101:32-34.)[17]

Lack of faith and lack of faithfulness are the sicknesses that create spiritual blindness. No one knew that better than Moroni, who had witnessed it to the fullest extent — in his own lifetime and vicariously through the records entrusted into his care. Using the faith of the brother of Jared as a standard, he recorded the Lord's words that challenge us to enlarge the boundaries of our own faith: "I will show unto you the greater things, the knowledge which is hid up because of unbelief. . . . When ye shall rend that veil of unbelief which doth cause you to remain in your awful state of wickedness, and hardness of heart, and blindness of mind, then shall the great and marvelous things which have been hid up from the foundation of the world" be made known. (Ether 4:13, 15.)

Those with such faith will not be kept within the veil that separates the holy from the earthly. They shall see what the prophets have seen and know what the prophets have known.

NOTES

1. The book of Omni contains a brief reference to a Jaredite matter, written by Amaleki before Ether's history was discovered. Sometime between the arrival of the Mulekites in the New World and their joining with king Mosiah and the Nephites (Omni 1:12-15), the Mulekites came upon a

large inscribed stone. It was written by a man named Coriantumr, who was alive at the time of the discovery and lived for nine months among the Mulekites. (Omni 1:20-22.) This was undoubtedly the same Coriantumr who was a contemporary of Ether and who played a major role in the final events in the history of the Jaredite nation. (See Ether 12-15; especially 15:29-34.)

2. We are not informed of Ether's sources for the compilation of his record, which covered over two thousand years. But knowing how other sacred histories were written, including that of Mormon and Moroni, it is certainly possible that Ether had earlier Jaredite writings from which he compiled his account.

3. I suppose that it would not be inappropriate to wish that Moroni had included the account of history from Adam's time to that of Jared. Since we know from the Joseph Smith Translation and the Book of Mormon that the Old Testament did not arrive in the latter days without suffering major omissions, it is likely that the Jaredite equivalent of Genesis 1-11 would reveal fascinating information to us that is not available elsewhere.

4. Without question, the book of Ether clearly substantiates the historicity of the Tower of Babel and the account of the confounding of the languages that took place because of it. Whatever the exact circumstances may have been, at least we know because of Ether's account—untainted by textual manipulation and uninspired tradition—that there was such a tower and that the Lord did indeed confound the languages of his children in order to scatter them throughout the earth. (Ether 1:33-37.)

5. Arab men frequently have secondary names constructed from "Abu" ("father of"), often followed by the name of the first-born son (i.e., Abu-Ibrahim, "father of Ibrahim," etc.).

6. The account was published in a footnote in the *Juvenile Instructor*, May 1, 1892, p. 282. It reads as follows: "While residing in Kirtland Elder Reynolds Cahoon had a son born to him. One day when President Joseph Smith was passing his door he called the Prophet in and asked him to bless and name the baby. Joseph did so and gave the boy the name of Mahonri Moriancumer. When he had finished the blessing he laid the child on the bed, and turning to Elder Cahoon he said, the name I have given your son is the name of the brother of Jared; the Lord has just shown [or revealed] it to me. Elder William F. Cahoon, who was standing near heard the Prophet make this statement to his father; and this was the first time the name of the brother of Jared was known in the Church in this dispensation."

7. *Juvenile Instructor*, May 1, 1892, p. 284, note. Elder Reynolds also wrote: "We have no direct information in regard to the locality of Morian-

cumer, but those who believe that the Jaredites traveled eastward through Central Asia, are of the opinion that it was near the mouth of one of the great rivers that flow through the Chinese empire into the Pacific Ocean." (*Juvenile Instructor*, May 1, 1892, note.)

8. Spencer W. Kimball, *The Teachings of Spencer W. Kimball*, ed. Edward L. Kimball (Salt Lake City: Bookcraft, 1984), pp. 439-40; see also Harold B. Lee, citing Bruce R. McConkie, in *Conference Report*, April 1973, pp. 6-7.

9. "How to Receive a Blessing from God," *Improvement Era*, October 1966, p. 862.

10. See Joseph Smith, *Teachings of the Prophet Joseph Smith*, selected by Joseph Fielding Smith (Salt Lake City: Deseret Book Company, 1938), p. 150.

11. Several explanations have been given for this passage. See Joseph Fielding Smith, *Answers to Gospel Questions*, 5 vols. (Salt Lake City: Deseret Book Company, 1957-66), 2:124-25; Bruce R. McConkie, *The Promised Messiah* (Salt Lake City: Deseret Book Company, 1978), pp. 47, 599-600; Sidney B. Sperry, *Answers to Book of Mormon Questions* (Salt Lake City: Bookcraft, 1967), pp. 47-51; Daniel H. Ludlow, *A Companion to Your Study of the Book of Mormon* (Salt Lake City: Deseret Book Company, 1976), p. 318.

12. See Kent P. Jackson, "Jesus and the Gospels," *Studies in Scripture, Vol. 5: The Gospels*, ed. Kent P. Jackson and Robert L. Millet (Salt Lake City: Deseret Book Company, 1986), pp. 2-5.

13. Joseph Fielding Smith, *Doctrines of Salvation*, 3 vols., comp. Bruce R. McConkie (Salt Lake City: Bookcraft, 1954-56), 1:27.

14. Ibid., p. 30, emphasis added.

15. It also helps clarify the identities in Isaiah 53 (see especially verse 10). For a detailed discussion of the role of Christ as Father, see Robert L. Millet, "The Ministry of the Father and the Son," in *The Book of Mormon: The Keystone Scripture*, ed. Paul R. Cheesman (Provo, Utah: Religious Studies Center, Brigham Young University, 1988), pp. 44-72.

16. Rodney Turner wrote concerning Moses' similar vision in Moses 1:27-28: "Nor did he simply view them en masse as one might look at a vast concourse of people without discerning any one individual. By the incomprehensible power of the Holy Ghost he perceived each man, woman, and child comprising the human race *at one and the same time!* In doing so, he experienced something of the omnipresent nature of the Spirit of the Lord." ("The Visions of Moses," *Studies in Scripture, Vol. 2: The Pearl of*

Great Price, ed. Robert L. Millet and Kent P. Jackson [Salt Lake City: Randall Book Company, 1985], p. 55.)

17. See Bruce R. McConkie, "The Doctrinal Restoration," in *The Joseph Smith Translation: The Restoration of Plain and Precious Things*, ed. Monte S. Nyman and Robert L. Millet (Provo, Utah: Religious Studies Center, Brigham Young University, 1985), pp. 15, 20-21.

23

PROMISES FULFILLED
(Ether 5–8)

ANDREW C. SKINNER

Long before the ancient patriarch Abraham, father of the Hebrews, went out from Ur and journeyed to his land of promise as part of the great covenant, others had already left the Near East and traveled thousands of miles in search of yet another promised land. Moroni's abridged account of the voyage and arrival of the Jaredites, found in Ether 5-8, is inspiring as well as instructive theologically, prophetically, historically, culturally, and politically. It provides us with many instances of prophecies and promises fulfilled by the Lord.

Perhaps God sends people to covenant lands so that they might establish a special relationship with him as they struggle in the midst of ungodliness. Five such examples immediately come to mind: the Jaredites, Abraham and his people, the Israelites under Moses, the Nephites, and the nineteenth-century Latter-day Saint pioneers.

That Deity takes seriously the giving of certain lands or territories, viewing them as *special* gifts and important symbols of favored status, seems certain. (See 2 Ne. 3:2; and 9:1-2, for example.) All the lands of the earth are God's, just as the psalmist wrote: "The earth is the Lord's, and the fulness thereof." (Ps. 24:1.) God may give *whatever* land he chooses to *whomever* he chooses. But those who receive come under strict requirements of righteous living, as the Jaredite record demonstrates: "But he would that they should come forth even unto the land of promise, which was choice above all other

_____

Andrew C. Skinner is instructor of history at Metropolitan State College, Denver, Colorado.

lands, which the Lord God had preserved for a righteous people. And he had sworn in his wrath unto the brother of Jared, that whoso should possess this land of promise, from that time henceforth and forever, should serve him, the true and only God, or they should be swept off when the fulness of his wrath should come upon them." (Ether 2:7-8.)

Thus, God may also sweep off from the face of his property whomever he chooses; and this he has done in the past. (See Gen. 6:7; Deut. 7:1-2; 1 Sam. 15:3, 8; Ether 15.)

Moroni interrupted the story of Jaredite travel and settlement in the land of promise by inserting some direct and personal instructions to the future translator of the record he had produced. Moroni warned him not to touch the portion of the record that was sealed up unless God so commanded him. (Ether 5:1.) According to Moroni, the sealed portion contained "the very things which the brother of Jared saw" (Ether 4:4) on Mount Shelem; in particular "all the inhabitants of the earth which had been, and also all that would be; and he withheld them not from his sight, even unto the ends of the earth" (Ether 3:25). These are some of the things other great prophet-patriarchs have also viewed, as attested to by Enoch (Moses 6:36), Abraham (Abr. 3:22), Moses (Moses 1:8, 28), and even our first father, Adam (D&C 107:56).

Having been instructed by the Lord that this "revelation from God, from the beginning of the world to the ending thereof" (2 Ne. 27:7) would not be given to other people until they became sanctified like Jared's brother (Ether 4:7), Moroni told the future prophet (Joseph Smith) that it was not to be translated. However, Moroni was able to promise him that the plates containing the record would be shown to three witnesses who would help him translate the appointed portion. Their testimony was to stand as evidence to the rest of the world of the record's reality and truth.

The Law of Witnesses

So it was in June 1829, some 1,400 years after Moroni's prophetic instructions to a future prophet, that three men asked Joseph Smith if they could be the special witnesses spoken of by Moroni in Ether 5:2-4. Joseph Smith's own words recount the episode:

> In the course of the work of translation, we ascertained that three special witnesses were to be provided by the Lord, to whom He would grant that they should see the plates from which this work (the Book of Mormon) should be translated; and that these witnesses should bear record of the same, as will be found recorded [2 Ne. 11:3; Ether 5:2-4]. Almost immediately after we had made this discovery, it occurred to Oliver Cowdery, David Whitmer and the aforementioned Martin Harris (who had come to inquire after our progress in the work) that they would have me inquire of the Lord to know if they might not obtain of him the privilege to be these three special witnesses; and finally they became so very solicitous, and urged me so much to inquire that at length I complied.[1]

The revelation that followed promised the fulfillment of Moroni's earlier prophecy; it is set forth in modern scripture as section 17 of the Doctrine and Covenants. It begins with these words: "Behold, I say unto you, that you must rely upon my word, which if you do with full purpose of heart, you shall have a view of the plates, and also of the breastplate, the sword of Laban, the Urim and Thummim, which were given to the brother of Jared upon the mount, when he talked with the Lord face to face." (D&C 17:1.)

According to the Prophet Joseph Smith, not many days after the revelation was received, the four men (Joseph Smith, Martin Harris, David Whitmer, and Oliver Cowdery) went into some woods near David Whitmer's house to try to obtain the actual fulfillment of the promises made in the revelations from God. (Ether 5; D&C 5; 17.) Each man, beginning with Joseph Smith, took a turn at praying vocally for an answer or divine manifestation. The same procedure was repeated after the first attempt failed to produce the desired result. After a second failure, Martin Harris withdrew himself, believing that he was the cause of the difficulty. The men, without Martin Harris, again prayed and in a matter of minutes received a glorious manifestation of the plates held by an angel. They also heard a voice from heaven that confirmed the very words Moroni had uttered many centuries earlier when he prophesied precisely that the plates would be "shown by the power of God." (Compare the wording in Ether 5:3 and *History of the Church* 1:55.)

Joseph Smith left the two in order to check on Martin Harris. Joseph and Martin joined in prayer with the following result, as reported by the Prophet himself: "Before we had yet finished, the same vision was opened to our view, at least it was again opened to me, and I once more beheld and heard the same things; whilst at the same moment, Martin Harris cried out, apparently in an ecstasy of joy, ' 'Tis enough; 'tis enough; mine eyes have beheld; mine eyes have beheld;' and jumping up, he shouted, 'Hosanna,' blessing God, and otherwise rejoiced exceedingly."[2]

These episodes constitute the final link in an ancient chain going all the way back to the Jaredites. For it is, in part, the things that happened to Jared, his brother, and their families, that the three witnesses attested to. Oliver Cowdery, David Whitmer, and Martin Harris were the physical, literal fulfillment of Moroni's promise. They became living witnesses not only of the things the Prophet Joseph Smith was doing but also of the importance of the law of witnesses itself. Because of this law of witnesses, Joseph Smith did not have to stand alone as he fielded the abuses and injuries inflicted by an apostate world. Thus, we may more fully appreciate his remarks made soon after his experience with the three witnesses: "Father, mother, you do not know how happy I am; the Lord has now caused the plates to be shown to three more besides myself. They have seen an angel, who has testified to them, and they will have to bear witness to the truth of what I have said, for now they know for themselves that I do not go about to deceive the people, and I feel as if I was relieved of a burden which was almost too heavy for me to bear, and it rejoices my soul that I am not any longer to be entirely alone in the world."[3]

At the time Moroni prepared his abridgment of the account of the people of Jared, circa A.D. 400, the law of witnesses was already a very ancient one. It was an integral part of the cultural, legal, and moral heritage carried by Moroni's ancestors from Jerusalem in 600 B.C. Though nothing is said in the Bible about qualification, it is likely that a witness in biblical times was considered to be any free man who had firsthand knowledge of a fact or an event.[4] During early Christian times, those who had firsthand knowledge of Jesus were called witnesses. Eventually the Greek word for witness, *martus*, came to denote those who had given up their lives or met violent deaths in pursuit of the Christian cause, martyrs.

Moroni's understanding of the law of witnesses parallels that of the Apostle Paul; that is, "In the mouth of two or three witnesses shall every word be established." (2 Cor. 13:1.) The knowledge of both Paul and Moroni regarding the law was undoubtedly based, in part, on several Mosaic prescriptions that required the testimony of at least two witnesses to establish with certainty any claim. (Num. 35:30; Deut. 17:6; 19:15.) It was the intention of the law in ancient Israel to establish as securely as possible any information being attested to. For this reason, three witnesses were preferable to two. Multiple witnesses decreased the possibility of shoddy, perverted, or "plotting witnesses" (*edim zummim*).[5] It is significant that where the plates and sacred records are concerned, the Lord provided, first, three witnesses and, later, many more for these latter days. Concerning the law of witnesses, Elder Bruce R. McConkie wrote:

> Whenever the Lord has established a dispensation by revealing his gospel and by conferring priesthood and keys upon men, he has acted in accordance with the *law of witnesses* which he himself ordained. This law is: "In the mouth of two or three witnesses shall every word be established." (2. Cor. 13:1; Deut. 17:6; 19:15; Matt. 18:15-16; John 8:12-29.) Never does a prophet stand alone in establishing a new dispensation of revealed truth, or in carrying the burden of such a message and warning to the world. In every dispensation, from Adam's to the present, two or more witnesses have joined their testimonies, thus leaving their hearers without excuse in the day of judgment should the testimony be rejected.[6]

A Miraculous Journey

After Moroni made an end of his prophecies and promises, he gave an account of the great voyage of the people of Jared. With the many necessary preparations finally completed, the people entered their barges and set forth into the sea, putting their trust in the Lord. We are told that they were in the water an incredible 344 days — almost a full year.

Moroni's abridgment gives us some small idea of the truly miraculous and spectacular nature of the Jaredite adventure, wherein the eight barges were propelled toward their destination by a furious wind, created by the Lord, which "did never cease to blow towards the promised land." (Ether 6:8.) While some may question the veracity of such a story, it should be remembered that God is Lord over all the elements of the earth. As he himself told Moroni, "At my command the heavens are opened and are shut; and at my word the earth shall shake." (Ether 4:9.)

Even those modern-day skeptics who most disbelieve maritime theories concerning the ancient peopling of the Americas admit that some early transoceanic voyages are probable due to oceanic currents and prevailing winds. From the work of one writer we read:

> The winds and current of the North Pacific trend eastward. Any craft caught helpless in their embrace can easily be carried across the ocean; in fact, there are records to show that, for example, between 1775 and 1875 about twenty Japanese junks were blown, against their will, to the west coast of America and deposited at various points between Alaska and Mexico. If Japanese vessels in the last century, why not Chinese or Indian or Malaysian during all the long centuries that preceded the arrival of Columbus? There must have been a certain number that ended a storm-tossed journey on this side of the Pacific. Perhaps a few of the hardier spirits among their crews risked the long sail back home, but most must have chosen to live on where they landed. Eventually they either died out or became wholly absorbed, leaving behind only tantalizing indirect reminiscences of their presence such as art motifs, pottery shapes, and the like.[7]

Other less skeptical scholars have long recognized the reality of transoceanic crossings but have opted to support Atlantic-route theories also based, in part, on the existence of "gentle climatic conditions and extremely favorable ocean currents and prevailing winds."[8]

In fact, journeys like that of the Jaredites are in harmony with ancient Near Eastern cultural and literary motifs as well as historical circumstances of the late fourth and early third millennium B.C., which is the time-frame posited by recent scholarship for the rise of Jaredite civilization in the New World.[9] Very early Near Eastern records abound with references to ships and voyages. "No motif is more common in the miniature art of the Mesopotamian cylinder seals than the reed boats used by the legendary heroes in the period of settlement."[10] Mesopotamia was known for its seagoing excursions, and it is also generally accepted as the land of the tower where the Jaredites originated. The earliest Mesopotamian people, known as the Sumerians, incorporated into their literature the episode of the great flood. Regarding the period of settlement after the flood, Sumerian writings indicate that the survivors landed in a big ship at a place called Dilmun and from there went to Mesopotamia, also by sea.[11] Thus, seagoing ventures were, early on, a significant part of the Mesopotamian cultural milieu. Some scholars have suggested that the oldest sign for *ship* in ancient Sumer was the same as the one used for the *marine* in the hieroglyphic script of Egypt.[12] These writing systems both date to before 3000 B.C..

The ancient Jaredite record gives us some idea concerning the construction of the barges, which were "tight like unto a dish." The record compares them to the ark of Noah. (Ether 6:7.)

Because the Jaredite barges were watertight, they could be "buried in the deep" without harm to their passengers. It was this construction that made necessary the special system of lighting (sixteen transparent stones) designed by the brother of Jared and put into operation by the finger of the Lord. The King James Version of the Old Testament reports that Noah's ark was to have a "window" for a light: "A window shalt thou make to the ark." (Gen. 6:16.) However, some modern Jewish translators of the Hebrew text render this passage: "A *light* shalt thou make to the ark." The word in question, *tsohar*, in the dual form means "noon" or "midday." Ancient Jewish legend relates that it was not just a light in the ark but was actually "a precious stone which illuminated the whole interior of the Ark."[13]

In another interesting parallel to the Jaredite barges found in ancient Near Eastern literature, one of the heroes of the Gilgamesh Epic is commanded to build a ship in the face of an impending flood. This hero (Utnapishtim) is told by one of the gods to build it according to proper specifications and to caulk or seal it. The boat will take him down into "the (watery) Deep . . . to dwell."[14]

Suffice it to say that nonscriptural sources provide an important historical and cultural context for the events recounted by Moroni. In Joseph Smith's day, such things as these were almost totally unknown. Nowadays we know that the Jaredite record fits the pattern of the ancient world. And yet our conviction of its truth is a matter of faith.

Jaredite Kingship

Perhaps we cannot appreciate from Moroni's brief account the great joy felt by the people of Jared when they finally landed in the promised land. They stood upon a land that was both promised and promising. It represented, in tangible form, the very fulfillment of the Lord's words: "I will go before thee into a land which is choice above all the lands of the earth." (Ether 1:42.) It represented, in tangible form, a covenant kept. We may only guess at the kind of powerful revelations the people received as they were "taught from on high" in their new home. (Ether 6:17.)

After not too long a time, as the record seems to indicate, the people of Jared voiced their desire to have a king rule over them. History confirms that monarchy has existed since the earliest periods of human culture. Some peoples have believed that kingship was instituted by, and serves as the agent of, divine will. The situation of the Jaredites at this juncture in their history immediately brings to mind the people of Israel, who also clamored for a king. They were told by Samuel the prophet the same thing the brother of Jared told his people centuries earlier: "Surely this thing leadeth into captivity." (Ether 6:23.)

Perhaps because they knew the risks associated with kingship, several of the Jaredites refused the office. Finally, one of the sons of Jared — Orihah — was anointed. He was a righteous and successful king because he "did walk humbly before the Lord, and did remember how great things the Lord had done for his father, and also taught his people how great things the Lord had done for their fathers." (Ether 6:30.)

Orihah is a perfect example of the Lord's teachings on righteous kingship as presented by Mosiah. If just rulers could always be chosen, then kingship would be an expedient form of government. However, not all leaders are just, and it is therefore usually not expedient to have kings rule. As Mosiah taught, "How much iniquity doth one wicked king cause to be committed, yea, and what great destruction!" (Mosiah 29:17.)

Clearly the brother of Jared well understood the Lord's teachings regarding kingship, for it was not long after the reign of Orihah that his prophetic words were fulfilled when Orihah's successor was brought into captivity. (Ether 7:5.) What followed was one of the bright spots in the history of the Jaredite people—a history filled with rebellion, treachery, warfare, and extreme wickedness. That bright spot was the reign of Shule, who "remembered the great things that the Lord had done for his fathers in bringing them across the great deep into the promised land; wherefore he did execute judgment in righteousness all his days." (Ether 7:27.)

Secret Combinations: Freedom Assaulted

Several things made Orihah and Shule successful and blessed rulers, bringing peace and prosperity to the Jaredites. These things include those important institutions to which all of us most owe our loyalties and allegiance: God, family, and fellow beings. After a time, when these things were rebelled against and forgotten, the Jaredite culture began to collapse. The steady slide of the Jaredite people toward destruction began in earnest with the rebellion of one Jared (son of Omer and grandson of Shule), who took his own father into captivity and sought, without moral restraint, "the kingdom and . . . the glory of the world." (Ether 8:7.)

It is significant that Jared's own daughter, following the wicked example he himself had set, provided the impetus to introduce into their society the most insidious and cunning of all Satan's wicked schemes, secret combinations. (Ether 8:9.) She reminded her father that part of the record brought by their ancestors to the promised land contained "an account concerning them of old, that they by their secret plans did obtain kingdoms and great glory." Eventually, one Akish was persuaded to become involved in these secret plans. "And it was the daughter of Jared who put it into his heart to search up these things of old; and Jared put it into the heart of Akish; wherefore, Akish administered it unto his kindred and friends, leading them away by fair promises to do whatsoever thing he desired." (Ether 8:17.)

As to what was contained in that part of the ancient record referred to by Jared's daughter, we have been given an outline from various sources. According to Ether, the secret plans consisted of "oaths which were given by them of old who also sought power, which had been handed down even from Cain, who was a murderer from the beginning." (Ether 8:15.) Nephi reported that these oaths were "administered by the devil, to combine against all righteousness." (3 Ne. 6:28.) The record of Moses confirms the veracity of the previous two statements in a graphic and frightening manner: "Satan said unto Cain: Swear unto me by thy throat, and if thou tell it thou shalt die; and swear thy brethren by their heads, and by the living God, that they tell it not; for if they tell it, they shall surely die; and this that thy father may not know it; and this day I will deliver thy brother Abel into thine hands." (Moses 5:29.)

Moroni testified that secret combinations lead to destruction—the destruction of life, property, and freedom. (Ether 8:25.) The overthrow of freedom or free agency was Satan's plan from the beginning. (Moses 4:1-4.) Thus, secret combinations can be found in many elements of society among all people. (Ether 8:20.) Perhaps this may frighten us in the latter days. But it may also make us more conscious of Moroni's warning for our times—which warning he was commanded to write (Ether 8:26): "Whatsoever nation shall uphold such secret combinations, to get power and gain, until they shall spread over the nation, behold they shall be destroyed.... Wherefore, O ye Gentiles, it is wisdom in God that these things should be shown unto you, that thereby ye may repent of your sins, and suffer not that these murderous combinations shall get above you, which are built up to get power and gain—and the work, yea, even the work of destruction come upon you, yea, even the sword of the justice of the Eternal God shall fall upon you, to your overthrow and destruction if ye shall suffer these things to be." (Ether 8:22-23.)

If there is one lesson we learn from reading Ether 5-8, it is that when the Lord makes a prophecy or promise it must surely come to pass. Latter-day Saints must resolve to fight against Satan through personal righteousness and by avoiding the very appearance of evil. Does something degrade rather than edify? Is it done solely to get gain? Or does it attempt to stay hidden from Deity? If so, we must leave it alone.

Conclusion

The book of Ether is a record of great importance. It teaches of righteous leaders who were surely among the noble and great souls seen by Abraham. (Abr. 3:22-23.) It discloses glimpses of unspeakably glorious matters reserved for a future time of great righteousness. (Ether 4:7.) It bears testimony of the prophet Joseph Smith and three other latter-day witnesses called by God. (Ether 5.) It describes the customs and culture of an ancient people. (Ether 6.) It is full of verifying traditions.

The book of Ether (especially chapters 5-8) is important as well as interesting because it contains a number of parallels to be found in other scriptures. These include a great ocean voyage, barges like Noah's ark, prayers and praises sung unceasingly (compare Enos and others), a great family gathering before the death of the patriarchs (compare Ether 6:19-20 and D&C 107:53), the request for kingship, and secret combinations.

However, the great value of Ether, in particular chapters 5-8, lies in the spiritual lessons it provides: The promises of God are sure and must be fulfilled, and if we are righteous we shall prosper in the land. Just as Moroni wrote these things in his record so that "evil may be done away," let us read and apply them for the same reason.

NOTES

1. Joseph Smith, *History of the Church of Jesus Christ of Latter-day Saints*, 2nd ed. rev. (Salt Lake City: The Church of Jesus Christ of Latter-day Saints, 1932-51), 1:52-53.

2. Ibid., p. 55.

3. Ibid., p. 56, footnote.

4. Josephus reported that women and slaves were disqualified as witnesses. Josephus, *Antiquities* 4:8, 15.

5. J. H. Hertz, ed., *The Pentateuch and Haftorahs*, 2nd ed. (London: Soncino Press, 1967), p. 830.

6. Bruce R. McConkie, *Mormon Doctrine*, 2nd ed. (Salt Lake City: Bookcraft, 1966), p. 436.

7. Jamake Highwater, *Native Land, Sagas of the Indian Americas* (Boston: Little, Brown and Company, 1986), p. 16.

8. Ross T. Christensen, ed., *Transoceanic Crossings to Ancient America* (Provo: Brigham Young University, 1970), p. 25.

9. John L. Sorenson, *An Ancient American Setting for the Book of Mormon* (Salt Lake City: Deseret Book Company, and Provo, Utah: Foundation for Ancient Research and Mormon Studies, 1985), pp. 116-18.

10. Thor Heyerdahl, *The Tigris Expedition* (Garden City, N.Y.: Doubleday and Company, 1981), p. 8.

11. Ibid., p. 23.

12. Ibid., p. 8.

13. Hertz, *Pentateuch and Haftorahs*, pp. 26-27.

14. James B. Pritchard, ed., *The Ancient Near East Volume 1, An Anthology of Texts and Pictures*, 2 vols. (Princeton: Princeton University Press, 1973), p. 66.

24

A MORE EXCELLENT WAY
(Ether 9–15)

CATHERINE THOMAS

The Book of Mormon belongs to that group of ancient religious records known as Two-Way documents. A number of other ancient records may be described as Two-Way documents: the Qumran Manual of Discipline, the early Christian Didache, the Epistle of Barnabas, and so on.[1] Two-Way literature presents a philosophy that describes life as consisting of only two ways, each antithetical to the other; it identifies only two inclinations in man, also antithetical. For example, 2 Nephi 10:23-24 describes two ways: "Therefore, cheer up your hearts, and remember that ye are free to act for yourselves — to choose the way of everlasting death or the way of eternal life. Wherefore ... reconcile yourselves to the will of God, and not to the will of the devil and the flesh." At the end of Ether 8, Moroni anticipated the reader's question as to why he occupied so much space with the grim, nearly unrelieved saga of the fall of the Jaredite nation. He answered with a two-way statement: "I ... am commanded to write these things that evil may be done away, and that the time may come that Satan may have no power upon the hearts of the children of men, but that they may be persuaded to do good continually, that they may come unto the fountain of all righteousness and be saved." (Ether 8:26.)

We could illustrate the Two Ways on a line, with *Evil/Satan's Will* on one end and *Righteousness/God's Will* on the other. The

---

Catherine Thomas is a doctoral student in ancient history at Brigham Young University.

Book of Mormon describes no in-between states. Moroni observed later in his own book that an evil person cannot do good, and a follower of Christ cannot do evil. (Moro. 7:6-11.) One's life is characterized either by directing his energies to the right side where he or she experiences abundant life, or toward the left where he or she suffers a diminution of life and, if undeterred, self-annihilation. A nation's life is characterized by the same polarity. Moroni presented this two-way energy principle in the rise and fall of the Jaredites.

War and Peace

Moroni compressed several hundred years in chapters 9-11 of Ether. We read 9:15-25 carefully because it describes an atypical period of over 225 years of peace, perhaps somewhat similar to that in 4 Nephi. Moroni supplied little description of these years except that the people enjoyed harmony and plenty, with even an appearance of the Son of Righteousness to Emer.

But we do not need Moroni to give us details. All righteous societies have energy flows in common. They direct their energies toward discerning the word of the Lord and supporting and nurturing one another. Their growth in the Lord is unhindered by ego-conflicts and contention. Peaceful societies never happen by accident. They result from steady devotion to selflessness: they take thought on what causes human beings to thrive; they speak to nurture one another; they act to develop each other. They have laid down their natural self-wills and have taken on the image of Christ. They experience loving, sustained closeness.

It is sobering how readily people trade inner peace for something less. These gospel societies would never cease if it were not that people begin to choose something other than peace. Akish, for example, chose power (Ether 9:11); Riplakish chose wives, concubines, and gold (Ether 10:5-8); Shiblom chose secret combinations (Ether 11:7). Before obvious signs of deterioration appear, people begin to think in terms, not of unity and mutual support, but of separateness.

Separation begins in such subtle ways. We unwittingly begin to look for trouble, picking at this, complaining at that. We take offense over a real or imagined slight; we get angry because people around us do not do what we want; we grow cold or irritable, or we retaliate to get what we want; we insist on being right at the expense of precious relationships; we reject others who seem to lack love, failing to perfect love in ourselves. We disturb ourselves with self-seeking. Thus keeping the water rippling around us, we are not still and at rest in the principles of tolerance and love, of overlooking, of letting go, of forgiving, of ceasing to expect anything—except tolerance and kindness in ourselves. In candid moments we may wonder if we would singlehandedly dismantle a Zion society.

In achieving separateness, people are left with emptiness and alienation. They try to fill the void with external things, or power, or self-gratification, when the cause of their emptiness is their spiritual death; what they are hungry for is the love of Christ and relationships built on loving commitment. Their misery drives them to create more misery, and finally to destroy life.

This pattern of the pursuit of misery recurs in Ether. By Ether 9:26 the murderous secret oaths had taken root again. From this point the Jaredites traced a familiar curve: up and down from obedient to depraved king, from peace to desperation. Each dip in the curve brought a more severe response from the Lord as the spiritual law of the harvest operated on each generation. The ancient oaths found willing hearts. They gained so great a grasp on the people that the Lord threatened a destruction "as never had been upon the face of the earth, and their bones should become as heaps of earth upon the face of the land except they should repent of their wickedness." (Ether 11:6.) Finally the Lord swore to execute judgment of utter destruction and to bring forth another people to possess the land. (Ether 11:20-21.) This prophecy was fulfilled with the final destruction of the Jaredites and the nearly simultaneous arrival of the Nephites and Mulekites.

As this once so-promising Jaredite world approached genocide, Ether found refuge in visions of a better world; the reader senses that Moroni too was brooding over his own Nephite brethren who faced the same fate. Moroni also gazed soberly forward into the world of latter-day Israel. He provoked his modern reader with this question: How shall *we* escape the Jaredite and Nephite fate?

How do any people halt their precipitous decline? Ether declared: "By faith all things are fulfilled—wherefore, whoso believeth in God might with surety hope for a better world." (Ether 12:3-4.) Deliverance hangs on a total reversal of mental, physical, and spiritual energy flows. But Ether's people would not believe because (1) they had chosen something other than peace and unity; they did not any longer want a better world, and (2) they could not *see* the evidence of Ether's promise. (Ether 12:5.)

Faith and Sight

"By faith all things are fulfilled." (Ether 12:3.) Moroni used Ether's thought as the springboard for his own discussion of faith. He illustrated with several examples that the fulfillment of heavenly promises comes only after people have demonstrated their faith. In every apostasy that ever developed on the earth, people declined to that state in which, like Korihor, they declared: "Ye cannot know of things which ye do not see; therefore ye cannot know that there shall be a Christ." (Alma 30:15.) They preferred their own power to God's power, since God's power required of them more than they wanted to give.

"Dispute not because ye see not, for ye receive no witness until after the trial of your faith." (Ether 12:6.) In the scriptures, *faith* assumes *faith in Jesus Christ*. (See Ether 12:18.) Why is it so important to have a trial—a period of proving—of one's faith in Jesus Christ? Why is one more blessed for believing in Jesus without having seen him? Here we come to an essential spiritual fact: one key purpose of earth life is to develop faith, to learn to "walk by faith, not by sight." (2 Cor. 5:7.) Moroni observed that people first had to have faith in Christ before he could show himself to them. But how can people have faith in that which they have not seen? Why should people believe in Christ more than in Buddha? Why should they believe in any God at all?

God can hold people responsible for faith in Christ for three reasons: (1) Jesus Christ *is* the Savior of all. (2) God created people such that they could discern truth from error. Their existence and progression involve the divine substances of light, spirit, truth, intelligence, and glory. (D&C 93.) This divinity underlies the nature of God and man. People may enlarge their portion of divinity until like Christ they obtain the fullness, at which point they too become gods. Another term for the divine element in mortals is "Spirit of Christ." (Moro. 7:16; John 1:4.) (3) God can hold people responsible for truth because faith implies a desire, a *choosing* to know. Many people have sensed spiritual truths but have not wanted to exert the effort leading to personal sanctification. Amulek said, "I knew . . . , yet I would not know." (Alma 10:6.)

Here is the distinction between testimony-seeking and sign-seeking: the sign-seeker wants to keep his disobedient life and still have spiritual power. He wants to reap where he has not sown. The testimony-seeker wants to submit to God, repent, and live by the light that the Lord gives through the Holy Ghost.

When a messenger of God teaches the gospel by the Holy Spirit, that spirit bears witness to the truth. The listener is now responsible; shall he or she accept or reject the witness? We recall that God held Korihor responsible for his deception. Korihor confessed that he chose Satan's lie because it was pleasing to his carnal mind. (Alma 30:53.) When gospel truth has been revealed, deception is a choice; spiritual blindness is self-induced. (Alma 13:4.)

If we have come to earth to develop this inner truth-discernment, then we understand why Jesus told his disciples that he must for their sakes go away. That is, if they were to develop this inner spiritual capacity independent of what they could see, spiritual realities had to be removed behind a veil. Moroni calls this spiritual organ of truth discernment the "eye of faith." (Ether 12:19.) We understand that after one's faith has developed through the power of the Holy Ghost, one may receive the Second Comforter or the tangible and visible presence of the Godhead. Thus one who has developed this inner capacity is more blessed spiritually than one who depends only on the senses for knowledge. Such a one *knows* more. Elder Bruce R. McConkie bore powerful personal witness to this spiritual knowing:

> As pertaining to Jesus Christ, I testify that he is the Son
> of the living God and was crucified for the sins of the world.
> He is our Lord, our God, and our King. This I know of myself

independent of any other person. I am one of his witnesses, and in a coming day I shall feel the nail marks in his hands and in his feet and shall wet his feet with my tears. But I shall not know any better then than I know now that he is God's Almighty Son, that he is our Savior and Redeemer, and that salvation comes in and through his atoning blood and in no other way.[2]

"[Christ] prepared a way that thereby others might be partakers of the heavenly gift, that they might hope for those things which they have not seen. Wherefore, ye may also have hope, and be partakers of the gift, if ye will but have faith. . . . In the gift of his Son hath God prepared a more excellent way; and it is by faith that it hath been fulfilled. For if there be no faith among the children of men God can do no miracle among them." (Ether 12:8-12.) Moroni presented another two-way concept: two kinds of life are available to mortals: natural life and spiritual life. (Cf. Mosiah 3:19.) He referred to this higher life as "the heavenly gift." He meant the quality of life given first through the Holy Ghost as the First Comforter and then through Christ himself.

Men of old, in the beginning having the same standing as their brethren, chose to live so righteously because of their strong confidence in Christ that they entered into the holy order of God, and into the *rest of God.* (Alma 13:12.) This state of rest does not always refer to some distant state for which we must wait until exaltation; rather, we obtain that state of rest here through our faith in Christ and take it with us into the kingdom. (See Moroni 7:3, where Mormon commended the members for having entered into the rest of the Lord; cf. Alma 33:23.)

Faith progresses from one's having confidence in God to God's having confidence in that person and permitting him or her to witness and even to administer divine power, as did Moses, Alma, Amulek, Nephi and Lehi, Ammon, the three Nephite disciples, and those— like the brother of Jared, whom Moroni described in Ether 12:19-21, whose inner spiritual capacity was so well-developed from obedience—who had obtained Christ's word (or mind of Christ, 1 Cor. 2:16) to such a degree that they could, with their immanent oneness in Christ, compel his presence. We will learn before the end of chapter 12 that Moroni himself was such a man.

Students of the scriptures ask how one closes the gap between where he or she is and where such people as Moroni and the brother of Jared were. Joseph Smith said: "Here, then, is eternal life — to know the only wise and true God; and you have got to learn how to be Gods yourselves, and to be kings and priests to God, the same as all Gods have done before you, namely, by going from one small degree to another, and from a small capacity to a great one; from grace to grace, from exaltation to exaltation, until you attain to the resurrection of the dead, and are able to dwell in everlasting burnings, and to sit in glory, as do those who sit enthroned in everlasting power."[3] Even Jesus "received not of the fulness at first, but continued from grace to grace, until he received a fulness." (D&C 93:13.)

One does not usually leap ahead from one capacity level to a level much farther away; we usually develop patiently by making small adjustments, gradually increasing our capacity, building a solid foundation on the most simple principles of the gospel: "Ye are not able to abide the presence of God now, neither the ministering of angels; wherefore, continue in patience until ye are perfected." (D&C 67:13.)

We make spiritual progress through two means: our own agency and God's timetable. He does not always reveal his timetable. To possess some capacities, we wait on the Lord. We make a mistake if we think that by going into some kind of spiritual overdrive, we can suddenly assume great spiritual capacity or compel spiritual experience.

Strength in Weakness

The truth is that we were born into an imperfect state in a fallen world. We chafe against our imperfection, but we cannot completely eradicate our humanity in this life. Here power is an attribute of God, not of man. We were created weak so that we would turn to the only source that could develop real spiritual stamina in us. Moroni recorded his conversation with the Lord on this subject in Ether 12:23-37. He feared that the Gentiles would not accept the precious records because of the weaknesses in their writing. (Ether 12:25.) The Lord comforted him with this wonderful principle: "My grace is sufficient for the meek, that they shall take no advantage of your weakness; and if men come unto me I will show unto them their weakness. I give unto men weakness that they may be humble; and my grace is sufficient for all men that humble themselves before me; for if they ... have faith in me, then will I make weak things become strong unto them." (Ether 12:26-27.) When the Lord told the Apostle Paul, "My grace is sufficient for thee: for my strength is made perfect in weakness," Paul declared, "Most gladly therefore will I rather glory in my infirmities, that the power of Christ may rest upon me." (2 Cor. 12:9.)

The idea of heavenly community continued to direct Moroni's thoughts. He remembered that Christ had said that he had prepared a house for man among the mansions of his Father for which a man must hope [a gift of the Holy Ghost] or he could not inherit that excellent place. (Ether 12:32.) He recalled that Christ secured this excellence by laying down his life. (Ether 12:33.) Moroni was moved by this charity that made the heavenly place possible. Charity is another spiritual gift given to mortals in increments called *grace*. The Greek word behind *grace* in the New Testament means "divine gift." It refers to divine gifts of power unlocked by the Atonement. Grace, like all divine gifts, is administered to mortals through the Holy Ghost. It helps them do what they could not do by themselves.[4]

Moroni prayed that God would endow the Gentiles with grace. Here the Lord taught Moroni another principle: "If they have not charity it mattereth not unto thee, thou hast been faithful; wherefore, thy garments shall be made clean. And because thou hast seen thy weakness thou shalt be made strong, even unto the sitting down in the place which I have prepared in the mansions of my Father." (Ether 12:37.)

The Lord confirmed Moroni's calling and election here as he reassured him that because Moroni in his weakness drew on God's strength, he would sit down in the mansion that Christ had prepared for him. (Ether 12:37.) Moroni sealed his prophecies with his witness that they were true because Christ had told him face to face, in plain humility, in his own language. He bade us to seek Jesus, that his grace, his heavenly gifts, would abide in us forever.

New Jerusalem and the End of the Jaredites

The thread of the heavenly community continues to weave through Ether's tale of dissolution. Moroni resumed his narrative (chapter 13) with Ether's description of a new heaven and earth, a world with two centers of heavenly power: the New Jerusalem, that holy sanctuary of the Lord that would descend to the new world, joining with the earthly New Jerusalem, and contain the seed of Joseph. The rebuilt, sanctified city of Jerusalem in the ancient world would be headquarters for other tribes of scattered Israel, gathered from the the whole earth. These heavenly-city dwellers are partakers of the fulfilling of the Abrahamic covenant, or the covenant of exaltation. These cities will stand during the Savior's millennial reign until the celestialization of the earth. (Ether 13:8; D&C 101:16-38; Moses 7:60-64.) Those offered the gospel first, the Jews, have been reserved for redemption last because they were so tardy in accepting their Savior; the Gentiles, last to be taught the gospel in ancient times, will have been saved first. (Ether 13:12.)

Ether witnessed these harmonious scenes with the eye of faith as the Jaredites clamored on in mutual extinction. By day he lived in a cave and at night went out to witness the days' destruction, gathering material to finish his record. War rose in terrible crescendo through the next four years. Besides the prophet Ether, only Coriantumr would survive his people. He would not fall by the sword but would be buried by the very people who would supplant the Jaredite nation in the Lord's favor. (Ether 13:21; 14:24.) The chosen people are only those who choose the Lord.

"The Spirit of the Lord had ceased striving with them, and Satan had full power over the hearts of the people; for they were given up unto the hardness of their hearts, and the blindness of their minds that they might be destroyed." (Ether 15:19.) Ether recorded, "All the people upon the face of the land were shedding blood, and there was none to restrain them." (Ether 13:31.) Civil order had collapsed. In reflection of the slipperiness and the utter perishability of their

279

lives and works, they held on to nothing but their swords; no security offered itself. The relentless law of the harvest rolled upon them, and they lived out their remaining days like specters in a terrifying nightmare of anger — sickness, howling, stench, and blood. The lives they had chosen had filled them, not with desire for peace and abundant, thriving life, but with hatred and self-destruction. The ultimate end of evil is death.

Coriantumr and Shiz shared the last scene together. Ether, looking on secretly from his hiding place, saw Coriantumr behead Shiz in a memorably gory scene, after which Coriantumr fell to the earth "as if he had no life." (Ether 15:32.) But he was not dead, as the Lord foresaw. Coriantumr appeared again among the Mulekites as one who pathetically straddled that transition from a fallen group to a new chosen people. (Omni 1:21.)

Conclusion

One of the greatest lessons of the Book of Mormon is that whatever the Lord prophesies is fulfilled every whit, in every specific detail, nothing omitted. One day not far hence we will read those pages that precede the annihilation of the Jaredites, or the destruction of the Nephites before the Lord's first appearance, or the extinction of the Nephites in Moroni's day, and understand that the Book of Mormon was given to us in our day as a manual by which we could read the signs of the times and escape the irrevocable judgments of God.

Between the lines, however, we learn about the qualities of a Zion people. Undoubtedly Zion will be built up with some grand gestures, with some dramatic acts, but by and large it will be built up and sustained by those who have learned how to overcome in the most simple issues of life: to live in sweet, tolerant, humble peace — not just absence of war — but real, deep peace and real love with those around them. Only those who practice inner peace will survive in Zion.

Earlier we observed that the Book of Mormon describes no states between God's will and man's self-will, even though we may think we ourselves occupy intermediate positions. The question does not concern position but direction. As simplistic as this two-way philosophy seems at first, we must finally conclude that there really are only two ways. Anyone who operates from the ego impulses of self-will must admit that he or she spends his or her energies in the one way. Only that energy spent to grasp and respond to Christ's voice allows us to claim the other way. When we feel inner disturbance, it is a blessing to be able to check our own energy flow and correct its course. Only Christ makes us alive; every other way of life results in death.

NOTES

1. For a discussion of Two-Way literature, see A.R.C. Leaney, *The Rule of Qumran and Its Meaning* (Philadelphia: Westminster Press, 1966) pp. 46f.

2. *Ensign*, May 1985, p. 11.

3. Joseph Smith, *Teachings of the Prophet Joseph Smith*, selected by Joseph Fielding Smith (Salt Lake City: Deseret Book Company, 1938), pp. 346-47.

4. See "Grace" in "Bible Dictionary," Holy Bible (Salt Lake City: The Church of Jesus Christ of Latter-day Saints, 1979).

25

THE PRACTICES OF THE CHURCH
(Moroni 1–6)

ROBERT E. PARSONS

This final book in the Book of Mormon was written by Moroni after his father's death and some fifteen to thirty-five years after the battle at Cumorah. Moroni's dangerous and lonely situation is expressed in the opening verses: "Now I, Moroni, after having made an end of abridging the account of the people of Jared, I had supposed not to have written more, but I have not as yet perished; and I make not myself known to the Lamanites lest they should destroy me. For behold, their wars are exceedingly fierce among themselves; and because of their hatred they put to death every Nephite that will not deny the Christ. And I, Moroni, will not deny the Christ; wherefore, I wander whithersoever I can for the safety of mine own life." (Moro. 1:1-3.)

The first six chapters of Moroni deal with procedures and practices of the Church in Moroni's day. What is written is somewhat "ordinary" for active Latter-day Saints because the procedures are so similar to Church practices today. Thus, there often is a tendency to skim these chapters quickly and move on to more exciting material. However, a different view is needed if we acknowledge that Moroni was writing to our generation and had seen our day and time:

> Behold, the Lord hath shown unto me great and marvelous
> things concerning that which must shortly come, at that day
> when these things shall come forth among you. Behold, I speak

Robert E. Parsons is associate professor of ancient scripture at Brigham Young University.

unto you as if ye were present, and yet ye are not. But behold, Jesus Christ hath shown you unto me, and I know your doing. And I know that ye do walk in the pride of your hearts; and there are none save a few only who do not lift themselves up in the pride of their hearts, unto the wearing of very fine apparel, unto envying, and strifes, and malice, and persecutions, and all manner of iniquities; and your churches, yea, even every one, have become polluted because of the pride of your hearts. (Morm. 8:34-36.)

In connection with seeing our day, I like to think that Moroni also saw the practices of modern-day Christianity. This makes it easier to understand his concern and interest in telling us the correct procedures for such basic practices as conferring the Holy Ghost, ordaining to offices in the priesthood, administering the sacrament, and conducting church meetings. If one were to visit Catholics, Baptists, Lutherans, Pentecostals, and Unitarians on successive Sundays, what would he or she observe regarding the sacrament, ordinations, and church meetings? In that framework, it is easy to understand Moroni's concern with basic procedure and why he wrote what he did to this generation.

Power to Minister for Christ

Moroni's straightforward explanation in chapters 2 and 3 clarifies the statement of Jesus in John: "Ye have not chosen me, but I have chosen you, and ordained you, that ye should go and bring forth fruit." (John 15:16.) What does it mean that Christ ordained the apostles? The Christian world lays on unauthorized hands, confers divinity degrees to bestow authority, or assumes power by simple desire. In clear, unmistakable words, Moroni stated:

The words of Christ, which he spake unto his disciples, the twelve whom he had chosen, as he laid his hands upon them—And he called them by name, saying: Ye shall call on the Father in my name, in mighty prayer; and after ye have done this ye shall have power that to him upon whom ye shall lay your hands, ye shall give the Holy Ghost; and in my name shall ye give it, for thus do mine apostles. (Moro. 2:1-2.)

The manner which the disciples, who were called the elders of the church, ordained priests and teachers—After they had prayed unto the Father in the name of Christ, they laid their hands upon them, and said: In the name of Jesus Christ I ordain you to be a priest, (or, if he be a teacher) I ordain you to be a teacher, to preach repentance and remission of sins through Jesus Christ, by the endurance of faith on his name to the end. Amen.

And after this manner did they ordain priests and teachers, according to the gifts and callings of God unto men; and they ordained them by the power of the Holy Ghost, which was in them. (Moro. 3:1-4.)

As we read these words, there can be no question as to how one is ordained with power to minister for Christ and how that power is used to bestow the Holy Ghost. Another plain and precious teaching has been restored in the Book of Mormon, and we can now read biblical statements on receiving the priesthood and bestowing the Holy Ghost without misunderstanding.

Verse 2 of Moroni chapter 2 ends, "for thus do mine apostles." Obviously the Nephites were familiar with this term as well as the sacred office, notwithstanding the constant use of the terms "twelve" or "disciple." Concerning the presence of apostles among the Nephites and the office in their church administration, Joseph Smith stated:

This book also tells us that our Saviour made His appearance upon this continent after His resurrection; that He planted the Gospel here in all its fullness, and richness, and power, and blessing; that they had Apostles, Prophets, Pastors, Teachers, and Evangelists; the same order, the same priesthood, the same ordinances, gifts, powers, and blessings, as were enjoyed on the eastern continent, that the people were cut off in consequence of their transgressions, that the last of their prophets who existed among them was commanded to write an abridgment of their prophecies, history, &c, and to hide it up in the earth and that it should come forth and be united with the Bible for the accomplishment of the purposes of God in the last days.[1]

Elder Joseph Fielding Smith added: "While in every instance the Nephite twelve are spoken of as disciples, the fact remains that they had been endowed with divine authority to be special witnesses for Christ among their own people. Therefore, they were virtually apostles to the Nephite race, although their jurisdiction was, as revealed to Nephi, eventually to be subject to the authority and jurisdiction of Peter and the twelve chosen in Palestine."[2]

Sacramental Prayers

As Moroni saw our day and observed a typical Christian Sabbath, he must have been amazed at the multitude of apostate practices surrounding the holy yet simple ordinance of the sacrament in the various Christian churches. Visiting the Catholics, Presbyterians, Congregationalists, or Pentecostals, one would see a variety of practices. No wonder Moroni wrote the prayers and manner of administering and said, "We know the manner to be true." (Moro. 4:1.)

Both of the sacramental prayers contain the phrase "always remember him." We learn something of the importance of this phrase in the account recorded in 3 Nephi 1-2. A plan had been made to slay the righteous, and a day had been set apart to do this if the sign spoken of by Samuel the Lamanite should not come to pass. As Nephi pleaded with God in mighty prayer, the Lord spoke, saying: "Lift up your head and be of good cheer; for behold, the time is at hand, and on this night shall the sign be given, and on the morrow come I into the world, to show unto the world that I will fulfil all that which I have caused to be spoken by the mouth of my holy prophets." (3 Ne. 1:13.)

The sign was given, and the effect of this sign on those in the promised land is recorded as follows: "From this time forth there began to be lyings sent forth among the people, by Satan, to harden their hearts, to the intent that they might not believe in those signs and wonders which they had seen; but notwithstanding these lyings and deceivings the more part of the people did believe, and were converted unto the Lord." (3 Ne. 1:22.)

Although it is common to say "signs do not convert," it is clear that this sign was so tremendous that "the more part of the people did believe, and were converted to the Lord."

A great lesson is now taught in the Book of Mormon, for we learn that after conversion one must continue in works of faith to retain this conversion. Only three or four years after the people were converted, we read: "Thus passed away the ninety and fifth year also, and the people began to forget those signs and wonders which they had heard, and began to be less and less astonished at a sign or a wonder from heaven, insomuch that they began to be hard in their hearts, and blind in their minds, and began to disbelieve all which they had heard and seen." (3 Ne. 2:1.)

How do people "begin to forget"? Could they actually forget they had seen a day, a night, and a day as one day? Certainly not, but they could forget the spiritual significance of that experience. They could forget their spiritual feelings and thus could lose their spiritual conversion. Unfortunately, we see the same thing in the lives of a few Church members today. For example, a returned missionary will never forget where he served his mission, but he may forget his spiritual feelings and conversion. How does this happen? By neglecting the sacred ordinance given that "we might always remember." If we always remember, we certainly cannot forget. If we neglect the sacred ordinance of the sacrament, or do not partake of the emblems worthily and with the proper attitude, it is not long until we do not "always remember him" and "always have his spirit to be with us." If we lose his spirit, we are no longer numbered with the faithful. Although the Nephites in 3 Nephi 2 did not have the ordinance of the sacrament (it had not yet been instituted among them), they obviously had sacrificial ordinances designed to point them to Christ and to help them always remember him. They lost the spirit that converted them and could keep them faithful. The necessity of faithful sacrament observance in remembering the Lord was discussed by President Spencer W. Kimball: "When you look in the dictionary for the most important word, do you know what it is? It could be remember. Because all of you have made covenants—you know what to do and you know how to do it—our greatest need is to remember. That is why everyone goes to sacrament meeting every Sabbath day, to take the sacrament and listen to the priests pray that they 'may always remember him and keep his commandments which he has given them.' Nobody should ever forget to go to sacrament meeting. Remember is the word. Remember is the program."[3]

Sacred Ordinances

Elder Boyd K. Packer said, "Good conduct without the ordinances of the gospel will neither redeem nor exalt mankind; covenants and the ordinances are essential."[4]

Elder Packer was speaking of the ordinances of salvation—beginning with baptism and progressing on to the sealing ordinances of the temple. Why should ordinances be so important? Certainly most Protestant churches place little saving value on them. The following four points may help solidify our understanding of their purpose and importance.

First, God has commanded them. This in and of itself should be sufficient: "Wherefore he that prayeth, whose spirit is contrite, the same is accepted of me if he obey mine ordinances. He that speaketh, whose spirit is contrite, whose language is meek and edifieth, the same is of God if he obey mine ordinances." (D&C 52:15-16.)

Second, ordinances are the legal means for the orderly accomplishment of stated purposes. Priesthood is used in God's kingdom so that the work performed is legal. So it continues with ordinances. God could remit sins through any means he decreed. If he said that one must read the Bible eight times to be forgiven of sins, that decree would stand. However, for good reasons he instituted the principle that sins are to be forgiven through faith in the Lord Jesus Christ, repentance of sins, and participation in the ordinance of baptism. Thus, this becomes the legal or authorized means for remitting sins. Performed under the direction of his priesthood, it is and remains an orderly procedure, without confusion, carefully and harmoniously regulated.

Third, ordinances are effective teaching symbols that clearly portray what is happening. The ordinance of baptism is a perfect example. How gracious of God to institute a procedure that portrays forgiveness. Water itself is a cleansing agent. The burial in the water symbolizes the burying of the man of sin in a watery grave. The rising of the person from immersion in water is analogous to the dead rising from an earthly grave. The rising or resurrection is to a new life—a spiritual life. As we wash away our sins in a watery grave and bury the man of sin in a watery tomb, so we also come forth to a new, spiritual life, cleansed and forgiven through the sacred ordinance of baptism.

Fourth, ordinances serve as witnesses to spiritual agreements between God and man. As one puts his signature to a document to bind himself to the written terms, so we bind ourselves to the terms of ordinances by participating in them. Such a seal of intent and participation is noted in heaven itself and is also recorded on earthly records kept by the Church. When the day of judgment arrives and the books are opened, records of our participation in and binding ourselves to the terms of ordinances will be brought forth. Both our making of these ordinances and our keeping of the terms entered into will play a major role in the judgment rendered upon us.

Nourishing New Members

Moroni 6 is most interesting and enlightening concerning Nephite church practices. We read: "After they had been received unto baptism, and were wrought upon and cleansed by the power of the Holy Ghost, they were numbered among the people of the church of Christ; and their names were taken, *that they might be remembered and nourished by the good word of God*, to keep them in the right way, to keep them continually watchful unto prayer, relying alone upon the merits of Christ, who was the author and the finisher of their faith." (Moro. 6:4; emphasis added.)

To illustrate the importance of nourishing new members, I would like to include excerpts from a lesson taught to a Book of Mormon class at Brigham Young University during the fall of 1987. I asked the class to indicate where they had family members serving on missions and then to estimate how many hours a day the missionary was working and how much the mission was costing per month.

Teacher: We have suggested time and cost of missionary work. Let us examine another question. Why do some converts not remain active in the Church? My own experience has been that if we were to pick the one central thing that causes more people to go inactive than anything else, the answer would have to be lack of fellowshipping. But that has ramifications. You can say, well they weren't really converted, but what that means is that as long as someone fellowshipped them they were converted enough to keep coming and to grow. But if you stop the fellowshipping, they weren't able to keep on by themselves. If we had fellowshipped them another one or two years, maybe they would have been strong enough to stand by themselves.

The reason we've discussed this is that I did a little calculating. Although these figures may not be exactly up to date, they are not too far off. These figures were worked out in the early 1980s. I took the number of converts we get in the Church per year, and the number of missionaries we have, and an estimated number of hours they work, and the estimated average cost. What I came up with was that it was taking about 468 hours of missionary work per convert, and it was costing about $540 per convert. If you go on a mission and know that it is going to take that many hours to make a convert and cost that much money, do you want to go or stay home? Do you find members objecting to spending that much money and that much time to convert somebody to the Church? We don't object to that. We say we would like to be more economical because we want more people to hear the gospel. But, if that is what it takes, we'll spend the time and the money. Now, isn't it a shame to spend all that time and all that money to bring somebody into the Church, and then lose him? And the main reason we lose him is what? Lack of fellowshipping. We should keep many more converts in the Church. We should be much more successful.

Have you ever gone to sacrament meeting, stood at the back of the hall for ten or fifteen minutes before the meeting began, watched people come in and sit down, and noticed who looked like he might be all alone? Have you ever watched for somebody sitting all by himself? Did you ever have enough compassion and spirit of fellowshipping to go sit down by that person and say, "I'm so-and-so and you're who?" Did you get acquainted and make that person feel at home and go through the meetings with him? No, we don't do that. That's as much a part of missionary work for this time and circumstances as to accept a full-time mission when the call comes.

Now, in the light of all I've said, let's read a passage from Moroni chapter 6. We want to pick it up in verse 4. We are talking about converts who come into the Church. "After they had been received unto baptism, and were wrought upon and cleansed by the power of the Holy Ghost, they were numbered among the people of the church of Christ; and their names were taken, that they might be remembered and nourished by the good word of God, to keep them in the right way."

We have a system for keeping track of people. Isn't that what Moroni was saying they did? They were numbered, and their names were taken. Now, they didn't have computers like we do today, but they kept track of people so they could be nourished and kept in the right way. They fellowshipped them to strengthen them in the kingdom.

We do a very good job in missionary work and are willing to spend money and time to convert people to the Church. We don't do a very good job currently in fellowshipping. There are some exceptions to that; once in a while you go to a ward where they really take care of strangers.

Student: Sometimes we, as missionaries, hated to take someone to a ward knowing how cold that ward was going to be. We had something so precious that we wanted to share with them, but we were afraid of what the members would do.

Teacher: That's not too flattering to us, is it? As we reflect on our efforts to strengthen converts and keep track of members in the Church today, it is edifying to read Moroni's statement of similar concern in his day and of the practices of the Church among the Nephites.

Is it not faith-promoting to know that the Church in earlier dispensations not only practiced faith, repentance, and baptism, but also recorded the names of members and watched over and nourished them that they might be kept in the faith? Today we call such practices fellowshipping, home teaching, or visiting teaching, but the purpose in each dispensation has been the same—first to convert and then to perfect members of Christ's Church. President Gordon B. Hinckley commented on the tragedy of losing souls after once having brought them into the kingdom: "The greatest tragedy in the Church . . . is the loss of those who join the Church and then fall away. With very few exceptions it need not happen. I am convinced that almost universally those who are baptized by the missionaries have been taught sufficiently to have received knowledge and testimony sufficiently to warrant their baptism. But it is not an easy thing to make the transition incident to joining this Church. It means cutting old ties. It means leaving friends. It may mean setting aside cherished beliefs. It may require a change of habits and a suppression of appetites. In so many cases it means loneliness and even fear of the unknown. There must be nurturing and strengthening during this difficult season of a convert's life. A tremendous price has been paid for his presence in the Church. The long efforts of the missionaries and the cost of their service, the separation from old relationship and the trauma associated with this makes it imperative that these precious souls be welcomed, reassured, helped in their times of weakness, praised for what they do, given responsibility under which they may grow strong, and encouraged and thanked for all they do."[5]

Conducting Meetings

Moroni 6 concludes: "The church did meet together oft, to fast and to pray, and to speak one with another concerning the welfare of their souls. . . . And their meetings were conducted by the church after the manner of the workings of the Spirit, and by the power of the Holy Ghost; for as the power of the Holy Ghost led them whether to preach, or to exhort, or to pray, or to supplicate, or to sing, even so it was done." (Moro. 6:5, 9.)

Those who preside over meetings today are concerned that what is done is under the influence of the Holy Ghost. Meetings should be planned under the inspiration of the Holy Spirit, and meetings should be conducted under that same spirit. This will necessitate, at times, that on-the-spot changes be made in the songs sung and those called upon to speak and the subjects spoken upon—all this that God may be glorified and that Church members may be watched over and strengthened as was done in the ancient church among the Nephites.

NOTES

1. Joseph Smith, *History of the Church of Jesus Christ of Latter-day Saints*, ed. B.H. Roberts, 7 vols. (Salt Lake City: The Church of Jesus Christ of Latter-day Saints, 1932-51), 4:538, March 1842.

2. Joseph Fielding Smith, *Answers to Gospel Questions* (Salt Lake City: Deseret Book Company, 1957), 1:122.

3. "Circles of Exaltation," *Charge to Religious Educators*, 2nd ed. [Salt Lake City], 28 June 1968.

4. *Conference Report*, Oct. 1984, p. 105.

5. President Gordon B. Hinckley, Regional Representatives' Seminar, April 3, 1987.

26

HOPE, FAITH, AND CHARITY
(Moroni 7–8)

MONTE S. NYMAN

Many members of the Church can quote some of the verses from Moroni 7, such as "All things which are good cometh of God" (v. 12); "The Spirit of Christ is given to every man" (v. 16); and "Charity is the pure love of Christ" (v. 47). However, few have ever seen the great overall message and the unity of the whole chapter. It is my opinion that Mormon's sermon ranks as one of the greatest, surpassed only by those of the Savior.

Mormon identified his audience as those "of the church, that are the peaceable followers of Christ, and that have obtained a sufficient hope by which [they] can enter into the rest of the Lord, from this time henceforth until [they] shall rest with him in heaven." (Moro. 7:3.) While we do not know exactly when Mormon delivered his sermon, we do know that it was in a period when great trials and afflictions were upon the Church. In A.D. 345, Mormon, who was then about thirty-four years old, lamented that "a continual scene of wickedness and abominations has been before mine eyes ever since I have been sufficient to behold the ways of man." (Morm. 2:18.)[1] As these conditions only worsened over the next forty years of his life, those whom Mormon addressed as the faithful members of the Church would have endured the sufferings and persecutions of their corrupt society.

When Mormon presented the sermon recorded in Moroni 7, he

Monte S. Nyman is professor of ancient scripture at Brigham Young University.

was a disciple of Jesus Christ (3 Ne. 5:12-13), a special witness, grounded in the knowledge of the gospel. His office not only gave him the authority but also the responsibility to declare the gospel "according to the power of the Holy Ghost." (D&C 18:32.) His message to the Nephites is as applicable to us today as it was to those who heard it in his own time. As will be shown, it represents a three-step plan of salvation: hope, faith, and charity. While these terms have become common in our modern Christian world, we may also have become complacent in really understanding them. That they are of universal importance is demonstrated by Paul's use of them in writing to the Corinthians. (1 Cor. 13.)[2]

Hope Produces Good Works

Those faithful members of the Church to whom Mormon spoke had been brought to their present spiritual status through the principle of hope — the hope of eternal life (Titus 1:2; 3:7) obtained through Jesus Christ (Jacob 2:19). This hope gives people the courage to follow the commandments, thereby producing good works in their lives. Both ancient and modern scriptures tell us all people will be judged of their works, whether they be good or evil. (2 Cor. 5:10; Morm. 3:20.) This is enlarged upon by Mormon.

Mormon commenced the body of his sermon by saying: "The word of God . . . [says] by their works ye shall know them . . . a man being evil cannot do that which is good." (Moro. 7:5-6.)[3] This statement serves as a warning or refutation of the idea of earning or buying salvation through a specified number of good deeds. As Mormon continued, "if [a man] offereth a gift, or prayeth unto God, except he shall do it with real intent it profiteth him nothing." (Moro. 7:6.) In other words, we must do the right thing for the right reason. After expounding upon the idea that it is impossible for an evil person to do good things, Mormon declared that this is because "all things which are good cometh of God; and that which is evil cometh of the devil." (Moro. 7:12.) Doing something for the right reason is doing it not only because it is what God would want us to do, but also because it is what we want to do. Consequently, work will demonstrate a love of God and be a service to humanity. It will further

God's work of bringing "to pass the immortality and eternal life of man." (Moses 1:39.) It will be inspired of God. (Moro. 7:13.)

Mormon added a further warning about how we perceive works. He cautioned us against judging what is good to be from the devil and what is evil from God. (Moro. 7:14.) As an answer to this dilemma of how we can know which is which, he reminded his congregation and us that "the Spirit of Christ is given to every man, that he may know good from evil." He then noted that the way to judge whether a thing is good or not is to determine whether it "inviteth to do good, and to persuade to believe in Christ." (Moro. 7:15-16.) If it does, it is good. After giving a similar but contrasting description of how the devil's operations entice us to do evil, Mormon cautioned that the way we judge will determine the way we will also be judged. (Moro. 7:17-18.)

Through a hope in Christ, we produce good works in this life and gain the right to receive the Spirit in our lives. This is one criterion for the judgment for every individual. By following the directions of the Spirit of Christ, given to everyone who is born into this world, we can make the proper selection of which good works to accomplish.

Faith Produces Ordinances

Mormon told his listeners that they could lay hold upon every good thing through their faith, for a good thing comes through Christ; and God, who knows all things, sent angels to minister to mortals and make known Christ's coming. (Moro. 7:19-22.) Mormon added that God also declared to prophets that Christ would come and that there were various ways that good things were manifest: "Wherefore ... men began to exercise faith in Christ; and thus by faith, they did lay hold upon every good thing; and thus it was until the coming of Christ." (Moro. 7:23-25.)

Mormon further attested that people were saved by faith in Christ, thus becoming the sons and daughters of God. (Moro. 7:26.) We become his sons and daughters through being born again. (Mosiah 5:7; Ether 3:14; Gal. 4:1-7.) As the Prophet Joseph Smith taught: "Being born again, comes by the Spirit of God through ordinances."[4] Thus faith produces ordinances necessary for salvation. Mormon equated these saving ordinances with miracles, which he said had not ceased since the coming of Christ in the flesh, neither had angels ceased to minister to God's children. (Moro. 7:27-29.) He noted that there are two prerequisites for angels to minister to mortals: first, angels must be commanded to come by Jesus; and second, the recipient must be "of strong faith and a firm mind." (Moro. 7:30.)

There are two basic purposes for which angels come: (1) to call people to repentance, and (2) to fulfill and to do the work of the covenants of the Father. (Moro. 7:31.) The calling of people to repentance is illustrated in various places in the Book of Mormon. (See, for example, 1 Ne. 3:29; Mosiah 27:11.) The appearance of angels to fulfill and to do the work of the covenants of the Father is the work of providing ordinances for salvation. For ordinances to be efficacious, they must be done by the authority of the priesthood. The keys of the priesthood are the directing power of the priesthood.[5] When apostasy has occurred and the keys of the priesthood have been lost, making it necessary to restore these keys again, God has used angels to restore them. In our own dispensation, John the Baptist restored the keys of the Aaronic Priesthood (D&C 13); Peter, James, and John restored the keys of the Melchizedek Priesthood (D&C 27:12-13); Moses brought back the keys of the gathering of Israel, Elias the keys of the Abrahamic covenant, Elijah the keys of sealing power (D&C 110:11-16); other angels from Adam to the present all declared their dispensation, their keys, and so on (D&C 128:21). Thus the way is once more prepared for individuals to attain salvation through the exercise of faith to receive the ordinances of the priesthood. The chosen vessels of the Lord (priesthood leaders) bear testimony of Christ, and the ordinances necessary for salvation through him (baptism, etc.), and the covenants of the Lord are fulfilled. (Moro. 7:31-32.) By faith, miracles are performed and angels minister to God's children. Without faith, these ordinances are not performed, angels do not minister, and individuals are not fit to be numbered among the people of the Church. (Moro. 7:37-39.)

Mormon proclaimed that such faith would not be obtainable without hope. This hope, which motivates us to do things, is a necessary companion of faith. We hope for eternal life, and because of our hope we have faith in Christ. Because of our faith in Christ, we do the works of the Father. We could not exercise faith to receive the ordinances if we did not hope for eternal life through the atonement. (Moro. 7:40-42.)

Charity Brings Grace

Through the humility required to obtain hope and faith, one is also able to obtain the essential quality for salvation, charity. This enables him or her to confess "by the power of the Holy Ghost that Jesus is the Christ." Without this celestial quality, Mormon says, mortals are considered as nothing. (Moro. 7:44.) Similar testimony of this concept was previously borne in the Book of Mormon by Nephi (2 Ne. 26:30) and Amulek (Alma 34:28-29). Mormon gave or quoted a lengthy definition of charity. The definition concludes with the familiar statement: "Charity is the pure love of Christ." (Moro. 7:45-47.)

Mormon bore witness that it will be well at the time of judgment for those who possess charity. (Moro. 7:47.) He then gave the formula for obtaining this gift of God: "Pray unto the Father with all the energy of heart," and the gift will be "bestowed upon all who are true followers of his Son, Jesus Christ; that [they] may become the sons [and daughters] of God." (Moro. 7:48.) The obtaining and maintenance of this pure love is possible through "diligence unto prayer, until the end shall come." (Moro. 8:26; see also 2 Ne. 33:6-9.) Therefore, charity is the pure love of God and is a gift from God based on prayer and true discipleship. Gaining it is required for salvation in the celestial kingdom, and it is bestowed through God's grace. As one shares the love, he or she receives more of God's grace—he or she receives "grace for grace." (D&C 93:12; John 1:16.)

Three Steps to Salvation

Basically, three things are required for salvation: works, faith, and grace. Some religions emphasize that salvation comes only through faith and the grace of God. Others emphasize that salvation comes from ordinances. Still others preach the necessity of works. The scriptures show that all three are required for salvation. Because hope for eternal life produces works, individuals will be judged according to their works. Through faith we gain the ordinances prerequisite for salvation. However, after we receive all of the ordinances and do all of the works, it is the grace of God that prepares and purifies us for salvation. This is what Nephi meant when he said, "It is by grace that we are saved, after all we can do." (2 Ne. 25:23.)

The Doctrine of Christ Concerning Children

The sermon we have just considered was placed in the record by Moroni as he concluded his engravings on the plates. He also included a letter he had received from his father concerning the baptism of little children, a pernicious doctrine that had been introduced into the Nephite church and seemed always to creep into the church as apostasy began to set in. (Moro. 8:4-6.)[6] The placement of Mormon's letter following his sermon does not seem to be accidental. Mormon testified to his son that those who suppose that little children need baptism are "in the gall of bitterness and in the bonds of iniquity; for he hath neither faith, hope, nor charity." (Moro. 8:14.)

Before considering Mormon's explanation of the relationship of Christ and little children, we should affirm the source of his reasoning. He had received the word of the Lord by the power of the Holy Ghost and had received the authority and responsibility from God to boldly declare his words. Therefore, we will not be considering merely the opinion of Mormon but the very "words of Christ" that came to him. (Moro. 8:7-8, 16.)

The Lord revealed three reasons to Mormon as to why children do not need to be baptized. The first is that little children are not capable of committing sin. The second is that the atonement of Christ has paid for the transgressions of little children. The third is that little children cannot repent. These three reasons will each be considered separately.

Mormon was told that little children were not capable of committing sin. After being reminded of Jesus' teaching that he came into the world not to call the righteous but sinners to repentance (cf. Mark 2:17), Mormon was told that the curse of Adam (the fall into an environment of sin) was taken from children and had no power over them. In other words, Satan has no power to tempt little children. (D&C 29:47.) Furthermore, Mormon was informed that the law of circumcision was done away or revoked by Christ (Moro. 8:8) because this law had served its purpose. Prior to the Savior's advent, circumcision at eight days typified the principle that children are not accountable until they are eight years old. (JST Gen. 17:11-12.) When the atonement was accomplished, circumcision, like Mosaic sacrifice, was done away. Thus Mormon concluded that it was solemn mockery to baptize little children when the atonement of Christ had taken care of whatever transgressions they may have committed.

Mormon next explained to Moroni that "little children are alive in Christ, even from the foundation of the world." The plan of salvation was based upon the foreknowledge of God. God, knowing that many little children would not live to the age of accountability, provided for their salvation through the atonement, without the necessity of baptism. (Moro. 8:11-12.) As revealed to Joseph Smith, "All little children who die before they arrive at the years of accountability are saved in the celestial kingdom of heaven." (D&C 137:10.) Not to have provided for these little children would have rendered God "a partial God," for "many little children have died without receiving baptism." (Moro. 8:12.) Based on his foreknowledge, God sent those spirits who were of a celestial character to the bodies of those who would die in their infancy. In the words of Joseph Smith:

> We have again the warning voice sounded in our midst, which shows the uncertainty of human life; and in my leisure moments I have meditated upon the subject, and asked the question, why it is that infants, innocent children, are taken away from us, especially those that seem to be the most intelligent and interesting. The strongest reasons that present themselves to my mind are these: This world is a very wicked world; and it is a proverb that the "world grows weaker and wiser"; if that is the case, the world grows more wicked and corrupt. In the earlier ages of the world a righteous man, and a man of God and of intelligence, had a better chance to do good, to be believed and received than at the present day; but in these days such a man is much opposed and persecuted

by most of the inhabitants of the earth, and he has much sorrow to pass through here. The Lord takes many away even in infancy, that they may escape the envy of man, and the sorrows and evils of this present world; they were too pure, too lovely, to live on earth; therefore, if rightly considered, instead of mourning we have reason to rejoice as they are delivered from evil, and we shall soon have them again.[7]

These children needed to receive a body, that they might go on in their eternal progression.[8] Of course other great and noble spirits were needed to administer the plan of salvation upon the earth and were also chosen in the premortal councils to be leaders on the earth at various times in mortality. (Abr. 3:22-23.) In the wisdom and foreknowledge of God, the assignments were made based upon the faith and good works of the spirits in the first estate, meaning the premortal life. (Alma 13:1-5.) Without an acceptance of the omniscience of God, the doctrine of salvation for little children is incompatible with God being unchangeable and no respecter of persons.

Mormon's final point that little children are unable to repent (Moro. 8:19) is also based upon the law of accountability. Repentance includes the recognition of sin, a remorse for mistakes, and a restitution for the damage or hurt that has been done. Until the child matures enough to be able to do this, he is not accountable; until the child is able to understand right and wrong and the effects of his actions, the Lord does not hold him accountable. To believe in the need for baptism of infants, in Mormon's words, "denieth the mercies of Christ, and setteth at naught the atonement of him and the power of his redemption." (Moro. 8:20.) Mormon invited the readers to give heed, for his words will stand for or against them at the judgment seat of Christ. (Moro. 8:21.)

Mormon added another dimension to his treatise on little children; he said that those who are without the law are also alive in Christ. This would include all people who are born into a situation where they are never taught,[9] as well as those who through some imparity are also incapable of understanding the law. (Moro. 8:22; see also D&C 29:50.)

Become Like Little Children

Mormon admonished his missionary son to teach "repentance and baptism unto those who are accountable and capable of committing sin; yea, teach parents that they must repent and be baptized, and humble themselves as their little children, and they shall all be saved with their little children." (Moro. 8:10.) Jesus taught similar things during his mortal ministry. (Matt. 18:2-6.) Paul taught the saints to be children in the sense that they were devoid of malice, but to be adults in regard to understanding. (1 Cor. 14:20.) Mormon further taught that the first fruit of repentance was baptism, "and baptism cometh by faith unto the fulfilling the commandments; and the fulfilling the commandments bringeth remission of sins; and the remission of sins bringeth meekness, and lowliness of heart; and because of meekness and lowliness of heart cometh the visitation of the Holy Ghost, which Comforter filleth with hope and perfect love, which love endureth by diligence unto prayer, until the end shall come, when all the saints shall dwell with God." (Moro. 8:25-26.) The plan of redemption is to fill all of us, like Christ, full of charity. Those who have hope and bring forth works unto repentance will receive a remission of their sins through their faith in accepting the ordinances. Through the ordinances they will receive the Holy Ghost, who will fill them with hope to do more and more good works in and through the love of Christ, which is charity. This charity will then enable them to endure to the end.

Mormon followed this plan and attained the desired goal. He was filled with everlasting charity for all people, and he especially loved little children. He urged his son Moroni to pray for the Lamanites, his enemies who were seeking his life. (Moro. 8:27-29.) With the exception of the Savior himself, we may have no better example of a charitable person than Mormon. Moroni took his father's advice and seems to have attained that same quality of love. As he later abridged the record of the Jaredites, he prayed for the Gentiles unto whom his record would come. (Ether 12:33-41.) As he added a few more chapters to the records of his father, he also did so for the benefit of the Lamanites. (Moro. 10:1-4.) With such examples and admonitions to follow, we should be encouraged to strive to attain the same quality of love in our lives, "for charity never faileth" and "all [other] things must fail." (Moro. 7:46.)

NOTES

1. Mormon was about ten years of age in A.D. 321, making him about thirty-four in the year A.D. 345. (4 Ne. 1:48-49; Morm. 1:2.)

2. Charges of plagiarizing have been leveled against the Prophet Joseph Smith because of the similarities between 1 Corinthians 13 and Moroni 7. There are several possibilities for these similarities: (1) The Holy Ghost inspired both men; (2) Jesus taught these things to both the Jews and the Nephites and they were not recorded (John 21:25; Acts 1:3; 3 Ne. 26:8-12); (3) Paul and Mormon both were quoting from an earlier source that was lost from the original text of the Bible with other plain and precious things (1 Ne. 13:24-29). Some support of the latter is given by references to charity in Old Testament times by Nephi. (2 Ne. 26:30.) The last two possibilities are supported by modern biblical critics who question Paul as the originator of the message of 1 Corinthians 13. For their theories and evidences, see Richard L. Anderson, *Understanding Paul* (Salt Lake City: Deseret Book Company, 1983), pp. 118-19 and notes.

3. Mormon's quotation is very similar to 3 Nephi 14:16-20 or Matthew 7:14-20. Because these sources use "fruits" instead of "works" and "a tree" rather than "a man," it is possible that Mormon was paraphrasing these teachings. Another possibility is that he was quoting from an Old Testament source that is no longer in the Bible because of the loss of plain and precious parts. (1 Ne. 13:24-29.) Further support for the latter possibility is that much of the so-called Sermon on the Mount was known to the Nephites before it was given as a collective sermon to the Nephites. (See Matt. 7:7 and 2 Ne. 32:4.)

4. *Teachings of the Prophet Joseph Smith*, comp. Joseph Fielding Smith (Salt Lake City: Deseret Book Company, 1976), p. 162.

5. Joseph F. Smith, *Gospel Doctrine*, 11th ed. (Salt Lake City: Deseret Book Company, 1959), p. 136.

6. The washing of little children was a false doctrine instituted in the days of Abraham and refuted by the Lord in a revelation. (JST Gen. 17:3-6.) The Lord on this same occasion made the covenant with Abraham that every male child should be circumcised when eight days old. (Gen. 17:9-

12.) The circumcision being performed at eight days was symbolic of the child becoming accountable at eight years. (JST Gen. 17:11-12; see also D&C 68:25-27.)

7. *Teachings*, pp. 196-97.

8. The Prophet Joseph Smith taught: "We came to this earth that we might have a body and present it pure before God in the celestial kingdom. The great principle of happiness consists in having a body. The devil has no body, and herein is his punishment. He is pleased when he can obtain the tabernacle of man, and when cast out by the Savior he asked to go into the herd of swine, showing that he would prefer a swine's body to having none." (*Teachings*, p. 181.) These little children, being pure, did not need to be tested further. Their gaining of earthly experience, another purpose for coming to mortality, will be provided for them in the millennium. (See *Gospel Doctrine*, pp. 453-54.) See also Joseph Fielding Smith, *Doctrines of Salvation*, 3 vols., comp. Bruce R. McConkie (Salt Lake City: Bookcraft, 1954-56), 2:56-57; Bruce R. McConkie, "The Salvation of Little Children," *Ensign*, April 1977, p. 6.

9. Paul taught that "where no law is, there is no transgression." (Rom. 4:15; see also 2 Ne. 9:25-26.) However, while those who have no law are not taught, it must also be remembered that without the law there is no progression. Those who die without the law are only terrestrial beings unless they accept the gospel in the spirit world. (D&C 76:72; see also Joseph Fielding Smith, *Answers to Gospel Questions*, 5 vols., compiled by Joseph Fielding Smith, Jr. [Salt Lake City: Deseret Book Company, 1957-66], 4:10.)

27

COME UNTO CHRIST
(Moroni 9–10)

S. BRENT FARLEY

"My beloved son, I write unto you again that ye may know that I am yet alive; but I write somewhat of that which is grievous." (Moro. 9:1.) Thus began the final known letter of Mormon to his son Moroni. The ravages of war threatened to annihilate an entire nation; yet the prophet-father reached his prophet-son with the news that he was yet alive. His only joy was the knowledge of their faithfulness. (See Moro. 9:6, 22, 25-26.)

Mormon's report on the condition of their people was appalling. They had, by choice, gone beyond the point of repentance. Inspired warnings were met with anger; they refused to repent. Their feelings for the dignity of the human race had dwindled from smoking embers to cold ash. They thirsted for blood and craved immorality. They had become so hardened that they delighted in torture and murder; they even ate the flesh of their victims as a token of bravery. They were without civilization, without principle, and beyond feeling.

The bleakness of the letter was broken by the hope of reunion and the transferral of sacred records. (Moro. 9:24.) The closing reflected the sacred trust that though a nation might perish, a faithful saint would be raised up to the glory of eternal life. (Moro. 9:25.) With a final "amen," Mormon disappeared from known history.

S. Brent Farley is an instructor at the LDS Institute of Religion at Utah State University.

Moroni's Promise

In the ensuing years, Moroni concluded his sacred commission with the golden plates. His final message to the world began with a promise that will help change the world as its inhabitants come unto Christ (a millennial destiny). It is called "the promise of the Book of Mormon."

"Behold, I would exhort you that when ye shall read these things . . . " (Moro. 10:3.) Moroni was referring specifically to the sacred records, a portion of which would be revealed in the restoration of the gospel to Joseph Smith. The portion would be translated and published for all the world to read. *"If it be wisdom in God that ye should read them."* The book could be read and laid aside as any other piece of literature. But if the reader sought wisdom about God and his kingdom, he would be taking a step upward in his relationship with the divine. It would be the wisdom of God ingested to one's spirit from the printed page. To further qualify for this great promise, the reader is encouraged, *"Remember how merciful the Lord hath been unto the children of men, from the creation of Adam even down until the time that ye shall receive these things."* This provides a perspective that spans time and races, and causes one to realize that God is a personal and loving individual who has been dealing with humanity for their salvation since time began on this planet. It implies a reference to the Bible, for it is the most commonly possessed scripture that provides knowledge of God's dealings with his children since the creation. Having an understanding of biblical accounts provides a foundation for an understanding and an acceptance of the Book of Mormon as another testament for Christ. *"And ponder it in your hearts."* Pondering is thinking seriously, thoughtfully considering something, or reflecting upon a topic. To ponder in the heart adds the dimension of the feelings of the soul, wherein heart and mind are combined in an effort to understand.

Such an attitude of consideration begins with the "reading" and leads to the "receiving." (Moro. 10:4.) As Alma explained, truth (applied in this case to the Book of Mormon—the experiment being tested) has an effect upon the soul, for truth "will begin to swell within your breasts; and when you feel these swelling motions, ye will begin to say within yourselves—It must needs be that this is a good seed, or that the word is good, for it beginneth to enlarge my soul; yea, it beginneth to enlighten my understanding, yea, it beginneth to be delicious to me." (Alma 32:28.) This is a gradual but very noticeable process. As one reads and receives, the admonition of the promise continues: *"I would exhort you that ye would ask God, the Eternal Father, in the name of Christ, if these things are not true; and if ye shall ask with a sincere heart, with real intent, having faith in Christ, he will manifest the truth of it unto you, by the power of the Holy Ghost."* (Moro. 10:4.) Nephi, an earlier Book of Mormon prophet, testified that "if ye shall believe in Christ ye will believe in these words, for they are the words of Christ." (2 Ne. 33:10.) A simpler deduction would be hard to obtain; the promise of the Book of Mormon is a guarantee that this logical point will be proven. The proof, however, is not an empirical test open to the view of all. It is open only to the view of all who perform the test in the specified way; it is a test that affects the soul and the mind. The heart must be "sincere"; the intent must be "real." The sincerity and intent must be of such a nature and force as to produce change in the heart of the reader upon verification of the truth. And it requires faith, a quality difficult to measure for mortals, but which is definitely measurable to God. When such conditions are adequately met, the grand promise is: *"He will manifest the truth of it unto you, by the power of the Holy Ghost."* (Moro. 10:4.) A direct communication from God through the Holy Ghost will occur.

The promise originates with God. Thousands upon thousands have tested the promise and obtained the blessing of positive and undeniable proof. Many are the witnesses who verify the validity of fulfillment. Such evidence is referred to as a testimony. Through varying degrees and in differing manners, one may, as Moroni testified, "know the truth of all things" by the power of the Holy Ghost. (Moro. 10:5.)

Gifts of the Spirit

Moroni prophetically declared: "Nothing that is good denieth the Christ, but acknowledgeth that he is. And ye may know that he is, by the power of the Holy Ghost." (Moro. 10:6-7.) He then rehearsed some of the gifts of God that come by the Spirit (much as Paul did in 1 Corinthians 12).

"To one is given by the Spirit of God, that he may teach the word of wisdom." (Moro. 10:9.) Wisdom is the ability to understand and use principles and ideas that are correct and true; it is the ability to incorporate those principles into life for the betterment of humanity. The greatest source of wisdom is God. James declared, "If any of you lack wisdom, let him ask of God, that giveth to all men liberally, and upbraideth not; and it shall be given him." (James 1:5.) It was this scripture that led Joseph Smith into the sacred grove and the presence of God. Wisdom embraces the use of principles both spiritual and temporal, great and small; but all wisdom results in the benefit of mankind and their ultimate progression toward God. The ability to teach the word of wisdom is the ability to emulate and propagate that which benefits and improves mankind.

"And to another, that he may teach the word of knowledge by the same Spirit." (Moro. 10:10.) Knowledge is attained when one grasps truth. "Truth is knowledge of things as they are, and as they were, and as they are to come." (D&C 93:24.) Knowledge is not a distorted grasp of the facts; it is a clear attainment and understanding of that which is. It is not the varying interpretations of mortals that produce knowledge most readily; it is the guidance of the Spirit of the Lord that brings things into view "as they really are, and . . . as they really will be." (Jacob 4:13.) The greatest knowledge is that which opens the way to exaltation. As with wisdom, there are varying degrees of knowledge, temporal and spiritual, greater and smaller. The ultimate and sublime purpose of knowledge is "for the salvation of our souls." (Jacob 4:13.)

Firsthand knowledge comes with the aid of the Spirit. To read the scriptures gives one knowledge of what others have said. That is secondhand knowledge. When the Spirit bears witness to the truth of what the prophets have written, it becomes the personal and firsthand knowledge of the reader. The knowledge thus obtained is a gift of God, and the ability to teach knowledge is the capacity to aid others in their grasp of truth.

"And to another, exceedingly great faith." (Moro. 10:11.) "Faith is the assurance of things hoped for, the evidence of things not seen." (JST Heb. 11:1.) Faith comes in varying degrees for a variety of situations, both temporal and spiritual, from the farmer who plants the seeds to the prophet who sees within the veil the things of God. Its exercise develops power and undying trust. Abel, Enoch, Noah, Abraham, and Sarah are cited for their faith. (Heb. 11:4-13; see also Ether 12:19.) Faith was the power that saved Israel when they were led through the waters of the Red Sea. (Heb. 11:29.) Faith in its perfection is embodied in God, who framed the worlds through this power. (Heb. 11:3.)

Faith is the ability to trust explicitly in someone or something. In its truest sense, it binds one to God and the principles of his kingdom. Great faith is a peak in spiritual development. The brother of Jared illustrated this when he saw the Savior. (Ether 3:4-13.)

"And to another, the gifts of healing by the same Spirit." (Moro. 10:11.) Healing is the process by which the sick are restored to health. The priesthood ordinance of administering to the sick by use of pure olive oil and the authority of God is designed for this purpose. Many could testify to the miracle of healing through priesthood ordinances. The scriptures are replete with examples of healing, the prime focus centering in Christ himself, who went about "healing all manner of sickness and all manner of disease among the people which believed on his name." (JST Matt. 4:22.) The gift of healing by the Spirit is a special and notable ability to perceive the situations in which the miracle of restoration of health may be called forth by faith and priesthood power.

The gift to heal is not limited solely to physical maladies; it also extends to the ability to restore health to the spirit. The sicknesses of sin and depression affect spirituality. Some have the ability to teach or speak in such a manner that hope and enlightenment are brought to those who are down in spirit; they are thereby able to grasp that healing balm provided in the word of another and work their way back to full spiritual health.

"And again, to another, that he may work mighty miracles." (Moro. 10:12.) A miracle is something perceived by others as "supernatural," or beyond the normal power of mortals to produce. It is a manifestation of divine power, usually in response to faith.[1] Miracles have affected the earth, the elements of nature, and the inhabitants of the world. Some miracles appear greater than others. The greatest miracle of all was the atoning sacrifice and resurrection of the Savior.

"To another, that he may prophesy concerning all things." (Moro. 10:13.) The ability to prophesy is the spiritual power to foresee and foretell events in the future. The greatest prophecies were the predictions of the prophets of the mission of Jesus Christ before it actually occurred.

To prophesy is greater than to predict; people predict weather and events based upon logic and consistency of occurrences. Often they are wrong. Prophecy is a gift of the Spirit, sure and validated by the workings of God. "The testimony of Jesus is the spirit of prophecy." (Rev. 19:10.) As judged appropriate by God, certain individuals have the gift to know of things in the future.

"To another, the beholding of angels and ministering spirits." (Moro. 10:14.) This gift enables one to see people who are normally beyond the veil limiting mortal sight. It is to behold heavenly beings. "Ordinarily the word *angel* means those ministering persons who have a body of flesh and bone, being either resurrected from the dead (re-embodied), or else translated, as were Enoch, Elijah, etc. (D&C 129). . . . Spirits are those beings who either have not yet obtained a body of flesh and bone (unembodied), or who have once had a mortal body and have died, and are awaiting the resurrection (disembodied)."[2]

"And again, to another, all kinds of tongues; and again, to another, the interpretation of languages and of divers kinds of tongues." (Moro. 10:15-16.) The gift of tongues applies to the understanding of various languages. It may come suddenly in the ability to speak in one language and be understood in another, as on the Day of Pentecost. (Acts 2:1-11.) More commonly, it is the ability given to missionaries to quickly acquire the skill to speak in and understand a foreign tongue spoken in the mission area to which they are called.

"And all these gifts come by the Spirit of Christ; and they come unto every man severally, according as he will." (Moro. 10:17.) The

Spirit of Christ is the "true light, which lighteth every man who cometh into the world" (JST John 1:9); it is the power that enlightens eyes and "quickeneth your understandings" (D&C 88:11). It is referred to by many as the "conscience." Through that medium, the gift of the Holy Ghost brings about the greater spiritual gifts to those who are obedient to God's commandments. Every person has a spiritual gift or gifts; they are determined and given by an all-wise God for the benefit of the individual and those with whom he or she relates. All gifts are designed to bring people to Christ.

Moroni testified to "all the ends of the earth—that if the day cometh that the power and gifts of God shall be done away among you, it shall be because of unbelief." (Moro. 10:24.) He had lived in such a society.

"And again I would exhort you that ye would come unto Christ, and lay hold upon every good gift, and touch not the evil gift, nor the unclean thing." (Moro. 10:30.) As the good gifts came from God and led to eternal happiness, so the evil gifts would refer to powers and abilities of wickedness derived from obedience to Satan, which would lead to eternal misery. Implied in the exhortation to "lay hold upon every good gift" is that all gifts from God may be enjoyed at some point in time—their fullness undoubtedly reserved for the next life for those who are exalted. To "lay hold" would imply not only the use of individual gifts, but also the enjoyment available from the emanation of gifts exercised by others.

Becoming Perfected in Christ

A concise and concluding formula for coming unto Christ is given by Moroni. (Moro. 10:32-33.) "Come unto Christ, and be perfected in him." In the records Moroni was about to seal was the recorded commandment of the Savior: "I would that ye should be perfect even as I, or your Father who is in heaven is perfect." (3 Ne. 12:48.) Being close to Christ carries this requirement: "Deny yourselves of all ungodliness." To become godlike is the supreme goal in gospel progression. Satan would thwart that goal by cloaking evil enticements in attractive garbs. To resist them requires denial. It requires saying no to the attractive show of Satan's wares. Success also requires the exertion to "love God with all your might, mind and strength." In turning away from Satan, one must turn to God. A complete commitment and devotion fosters a love that takes on a divine characteristic, for it transcends all other relationships. It moves more and more toward charity, which is "the pure love of Christ." (Moro. 7:47.) It becomes more and more a privilege than a command as one grows in love of God. As that occurs, "then is his grace sufficient for you, that by his grace ye may be perfect in Christ." That which is beyond the capability of an individual to achieve on his or her own is granted by divine providence. The power of increased spiritual strength brings one closer to the attributes of godliness, and thus closer to the eternal goal of perfection. Perfection in mortality is possible in a limited way; that is, one does the best in gospel progression of which he or she is capable within the confines of mortality. It is to gain the triumph over sin. Thus it was recorded that "Noah found grace in the eyes of the Lord; for Noah was a just man, and perfect in his generation." (Moses 8:27.) Ultimately, perfection is attained in the eternal sense when one becomes like God: "He that receiveth my Father receiveth my Father's kingdom; therefore all that my Father hath shall be given unto him." (D&C 84:38.) These, Christ said, will "sit with me in my throne, even as I also overcame, and am set down with my Father in his throne." (Rev. 3:21.)

The perfection in mortality involves qualifying to be "sanctified in Christ by the grace of God, through the shedding of the blood of Christ, which is in the covenant of the Father unto the remission of your sins, that ye become holy, without spot." (Moro. 10:33.) To be sanctified is to be cleansed by the spirit of the Holy Ghost because of the efficacy of the atonement of Jesus Christ, made possible by baptism into the Lord's church. It leaves one pure and clean. In mortality, it is an ongoing and renewable process, for throughout mortality one keeps overcoming mistakes and progressing. Sins are repented of quickly and regularly, and the seriousness is less and less when compared with the mistakes of earlier development. The cleansing is a type of that which becomes permanent when one enters the kingdom of God in eternity. Then that which was known in part is achieved in a fullness, that the one so sanctified may remain in that state forever.

Moroni knew by the spirit of prophecy that such would be his case after death. "I soon go to rest in the paradise of God, until my spirit and body shall again reunite, and I am brought forth triumphant through the air, to meet you before the pleasing bar of the great Jehovah, the Eternal Judge of both quick and dead. Amen." (Moro. 10:34.)

NOTES

1. See "Bible Dictionary," Holy Bible (Salt Lake City: The Church of Jesus Christ of Latter-day Saints, 1979), p. 732.

2. Bible Dictionary, p. 608.

Scripture Index

THE OLD TESTAMENT

THE DOCTRINE AND COVENANTS

THE PEARL OF GREAT PRICE

Subject Index

Abinadi, 59

Abraham: lawful heirs of, 169; covenant of, 188-19, 193

Accountability, 300

Actions, thoughts precede, 156

Adultery, 155-56

Agency: as part of plan of salvation, 31-32; involves accepting consequences, 107; role of, in receiving blessings, 182-83 n. 9; Satan desires to overthrow, 268

Alma: Korihor is brought before, 1; testifies of God to Korihor, 5; undertakes Zoramite mission, 19; gives discourse on faith, 22-25; departs out of land forever, 37, 125-26; counsels his sons, 41-42; conversion and testimony of, 43-44; entrusts Helaman with records, 45-46; calls Corianton to resume mission, 54; discussion by, of resurrection, 59-60; is compared with Nephi, son of Helaman, 136 n. 1

Alms, 156

Amalickiah, 75-76, 81

Americas as promised land, 249

Aminadab, 102

Ammaron, 233

Ammon, people of: outcast Zoramites join, 36; withdraw from Jershon to Melek, 36; nearly break oath of peace, 84-85; two thousand sons of, go to war, 85-87

Ammoron, 81, 83-84, 90, 129-30

Amlulek, teachings of, to Zoramites, 29-34

Angels: sent to Alma, 44; ministering of, 296; definition of, 309

Anger, sin of, 155

Annalistic writing, 92, 104 n. 1

Anti-Christ, Korihor as, 1, 10-11, 18, 26 n. 2

Antipus, 86

Apostasy: of Nephites, 103, 108, 117-18, 127; resulting from pride, 141; first mistakes of, involve nature of God, 173-74; classic study of, 218; steps into, after Golden Era, 226

Apostles, 284-85

Ark of Noah, 265

Ashton, Marvin J., 229

Assassins, 94, 104 n. 3

Atonement: Korihor denied need for, 9-10; Amulek explains necessity of, 30; as part of plan of salvation, 32, 37; required infinite sacrifice, 32; infinite effects of, 39 n. 10, 53; repentance depends on, 53; makes mercy possible, 64, 120

Augustine, 30-31

Authority: Jesus bestows, on Nephite Twelve, 151-52, 178; Jesus proclaims his, 162; Moroni reemphasizes, 283-84

Ballard, Melvin J., 40 n. 21, 180-81